Adolescence

Development, Diversity, and Context

Series Editor

Richard M. Lerner
Tufts University

A GARLAND SERIES

Series Contents

1. Theoretical Foundations and Biological Bases of Development in Adolescence
2. Cognitive and Moral Development and Academic Achievement in Adolescence
3. The Development of Personality, Self, and Ego in Adolescence
4. Adolescents and Their Families
5. Risks and Problem Behaviors in Adolescence
6. Social Interactions in Adolescence and Promoting Positive Social Contributions of Youth

The Editors of this series are grateful to the several colleagues who facilitated our work on this series. Foremost, we are grateful to the authors of the selections reprinted in this volume. Their scholarship has shaped the study of adolescent development and we appreciate greatly their allowing us to include their work in this book.

We are especially grateful to Sofia T. Romero, Editor at the Boston College Center for Child, Family, and Community Partnerships, and to Imma De Stefanis, Graduate Research Assistant at the Center, for all their many contributions. Ms. Romero provided us with sage and professional editorial advice. Her wisdom, judgment, and skills enhanced the quality of our work and made it much more productive. Sr. De Stefanis collaborated extensively with us in the selection and organization of the scholarship included in the series. Her knowledge of and enthusiasm for the study of adolescence was an invaluable asset in our work.

We appreciate as well the excellent work of Carole Puccino, Editor at Garland Publishing. Her productivity and organizational skill enabled the volume to be produced with efficiency and quality. Finally, we thank Leo Balk, Vice President of Garland, for his enthusiasm for this project and for his support, encouragment, and guidance.

The Development of Personality, Self, and Ego in Adolescence

Edited, with an introduction by

Richard M. Lerner
Tufts University

Laura E. Hess
Purdue University

GARLAND PUBLISHING, INC.
A MEMBER OF THE TAYLOR & FRANCIS GROUP
New York & London
1999

Library of Congress Cataloging-in-Publication Data

The development of personality, self, and ego in adolescence / edited, with an introduction by Richard M. Lerner, Laura E. Hess.
p. cm. — (Adolescence : development, diversity, and context ; 3)
Includes bibliographical references.
ISBN 0-8153-3292-0 (alk. paper)
1. Self-perception in adolescence. 2. Ego (Psychology) in adolescence. 3. Personality in adolescence. I. Lerner, Richard M. II. Hess, Laura E. III. Series: Adolescence (New York, N.Y.) ; 3.
BF724.3.S35D48 1999
155.5'1825—dc21 99-33730
CIP

Printed on acid-free, 250-year-life paper
Manufactured in the United States of America

Contents

ix Introduction
The Development of Personality, Self, and Ego in Adolescence:
A View of the Issues
Richard M. Lerner and Laura E. Hess

PERSONALITY

2 Cultural Change and Adolescent Personality Development:
An Application of Longitudinal Sequences
Paul B. Baltes and John R. Nesselroade

16 Continuity and Discontinuity in the
Affective Experiences of Parents and Children:
Evidence from the New York Longitudinal Study
Jonathan G. Tubman and Richard M. Lerner

30 Temperament and Adjustment in Young Adulthood:
A 15-Year Longitudinal Analysis
Jonathan G. Tubman, et al.

SELF

41 The Development of Self-Understanding
from Infancy Through Adolescence
William Damon and Daniel Hart

65 Perceived Self-Efficacy in the Exercise of Personal Agency
Albert Bandura

79 Stability of Global Self-Evaluations in Early Adolescence:
A Cohort Longitudinal Study
Françoise D. Alsaker and Dan Olweus

103 A Longitudinal Study of Consistency and Change in Self-Esteem
from Early Adolescence to Early Adulthood
Jack Block and Richard W. Robins

119 Factors Related to Self-Esteem among African American Youths:
A Secondary Analysis of the High/Scope Perry Preschool Data
Tom Luster and Harriette Pipes McAdoo

137 Self-Concept, Self-Esteem, and Body Attitudes Among Japanese Male and Female Adolescents
Richard Lerner, et al.

147 Masculinity, Femininity, and Sex Role Attitudes in Early Adolescence: Exploring Gender Intensification
Nancy L. Galambos, David M. Almeida, and Anne C. Petersen

157 The Perceived Directionality of the Link Between Approval and Self-Worth: The Liabilities of a Looking Glass Self-Orientation Among Young Adolescents
Susan Harter, Clare Stocker, and Nancy S. Robinson

182 An Exploratory Study of Pubertal Maturation Timing and Self-Esteem Among Gay and Bisexual Male Youths
Ritch C. Savin-Williams

191 Adolescents' Affective Experience of Family Behaviors: The Role of Subjective Understanding
Sally I. Powers, Deborah P. Welsh, and Virginia Wright

208 Contributions of Parental Attachments to View of Self and Depressive Symptoms among Early Adolescents
Maureen E. Kenny, et al.

232 Ethnicity, Ethnic Identity, and Competence Formation: Adolescent Transition and Cultural Transformation
Margaret Beale Spencer, Dena Phillips Swanson, and Michael Cunningham

EGO

255 Identity Development from Adolescence to Adulthood: An Extension of Theory and a Review of Research
Alan S. Waterman

273 Development and Validation of Ego-Identity Status
James E. Marcia

281 A Longitudinal Study of Changes in Ego Identity Status During the Freshman Year at College
Alan S. Waterman and Caroline K. Waterman

288 Identity Processes Among Racial and Ethnic Minority Children in America
Margaret Beale Spencer and Carol Markstrom-Adams

309 Adolescent Ego Development within the Family: Family Styles and Family Sequences
Stuart T. Hauser, et al.

339 Ego Development and Adolescent Emotions
Stuart T. Hauser and Andrew W. Safyer

355 Acknowledgments

Introduction

The Development of Personality, Self, and Ego in Adolescence: A View of the Issues

*Richard M. Lerner, **Laura E. Hess

Adolescence is a period in which youth make a transition from the innocence and security of childhood to the responsibility and autonomy of adulthood (Hess, Petersen, and Mortimer, 1994). Although the biological changes associated with puberty may be the most visible and universal features of this period, cognitive, psychological, and social characteristics are also undergoing profound and interrelated transformations during adolescence (Lerner and Spanier, 1980). These multidimensional and complex transitions both influence and are influenced by the adolescent's development of their identity, or their unique sense of self.

While rooted in distinct theoretical traditions, the concepts of personality, self, and ego, in combination, capture the core aspects of the formation of the young person's individually unique sense of self or identity, a psychosocial development fundamentally associated with, and undergoing significant transformation during, adolescence. Consistent with the developmental-systems models of person-context relations at the forefront of current human development theory and research (Lerner, 1998), the articles within this volume underscore the importance of dynamic, reciprocal relations between youth and key socializing agents within their ecologies for the development of personality, self, and ego. Nevertheless, the articles represented in this volume illustrate that when attempting to understand the development of personality- and self-systems, scholars differ in the extent to which they place primary emphasis on the individual, on the context, or on the relationship between the two.

Theoretical Orientations about Adolescent Personality, Self, and Ego

The concepts of personality, self, and ego are rooted in unique and long-standing theoretical traditions within such fields as human development, psychology, and sociology (Lerner, 1986). For instance, while Bandura (1989), writing from a cognitive social learning orientation, stresses the importance of the individual's sense of self-efficacy in creating beliefs about personal agency, he also underscores the importance of reciprocal relations between person and environment in understanding the development of self. Similarly, Harter (1998) recognizes that the development of self is inextricably linked to interactions with and feedback from significant people in the individual's context. Accordingly, Harter et al. (1996) adopt a more person-context relational orientation in their examination of the link between approval from others (e.g., peers and key adults) and perceived self-worth. Other articles in this volume that adopt a comparable relational view regarding the development of the self include Alsaker and Olweus (1992), Block and Robins (1993), Galambos et al. (1990), Lerner et al. (1980), Luster and McAdoo (1995), Savin-Williams (1995), and Kenny et al. (1993).

The latter article illustrates the integrative use of ideas from different theoretical traditions, in that the Kenny et al. (1993) study uses a model influenced by organismic, attachment theory (e.g., Bowlby, 1969) as well as by relational models of development to study the impact of emotional attachment to parents on adolescents' self concepts and depressive symptomatology. Other articles reflect also the combined use of different theoretical orientations. For instance, differential developmental theory (Lerner, 1986) uses the idea of personality traits; this concept is integrated with person-context relational ideas pertinent to the life-span study of developmental systems in the articles by Baltes and Nesselroade (1972), Tubman and Lerner (1994), and Tubman et al. (1992). In turn, the organismic approach to the study of development, in regard to the development of cognitive or ego processes (Marcia, 1966; Waterman, 1982), is pursued within a sensitivity to the importance of contextual (e.g., interpersonal, peer or familial) relations in the articles by Damon and Hart (1982), Hauser et al. (1991), Hauser and Sayfer (1994), Powers et al. (1994), Spencer and Markstrom-Adams (1990), and Waterman and Waterman (1971).

In sum, the theoretical approaches represented in this volume underscore the use of integrating ideas from multiple theories in attempting to account for the features of adolescent development. Nevertheless, all approaches point to the importance of focusing on both the diverse dimensions of the individual and of his or her ecology in the study of personality, self, and ego.

Levels of Contextual Analysis in the Study of Adolescent Personality, Self, and Ego

The ecology of adolescent development is composed of multiple, integrated levels of organization (Bronfenbrenner and Morris, 1998), including the biological, psychological, interpersonal, institutional, cultural, and historical. Thus, the period of adolescence is one of continual exchange and transition between individuals and their multi-level context (Lerner, 1995).

Articles in this volume depict the diversity of ecological variables impacting personality, self, and ego development in adolescence. For example, the research represented in this volume illustrates how the development of the self system is associated with variation in ethnic and racial background (Lerner et al., 1980; Luster and McAdoo, 1995; Spencer and Markstrom-Adams, 1990), gender (Galambos, Almeida, and Petersen, 1980), sexual orientation (Savin-Williams, 1995), and family structure and function (Hauser et al., 1991; Powers, Welsh, and Wright, 1994).

The range and richness of the relations linking adolescents and their contexts represent a challenge for the design of both descriptive and explanatory research as well as for the planning and implementation of policies aimed at enhancing personality, self, or ego characteristics of youth. The importance and complexity of person-context relations mean that interventions, if they are to be effective, should be tailored to fit a given group of adolescents' specific developmental and contextual circumstances (Lerner, 1995).

Simply, the complex, bidirectional features of the person-context relations involved in the development of personality, self, and ego suggests that both basic and applied research be designed in manners sufficient to capture this complexity. The articles in this volume illustrate some of the variations in research designs that may be particularly useful in attempting to understand this complexity and/or capitalize on it to promote positive youth development.

Research Designs in the Study of Adolescent Personality, Self, and Ego

Several articles employ longitudinal designs to study continuities and discontinuities in personality, self, and ego development. These articles emphasize the changes in personality and self that accompany the transitions of adolescence. For instance, Tubman et al. (1992) examine stability and change in temperament, or behavioral style, while Block and Robins (1993) focus on consistencies and variations in self-esteem. Such longitudinal investigations give primacy to age-related changes in youth. In addition, articles by Baltes and Nesselroade (1972) and Alsaker and Olweus (1992) employ cohort-longitudinal designs which enable changes in personality that are associated with historical time, age, and birth cohort to be disentangled.

Such designs hold considerable promise for capturing the complex variation that is involved in the development of adolescent personality, self, and ego. Given that other articles in the volume employ designs that afford elucidation of the import for adolescent development of variation in ethnic and racial background (Lerner et al., 1980; Luster and McAdoo, 1995; Spencer and Markstrom-Adams, 1990), gender (Galambos et al., 1990), sexual orientation (Savin-Williams, 1995), and family diversity (Hauser et al., 1991; Powers et al., 1994), the need is underscored for methodologies sensitive to the complex and changing world of adolescents and their ecology. Knowledge based on such sensitivity is critical for advancing understanding of when and at what levels we should intervene to promote positive youth development.

Conclusions

The articles in this volume illustrate that adolescence is a dynamic developmental period. Despite the variation that exists in regard to theoretical orientation; emphasis on changes in the individual, the context, or person-context interactions; and research designs pertinent to understanding complex, dynamic person-context relations, the articles, in combination, indicate that diversity in adolescent personality and self concept results from complex — reciprocal and systemic relations — between youth and their contexts. The articles underscore the view that a developmental systems orientation has considerable use in the study of adolescence.

The articles suggest that through such scholarship substantial progress can be made in both understanding the development of individuality in adolescence and in promoting healthy variation in, and later-life outcomes of, this development. The research in this volume lays the groundwork for application of developmental knowledge to people and their contexts in order to promote positive individual developments that serve to further civil society.

*Richard M. Lerner holds the Bergstrom Chair in Applied Developmental Science at Tufts University. A developmental psychologist, Lerner received a Ph.D. in 1971 from the City University of New York. He has been a fellow at the Center for Advanced Study in the Behavioral Sciences and is a fellow of the American Association for the Advancement of Science, the American Psychological Association, the American Psychological Society, and the American Association of Applied and Preventive Psychology. Prior to joining Tufts University, he was on the faculty and held administrative posts at Michigan State University, Pennsylvania State University, and Boston College, where he was the Anita L. Brennan Professor of Education and the director of the Center for Child, Family, and Community Partnerships. During the 1994–95 academic year Lerner held the Tyner Eminent Scholar Chair in the Human Sciences at Florida State University. Lerner is the author or editor of 40 books and more than 275 scholarly articles and chapters, including his 1995 book, *America's Youth in Crisis: Challenges and Options for Programs and Policies*. He edited Volume 1, on "Theoretical models of human development," for the fifth edition of the *Handbook of Child Psychology*. He is known for his theory of, and research about, relations between life-span human development and contextual or ecological change. He is the founding editor of the *Journal of Research on Adolescence* and of the new journal, *Applied Developmental Science.'*

**Laura E. Hess is an Assistant Professor of Child Development at Purdue University. She received a Ph.D. in Human Development and Family Studies from the Pennsylvania State University in 1990. Building upon her experiences as a Postdoctoral Fellow at the Max Planck Institute for Human Development and Education in Berlin, Germany (1990–92), and a Pediatric Psychology Fellow at the University of Pennsylvania School of Medicine (1992–94), Hess joined the faculty of the Department of Child Development and Family Studies at Purdue University in 1994. She teaches undergraduate courses in the areas of child and family health and life-span development, as well as graduate courses in child development, applied research methods, and school violence. Her research interests focus on individual, family, and school ecology factors which may impact the development of social and self competence during childhood and adolescence. Her most recently published work has examined factors associated with victimization of and aggression by children at school, as indexed by teacher-, peer-, and self-perceptions. She also serves as scientific secretary for the Board of Trustees of the Johann Jacobs Foundation (Zurich, Switzerland), which promotes applied research and supports international scientist/policy-maker/practitioner interactions that will enhance social policies and programs directed towards at-risk youth.

References[1]

Bowlby, J. (1969). *Attachment and loss: Vol. 1 Attachment.* New York: Basic Books.

Bronfenbrenner, U., and Morris, P.A. (1998). The ecology of developmental process. In R.M. Lerner (Ed.), *Theoretical models of human development.* Volume 1 of the *Handbook of child psychology* (5th ed., pp. 993–1028). Editor in chief: W. Damon. New York: Wiley.

Harter, S. (1998). The development of self-representations. In N. Eisenberg (Ed.), *Social, emotional, and personality development.* Volume 3 of the *Handbook of child psychology* (5th ed., pp. 553–617). Editor in chief: W. Damon. New York: Wiley.

Hess, L.E., Petersen, A.C., and Mortimer, J.T. (1994). Youth, unemployment and marginality: The problem and the solution. In A.C. Petersen and J.T. Mortimer (Eds.), *Youth unemployment and society* (pp. 3–33). New York: Cambridge University Press.

Lerner, R.M. (1986). *Concepts and theories of human development.* (2nd ed.). New York: Random House.

Lerner, R.M. (1995). *America's youth in crisis: Challenges and options for programs and policies.* Thousand Oaks, CA: Sage.

Lerner, R.M. (1998). Theories of human development: Contemporary perspectives. In R.M. Lerner (Ed.), *Theoretical models of human development.* Volume 1 of the *Handbook of child psychology* (5th ed., pp. 1–24). Editor in chief: W. Damon. New York: Wiley.

Lerner, R.M., and Spanier, G.B. (1980). A dynamic interactional view of child and family development. In R.M. Lerner and G.B. Spanier (Eds.), *Child influences on marital and family interaction: A life-span perspective* (pp. 1–20). New York: Academic Press.

Footnote

[1]This list provides reference only to citations not included in this volume.

The Development of Personality, Self, and Ego in Adolescence

Developmental Psychology
1972, Vol. 7, No. 3, 244–256

Cultural Change and Adolescent Personality Development:

An Application of Longitudinal Sequences[1]

PAUL B. BALTES[2] AND JOHN R. NESSELROADE
West Virginia University

The relative contribution of ontogenetic versus generational change to adolescent personality development from 1970 to 1971 was examined. Using a series of 1-year longitudinal sequences as the basic design, a stratified random sample of 1,249 adolescents (cohorts 1953–1957) was measured both in 1970 and 1971 with Cattell's High School Personality Questionnaire. A 5 (Cohort) × 2 (Time) × 2 (Sex) analysis of variance was performed on each of the 14 trait dimensions. Results strongly support the conclusion that cross-sectional age differences are fallacious indicators of ontogenetic age change and that sequential strategies must be employed to disentangle ontogenetic from generational change components. Moreover, the data suggest that age-stage models are not appropriate for describing contemporary personality change during adolescence. On the contrary, the nature of adolescent trait change appears less dictated by age-related components than by the type of social change patterns which are setting the environmental milieu for adolescents of all ages over a given period of time.

In the past 10 years developmental psychologists have witnessed an increasing concern with analyzing the relationships between individual (ontogenetic) and historical (generational) development (e.g., Baltes, 1968; Schaie, 1965). Earlier developmental research was assumed to provide, for the most part, relatively robust information on ontogenetic patterns that held up in subsequent decades. Present cultural change, however, appears so rapid and pervasive that results from particular cross-sectional or longitudinal studies are threatened with obsolescence before they can be marketed for the scientific consumer. In fact, whereas such cultural acceleration phenomena were previously treated under the heading of secular trends (e.g., Bakwin, 1964; Muuss, 1970), present day evidence on the rate of changing ontogeny indicates that terms like "yearly" or "decennial" trends may be more appropriate (e.g., Baltes, Baltes, & Reinert, 1970; Baltes & Reinert, 1969; Nesselroade, Schaie, & Baltes, 1972; Schaie, 1972).

For two primary reasons, the area of adolescence seems to be a prime candidate for further study of the relationships between ontogenetic and generational change patterns. First, there is a rich body of data on secular trends in the rate of biological development during adolescence (e.g., Meredith, 1963; Muuss, 1970; Tanner, 1962) which indicates a general process of secular acceleration. Although these data are based on long-range comparisons of biological attributes, they suggest the existence of parallel phenomena in behavioral characteristics. In

[1] This study was supported by United States Office of Education Grant No. 09-580289-4415. The authors gratefully acknowledge the generous cooperation given by the county school superintendents and their assistants, by the school principals and teachers, and, certainly, by the students in the West Virginia counties of Harrison, Wetzel, and Wood. The authors also wish to express their appreciation for a job well done to Margret M. Baltes, John C. Friel, Erich W. Labouvie, and Nancy Reese who supervised the data collection and assisted in various phases of the data analysis.

[2] Requests for reprints should be sent to Paul B. Baltes, Division of Individual and Family Studies, Pennsylvania State University, University Park, Pennsylvania 16802

fact, researchers using time-lag designs (e.g., Broderick & Fowler, 1961; Greenstein, 1964; Harris, 1959; Jones, 1960) reported marked generational differences in adolescent attitudes and values. None of these studies, however, was based on the type of sequential designs necessary to disentangle ontogenetic from generational change components.

Second, a variety of propositions concerning the nature of adolescent development not only support the necessity of obtaining longitudinal data but also imply a marked sensitivity of adolescent change to environmental conditions. On the one hand there is the widely publicized, though inadequately supported, conception of adolescence as a period of intensive quantitative and qualitative change (e.g., Bandura, 1964). In a similar vein, it is sometimes argued that an age-stage model (e.g., Rogers, 1969), implying a fixed sequence of behavior changes and transitional periods, is useful in describing adolescent personality. On the other hand, various socioculturally oriented theorists (e.g., Coleman, 1970; Keniston, 1970; Muuss, 1962) emphasize an intricate relationship between societal and individual development throughout adolescence. Such a vantage point not only suggests that environmental conditions are important factors in shaping the nature of adolescence at a given point in time, but it also implies that historical change in cultural conditions may result in marked cohort differences in adolescent behavior.

In line with this reasoning, the present study is aimed at providing an initial examination of the effects of current cultural or societal change on adolescent personality development. Specifically, incorporating a strategy termed longitudinal sequences, the purpose of the research is to separate the relative contribution of ontogenetic (age-related) and generational (cohort-related) change during the period 1970–1971 in adolescents observed both in 1970 and 1971. The evidence obtained from the present investigation is also compared with that on adolescent personality development (e.g., Sealy & Cattell, 1966) based on cross-sectional methodology. Further, the findings presented will have significant bearing on assessing the general usefulness of age-stage hypotheses for describing personality development during adolescence.

Method

Design

The results reported here are based on a retest design (see Table 1) involving a 1-year longitudinal study (1970–1971) for each of five successive cohorts (1953, 1954, 1955, 1956, 1957). In addition, two groups of subjects were included to control for selective dropout and testing effects.

The first control group, whose data were used to examine the effect of repeated testing by means of a posttest-control design, consisted of a stratified random sample tested at the second occasion of measurement (1971) only. The second control group, necessary for assessing potential selective dropout effects and the generalizability of the findings, consisted of those subjects who participated in the 1970 but not in the 1971 occasion of measurement. Details on the age and sex distributions of the various subsamples are presented in Table 1.

Subjects and Procedure

The base population of subjects included some 20,000 students from all 32 junior high and high schools in three West Virginia counties located in the northwest area of the state. Selection of these counties was based on proximity to the authors' institution, cooperation of the school authorities involved, and general demographic characteristics. Census data suggest that none of the counties are considered part of West Virginia's underdeveloped region. The ratio of Caucasian to Negro population is about 95:5. A stratified (grade, homeroom unit, sex) random sample of about 2,100 students was drawn from the rosters in all 32 schools and asked (by letter) to volunteer for a study on the relationship between social change and personality development.

A total of 1,927 students participated in various phases of the study. The intact longitudinal sample consisted of 1,249 students or 75.9% of the sample ($N = 1,646$) asked to participate both in 1970 and 1971. Correspondingly, the dropout sample which served as a control group involved 24.1% of the students who, for various reasons, were not retested in 1971 (see Labouvie, Bartsch, Nesselroade, & Baltes, 1972, for an extensive discussion of testing and dropout effects). Finally, an additional 281 students formed the other control group tested for the first time at the second occasion of measurement (1971).

The 1970 and 1971 occasions of measurement each extended over a period of approximately 4 months (late fall till early spring). Thus, January 1 was taken as the approximate mean testing date for both occasions. Testing was done in classrooms during regular school periods. The testers were carefully trained and continuously supervised

TABLE 1

Distribution of Subjects by Cohort, Sex, and Condition

Cohort	Longitudinal sample 1970–1971				Dropout 1970–1971				Control 1971		Total N
	Male		Female		Male		Female		Male	Female	
	N	1970 age	N	1970 age	N	%	N	%	N	N	
1950					2						2
1951	4		1		4		5				14
1952	15		12		14		7		9	2	59
1953[a]	91	16-5	83	16-5	38	42	51	61	19	11	293
1954[a]	138	15-5	117	15-5	43	31	39	33	28	29	394
1955[a]	137	14-6	149	14-6	41	30	42	28	38	33	440
1956[a]	136	13-6	156	13-6	42	31	27	17	30	39	430
1957[a]	92	12-6	118	12-6	23	25	18	15	17	26	294
1958					0		1				1
Total N	613		636		207		190		141	140	1927

Note.—Ages (in years and months) are computed for 1970 time of measurement. Standard deviations range 3–4 months.
[a] Subjects used in the present cross-sequential analysis.

by either the project directors or their graduate research assistant. Total testing time was 4 hours, divided into one morning and one afternoon session.

Measurement Variables

The focus in selecting the measurement variables was on comprehensively mapping the personality sphere as conceptualized in trait models. Subjects were asked to respond both to Cattell's (1964) High School Personality Questionnaire (HSPQ, Form A) and Jackson's (1968) Personality Research Form (PRF, Form E). In addition, to mark the major dimensions of the ability domain, Thurstone and Thurstone's (1962) Primary Mental Abilities (PMA) battery was administered. Tests were always given in the order PMA, HSPQ, PRF, with the PRF using the second of the two 2-hour sessions.

The present report is restricted to the HSPQ results only. The HSPQ is the adolescent version of the Sixteen Personality Factor Questionnaire (16 PF, Cattell, Eber, & Tatsuoka, 1970), the latter being generally recognized as representing most distinctly the notion of convergence between a theory of personality structure and a corresponding set of measurement instruments. The HSPQ includes scales for 14 of the 16 PF dimensions, 8 of which are regarded as being affected by age development in late childhood and adolescence (Cattell & Cattell, 1969; Sealy & Cattell, 1966). Some evidence is also available on estimates of the relative contribution of hereditary versus environmental sources to observed variance in HSPQ dimensions (Cattell, Blewett, & Beloff, 1955). For example I, C, F, Q_2, and Q_4 were shown to be predominantly environmentally determined dimensions. Accordingly, one might hypothesize them to be particularly susceptible to social change, given the comparative stability of putative genetic determinants over the time span covered in the present research.

Data Analysis

Schaie (1965) proposed that data such as that reported here be analyzed by successive application of three sequential models (time sequential, cross-sequential, cohort sequential) in order to specify the relative contribution and substantive nature of the components (age, cohort, and time of measurement) involved in terms of either genetic (cohort), cultural (time of measurement), or maturational (age) correlates. Baltes (1968), however, has argued that such an analysis is not appropriate for two reasons: First, the three components are totally confounded. Second, variation of time characteristics per se does not allow for a specification of the substantive correlates producing the obtained component effects. In the same article it was proposed, therefore, that data collected by means of sequential strategies should not be analyzed with a focus on Schaie's (1965) "explanatory" developmental model. It was suggested, rather, that Schaie's model be regarded as a general design permitting only descriptive information on the relative impact of age- and cohort-related change patterns. From a data analysis perspective, unconfounded information about age and cohort effects can be obtained if data from at least three times of measurement are available.

In principle, the present data (representing only two occasions of measurement) would allow for either a cross-sequential (variation of cohort and time of measurement while confounding age) or a time-sequential (variation of age and time of measurement while confounding cohort) analysis. Since it has been argued previously (Baltes, 1968) that none of these models is necessarily superior in terms of substantive interpretations, additional criteria were examined, in choosing between the two options. One important aspect of the data which is particularly relevant to the study of change is the availability of 1-year longitudinal measurements which permits the use of within-subjects statistics and the computation of stability coefficients. Since use of a time-sequential model (holding age constant) would not permit taking advantage of repeated-measurement characteristics, it was decided to apply a cross-sequential model involving the cohorts 1955–1957 as shown in Table 1.

Specifically, the major analysis conducted on the longitudinal sample (see Table 1) consisted of 5 (Cohorts: 1953, 1954, 1955, 1956, 1957) × 2 (Time of Measurement: 1970, 1971) × 2 (Sex) analyses of variance performed for each of the 14 HSPQ dimensions (with repeated measurement on the time factor). Furthermore, 1-year stability coefficients (separately for cohort and sex levels) were computed for each of the 14 HSPQ dimensions.

Two additional analyses were conducted to assess potential selective dropout and testing effects. First, for the 1970 data only, 2 (Dropout versus Retestees) × 5 (Cohort) × 2 (Sex) designs were used to determine whether or not the longitudinal sample differed from the dropout sample on any of the 14 HSPQ dimensions. Second, an examination was conducted to ascertain whether apparent changes observed from 1970–1971 might be attributed to the effects of repeated testing. This involved comparing the second control group with the longitudinal sample, using only the 1971 data, in a series of 2 (Retestees versus Control) × 5 (Cohort) × 2 (Sex) analyses of variance; one for each of the 14 HSPQ dimensions.

Results

Overview

The principal results of the 14 analyses of variance are summarized in Table 2 which contains information on the main effects only, since just one of the interactions reached significance (Factor C). In addition, outcomes particularly relevant to an examination of the relative contribution of ontogenetic and generational change components (as indicated by cohort and/or time effects) are shown in Figures 1–7. In these figures are displayed (*a*) the two cross-sectional gradients derived from the 1970 and 1971 times of measurement and (*b*) the 1-year longitudinal gradients obtained for each of the five cohorts. Although this form of representation is not an exact replica of the analytic scheme, it provides a conveneint graphic framework in which the present findings can be related to research using simple cross-sectional or longitudinal methodology only. Keeping this restriction in mind (see Baltes, 1968, for an extensive discussion), what then is the relationship of the present effects to components of age- and generation-related change?

In the present design, time differences (between 1970 and 1971) are seen as the most acceptable indicators of "true" longitudinal, cohort-specific age change occurring over 1-year periods (12 years 6 months (12-6)–13-6, 13-6–14-6, etc.) for each of the five cohorts. Significant main effects of time were obtained for 7 (B, C, F, G, I, O, Q_3) of the 14 HSPQ dimensions. The interpretation of cohort differences is less satisfactory since the variation of cohort involves both 4-year differences in cohort (1953–1957) and age (13–17). Such cohort effects—indicative then of both generational and cross-sectional age differences—were obtained for a somewhat smaller number of

TABLE 2

F VALUES FROM ANALYSES OF VARIANCE OF LONGITUDINAL DATA

Dimension	Cohort	Sex	Time
A	1.3	166.5*	.4
B	7.1*	33.4*	46.7*
C	.8	136.8*	7.2*
D	2.4	.4	2.7
E	.8	700.5*	1.9
F	1.5	27.4*	36.5*
G	.5	39.2*	10.0*
H	.4	85.3*	.1
I	3.5*	1678.0*	12.9*
J	3.7*	79.5*	.0
0	2.1	31.0*	12.1*
Q_2	4.9*	211.5*	6.4
Q_3	.9	4.2	7.5*
Q_4	1.2	27.9*	1.2

Note.—The degrees of freedom associated with the various tests were 4 (cohort), 1 (sex), 4 (Cohort × Sex), 1 (time), 4 (Cohort × Time), 1 (Sex × Time), 4 (Cohort × Sex × Time), all tested against $df = 1{,}207$.
* $p < .01$.

dimensions (B, I, J, Q_2). None of the Cohort × Time interactions, nor any of the triple interactions, reached significance. The major share of accountable variance is clearly due to sex main effects which were significant for 12 of the 14 dimensions. This is an interesting developmental finding, but it is of secondary importance in the present report, except for the case of Factor C where a significant Sex × Time interaction was found.

In the following sections, the 14 HSPQ factors are briefly characterized. Each is designated by the descriptions for both their low (−) and high (+) pole. The specifications are taken from Cattell and Cattell (1969) who, in addition to the technical names, give popular terms to assist the less familiar reader with the meaning of the HSPQ factors. Subsequently, the results of the control analyses are presented which, for the most part, substantiate the internal validity of the main results.

Scale-Specific Results

Factor A. Factor A (A− = sizothymia: reserved, detached; A+ = affectothymia: warmhearted, outgoing) shows a strong main effect of sex only. Male adolescents are significantly lower ($\bar{X}$ = 9.65) than female adolescents ($\bar{X}$ = 11.96) on this dimension. The important implication for the present study is that this finding can be generalized to all ages and all cohorts. From a developmental perspective, this outcome suggests that strong sex differences on sizothymia-affectothymia emerge prior to age 12 and that these sex differences are maintained throughout adolescence.

Factor B. Factor B (B− = low intelligence: dull; B+ = high intelligence: bright) is a brief measure of general ability. It exhibits significant main effects of cohort, sex, and time. The main sex effect gives the females ($\bar{X}$ = 7.20) an edge over the males ($\bar{X}$ = 6.66). The relationship between cohort and time of testing is illustrated in Figure 1.

As expected, both cross-sectional gradients exhibit a systematic age-related "increase" in general intelligence which is a reflection of the significant main effect of cohort. Note, however, that the 1-year longitudinal gradients (reflecting a significant time effect) display

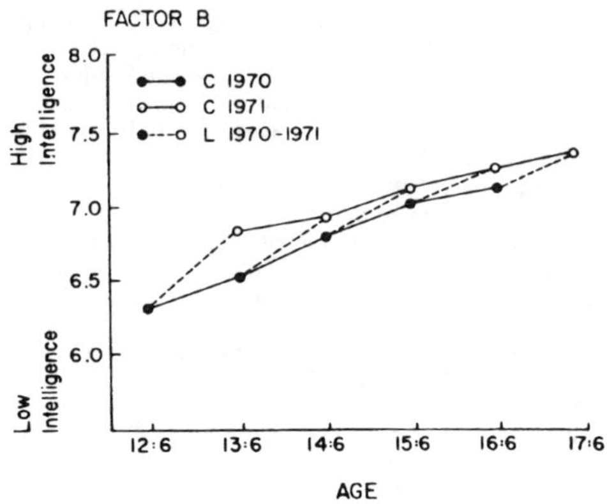

FIG. 1. Comparisons of cross-sectional with longitudinal gradients for Factor B.

sharper increments than the cross-sectional data as a result of the fact that all 1971 subjects excel their 1970 same-age counterparts.

These results are especially remarkable since the magnitude of 1-year longitudinal, cohort-specific age changes is comparable to the magnitude of about 2-year cross-cohort age differences. Consider, for example, the phenomenon that subjects at age 13-6 in 1971 perform on par with subjects at age 14-6 in 1970.

Factor C. Factor C (C− = low ego strength: affected by feelings, emotionally less stable; C+ = high ego strength: emotionally stable, mature) manifests three significant effects. The sex main effect gives evidence that male adolescents ($\bar{X}$ = 9.37) have significantly higher ego strength than females ($\bar{X}$ = 7.49). The time main effect indicates that, overall, adolescents in 1971 were more emotionally stable ($\bar{X}$ = 8.53) than in 1970 ($\bar{X}$ = 8.27).

In Figure 2, the cross-sectional and longitudinal gradients are shown separately for male and female adolescents to illustrate the significant Sex × Time interaction. It can be seen that the significant time effect (again reflecting 1-year longitudinal, cohort-specific age changes) holds true consistently only for males, for whom all five cohorts exhibit systematic age-related increments in ego strength. Female adolescents, however, except for those at ages 15-6 and 16-6 (born in 1954 and 1953, respectively), do not show

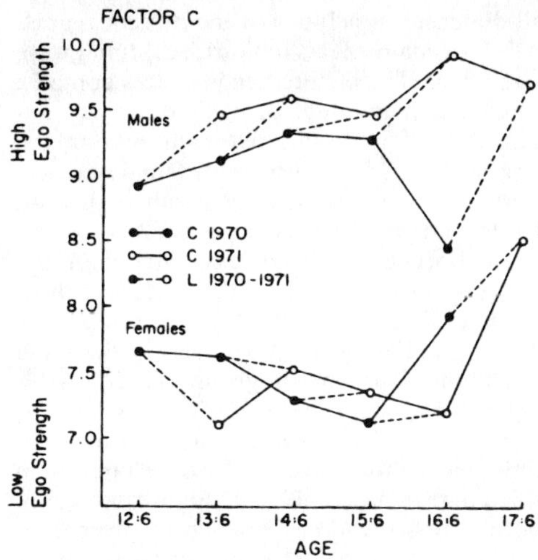

FIG. 2. Comparison of cross-sectional with longitudinal gradients for Factor C.

such age-related increments. Once more the cross-sectional gradients do not appear to be good indicators of longitudinal age changes. This conclusion is most clearly supported by the fact that no significant cohort effect was obtained, although the cohort levels comprise cross-sectional age differences between five yearly age groups (12-6–17-6).

Factor D. It is surprising that Factor D (D− = phlegmatic temperament: undemonstrative, deliberate; D+ = excitability: excitable, impatient) is not affected by any of the three design components. Most theoretical positions concerning adolescent development (e.g., Muuss, 1962) seem to imply that this period would show some changes on a dimension of phlegmatic temperament-excitability paralleling the reputed emotional crises associated with transitional periods and the acquisition of new social roles, etc. Apparently, however, the adolescent period is not the main normative period for the formation of individual differences in behaviors defining Factor D.

Factor E. Factor E (E− = submissiveness: obedient, mild; E+ = dominance: assertive, aggressive) shows a surprisingly similar picture. Although the highly significant main effect of sex, indicating that male adolescents ($\bar{X}$ = 10.38) are much more dominant than their female counterparts ($\bar{X}$ = 6.79), fits the standardization data and previous knowledge about sex differences on this dimension, it was unexpected that the age range 12-6–17-6 would show neither systematic ontogenetic nor generational change. Again, a possible interpretation is that the critical socialization period for the emergence of sex differences in this class of behavior lies before age 12.

Factor F. Factor F (F− = desurgency: sober, taciturn; F+ = surgency: enthusiastic, heedless) displays both a main effect of sex and time of measurement. The sex difference indicates that male adolescents exhibit more surgency ($\bar{X}$ = 10.43) than females ($\bar{X}$ = 9.49).

The main effect of time which again points to marked discrepancies between cross-sectional and longitudinal gradients is shown in Figure 3. Whereas both cross-sectional gradients give no evidence of age-related differences (as indicated by the absence of significant cohort effects), the five longitudinal gradients (reflecting the significant main effect of time of measurement) show a fairly consistent pattern in that all five cohorts display increments in Factor F over 1-year periods.

Factor G. Factor G (G− = weak superego stength: disregards rules, expedient; G+ = strong superego strength: conscientious, persistent) has the same statistical pattern as Factor F, that is, significant main effects

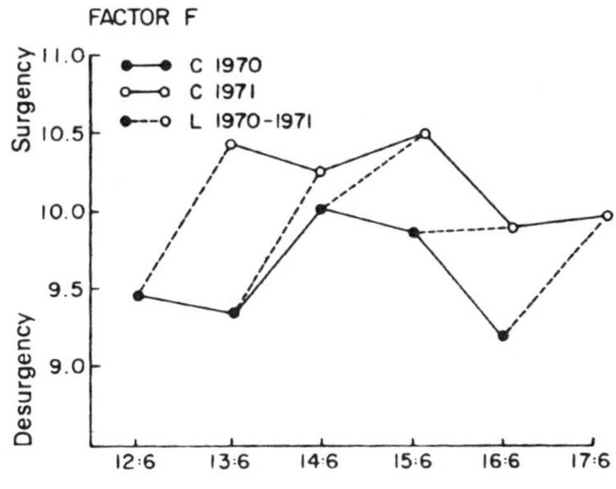

FIG. 3. Comparison of cross-sectional with longitudinal gradients for Factor F.

of both sex and time. The sex effect indicates that female adolescents ($\bar{X}$ = 11.27) have higher superego strength than male adolescents ($\bar{X}$ = 10.25).

Discrepancies between the two cross-sectional gradients (lack of cohort effects suggests no age differences) and the five 1-year longitudinal trends are illustrated in Figure 4. The latter, with the exception of the age period 15-6–16-6 (Cohort 1954), exhibit a fairly consistent pattern of age decrements in superego strength. This is particularly true for the two youngest cohort and/or age groups, although this inference is not supported statistically due to a lack of a significant Cohort × Time interaction.

Factor H. Factor H (H− = threctia: shy, timid; H+ = parmia: adventurous, thick-skinned) is another of those dimensions that, in contrast to common speculations about adolescents, does not show any significant cohort or time effects but only a strong main effect of sex. In line with socialization expectancies, higher values for male ($\bar{X}$ = 10.31) than for female ($\bar{X}$ = 8.69) adolescents obtain. Again, the absence of sex interactions and of other main effects implies that this sex difference develops prior to the youngest age level included in this study.

Factor I. Factor I (I− = harria: tough-minded, rejects illusions; I+ = premsia: tender-minded, sensitive), from the standpoint of significant effects, is the most complex of

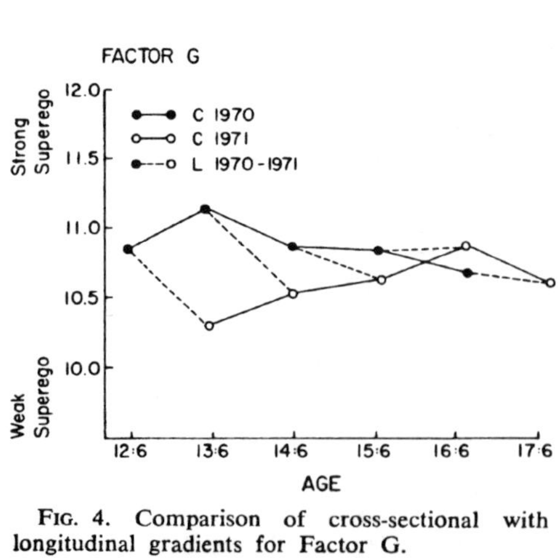

FIG. 4. Comparison of cross-sectional with longitudinal gradients for Factor G.

all dimensions included in the present report. All three main effects (cohort, sex, time) were significant. The picture becomes less complex when the magnitude of each effect is considered. Sex is associated with by far the largest share of variance, with female adolescents ($\bar{X}$ = 14.10) scoring much higher on Factor I than their male peers ($\bar{X}$ = 6.78). The cohort effect, though less strong than that for sex, indicates that the oldest cohort (16-6–17-6, born in 1953) exhibits a higher degree of Factor I ($\bar{X}$ = 11.03) than the remaining four cohort groups (1954, $\bar{X}$ = 9.97; 1955, $\bar{X}$ = 10.51; 1956, $\bar{X}$ = 10.73; 1957, $\bar{X}$ = 10.52). The relationship between time and cohort effects, of prime interest in this context, is graphed in Figure 5. Again, both cross-sectional gradients present a confusing picture. The longitudinal 1-year gradients, however, give a systematic and consistent pattern. All cohorts display an age-related decline on Factor I over this period indicating that, from 1970 to 1971, all subjects became more tough-minded.

Factor J. Factor J (J− = zeppia: zestful, liking group action; J+ = coasthenia: circumspect individualism, reflective) shows significant main effects of cohort and sex. The cohort effect signifies that the oldest cohort (1953 at ages 16-6–17-6) exhibits more coasthenia ($\bar{X}$ = 9.26) than all remaining cohorts (1954, $\bar{X}$ = 8.59; 1955, $\bar{X}$ = 8.35; 1956, $\bar{X}$ = 8.61; 1957, $\bar{X}$ = 8.50). However, the absence of any time effects would suggest that this difference is less due to adolescent age change than to generational differences. Not in line with common socialization expectations is the strong sex effect, with female adolescents lower ($\bar{X}$ = 7.89) on Factor J (i.e., more zestful, etc.) than their male peers ($\bar{X}$ = 9.29). Note again that the absence of any significant time effects implies that sex typing for Factor J occurs prior to age 12.

Factor O. Factor O (O− = untroubled adequacy: self-assured, placid; O+ = guilt proneness: apprehensive, self-reproaching) is another dimension that most adolescent theorists would assign a central role in adolescent development. The main effects of both sex and time were significant. The main effect of sex reflects the finding that females are higher ($\bar{X}$ = 9.97) on Factor O (more

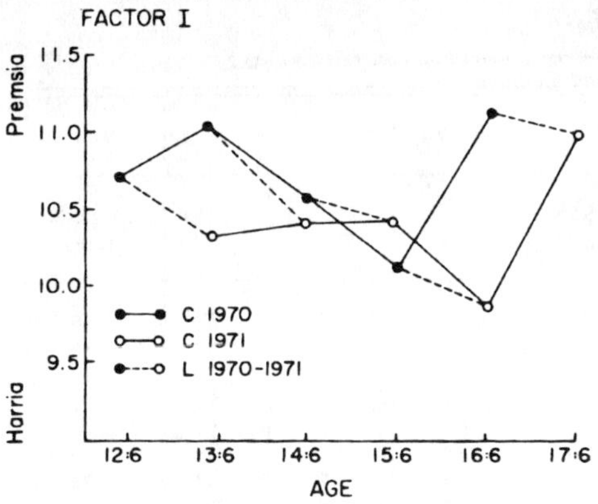

FIG. 5. Comparison of cross-sectional with longitudinal gradients for Factor I.

guilt prone) than males ($\bar{X}$ = 9.08). This is in agreement with most theoretical positions and empirical findings.

Figure 6, summarizing the time effect, shows a clear-cut pattern. Although the cross-sectional cohort/age differences were not significant, the five short-term longitudinal trends present convincing evidence for a systematic, cohort-specific, age-related change in the direction of adolescents becoming more self-assured than they were in the previous year.

Factor Q_2. Factor Q_2 (Q_2- = group dependency: socially group dependent; Q_2+ = self-sufficiency: self-sufficient, resourceful) produced main effects of both cohort and sex. Whereas the sex effect (males, $\bar{X}$ = 9.75; females, $\bar{X}$ = 7.37) is in accord with socialization goals in assigning higher priority for self-sufficiency to male adolescents than to females, Figure 7, in which the cohort effect is illustrated, is less consistent. On a descriptive level, the cohort effect suggests that the oldest cohort (1953 at ages 16-6 and 17-6) shows more self-sufficiency than the remaining cohorts. Although this effect makes sense in an ontogenetic framework, the lack of significant 1-year changes (time effect) seems to indicate again that this effect may be more a reflection of historical than ontogenetic components. This conclusion is supported by the fact that none of the cohorts exhibits a longitudinal trend that would suggest that the younger adolescents are "on their way up" to the level of self-sufficiency displayed by the oldest cohort.

Factor Q_3. Factor Q_3 (Q_3- = low self-sentiment integration: uncontrolled, lax; Q_3+ = high self-sentiment: controlled, exacting will power) exhibits a significant time effect only. The means indicate a decrease (adolescents became more lax and uncontrolled) from 1970 ($\bar{X}$ = 10.03) to

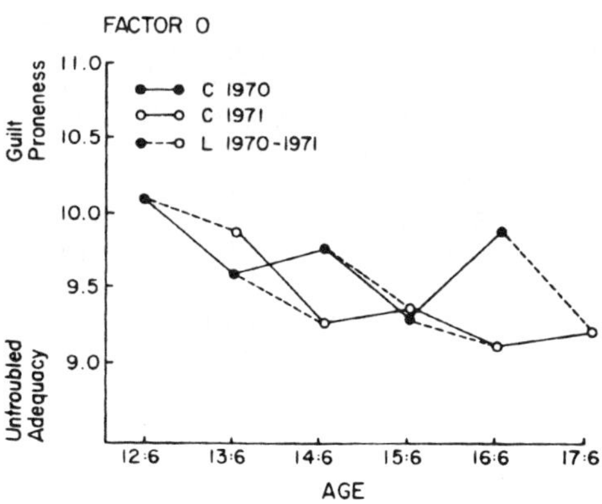

FIG. 6. Comparison of cross-sectional with longitudinal gradients for Factor O.

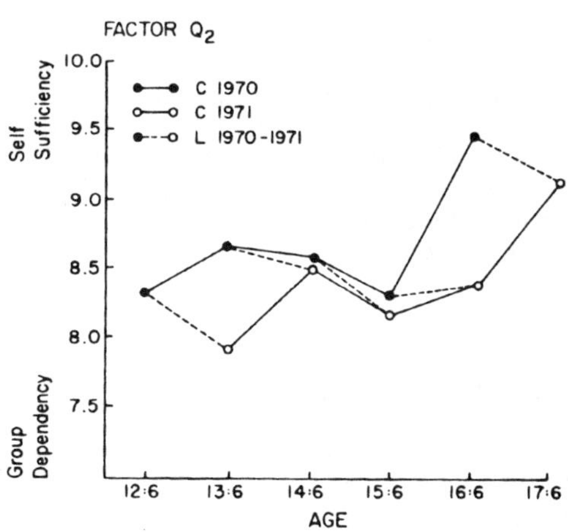

FIG. 7. Comparison of cross-sectional with longitudinal gradients for Factor Q_2.

TABLE 3

ONE-YEAR STABILITY COEFFICIENTS COMPUTED ACROSS COHORT (AGE) AND SEX

Dimension	Sex		Cohort					Criterion[a]
	Male	Female	1957 (12-6)	1956 (13-6)	1955 (14-6)	1954 (15-6)	1953 (16-6)	Immediate retest
A	50	55	47	54	58	64	62	86
B	54	53	48	53	58	54	58	85
C	43	49	49	40	51	58	52	79
D	46	50	44	47	45	54	51	81
E	35	40	53	56	54	59	56	76
F	47	56	47	49	54	58	55	82
G	49	53	48	48	50	57	62	74
H	41	56	43	45	49	61	64	89
I	57	58	76	80	78	81	83	90
J	37	40	40	43	34	44	49	82
O	33	44	41	47	30	47	31	84
Q_2	50	52	46	54	57	62	62	85
Q_3	34	46	35	39	40	44	49	80
Q_4	51	49	48	47	45	60	53	91

Note.—Decimal points are omitted. Mean ages are given for 1970 occasion of measurement. Levels of cohort and age comprise 1-year intervals.

[a] Immediate retest coefficients are based on 292 eleventh graders (from Cattell & Cattell, 1969).

1971 ($\bar{X}$ = 9.76). The resulting pattern of cross-sectional versus longitudinal gradients is similar to the results for Factor F shown in Figure 3.

Factor Q_4. For Factor Q_4 (Q_4- = low ergic tension: relaxed, tranquil; Q_4+ = high ergic tension: tense, driven) the only significant effect is sex, with female adolescents being more tense ($\bar{X}$ = 11.09) than the males ($\bar{X}$ = 10.18). Although this finding suggests that adolescence may be a more stressful period for girls than boys, the lack of any significant time or cohort effect implies that this sex difference exists for all age levels during adolescence and that the formation of such differences occurred prior to age 12.

Stability Coefficients

One-year stability (test-retest) coefficients, computed separately for each of the five cohorts (across sex) and each sex (across cohorts), are presented in Table 3. Cattell and Cattell (1969) reported fairly high immediate retest coefficients for the 14 HSPQ factors ranging from .74 (G) to .91 (Q_4). In Table 3 the 1-year stability coefficients may be compared with immediate retest coefficients contained in the HSPQ manual. It is obvious that 1-year stabilities are sufficiently lower than immediate retest coefficients to suggest that individual differences in HSPQ traits have not yet stabilized during adolescence. The degree of stability obtained varies with the traits and subsamples considered. Contrast, for example, the large discrepancy for immediate versus 1-year stabilities for Factor 0 with that for Factor I, where 1-year stabilities (when cohorts are considered) are barely distinguishable from immediate retest effects. A clear sex difference may be noted in that female adolescents (across cohorts) show higher stability coefficients than males on 12 of the 14 dimensions. Further, there is a pattern evident for subjects to exhibit slightly higher stability with increasing age, although this trend is less pronounced than expected and is restricted to a subset of traits (e.g., A, H, Q_3).

Control Analyses

A comprehensive treatment of the analyses for testing and dropout effects is presented elsewhere (Labouvie et al., 1972). The present discussion is restricted to salient and pertinent findings only.

The first examination of control group data involved comparing retest (1971) scores for the longitudinal group and initial scores for a control group in order to examine potential testing effects. The outcome of these comparisons was that for none of the 14 HSPQ scales was there a significant difference between the longitudinal and control group. Further, none of the possible interactions attained significance. Thus, these data support the conclusion that the differences between occasions of measurement exhibited by the longitudinal group are not attributable to testing effects.

The second control analysis was aimed at assessing potential selective dropout effects. The results of comparing the 1970 data of the longitudinal sample with the 1970 data of the dropout sample indicated a significant difference for only 3 of the 14 scales. Examination of means revealed that the dropouts are less intelligent (B), lower on superego strength (G), and lower on self-sentiment (Q_3) than their contemporaries in the longitudinal group. In addition, only 3 of the possible 42 interactions (Group × Sex, Group × Cohort, Group × Sex × Cohort) reached significance. Although these significant effects require that generalization from the longitudinal sample to the base population be appropriately qualified (primarily for B, G, and Q_3), the analysis suggests that the overall dropout effect is not strong enough to generally restrict the external validity of the findings.

Discussion

Since the investigation of the relationship between ontogenetic and generational change components is the primary objective of this study, the following discussion deals primarily with that issue. Although additional times of measurements are necessary to provide more complete and unconfounded information on the directionality and stability of the individual and historical change patterns observed, a number of conclusions appear warranted at the present time.

Cross-Sectional versus Longitudinal Data

In our judgment, the study presents convincing evidence that cohort differences play a major role in the development of adolescent personality. This outcome further substantiates the available evidence on cohort differences obtained with adult subjects (e.g., Nesselroade et al., 1972; Schaie & Strother, 1968). Correspondingly, the present results demonstrate that cross-cohort (cross-sectional) age gradients are fallacious indicators of true age changes.

In the present study, in all cases (Factors B, C, F, G, I, J, O, Q_2, and Q_3) where significant ontogenetic trends were found (in terms of either main or interaction effects of cohort and time of measurement), the cross-sectional gradients did not coincide with longitudinal trends. This outcome, however disconcerting to those developmentalists interested in the quick results obtainable from cross-sectional studies, very clearly supports the conclusion that the cross-sectional method is not an acceptable shortcut when describing developmental *change*. Instead, cross-sectional, cross-cohort age differences represent a confounding of ontogenetic and generational change and convey information about ontogenetic patterns that is clearly misleading. For example, the present data on 1-year longitudinal change in several cohorts contain little evidence to support either the usefulness of linear trend models espoused in the Sealy and Cattell (1966) article or the age correlations reported in the 1969 HSPQ manual, both of which are based on cross-sectional data.

Implications for Conceptions of Adolescent Personality

What is the relevance of the present results for conceptions of adolescent personality development?

Sex effects. Main effects of sex, attaining significance on 12 of the 14 dimensions, contributed the major accountable share of the observed variance. An interesting byproduct, however, is that only 1 of the 28 Sex × Cohort or Sex × Time interactions reached significance, indicating that the adolescent period (1970–1971) did not contain significant influences in the shaping (accentuating or redirecting) of sex differences in personality traits. In fact, the pervasiveness of the observed sex differences suggests that the major normative period for the emergence of sex differences lies somewhere before age 12. Recognition of historical change components, however, alerts us to add that this phenomenon may be restricted to the cohorts (1953–1957) and time period (1970–1971) considered.

Stability coefficients. Sex- and cohort (age)-related differences in trait stability coefficients were not as conspicuous as expected. The more salient information appears to involve the marked differences in the degree of 1-year trait stability, despite satisfactory short-term stability indexes.

The authors (Baltes & Nesselroade, 1972) view stability not as a phenomenon that is necessarily desirable from a statistical viewpoint but, rather, as one that conveys important substantive information for developmental considerations (see also Bloom, 1964). Neglecting issues involved in age-correlated activation of genetic mechanisms, the authors have argued that the degree of stability of a given class of behavior provides information about the stability of the environmental fields to which individuals are exposed during the time interval considered. In the present context, such an environment-oriented approach to the interpretation of stability coefficients leads to two conclusions. First, the moderate degree of stability and the lack of any substantial age-related increase in stability suggests that subject-related differences in environmental fields associated with personality trait formation do not show further developmental (age-related) accentuation during adolescence. Second, the marked differences in trait stability (despite comparable and satisfactory short-term stability) points to the notion that the environment consists of multiple fields that differ in degree of stability. Despite the presence of significant ontogenetic and generational change components, Factor I (tough-minded), for example, is the most stable of all traits considered, suggesting high stability of subject-related environmental field differences. Yet other dimensions (e.g., D, E, H), exhibiting no significant ontogenetic or generational trends, show lower stabilities which reflect in our view, greater subject-related variation in socialization influences. It appears worthwhile to consider such stability differentials in future searches for the key antecedents underlying the developmental history of trait patterns during adolescence. Unfortunately, since the present study does not contain any information on time-related changes in environmental conditions, we could only speculate about the general nature of the social ecology characterizing the time period from 1970 to 1971.

Age-stage models. Finally, the impact of generational differences argues strongly against the usefulness of universal, stagelike models of adolescent personality development, at least within Cattell's framework of personality structure. Thus, there is no evidence for invariant and robust adolescent trends characteristic of conceptions that favor stage-type approaches in the organization of adolescent development. In contrast, the present results suggest that the average standing of adolescents on personality dimensions is less dependent upon their chronological age than upon the time (cultural moment) at which they are measured. Witness, for example, that in many cases same-age subjects measured in different years are less similar than different-age subjects measured in the same year.

This position, delegating a lesser role to the age sequence per se but a major role to patterns of cultural change, is in agreement with a number of heretofore largely speculative propositions. There are various social and anthropological interpretations of adolescence (see Muuss, 1962, for review) which focus on the cultural specificity and sociological determination of adolescent change phenomena. The authors feel, however, that none of these theoretical propositions would have assumed that 1-year cohort differences would be of the magnitude reported here. Indeed, the present results present a serious challenge to those conceptions of adolescence that (*a*) decree development to be a largely invariant sequence of systematic transitions in personality and (*b*) represent adolescence as a period that implies invariant, normative developmental determinants for later ontogeny.

We realize, of course, that only further research (involving additional occasions, alternative measurement frameworks, disparate cultural milieus, etc.) will provide critical information about the generality of the conclusions. It is hoped, however, that the present findings will stimulate such research and also be helpful in guiding future endeavors aimed at more fine-grained analyses of the mechanisms involved in the developmental linkage of ontogenetic and historical change components.

REFERENCES

BAKWIN, H. The secular change in growth and development. *Acta Paediatrica,* 1964, **53,** 79–89.

BALTES, P. B. Longitudinal and cross-sectional sequences in the study of age and generation effects. *Human Development,* 1968, **11,** 145–171.

BALTES, P. B., BALTES, M. M., & REINERT, G. The relationship between time of measurement and age in cognitive development of children: An application of cross-sectional sequences. *Human Development,* 1970, **13,** 258–268.

BALTES, P. B., & NESSELROADE, J. R. The developmental analysis of individual differences on multiple measures. In J. R. Nesselroade & H. W. Reese (Eds.), *Life-span developmental psychology: Methodological issues.* New York: Academic Press, 1972.

BALTES, P. B., & REINERT, G. Cohort effects in cognitive development of children as revealed by cross-sectional sequences. *Developmental Psychology,* 1969, **1,** 169–177.

BANDURA, A. The stormy decade: Fact or fiction? *Psychology in the Schools,* 1964, **1,** 224–231.

BLOOM, B. S. *Stability and change in human characteristics.* New York: Wiley, 1964.

BRODERICK, C. B., & FOWLER, S. E. New patterns of relationships between the sexes among preadolescents. *Marriage and Family Living,* 1961, **23,** 27–30.

CATTELL, R. B. *The High School Personality Questionnaire.* Champaign, Ill.: Institute for Personality and Ability Testing, 1964.

CATTELL, R. B., BLEWETT, D. B., & BELOFF, J. R. The inheritance of personality: A multiple variance analysis determination of approximate nature-nurture ratios for primary personality factors in Q-data. *American Journal of Human Genetics,* 1955, **7,** 122–146.

CATTELL, R. B., & CATTELL, M. D. L. *Handbook for the Jr.-Sr. High School Personality Questionnaire "HSPQ."* Champaign, Ill.: Institute for Personality and Ability Testing, 1969.

CATTELL, R. B., EBER, H. W., & TATSUOKA, M. M. *Handbook for the Sixteen Personality Factor Questionnaire.* Champaign, Ill.: Institute for Personality and Ability Testing, 1970.

COLEMAN, J. S. Interpretations of adolescent culture. In J. Zubin & A. M. Freedman (Eds.), *The psychopathology of adolescence.* New York: Grune & Stratton, 1970.

GREENSTEIN, F. I. New light on changing American values: A forgotten body of survey data. *Social Forces,* 1964, **42,** 441–450.

HARRIS, D. B. Sex differences in the life problems and interests of adolescents, 1935 and 1957. *Child Development,* 1959, **30,** 453–459.

JACKSON, D. N. *Personality research form.* Goshen, N. Y.: Research Psychologists Press, 1968.

JONES, M. C. A comparison of the attitudes and interests of ninth grade students over two decades. *Journal of Educational Research,* 1960, **51,** 175–186.

KENISTON, K. Postadolescence (youth) and historical change. In J. Zubin & A. M. Freedman (Eds.), *The psychopathology of adolescence.* New York: Grune & Stratton, 1970.

LABOUVIE, E. W., BARTSCH, T. W., NESSELROADE, J. R., & BALTES, P. B. The effects of testing and selective drop-out on longitudinal measures of intelligence and personality in adolescence. Unpublished manuscript West Virginia University, 1972.

MEREDITH, H. V. Change in the stature and body weight of North American boys during the last 80 years. In L. P. Lipsitt & C. C. Spiker (Eds.), *Advances in child development and behavior.* Vol. 1. New York: Academic Press, 1963.

MUUSS, R. E. *Theories of adolescence.* New York: Random House, 1962.

MUUSS, R. E. Adolescent development and the secular trend. *Adolescence,* 1970, **5,** 267–284.

NESSELROADE, J. R., SCHAIE, K. W., & BALTES, P. B. Ontogenetic and generational components of structural and quantitative change in adult cognitive behavior. *Journal of Gerontology,* 1972, **27,** 222–228.

ROGERS, D. Stage theory and critical period as related to adolescence. In D. Rogers (Ed.), *Issues in adolescent psychology.* New York: Appleton-Century-Crofts, 1969.

SCHAIE, K. W. A general model for the study of developmental problems. *Psychological Bulletin,* 1965, **64,** 92–107.

SCHAIE, K. W. Limitations on the generalizability of growth curves of intelligence: A re-analysis of some data from the Harvard Growth Study. *Human Development,* 1972, **15,** in press.

SCHAIE, K. W., & STROTHER, C. R. A cross-sectional study of age changes in cognitive behavior. *Psychological Bulletin,* 1968, **70,** 671–680.

SEALY, A. P., & CATTELL, R. B. Adolescent personality trends in primary factors measured on the 16 PF and the HSPQ Questionnaires through ages 11–23. *British Journal of Social and Clinical Psychology,* 1966, **5,** 172–184.

TANNER, J. M. *Growth at adolescence.* Oxford: Blackwell Publications, 1962.

THURSTONE, L. L., & THURSTONE, T. G. *SRA Primary Mental Abilities.* Chicago: Science Research Associates, 1962.

(Received March 27, 1972)

Amer. J. Orthopsychiat. 64(1), January 1994

CONTINUITY AND DISCONTINUITY IN THE AFFECTIVE EXPERIENCES OF PARENTS AND CHILDREN: Evidence From the New York Longitudinal Study

Jonathan G. Tubman, Ph.D., and Richard M. Lerner, Ph.D.

Canonical correlation described continuity and discontinuity in salient covariates of emotional and interactional components in parent-child relationships among NYLS participants from middle adolescence to young adulthood. The results underscore the importance of multiple indicators of parent-child relationship quality, and their implications for assessment and intervention efforts are discussed.

An extensive body of research has sought, across a wide variety of disciplinary orientations and investigative methodologies, to examine systematically the quality of parent-child relations in adolescence *(Montemayor, 1983; Steinberg, 1989)*. Many have equated relationship quality with parent-adolescent conflict. Descriptive studies of the course or content of parent-adolescent conflict have examined facets of the same phenomenon via such methods as large-scale social surveys of attitudes *(Bengtson & Black, 1973; Kandel & Lesser, 1969; Offer, Ostrov, & Howard, 1981)*, questionnaires regarding sources of conflict *(Caplow, Bahr, Chadwick, Hill, & Williamson, 1982; Eyberg & Robinson, 1983; Harris & Howard, 1984)*, observation of connections among sequences of behavior and conflict *(Forehand, 1990; Patterson, 1982; Steinberg, 1981)*, and observation of processes of communication and negotiation in conflict situations *(Grotevant & Cooper, 1985; Hauser et al., 1984; Kendall, 1991)*. Thus, parent-adolescent conflict has been measured via a variety of methods and levels of analysis.

Normative developmental transformations in parent-child relationships as children attempt to develop their own identities or "individuate" from their parents in late adolescence have been portrayed as sources of conflict. Traditional psychodynamic formulations of the development of autonomy among adolescents have emphasized the importance of establishing independent emotional relationships with parents after puberty and the intensification of relationships with peers, especially those of the opposite sex *(Blos, 1967; Freud, 1958; Murphy, Silber, Coelho, Hamburg, & Greenberg, 1963)*. In contrast, Stierlin *(1981)* developed a more balanced formula that integrated parents' desires for continuity in relationships with adolescents' desires for separation. Other investigators have sought formulations of normative developmental processes that would accommodate both growing psychological and physical separation between parents and children and

A revised version of a paper submitted to the Journal in November 1992. Research was supported in part by grant MH39957 from the National Institute of Mental Health. Authors are at: Florida International University, Miami (Tubman); and Institute for Children, Youth, and Families, Michigan State University, East Lansing (Lerner).

continuity in processes of mutual influence, affection, association, and respect *(Grotevant & Cooper, 1986; Hill & Holmbeck, 1986; Smollar & Youniss, 1989)*. These formulations took into account continuity and discontinuity in various aspects of social relations as they are renegotiated, as well as reciprocal relations between parents and children.

Research regarding continuity-discontinuity in the process of individuation of adolescents from parents has considered the functional significance of conflict in parent-child relations *(Cooper, 1988; Steinberg, 1989)*. Some studies have suggested that family communication processes, e.g., expression of viewpoints and disagreements, predict adolescent identity formation, perspective-taking, and conflict-resolution skills *(Cooper, 1988; Grotevant & Cooper, 1985, 1986)*. Other research has documented associations between progressive discourse change among family members and adolescents' levels of ego development *(Hauser et al., 1984)*, links between parenting styles and adolescent social competence *(Baumrind, 1978)*, and relationships between the renegotiation of parent-child relations and adolescents' cognitive development and level of reasoning *(Smetana, 1988)*. In addition, Steinberg *(1989)* has speculated that parent-child conflict in adolescence may have an evolutionary basis in that it forces adolescents to seek sexual partners outside of the family of origin and encourages autonomy among adolescent males. While conceptualizations of individuation and its functional significance may differ among these researchers, adolescent development is typically seen as occurring in the context of ongoing parent-child relations within which "individuality and connectedness" are negotiated *(Grotevant & Cooper, 1986; Smollar & Youniss, 1989)*.

To the extent that contemporary research on parent-adolescent relations has focused on conflict between parents and children, it has given greater priority to the developmental course of parent-adolescent conflict and to categorizing families in terms of their level of conflict. Assessing the quality of parent-child relationships as a whole has been given less priority. However, as Montemayor *(1986)* has argued, families cannot simply be dichotomized on the dimension of parent-child conflict because parent-child dyads vary in the amount of conflict expressed. Parent-adolescent conflict has been found to vary systematically with family social context and structure, parent and child characteristics, and styles of parent-child interaction *(Montemayor, 1986; Smetana, Yau, Restrepo, & Braeges, 1991)*. In contrast, the issues about which parents and children generally experience conflict have remained essentially the same for decades *(Montemayor, 1983)*. Therefore, while distinctions on the basis of conflict may be useful in contrasting clinical and nonclinical samples, they accord too much importance to conflict as a component of the normative developmental course of parent-adolescent relations. This observation may be particularly pertinent if parent-child relations are to be studied into young adulthood when the likelihood of conflict over "normal, everyday, mundane family matters" *(Montemayor, 1983)* decreases due to the increasing physical and psychological separation between parents and children.

Thus, in describing the normative developmental course of parent-child relations from adolescence to young adulthood, it may be more fruitful to assess parent and child perceptions of relationships than to classify families by preexisting monolithic definitions. Frank, Avery, and Laman *(1988)* employed in-depth interviewing techniques to obtain multivariate assessments of autonomy and relatedness in relationships between young adults and their parents. This study derived several dimensions of relationship experiences in reports by the young adults; significant associations between these dimensions and children's age, sex, and marital status; and the identification of several theoretically relevant types of parent-child relationships. This study is an excellent example of how participants' own perceptions can be used to explore individual differences in multiple dimensions of parent-child relationships.

Unfortunately, most extant studies of self-perceptions of parent-child relationships in middle to late adolescence are cross-sectional or short-term longitudinal in design. This may limit the description of continuity-discontinuity in relationship ratings, the identification of concurrent or antecedent covariates of these ratings, and the description of parent or child characteristics associated with relationship quality. By further exploring individual differences in parents' and adolescent children's ratings of their relationships, using the resources of the New York Longitudinal Study (NYLS), the present report seeks to provide initial long-term longitudinal data about the continuity-discontinuity of parent and child perceptions, concurrent-antecedent covariates, and the clinical relevance of identified covariates. Variables used in this report were identified as relevant to the quality of parent-child relationships in earlier qualitative treatments of NYLS data; they include child temperament, childhood negative emotional-behavioral states, early parent-child relationship problems, and young adult psychiatric symptoms *(Chess & Thomas, 1984; 1986; Thomas & Chess, 1977)*.

METHOD

Participants

Participants were the 133 middle-class children from the NYLS sample *(Thomas & Chess, 1977)*. The sample is over 99% white and predominantly (78%) Jewish. All participants were initially studied in their first weeks of life, and have been followed at regular intervals since *(Chess & Thomas, 1984)*. The NYLS employs a sample of convenience, as all participant families were previously acquainted with the study's founders or with their professional colleagues. Of importance to the present report are the adolescent interviews at 16–17 years, the college-age interviews at 18–23 years, and the young-adult interviews at 25–31 years. Sample recruitment began in 1956 and ended in 1962. By 1984, 24 of the original 84 families had experienced divorce, affecting 34 of the 133 target children (25.6%). The sample has remained intact throughout the study, with a participation rate among target children of 97% (N=129) in the latest wave of data collection, completed in 1987.

Measures

Affective experience ratings. Ratings of parent-child relationships were constructed for mothers and fathers separately, and for both parents combined (see below) at the adolescent and college-age interviews; parents were not systematically interviewed at the time of the young-adult interviews. Children's relationship ratings were constructed at the adolescent, college-age, and young-adult interviews. Ratings of or by both parents differ from those of or by mothers and fathers separately in that they were constructed from statements attributed to both parents in an interview or from statements made by a child about both parents. Emotional Quality was rated on a three-point scale: positive (3); mixed, variable, ambivalent, or neutral (2); and negative (1). Interaction Quantity was also rated on a three-point scale: high (3), medium (2), and low (1).

Data were generated following a method employed by Thomas, Chess, Birch, Hertzig, and Korn *(1963)*. At each time of testing, statements were excerpted as thematic units from interviews if they contained any text that referred either to emotional aspects of parent-child relations (e.g., closeness or distance, love or hate, conflict and tension, or evaluations of the other person that included an emotional component) or to the interactional aspects of these relationships (e.g., giving advice, sharing problems, expressing feelings, making decisions, and the performance of joint activities).

Other than those referring to a change in a relationship between past and present, all statements pertained to the present, or to the past month. All generated statements were rendered anonymous and gender-nonspecific in references to NYLS children.

Reliability estimates of the thematic statement generation process were based on a randomly selected 15% of the five waves of transcripts, as measured by the number of times two individuals generated the same thematic statements; estimates ranged from 86% to 94%. A total of 7,912 thematic statements were generated and were then rated randomly by three of five raters. If two of the three raters did not rate a statement for at least one dimension, as happened with 2.2% of statements, it was discarded. Interrater reliability, the number of times at least two of the three raters agreed for each dimension, was 89.6% for emotional quality and 88.2% for interaction quantity for a randomly selected sample of 20% of the statements. Summary scores for each dimension were constructed by averaging across statements the modal ratings (by the three raters) for each child and parent at each time of data collection.

Missing data from parent and child ratings, which stemmed primarily from the process of statement generation (i.e., participants' lack of elaboration about parent-child relations) rather than from missing subjects, were estimated using least-squares estimates *(Little & Rubin, 1987; Rovine & Delaney, 1990)*. The amount of data estimated varied by time of measurement and by source of rated statements, ranging from 3.6% to 35.4%, with an average of 16.2%. Emotional quality and interaction quantity rating means, standard deviations, and intercorrelations did not differ statistically before and after data estimation.

Temperament. Through scores derived from coded interview responses, each participant's temperament, or behavioral style, was measured in middle adolescence, at college age, and in young adulthood. Nine dimensions of temperament were assessed at each point, following Thomas and Chess *(1977)*. The temperament domains and their definitions from Chess and Thomas *(1984)* were: *1)* Activity Level, the motor component present in functioning and the diurnal proportion of active and inactive periods; *2)* Rhythmicity, the predictability of biological functioning; *3)* Adaptability, responses to new or altered situations, and the ease with which those responses are modified; *4)* Approach/Withdrawal, the nature of an initial response to a new stimulus, be it a person, place, or thing; *5)* Threshold of Responsiveness, the intensity level of stimulation that is necessary to evoke a discernible response; *6)* Intensity of Reaction, the energy level of response, regardless of its quality or direction; *7)* Quality of Mood, the amount of pleasant versus unpleasant behavior; *8)* Distractibility, the effectiveness of extraneous environmental stimuli in interfering with or altering ongoing behavior; and *9)* Persistence, the continuation of an activity direction in the face of obstacles to its continuation.

At each time of testing relevant to this report, temperament scores were obtained for each participant from responses to standard questions posed in face-to-face interviews with an NYLS psychiatrist (e.g., Thomas, Chess, or others). The interviews were standard across the three points of measurement and followed a semistructured, two- to three-hour protocol, generally conducted in a participant's home or the interviewer's office. Temperament scores ranged from low (1) to high (7), and reflected clinicians' ratings of participants' temperament determined from their responses to questions in the face-to-face interview. The exact procedures for these interviews and the techniques used for coding and for establishing reliability have been reported in numerous publications *(Chess & Thomas, 1984; Lerner, Hertzog, Hooker, Hassibi, & Thomas, 1988; Thomas & Chess, 1977)*. For the college-age interviews, an analysis of pooled interrater reliabilities (within time correlations) for

24 randomly selected interviews found moderate reliabilities (range .54 to .76) for eight of the nine temperament dimensions. One attribute (intensity), however, had a low (.33) pooled reliability *(Chess & Thomas, 1984)*. In young adulthood, an analysis of 24 randomly selected interviews found simple (i.e., uncorrected) interrater reliabilities in the moderate range (.42 to .78) for seven temperament attributes and low uncorrected interrater reliabilities for Activity Level (.30) and Distractibility (.26) *(Thomas, Chess, Lerner, & Lerner, 1989)*.

Adjustment in childhood. Evidence of poor psychological adjustment of the sample was rated by NYLS psychiatrists on a five-point scale for 11 dimensions at age three, from insignificant (1) to severe (5). The 11 dimensions from the age-three parent interviews were: sleeping; eating; elimination; fears, tics, and rituals; speech and communication; motor activity; relationship with parents; discipline; relationship with siblings; relationship with nonfamily persons; and coping and task mastery. Relationship to school was added as a twelfth dimension at the age-five parent interview. Each dimension was composed of a series of items rated individually and then averaged. Global adjustment scores at ages three and five were derived by adding the average score for each dimension and dividing by the number of dimensions. Therefore, the scores for global adjustment at ages three and five may be decomposed into scores for more specific domains of adjustment. Scores generated for the 11 adjustment dimensions at age three had interrater reliabilities (within time correlations) above .80 for seven of the dimensions, and reliabilities of .75 for sleep; .68 for fears, tics, and rituals; .64 for sleeping; and .32 for coping. At age five, all 12 adjustment dimensions had interrater reliabilities above .88 *(Chess & Thomas, 1984)*.

Negative emotional or behavioral states. Negative emotional or behavioral states (NEBS) for the childhood years were coded by an independent psychiatrist employing an inductive content analysis of the NYLS childhood interviews with parents and teachers; for details of procedure and scoring see Chess and Thomas *(1984)*, Lerner et al. *(1988)*, and Thomas and Chess *(1977)*. These interviews contained detailed descriptions of the child's behavior in the home and in school. For ages one through six, ratings were made for anxiety, aggressiveness, undercompliance, dissatisfaction, and problematic peer relations. For ages seven through 12, ratings were assigned for anxiety, depressive mood, aggressiveness, disobedience in the home, academic difficulties, and excessive parental physical punishment. Each behavior was scored as not present (0), mild (1), moderate (2), or severe (3). When a negative emotional or behavioral state was indicated in two interviews over a six-month interval by parents, it was given a score of one. When, in addition to reports by parents, teachers also indicated the presence of a negative state, the intensity was given a score of two. Finally, when both parents and teachers reported negative emotional behavioral states in interviews from two consecutive years, the intensity was given a score of three *(Lerner et al., 1988)*. These NEBS ratings have shown considerable internal predictive validity in prior analyses. For example, the NEBS categories of anxiety and aggression have stability coefficients of .97 and .91, respectively, for ages one through six and seven through 12. In terms of external validity, childhood problems such as high anxiety and high aggressiveness were predictive of adjustment problems in adolescence *(Lerner et al., 1988)*.

Young adult psychiatric symptoms. In the young-adult interview, participants were asked to describe any psychological symptoms, psychosomatic symptoms, or thought disturbances they were currently experiencing. Reported symptoms were placed by a psychiatrist in the following categories: anxiety, depression, thought disorders, passive-dependency, aggressiveness, mood disorders, motor disturbances, speech disorders, psychosomatic symptoms, and other symptoms. Like the childhood NEBS ratings, psychiatric symptom ratings in young adulthood were meant to index serious underlying adjustment problems. Symptom categories were rated on a four-point scale as not present (0), mild (1), moderate (2), or severe (3). Motor disturbances were not included in this study because none of the participants reported them in young adulthood.

Analyses

Canonical correlation was used to assess multivariate associations among sets of *a)* affective experience ratings and *b)* clinically relevant variables at occasions of measurement from early childhood to young adulthood. This technique was selected to identify features of parents and children that were linked to specific relationship ratings by mothers, fathers, or children both within and across times of measurement *(Tatsuoka, 1988)*. Canonical correlation determines linear combinations (underlying dimensions, or canonical variates) in each of two sets of variables that are most highly correlated with one another without being correlated with additional, smaller linear combinations within either set of variables. The meaning of each canonical variate can be indirectly interpreted by examining the degree to which the original observed variables are correlated with their canonical variates, i.e., via canonical structure *(Levine, 1977)*.

TABLES 3 through 6 summarize canonical correlations between sets of relationship ratings during adolescence and sets of parent or child characteristics. These tables show canonical correlations and all variables correlated .40 or greater with their canonical variates; for each significant canonical correlation analysis, only one canonical correlation was significant. These tables also contain summary data from redundancy analyses of each canonical correlation. Total redundancy coefficients indicate the amount of variance in each set of variables that may be accounted for by all canonical variates, significant and insignificant, of the opposite set of variables *(Levine, 1977)*. Therefore, for each of two variable sets, each table contains the structure of an underlying dimension, the correlation between these underlying dimensions, and the amount of variance in each dimension that may be accounted for by the other.

RESULTS

Relationship Ratings

Content. TABLES 1 and 2 summarize the means and standard deviations in relationship ratings of mothers, fathers, parents, and children from middle adolescence to

Table 1

CHILD AND PARENT AFFECTIVE EXPERIENCE RATINGS: EMOTIONAL QUALITY

	CHILD RATINGS			PARENT RATINGS		
EMOTIONAL QUALITY	*N*	*M*	*SD*	*N*	*M*	*SD*
Mothers						
Adolescence	101	1.99	0.59	101	1.98	0.45
College age	131	1.96	0.61	131	1.98	0.55
Young adulthood	119	2.10	0.60			
Fathers						
Adolescence	96	2.05	0.65	96	2.03	0.59
College age	122	1.95	0.60	122	2.06	0.56
Young adulthood	110	2.02	0.69			
Parents						
Adolescence	96	2.16	0.45	96	1.99	0.46
College age	121	1.99	0.52	120	1.86	0.50
Young adulthood	107	1.81	0.42			

Note. Emotional Quality statements rated 1 (negative), 2 (mixed, variable, ambivalent, or neutral), or 3 (positive).

college age. In general, the means of these ratings may be characterized as stable. Between the adolescent and the college-age interviews none of the mean ratings of mothers, fathers, or parents fluctuated more than 0.14 on a scale of 1 to 3. Differences of this magnitude did not appear to be psychosocially significant. In addition, within times of measurement, mean ratings of emotional quality and interaction quantity of mothers, fathers, and parents did not vary by more than 0.20. Across target parent(s) within occasions of measurement, mean ratings by children ranged between 0.04 and 0.29. Across times of measurement, mean ratings did not range widely. The greatest difference across time was 0.35 for emotional quality ratings of children's statements about parents. However, differences were generally 0.20 or less. Few (two out of ten) significant gender differences were found in parents' ratings of children or in children's ratings of parents (two out of 18) *(Tubman, 1990)*. Therefore, additional analyses were conducted using the total sample rather than by child's gender.

Covariates. TABLE 3 summarizes information about significant associations among children's temperamental characteristics and parent and child relationship ratings in adolescence and at college age. Several temperamental characteristics, in particular adaptability and mood quality, were associated with emotional quality and interaction quantity ratings. Positive mood quality and higher adaptability were consistently associated with higher relationship ratings. Canonical variates representing emotional quality in adolescence and at young adulthood and interaction quantity in adolescence were most highly correlated with fathers' and parents' ratings of children and with children's ratings of fathers in adolescence, as well as with nearly all relationships ratings at college age. Therefore, two dimensions of temperament can be identified as significant covariates in adolescence and at college age of child and parent reports, especially those of fathers, of the emotional and interactional components of parent-child relationships.

Significant relationships among childhood NEBS ratings and parent-child relationship ratings in adolescence and at college age are summarized in TABLE 4. NEBS ratings for anxiety, aggressiveness, disobedience, and academic difficulties for years seven through 12 were significantly intercorrelated. A similar cluster of preschool emotional and behavioral symptoms was identified among NEBS ratings for years one to six (i.e., anxiety, aggressiveness, peer relations, and under-compliance). These clus-

Table 2

CHILD AND PARENT AFFECTIVE EXPERIENCE RATINGS: INTERACTION QUANTITY

	CHILD RATINGS			PARENT RATINGS		
EMOTIONAL QUANTITY	*N*	*M*	*SD*	*N*	*M*	*SD*
Mothers						
Adolescence	101	1.74	0.50	101	1.73	0.39
College age	131	1.68	0.53	131	1.73	0.50
Young adulthood	119	1.84	0.56			
Fathers						
Adolescence	95	1.60	0.45	96	1.76	0.59
College age	122	1.58	0.47	122	1.90	0.59
Young adulthood	110	1.71	0.60			
Parents						
Adolescence	96	1.90	0.36	96	1.82	0.43
College age	121	1.70	0.50	120	1.73	0.48
Young adulthood	71	1.75	0.48			

Note. Interactional Quality statements rated 1 (low), 2 (medium), or 3 (high).

Table 3

SIGNIFICANT CANONICAL CORRELATIONS (CC) OF TEMPERAMENT AND CONCURRENT RELATIONSHIP RATINGS: ORIGINAL VARIABLES AND CANONICAL VARIATES

TEMPERAMENT	PEARSON'S *r*	CC	RELATIONSHIP	PEARSON'S *r*
Adolescence		0.68**	Emotional Quality	
Adaptablility	0.75		Child/Mother	0.48
Approach/Withdrawal	0.41		Child/Father	0.70
Intensity	-0.45		Child/Parents	0.59
Mood quality	0.91		Mother/Child	0.46
Persistence	0.44		Father/Child	0.67
Distractibility	-0.40		Parents/Child	0.93
Factor redundancy, 0.13			Factor redundancy, 0.20	
Total redundancy, 0.17			Total redundancy, 0.26	
Adolescence		0.69**	Interaction Quantity	
Adaptability	0.63		Child/Father	0.50
Approach/Withdrawal	0.55		Child/Parents	0.47
Intensity	-0.53		Father/Child	0.71
Mood quality	0.82		Parents/Child	0.87
Persistence	0.42			
Distractibility	-0.42			
Factor redundancy, 0.12			Factor redundancy, 0.14	
Total redundancy, 0.19			Total redundancy, 0.22	
College Age		0.52*	Emotional Quality	
Adaptability	0.63		Child/Mother	0.56
Intensity	-0.40		Child/Father	0.59
Mood quality	0.84		Child/Parents	0.69
			Father/Child	0.63
			Parents/Child	0.71
Factor redundancy, 0.05			Factor redundancy, 0.10	
Total redundancy, 0.08			Total redundancy, 0.14	

Note. Labels for emotion and interaction ratings refer to person making statement/person to whom statement refers. **p*<.05; ***p*<.001.

ters of problem behavior were consistently related to negative ratings of parent-child relationships, in particular, parents' ratings of children in adolescence and fathers' ratings at college age. Therefore, NEBS ratings of preschool and school-age children were significant distal covariates of ratings of affective experiences of parents and children in adolescence and at college age. Parental reactions to types of child behavior associated with NEBS ratings may have reinforced child behavior patterns, resulting in negative reciprocal patterns of parent-child interaction *(Patterson, 1982)*. Alternatively, as suggested by Lerner et al. *(1988)*, NEBS ratings may have been early indicators of adjustment problems in adolescence and at college age that would be concurrent correlates of ratings of parent-child relationship quality.

Associations among indices of early childhood adjustment and relationship ratings at college age are summarized in TABLE 5. Several childhood adjustment problems were significantly correlated with their canonical variates, including discipline problems, parental attitudes, parent-child relationship quality, and global adjustment. Ratings of statements by mothers, fathers, and parents about their children were consistently correlated with the relationship variates at college age. Ratings of early childhood relationship and adjustment problems were negatively associated with parent reports of the emotional quality of and the amount of interaction in parent-child relationships at college age. These data may reflect associations between indices of early parent-child conflict and correlates of conflict at college age. Conflict in early parent-child

Table 4

SIGNIFICANT CANONICAL CORRELATIONS (CC) AMONG NEGATIVE EMOTIONAL/BEHAVIORAL STATES (NEBS) RATINGS AND RELATIONSHIP RATINGS: ORIGINAL VARIABLES AND CANONICAL VARIATES

NEBS RATING		PEARSON'S *r*	CC	RELATIONSHIP		PEARSON'S *r*
Years 7–12			0.49*	Emotional Quality		Adolescence
Anxiety		-0.54		Child/Mother		0.52
Aggressiveness		-0.75		Child/Father		0.49
Disobedience		-0.66		Child/Parents		0.56
Academic difficulties		-0.66		Mother/Child		0.65
Parental punishment		-0.66		Parents/Child		0.96
Factor redundancy,	0.09			Factor redundancy,	0.09	
Total redundancy,	0.14			Total redundancy,	0.14	
Years 7–12			0.55*	Interaction Quantity		Adolescence
Anxiety		-0.78		Child/Parents		0.40
Aggressiveness		-0.68		Mother/Child		0.50
Disobedience		-0.68		Parents/Child		0.94
Academic difficulties		-0.61				
Factor redundancy,	0.11			Factor redundancy,	0.08	
Total redundancy,	0.15			Total redundancy,	0.13	
Years 1–6			0.58*	Interaction Quantity		Adolescence
Anxiety		-0.56		Child/Mother		0.42
Aggressiveness		-0.69		Child/Parents		0.56
Undercompliance		-0.73		Parents/Child		0.91
Peer relations		-0.54				
Factor redundancy,	0.11			Factor redundancy,	0.09	
Total redundancy,	0.14			Total redundancy,	0.11	
Years 1–6			0.56**	Emotional Quality		College Age
Anxiety		-0.89		Child/Mother		0.58
Aggressiveness		-0.52		Child/Father		0.50
Peer relations		-0.72		Father/Child		0.82
				Parents/Child		0.46
Factor redundancy,	0.11			Factor redundancy,	0.09	
Total redundancy,	0.14			Total redundancy,	0.11	

Note. Labels for emotion and interaction ratings refer to person making statement/person to whom statement refers. *$p<.05$; **$p<.01$.

relationships may have initiated negative reciprocal interaction patterns between parents and children, a mechanism potentially capable of maintaining maladaptive levels of emotional quality and interaction quantity over long periods. These findings suggest that, although parent-child relationships undergo a process of renegotiation in middle to late adolescence, there may be substantial continuity in the affective experiences of both parents and children based on indicators of adjustment and behavior problems in early childhood. These distal influences appear to be more salient for parents than for children as parental, but not children's, relationship ratings at college age are significantly associated with the early childhood behavior and adjustment ratings in canonical correlation analyses.

Significant associations among psychiatric symptoms and young adult ratings of relationships with mothers, fathers, and parents are summarized in TABLE 6. The psychiatric symptoms of young adults were one of the few variable sets demonstrating significant associations with children's ratings of concurrent parent-child relationships. The psychiatric symptom variate was significantly correlated with several original variables, including mood disorders and aggressiveness, that were conceptually similar to several of the childhood NEBS ratings. The young adult psychiatric symp-

Table 5

SIGNIFICANT CANONICAL CORRELATIONS (CC) AMONG EARLY CHILDHOOD PARENT-CHILD PROBLEMS AND RELATIONSHIP RATINGS: ORIGINAL VARIABLES AND CANONICAL VARIATES

CHILD PROBLEMS	PEARSON'S *r*	CC	RELATIONSHIP	PEARSON'S *r*
Age 3		0.40*	Emotional Quality	College Age
Discipline	0.45		Mother/Child	-0.79
Parental attitude	0.66		Father/Child	-0.63
Global problems	0.83		Parents/Child	-0.49
Factor redundancy, 0.06			Factor redundancy, 0.04	
Total redundancy, 0.09			Total redundancy, 0.06	
Age 3 and Age 5		0.47*	Interaction Quantity	College Age
Relationship: Age 5	0.78		Mother/Child	-0.48
Discipline: Age 5	0.50		Father/Child	-0.66
Parent attitude: Age 3	0.57		Parents/Child	-0.46
Global problems: Age 3	0.60			
Global problems: Age 5	0.68			
Factor redundancy, 0.06			Factor redundancy, 0.04	
Total redundancy, 0.10			Total redundancy, 0.12	

Note. Labels for emotion and interaction ratings refer to person making statement/person to whom statement refers.
*$p<.05$.

tom ratings may have indexed problem behavior that was negatively associated with relationship ratings, much as the NEBS ratings did. This significant association in young adulthood was another example of coexisting continuity and discontinuity in the affective experiences of parents and children through adolescence into young adulthood. First, this association in young adulthood paralleled associations between NEBS ratings and affective experience ratings in adolescence and at college age. Second, by young adulthood their lives had sufficiently individuated from those of their parents that only indicators of severe intrapersonal and interpersonal dysfunction were associated with the emotional quality of their parent-child relationships.

DISCUSSION

This report employed NYLS data to assess continuity and discontinuity in covariates of emotional quality and interaction quantity ratings of parent-child relations from adolescence to young adulthood. The findings allowed several conclusions. First, the mean levels of the relationship ratings were moderately high and did not fluctuate

Table 6

SIGNIFICANT CANONICAL CORRELATIONS (CC) OF YOUNG ADULT PSYCHIATRIC SYMPTOMS AND CONCURRENT RELATIONSHIP RATINGS: ORIGINAL VARIABLES AND CANONICAL VARIABLES

SYMPTOMS	PEARSON'S *r*	CC	RELATIONSHIP	PEARSON'S *r*
Psychiatric		0.53*	Emotional Quality	
Thought disorders	0.48		Child/Father	-0.45
Passive-dependency	0.53		Child/Parents	-0.93
Aggressiveness	0.47			
Mood disorders	0.87			
Other symptoms	0.54			
Factor redundancy, 0.06			Factor redundancy, 0.06	
Total redundancy, 0.10			Total redundancy, 0.14	

Note. Labels for emotion and interaction ratings refer to person making statement/person to whom statement refers.
*$p<.05$.

markedly between occasions of measurement. Second, canonical correlation analyses revealed significant associations between parent and child ratings of affective experiences and a range of clinically relevant variables including concurrent temperament ratings, NEBS ratings from early and middle childhood, early childhood adjustment ratings, and young adult psychiatric symptoms. Third, the number and magnitude of significant canonical correlations was highest in adolescence and dropped steadily to young adulthood, suggesting increasing individuation of adolescents from their parents across this period. Fourth, certain associations in canonical correlation analyses indicated significant degrees of substantive continuity in covariates of parent and child ratings of affective experiences.

These findings support those of contemporary research literature in locating associations among ratings of parent and child affective experiences and variables that appeared to be clinically relevant in earlier qualitative analyses of NYLS data (*Chess & Thomas, 1984, 1986*). For example, mood quality and adaptability have been cited previously as temperamental risk factors for poor fit between infants or children and their social environments, with implications for parent-child relationships *(Bates, 1989; Carey, 1989; Hubert & Wachs, 1985)*. In addition, aggressive, antisocial, or noncompliant behavior by children and adolescents has been shown to elicit coercive parental behavior. Repeated experiences of high rates of coercive exchanges between parents and children may function to instigate and maintain mutually reinforcing patterns of negative interactions *(Forehand, 1990; Forehand & Long, 1988; Patterson, 1986)*. In the NYLS sample, these temperamental and behavioral characteristics from early childhood to young adulthood were consistently associated with the emotional quality of and the amount of interaction in parent-child relationships throughout adolescence.

Data presented in this report support the notion of discontinuity in affective relationships between parents and children from middle adolescence to young adulthood. Declining numbers and magnitudes of significant canonical correlations between relationship ratings and child or parent variable sets across this period suggested ongoing individuation, i.e., the physical and psychological separation of parents and children *(Grotevant & Cooper, 1986; Smollar & Youniss, 1989)*. Temporal decreases in significant associations between parent or child variable sets and relationship ratings were noted for canonical correlation analyses presented in this report. They have also been noted for other analyses that linked relationship ratings to concurrent ratings of child adjustment, substance use, and demographic variables *(Tubman, 1990)*.

The majority (eight out of 14) of the canonical correlation analyses were statistically significant at adolescence, and the proportion dropped at college age (six out of 14) and again in young adulthood (three out of eight). The decreasing number and magnitude of significant canonical correlations underscored two points. First, as children separated both psychologically and geographically from parents, the emotional quality and the amount of interaction between parents and children were less likely to be influenced by "normal, everyday, mundane family matters" than by serious adjustment problems *(Montemayor, 1983)*. Second, classifying parent-child relationships as conflicted or nonconflicted is less useful than is identifying characteristics of parents, children, or families that are associated with the quality of parent-child relationships *(Montemayor, 1986)*.

These data also document significant degrees of continuity in several aspects of the affective relationships of parents and children. Indices of mood quality, adaptability, and aggressive or antisocial behavior were consistently associated with poorer-quality parent-child relationships from middle adolescence to young adulthood. These affective and behavioral covariates of relationship ratings were assessed both concurrently and in early to middle childhood. Of particular interest were the associations between early childhood NEBS ratings or early adjustment ratings and relationship ratings 15 to 20 years later at college age. These findings suggest that interactions in early parent-child relationships remain a salient distal influence upon the affective experiences of parents and children beyond middle adolescence. However, the relative influence of several factors—including stability of children's personality traits, stability of specific antisocial behavior, or stability of parental reaction patterns—for continuity in the covariates of the quality of parent-child relationships is not clear. Each of these factors may contribute to the continuity of experiences within parent-child relationships as data suggest less adaptive life-course patterns of ill-tempered children *(Caspi, Elder, & Bem, 1987; Caspi, Elder, & Herbener, 1990)*; the stability of children's conduct disorders and significant associations with adult psychiatric diagnoses *(Farrington, Loeber, & van Kammen, 1990; Robins, 1978)*; and consistent associations between child and adolescent conduct disorders and parental warmth, support, or communication style *(Hanson, Henggeler, Haefele, & Rodick, 1984; Loeber & Dishion, 1984)*.

For clinicians and clinical researchers, these data have several implications. First, they suggest the value of moving beyond the unidimensional assessment of parent-child conflict to the identification of multiple covariates of the quality of parent-child relationships. Second, it appears to be useful to include several constructs in assessment and intervention efforts with parent-child relationships, including temperament, antecedent and concurrent problem behavior, and antecedent relationship quality. Third, it may be more useful to assess the degree of coexisting continuity and discontinuity in elements of parent-child relationships during adolescence than to focus on global stability or change in these relationships.

While both the internal and external validity of the present report were limited because it analyzed archival data *(Tubman & Lerner, in press)*, it was intended as an initial exploration of the covariates of parent-child relationship ratings from adolescence to young adulthood. The value of these NYLS data lies not in their representativeness, but in their illumination of the scope of efforts needed to investigate continuity-discontinuity in parent-child relationships as children move from adolescence into young adulthood.

REFERENCES

Bates, J.E. (1989). Concepts and measures of temperament. In G.A. Kohnstamm, J.E. Bates, & M.K. Rothbart (Eds.), *Temperament in childhood* (pp. 3–26). New York: John Wiley.

Baumrind, D. (1978). Parental disciplinary patterns and social competence in children. *Youth and Society, 9*, 239–276.

Bengtson, V.L., & Black, K.D. (1973). Intergenerational relations and continuities in socialization. In P.B. Baltes & K.W. Schaie (Eds.), *Life-span developmental psychology* (Vol. 1, pp. 207–234). New York: Academic Press.

Blos, P. (1967). The second individuation process of adolescence. *Psychoanalytic Study of the Child, 22*, 162–186.

Caplow, T., Bahr, H.M., Chadwick, B.A., Hill, R., & Williamson, M.H. (1982). *Middletown families*. Minneapolis: University of Minnesota Press.

Carey, W.B. (1989). Practical applications in pediatrics. In G.A. Kohnstamm, J.E. Bates, & M.K. Rothbart (Eds.), *Temperament in childhood* (pp. 405–419). New York: John Wiley.

Caspi, A., Elder, G.H. Jr., & Bem, D.J. (1987). Moving against the world: Life course patterns of explosive children. *Developmental Psychology, 23*, 308–313.

Caspi, A., Elder, G.H. Jr., & Herbener, E.S. (1990). Childhood personality and the prediction of life-course patterns. In L. Robbins & M. Rutter (Eds.), *Straight and devious pathways from childhood to adulthood* (pp. 13–35). New York: Cambridge University Press.

Chess, S., & Thomas, A. (1984). *Origins and evolution of behavior disorders from infancy to early adult life*. New York: Brunner/Mazel.

Chess, S., & Thomas, A. (1986). *Temperament in clinical practice*. New York: Guilford.

Cooper, C.R. (1988). Commentary: The role of conflict in adolescent-parent relationships. In M.R. Gunnar & W.A. Collins (Eds.), *Development during the transition to adolescence: 21st Minnesota Symposium on child psychology* (pp. 181–187). Hillsdale, NJ: Lawrence Erlbaum.

Eyberg, S.M., & Robinson, E.A. (1983). Conduct problem behavior: Standardization of a behavioral rating scale with adolescents. *Journal of Clinical Child Psychology, 12,* 347–354.

Farrington, D.P., Loeber, R., & van Kammen, W.B. (1990). Long-term criminal outcomes of hyperactivity-impulsivity-attention deficit and conduct problems in childhood. In L. Robins & M. Rutter (Eds.), *Straight and devious pathways from childhood to adulthood* (pp. 62–81). New York: Cambridge University Press.

Forehand, R. (1990). Families with a conduct problem child. In G.H. Brody & I.E. Sigel (Eds.), *Methods of family research: Biographies of research projects: Vol. 2. Clinical populations* (pp. 1–30). Hillsdale, NJ: Lawrence Erlbaum.

Forehand, R., & Long, N. (1988). Outpatient treatment of the acting out child: Procedures, long term follow-up data, and clinical problems. *Advances in Behaviour Therapy and Research, 10,* 129–178.

Frank, S.J., Avery, C.B., & Laman, M.S. (1988). Young adults' perceptions of their relationships with their parents: Individual differences in connectedness, competence, and emotional autonomy. *Developmental Psychology, 24,* 729–737.

Freud, A. (1958). Adolescence. *Psychoanalytic Study of the Child, 13,* 255–278.

Grotevant, H.D., & Cooper, C.R. (1985). Patterns of interaction in family relationships and the development of identity formation in adolescence. *Child Development, 56,* 415–428.

Grotevant, H.D., & Cooper, C.R. (1986). Individuation in family relationships. *Human Development, 29,* 82–100.

Hanson, C.L., Henggeler, S.W., Haefele, W.F., & Rodick, J.D. (1984). Demographic, individual, and family relationship correlates of serious and repeated crime among adolescents and their siblings. *Journal of Consulting and Clinical Psychology, 52,* 528–538.

Harris, I.D., & Howard, K.I. (1984). Parental criticism and the adolescent experience. *Journal of Youth and Adolescence, 13,* 113–121.

Hauser, S.T., Powers, S.I., Noam, G.G., Jacobson, A.M., Weiss, B., & Follansbee, D.J. (1984). Familial contexts of adolescent ego development. *Child Development, 55,* 195–213.

Hill, J.P., & Holmbeck, G.N. (1986). Attachment and autonomy during adolescence. In G. Whitehurst (Ed.), *Annals of child development* (Vol. 3, pp. 145–189). Greenwich, CT: JAI Press.

Hubert, N.C., & Wachs, T.D. (1985). Parental perception of the behavioral components of infant easiness/difficultness. *Child Development, 56,* 1525–1537.

Kandel, D., & Lesser, G.S. (1969). Parent-adolescent relationships and adolescent independence in the United States and Denmark. *Journal of Marriage and the Family, 31,* 348–358.

Kendall, P.C. (1991). *Child and adolescent therapy: Cognitive-behavioral procedures.* New York: Guilford.

Lerner, J.V., Hertzog, C., Hooker, K.A., Hassibi, M., & Thomas, A. (1988). A longitudinal study of negative emotional states and adjustment from early childhood through adolescence. *Child Development, 59,* 356–366.

Levine, M.S. (1977). *Canonical analysis and factor comparison.* Newbury Park, CA: Sage Publications.

Little, R.J.A., & Rubin, D.B. (1987). *Statistical analysis with missing data.* New York: John Wiley.

Loeber, R., & Dishion, T.J. (1984). Boys who fight at home and school: Family conditions influencing cross-setting consistency. *Journal of Consulting and Clinical Psychology, 52,* 759–768.

Montemayor, R. (1983). Parents and adolescents in conflict: All families some of the time and some families all of the time. *Journal of Early Adolescence, 3,* 83–103.

Montemayor, R. (1986). Family variation in parent-adolescent storm and stress.*Journal of Adolescent Research, 1,* 15–31.

Murphy, E.B., Silber, E., Coelho, G.V., Hamburg, D.A., & Greenberg, I. (1963). Development of autonomy and parent-child interaction in late adolescence. *American Journal of Orthopsychiatry, 33,* 643–652.

Offer, D., Ostrov, E., & Howard, K.I. (1981). *The adolescent:A psychological self-portrait.* New York: Basic Books.

Patterson, G.R. (1982). *Coercive family process.* Eugene, OR: Castalia.

Patterson, G.R. (1986). Performance models for antisocial boys. *American Psychologist, 41,* 432–444.

Robins, L.N. (1978). Sturdy childhood predictors of adult antisocial behavior: Replications from longitudinal studies. *Psychological Medicine, 8,* 611–622.

Rovine, M.J., & Delaney, M. (1990). Missing data estimation in developmental research. In A. von Eye (Ed.), *Statistical methods for longitudinal research* (Vol. 1, pp. 35–80). New York: Academic Press.

Smetana, J.G. (1988). Concepts of self and social convention: Adolescents' and parents' reasoning about hypothetical and actual family conflicts. In M. Gunnar & W.A. Collins (Eds.), *Development during the transition to adolescence: 21st Minnesota svmposium on child psychology* (pp. 79–122). Hillsdale, NJ: Lawrence Erlbaum.

Smetana, J.G., Yau, J., Restrepo, A., & Braeges, J. (1991). Parent-adolescent conflict in married and divorced families. *Developmental Psychology, 27,* 1000–1010.

Smollar, J., & Youniss, J. (1989). Transformations in adolescents' perceptions of parents. *International Journal of Behavioral Development, 12,* 71–84.

Steinberg, L.D. (1981). Transformations in family relations at puberty. *Developmental Psychology, 17,* 833–840.

Steinberg, L.D. (1989). Pubertal maturation and parent-adolescent distance: An evolutionary perspective. In G.R. Adams, R. Montemayor, & T.P. Gullotta (Eds.), *Advances in adolescent development: Vol. 1. Biology of adolescent behavior and development* (pp. 71–97). Newbury Park, CA: Sage Publications.

Stierlin, H. (1981). *Separating parents and adolescents.* Northvale, NJ: Aronson.

Tatsuoka, M.M. (1988). *Multivariate analysis* (2nd ed.). New York: Macmillan.

Thomas, A., & Chess., S. (1977). *Temperament and development.* New York: Brunner/Mazel.

Thomas, A., Chess, S., Birch, H.G., Hertzig, M., & Korn, S. (1963). *Behavioral individuality in early childhood.* New York: New York University Press.

Thomas, A., Chess, S., Lerner, R.M., & Lerner, J.V. (1989). *Behavioral individuality in adult life.* Unpublished manuscript, New York University Medical Center. New York.

Tubman, J.G. (1990). *Affective experiences of children and parents: Their stability and covariates.* Unpublished doctoral dissertation, Pennsylvania State University, University Park.

Tubman, J.G., & Lerner, R.M. (in press). Affective experiences of parents and their children from adolescence to young adulthood: Stability of affective experiences. *Journal of Adolescence.*

For reprints: Jonathan G. Tubman, Department of Psychology, Florida International University, University Park Campus, Miami, FL 33199.

Amer. J. Orthopsychiat. 62(4), October 1992

TEMPERAMENT AND ADJUSTMENT IN YOUNG ADULTHOOD: A 15-Year Longitudinal Analysis

Jonathan G. Tubman, Ph.D., Richard M. Lerner, Ph.D., Jacqueline V. Lerner, Ph.D., Alexander von Eye, Ph.D.

The relationship between easy/difficult temperament and adjustment from middle adolescence to young adulthood was examined. Cluster analysis revealed four groups of individuals via composite temperament scores over three points of measurement. Multivariate analyses indicated that extremely difficult temperament was associated with poorer psychosocial functioning in childhood and young adulthood.

The concept of the "difficult child" was introduced a quarter century ago as a constellation of temperamental characteristics that functioned, in the New York Longitudinal Study (NYLS), to predispose children to reactive behavior disorders *(Thomas, Chess, & Birch, 1968)*. The five characteristics indicative of temperamental difficulty in early childhood included low rhythmicity, low approach, low adaptability, negative mood, and high intensity. Since its introduction, the use of the concept of temperamental difficulty has been expanded to encompass a greater range of settings, ages, and outcomes, prompting calls for the use of more general terms, e.g., temperamental risk factors, to encompass any temperamental characteristics that are associated with poor match or "fit" between children and their environments *(Carey, 1989)*.

Several contemporary investigators, citing the imprecise definition of the original formulation of temperamental difficulty, have opted for narrower definitions, including frequent, intense expressions of negative affect, or, alternatively, negative mood and low adaptability *(Bates, 1987, 1989a; Hubert & Wachs, 1985; Maziade, Boutin, Cote, & Thivierge, 1986)*. Nonetheless, the concept of difficult temperament has been identified across cultures and socioeconomic groups as developmentally relevant, as well as empirically replicable from infancy to middle childhood *(deVries, 1989; Matheny, Wilson, & Nuss, 1984; Maziade, Cote, Boudreault, Thivierge, & Caperaa, 1984; Persson-Blennow & McNeill, 1982)*. It is also generally accepted that individual differences in temperamental difficulty in children have functional significance for the development of emotional and behavioral disorders in both normal and high-risk samples *(Maziade, 1989a; Rutter, 1987)*.

A revised version of a paper submitted to the Journal in August 1991. Work was supported in part by NIMH Grant MH39957 and NICHD Grant HD23229. Authors are at: Research Institute on Addictions, Buffalo, N.Y. (Tubman); Institute for Children, Youth, and Families (R.M. Lerner) and Department of Psychology (J.V. Lerner), Michigan State University, East Lansing; and Department of Human Development and Family Studies, Pennsylvania State University, University Park (von Eye).

There is, however, only limited evidence that moderate levels of temperamental difficulty function to alter socioemotional functioning substantially in infancy and childhood in "normal" populations *(Bates, 1989b)*. The evidence that difficulty in infancy or in early childhood directly influences the quality of observed mother–child interaction is limited, inconsistent, and possibly a methodological artifact of child effects research *(Bates, 1987; Crockenberg, 1986; Rothbart, 1986)*. It has been suggested that indirect negative influences upon the quality of parent–child interaction exist after toddlerhood, as socialization efforts increase, via the degree of fit of children's temperamental style to parental demands *(Bates, 1989b; Crockenberg, 1986)*.

Similarly, difficult temperament in children is not thought to be predictive of psychopathology unless this temperamental style is manifested after age three *(Thomas et al., 1968; Maziade, 1989a)*. Other research has found significant associations between maternal ratings of early childhood temperamental difficulty and of children's behavior problems between the ages of three and six *(Bates & Bayles, 1988; Bates, Maslin, & Frankel, 1985)*, but not with teacher reports of social competence in this same age period *(Bates, 1989b)*. Therefore, the functional significance of temperamental difficulty in infancy and early childhood for later behavioral and socioemotional functioning remains unclear, obscured in part by the wide scope of relevant, complex, child–context interactions to be investigated and potential confounds in early parent–child interaction research *(Bates, 1989b; Lerner & Lerner, 1983; Lerner, Nitz, Talwar, & Lerner, 1989)*.

Significant associations between difficult temperament and behavioral and socioemotional functioning in middle childhood or in later developmental periods have been documented *(Chess & Thomas, 1984, 1986; Maziade, 1989a, 1989b; Thomas & Chess, 1984; Windle, 1991, 1992)*. In a cross-sectional analysis of adolescents dwelling in the community, a linear relationship has been described between the number of difficult temperament factors and levels of substance use, childhood behavior problems, delinquent activity, depressive symptoms, and family social support *(Windle, 1991)*. Further analyses of the total sample ($N = 975$) demonstrated partial support for structural equation models in which the influence of difficult temperament on depressive symptoms and delinquent activities was mediated by perceived friend and family support. In these models, difficult temperament also had direct influences on depression and delinquency *(Windle, 1992)*.

Studies of clinical and nonclinical community-dwelling populations have demonstrated concurrent and predictive relationships between extremely difficult temperament and psychiatric symptomatology. One research group has documented that clinical behavior disorders are associated with this temperament constellation after four or five years of age *(Maziade, Cote, & Thivierge, 1989)*. Extremely difficult temperament has been shown to be associated with specific types of concurrent behavior disorder (e.g., oppositional, conduct, or attention-deficit disorders) in a large sample of consecutive admissions to a children's psychiatric center *(Maziade, Caron, Cote, Boutin, & Thivierge, 1990)*. In addition, in subgroups from a general population sample, extreme temperament at age seven predicted psychiatric status at age 12 and at age 16 when level of family functioning was taken into account *(Maziade, Caron, Cote, Merette, et al., 1990)*. Therefore, extreme temperamental difficulty has been associated with lower adjustment, as well as with psychiatric symptomatology from childhood to middle adolescence.

Longitudinal analyses of temperament–adjustment relations remain, however, the exception rather than the rule, especially in subjects beyond adolescence *(Windle, 1988)*. Investigations of the functional significance of temperamental difficulty after childhood raise issues of the measurement equivalence of temperamental attributes across developmental periods, as well as of the impact of shifts in person–context relations on associations between difficult temperament and psychosocial functioning. For the purposes of the present report, definitional constancy and measurement equivalence of temperament have been sought, a strategy that has precedent in other temperament research aimed at assessing temperament–context relations *(Windle & Lerner, 1986a, 1986b)*. Implementation of this approach required drawing on temperament constructs (i.e., the easy/difficult constellation) that can be indexed comparably across developmental periods.

Using data from the NYLS, this report examined relationships between easy/difficult temperament and psychological adjustment from middle adolescence to young adulthood. First, easy/difficult temperament ratings were categorized into distinct, meaningful, longitudinal patterns. Second, adjustment differences by temperament category were described in young adulthood. Third, adjustment differences among the longitudinal temperament categories preceding adolescence were described. These analyses provided longitudinal information about the functional significance of the easy/difficult temperament profiles beyond middle adolescence.

METHOD

Participants

Participants were the 133 middle-class children (66 males, 67 females) from the NYLS sample *(Thomas & Chess, 1977, 1986)*. The sample is over 99% white and predominantly (78%) Jewish. All participants were initially studied in their first weeks of life, and have since been followed at regular intervals *(Chess & Thomas, 1984)*. Sample recruitment began in 1956 and ended in 1962. The most recent wave of data collection was completed in 1987, when the sample ranged in age from 25 to 31 years. The sample has remained intact throughout the study, with a participation rate of 97% ($N=129$) in the latest wave of data collection.

Measures

In the NYLS, temperament and adjustment have been conceptualized and derived as independent constructs. Temperament has been defined as the *style* of behavior, that is, how a person performs a given behavior *(Lerner & Lerner, 1983; Thomas & Chess, 1977)*. Adjustment has referred to outcomes of behavioral functioning, reflecting the adequacy or "fit" of behavior with respect to normative or situational criteria. Data used to rate a participant's temperament dealt solely with the stylistic aspects of ongoing behavior. In turn, psychological adjustment was rated by NYLS psychiatrists on the basis of either the parents' or the participants' responses during an open-ended interview involving questions about behavioral adequacy in regard to a given area of functioning.

Easy vs difficult temperament. Temperament scores for the five dimensions relevant to the easy/difficult temperament composite were derived from responses to standardized questions in semistructured face-to-face interviews with NYLS psychiatrists in middle adolescence (16–17 years), at college age (18–23 years), and in young adulthood (25–31 years). These temperament domains and their definitions from Chess and Thomas *(1984)* were: *Rhythmicity,* the predictability of biological functioning; *Adaptability,* responses to new or altered situations, and the ease with which those responses are modified; *Approach/Withdrawal,* the nature of an initial response to a new stimulus, be it a person, place, or thing; *Intensity of Reaction,* the energy level of response, regardless of its quality or direction; and *Quality of Mood,* the amount of pleasant versus unpleasant behavior.

The scores for each temperament dimension ranged from low (1) to high (7). The easy/difficult composite score was calculated by subtracting the sum of the scores for Approach/Withdrawal, Mood Quality, Rhythmicity, and Adaptability from the score for Intensity. This composite score ranged from 3 to −27, with high scores indicating greatest difficulty. The composite score demonstrated significant normative stability ($p<.001$). Pearson correlations were .55 between middle adolescence and college age and .52 between college age and young adulthood *(Thomas, Chess, Lerner, & Lerner, 1989)*.

The exact procedures for these interviews and the techniques used for coding and for establishing reliability have been reported in numerous publications *(Chess & Thomas, 1984; Lerner, Hertzog, Hooker, Hassibi, & Thomas, 1988; Thomas & Chess, 1977)*. An analysis of pooled interrater reliabilities for 24 randomly selected interview protocols found moderate reliabilities for four of the five temperament dimensions (range 0.68 to 0.76) for the college-age interviews *(Chess & Thomas, 1984)*. However, one attribute—Intensity—had a low pooled reliability (0.33). An analysis of 24 randomly selected interview protocols in young adulthood revealed simple (i.e., uncorrected) interrater reliabilities in the moderate range for the five temperament attributes (range 0.42 to 0.78) *(Thomas et al., 1989)*.

Psychological adjustment. The psychological adjustment of NYLS participants was assessed in early and middle childhood, as well as in young adulthood. The procedures for obtaining these scores have been detailed elsewhere *(Chess & Thomas, 1984; Lerner et al., 1988; Thomas & Chess, 1977)* and involved the coding of responses by participants to standard interview questions. During young adulthood, psychological adjustment was rated in the following areas: self-evaluation, family relationships, school functioning, social functioning, sexual functioning, goals, implementation of goals, coping patterns, work functioning, communication, emotional expressiveness, and routines. These 12 dimensions of adjustment were rated on a seven-point scale, from poor adjustment (1) to excellent adjustment (7). A rating of global adjustment was also assigned to each participant ranging from poor adjustment (1) to excellent adjustment (9). School functioning was not used in this report because many of the participants had completed formal schooling. Interrater reliabilities for adjustment ratings obtained in young adulthood ranged widely. An analysis of 24 randomly selected interview protocols reported simple (i.e., uncorrected) interrater reliabilities in the moderate to high range for the adjustment ratings (range 0.53 to 0.79) *(Thomas et al., 1989)*.

Negative emotional/behavioral states (NEBS) in childhood were coded by an independent psychiatrist, employing an inductive content analysis of NYLS interviews with parents and teachers. These interviews described children's behavior at home and in school. For years one through six, children were rated for displays of anxiety, difficulty with peers, dissatisfaction, aggressiveness, and undercompliance. For years seven through 12, ratings were assigned for anxiety, depressive mood, aggressiveness, disobedience in the home, academic difficulties, and excessive parental physical punishment.

Each NEBS variable was scored from not present (0) to severe (3). When a target behavior or state was indicated in two interviews over a six-month interval by parents, it was scored 1 (mild). When, in addition to reports by parents, teachers reported a NEBS variable, the intensity was scored 2 (moderate). Finally, when parents and teachers reported NEBS variables in interviews for two consecutive years, the intensity was rated 3 (high) *(Chess & Thomas, 1984; Lerner et al., 1988; Thomas & Chess, 1977)*. The NEBS categories of anxiety and aggression had stability coefficients of .97 and .91 respectively for the ages 1–6 and

7–12. Early NEBS ratings (e.g., anxiety and aggressiveness) predicted adjustment problems in adolescence *(Lerner et al., 1988)*.

Design of Analyses

Cluster analysis was employed for constructing longitudinal group profiles of easy/difficult temperament ratings to obtain a powerful indicator of cross-temporal behavioral individuality, i.e., the stability of this temperament constellation. Ward's *(1963)* method was selected for the cluster analysis, since its properties included nonoverlapping clusters, distance rather than a correlational measure, and preservation of unequal cluster sizes. An optimal number of clusters for the easy/difficult temperament scores was determined using Ward's method and was verified by another clustering technique, K-means, as implemented in the FASTCLUS algorithm *(SAS Institute, 1985)*. The solutions were essentially identical. FASTCLUS also estimated easy/difficult scores for the four NYLS participants who were not interviewed in young adulthood.

Multivariate analysis of variance (MANOVA) was employed to investigate relationships between easy/difficult temperament groups and concurrent and antecedent indices of psychological adjustment. Young adult adjustment ratings were entered as two sets of dependent variables in MANOVA equations, that is, as measures of individual functioning or social functioning. MANOVAs were also employed to determine the amount of variance accounted for in NEBS ratings by longitudinal temperamental profiles or "pathways" *(Magnusson & Bergman, 1990)* to indicate ways in which adjustment levels of the temperament cluster members differed prior to adolescence. Differences in mean group levels for each measure of adjustment in young adulthood and childhood were tested for significance using the Kramer version of the Newman-Keuls statistic to take into account differences in the size of temperament groups.

RESULTS

Patterns of Easy/Difficult Temperament

Results of the cluster analysis suggested a four-group solution for the standardized easy/difficult temperament scores over the three points of measurement. Cluster mean profiles for the easy/difficult temperament scores are presented in FIGURE 1. Cluster 1 ($N=6$) had a high mean score for easy/difficult temperament in adolescence that increased at the two subsequent points of measurement. Cluster 2 ($N=33$) had a low mean easy/difficult score in adolescence that also increased steadily over time. Cluster 3 ($N=56$) had a moderately low initial mean easy/difficult score in adolescence that decreased steadily over time. Cluster 4 ($N=38$) had an above-average initial easy/difficult temperament score that increased at college age and subsequently declined at young adulthood. Higher easy/difficult scores indicated more difficult temperament. Therefore, members of Cluster 1 had the most difficult temperament profiles, while members of Cluster 3 had the easiest.

Adjustment in Young Adulthood

Two MANOVAs conducted to determine the amount of variance accounted for by the longitudinal easy/difficult temperament clusters in psychological adjustment ratings in young adulthood are summarized in TABLE 1. The MANOVA containing the individual adjustment variables indicated that cluster membership accounted for significant amounts of variance in several psychological adjustment ratings: self-evaluation, emotional adjustment, goals adjustment, implementation of goals, coping adjustment, and adjustment to routines. This MANOVA resulted in a significant overall effect, $F(18,331)=4.00, p<.001$. The MANOVA containing the social adjustment variables also resulted in a significant overall effect, $F(18,326)=2.82, p<.001$. This MANOVA indicated that cluster membership accounted for significant amounts of variance in the ratings for work adjustment, social ad-

Figure 1

CLUSTER MEANS FOR STANDARDIZED TEMPERAMENT SCORES

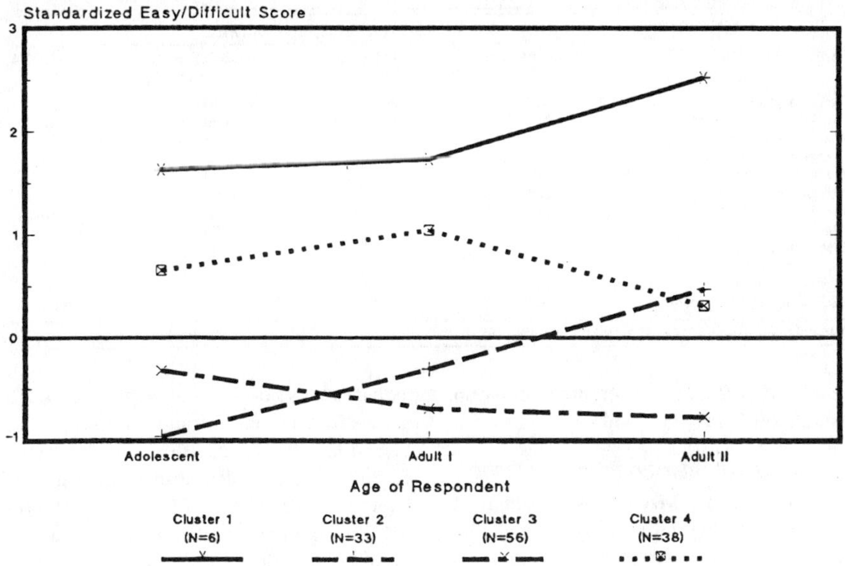

Note. Higher score indicates higher level of difficult temperament.

justment, sexual adjustment, and global adjustment.

TABLE 2 summarizes cluster means for all young-adult adjustment ratings. These results are congruent with research findings that link difficult temperament to poorer adjustment outcomes in childhood *(Bates, 1989b; Maziade, 1989a; Maziade, Caron, Cote, Boutin, & Thivierge, 1990)*. The individuals with the highest difficult temperament scores in middle adolescence through young adulthood (Cluster 1) had significantly lower mean scores for adjustment ratings in which cluster membership accounted for significant amounts of variance. In addition, Cluster 1 had a significantly lower mean rating for communication adjustment. The individuals reporting consistently low difficult temperament scores in adolescence through young adulthood (Cluster 3) had the highest ratings for all these same measures of adjustment, although not significantly higher than those for the groups rated as having intermediate

Table 1

MANOVAs OF YOUNG ADULT ADJUSTMENT RATINGS BY TEMPERAMENT CLUSTERS

DEPENDENT VARIABLE	UNIVARIATE *F*
Psychological Adjustment[a]	
Self-evaluation	15.51(3,125)**
Emotional adjustment	2.74(3,125)*
Goals adjustment	13.92(3,125)**
Implementation of goals	15.08(3,125)**
Coping adjustment	11.33(3,125)**
Adjustment to routines	13.94(3,125)**
Social Adjustment[b]	
Family relationships	2.54(3,123)
Work adjustment	9.20(3,123)**
Social adjustment	8.87(3,123)**
Sexual adjustment	6.98(3,123)**
Communications adjustment	2.56(3,123)
Global adjustment	10.40(3,123)**

[a] Overall $F=4.00(18,331)$, $p<.001$.
[b] Overall $F=2.82(18,326)$, $p<.001$.
* $p<.05$; ** $p<.001$.

Table 2

SUMMARY OF TEMPERAMENT CLUSTER MEANS FOR SIGNIFICANT YOUNG ADULT ADJUSTMENT VARIABLES

	TEMPERAMENT SCORES			
DEPENDENT VARIABLE	CLUSTER 1	CLUSTER 2	CLUSTER 3	CLUSTER 4
Self-evaluation	3.00[a]	5.87	6.15	5.24
Emotional adjustment	4.17[a]	5.48	5.59	5.40
Goals adjustment	2.67[a]	5.56	6.13	5.70
Implementation of goals	2.67[a]	5.77	6.46	5.78
Coping adjustment	3.00[a]	5.62	6.08	5.22
Adjustment to routines	2.50[a]	5.42	5.60	5.32
Family relations	4.00	4.93	5.33	4.76
Work adjustment	4.00[a]	5.87	6.31	6.16
Social adjustment	3.38[a]	5.17	5.86	5.14
Sexual adjustment	3.17[a]	4.97	5.59	4.65
Communication	4.33[a]	5.33	5.63	5.27
Global adjustment	3.50[a]	6.37	7.19	6.38

[a] Means significantly lower than all other means.

levels of difficult temperament in young adulthood (Clusters 2 and 4).

Psychological Adjustment in Childhood

Two additional MANOVAs conducted to determine if longitudinal easy/difficult cluster membership was associated with levels of childhood adjustment ratings are summarized in TABLE 3. The MANOVA containing the NEBS ratings for years one through six resulted in a significant overall effect, $F(15,345)=2.55$, $p<.01$. Significant univariate F tests in this MANOVA included those for anxiety, aggressiveness, dissatisfaction, and difficulties with peers. The MANOVA for NEBS ratings for years seven through 12 also resulted in a significant overall effect, $F(18,292)=1.66$, $p<.05$. Significant univariate F tests in this MANOVA included those for anxiety, aggressiveness, depressive mood, disobedience, and excessive parental physical punishment.

Table 3

MANOVAs OF NEBS RATINGS BY LONGITUDINAL EASY/DIFFICULT TEMPERAMENT CLUSTERS

DEPENDENT VARIABLE	UNIVARIATE F
Years 1–6[a]	
Anxiety	5.74(3,132)***
Aggressiveness	5.38(3,132)**
Dissatisfaction	3.22(3,132)*
Undercompliance	2.39(3,132)
Difficulties with peers	5.07(3,132)**
Years 7–12[b]	
Anxiety	3.96(3,111)*
Aggressiveness	3.28(3,111)*
Depression	4.50(3,111)**
Disobedience	3.56(3,111)*
Academic difficulties	1.59(3,111)
Excess parental punishment	2.74(3,111)*

[a] Overall $F=2.55(15,345)$, $p<.01$.
[b] Overall $F=1.66(18,292)$, $p<.05$.
* $p<.05$; ** $p<.01$; *** $p<.001$.

TABLE 4 summarizes cluster means for all NEBS ratings. The individuals reporting the highest difficult temperament scores in adolescence through young adulthood (Cluster 1) were rated significantly higher than all other clusters on the NEBS ratings at years one through six for anxiety, aggressiveness, undercompliance, and difficulties with peers, as well as for anxiety during years seven through twelve. Cluster 1 also had the highest group mean for the other five NEBS ratings at ages seven through 12. The individuals reporting consistently low difficult scores in adolescence through young adulthood (Cluster 3) were rated lowest, although not significantly so, at years one through six for NEBS ratings of anxiety and dissatisfaction, as well as at years seven through 12 for NEBS ratings of anxiety, depressive mood, academic difficulties, and excessive parental physical pun-

Table 4

SUMMARY OF TEMPERAMENT CLUSTER MEANS FOR CHILDHOOD NEBS RATINGS

	TEMPERAMENT SCORES			
DEPENDENT VARIABLE	CLUSTER 1	CLUSTER 2	CLUSTER 3	CLUSTER 4
Years 1–6				
Anxiety	1.50[a]	0.48	0.39	0.79
Aggressiveness	1.50[a]	0.36	0.50	0.76
Dissatisfaction	0.67	0.48	0.36	0.82
Undercompliance	1.33[a]	0.52	0.55	0.74
Peer difficulties	1.17[a]	0.21	0.25	0.63
Years 7–12				
Anxiety	1.67[a]	0.69	0.53	0.83
Aggressiveness	1.00	0.31	0.38	0.77
Depressive mood	1.33	0.54	0.38	0.86
Disobedience	0.83	0.15	0.31	0.68
Academic difficulties	0.67	0.42	0.22	0.54
Parental punishment	0.83	0.31	0.29	0.63

[a] Means significantly higher than all other means.

ishment. Therefore, prior to adolescence, adjustment differences existed in the NYLS sample on the basis of longitudinal easy/difficult cluster membership.

DISCUSSION

This report employed NYLS data to address questions of longitudinal relationships among temperamental ease or difficulty from middle adolescence to young adulthood and adjustment both in young adulthood and in prior, early and middle childhood years. Patterns of easy/difficult temperament scores previously described in earlier developmental periods by this and other studies existed over the period covered by this report. The most significant of these profiles of temperament stability was the identification of a small, extremely difficult group of NYLS participants, since the majority of individuals remained within one standard deviation of the mean for the standardized easy/difficult scores. The functional significance of membership in this group (Cluster 1) included significantly lower functioning in 11 of 12 adjustment domains rated in young adulthood.

Data regarding the functional significance of extreme temperament in the NYLS reflected other findings dealing with childhood and adolescence *(Maziade, 1989a; Maziade, Caron, Cote, Boutin, & Thivierge, 1990; Maziade, Caron, Cote, Merette, et al., 1990; Windle, 1992)*. Not only did members of the highly difficult cluster (1) report lower levels of adjustment in young adulthood, but their case files also detailed a range of clinical behavior disorders in young adulthood; these included avoidant personality disorder, major depression, narcissistic personality disorder, obsessive compulsive disorder, panic state, and substance abuse, as well as psychiatric hospitalizations. Extremely difficult temperament should not, however, be assumed to be synonymous with clinical status, as noted by Maziade, Caron, Cote, Boutin, and Thivierge *(1990)*. One of the six NYLS participants in the extremely difficult group had no clinical diagnosis in young adulthood. Distinguishing features between this case and the other five cases included the active selection of contextual features to promote "goodness of fit," positive self-concept, and the capacity for self-insight *(Chess & Thomas, 1990; Thomas & Chess, 1989)*.

The results of this report suggest that relationships between extremely difficult temperament and psychological adjustment may be interactive in nature. The group of NYLS participants with extremely difficult temperament had significantly lower levels of psychosocial adjustment in early and middle childhood, in addition to those described in young adulthood. The seeming continuity in difficult temperament–adjustment relations suggested that children or young adults with extremely difficult temperaments may find it particularly hard to achieve a good fit within the multiple contexts where they live and interact *(Rutter, 1989)*. For example, five of the six members of the NYLS extremely difficult temperament group experienced great conflict in relationships with their families, a condition cited by Maziade, Caron, Cote, Merette, et al. *(1990)* as a mechanism in the development of psychopathology in temperamentally extreme subgroups of a general population sample. Without extensive personal resources (e.g., the capacity for context selection, positive self-concept, and self-insight) temperamentally difficult individuals may lack tools to modify the degree of fit between self and context either through selecting more appropriate contexts or by shaping the expression of temperamental attributes in response to given contexts *(Chess & Thomas, 1990; Thomas & Chess, 1989)*.

This report was generally congruent with and expanded upon links between difficult temperament and adjustment found in studies involving infants and children *(Maziade, 1989a; Maziade, Caron, Cote, Boutin, & Thivierge, 1990; Maziade, Caron, Cote, Merette, et al., 1990)*. The NYLS easy/difficult temperament constellation has been replicated in a wide variety of samples *(deVries, 1989; Matheny et al., 1984; Maziade et al., 1984; Persson-Blennow & McNeill, 1982)*. The fact that the NYLS contains a sample of convenience *(Chess & Thomas, 1984)* does not diminish its utility as a forum in which longitudinal relations between temperament and adjustment can be explored. Findings from the NYLS must be qualified, however, due to potential biases in ratings of temperament and adjustment; these include identical raters at consecutive points of measurement, and the development of response sets due to the use of a standardized interview protocol.

These findings, while exploratory, are provocative and point to future directions in investigations of relationships between temperamental difficulty and psychosocial adjustment from middle adolescence to young adulthood. Future issues to be resolved include delineation of the degree of fit between different temperament constellations and a variety of contexts throughout adolescence into young adulthood, the continuity of difficult temperament across this developmental period, and the predictive power of temperamental difficulty for young adult adjustment beyond that exercised by childhood adjustment *(Chess & Thomas, 1990; Rutter, 1989)*. While many issues remain unresolved regarding the mechanisms by which extreme temperamental difficulty predisposes adolescents or young adults to psychopathology, and regarding the mediators of these developmental processes, additional person-oriented research will further disentangle these relationships *(Magnusson & Bergman, 1990)*.

The systematic application of a pattern approach to difficult temperament–adjustment relations would attempt to identify links among particular sets of participant attributes and maladaptive or psychopathological outcomes. This report was an initial attempt to employ methods derived from a pattern approach to construct profiles or pathways depicting difficult temperament–adjustment relationships from middle adolescence to young adulthood. Future investigations with larger, more representative samples will provide additional details concerning the functional significance of difficult temperament in young adulthood, as well as the different paths to adaptive and maladaptive outcomes.

REFERENCES

Bates, J.E. (1987). Temperament in infancy. In J.D. Osofsky (Ed.), *Handbook of infant development* (2nd ed., pp. 1101–1149). New York: John Wiley.

Bates, J.E. (1989a). Concepts and measures of temperament. In G.A. Kohnstamm, J.E. Bates, & M.K. Rothbart (Eds.), *Temperament in childhood* (pp. 3–26). New York: John Wiley.

Bates, J.E. (1989b). Applications of temperament concepts. In G.A. Kohnstamm, J.E. Bates, & M.K.

Rothbart (Eds.), *Temperament in childhood* (pp. 321–355). New York: John Wiley.

Bates, J.E., & Bayles, K. (1988). The role of attachment in the development of behavior problems. In J. Belsky & T. Nezworski (Eds.), *Clinical implications of attachment* (pp. 253–299). Hillsdale, NJ: Lawrence Erlbaum.

Bates, J.E., Maslin, C.A., & Frankel, K.A. (1985). Attachment security, mother–child interaction, and temperament as predictors of behavior problem ratings at age three years. In I. Bretherton & E. Waters (Eds.), Growing points of attachment theory and research (pp. 167–193). *Monographs of the Society for Research in Child Development, 50* (1–2, Serial No. 209).

Carey, W.B. (1989). Practical applications in pediatrics. In G.A. Kohnstamm, J.E. Bates, & M.K. Rothbart (Eds.), *Temperament in childhood* (pp. 405–419). New York: John Wiley.

Chess, S., & Thomas, A. (1984). *The origins and evolution of behavioral disorders*. New York: Brunner/Mazel.

Chess, S., & Thomas, A. (1986). *Temperament in clinical practice*. New York: Guilford Press.

Chess, S., & Thomas, A. (1990). Continuities and discontinuities in temperament. In L. Robins & M. Rutter (Eds.), *Straight and devious pathways from childhood to adulthood* (pp. 205–220). New York: Cambridge University Press.

Crockenberg, S.B. (1986). Are temperamental differences in babies associated with predictable differences in care giving? In J.V. Lerner & R.M. Lerner (Eds.), *New directions for child development: Temperament and social interaction in infancy and childhood* (pp. 53–73). San Francisco: Jossey-Bass.

deVries, M.W. (1989). Difficult temperament: A universal and culturally embedded concept. In W.B. Carey & S.C. McDevitt (Eds.), *Clinical and educational applications of temperament research* (pp. 81–85). Amsterdam: Swets & Zeitlinger B.V.

Hubert, N.C., & Wachs, T.D. (1985). Parental perception of the behavioral components of infant easiness/difficultness. *Child Development, 56*, 1525–1537.

Lerner, J.V., Hertzog, C., Hooker, K.A., Hassibi, M., & Thomas, A. (1988). A longitudinal study of negative emotional states and adjustment from early childhood through adolescence. *Child Development, 59*, 356–366.

Lerner, J.V., & Lerner, R.M. (1983). Temperament and adaptation across life: Theoretical and empirical issues. In P.B. Baltes & O.G. Brim, Jr. (Eds.), *Life-span development and behavior* (Vol. 5, pp. 197–230). New York: Academic Press.

Lerner, J.V., Nitz, K., Talwar, R., & Lerner, R.M. (1989). On the functional significance of temperamental individuality: A developmental contextual view of the concept of goodness of fit. In G.A. Kohnstamm, J.E. Bates, & M.K. Rothbart (Eds.), *Temperament in childhood* (pp. 509–522). New York: John Wiley.

Magnusson, D., & Bergman, L.R. (1990). A pattern approach to the study of pathways from childhood to adulthood. In L. Robins & M. Rutter (Eds.), *Straight and devious pathways from childhood to adulthood* (pp. 101–115). New York: Cambridge University Press.

Matheny, A.P., Jr., Wilson, R.S., & Nuss, S.M. (1984). Toddler temperament: Stability across settings and over ages. *Child Development, 55*, 1200–1211.

Maziade, M. (1989a). Should adverse temperament matter to the clinician? An empirically based answer. In G.A. Kohnstamm, J.E. Bates, & M.K. Rothbart (Eds.), *Temperament in childhood* (pp. 421–435). New York: John Wiley.

Maziade, M. (1989b). Child temperament as an epidemiological concept. In W.B. Carey & S.C. McDevitt (Eds.), *Clinical and educational applications of temperament research* (pp. 175–186). Amsterdam: Swets & Zeitlinger B.V.

Maziade, M., Boutin, P., Cote, R., & Thivierge, J. (1986). Empirical characteristics of the NYLS temperament in middle childhood: Congruities and incongruities with other studies. *Child Psychiatry and Human Development, 17*, 38–52.

Maziade, M., Caron, C., Cote, R., Boutin, P., & Thivierge, J. (1990). Extreme temperament and diagnosis: A study in a psychiatric sample of consecutive children. *Archives of General Psychiatry, 47*, 477–484.

Maziade, M., Caron, C., Cote, R., Merette, C., Bernier, H., Laplante, B., Boutin, P., & Thivierge, J. (1990). Psychiatric status of adolescents who had extreme temperament at age 7. *American Journal of Psychiatry, 147*, 1531–1536.

Maziade, M., Cote, R., Boudreault, M., Thivierge, J., & Caperaa, P. (1984). The New York Longitudinal Studies model of temperament: Gender differences and demographic correlates in a French-speaking population. *Journal of the American Academy of Child Psychiatry, 23*, 582–587.

Maziade, M., Cote, R., & Thivierge, J. (1989). Significance of extreme temperament in infancy for clinical status in preschool years, I: Value of extreme temperament at 4–8 months for predicting diagnosis at 4.7 years. *British Journal of Psychiatry, 154*, 535–543.

Persson-Blennow, I., & McNeill, T.F. (1982). Factor analysis of temperament characteristics in children at 6 months, 1 year and 2 years of age. *British Journal of Educational Psychology, 52*, 51–57.

Rothbart, M.K. (1986). Longitudinal observation of infant temperament. *Child Development, 52*, 569–578.

Rutter, M. (1987). Temperament, personality, and personality disorder. *British Journal of Psychiatry, 150*, 443–458.

Rutter, M. (1989). Temperament: Conceptual issues and clinical implications. In G.A. Kohnstamm, J.E. Bates, & M.K. Rothbart (Eds.), *Temperament in childhood* (pp. 463–479). New York: John Wiley.

SAS Institute Inc. (1985). *SAS user's guide: Statistics, version 5 edition*. Cary, NC: Author.

Thomas, A., & Chess, S. (1977). *Temperament and development*. New York: Brunner/Mazel.

Thomas, A., & Chess, S. (1984). Genesis and evolution of behavioral disorders: From infancy to early adult life. *American Journal of Psychiatry, 141*, 1–9.

Thomas, A., & Chess, S. (1986). The New York Longitudinal Study: From infancy to early adult life. In R. Plomin & J. Dunn (Eds.), *The study of temperament: Changes, continuities, and challenges* (pp. 39–52). Hillsdale, NJ: Lawrence Erlbaum.

Thomas, A., & Chess, S. (1989). Temperament and personality. In G.A. Kohnstamm, J.E. Bates, & M.K. Rothbart (Eds.), *Temperament in childhood* (pp. 249–261). New York: John Wiley.

Thomas, A., Chess, S., & Birch, H.G. (1968). *Temperament and behavior disorders in children*. New York: New York University Press.

Thomas, A., Chess, S., Lerner, R.M., & Lerner, J.V. (1989). *Behavioral individuality in adult life*. Unpublished manuscript, New York University Medical Center.

Ward, J. (1963). Hierarchical grouping to optimize an objective function. *Journal of the American Statistical Association, 58,* 236–244.

Windle, M. (1988). Psychometric strategies of measures of temperament: A methodological critique. *International Journal of Behavioral Development, 11,* 171–201.

Windle, M. (1991). The difficult temperament in adolescence: Associations with substance use, family support, and problem behaviors. *Journal of Clinical Psychology, 47,* 310–315.

Windle, M. (1992). Temperament and social support in adolescence: Interrelations with depressive symptoms and delinquent behaviors. *Journal of Youth and Adolescence, 21,* 1–21.

Windle, M., & Lerner, R.M. (1986a). Reassessing the dimensions of temperamental individuality across the life span: The Revised Dimensions of Temperament Survey (DOTS-R). *Journal of Adolescent Research, 1,* 213–230.

Windle, M., & Lerner, R.M. (1986b). The goodness of fit model of temperament–context relations: Interaction or correlation? In J.V. Lerner & R.M. Lerner (Eds.), *New directions for child development: Temperament and psychosocial interaction in infancy and childhood* (pp. 109–120). San Francisco: Jossey-Bass.

For reprints: Jonathan G. Tubman, Ph.D., Research Institute on Addictions, 1021 Main Street, Buffalo, NY 14203

Review

The Development of Self-Understanding from Infancy through Adolescence

William Damon and Daniel Hart
Clark University

DAMON, WILLIAM, and HART, DANIEL. *The Development of Self-Understanding from Infancy through Adolescence.* CHILD DEVELOPMENT, 1982, **53,** 841–864. This review focuses on self-understanding, the cognitive basis for self-conception. Its purpose is to construct from the psychological literature a descriptive account of self-understanding development between infancy and adolescence. The paper begins by distinguishing self-understanding from other aspects of self-concept, in particular self-esteem. It is argued that a developmental model of self-understanding is a necessary step in the assessment and study of children's self-esteem. Next, the review presents a justification for studying self-understanding separately from other social cognitive achievements (such as understanding other people). With reference to William James's theory, the self as a cognitive concept is analyzed into its diverse components. Empirical studies of self-understanding in infants, children, and adolescents are then summarized and placed within the theoretical framework of this conceptual analysis. The review identifies the developmental trends consistently uncovered by empirical studies and presents a chronological account based on these trends. Finally, the review proposes a developmental model that outlines genetic and conceptual relations among different aspects of self-understanding. This model is extrapolated from the available literature, which is still in a germinal phase; therefore, the model is considered speculative at this point. It is hoped that the model will be subject to further empirical testing in time and will provide a theoretical basis for more precise definition of developmental patterns in self-understanding between infancy and adolescence.

Psychological studies of concept formation generally analyze how people understand a problematical issue representing some important feature of human life. Developmental studies are similar in intent, except that they examine people's conceptual understanding at different life periods, since developmentalists assume that with time the cognitive bases for people's conceptual understanding undergo substantial changes. In both developmental and nondevelopmental studies, the investigator's focus is on the intellectual strategies, considerations, and procedures by which a subject arrives at an understanding of the problematic issue, and on the nature of the conception ultimately expressed by a subject while reasoning about the issue.

This paradigm for concept-formation research has dominated studies of both physical and social intelligence from the earliest days of experimental psychology to the present. It is common to the logical reasoning studies of Piaget, Vygotsky, Bruner, and their followers; to the moral judgment studies of Kohlberg and his followers; and to most contemporary lines of research in cognitive development, including memory, perception, and social cognitive research. However, although pervasive, this paradigm has not been universal. For the concept of the self, an area that many consider to be focal for all others, a very different approach has been followed.

Self-concept research in psychology has followed a course all its own. Unlike research in other areas of concept formation, studying self-concept development usually has meant studying an evaluative orientation to the self called "self-esteem." This is true of the vast majority of both developmental and nondevelopmental studies considered by Wylie in her thorough review (Wylie 1979). For example, of the 151 "developmental" studies cited by

Preparation of this manuscript was supported in part by a grant to the first author from the Spencer Foundation. We gratefully acknowledge the help of Wendy Praisner and Jaye Shupin. Requests for reprints should be sent to William Damon, Department of Psychology, Clark University, Worcester, Massachusetts 01610.

[*Child Development*, 1982, 53, 841–864. 0009-3920/82/5304-0034$01.00]

Wylie, over 80% focus on self-evaluation. In other words, psychological research on self-concept development generally has been limited to research on children's self-esteem. Studies examining the changing nature of self-understanding during development have been so rare that recent commentators have expressed surprise and dismay over their scarcity (Brim 1976).

Esteem, unlike conceptual understanding, is an affective orientation and can be assessed according to its positive or negative valence. That is, measures of esteem determine the extent to which a subject positively or negatively values an object. The assessed variable therefore is the subject's affective orientation toward an object; once the positive or negative direction of the subject's orientation has been established, the measurement indexes are essentially quantitative. Conceptual understanding, on the other hand, is a cognitive activity that must be assessed in qualitative terms. A subject does not achieve positive or negative understanding of an object, and there can be no way of determining how much understanding a subject has in a quantitative sense. Rather, the analysis of understanding relies on descriptive accounts of cognitive processes that people use in their search for comprehension.

Why have psychologists approached the study of self-concept through an affective and quantitative dimension like esteem rather than, as is more typical in concept-formation research, through a cognitive framework, like understanding? Part of the answer is, no doubt, the shared assumption among child psychologists and educators that children's positive and negative self-feelings are implicated in children's social relations, school performances, mental health, and successful adaptation to the world in general (Jersild 1952; Rosenberg 1979). The suspected practical importance of self-esteem no doubt has encouraged many psychologists to design ways of measuring it quantitatively and determining its antecedents and correlates.

Despite the practical appeal of self-esteem as a research topic, psychologists have not generally met with success in using self-esteem as an explanatory factor. Wylie concludes her review with a complaint that "the most impressive thing which emerges from an overview of this book" is "the widespread occurrence of null or weak findings" in studies relating self-esteem to achievement, ability, and interpersonal relations, as well as a host of other antecedent or consequent variables (Wylie 1979, p. 690). A perusal of Wylie's review reveals that this is even more true of the child studies than of the adult studies. As Wylie points out, these null and weak results fly in the face of common sense, since we have many intuitive reasons to believe that self-regard should be importantly connected with successful adaptation to life. These are areas, she writes, in which "theory and conventional wisdom very confidently predict strong trends" (Wylie 1979, p. 690). What, then, has interfered with what should be a straightforward attempt to establish empirical relations between self-esteem and other critical life variables? Wylie's own speculations concern the methodological inadequacies inherent in existing self-esteem scales. We are in accord with this concern, but also believe that these inadequacies stem from a deeper problem not solvable by a piecemeal correction of self-esteem instruments.

There are many self-esteem scales, reflecting a variety of assumptions concerning the nature of the self-concept. Some measures (e.g., Rosenberg 1965) are based upon subjects' global assessments of their own self-worth, as reflected by how strongly subjects agree or disagree with statements like, "On the whole I am satisfied with myself." Other measures (e.g., Coopersmith 1967; Piers & Harris 1964) assess subject's feelings about a range of self-attributes, some specific and some quite general ("I am popular"; "I am a good person"). Some scale designers have consciously attempted to select items that are at least comprehensible across wide age ranges, thus avoiding the too common mistake of blindly applying items developed for adults to populations of children (see Wylie [1974] for a critical review). But of all the self-esteem scales in the current literature, none anticipates or "corrects for" developmental transformations in the conception of self. In other words, there is no measure of self-esteem that includes in its determination of scores a recognition that the conceptual bases of a subject's self-evaluations may be differently construed and differently weighed at different periods in the subject's development.

In order to accomplish this, self-esteem measurement would require as a prerequisite a developmental model of self-understanding to ensure that the test items of a self-esteem inventory reflected the major ways in which self-understanding is organized and reorganized throughout the life span. Failing such a developmental model, there can be no valid measures of self-esteem for children, adolescents, or adults (see also Brim [1976] and Keller, Ford, & Meacham [1978] for further discussion of this point). Even though self-esteem may appear to be the central practical issue requiring study, self-esteem cannot be assessed independently of self-understanding, as psychologists have traditionally attempted to do.

A developmental model of self-understanding is important for reasons beyond the valid assessment of self-esteem. Recent studies in social cognitive development have shown that social concepts require their own developmental analyses (Damon 1977, 1979; Flavell & Ross 1981; Turiel 1978). Self-understanding is a crucial constituent of a person's understanding of his or her social world. Unlike concepts of relations (friendship, authority) or concepts of regulations (fairness, social rules, conventions), all of which serve to connect the individual with society, the concept of self provides one with an understanding of one's differentiation from others in society. In this way, it establishes the cognitive basis for one's identity as a unique individual and for one's special position, status, and role within the social network. Though not synonymous with personality, it is the conceptual underpinning of it. But despite its importance as a social concept with developmental significance, self-understanding has received relatively little attention from researchers studying social cognitive development (Shantz 1975; in press).

Understanding Self in Comparison and Contrast with Understanding Others

The relative lack of interest in studying self-conception developmentally may be due in part to a long tradition that asserts the similarity between understanding self and understanding others (Baldwin 1902; Kohlberg 1969; Lewis & Brooks-Gunn 1979; Mead 1934; Piaget 1932/1965). If the two conceptual systems are structured the same, why study their development separately? Baldwin initiated this view in his discussion of the developmental processes that produce self-understanding. Baldwin believed that one comes to know the self only as one comes to know others and vice versa. In other words, both self and others are discovered simultaneously, in the course of interactions between self and others. From such interactions, a person eventually makes inferences about the nature of self and others. Both types of inferences—self-inferences and other-inferences—must be organized identically, since they share a common source in the social interactions that the person has experienced. In particular, Baldwin emphasized two social interactional processes that ensure the similarity between self- and other-knowledge: imitation and ejection. Through imitation, one takes onto the self the features that one observes in the other; and through ejection (imitation projected outward), one endows the other with characteristics that one observes in the self. So Baldwin wrote, "My sense of myself grows by imitation of you, and my sense of yourself grows in terms of myself" (Baldwin 1902, p. 185); and, elsewhere, "So the dialectic may be read thus: my thought is in the main, as to its character, a personal self, filled up with my thought of others, distributed variously as individuals; and my thought of others, as persons, is mainly filled up with myself" (1902, p. 18). A number of empirical studies have demonstrated that, in many respects, the two types of knowledge do indeed develop in parallel fashion in the individual (Livesly & Bromley 1973; Mullener & Laird 1971; Secord & Peevers 1974).

But despite the important parallels pointed out by Baldwin and his followers, there are also many obvious differences between self- and other-understanding. In fact, these differences often overshadow the similarities, and may lead us to question whether statements made by Baldwin, Lewis and Brooks-Gunn, and others, have too strongly stressed the similarities while neglecting the distinctions between self- and other-knowledge.

For one thing, there is the distinction mentioned by Baldwin himself between "that which is immediate and that which is objective" (1902, p. 18). Although Baldwin chose to ignore this issue, it hardly seems a minor point as far as the development of cognitive structures is concerned. It is difficult to imagine that the entire range of affect and cognition to which one has access in the "immediate" experience of self can be wholly and adequately represented through ejection or any other means for the sake of knowledge about others. An equally serious problem applies to the converse effort of gaining "objective" knowledge about the self. As Taylor and Fiske have pointed out, a person's perceptual orientation is "focussed on the situation in which he is behaving, and he literally cannot see himself performing his actions" (Taylor & Fiske 1975, p. 439). In contrast, a person often can observe others' actions with little difficulty. In Taylor and Fiske's own studies, they have found that ". . . point of view does indeed markedly determine causal interpretations of social situations" (p. 445). This permanent difference in perceptual orientations toward self and other seems certain to create differences in how self and other are conceived. Finally, there may be profound affective differences between how one receives feedback on the self versus how one receives feedback on others. One simply is emotionally invested in the nature of one's own identity in a different way than in the nature of others' identities, and this may well lead to differences in how personal information on self and other is cognitively processed.

The small bit of empirical research that bears on this issue contains some indications that self and other may indeed be construed in significantly different ways. Taylor and Fiske's studies have been noted above. Nisbett, Caputo, Legant, and Maracek (1973) report that one is likely to attribute one's own behavior in experimental situations to situational causes and free will, while one is likely to attribute another's behavior in the same situations to personality traits and dispositions. This phenomenon has been replicated in a number of studies reviewed by the same authors. Kuiper and Rogers (1979) report that subjects more easily and more confidently assess the applicability of a particular character adjective for themselves than for other persons. Livesly and Bromley (1973) found that one is more likely to use categories referring to inner experiences (such as motivation) when describing self than when describing others, suggesting that the two types of understanding may have a different emphasis if not different conceptual bases.

Self-understanding in itself is worthy of social cognitive investigation because of its unique role in social development and because of the likelihood that it has properties distinguishing it from other social concepts.

Historical Roots of Self-Understanding: William James's Theory

James contributed one of the most insightful and influential theoretical analyses of the self found in the psychological literature, and his discussion of self-understanding will serve as the framework within which we will organize and integrate a diverse body of research.

For James, the self was divided into two main components, the "Me" and the "I."

The "Me" aspect is "the sum total of all a person can call his" (James 1892/1961, p. 44). The primary elements of the "Me" were what James called the "constituents." These constituents are the actual qualities that define the self as known. They include all the material characteristics (body, possessions), all the social characteristics (relations, roles, personality), and all the "spiritual" characteristics (consciousness, thoughts, psychological mechanisms) that identify the self as a unique individual. Because of a consistent trend in the studies to be reviewed, we will add a fourth constituent: the active qualities of self (capabilities, typical activities). James analyzed his three primary constituents qualitatively in terms of their nature and relation to one another. His suggestion was that each individual organizes the constituents of the "Me" into a hierarchical structure that assigns differential values to each of the various material, social, and spiritual constituents. James's assumption was that all individuals hierarchize the basic constituent "Me" categories similarly, with "the bodily me at the bottom, the spiritual me at the top, and the extracorporeal material selves and the various social selves between" (p. 57). Although James admitted to some individual variation in how the constituents were formulated, he did not recognize the possibility that their hierarchical interrelations might vary, both across individuals and within one individual over time. This is the same error by omission found in recent self-esteem research, as we have noted above. James's theory may in fact have led later researchers astray in this regard, particularly since James himself offered some speculations about how to measure self-esteem.

The "I" is the "self-as-knower," the aspect of self that continually organizes and interprets experience in a purely subjective manner. The individual is aware of the "I" through three types of experiences: *continuity, distinctness,* and *volition.* A stable self-identity derives from a sense of the continuity of the self-as-knower. As James wrote, ". . . each of us spontaneously considers that by 'I' he means something always the same" (p. 63). A feeling of individuality, of distinctness from others, also derives from the subjective nature of the self-as-knower: "Other men's experiences, no matter how much I may know about them, never bear this vivid, this peculiar brand" (p. 71). A sense of personal volition is perhaps the quintessential experience of the self-as-knower. The very notion of subject denotes an active processor of experience. Through one's own thoughts and interpretations of the world, one exerts agency of the most fundamental kind over self. Finally, implicit in the experience of each of these self-features (continuity, distinctness, and volition) is the additional second-order awareness of the *self-reflectivity* that knows the nature of self.

James predicted that the "I" aspect of the self-duality would prove elusive to empirical study precisely because of its indeterminate nature. It is difficult to observe or characterize a phenomenon that is totally subjective and that, therefore, may change unpredictably from moment to moment. Also, unlike the somewhat circumscribed nature of the "Me" (which is mainly the collection of definitions that one and others construct for one's self), the "I" potentially incorporates all of a person's interactions with the world. The "I" enters into all of a person's experience since it determines the unique nature of all the person's interpretations of events, people, and things. It determines the very meaning of life events, providing itself even with a perspective on itself. James's conclusion was that inquiry into the "I" was best left to philosophical rather than psychological analysis, and that psychologists interested in the self-concept should focus on the "Me."

But Mead offered a constructive solution for psychologists who would hesitate to deny their discipline access to the aspect of self responsible for such essential sensibilities as continuity and volition. Mead suggested approaching the "I" through the "Me" by studying individuals' *knowledge* of both their objective and subjective selves. This amounts to a suggestion to focus the empirical study of self not on self in all its duality but, rather, on one's *self-understanding* of both the "Me" and "I." The "Me" is, by definition, the understanding of self as object, so that the study of the "Me" is by nature the study of self-understanding in one of its components. Extending such study to the "I" means, in addition, exploring individuals' understanding of self-as-subject. *Self-understanding*, then, includes in this comprehensive definition an individual's knowledge and reflections on the self-as-known as well as on the self-as-knower. It includes, in other words, an individual's conception of "I" characteristics such as continuity, distinctness, volition, and self-reflection. It also includes the rest of the individual's self-definition, the main body of the "Me." It does not include the actual "I" in the Jamesian sense, because this extends beyond self-understanding to the entire domain of psychological functioning. Our definition of self-understanding as the totality of a person's conceptions of the "I" and the "Me" is the definition that we shall use throughout this review.

Chronology of Self-Understanding from Infancy to Adulthood: A Review of Empirical Studies

The following review draws on a range of studies conducted with differing purposes, methodologies, and theoretical orientations. Many of the studies were not originally intended to provide developmental accounts of self-understanding. But, regardless of a researcher's own goals, a piece of research often sheds light on phenomena of interest to other researchers. The studies are described in detail to reveal the diversity of methods and results found in the literature; we shall, however, try to indicate how each study fits into James's analysis, presented earlier. The consistent thread uniting all the studies selected for this review is that they illuminate the nature of self-understanding during at least one period of human development. The overall aim of the review is to sketch a broader developmental picture out of a diversity of separate studies, all of which in themselves may be relatively narrow in scope. A final caveat: the subjects in these studies are limited to American schoolchildren, and the ontogenetic trends to be outlined in the review may be descriptive of only this population.

Infancy.—Infants cannot reflect verbally on the nature of self, nor can they understand the complex instructions required for engagement in most psychologists' tasks. Because of these and other similar methodological considerations, studies of infant self-understanding have been narrower in scope than studies during later periods. In fact, there has been only one experimental paradigm that consistently has yielded data on self-understanding during infancy: testing for self-recognition by showing images of themselves through pictures, mirrors, or other visual media. The monopolistic dominance of this paradigm has limited our knowledge of infant self-understanding to the domain of visual self-recognition. We do not know whether other modes of self-recognition (such as through touch, hearing, and smell) might provide better indexes of infant self-understanding. Nor do we know whether self-recognition in general is a good representative of the full range of infant self-understanding. Most important, we do not even know whether this limitation is due to shortcomings in our experimental ingenuity, or whether it is an inevitable result of infants' limited conceptual abilities (implying, in the latter case, that visual self-recognition does fairly represent the extent of infant self-understanding).

Its limitations aside, the visual self-recognition paradigm has been used successfully by investigators and has produced several mutually supporting accounts of developmental trends. The most common—and the oldest technique—for studying visual self-recognition is observing subjects' reactions to their own mirror images.

The scientific use of this technique with infants dates back to Charles Darwin, who noted in his diary descriptions of his 9-month-old son that the boy would look at a mirror and exclaim "Ah!" when his name was spoken (Darwin 1877). Darwin concluded that this act signified his son's first act of conscious self-recognition. In a nineteenth-century observation of an infant looking in the mirror, Preyer reported a similar "conscious" self-recognition first appearing at 14 months in his infant subject (Preyer 1893).

Modern investigators have also turned to the mirror as a tool for exploring infants' self-recognition. The first of these modern efforts was Dixon's observations of five infants followed longitudinally from ages 4 months to 12 months (Dixon 1957). Dixon recorded the infants' reactions to mirrors placed at one end of their cribs, focusing particularly on "behavioral sequences" like smiling at the image, talking to it, trying to touch it, and so on. In addition, Dixon rigged an experimental setup of one- and two-way mirrors and special lighting that presented to the infants images of self, another infant, and the mother, sometimes simultaneously and sometimes alternately.

On the basis of his observations, Dixon reported a developmental sequence of self-recognition that remained constant for all five subjects. Dixon's developmental sequence consisted of four stages, the order of which did not vary across infants, although the ages associated with each stage did. The first stage, which Dixon observed in infants' behavior at 4 months, he called "Mother": the infant shows no sustained interest in its own reflection, but does show immediate recognition of its mother's reflection; the infant smiles, looks, and vocalizes at the mother's image as soon as it is presented. At stage 2, called "Playmate" by Dixon, the infant becomes interested in its own reflection, but ". . . his behavior toward his mirror image is indistinguishable from that when placed before another infant" (p. 253). Stage 2 lasts until about 6 months. Beginning at around 7 months, according to Dixon, the infant "relates the mirror image to himself" by repeating simple actions (opening the mouth) while gazing in the mirror. This is stage 3, which Dixon calls "Who dat do dat when I do dat?" The infant is now capable of distinguishing between its own mirror image and that of another infant and prefers to interact with the image of the other rather than that of the self. At stage 4, beginning at 12 months, the infant may even cry or turn away from its own reflection, supposedly for this same reason. The infant now unambiguously demonstrates recognition of self and other, shifting its gaze appropriately when asked, "Where is (X)?" "Where are you?"

Although Dixon's study established the fact of self-recognition in young infants and offered some preliminary indications of developmental trends, it left a number of unanswered questions concerning the basis of self-recognition at this early age. From Dixon's observational procedure, it is impossible to determine what the young infant recognizes in its own reflection. This is because, as Lewis and Brooks-Gunn (1979) later pointed out, mirror images contain at least two kinds of clues for self-recognition: contingency clues and feature clues. In the case of the former, a person looking in a mirror sees an image that moves immediately in tandem to the person's own physiological sensations of movement. In the case of the latter, a person looking in a mirror can observe images of particular facial and bodily features, some of which may become familiar to the person through repeated observation. It is easy to see how an infant could use either contingency or feature clues to distinguish the mirror images of self and other. Or the infant might use both types of clues. Dixon's experimental design offered no means of isolating or disconfounding these two types of self-recognition clues. The only "feature" of self to which we know Dixon's infants responded was their names, beginning at around 18 months (at the end of Dixon's stage 4), which is most nearly categorized as a material constituent of the "Me." In addition Dixon's study is weakened by its small sample size and lack of reliability and other psychometric procedures.

Using an ingenious technique similar to one introduced by Gallup (1970) in chimpanzee research, Amsterdam (1972) was able to isolate a type of facial feature that young infants can use in self-recognition. In Amsterdam's experiment, infants' noses were surreptitiously dabbed with rouge, and the infants were placed in front of mirrors and asked, "See?" and "Who's that?" Amsterdam recorded responses similar to those noted by Dixon (smiling, vocalizing, gazing, touching), although in more systematic fashion, with traditional reliability checks. Also, Amsterdam's study had a full sample size of 88 infants ages 3 through 24 months, including two infants followed longitudinally from 12 to 24 months.

Amsterdam defined full self-recognition as self-directed behavior indicating awareness of the red spot on the nose. Her assumption was that "the child's ability to locate a red spot on the face shows that he associates his own face with the face in the mirror . . ." (p. 304). In addition, of course, special attention to the red spot indicates an awareness that the self has stable facial features that do not include a reddened nose. Amsterdam reported that this type of "full" self-recognition was found only at 20–24 months. In addition, it was not until this age that Amsterdam's infants showed other conscious signs of self-recognition, such as "self-admiring" behavior (strutting, preening) and embarrassed behavior (blushing, coyness). Amsterdam's conclusion, contrary to those of Darwin, Preyer, and Dixon before her, was that conscious self-recognition, based on stable features of self, does not normally occur until the end of the second year of life. Prior to this, Amsterdam found two of the phases described by Dixon: (1) the "playmate" phase (6–12 months), in which the child treats the image as an interacting peer; and (2) a "withdrawal" phase (13–24 months), in which the child expresses weariness of the mirror image. But, unlike Dixon, Amsterdam doubts that during either of these phases the infant "relates the mirror image to the self." Amsterdam suggests that Dixon wrongly inferred self-recognition from the infant's particular concern with the contingency aspects of its own mirror image; and, despite this particular concern, the infant younger than 20 months sees only the image of a strange peer in the mirror.

Amsterdam's focus on feature recognition provides a methodologically valuable means of separating out distinguishable components of self-recognition, but one wonders whether she has dismissed the significance of early contingency awareness too lightly. Missing from her design is a means of determining whether contingency awareness, either independent from or in combination with feature recognition, is an index of self-recognition; however, she does demonstrate that at 20 months the infant does have some knowledge of the bodily constituents of the "Me" and an awareness that these constituents are continuous over time.

In a systematic series of studies, Lewis and Brooks-Gunn (1979) were able to present both contingency and feature clues to infants in an orderly and disconfounded way. They separated the two types of clues by using a variety of mediums to present the child with the self's image, such as mirrors, photographs, and videotapes: mirror images always move contingently with the self, photographed images never do, and videotape images can be either contingent or noncontingent. In one of their studies using a mirror to present infants with their images, Lewis and Brooks-Gunn followed the same procedure used by Amsterdam with infants from 9 months to 24 months of age. Their results basically parallel those of Amsterdam. However, the authors found infants as young as 15 months responded to their reddened noses. This is a younger age for the behavior than that reported by Amsterdam.

Lewis and Brooks-Gunn's videotape studies were designed to further investigate the development of self-recognition by separating contingency and feature clues. Infants' responses to three types of TV images were compared: (1) "live" images of themselves; (2) images of themselves shot 1 week earlier; and (3) images of another infant. In assessing their subjects' responses to the TV images, Lewis and Brooks-Gunn made special note of the infants' tendencies to imitate and to "play with" the image on the TV screen. In addition, the infants' facial and vocal expressions were recorded as well as their movements toward and away from the image.

Subjects in the TV studies were the same ages as those in the mirror study (9 months and up), and the TV results nicely supplemented the mirror-study findings. Infants as young as 9 months distinguished the live TV image of self from the other images presented, which they indicated by playing more with it and by generally responding more positively to it than to the other images. These results confirm Dixon's tentative findings and indicate that initial visual self-recognition is present at least as early as 9 months and is based on the principle of contingency: when an image moves along with the self, it is possible at a very early age to recognize the self in that image. It should be noted that other researchers (e.g., Papousek & Papousek 1974) have found signs of such self-recognition even prior to 9 months, although their techniques do not confirm this as convincingly as Lewis and Brooks-Gunn's.

Although the ability to use contingency as a clue to self-recognition is present in the child as young as 9 months, infants develop a greater responsiveness to contingency as they grow older. Lewis and Brooks-Gunn found a steady increase in infants' awareness of contingency through the second year of life. But the most striking developmental advance was not in the infants' use of contingency but in their use of physical appearance in recognizing the self. To uncover this developmental advance, Lewis and Brooks-Gunn compared their subject's responses with the noncontingent televised self-image (shot a week ago) with their subjects' responses to the televised image of another baby. It was not until 15 months of age that infants distinguished their own pretaped images from images of another child on the TV screen. When they were able to make this distinction, they smiled at and moved toward the other baby's image more than toward their own image, and they imitated and played with their own image more than with the other baby's image. These differences in behavior, which began at about 15 months, increased further as the infants grew older. Lewis and Brooks-Gunn speculate that the infants of 15 months and older were able to distinguish their own images from the images of other babies by referring to differences in the facial features of the two, meaning that at about 15 months infants begin to know what their faces look like.

This developmental progression is confirmed further by the findings of Lewis and Brooks-Gunn's picture study. By showing infants pictures of themselves and other babies, the researchers found the first clear feature recognition of self in infants aged 15–18 months. Signs of this recognition included smiling, gazing, and pointing to one's picture when one's name was called, as opposed to ignoring or frowning at the picture of peers. (In one small pilot sample, the researchers found the smiling sign in infants as young as 9 months, but only occasionally and sporadically.) Since pictoral images are noncontingent on a subject's actions but do reveal facial and other physical cues, age trends from the picture study coincide with the age trends from Lewis and Brooks-Gunn's TV and mirror studies.

Further findings from the picture study suggest some of the basic categories that infants, beginning at 15 months or so, use to identify themselves. These categories are sex and age. When infants of 15 months begin distinguishing themselves from others on the basis of noncontingent cues, they are particularly attuned to physical features associated with their sex and their age. They find it especially easy to tell themselves apart from opposite-sex babies and from older persons. The researchers believe that infants are able to discern the distinctive facial features that accompany sex and age: females have different-shaped faces (as well as different hair styles) from males, and babies have faces and heads that are shaped differently from those of older people. In their initial constructions of the self-as-object (the "Me"), infants focus particularly on facial features, as the Lewis and Brooks-Gunn studies indicate. Of all facial features, those associated with sex and age are particularly apparent to infants as they begin constructing "categorical" knowledge of themselves.

Surveying the preceding literature as well as the results of their own studies, Lewis and Brooks-Gunn postulate that there are four major advances in infants' self-knowledge during the first 2 years of life. The first of these advances is seen in infants younger than 3 months. Since the infants in Lewis and Brooks-Gunn's studies were all 6 months or older, the authors' description of this first infant self-knowledge advance is conjectural, based on informal observation and outside sources in the psychological literature. From birth to 3 months of age, the initial organizing principle to appear in infants' self-knowledge is an unlearned attraction to the images of other people and especially to the images of young babies. This attraction shows up in a young infant's fascination with mirror images, drawings, and pictures of faces, especially when the face is that of the self or of another young infant. The second advance occurring between 3 and 8 months of age in infant self-knowledge is the ability to recognize the self through contingency cues. The essence of this ability is the understanding that the self is the origin and cause of the moving visual image that the subject sees in the mirror or on the TV screen.

The third self-knowledge advance, between the infancy ages of 8 and 12 months, is the association of certain stable categorical features with the self. The infant now can go beyond recognizing the self merely as the origin of paired causes and effects in the world and can begin constructing the self as a permanent object with enduring qualities. In this manner, the permanence of the self is realized and becomes an important organizing principle for the infant's knowledge of both self-as-subject and self-as-object. Finally, the fourth infancy advance, occurring throughout the second year of life, is the defining of the self through categorical features alone, independent of any contingency knowledge that the subject may have.

Although Lewis and Brooks-Gunn are referring to the physical constituents of the "Me" when they write of the development of knowledge of the categorical features of self, there is evidence indicating that the child is aware of other characteristics of the "Me."

As part of a larger study of cognitive development in the second and third years of life, Kagan (1981) investigated the child's willingness and ability to imitate an action performed by an experimenter with a variety of toys. Each child was first allowed to play with a variety of toys for about 15 min. The experimenter then approached the child, gained the child's attention, and demonstrated a symbolic act using several of the toys the child had been playing with (the specific act to be performed was de termined ahead of time). Kagan found that some of the infants cried after observing the experimenter's act, a reaction Kagan claims is due to the infant's recognition that he or she is not capable of performing that act. Consequently, the child must be aware of the self's limitations. Crying following an act was absent in infants 20 months old. It peaked to 31% of the infants at 23, 24, and 25 months. At 29 months, no child cried following the act. The data indicate that the child becomes aware of the self's action capabilities at around 24 months of age. The decline in crying shortly thereafter, according to Kagan, is due to the child's increased ability to perform the act or to deal with the self's limitations without crying. It does not represent a decline in self-awareness.

The assumption that self-awareness appears around 24 months is further buttressed by Kagan's finding that children's self-descriptive statements ("I play"; "I can do this") increase in frequency around this age. Self-descriptive statements reflect self-awareness because a child could not make meaningful statements about the self if the child were not aware of the self's qualities. Kagan's research reveals that, in addition to knowledge about the self's physical constituents, the child is aware of the self's actions and capabilities, or active constituents. Active constituents of the "Me" (e.g., "I play"; "I can tie my shoe") are qualitatively different from the physical constituents of the "Me" (e.g., "I have red hair"; "I have a big bicycle") and must be treated as distinct areas in an accurate depiction of self-understanding development. We shall return to this point in the next section.

Column 1 in table 1 summarizes the trends revealed by the infant research. The remaining three columns summarize trends from the childhood and adolescent studies reviewed in the following two sections.

Childhood.—Research on children's self-knowledge is different in character from infant self research for the simple reason that children are able to communicate their self-conceptions verbally. Because of this, the study of childhood self-knowledge is not limited to the study of visual self-recognition, as it was during infancy. Indeed, through the use of interview and other verbal procedures, researchers have been able to probe children's conceptions of many psychological issues related to self. These issues include the nature of the self's basic components (including mind and body), one's awareness of self, one's definition of self, self in comparison to others, self in relation to others, and points of pride and shame in self. From all these diverse efforts, we can piece together a chronology of self-knowledge as it develops in the childhood years.

In a broad-based study of children's "naive epistemologies" (i.e., their spontaneous philosophical analyses of the world), Broughton asked children a number of open-ended questions concerning the self, particularly focusing on "I" conceptions such as volition and distinctness from others (Broughton 1978). Broughton's questions were in the form of direct interrogations, like: "What is the self?" "What is the mind?" "What is the difference between the mind and the body?" As is traditional in clinical interviews with children, Broughton probed the child's responses with a series of follow-up questions. From subjects' answers, Broughton derived a developmental progression of naive epistemologies that covers the period from childhood through middle adulthood. We shall consider only the aspects of Broughton's outline that concern self-knowledge. In this section, we describe Broughton's two childhood levels; in the next section, his two adolescent levels.

In early childhood, according to Broughton, the self is conceived strictly in physical terms. The self is believed to be part of the body. Usually this means the head, although other body parts are also cited, including the whole body. Accordingly, the child confuses self, mind, and body. Because of this type of reasoning, young children typically express a number of peculiar opinions unique to this early level. For example, because young children believe that self and mind are simply parts of the body, they often say that any body may have a self and a mind, including animals, plants, and dead people. Further, since self is a body part, it can be described in terms of material dimensions such as size, shape, or color. Thus children at this level distinguish themselves from others on the basis of their physical appearances and other material attributes: I am different from Johnny because I have blond hair, different

TABLE 1

Summary of Research Findings on Self-understanding Development from Infancy through Adolescence

Aspect of Self-understanding	Infancy and Childhood (1)	Late Childhood (2)	Early Adolescence (3)	Late Adolescence (4)
The "Me":				
Physical	Knowledge of physical features and name (Amsterdam 1972; Broughton 1978; Dixon 1957; Lewis & Brooks-Gunn 1979; Selman 1980)	Physical aspects of self are less important than psychological aspects (Selman 1980)	Unknown	Unknown
Active	Awareness of self's action capabilities (Kagan 1981) Activities are a dominant aspect of self (Keller, Ford, & Meacham 1978; Secord & Peevers 1974)	Self's comparative ability becomes important (Secord & Peevers 1974; Ruble, in press); self acts as result of surrounding physical & emotional environs (Bernstein 1980)	Unknown	Unknown
Social	Unknown	Membership in group & familial relationships (Livesly & Bromley 1973)	Social personality begins to become important (Rosenberg 1979)	Social personality traits are roots of self's actions (Bernstein 1980)
Psychological	Knowledge of self's preferences and aversions (Keller, Ford, & Meacham 1978)	Self's subjective, psychological experience is distinguished from material experience (Broughton 1978; Selman 1980)	Conception of mind as processor of experience (Broughton 1978)	Belief systems characterize self (Secord & Peevers 1974); beliefs are roots of self's actions (Bernstein 1980); development of notion of unconscious (Selman 1980); mental world has own system of internal regulation (Broughton 1978)

TABLE 1 (*Continued*)

Aspect of Self-understanding	Infancy and Childhood (1)	Late Childhood (2)	Early Adolescence (3)	Late Adolescence (4)
The "I":				
Continuity	Continuity based on physical features and name (Amsterdam 1972; Guardo & Bohan 1971; Lewis & Brooks-Gunn 1979)	Continuity asserted on basis of bodily and psychological attributes (Guardo & Bohan 1971)	Past and future of self becomes increasingly important (Secord & Peevers 1974)	Unknown
Distinctness	Contingent action, physical features, and name distinguish self from others (Broughton 1978; Guardo & Bohan 1971; Lewis & Brooks-Gunn 1979)	Psychological attributes emerge as criterion of distinctness (Broughton 1978; Guardo & Bohan 1971)	The privacy and immediacy of self-knowledge, as opposed to the difficulty of knowing others, distinguishes self from other (Broughton 1978)	Distinctness from others increasingly mentioned in self-definition (Montemayor & Eisen 1977)
Volition	Volition located in body part (Broughton 1978; Selman 1980)	Self can manipulate correspondence between external behavior and internal feelings, and therefore can deceive others (Selman 1980)	Mind, as active processor of self's experience, can manipulate the self's experience (Selman 1980)	Mind controls only conscious experience, while unconscious experience can affect behavior (Selman 1980); self judges self's actions (Broughton 1978; Secord & Peevers 1974); feeling of self-direction connected with a sense of pride (Rosenberg 1979)
Self-reflection	Unknown	Beginning distinction between subjective and objective (Broughton 1978; Selman 1980)	Awareness of self-awareness (Selman 1980); self-knowledge is immediate and complete because self reflects on itself (Broughton 1978)	Recognition that there are some experiences of which the self is not aware (Selman 1980); belief in real and phony selves (Broughton 1980)
Organization and integration of disparate aspects of self	Unknown	Statements about self are segregated from one another (Bernstein 1980)	Superficial integration of self-statements (Bernstein 1980)	Self-statements are organized into self-system (Bernstein 1980)

from that tree because I am smaller, different from my sister because I have a bike. Even the volitional aspects of self—that is, one's motivations and "free will"—are attributed to physical body parts. The child might say, for example, that the self is the brain, and the brain tells you what to do.

Later, when the child is about 8 years old, Broughton's second level of self-knowledge emerges. Children now begin to understand the mental and volitional aspects of self on their own terms, removed from their direct links to any particular body parts. In other words, children now begin to distinguish between mind and body, although this distinction is not as finely articulated as it will be in the adolescent years. The beginning distinction between mental and physical enables children to appreciate the subjective nature of self. One is distinct from others not simply because one looks different or has different material possessions but because one has different thoughts and feelings. The self's essential nature is therefore defined internally rather than externally and becomes a matter of psychological rather than physical attributes. Broughton quotes from a 10-year-old at this level: "I am one of a kind . . . There could be a person who looks like me or talks like me, but no one who has every single detail I have. Never a person who thinks exactly like me" (p. 86).

Using different types of interview procedures, Selman (1980) replicated much of Broughton's developmental progression, investigating both the changing understanding of the "I," such as volition, and the constituents of the "Me." Rather than asking children direct questions, Selman posed the following dilemma: "Eight-year-old Tom is trying to decide what to buy his friend, Mike, for a birthday party. By chance, he meets Mike on the street and learns that Mike is extremely upset because his dog, Pepper, has been lost for two weeks. In fact, Mike is so upset that he tells Tom, 'I miss Pepper so much that I never want to look at another dog again.' Tom goes off, only to pass a store with a sale on puppies. Only two are left, and these will soon be gone." Children are then asked whether or not Tom should buy Mike the puppy as a birthday present. Follow-up questions probe a number of psychological issues revolving around the perspectives of self and other. For example, sample questions are, "Can you ever fool yourself into thinking that you feel one way when you really feel another?" and "Is there an inside and an outside to a person?" From children's responses to this dilemma, Selman has outlined three childhood levels of self-awareness.

Selman's first level, which he calls "physicalistic conceptions of self," is almost identical with Broughton's first level. At this level, the child makes no distinction between inner psychological experience and outer material experience. In response to the Mike dilemma, children at this level typically will deny that a person's statements and behavior can be distinguished from the person's feelings: "If I say that I don't want to see a puppy ever again, then I really won't ever want to." Since the child is not aware of psychological experience apart from overt physical attributes and acts, the child views the self only in physical terms. The self's volitional tendencies are tied to specific body parts and derive strictly from the functioning of these parts; for instance, "I am the boss of myself . . . [because] my mouth told my arm and my arm does what my mouth tells it to do" (p. 95).

Later in childhood, according to Selman, children recognize differences between inner and outer states, and define the "true self" in terms of subjective inner states rather than material outer states. Unlike Broughton, Selman believes that this developmental transformation in children's self-knowledge occurs in two levels rather than in one. First, writes Selman, children by age 6 or so realize that psychological experience is not the same as physical experience, but they still believe that the two types of experience are consistent with one another. Then, by age 8 or so, the child realizes that the self can fool oneself as well as others because of discrepancies between one's inner experience and one's outer appearance. Thus, Mike might really feel that he wants another puppy (psychological experience) even though he might say he does not (behavioral appearance). At this point, conscious deception becomes a possibility for the child, because the child is able to manipulate the relation between internal and external reality. The child now sees that the self can monitor its own thoughts in a more direct way than others can. This means that one can put on a facade that others may not be able to penetrate. While the child admits that sometimes one's facade will fool the self as well as others, the child is also aware that generally the self has better access to one's own psychological experience than do others. This appreciation of the private, subjective nature of self, according to Selman, leads the child to a "reflective understanding that the self is capable of gaining inner strength by having confidence in its own abilities" (p. 100).

Although Selman's three levels add some intricacies to Broughton's two-level progression, the two researchers agree on the basic childhood shift from physicalistic to psychological conceptions of self. Research by Guardo and Bohan (1971) on the cognitive bases for self-identity in children ages 6 through 9 provides further evidence of this shift. Guardo and Bohan focused specifically on children's knowledge of four dimensions of self: humanity, sexuality, individuality, and continuity. Humanity refers to the sense that one has human qualities distinct from other life forms. Sexuality is the awareness of one's own sex and sex role. Individuality is the sense that one is unique in the world. Continuity refers to one's belief that one is connected with one's past and future self. Guardo and Bohan assert that, taken together, these dimensions provide the individual with a sense that he or she "is one being with a unique identity who has been, is, and will be a male (or female) human person separate from and entirely like no other" (p. 1911). The reader will recognize in this assertion the major elements of James's "I." Concordant with James and his many followers, Guardo and Bohan approach the study of self with the point of view that the self is a psychological construct whose major function is to provide one with a cognitive sense of one's individuality. Guardo and Bohan's findings tell us how children between 6 and 9 do this.

In order to test for children's senses of self, Guardo and Bohan asked their subjects if they believed that they could assume the identity of another being. Three types of being were specifically mentioned by the interviewer: a pet (testing for humanity), an opposite-sex peer (testing for sexuality), and a same-sex peer (testing for individuality). The researcher's assumption was that, if children believe that they can assume the identity of another being, they lack the dimension of self on which the question focused. In addition to these identity tests, the researchers tested for continuity by asking subjects whether they were the same persons in the past and future. Follow-up questions for all items for children's understanding of the four dimensions were asked. For example, a typical probe question was, "Why do you think you could never become a dog?" In this manner the researchers could determine not only whether the child had a sense of humanity but also the cognitive basis of that sense.

Guardo and Bohan found that all children in the 6–9 age range had a definite sense of all four self-dimensions. That is, virtually all subjects expressed belief in their own immutable humanity, sexuality, individuality, and continuity. This, of course, should come as no surprise to us, considering that Lewis and Brooks-Gunn found some awareness of at least the last three of these dimensions in infants younger than 2. More revealing, from a developmental point of view, was Guardo and Bohan's finding that the conceptual basis for children's belief in these dimensions changes with age. Six- and 7-year-olds base their beliefs on their physical and behavioral characteristics. For example, a 7-year-old might say that it would be impossible to become just like a particular peer because that peer is shorter and not as good at basketball. Or the child might say that he will be the same as an adult because he will have the same name. Eight- and 9-year-olds use many similarly physicalistic notions but also add to their explanations some psychological ones as well. For example, a 9-year-old might say that it would be impossible to assume a friend's identity because the friend has different likes and dislikes. Guardo and Bohan's study focuses more directly on the understanding of the "I" than do Broughton or Selman's studies, the main thrust of the findings from all these investigations is basically the same: during middle childhood there is a developmental shift in self-knowledge—from physicalistic to psychological conceptions.

One recent study, however, has given us reason to modify the developmental sequence suggested by the writings of Broughton, Selman, and Guardo and Bohan. In this study, Keller et al. (1978) showed that very young children (ages 3–5) think of the self more in terms of activities than in terms of body parts or material attributes. The researchers used several techniques to arrive at this conclusion. First, children were asked to spontaneously say up to 10 things about themselves. Second, they were asked to complete the following sentences: "I am a ———." "I am a boy/girl who ———." On these items, children responded most frequently with action statements, such as, "I play baseball" or, "I walk to school." Body image answers ("I am big"; "I have blue eyes") were far less common. In fact, other than action statements, which constituted over 50% of children's responses, no other category of response occurred more than 10% of the time, although it is interesting to note that about 5% of even the youngest children's responses referred to their likes and dislikes, a psychological aspect of self. In a further confirmation of this trend, the researchers gave children direct choices between action and body image statements. To do this, the researchers asked subjects which of the following types of statements subjects would rather have written about themselves: "Johnny has a nice face"; "Johnny can brush his teeth." Children overwhelmingly chose the latter type of statement, indicating again their preference for action descriptions of the self.

The results of Keller, Ford, and Meachum's study add a new dimension to our understanding of self-knowledge in early childhood. These results need not be taken as a contradiction of the physicalistic level proposed by the researchers cited above, as long as the notion physicalistic is conceived broadly enough to include physical actions as well as body image and material possessions. In fact, this is in line with Selman's use of the word physicalistic: Selman's illustrative examples of his first self-awareness level include instances of children speaking about their actions. However, for the sake of precise developmental description, it may be wisest to separate the notion of active self-constituents from the notion of physical self-constituents, as we alluded to earlier in our discussion of James. In fact, in light of Keller, Ford, and Meachum's study, we might conclude that the active self predominates in the preschool years. This conclusion also accords with earlier research by Secord and Peevers (1974), who claimed, on the basis of free-response data, that kindergarten children describe themselves almost exclusively in terms of activities like play. However, we must give some recognition to Broughton's and others' consistent evidence in favor of bodily and material self-definitions in very young children. Even if action does dominate self-knowledge at early developmental levels, it is clearly used along with more blatantly physical notions like body image and material possessions. It seems that elements of both active and physical self can be found in the preschool years. As long as we do not conflate action with other physicalistic notions, we can see that self may be conceived in multiple dimensions even in the early phases of development.

There are also reasons to believe that action continues to be an important element in older children's self-knowledge, only in a somewhat different way. In their study of children's free responses to self-questions, Secord and Peevers report that, even by third grade, children describe the self primarily in terms of activities. But there is a new quality in the third-graders' active self-statements: unlike preschoolers, who describe self in terms of its typical activities ("I ride a bike"), older children describe themselves in terms of their active abilities relative to others ("I can ride a bike better than my brother"). Secord and Peevers describe this as a shift from a focus on the self's habitual action to a focus on the self's action competencies. It indicates that children are now distinguishing themselves from others on comparative rather than absolute terms. That is, the issue is no longer what I do (or do not do) but what I can do well in comparison with others. This developmental shift serves the differentiating function of self, since it provides a sharper means of establishing one's differences as an individual from others.

A recent set of findings in social psychological research confirms the developmental shift noted by Secord and Peevers. In a programmatic series of studies, Ruble (in press) has investigated children's use of social comparisons in their self-evaluations. The basic design of these studies was to give children a difficult task and then to offer them feedback on their own performances as well as information about the performances of other children their age. Subjects were then asked for self-evaluations. Ruble found that children younger than 7 made almost no reference to the information about other children's performances. Rather, they based their self-evaluations on the "absolute standard" of whether they completed the tasks. In contrast, children over 7 frequently compared their performances against those of others and based their self-evaluations on such social comparisons. Interestingly, Lively and Bromley (1973) report remarkably similar quantitative results in their study of self-descriptions: at around age 7, children's use of comparative competence notions in their descriptions of self and other triples.

We can see from the combined results of studies reviewed in this section the early use and later transformation of active knowledge of the self. In addition, we know that the self is often defined physically at early ages, and that psychological self-notions emerge toward the end of childhood. There is also one further aspect of self-knowledge that can be found in children's statements: the social self-constituents. Livesly and Bromley (1973) have noted that in childhood children refer to social group memberships in their self-descriptions. A child might say, for example, that he is a Boy Scout or a Catholic. This indicates that, although the social self does not seem to be as dominant during childhood as either the active or the physical self, it is occasionally present in the self-awareness of children at all ages, as is the psychological self. These are indications of the multiple bases of self-knowledge during all phases of childhood development (see cols. 2 and 3, table 1).

Adolescence.—There is noteworthy convergence in findings from several independently conducted studies of adolescent self-understanding. Virtually all researchers have found that, with development, adolescent self-understanding shows an increasing use of psychological and social relational concepts for describing the "Me," a more prominent belief in the "I" 's agency and volitional power, and a tendency toward integration of the disparate aspects of self into an internally consistent construct system. In addition to these areas of agreement, some researchers have also reported other special features of adolescent thinking, such as an awareness of self-reflection (again a part of the "I" conception), that are not always apparent in every study because of methodological considerations. Accordingly, despite a wide overall consensus concerning general developmental trends, there do exist some important differences among studies in their emphasis on particular qualities that characterize adolescent self-understanding. In this section, we shall first review those studies which investigate childhood as well as adolescent development and which, therefore, have been in part summarized in the previous section. Then we shall review studies that confine themselves mostly to populations of adolescents and which we have not covered above.

Selman's developmental sequence of self-awareness continues into the adolescent years, with its final two levels emerging in early and late adolescence, respectively. Selman's fourth level (his first in adolescence) is defined by the self's awareness of its own self-awareness. This implies that the young adolescent knows that one can consciously monitor one's own self-experience. Not only does this new awareness explain the increased self-consciousness of young adolescents, commonly observed in the personality development literature (e.g., White 1972) but it also accounts for the increased sense of personal agency that most researchers have found during this age period. Because the adolescent now knows the possibility of self-reflection, the adolescent conceives of the mind as an active processor of experience and ultimately as a potential manipulator of one's experience. This establishes a new mode of self-control generated by one's mental powers of self-reflective self-awareness. Selman offers the following example: in response to a question asking about one's reactions to the loss of the puppy in Selman's dilemma, a young adolescent might say, "I can fool myself into not wanting to see another puppy if I keep on saying to myself, 'I don't want a puppy; I don't ever want to see another puppy.' "

Although the adolescent at Selman's fourth level generally believes that one has control over one's thoughts and emotions, there is also some awareness that certain mental experience is beyond one's volitional reach. For example, Selman quotes one young adolescent who said, "If I did something wrong, I really can't forget about it because of time. I really can't make myself forget; I will always remember it" (p. 103). But this apparent incongruity with the notion of self-reflective self-control poses an unresolvable contradiction to the young adolescent, who simply segregates the two irreconcilable notions of self in disparate, unrelated statements. Only at level 5, according to Selman, does the older adolescent resolve this problem by constructing the notion of conscious and nonconscious levels of experience (or some parallel version of this notion). The level 5 solution is that there are mental experiences that can influence one's actions but which are not available for conscious inspection. For example, Selman quotes one level 5 response to the question "Why did Mike say he didn't want to ever see another puppy again?" The adolescent replies, "He may not want to admit to himself that another dog could take Pepper's place. He might feel at some level that would be unloyal to Pepper to just go out and replace the dog. He may feel guilty about it. He doesn't want to face these feelings, so he says, no dog." (Is he aware of this?) "Probably not" (p. 106).

According to Selman, therefore, self-understanding in adolescence begins with a global notion of the "I" as a self-reflective, active controller of one's experience, with some uncoordinated recognition that there are limits to this awareness and control. Later in adolescence one develops the notion of two different levels of mental experience, one conscious and one nonconscious, both of which can influence one's thoughts and actions. In this manner, the adolescent conceptually constructs a unified self-system while still preserving the notion that self-awareness and conscious self-control have their boundaries.

Selman's self-understanding research is somewhat limited by his exclusive focus on self-awareness and by his consequent reliance on perspective taking as the "underlying" explanation for conceptual development in this area. Broughton's research, more broadly based and more directly aimed at self-specific issues, reveals some further trends in adolescent self-understanding development, in addition to replicating the basic findings reported by Selman. Broughton, like Selman, proposes two levels of self-knowledge in adolescence (levels 3 and 4 in Broughton's scheme). During early adolescence, an initial distinction is made between mental and physical reality. According to Broughton, this level 3 distinction has several important implications for young adolescents' self-conceptions. First, the mind, now seen as an entity in its own right, takes on volitional characteristics independent of the self's physical activity. For example, the "I" is seen as capable of evaluating the self's actions, as in this example from one of Broughton's teenage subjects: "With our minds we can make our own judgments and do what we feel is right" (p. 87). Second, the young adolescent sees the self as "I" as a stable way of mentally processing information, as a characteristic mode of knowing the world. One of Broughton's subjects replied that the self is "the way your thoughts go" (p. 88). Third, since the mental functions of self are recognized, the "I" is seen as having complete and private access to its own inner processes. The "I" knows itself, and this knowledge neither is shared by anyone else nor extends to others. That is, the "I" is seen as totally self-aware in a way special to itself: as an example, one young adolescent told Broughton, "I know what I feel about things, and I don't know someone else" (p. 88).

Although the young adolescent recognizes the distinction between mental and physical and bases a new understanding of self on this recognition, there is still little appreciation of the mental self's unique qualities. Broughton believes that such an appreciation develops late in adolescence, and this development defines Broughton's level 4. The adolescent at this point has some understanding of the mental world's internal system of relations and regulations. This enables the adolescent to conceive of the mental self as a system of distinct elements, sometimes operating concordantly and sometimes "divided." For example, Broughton quotes one adolescent who speaks of two inner mental selves, one of which is "natural" and one of which "imitates" its ideal (Broughton 1980). This, writes Broughton, is one typical version of this reasoning level, since it represents an attempt to understand both the complexity and the unity of the "I." Other examples include adolescents who introspect about the logical mechanisms that characterize their thought processes, posit real and phony mental activities, logical and irrational ones, and so on. In later levels of Broughton's developmental sequence (levels 5 and 6), Broughton describes further changes in individuals' understanding of the "I," but these changes occur during adulthood and are beyond the scope of this review.

Broughton's analysis of adolescent self-understanding converges with Selman's on the following points. First, both authors agree that the young adolescent views the self in primarily mental terms, as an active processor of experience. Both also agree that this conception is associated with the adolescent's new respect for the volitional powers either in the sense of monitoring and manipulating its own thoughts and actions (Selman) or in the sense of evaluating itself (Broughton). The adolescent tendency toward self-reflection is thus connected by both authors to a new and stronger sense of personal agency. Finally, both authors agree that a more realistic and adequate view of mental processes develops later in adolescence. Selman and Broughton both believe that this change enables the adolescent to understand the uneven and sometimes divided workings of mental life while at the same time maintaining a belief in the unity of the self-system. Selman stresses the adolescent's construction of conscious and nonconscious levels of mental experience, whereas Broughton stresses the adolescent's construction of such notions as the real mental self versus the imitative or phony mental self. But both authors portray the effects of the change similarly: as a move away from the notion of a global mental self with mysterious, unexplored working to a view of a systematic mental self consisting of distinct elements that operate according to definable laws and regularities.

Secord and Peevers's (1974) study of self-understanding in children and adolescents found the same developmental patterns reported by Selman and Broughton. The authors used a free-response method of questioning subjects and analyzed responses intuitively rather than with the aid of a formal coding scheme; but the authors' impressionistic account of their data not only dovetails nicely with Selman and Broughton's findings but also suggests some further features of adolescent self-understanding. The first developmental shift noted by Secord and Peevers occurs at the beginning of adolescence. At this age, the young adolescent describes the self in terms of abstractions and general evaluations, rather than in terms of specific acts and qualities as during childhood. Also, Secord and Peevers report that young adolescents are likely to describe themselves in terms of their past and future selves, the sense of continuity (an aspect of the "I"), whereas younger children almost invariably describe themselves in terms of the immediate present.

The next shift noted by Secord and Peevers occurs in middle adolescence (as revealed by the authors' sample of eleventh graders). Here we see many of the qualities reported by Selman and Broughton, though at a somewhat earlier age (during the *first* of the other two researchers' adolescent levels). This discrepancy could result from either differences in research populations or the relative informality and open-endedness of the Secord-Peevers testing procedure when compared with the more intensively probed interviews of Selman and Broughton. In any event, Secord and Peevers found that their adolescent subjects developed notions of self-reflectivity, volition, and self-evaluation as critical components of their self-understanding. For example, one typical self-reflective statement quoted by the authors was, "I saw myself back in high school—just like I could sit back and watch myself go to school" (Secord & Peevers 1974, p. 136). As an example of the awakened sense of adolescent volition, another subject said, "If I don't like a subject, I won't do anything in the subject . . . and, on the other hand, the subjects I do like—my science and mathematics—I really work" (p. 139). This, the authors write, demonstrates a recognition that inner processes like motivation determine the course of one's life events. Thus, the self is seen as active and self-generating: "There is a kind of projection of activities [at this age]—self as agent enacting various scenes, rather than as a being with qualities" (p. 138). In adolescence, then, the emphasis on self-understanding shifts away from the constituents of the "Me" and toward the aspects of the "I." Finally, in another manifestation of self-reflection and self-determinacy, the self is seen as its own evaluator. This, according to Secord and Peevers, takes place mostly on moral grounds, as in the following example: "But I still think that I consider popularity too important above other things more than I should . . . I don't like people who talk about other people behind their backs because it's—they wouldn't like it if they were talked about, and I don't think it's right" (p. 138).

A study by Bernstein (1980) elaborates some of the trends noted by Secord and Peevers, particularly the early adolescent trends not mentioned by Selman or Broughton. Bernstein asked 10-, 15-, and 20-year-olds three types of questions designed to reveal their conceptions of the "self-system". The first type of question was directed at differentiation in self-system conceptions. A typical question was, "Everyone behaves differently in different situations with different people. List all the ways that you act." The second type of question, directed at abstractness in self-system conceptions, was of the following sort: "You have listed a number of different ways that you act. What does each of these tell you about yourself?" The third type of question was aimed at integration and asked the subject to "Put all of this together in a statement about yourself."

Bernstein expected that older subjects would demonstrate greater differentiation in their self-system conceptions than younger subjects by making statements from a larger number of self categories. This expectation was unconfirmed. But Bernstein did find an age-related difference in the types of categories that subjects used. Children at age 10 were likely to refer to situational, behavioral, and emotional aspects of self (e.g., "I play at the playground"; "I hit my brother"; "I get mad at my mother"; as respective examples of statements from situational, behavioral, and emotional categories). Adolescents at ages 15 and 20 were likely to refer to their social personality characteristics, their beliefs, and their acceptance of social rules, as in, respectively, "I am really friendly, so I can make new friends easily"; "I think being a good sport is important, so if we lose a game, I am never a spoilsport"; "My mother thinks that it is wrong to cheat, so I don't."

As for abstraction in self-system conceptions, Bernstein reports that his youngest subjects generally were quite concrete, linking the self to direct action in most of their statements (e.g., "I mow the lawn at home"). Subjects in mid-adolescence linked together a variety of self-actions according to one common theme, thus demonstrating an initial abstracting from self-system characteristics; an example might be, "Going to the drive-in with my friends is just something I do with them, like I also play basketball with them." In his oldest subjects, Bernstein found some abstracting on the basis of "an underlying dimension which provides internal consistency for behaviors which appear discrepant" (p. 237). For example, a 20-year-old might say, "I help my brother with his homework, but I don't help my sister with hers because my brother really needs the help, while my sister is lazy. I mean it's fair to help him and not her."

Bernstein found a similar developmental trend in adolescent tendencies toward conceptual integration of the self-system. Integrating statements of 10-year-olds were generally confined to a simple reiteration of previous self-definitions, without recognition of possible contradiction in diverse definitions. By mid-adolescence, diversity of self-definition is recognized, but no coordinating principle between discrepant elements is yet constructed. For example, one such response might be, "Well, when I am around my friends, I am really talkative and animated, but just around my family I sort of keep to myself. It's sort of like I am two different people; I don't know why." By the end of adolescence, according to Bernstein, integrating principles that recognize diversity yet maintain the coherence of the self-system are found. An example of an amended version of the above statement might be, "When I am around my friends, I am really talkative because I feel like they are treating me like a person who has something interesting and important to say. My family doesn't listen to what I say, so I just don't feel like talking to hear myself speak." The principle that coordinates here between the two contradictory self-statements (talkativeness and silence) is the self's desire to engage in meaningful communication when talking.

Like the research summarized above, Bernstein's work shows the adolescent transition from action-based conceptions of self to conceptions based on psychological characteristics, such as beliefs. Bernstein's research also taps into the divided self of adolescence as portrayed by Broughton and, like Broughton and Selman, shows how older adolescents resolve the contradictions of this division by constructing conceptual principles that coordinate the various features of self into a coherent system. Like Secord and Peevers, Bernstein stresses the adolescent tendency toward abstraction around stable, unifying qualities of self. One such quality that emerges as primary in Bernstein's work is the social personality aspect of self. Bernstein shows how the young adolescent moves from a definition of the "Me" in terms of transient actions and emotions to a definition of the "Me" in terms of stable personality traits with social implications. When, in later adolescence, the notion of stable personality becomes combined with the notion of characteristic belief systems, the adolescent is able to establish an understanding of self that is self-reflective, complex, and systematic.

Two studies asking children and adolescents for their free descriptions of themselves have uncovered many of the same age trends reported by Bernstein and others. The first, by Montemayor and Eisen (1977), used Gordon's self-concept coding system (Gordon 1968) to analyze the free self-descriptions of subjects between the ages of 9 and 18. The researchers found that, with age, adolescents more frequently used the following categories from Gordon's system in their self-descriptions (the proportional frequencies of youngest subjects versus oldest who used each of the following categories at least once are given in parentheses): ideological beliefs (4%–39%), interpersonal style (42%–91%), psychic style (27%–72%), existential individuating (0%–54%), sense of self-determination (5%–49%), and sense of unity (0%–21%). Although the nominal labels of Gordon's categories differ somewhat from the language other authors have used, the concordance of results becomes apparent when we translate "existential" into "self-reflective," "sense of self-determination" into "sense of volition (or personal agency)," "interpersonal style" into "social personality characteristics," and "psychic style" into "manner of mentally processing experience"—all aspects of the sense of "I." Also in accord with other studies, Montemayor and Eisen found that with age adolescents use the following categories *less* frequently: territoriality-citizenship (11%–8%), possessions (50%–8%), and body image (87%–16%). The other free-response study of children and adolescents' self-descriptions was a similar, though less comprehensive, effort by Livesly and Bromley (1973). Age trends for categories like general personality attributes and beliefs, attitudes, and values were compatible with the findings of Montemayor and Eisen regarding similar categories.

It is noteworthy that even studies primarily focusing on self-esteem have tapped essentially identical developmental patterns in adolescent self-understanding. Rosenberg's broad-based series of studies into self-concept included three components relevant to the issue in this review (Rosenberg 1979). In Rosenberg's investigation tapping most directly into the development of self-understanding, he asked subjects aged 8 through 18 questions on the following areas of concern: points of pride and shame in self ("Could you tell me what things are really best about you?" "Do you have any weak points, that is, any things not as good about you?"), sense of distinctiveness and commonality ("In what ways are you different from most other kids you know?" "In what ways are you the same?"), and ideal self ("What kind of person would you like to be when you grow up?"). Rosenberg found that, in response to these questions, children generally describe the constituents of the "Me" in terms of physical and active qualities, whereas adolescents refer to psychological aspects of the "Me." In addition, Rosenberg reports the rising importance of the self's social personality characteristics during adolescence. When questioned about points of pride, 9% of the 8-year-olds' responses were interpersonal traits (e.g., friendly, shy) while 17% of the 14-year-olds' and 28% of the 16-year-olds' responses were interpersonal traits. When asked about the person the subject would like to become, 36% of the 8-year-olds' responses were interpersonal traits, while 69% of the 14–16-year-olds' responses were interpersonal traits. Finally, Rosenberg found that the self's ability to control itself becomes much more prominent during adolescence. When questioned about points of shame, only 14% of the 8-year-olds' responses were general traits reflecting self-control, while 32% of the 14–16-year-olds' responses were these kinds of general traits.

In a second aspect of his study, Rosenberg investigated the locus of both "interior" and "exterior" self-knowledge, that is, who knows the self best. The exterior self was operationalized as attitudes about intelligence, morality, and aesthetics: for example, "If I asked you and your mother how smart you were, and you said one thing and she said another, who would be right—you, or your mother?" A corresponding question for the interior self probed emotions and feelings in the following way: "Now who knows best what kind of person you really are deep down inside—your mother, your father, yourself, or your best friend?"

Rosenberg found that locus of self-knowledge shifts, with age, from the other, especially the parent, to the self. Concerning the exterior self, Rosenberg reports, "Almost half of the older children, but less than one-sixth of the younger children, placed the locus of exterior self-knowledge within the self" (Rosenberg 1979, pp. 243–244). Locus of interior self-knowledge followed a similar trend: about half of the younger children thought the parent knew the child better than did the child, while only 36% of the 12–14-year-olds believed the parent knew one better than did oneself. These findings, of course, agree with Broughton's description of the consequences of the distinction between mental and physical. Once the mental is seen to be unique, according to Broughton, the self is seen to be a privileged and omniscient processor of the self's experience, leading to an awareness that no one can ever understand one's experience as fully as can oneself.

Conclusion: A Model of Self-Understanding Development from Infancy to Adolescence

Our summary of research findings on self-understanding from infancy through adolescence reveals some widely replicated ontogenetic patterns, such as (1) the shift from physicalistic to psychological self-conceptions, (2) the emergence of stable social personality characterizations of self, (3) the increasingly volitional and self-reflective nature of self-understanding, and (4) the tendency toward the conceptual integration of diverse aspects of self into a unified self-system. Some of these trends are in line with general cognitive changes that have been documented for this age period. For example, the physical-psychological shift can be seen as another example of the "surface to depth" trend that Flavell and others have noted (Flavell 1977; Higgins, Ruble, & Hartup, in press). Similarly, the systematization of self can be seen as another example of the formalization of reasoning during adolescence (Inhelder & Piaget 1958; Keating 1975).

Nevertheless, we would resist the temptation to reduce a developmental account of self-understanding to a list of changes along a few general cognitive dimensions. Such an account would not only fail to capture the substance of self-understanding development but would also underrepresent the complexity of the ontogenetic patterns. For example, neither the physical to psychological nor the more general surface to depth notions define the developmental sequence in a totally accurate way. This is because (1) there is much in early self-understanding that does not meet the criterion of physicalistic, and (2) there is much in advanced self-understanding that does not meet the criteria of psychological. As examples of the first point: very young children express self-conceptions that are primarily active rather than physical; and they sometimes also make self-statements that are social (e.g., group membership) and even psychological (e.g., emotional states). As an example of the second point: the physical, social, and active self all remain important to most individuals throughout life, long after they are capable of predominantly psychological self-conceptions. In fact, psychologists have long noted that the physical self, after a period of relative neglect, once again waxes in significance for a person's self-concept at the end of adolescence (Freud 1922; Kohlberg & Gilligan 1971).

The solution to such complexity, we believe, is to abandon the attempt to analyze self-understanding development along a number of unrelated, unilateral dimensions and, rather, to posit a systematic developmental model in which changes along multiple dimensions are shown to interact with one another in the course of ontogenesis. Such a model of self-understanding development from infancy to adolescence is schematized in figure 1.

The logic of the model is as follows. The front face of the cube represents the self-as-object (James's "Me") divided into its four basic constituents (the physical, active, social, and psychological self). At all ages, children have some knowledge of each of these four constituent self-schemes, however cursory and primitive this knowledge may be. In the course of development, knowledge of each self-scheme changes in character. These changes are represented along the vertical dimensions (the columns of the model's front face). These developmental changes are the trends described in this review. Within the 16 boxes of the model's front face, we have offered abbreviated descriptions of these main developmental trends.

In addition to these vertical developmental trends within each of the four self-schemes, there is another important ontogenetic trend in children's understanding of the self-as-object. This is an age-related shift that favors, respectively, the physical, active, social, and then psychological aspects of self as the child becomes the adolescent. This movement is represented along the darkly outlined diagonal boxes of the model's front face. It is this movement that has seen the focus of previous unidimensional accounts of self-concept development. Although we believe that these previous accounts have erred in their too exclusive focus on this one ontogenetic movement, we do believe that it is a dominant dimension within a multidimensional developmental progression. For this reason this movement occupies the central position on the front face of our model. The four boxes along the darkened diagonal represent the prototypical conceptions of self at each of the four general self-understanding levels (rows 1, 2, 3, and 4 along the front face).

As for these four self-understanding levels,

Fig. 1.—Conceptual foundations of the "Me" (physical, active, social, and psychological self-constituents) and the "I" (continuity, distinctness, volition, and self-reflection) at four developmental levels during childhood and adolescence.

they are represented by the model's horizontal dimensions (the rows), cutting across each of the four constituent self-schemes. These overall levels consist of general features that the parallel developmental levels of the four self-schemes have in common. In other words, the four aspects of self-knowledge are linked at each developmental level because they share characteristics deriving from the dominant conception of self at that level. This dominant conception at each level is, as noted above, shown in the box along the diagonal. Thus, at each new level, a new aspect of self assumes dominance and lends its characteristics to parallel-level conceptions of other aspects of self. These characteristics become, in essence, the organizing principles of self-understanding at that level.

Thus the four general developmental levels of self-understanding with respect to the "Me" are organized as follows. At level 1, all self-understanding is to some extent physicalistic in the sense that it is chiefly descriptive of surface features. That is, even when concerned with the self's actions, social interactions, or emotions, it treats these only taxonomically and descriptively, as if they were physical objects. Similarly, at level 2 each of the four aspects is to some extent treated actively, at level 3 socially, and at level 4 psychologically. The qualifier "to some extent" is necessary here because each of the four aspects still retains its unique substance at each level. For this reason, our model does not "collapse" the four sequences into one sequence, as has been done previously; although it does recognize that there are conceptual and developmental connections among the four sequences.

The side face of the model shows the understanding of self-as-subject (James's "I"), especially with regard to the understanding of continuity, distinctness from others, volition, and self-reflection. Development here is represented as a shift from one pole to the other along the four respective dimensions, rather than as a progression from level to level (as is the case with understanding the "Me" aspect of the self). This is because there is nothing in the self-understanding literature to indicate that, between childhood and adolescence, there are a series of qualitatively distinct levels in the awareness of the "I." Rather, the literature indicates that during this age range there is a gradual emergence of some new notions in each of these four dimensions. Figure 1's side face, along the top pole of each dimension, briefly describes the nature of these new notions.

The cubical shape of the model indicates that, during the transition from childhood to adolescence, changes in understanding the "Me" interact with changes in understanding the "I" all throughout the development of self-understanding. It is not possible to determine whether, for example, a more advanced understanding of volition transforms one's understanding of various "Me" constituents, or whether, in contrast, a new mode of defining the "Me" makes possible the understanding of "I" dimensions like volition. Probably the wisest guess is that all throughout ontogenesis there is mutual influence between the two basic aspects of self-understanding. Although the "I" and the "Me" are structured around distinct conceptual issues, developmental progress in either seems to inform and encourage developmental progress in the other.

At this point, the model in figure 1 is largely speculative. The contents of the boxes in the model and the processes indicated by the model's configuration await more extensive and precise empirical documentation. Even if the fundamental structure of the model is sound, further research may prove the need to revise some of its features, such as the exact nature of the box descriptions.

The model leads to certain empirical expectations that can be easily confirmed or disconfirmed by a systematic study of self-understanding in children and adolescents. For example, with regard to self-definitional "Me" statements (represented by the cube's front face): the greatest frequency of such statements should fall along the diagonal, and upward movement along the diagonal should be closely associated with age during the period from childhood to adolescence. There also should be a positive horizontal correlation across the four aspects of self for any given subject. On the other hand, there also should be some individual variation in these patterns because of particular histories, talents, or interests of individual subjects. Such variation may translate into sex, cohort, or social contextual differences, or into some interaction of these, because of specific self-related considerations linked to these variables. Overall, however, the normative developmental trend should be upward along the diagonal, at least for children living in social cultural contexts similar to those in which the currently reviewed studies were set.

Accepting, for a moment, the general validity of the model described in this paper, at least one implication is clear. It must be concluded that existing instruments for measuring self-concept and self-esteem in children and adolescents are gravely in error, since none of these instruments takes into account the developmental transformations outlined in this review. This is not a conclusion that is totally new to this review. In fact, in at least two cases (Harter 1982; Rosenberg 1979), researchers who themselves construct scales to assess children's self-esteem have acknowledged this problem, although these researchers have not modified their own scales accordingly. Rosenberg asserts that self-esteem measurement ought to take account of his finding that children emphasize physical and active characteristics in their self-reports, whereas adolescents emphasize inner psychological characteristics (like emotions and thoughts). But Rosenberg does not adapt his own global self-esteem scale to these developmental insights. Harter, in recognition of similar possible developmental changes in orientation towards self, separates her "perceived competence" scale into physical, cognitive, and social subscales, assuming that each of these "factor structures" may be weighed differently by older than by younger children. Harter also uses different items and item formats for testing persons at different ages. But in her test construction, Harter does not go as far as to assume that self-concept may be radically reorganized with development. She maintains as a major criterion of her scales a factor structure that stays stable across age level (Harter 1980, p. 16), whereas developmental theory and research, as outlined in this review, shows that age change implies a reordering of factors. Similarly, the validity of other child and adolescent measures that rely on factor continuity across this broad age range (see Dusek & Flaherty [1981] on Monge's self-concept measure; Kokenes [1974] on Coopersmith) must be questioned, because of the indisputable fact of developmental transformation in self-understanding from childhood to adolescence. In the future, self-concept measures designed for use with children or adolescents must incorporate the changing nature of self-understanding. For instance, when young children are involved, test items should focus on the body and its typical activities; whereas, with adolescents, items must focus on the social and psychological aspects of self, and on notions of the self's unique, volitional, and self-reflective experience.

Finally, models of social cognitive development must integrate the acquisition of self-understanding into their formulations. Clearly, the developmental transformations that occur in understanding the self are parallel to certain general features of social cognitive development, such as the much-noted movement from surface to depth. But there are many developmental trends in children's and adolescents' self-understanding that are unique to this particular conceptual system. Among these trends are the emerging notions of personal volition and self-reflection that transform the adolescent's conception of both "Me" and "I" as well as the constantly increasing focus on the continuity and uniqueness of the self's experience. These and other special features of self-understanding require recognition from any comprehensive theory of social cognitive development.

References

Amsterdam, B. Mirror self-image reactions before age two. *Developmental Psychobiology*, 1972, **5**, 297–305.

Baldwin, J. M. *Social and ethical interpretations in mental development*. New York: Macmillan, 1902.

Bernstein, R. M. The development of the self-system during adolescence. *Journal of Genetic Psychology*, 1980, **136**, 231–245.

Brim, O. G. Life-span development of the theory of oneself: implications for child development. In H. W. Reese (Ed.), *Advances in child development and behavior*. Vol. **2**. New York: Academic Press, 1976.

Broughton, J. Development of concepts of self, mind, reality, and knowledge. *New Directions for Child Development*, 1978, **1**, 75–100.

Broughton, J. The divided self in adolescence. *Human Development*, 1980, **24**, 13–32.

Coopersmith, S. *The antecedents of self-esteem*. San Francisco: W. H. Freeman, 1967.

Damon, W. *The social world of the child*. San Francisco: Jossey-Bass, 1977.

Damon, W. Why study social-cognitive development? *Human Development*, 1979, **22**, 206–211.

Darwin, C. A biographical sketch of an infant. *Mind*, 1877, **2**, 285–294.

Dixon, J. C. Development of self-recognition. *Journal of General Psychology*, 1957, **91**, 251–256.

Dusek, J. B., & Flaherty, J. F. The development of the self-concept during the adolescent years. *Monographs of the Society for Research in Child Development*, 1981, **46**(4, Serial No. 191).

Flavell, J. H. *Cognitive development*. Englewood Cliffs, N.J.: Prentice-Hall, 1977.

Flavell, J. H., & Ross, L. (Eds.). *Social cognitive development: frontiers and possible futures.* Cambridge: Cambridge University Press, 1981.

Freud, S. *Group psychology and the development of the ego.* New York: Norton, 1922.

Gallup, G. G., Jr. Chimpanzees: self-recognition. *Science,* 1970, **167,** 86–87.

Gordon, C. Self-conceptions: configurations of content. In C. Gordon & K. J. Gergen (Eds.), *The self in social interaction.* Vol. **1.** New York: Wiley, 1968.

Guardo, C. J., & Bohan, J. B. Development of a sense of self-identity in children. *Child Development,* 1971, **42,** 1909–1921.

Harter, S. A model of intrinsic mastery motivation in children: individual differences and developmental change. In A. Collins (Ed.), *Minnesota symposium on child psychology.* Vol. **14.** Hillsdale, N.J.: Erlbaum, 1980.

Harter, S. The perceived competence scale for children. *Child Development,* 1982, **53,** 87–97.

Higgins, E. T.; Ruble, D.; & Hartup, W. W. (Eds.). *Social cognition and social behavior: developmental perspectives,* in press.

Inhelder, B., & Piaget, J. *The growth of logical thinking from childhood to adolescence.* New York: Basic, 1958.

James, W. *Psychology: the briefer course.* New York: Harper & Bros., 1961. (Originally published 1892.)

Jersild, A. T. *In search of self.* New York: Teachers College, Columbia University, Bureau of Publications, 1952.

Kagan, J. *The second year: the emergence of self-awareness.* Cambridge, Mass.: Harvard University Press, 1981.

Keating, D. P. Precocious cognitive development at the level of formal operations. *Child Development,* 1975, **46,** 276–280.

Keller, A.; Ford, L. H., Jr.; & Meacham, J. A. Dimensions of self-concept in preschool children. *Developmental Psychology,* 1978, **14,** 483–489.

Kohlberg, L. Stage and sequence: the cognitive-developmental approach to socialization. In D. A. Goslin (Ed.), *Handbook of socialization theory and research.* Chicago: Rand McNally, 1969.

Kohlberg, L., & Gilligan, C. The adolescent as a philosopher: the discovery of the self in a postconventional world. *Daedalus,* 1971, **100,** 1051–1086.

Kokenes, B. Grade level differences in factors of self-esteem. *Developmental Psychology,* 1974, **10,** 954–958.

Kuiper, N. A., & Rogers, T. B. Encoding of personal information: self-other differences. *Journal of Personality and Social Psychology,* 1979, **37,** 499–514.

Lewis, M., & Brooks-Gunn, J. *Social cognition and the acquisition of self.* New York: Plenum, 1979.

Livesly, W. J., & Bromley, D. B. *Person perception in childhood and adolescence.* New York: Wiley, 1973.

Mead, G. H. *Mind, self, and society.* Chicago: University of Chicago Press, 1934.

Montemayor, R., & Eisen, M. The development of self-conceptions from childhood to adolescence. *Developmental Psychology,* 1977, **13,** 314–319.

Mullener, N., & Laird, J. D. Some developmental changes in the organization of self-evaluations. *Developmental Psychology,* 1971, **5,** 233–236.

Nisbett, R.; Caputo, C.; Legant, P.; & Maracek, J. Behavior as seen by the actor and as seen by the observer. *Journal of Personality and Social Psychology,* 1973, **27,** 154–164.

Papousek, H., & Papousek, M. Mirror-image and self-recognition in young human infants, I: A new method of experimental analysis. *Developmental Psychobiology,* 1974, **7,** 149–157.

Piaget, J. *The moral judgment of the child.* New York: Free Press, 1965. (Originally published 1932.)

Piers, E. V., & Harris, D. B. Age and other correlates of self-concept in children. *Journal of Educational Psychology,* 1964, **55,** 91–95.

Preyer, W. *Mind of the child.* Vol. **2.** New York: Appleton, 1893.

Rosenberg, M. *Society and the adolescent self-image.* Princeton, N.J.: Princeton University Press, 1965.

Rosenberg, M. *Conceiving the self.* New York: Basic, 1979.

Ruble, D. The development of social comparison processes and their role in achievement-related self-socialization. In E. T. Higgins, D. Ruble, & W. W. Hartup (Eds.), *Social cognition and social behavior: developmental perspectives,* in press.

Secord, P., & Peevers, B. The development and attribution of person concepts. In T. Mischel (Ed.), *Understanding other persons.* Oxford: Blackwell, 1974.

Selman, R. *The growth of interpersonal understanding.* New York: Academic Press, 1980.

Shantz, C. U. The development of social cognition. In E. M. Hetherington (Ed.), *Review of child development research.* Vol. **5.** Chicago: University of Chicago Press, 1975.

Shantz, C. U. Social-cognition. In J. H. Flavell & E. Markman (Eds.), *Carmichael's handbook* of *child psychology*. Vol. **2.** New York: Wiley, in press.

Taylor, S., & Fiske, S. Point of view and perceptions of causality. *Journal of Personality and Social Psychology*, 1975, **32,** 439–445.

Turiel, E. Social regulations and domains of social concepts. *New Directions for Child Development*, 1978, **1,** 45–75.

White, R. W. *The enterprise of living: growth and organization in personality*. New York: Holt, Rinehart & Winston, 1972.

Wylie, R. C. *The self concept: a review of methodological considerations and measuring instruments* (Rev. ed.). Vol. **1.** Lincoln: University of Nebraska Press, 1974.

Wylie, R. C. *The self concept: theory and research on selected topics* (Rev. ed.). Vol. **2.** Lincoln: University of Nebraska Press, 1979.

Perceived Self-Efficacy in the Exercise of Personal Agency

Albert Bandura

The recent years have witnessed a resurgence of interest in self-referent phenomena. One can point to several reasons why self processes have come to pervade the research in many areas of psychology. Self-generated activities lie at the very heart of causal processes. They not only give meaning and valence to most external influences, but they function as important proximal determinants of motivation and action. People make causal contributions to their own psychosocial functioning through mechanisms of personal agency. Among the mechanisms of agency, none is more central or pervasive than people's beliefs about their capabilities to exercise control over events that affect their lives. Self-beliefs of efficacy influence how people feel, think, and act. The present article analyses the causal function of self-percepts of efficacy and the diverse processes through which they exert their effects.

Self-efficacy causality

A central question in any theory of cognitive regulation of motivation and action concerns the issue of causality. Do self-efficacy beliefs operate as causal factors in human functioning? This issue has been investigated by a variety of experimental strategies. Each approach tests the dual-causal link in which instating conditions affect efficacy beliefs, and efficacy beliefs, in turn, affect action. In one approach, perceived self-efficacy is raised in phobics from virtually non-existent levels to preselected low, moderate, or high levels by providing them with mastery experiences or simply by modelling coping strategies for them until the desired level of efficacy was attained (Bandura, Reese & Adams, 1982).

As shown in Figure 1, higher levels of perceived self-efficacy are accompanied by higher performance attainments. The efficacy-action relationship is replicated across different dysfunctions and in both intergroup and intrasubject comparisons, regardless of whether perceived self-efficacy was raised by mastery experiences or solely by vicarious influence. Microanalysis of efficacy-action congruences reveals a close fit between perceived self-efficacy and performance on individual tasks.

Another approach to the test of causality is to control, by selection, level of ability but to vary perceived self-efficacy within each ability level. Collins (1982) selected children who judged themselves to be of high or low mathematical effi-

The Psychologist: Bulletin of the British Psychological Society (1989), **10**, 411-424.

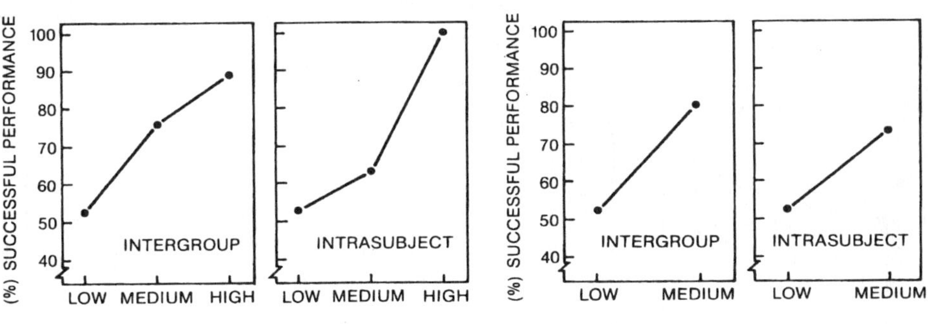

Figure 1. Mean performance attainments as a function of differential levels of perceived self-efficacy. The two left panels present the relationship for perceived self-efficacy raised by mastery experiences; the two right panels present the relationship for perceived self-efficacy raised by vicarious experiences. The intergroup panels show the performance attainments of groups of subjects whose self-percepts of efficacy were raised to differential levels; the intrasubject panels show the performance attainments for the same subjects after their self-percepts of efficacy were successively raised to different levels (Bandura, Reese & Adams, 1982).

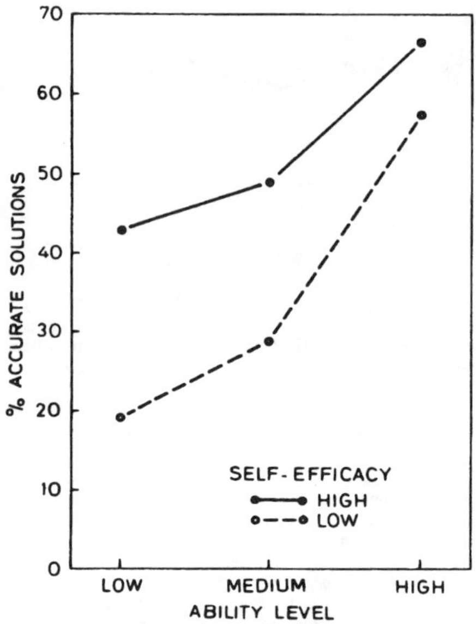

Figure 2. Mean levels of mathematical solutions achieved by students as a function of mathematical ability and perceived mathematical self-efficacy. Plotted from data of Collins, 1982.

cacy at each of three levels of mathematical ability. They were then given difficult problems to solve. Within each level of mathematical ability, children who regarded themselves as efficacious were quicker to discard faulty strategies, solved more problems (Figure 2), chose to rework more of those they failed, and did so more accurately. Perceived self-efficacy thus exerted a substantial independent effect on performance.

A third approach to causality is to introduce a trivial factor devoid of information to affect competency, but that can alter perceived self-efficacy. The impact of the altered perceived efficacy on level of motivation is then measured. Studies of anchoring influences show that arbitrary reference points from which judgements are adjusted either upward or downward can bias the judgements because the adjustments are usually insufficient. Cervone and Peake (1986) used arbitrary anchor values to influence self-appraisals of efficacy. Self-appraisals made from an arbitrary high starting point biased students' perceived self-efficacy in the positive direction, whereas an arbitrary low starting point lowered students' appraisals of their efficacy (Figure 3). The initial reference points in a sequence of performance descriptors similarly biased self-efficacy appraisal (Peake & Cervone, 1989). In a further study, Cervone (1989) biased self-efficacy appraisal by differential cognitive focus on things about the task that might make it troublesome or tractable. Dwelling on formidable aspects weakened people's belief in their efficacy, but focussing on doable aspects raised self-judgement of capabilities. In all of these experiments, the higher the instated perceived self-efficacy, the longer individuals persevere on difficult and unsolvable problems before they quit. Mediational analyses reveal that neither anchoring influences nor cognitive focus has any effect on motivation when perceived self-efficacy is partialled out. The effect of the external influences on performance motivation is thus completely mediated by perceived self-efficacy.

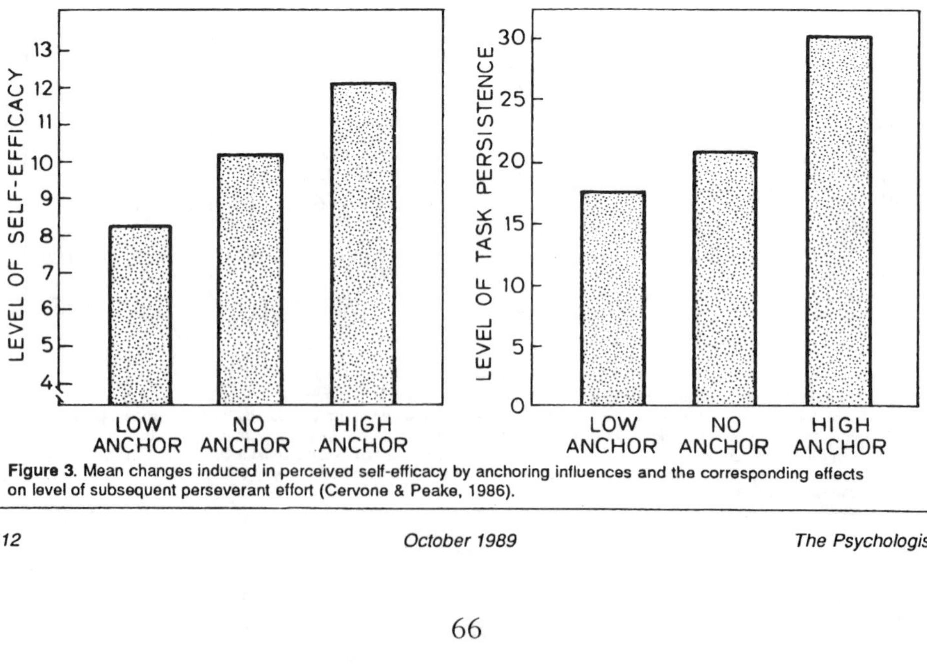

Figure 3. Mean changes induced in perceived self-efficacy by anchoring influences and the corresponding effects on level of subsequent perseverant effort (Cervone & Peake, 1986).

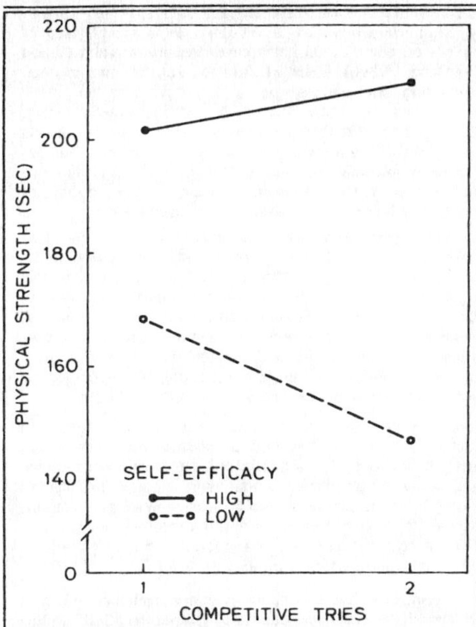

Figure 4. Mean level of physical stamina mobilised in competitive situations as a function of illusorily instated high or low self-percepts of physical efficacy (Weinberg, Gould & Jackson, 1979).

A number of experiments have been conducted in which self-efficacy beliefs are altered by bogus feedback unrelated to one's actual performance. People partly judge their capabilities through social comparison. Using this type of induction procedure, Weinberg, Gould and Jackson (1979) showed that physical stamina in competitive situations is mediated by perceived self-efficacy. They raised the self-efficacy beliefs of one group by telling them that they had triumphed in a competition of muscular strength. They lowered the self-efficacy beliefs of another group by telling them that they were outperformed by their competitor. The higher the illusory beliefs of physical strength, the more physical endurance subjects displayed during competition on a new task measuring physical stamina (Figure 4). Failure in a subsequent competition spurred those with a high sense of perceived self-efficacy to even greater physical effort, whereas failure further impaired the performance of those whose perceived self-efficacy had been undermined. Self-beliefs of physical efficacy illusorily heightened in females and illusorily weakened in males obliterated large preexisting sex differences in physical strength.

Another variant of social self-appraisal - bogus normative comparison - has also been used to raise or weaken beliefs of cognitive self-efficacy. Individuals are led to believe that they performed at the highest or lowest percentile ranks of the reference group, regardless of their actual performance (Jacobs, Prentice-Dunn & Rogers, 1984). Perceived self-efficacy heightened by this means produces stronger perseverant effort (Figure 5). The regulatory role of self-belief of efficacy instated by unauthentic normative comparison is replicated in a markedly different domain of functioning, namely pain tolerance (Litt, 1988). The higher the instated belief in one's capabilities, the greater the pain tolerance.

Still another approach to the verification of causality employs a contravening experimental design in which a procedure that can impair functioning is applied, but in ways that raise perceived self-efficacy. The changes accompanying psychological ministrations may result as much, if not more, from instilling beliefs of personal efficacy as from the particular skills imparted. If people's beliefs in their coping efficacy are strengthened, they approach situations more assuredly and make better use of the skills they have. Holroyd and his colleagues (Holroyd, *et al.*, 1984), demonstrated with sufferers of tension headaches that the benefits of biofeedback training may stem more from enhancement of perceived coping efficacy than from the muscular exercises themselves. In biofeedback sessions, they trained one group to become good relaxers. Unbeknownst to another group, they received feedback signals that they were relaxing whenever they tensed their muscles. They became good tensers of facial muscles, which, if anything, would aggravate tension headaches. Regardless of whether people were tensing or relaxing their musculator, bogus feedback that they were exercising good control over muscular tension instilled a strong sense of efficacy that they could prevent the occurrence of headaches in different stressful situations. The higher their perceived self-efficacy, the fewer headaches they experienced. The actual amount of change in muscular activity achieved in treatment was unrelated to the incidence of subsequent headaches.

These diverse causal tests conducted with different modes of efficacy induction, varied populations, and all sorts of domains of functioning provide supporting evidence that perceived self-efficacy contributes significantly to level of motivation and performance accomplishments. Evidence that divergent procedures produce convergent results add to the explanatory and predictive generality of the efficacy mediator.

The findings of the preceding experiments should not be taken to mean that arbitrary persuasory information is a good way of enhancing self-efficacy beliefs in the pursuits of everyday life. Rather, these studies have special bearing on the issue of causality because self-efficacy beliefs are

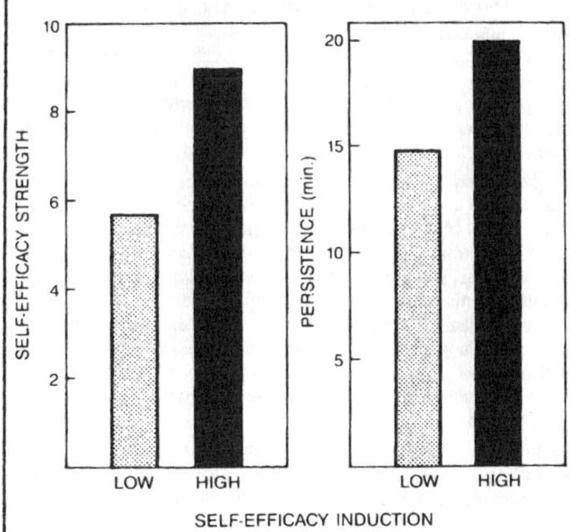

Figure 5. Mean changes in perceived self-efficacy induced by arbitrary normative comparison and the corresponding effects on level of subsequent perseverant effort. (Jacobs, Prentice-Dunn & Rogers, 1984).

altered independently of a performance modality and, therefore, cannot be discounted as by-products of performance. They demonstrate that changes in self-beliefs of efficacy affect motivation and action. In actual social practice, personal empowerment through mastery experiences is the most powerful means of creating a strong, resilient sense of efficacy (Bandura, 1986, 1988a). This is achieved by equipping people with knowledge, subskills and the strong self-belief of efficacy needed to use one's skills effectively.

Efficacy-activated processes

Self-efficacy beliefs regulate human functioning through four major processes. They include cognitive, motivational, affective and selection processes. Some of these efficacy-activated events are of interest in their own right rather than merely intervening influencers of action. These processes are analysed in some detail in the sections that follow.

Cognitive processes

Self-beliefs of efficacy affect thought patterns that can enhance or undermine performance. These cognitive effects take various forms. Much human behavior, being purposive, is regulated by forethought embodying cognised goals. Personal goal setting is influenced by self-appraisal of capabilities. The stronger the perceived self-efficacy, the higher the goals people set for themselves and the firmer their commitment to them (Bandura & Wood, 1989; Locke, Frederick, Lee & Bobko, 1984; Taylor, Locke, Lee & Gist, 1984). Challenging goals raise the level of motivation and performance attainments (Locke, Shaw, Saari & Latham, 1981; Mento, Steel & Karren, 1987).

People's perceptions of their efficacy influences the types of anticipatory scenarios they construct and reiterate. Those who have a high sense of efficacy visualise success scenarios that provide positive guides for performance. Those who judge themselves as inefficacious are more inclined to visualise failure scenarios which undermine performance by dwelling on how things will go wrong. Numerous studies have shown that cognitive simulations in which individuals visualise themselves executing activities skilfully enhance subsequent performance (Bandura, 1986; Corbin, 1972; Feltz & Landers, 1983; Kazdin, 1978). Perceived self-efficacy and cognitive simulation affect each other bidirectionally. A high sense of efficacy fosters cognitive constructions of effective actions and cognitive reiteration of efficacious courses of action strengthens self-percepts of efficacy (Bandura & Adams, 1977; Kazdin, 1979).

A major function of thought is to enable people to predict the occurrence of events and to create the means for exercising control over those that affect their daily lives. Many activities involve inferential judgements about conditional relations between events. Discovery of such predictive rules requires effective cognitive processing of multidimensional information that contains ambiguities and uncertainties. The fact that the same predictor may contribute to different effects and the same effect may have multiple predictors creates uncertainty as to what is likely to lead to what in probabilistic environments.

In ferreting out predictive rules people must draw on their pre-existing knowledge to generate hypotheses about predictive factors, to weight and integrate them into composite rules, to test their judgements against the results of their actions, and to remember which notions they had tested and how well they had worked. It requires a strong sense of efficacy to remain task oriented in the face of pressing situational demands and judgement failures that can have important repercussions.

The powerful influence of self-efficacy beliefs on self- regulatory cognitive processes is revealed in a programme of research on complex organisational decision-making (Wood & Bandura, 1989b). Much of the research on human decision-making involves single trial judgements in static environments (Beach, Barnes & Christensen-Szalanski, 1986; Hogarth, 1981). Judgements under such conditions may not provide a sufficient basis for developing either descriptive or normative models of decision-making in dynamic naturalistic environments which involve repeated judgements governed by learning and motivational mechanisms.

The mechanisms and outcomes of organisational decision-making do not lend themselves readily to experimental analysis in actual organisational settings. Advances in this complex field can be achieved by experimental analyses of decision making in simulated organisational environments. A simulated environment permits systematic variation of theoretically relevant factors and precise assessment of their impact on organisational performance and the psychological mechanisms through which they achieve their effects.

In this research, executives managed a computer-simulated organisation in which they had to allocate resources and to learn and implement managerial rules to achieve organisational levels of performance that were difficult to fulfil. At periodic intervals we measured their perceived self-efficacy, the goals they sought to achieve, the adequacy of their analytic thinking for discovering managerial rules, and the level of organisational performance they realised.

Social cognitive theory explains psychosocial functioning in terms of triadic reciprocal causation (Bandura, 1986). In this model of reciprocal determinism, cognitive and other personal factors, behaviour, and environmental events all operate as interacting determinants that influence each other bidirectionally. Each of the major interactants in the triadic causal structure - cognitive, behavioural, and environmental - functions as an important constituent in the dynamic simulated environment. The cognitive determinant is indexed by self-beliefs of efficacy, personal goal-setting, and quality of analytic thinking. The managerial choices that are actually executed constitute the behavioural determinant. The properties of the organisational environment, the level of challenge it prescribes, and its responsiveness to managerial interventions represent the environmental determinant. Analyses of ongoing processes clarify how the interactional causal structure operates and changes over time.

The interactional causal structure was tested in conjunction with experimentally varied organisational properties and belief systems that can enhance or undermine the operation of self- regulatory determinants. One important belief system is concerned with the conception of ability (M. Bandura & Dweck, 1988; Dweck & Elliott, 1983; Nicholls, 1984). Some people regard ability as an *acquirable skill* that can be increased by gaining knowledge and perfecting competencies. They adopt a learning goal. They seek challenges that provide opportunities to expand their knowledge and competencies. They regard errors as a natural part of an acquisition process. One learns from mistakes. They judge their capabilities more in terms of personal improvement than by comparison against the achievement of others. For people who view ability as a more or less *fixed capacity*, performance level is regarded as diagnostic of inherent cognitive capacities. Errors and deficient performances carry high evaluative threat. Therefore, they prefer tasks that minimise errors and permit ready display of intellectual proficiency at the expense of expanding their knowledge and competencies. High effort is also threatening because it presumably reveals low ability. The successes of others belittle their own perceived ability.

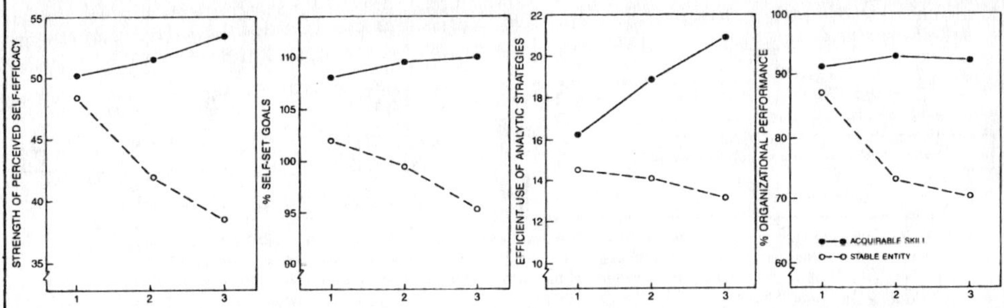

Figure 6. Changes in perceived managerial self-efficacy, the performance goals set for the organisation relative to the preset standard, effective use of analytic strategies, and achieved level of organisational performance across blocks of production orders under acquirable skill and entity conceptions of capability. Each trial block comprises six different production orders (Wood & Bandura, 1989a).

We induced these different conceptions of ability and then examined their effects on the self-regulatory mechanisms governing the utilisation of skills and performance accomplishments (Wood & Bandura, 1989a). Managers who viewed decision-making ability as reflecting basic cognitive aptitude were beset by increasing self-doubts about their managerial efficacy as they encountered problems (Figure 6). They became more and more erratic in their analytic thinking, they lowered their organisational aspirations, and they achieved progressively less with the organisation they were managing. In contrast, construal of ability as an acquirable skill fostered a highly resilient sense of personal efficacy. Under this belief system, the managers remained steadfast in their perceived managerial self-efficacy, they continued to set themselves challenging organisational goals, and they used analytic strategies in efficient ways that aided discovery of optimal managerial decision rules. Such a self-efficacious orientation paid off in high organisational attainments.

Another important belief system that affects how efficacy-relevant information is cognitively processed is concerned with people's beliefs about the extent to which their environment is influenceable or controllable. This aspect to the exercise of control represents the level of system constraints, the opportunity structure to exercise personal efficacy, and the ease of access to those opportunity structures. Our organisational simulation research underscores the strong impact of perceived controllability on the self-regulatory factors governing decision making that can enhance or impede performance (Bandura & Wood, 1989). People who managed the simulated organisation under a cognitive set that organisations are not easily changeable quickly lost faith in their decision-making capabilities even when performance standards were within easy reach (Figure 7). They lowered their aspirations. Those who operated under a cognitive set that organisations are controllable displayed a strong sense of managerial efficacy. They set themselves increasingly challenging goals and used good

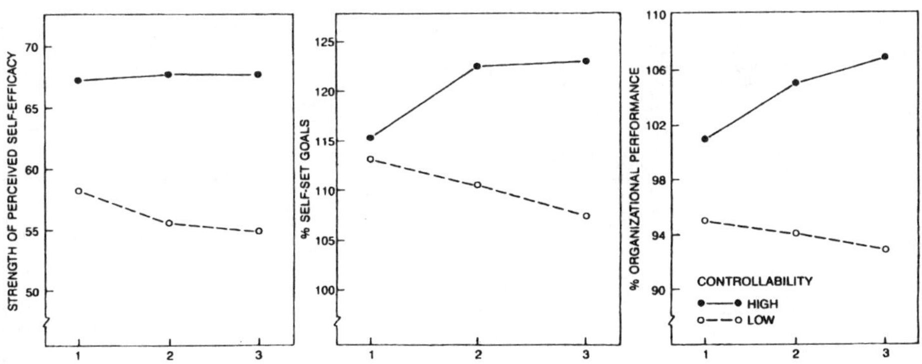

Figure 7. Changes in strength relative to perceived managerial self-efficacy, the performance goals set for the organization, and level of organizational performance for managers who operated under a cognitive set that organisations are controllable or difficult to control. Each trial block comprises six different production orders (Bandura & Wood, 1989).

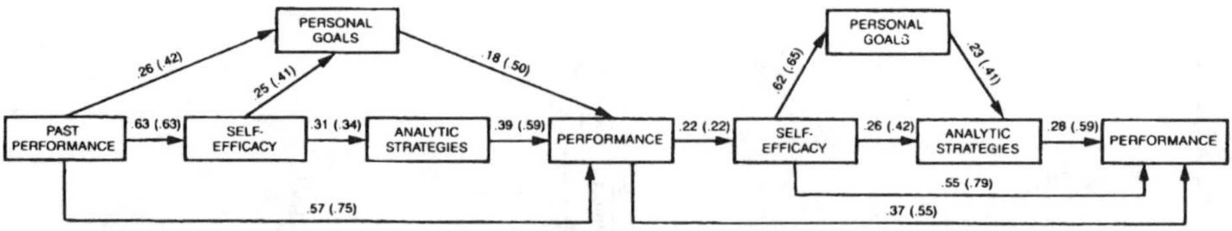

Figure 8. Path analysis of causal structures. The initial numbers on the paths of influence are the significant standardised path coefficients (*ps*<.05); the numbers in parentheses are the first-order correlations. The network of relations on the left half of the figure are for the initial managerial efforts, and those on the right are for later managerial efforts (Wood & Bandura, 1988b).

analytic thinking for discovering effective managerial rules. They exhibited high resiliency of self-efficacy even in the face of numerous difficulties. The divergent changes in the self-regulatory factors are accompanied by large differences in organisational attainments.

Path analyses confirm the postulated causal ordering of self-regulatory determinants. When initially faced with managing a complex unfamiliar environment, people relied heavily on their past performance in judging their efficacy and setting their personal goals. But as they began to form a self-schema concerning their efficacy through further experience, the performance system is powered more strongly and intricately by self-perceptions of efficacy (Figure 8). Perceived self-efficacy influences performance both directly and through its strong effects on personal goal setting and proficient analytic thinking. Personal goals, in turn, enhance performance attainments through the mediation of analytic strategies.

Motivational processes

Self-beliefs of efficacy play a central role in the self-regulation of motivation. Most human motivation is cognitively generated. In cognitive motivation, people motivate themselves and guide their actions anticipatorily through the exercise of forethought. They anticipate likely outcomes of prospective actions, they set goals for themselves and plan courses of action designed to realise valued futures.

One can distinguish three different forms of cognitive motivators around which different theories have been built. These include *causal attributions, outcome expectancies,* and *cognised goals.* The corresponding theories are attribution theory, expectancy-value theory, and goal theory, respectively. Figure 9 summarises schematically these alternative conceptions of cognitive motivation. Outcome and goal motivators clearly operate through the anticipation mechanism. Causal reasons conceived retrospectively for prior attainments can also affect future actions anticipatorily by altering self-appraisal of capability and perception of task demands.

The self-efficacy mechanism of personal agency operates in all of these variant forms of cognitive motivation. Causal attributions and self-efficacy appraisals involve bidirectional causation. Self-beliefs of efficacy bias causal attribution (Collins, 1982; Silver, Mitchell & Gist, 1989). The relative weight given to information regarding adeptness, effort, task complexity, and situational circumstances affects self-efficacy appraisal. Causal analyses indicate that the effects of causal attributions on performance attainments are mediated through self-efficacy beliefs rather than operate directly on performance (Relich, Debus & Walker, 1986; Schunk & Cox, 1986; Schunk & Gunn, 1986; Schunk & Rice, 1986). The stronger the self-efficacy belief, the higher the subsequent performance attainments.

In expectancy-value theory, strength of motivation is governed jointly by the expectation that particular actions will produce specified outcomes and the value placed on those outcomes (Atkinson, 1964; Feather, 1982; Fishbein, 1967; Rotter, 1954). However, people act on their beliefs about what they can do, as well as their beliefs about the likely outcomes of various actions. The effects of outcome expectancies on performance motivation are partly governed by self-beliefs of efficacy. There are many activities which, if done well, guarantee valued outcomes, but they are not pursued by people who doubt they can do what it takes to succeed (Beck & Lund, 1981; Betz & Hackett, 1986). The predictiveness of expectancy-value theory can be enhanced by including the self-efficacy determinant (McCaul, O'Neill & Glasgow, 1988; Wheeler, 1983).

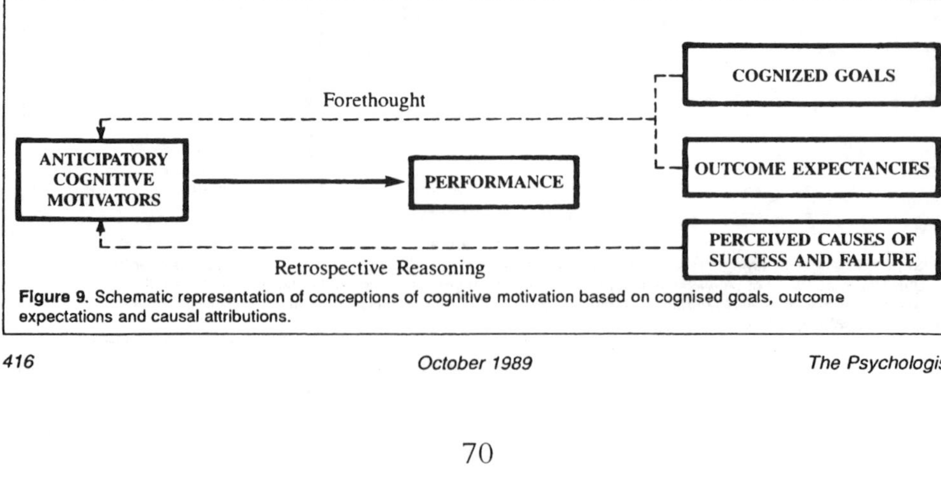

Figure 9. Schematic representation of conceptions of cognitive motivation based on cognised goals, outcome expectations and causal attributions.

The degree to which outcome expectations contribute independently to performance motivation varies depending on how tightly contingencies between actions and outcomes are structured, either inherently or socially, in a given domain of functioning. For many activities, outcomes are determined by level of competence. Hence, the types of outcomes people anticipate depend largely on how well they believe they will be able to perform in given situations. In most social, intellectual and physical pursuits, those who judge themselves highly efficacious will expect favourable outcomes, whereas those who expect poor performances of themselves will conjure up negative outcomes. Thus, in activities in which outcomes are highly contingent on quality of performance, self-judged efficacy accounts for most of the variance in expected outcomes. When variations in perceived self-efficacy are partialled out, the outcomes expected for given performances do not have much of an independent effect on behaviour (Barling & Abel, 1983; Barling & Beattie, 1983; Godding & Glasgow, 1985; Lee, 1984a,b; Williams & Watson, 1985).

Self-efficacy beliefs account for only part of the variance in expected outcomes when outcomes are not completely controlled by quality of performance. This occurs when extraneous factors also affect outcomes, or outcomes are socially tied to a minimum level of performance so that some variations in quality of performance above and below the standard do not produce differential outcomes. And finally, expected outcomes are independent of perceived self-efficacy when contingencies are discriminatively structured so that no level of competence can produce desired outcomes. This occurs in pursuits that are rigidly segregated by sex, race, age or some other factor. Under such circumstances, people in the disfavoured group expect poor outcomes however efficacious they judge themselves to be.

The capacity to exercise self-influence by personal challenge and evaluative reaction to one's own attainments provides a major cognitive mechanism of motivation and self-directedness (Bandura, 1988a). A large body of evidence is consistent in showing that explicit challenging goals enhance and sustain motivation (Latham & Lee, 1986; Locke, Shaw, Saari & Latham, 1981; Mento, Steel & Karren, 1987). Goals operate largely through self-referent processes rather than regulate motivation and action directly. Motivation based on aspirational standards involves a cognitive comparison process. By making self-satisfaction conditional on matching adopted goals, people give direction to their actions and create self incentives to persist in their efforts until their performances match their goals. They seek self-satisfactions from fulfilling valued goals and are prompted to intensify their efforts by discontent with substandard performances.

Activation of self-evaluation processes through cognitive comparison requires both comparative factors - a personal standard and knowledge of one's performance level. Simply adopting a goal, without knowing how one is doing, or knowing how one is doing in the absence of a goal, has no lasting motivational impact (Bandura & Cervone, 1983; Becker, 1978; Strang, Lawrence & Fowler, 1978). But the combined influence of goals with performance feedback heightens motivation substantially.

Cognitive motivation based on goal intentions is mediated by three types of self influences: affective self-evaluative reactions to one's performance, perceived self-efficacy for goal attainment, and adjustment of personal standards in light of one's attainments. Perceived self-efficacy contributes to motivation in several ways. It is partly on the basis of self-beliefs of efficacy that people choose what challenges to undertake, how much effort to expend in the endeavour, and how long to persevere in the face of difficulties (Bandura,1986; 1988b). When faced with obstacles and failures, people who have self-doubts about their capabilities slacken their efforts or abort their attempts prematurely and settle for mediocre solutions, whereas those who have a strong belief in their capabilities exert greater effort to master the challenge (Bandura & Cervone, 1983; Cervone & Peake, 1986; Jacobs, Prentice-Dunn & Rogers, 1984; Peake & Cervone, 1989; Weinberg, Gould & Jackson, 1979). Strong perseverance usually pays off in performance accomplishments.

Perceived self-efficacy contributes to motivation at different levels of discrepancy between personal standards and at-

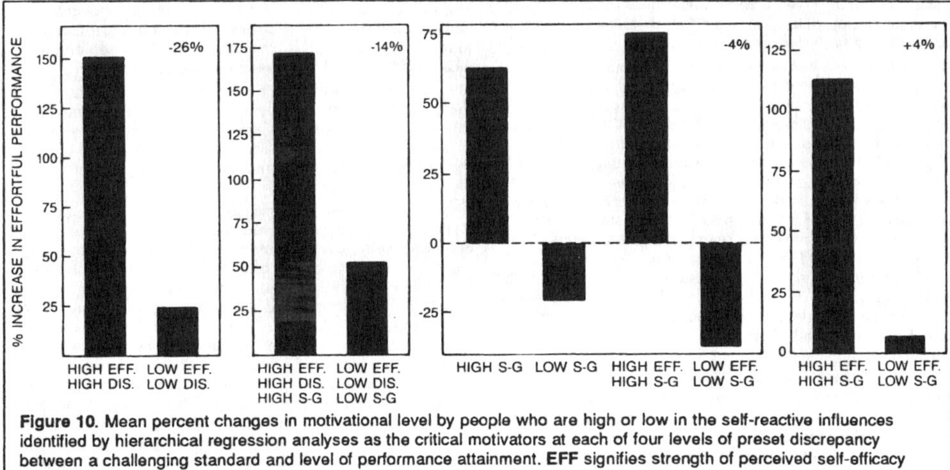

Figure 10. Mean percent changes in motivational level by people who are high or low in the self-reactive influences identified by hierarchical regression analyses as the critical motivators at each of four levels of preset discrepancy between a challenging standard and level of performance attainment. **EFF** signifies strength of perceived self-efficacy to attain a 50% increase in effort; **DIS** the level of self-dissatisfaction with the same level of attainment as in the prior attempt; and **S-G** the goals people set for themselves for the next attempt. The second set of graphs at the -4% discrepancy level summarise the results of the regression analysis performed with perceived self-efficacy averaged over the 30-70% goal attainment range (Bandura & Cervone, 1986).

tainments (Bandura & Cervone, 1986). The stronger the people's self-efficacy beliefs that they can meet challenging standards, the more they intensify and sustain their efforts (Figure 10). Discontent operates as an affective motivator when attainments fall substantially or moderately short of a comparative standard. The more self-dissatified people are with substandard attainments, the more they heighten their efforts. As people approach or surpass the adopted standard, they set new goals for themselves that serve as additional motivators. The higher the self-set goals, the more effort invested in the endeavour. Thus, notable attainments bring temporary satisfaction, but people who are assured of their capabilities enlist new challenges as personal motivators for further accomplishment. Taken together this set of self-reactive influences accounts for the major share of variation in motivation.

Many theories of motivation and self-regulation are founded on a negative feedback control model. This type of system functions as a motivator and regulator of action through a discrepancy reduction mechanism. Perceived discrepancy between performance and a reference standard motivates action to reduce the incongruity. Discrepancy reduction clearly plays a central role in any system of self-regulation. However, in the negative feedback control system, if performance matches the standard the person does nothing. Such a feedback control system would produce circular action that leads nowhere.

Human self-motivation relies on both *discrepancy production* and *discrepancy reduction* (Bandura, 1988b). It requires *proactive* control as well as *reactive* control. People initially motivate themselves through proactive control by setting themselves valued challenging standards that create a state of disequilibrium and then mobilising their effort on the basis of anticipatory estimation of what it would take to reach them. As previously shown, after people attain the standard they have been pursuing, those who have a strong sense of efficacy generally set a higher standard for themselves. The adoption of further challenges creates new motivating discrepancies to be mastered. Similarly, surpassing a standard is more likely to raise aspiration than to lower subsequent performance to conform to the surpassed standard. Self-motivation thus involves a hierarchical dual control process of disequilibrating discrepancy production followed by equilibrating discrepancy reduction.

There is a growing body of evidence that human attainments and positive well-being require an optimistic sense of personal efficacy (Bandura, 1986). This is because ordinary social realities are strewn with difficulties. They are full of impediments, failures, adversities, setbacks, frustrations, and inequities. People must have a robust sense of personal efficacy to sustain the perseverant effort needed to succeed. Self-doubts can set in fast after some failures or reverses. The important matter is not that difficulties arouse self-doubt, which is a natural immediate reaction, but the speed of recovery of perceived self-efficacy from difficulties. Some people quickly recover their self-assurance; others lose faith in their capabilities. Because the acquisition of knowledge and competencies usually requires sustained effort in the face of difficulties and setbacks, it is resiliency of self-belief that counts.

In his informative book, titled *Rejection*, John White (1982) provides vivid testimony that the striking characteristic of people who have achieved eminence in their fields is an inextinguishable sense of efficacy and a firm belief in the worth of what they are doing. This resilient self-belief system enabled them to override repeated early rejections of their work.

Many of our literary classics brought their authors repeated rejections. The novelist, Saroyan, accumulated several thousand rejections before he had his first literary piece published. James Joyce's, the *Dubliners*, was rejected by 22 publishers. Gertrude Stein continued to submit poems to editors for about 20 years before one was finally accepted. Now that is invincible self-efficacy. Over a dozen publishers rejected a manuscript by E.E. Cummings. When he finally got it published by his mother the dedication, printed in upper case, read: *With no thanks to ...* followed by the long list of publishers who had rejected his offering.

Early rejection is the rule, rather than the exception, in other creative endeavours. The Impressionists had to arrange their own art exhibitions because their works were routinely rejected by the Paris Salon. A Paris art dealer refused Picasso shelter when he asked if he could bring in his paintings from out of the rain. Van Gogh sold only one painting during his life. Rodin was rejected three times by the Ecole des Beaux-Arts. The musical works of most renowned composers were initially greeted with derision. Stravinsky was run out of town by an enraged audience and critics when he first served them the *Rite of Spring*. Many other composers suffered the same fate, especially in the early phases of their career. The brilliant architect, Frank Lloyd Wright, was one of the more widely rejected architects during much of his career.

To turn to more familiar examples, Hollywood initially rejected the incomparable Fred Astaire for being only *"a balding, skinny actor who can dance a little"*. Decca Records turned down a recording contract with the Beatles with the non-prophetic evaluation, *"We don't like their sound. Groups of guitars are on their way out."* Whoever issued that rejective pronouncement must cringe at each sight of a guitar.

It is not uncommon for authors of scientific classics to experience repeated initial rejection of their work, often with hostile embellishments if it is too discordant with what is in vogue at the time. For example, John Garcia, who eventually won well-deserved recognition for his fundamental psychological discoveries, was once told by a reviewer of his oft rejected manuscripts that one is no more likely to find the phenomenon he discovered than bird droppings in a cuckoo clock. Verbal droppings of this type demand tenacious self-belief to continue the tortuous search for new Muses. Scientists often reject theories and technologies that are ahead of their time. Because of the cold reception given to most innovations, the time between conception and technical realisation typically spans several decades.

The findings of laboratory investigations are in accord with these records of human triumphs regarding the centrality of the motivational effects of self-beliefs of efficacy in human attainments. It takes a resilient sense of efficacy to override the numerous dissuading impediments to significant accomplishments.

It is widely believed that misjudgement breeds dysfunction. Certainly, gross misjudgements can get one into trouble. But optimistic self-appraisals of capability that are not unduly disparate from what is possible can be advantageous, whereas veridical judgements can be self-limiting. When people err in their self-appraisal they tend to overestimate their capabilities. This is a benefit rather than a cognitive failing to be eradicated. If self-efficacy beliefs always reflected only what people can do routinely, they would rarely fail but they would not mount the extra effort needed to surpass their ordinary performances. The emerging evidence indicates that the successful, the innovative, the sociable, the nonanxious, the nondespondent, and the social reformers take an optimistic view of their personal efficacy to exercise influence over events that affect their lives (Bandura, 1986). If not unrealistically exaggerated, such self-beliefs enhance and sustain the level of motivation needed for personal and social accomplishments.

Affective processes

People's beliefs in their capabilities affect how much stress and depression they experience in threatening or taxing situations, as well as their level of motivation. In social cognitive theory (Bandura, 1986), perceived self-efficacy to exercise control over potentially threatening events plays a central role in anxiety arousal. Threat is not a fixed property of situational events. Nor does appraisal of the likelihood of aversive happenings rely solely on reading external signs of danger or safety. Rather, threat is a relational property concerning the match between perceived coping capabilities and potentially hurtful aspects of the environment. Therefore, to understand people's appraisals of external threats and their affective reactions to them it is necessary to analyse their judgements of their coping capabilities which, in large part, determine the subjective perilousness of environmental events.

People who believe they can exercise control over potential threats do not conjure up apprehensive cognitions and, hence, are not perturbed by them. But those who believe they cannot manage potential threats experience high levels of anxiety arousal. They tend to dwell on their coping deficiencies and view many aspects of their environment as fraught with danger. Through such inefficacious thought they distress themselves and constrain and impair their level of functioning (Beck, Emery & Greenberg, 1985; Lazarus & Folkman, 1984; Meichenbaum, 1977; Sarson, 1975).

That perceived coping efficacy operates as a cognitive mediator of anxiety and stress reactions has been tested by creating different levels of perceived self-efficacy and relating them at a microlevel to different manifestations of anxiety. People display little affective arousal while coping with potential threats they regard with high efficacy. But as they cope with threats for which they distrust their coping

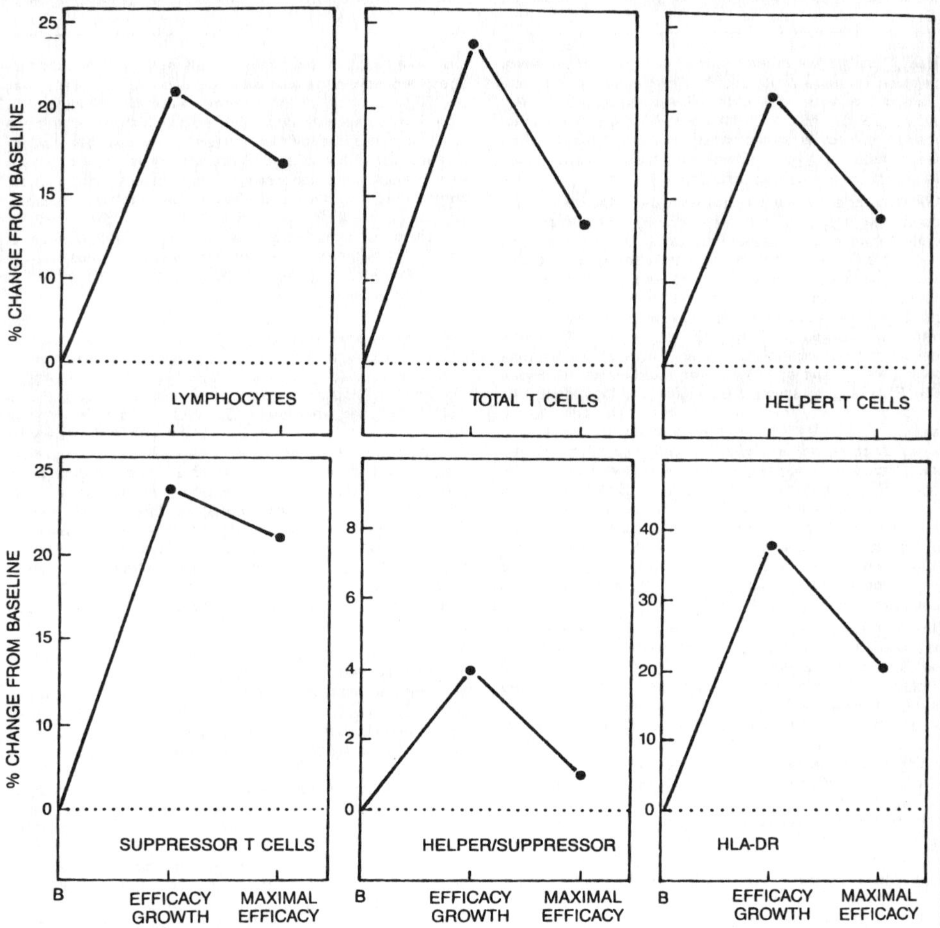

Figure 11. Changes in immune function experienced as percent of baseline values during exposure to the phobic stressor while aquiring perceived coping self-efficacy (**Efficacy Growth**) and after perceived coping self-efficacy had been developed to the maximal level (**Maximal Efficacy**) (Wiedenfeld, O'Leary, Bandura, Brown, Levine & Raska, 1989).

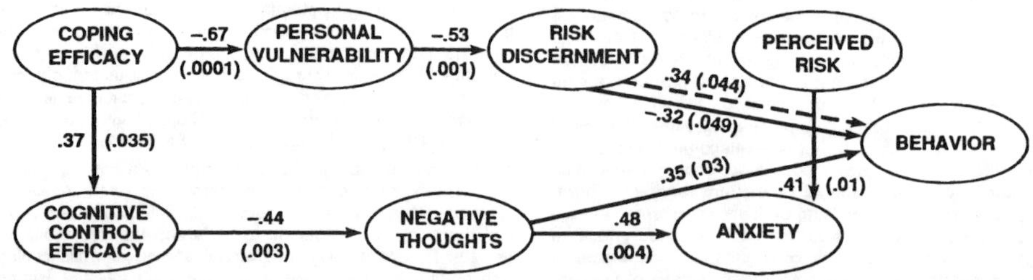

Figure 12. Path analysis of the causal structure. The numbers on the paths of influence are the significant standardised path coefficients; the numbers in parentheses are the significance levels. The solid line to behavior represents different activities pursued outside the home, the hatch line represents avoided activities because of concern over personal safety (Ozer & Bandura, 1989).

efficacy, their stress mounts, their heart rate accelerates, their blood pressure rises, and they display increased catecholamine secretion (Bandura, Reese & Adams, 1982; Bandura, Taylor, Williams, Mefford & Barchas, 1985). After perceived efficacy is strengthened to the maximal level by guided mastery, previously intimidating tasks no longer elicit differential autonomic or catecholamine reactions.

Other efficacy activated processes in the affective domain concern the impact of perceived coping efficacy on biochemical mediators of health functioning. Stress has been implicated as an important contributing factor to many physical dysfunctions. Controllability appears to be a key organising principle regarding the nature of these stress effects. Exposure to stressors with controlling efficacy has no adverse physiological effects. But exposure to the same stressors without controlling efficacy impairs the immune system (Coe & Levine, 1989; Maier, Laudenslager & Ryan, 1985). Physiological systems are highly interdependent. The types of biochemical reactions that have been shown to accompany a weak sense of coping efficacy are involved in the regulation of immune systems. For example, perceived weak efficacy in exercising control over stressors activate endogenous opioid systems (Bandura, Cioffi, Taylor & Brouillard, 1988). There is evidence that some of the immunosuppressive effects of inefficacy in controlling stressors are mediated by release of endogenous opioids. When opioid mechanisms are blocked by opiate antagonists, the stress of weak coping efficacy loses its immunosuppressive capabilities (Shavit & Martin, 1987).

In the laboratory research demonstrating immunosuppression through stress mediation, controllability is studied as a fixed dichotomous property in which animals either exercise complete control over physical stressors, or they have no control, whatsoever. They remain completely powerless in the face of unremitting bombardment by stressors. In contrast, most human stress is activated in the course of learning how to exercise control over recurring stressors. Stress aroused while gaining coping mastery may have very different effects than stress in aversive situations with no prospect in sight of ever gaining any self-protective efficacy. It would not be evolutionarily advantageous if acute stressors invariably impaired immune function, because of their prevalence in everyday life. If this were the case, people would experience continuous high vulnerability to infective agents.

There would be evolutionary benefits to experiencing a boost in immune function while one is acquiring coping mastery. But intense and prolonged stress of coping inefficacy may take its toll on the immune system. Indeed, we find that stress aroused in the process of gaining coping efficacy over phobic stressors enhances immune function (Figure 11). However, some individuals exhibit suppression of immune function during the efficacy acquisition phase. The rate of efficacy acquisition is a good predictor of whether exposure to acute stressors enhances or suppresses various components of the immune system (Wiedenfeld, O'Leary, Bandura, Brown, Levine & Raska, 1989). The slower the growth of perceived coping efficacy, the greater the immunoattenuation. High autonomic arousal and neuroendocrine activity also attenuated immune system status, but their impact is somewhat weaker.

Anxiety arousal in situations involving some risks is affected not only by perceived coping efficacy, but also by perceived efficacy to control distressing cognitions. The exercise of control over one's own consciousness is summed up well in the proverb: *"You cannot prevent the birds of worry and care from flying over your head. But you can stop them from building a nest in your head"*. Perceived self-efficacy in thought control is a key factor in the regulation of cognitively-generated arousal. It is not the sheer frequency of disturbing cognitions, but the perceived inability to turn them off that is the major source of distress (Kent, 1987; Salkovskis & Harrison, 1984). Thus, the incidence of aversive cognitions is unrelated to anxiety level when variations in perceived thought control efficacy are controlled for, whereas perceived thought control efficacy is strongly related to anxiety level when extent of frightful cognitions is controlled (Kent & Gibbons, 1987).

The dual control of anxiety and behaviour by perceived coping efficacy and thought control efficacy is revealed in a study of the mechanisms governing personal empowerment over pervasive social threats (Ozer & Bandura, 1989). Sexual violence toward women is a prevalent problem. Because any woman may be a potential victim, the lives of many women are distressed and constricted by a sense of inefficacy to cope with the threat of sexual assault. To address this problem at a self-protective level, women participated in a mastery modelling programme in which they mastered the physical skills to defend themselves successfully against sexual assailants. Mastery modelling enhanced perceived coping efficacy and cognitive control efficacy, decreased perceived vulnerability to assault and reduced the incidence of intrusive aversive thoughts and anxiety arousal. These changes were accompanied by increased freedom of action and decreased avoidant social behavior. Path analysis of the causal structure.revealed a dual path of regulation of behaviour by perceived self-efficacy: One path was mediated through the effects of perceived coping self-efficacy on perceived vulnerability and risk discernment, and the other through the impact of perceived cognitive control self-efficacy on intrusive aversive thoughts (Figure 12). A strong sense of coping efficacy rooted in performance capabilities has substantial impact on perceived self-efficacy to abort the escalation or perseveration of perturbing cognitions.

Perceived coping efficacy regulates avoidance behaviour in risky situations, as well as anxiety arousal. The stronger the perceived coping efficacy the more venturesome the behaviour, regardless of whether self-beliefs of efficacy are strengthened by mastery experiences, modelling influences, or cognitive simulations. The role of perceived self-efficacy and anxiety arousal in the causal structure of avoidant behaviour has been examined in a number of studies. The results show that people base their actions on self-percepts of efficacy in situations they regard as risky. Williams and his colleagues (Williams, Kinney & Falbo, 1989; Williams, Dooseman & Kleifield, 1984; Williams, Turner & Peer, 1985) have analysed by partial correlation numerous data sets from studies in which perceived self-efficacy, anticipated anxiety, and phobic behaviour were measured. Perceived self-efficacy accounts for a substantial amount of variance in phobic behaviour when anticipated anxiety is partialled out, whereas the relationship between anticipated anxiety and phobic behaviour essentially disappears when perceived self-efficacy is partialed out (Table 1). Studies of other threatening activities similarly demonstrate the predictive superiority of perceived self-efficacy over perceived dangerous outcomes in level of anxiety arousal. (Hackett & Betz, 1984; Leland, 1983; McAuley, 1985; Williams & Watson, 1985).

The data taken as a whole indicate that anxiety arousal and avoidant behaviour are largely coeffects of perceived coping inefficacy rather than causally linked. People avoid poten-

Table 1

	COPING BEHAVIOR	
	ANTICIPATED ANXIETY with Self-Efficacy Controlled	PERCEIVED SELF-EFFICACY with Anticipated Anxiety Controlled
Williams & Rappoport (1983)		
Pretreatment 1	-.12	.40*
Pretreatment 2	-.28	.59**
Posttreatment	.13	.45*
Follow-up	.06	.45*
Williams et al. (1984)		
Pretreatment	-.36*	.22
Posttreatment	-.21	.59***
Williams et al. (1985)		
Pretreatment	-.35*	.28*
Posttreatment	.05	.72***
Follow-up	-.12	.66***
Telch et al. (1985)		
Pretreatment	-.56***	-.28
Posttreatment	.15	.48**
Follow-up	-.05	.42*
Kirsch et al. (1983)		
Pretreatment	-.34*	.54***
Posttreatment	-.48**	.48**
Arnow et al. (1985)		
Pretreatment	.17	.77***
Posttreatment	-.08	.43*
Follow-up	-.06	.88**
Williams et al. (1989)		
Midtreatment	-.15	.65***
Posttreatment	.02	.47**
Follow-up	-.03	.71***

*p < .05
**p < .01
***p < .001

tially threatening situations and activities, not because they experience anxiety arousal or anticipate they will be anxious, but because they believe they will be unable to cope successfully with situations they regard as risky. They take self-protective action regardless of whether or not they happen to be anxious at the moment. They do not have to conjure up an anxious state before they can take action. They commonly perform risky activities at lower strengths of perceived self-efficacy despite high anxiety arousal (Bandura, 1988a or b).

Perceived self-efficacy to exercise control can give rise to despondency as well as anxiety. The nature of the outcomes over which personal control is sought operates as an important differentiating factor. People experience anxiety when they perceive themselves ill equipped to control potentially injurious events. Attenuation or control of aversive outcomes is central to anxiety. People are saddened and depressed by their perceived inefficacy in gaining highly valued outcomes. Irreparable loss or failure to gain valued outcomes figures prominently in despondency.

Several lines of evidence support the role of perceived self-inefficacy in depression. Perceived inefficacy to fulfil goals that affect evaluation of self-worth and to secure things that bring satisfaction to their life can give rise to bouts of depression (Bandura, 1988a; Holahan & Holahan, 1987a,b; Kanfer & Zeiss, 1983). When the perceived self-inefficacy involves social relationships, it can induce depression both directly and indirectly by curtailing the cultivation of the very interpersonal relationships that can provide satisfactions and buffer the effects of chronic daily stressors (Holahan & Holahan, 1987a). A low sense of efficacy to fulfill role demands that reflect on personal adequacy also contributes to depression (Cutrona & Troutman, 1986). When the valued outcomes one seeks also protect against future aversive circumstances, as when failure to secure a job jeopardises one's livelihood, perceived self-inefficacy is both distressing and depressing. Because of the interdependence of outcomes, both anxiety and despair often accompany perceived personal efficacy.

Self-regulatory theories of motivation and of depression make seemingly contradictory predictions regarding the effects of negative discrepancies between attainments and standards. Standards that exceed attainments are said to enhance motivation through goal challenges, but negative discrepancies are also invoked as activators of despondent mood. Moreover, when negative discrepancies do have adverse effects, they may give rise to apathy rather than to despondency. A conceptual scheme is needed that differentiates the conditions under which negative discrepancies will be motivating, depressing, or induce apathy.

In accord with social cognitive theory, the directional effects of negative goal discrepancies are predictable from the relationship between perceived self-efficacy for goal attainment and level of personal goals (Bandura & Abrams, 1986). Whether negative discrepancies are motivating or depressing depends on beliefs on one's efficacy to match them. Negative disparities give rise to high motivation and low despondency when people believe they have the efficacy to fulfil difficult goals and continue to strive for them. Negative disparities diminish motivation and generate despondency for people who judge themselves as inefficacious to attain difficult goals but continue to demand them of themselves. People who view difficult goals as beyond their capabilities and abandon them as unrealistic for themselves become apathetic rather than despondent.

Much human depression is cognitively generated by dejecting thought patterns. Therefore, perceived self-efficacy to exercise control over ruminative thought figures prominently in the occurrence, duration and recurrence of depressive episodes. Kavanagh and Wilson (1988) found that the weaker the perceived efficacy to terminate ruminative thoughts the higher the depression ($r = -.51$), and the stronger the perceived thought control efficacy instilled through treatment the greater the decline in depression ($r = .71$) and the lower the vulnerability to recurrence of depressive episodes ($r = -.48$). Perceived self-efficacy retains its predictiveness of improvement and reduced vulnerability to relapse when level of prior depression is controlled.

Selection processes

People can exert some influence over their life paths by the environments they select and environments they create. Thus far, the discussion has centred on efficacy-related processes that enable people to create beneficial environments and to exercise control over them. Judgements of personal efficacy also shape developmental trajectories by influencing selection of activities and environments. People tend to avoid activities and situations they believe exceed their coping capabilities, but they readily undertake challenging activities and pick social environments they judge themselves capable of handling. Any factor that influences choice behaviour can profoundly affect the direction of personal development. This is because the social influences operating in selected environments continue to promote certain competencies, values, and interests long after the decisional determinant has rendered its inaugurating effect (Bandura, 1986; Snyder, 1986). Thus, seemingly inconsequential efficacy determinants can initiate selective associations that produce major and enduring personal changes.

The power of self-efficacy beliefs to affect the course of life paths through choice-related processes is most clearly revealed in studies of career decision-making and career development (Betz & Hackett, 1986; Lent & Hackett, 1987). The stronger people's self-belief in their capabilities, the more career options they consider possible, the greater the interest they show in them, and the better they prepare themselves educationally for different occupational pursuits.

Biased cultural practices, stereotypic modelling of gender roles, and dissuading opportunity structures eventually leave their mark on women's beliefs about their occupational efficacy (Hackett & Betz, 1981). Women are especially prone to limit their interests and range of career options by self-beliefs that they lack the necessary capabilities for occupations traditionally dominated by men, even though they do not differ from men in actual ability. The self-limitation of career development arises from perceived inefficacy, rather than from actual inability. By constricting choice behaviour that can cultivate interests and competencies, self-disbeliefs create their own behavioural validation and protection from corrective influence. However, changes in cultural attitudes and practices may be weakening self-efficacy barriers. Students currently coming through the school ranks reveal a much smaller disparity between males and females in their beliefs about their efficacy to pursue successfully different types of careers (Post-Kammer & Smith, 1985).

Self-efficacy beliefs contribute to the course of social development as well as occupational pursuits (Perry, Perry & Rasmussen, 1986). The developmental processes undoubtedly involve bidirectional causation. Beliefs of personal capabilities determine choice of associates and activities, and affiliation patterns, in turn, affect the direction of self-efficacy development.

Concluding remarks

The multiple benefits of a sense of personal efficacy do not arise simply from the incantation of capability. Saying something should not be confused with believing it to be so. Simply saying that one is capable is not necessarily self-convincing, especially when it contradicts pre-existing beliefs. No amount of reiteration that I can fly, will persuade me that I have the efficacy to get myself airborne. Efficacy beliefs are the product of a complex process of self-persuasion that relies on cognitive processing of diverse sources of efficacy information conveyed enactively, vicariously, socially, and physiologically (Bandura, 1986).

The converging lines of evidence I have reported indicate that the self-efficacy mechanism plays a central role in the exercise of personal agency. The value of a psychological theory is judged not only by its explanatory and predictive power, but also by its operational power to enhance the quality of human functioning. Social cognitive theory provides prescriptive specificity on how to empower people with the competencies, self-regulatory capabilities and resilient self-belief or efficacy that enables them to enhance their psychological well-being and accomplishments.

References

Atkinson, J.W. (1964). *An Introduction to Motivation.* Princeton, NJ: Van Nostrand.

Bandura, A. (1986). *Social Foundations of Thought and Action: A social cognitive theory.* Englewood Cliffs, NJ Prentice-Hall.

Bandura, A. (1988a). Perceived self-efficacy: exercise of control through self-belief. In J.P. Dauwalder, M. Perrez & V. Hobi (Eds) *Annual Series of European Research in Behavior Therapy.* (Vol. 2, pp.27-59) Lisse(NL): Swets & Zeitlinger.

Bandura, A. (1988b). Self-regulation of motivation and action through goal systems. In V. Hamilton, G.H. Bower & N.H. Frijda (Eds) *Cognitive Perspectives on Emotion and Motivation.* Dordrecht: Kluwer Academic Publishers.

Bandura, A. & Abrams, K. (1987). Self-regulatory mechanisms in motivating, apathetic, and despondent reactions to unfulfilled standards. Unpublished manuscript, Stanford University, Stanford.

Bandura, A. & Adams, N.E. (1977). Analysis of self-efficacy theory of behavioral change. *Cognitive Therapy and Research,* **1**, 287-308.

Bandura, A. & Cervone, D. (1983). Self-evaluative and self-efficacy mechanisms governing the motivational effects of goal systems. *Journal of Personality and Social Psychology,* **45**, 1017-1028.

Bandura, A. & Cervone, D. (1986). Differential engagement of self-reactive influences in cognitive motivation. *Organizational Behavior and Human Decision Processes,* **38**, 92-113.

Bandura, A., Cioffi, D., Taylor, C.B. & Brouillard, M.E. (1988). Perceived self-efficacy in coping with cognitive stressors and opioid activation. *Journal of Personality and Social Psychology,* **55**, 479-488.

Bandura, A., Reese, L. & Adams, N.E. (1982). Microanalysis of action and fear arousal as a function of differential levels of perceived self-efficacy. *Journal of Personality and Social Psychology,* **43**, 5-21.

Bandura, A., Taylor, C.B., Williams, S.L., Mefford, I.N. & Barchas, J.D. (1985). Catecholamine secretion as a function of perceived coping self-efficacy. *Journal of Consulting and Clinical Psychology,* **53**, 406-414.

Bandura, A. & Wood, R.E. (1989). Effect of perceived controllability and performance standards on self-regulation of complex decision-maing. *Journal of Personality and Social Psychology,* **56**, 805-814.

Bandura, M.M. & Dweck, C.S. (1988). The relationship of conceptions of intelligence and achievement goals to achievement-related cognition, affect and behavior. Manuscript submitted for publication.

Barling, J. & Abel, M. (1983). Self-efficacy beliefs and performance. *Cognitive Therapy and Research,* **7**, 265-272.

Barling, J. & Beattie, R. (1983). Self-efficacy beliefs and sales performance. *Journal of Organizational Behavior Management,* **5**, 41-51.

Beach, L.R., Barnes, V.E. & Christensen-Szalanski, J.J.J. (1986). Beyond heuristics and biases: A contingency model of judgmental forecasting. *Journal of Forecasting,* **5**, 143-157.

Beck, A.T., Emery, G. & Greenberg, R.L. (1985). *Anxiety Disorders and Phobias.* New York: Basic Books.

Beck, K.H. & Lund, A.K. (1981). The effects of health threat seriousness and personal efficacy upon intentions and behaviour. *Journal of Applied Social Psychology,* **11**, 401-415.

Becker, L.J. (1978). Joint effect of feedback and goal setting on performance: a field study of residential energy conservation. *Journal of Applied Psychology,* **63**, 428- 433.

Betz, N.E. & Hackett, G. (1986). Applications for self-efficacy theory to understanding career choice behavior. *Journal of Social and Clinical Psychology,* **4**, 279-289.

Cervone, D. (1989) Effects of envisioning future activities on self-efficacy judgments and motivation: an availability heuristic interpretation. *Cognitive Therapy and Research,* **13**, 247-261.

Cervone, D. & Peake, P.K. (1986). Anchoring, efficacy, and action: the influence of judgmental heuristics on self-efficacy judgments and behavior. *Journal of Personality and Social Psychology,* **50**, 492-501.

Coe, C.L. & Levine, S. (1989, in press). Psychoimmunology: an old idea whose time has come. In P.R. Barchas (Ed) *Social Physiology of Social Relations.* Oxford: Oxford University Press.

Collins, J.L. (1982, March). *Self-efficacy and ability in achievement behavior.* Paper presented at the annual meeting of the American Educational Research Association, NY.

Corbin, C. (1972). Mental practice. In W. Morgan (Ed) *Ergogenic aids and muscular performance.* New York: Academic Press.

Cutrona, C.E. & Troutman, B.R. (1986). Social support, infant temperament, and parenting self-efficacy: a mediational model of postpartum depression. *Child Development,* **57**, 1507-1518.

Dweck, C.S. & Elliott, E.S. (1983). Achievement motivation. In P.H. Mussen (General Ed) & E.M. Heatherington (Vol eds) *Handbook of Child Psychology: Socialization, personality & social development.* (4th Ed. vol. 4, 644-691). New York: John Wiley.

Feather, N.T. (Ed) (1982). *Expectations and Actions: Expectancy-value models in psychology.* Hillsdale, NJ: Erlbaum.

Feltz, D.L. & Landers, D.M. (1983). Effects of mental practice on motor skill learning and performance: a meta-analysis. *Journal of Sport Psychology,* **5**, 25-57.

Fishbein, M. (Ed) (1967). *Readings in Attitude Theory and Measurement.* New York: Wiley.

Godding, P.R. & Glasgow, R.E. (1985). Self-efficacy and outcome expectations as predictors of controlled smoking status. *Cognitive Therapy and Research,* **9**, 583-590.

Hackett, G. & Betz, N.E. (1981). A self-efficacy approach to the career development of women. *Journal of Vocational Behavior,* **18**, 326-339.

Hackett, G. & Betz, N.E. (1984). Mathematics performance, mathematics self-efficacy, and the prediction of science-based college majors. Unpublished manuscript, University of California, Santa Barbara.

Hogarth, R. (1981). Beyond discrete biases: functional and dysfunctional aspects of judgmental heuristics. *Psychological Bulletin,* **90**, 197-217.

Holahan, C.K. & Holahan, C.J. (1987a). Self-efficacy, social support, and depression in aging: a longitudinal analysis. *Journal of Gerontology,* **42**, 65-68.

Holahan, C.K. & Holahan, C.J. (1987b). Life stress, hassles, and self-efficacy in aging: a replication and extension. *Journal of Applied Social Psychology,* **17**, 574-592.

Holroyd, K.A., Penzien, D.B., Hursey, K.G., Tobin, D.L., Rogers, L., Holm, J.E., Marcille, P.J., Hall, J.R. & Chila, A.G. (1984). Change mechanisms in EMG biofeedback training: cognitive changes underlying improvements in tension headache. *Journal of Consulting and Clinical Psychology,* **52**, 1039-1053.

Jacobs, B., Prentice-Dunn, S. & Rogers, R.W. (1984). Understanding persistence: an interface of control theory and self-efficacy theory. *Basic and Applied Social Psychology,* **5**, 333-347.

Kanfer, R. & Zeiss, A.M. (1983). Depression, interpersonal standard-setting, and judgments of self-efficacy. *Journal of Abnormal Psychology,* **92**, 319-329.

Kavanagh, D.J. & Wilson, P.H. (1988). Prediction of outcome with a group version of cognitive therapy for depression. Unpublished manuscript, University of Sydney.

Kazdin, A.E. (1978). Covert modeling - therapeutic application of imagined rehearsal. In J.L. Singer & K.S. Pope (Eds) *The Power of Human Imagination: New methods in psychotherapy. Emotions, personality and psychotherapy.* New York: Plenum.

Kazdin, A.E. (1979). Imagery elaboration and self- efficacy in the covert modeling treatment of unassertive behavior. *Journal of Consulting and Clinical Psychology,* **47**, 725-733.

Kent, G. (1987). Self-efficacious control over reported physiological, cognitive and behavioural symptoms of dental anxiety. *Behaviour Research and Therapy,* **25**, 341-347.

Kent, G. & Gibbons, R. (1987). Self-efficacy and the control of anxious cognitions. *Journal of Behavior Therapy & Experimental Psychiatry,* **18**, 33-40.

Latham, G.P. & Lee, T.W. (1986). Goal setting. In E.A. Locke (Ed) *Generalizing from Laboratory to Field Settings.* Lexington, MA: Heath.

Lazarus, R.S. & Folkman, S. (1984). *Stress, Appraisal and Coping.* New York: Springer.

Lee, C. (1984a). Accuracy of efficacy and outcome expectations in predicting performance in a simulated assertiveness task. *Cognitive Therapy and Research*, **8**, 37-48.

Lee, C. (1984b). Efficacy expectations and outcome expectations as predictors of performance in a snake-handling task. *Cognitive Therapy and Research*, **8**, 509-516.

Leland, E.I. (1983). Self-efficacy and other variables as they relate to precompetitive anxiety among male interscholastic basketball players. (Doctoral dissertation, Stanford University, 1983). *Dissertation Abstracts International*, **44**, 1376A.

Lent, R.W. & Hackett, G. (1987). Career self-efficacy. Empirical status and future directions. *Journal of Vocational Behaviour*, **30**, 347-382.

Litt, M.D. (1988). Self-efficacy and perceived control: cognitive mediators of pain tolerance. *Journal of Personality and Social Psychology*, **54**, 149-160.

Locke, E.A., Frederick, E., Lee, C. & Bobko, P. (1984). Effect of self-efficacy, goals, and task strategies on task performance. *Journal of Applied Psychology*, **69**, 241-251.

Locke, E.A., Shaw K.N., Saari, L.M. & Latham, G.P. (1981). Goal setting and task performance: 1969-1980. *Psychological Bulletin*, **90**, 125-152.

Maier, S.F., Laudenslager, M.L. & Ryan, S.M. (1985). Stressor controllability, immune function, and endogenous opiates. In F.R. Brush & J.B. Overmier (Eds) *Affect, Conditioning, and Cognition: essays on the determinants of behavior.* Hillsdale, NJ: Erlbaum.

McAuley, E. (1985). Modeling and self-efficacy: a test of Bandura's model. *Journal of Sport Psychology*, **7**, 283-295.

McCaul, K.D., O'Neill, K. & Glasgow, R.E. (1988). Predicting the performance of dental hygiene behaviors: an examination of the Fishbein and Ajzen model and self-efficacy expectations. *Journal of Applied Social Psychology*, **18**, 114-128.

Meichenbaum, D.H. (1977). *Cognitive-Behavior Modification: An integrative approach.* New York: Plenum Press.

Mento, A.J., Steel, R.P. & Karren, R.J. (1987). A meta-analytic study of the effects of goal setting on task performance: 1966-1984. *Organizational Behavior and Human Decision Processes*, **39**, 52-83.

Nicholls, J.G. (1984). Achievement motivation: conceptions of ability, subjective experience, task choice, and performance. *Psychological Review*, **91**, 328-346.

Ozer, E. & Bandura, A. (1989, in press). Mechanisms governing empowerment effects: a self-efficacy analysis. *Journal of Personality and Social Psychology.*

Peake, P.K. & Cervone, D. (1989). Sequence anchoring and self-efficacy: primacy effects in the consideration of possibilities. *Social Cognition*, **7**, 31-50.

Perry, D.G., Perry, L.C. & Rasmussen, P. (1986). Cognitive social learning mediators of aggression. *Child Development*, **57**, 700-711.

Post-Kammer, P. & Smith, P. (1985). Sex differences in career self-efficacy, consideration, and interests of eighth and ninth graders. *Journal of Counseling Psychology*, **32**, 551-559.

Relich, J.D., Debus, R.L. & Walker, R. (1986). The mediation role of attribution and self-efficacy variables for treatment effects on achievement outcomes. *Contemporary Educational Psychology*, **11**, 195-216.

Rotter, J.B. (1954). *Social Learning and Clinical Psychology.* Englewood Cliffs, NJ: Prentice-Hall.

Salkovskis, P.M. & Harrison, J. (1984). Abnormal and normal obsessions - a replication. *Behaviour Research and Therapy*, **22**, 549-552.

Sarason, I.G. (1975). Anxiety and self-preoccupation. In I.G. Sarason & D.C. Spielberger (Eds) *Stress and Anxiety.* Washington, DC: Hemisphere.

Schunk, D.H. & Cox, P.D. (1986). Strategy training and attributional feedback with learning disabled students. *Journal of Educational Psychology*, **78**, 201-209.

Schunk, D.H. & Gunn, T.P. (1986) Self-efficacy and skill development: influence of task strategies and attributions. *Journal of Educational Research*, **79**, 238-244.

Schunk, D.H. & Rice, J.M. (1986). Extended attributional feedback: sequence effects during remedial reading instruction. *Journal of Early Adolescence*, **6**, 55-66.

Shavit, Y. & Martin, F.C. (1987). Opiates, stress and immunity: animal studies. *Annals of Behavioural Medicine*, **9**, 11-20.

Silver, W.S., Mitchell, T.R. & Gist, M.E. (1989). The impact of self-efficacy on causal attributions for successful and unsuccessful performance. Unpublished manuscript, University of Washington, Seattle, Washington.

Snyder, M. (1986). *Public Appearances, Private Realities: The psychology of self-monitoring.* New York: W.H. Freeman.

Strang, H.R., Lawrence, E.C. & Fowler, P.C. (1978). Effects of assigned goal level and knowledge of results on arithmetic computation: laboratory study. *Journal of Applied Psychology*, **63**, 446-450.

Taylor, M.S., Locke, E.A., Lee, C. & Gist, M.E. (1984). Type A behaviour and faculty research productivity: what are the mechanisms? *Organizational Behavior and Human Performance*, **34**, 402-418.

Weinberg, R.S., Gould, D. & Jackson, A. (1979). Expectations and performance: an empirical test of Bandura's self-efficacy theory. *Journal of Sport Psychology*, **1**, 320-331.

Wheeler, K.G. (1983). Comparisons of self-efficacy and expectancy models of occupational preferences for college males and females. *Journal of Occupational Psychology*, **56**, 73-78.

White, J. (1982). *Rejection.* Reading, MA: Addison-Wesley.

Wiedenfeld, S.A., O'Leary, A., Bandura, A., Brown, S., Levine, S. & Raska, K. (1989). *Impact of perceived self-efficacy in coping with stressors on components of the immune system.* Manuscript submitted for publication.

Williams, S.L., Dooseman, G. & Kleifield, E. (1984). Comparative power of guided mastery and exposure treatments for intractable phobias. *Journal of Consulting and Clinical Psychology*, **52**, 505-518.

Williams, S.L., Kinney, P.J. & Falbo, J. (1989). Generalization of therapeutic changes in agoraphobia: the role of perceived self-efficacy. *Journal of Consulting and Clinical Psychology*, **57**, 436-442.

Williams, S.L., Turner, S.M. & Peer, D.F. (1985). Guided mastery and performance desensitization treatments for severe acrophobia. *Journal of Consulting and Clinical Psychology*, **53**, 237-247.

Williams, S.L. & Watson, N. (1985). Perceived danger and perceived self-efficacy as cognitive mediators of acrophobic behavior. *Behavior Therapy*, **16**, 136-146.

Wood, R.E. & Bandura, A. (1989a). Impact of conceptions of ability on self-regulatory mechanisms and complex decision making. *Journal of Personality and Social Psychology*, **56**, 407-415.

Wood, R.E. & Bandura, A. (1989b). Social cognitive theory of organizational management. *Academy of Management Review*, **14**, 361-384.

This article was presented as an invited address at the annual meeting of The British Psychological Society, St Andrews, Scotland, April 1989. Some sections of this article contain revised and expanded material from my article entitled, Human agency in social cognitive theory, *American Psychologist*, in press.

Requests for reprints should be addressed to:

Professor A. Bandura, Department
of Psychology, Jordan Hall,Building 420,
Stanford University,
Stanford,
California, 94305, USA.

Received 30 May 1989

JOURNAL OF RESEARCH ON ADOLESCENCE, 2(2), 123–145

Stability of Global Self-Evaluations in Early Adolescence: A Cohort Longitudinal Study

Françoise D. Alsaker and Dan Olweus*
Department of Psychosocial Science
University of Bergen

This study is mainly concerned with the stability (i.e., relative longitudinal consistency) of individual differences in global self-esteem in early adolescence. In the first part, stability data from a large cohort longitudinal study were presented. Approximately 2,400 subjects were followed over 2½ years, yielding a total of 42 stability coefficients. These coefficients were then compared with 21 stability coefficients from previously published studies. We concluded that the expected stability of global self-esteem is high for relatively short time intervals (up to 1 year or so), but it declines somewhat rapidly and is considerably lower at intervals of approximately 3 years. There was also a trend for stability coefficients with a fixed time interval to be higher in older than in younger subjects. These results were interpreted as providing support for a gradual consolidation hypothesis, implying that experiences are likely to have decreasing impact with age. In all, approximately 70% of the variance in stability coefficients could be predicted with time interval, age, sex, and the Sex × Time Interval interaction as predictors.

Despite a wealth of studies devoted to self-esteem (about 7,000 in 1982, according to Rosenberg, 1986), only a few have centrally addressed the issue of stability of this aspect of personality. Some writers, such as Morse and Gergen (1970), have argued that the self-concept is highly mutable and dependent on the situational context. On the other hand, proponents of consistency or self-maintenance theories (e.g., Lecky, 1945) assume that there is a motive to act or to interpret events in

*Françoise D. Alsaker and Dan Olweus contributed equally to this article.
Requests for reprints should be sent to Françoise D. Alsaker or Dan Olweus, Division of Personality and Developmental Psychology, Øysteinsgt. 3, N 5007 Bergen, Norway.

accordance with one's self-concept in order to maintain the self-concept unchanged. The stability of self-attitudes has also been emphasized both by writers primarily concerned with theory building, such as Coopersmith (1967) and Shavelson, Hubner, and Stanton (1976), and those interested in applications, such as Rogers (1961).

When the stability or consistency of self-perceptions (or any other characteristic) is discussed in the psychological or educational literature, the terms tend to be defined differently by different authors; in some cases, they are not defined at all. Before proceeding any further, we point out some important terminological distinctions. First, it is useful to distinguish between absolute and relative consistency. *Absolute consistency* indicates the extent to which an individual's behavior or "absolute" level on a certain dimension remains the same across various situations or time periods. *Relative consistency* concerns the extent to which individuals in a group retain their relative positions on a dimension across situations or measurement occasions (i.e., relative to the average value of the group studied). The degree of relative consistency for a group is usually indexed by some measure of association such as Pearson's product–moment correlation (in which differences in means and standard deviations among contexts or occasions are automatically removed) or the intraclass correlation.

In the person–situation or "consistency" debate (e.g., Block, 1977; Epstein, 1977; Magnusson & Endler, 1977; Mischel, 1968, 1969; Olweus, 1979, 1980), it was also common to make a distinction between cross-situational and longitudinal consistency (Olweus, 1974, 1980). *Cross-situational consistency* concerns the extent to which individuals in a group retain their relative positions on a certain dimension across various situations at approximately the same point in time. *Longitudinal relative consistency*, more often referred to as the *stability* of individual differences over time, indicates the extent to which individuals in a group retain their relative positions at different time periods.

In this article, we focus on the issue of longitudinal relative consistency or stability in the area of global self-perceptions. Using our terminology, the words *longitudinal relative consistency* and *stability* have the same meaning but, to simplify reading, we mainly use the term *stability*.

Most contemporary writers on the self agree on defining *self-concept* as a multidimensional construct, including a global component and several specific facets (Harter, 1982; Marsh, 1986; Rosenberg, 1979; Shavelson & Bolus, 1982; Shavelson et al., 1976). Within our framework, self-concept is conceived as an organization of mostly evaluative representations and beliefs about oneself as a person in terms of characteristics, behaviors, feelings, and thoughts (Alsaker, 1987). The person as a whole is the target of what we refer to as *global self-evaluation* or global self-esteem. We concentrate on the stability of this global component.

As just noted, there have been relatively few studies on the stability of self-esteem. With some exceptions (e.g., Drummond, McIntire, & Ryan, 1977; Mortimer & Lorence, 1981; O'Malley & Bachman, 1983), relevant findings have tended to be presented as minor parts of larger studies or as test–retest coefficients for relatively short periods. Many authors, nevertheless, seem to regard it as that established fact that self-esteem remains quite stable over time. Coopersmith's (1967) results are often referred to as an empirical basis for such a view. Using his own Self-Esteem Inventory (SEI), Coopersmith reported a test–retest (raw) correlation of .70 for preadolescent males and females (in Grades 5 and 6) followed over a 3-year period. Note, however, that the analysis was based on a sample of only 56 children, and no information was provided on how this subsample was drawn from the original population of 1,748 children. Accordingly, the reported coefficient should be interpreted with considerable caution. Given the fact that Coopersmith's results are repeatedly cited, it is important to find out to what extent they can be replicated in other studies using larger and maybe more representative samples.

In the consistency debate, it was argued (Mischel, 1968, 1969) that self-perceptions show considerable stability over time, whereas most noncognitive psychological dimensions display little or no continuity. Therefore, it is interesting to compare our results on stability of global self-evaluation with results from other domains. Unfortunately, there are very few noncognitive dimensions that have been carefully reviewed and that would permit meaningful comparison with the data in this article. The stability of aggression, however, has been reviewed in some detail and was also specifically mentioned by Mischel (1968, 1969) in his critique (see also Olweus, 1979, 1984). Accordingly, it is appropriate to relate our findings on global self-esteem to those on aggression.

In his review of research on aggression, Olweus (1979) found a substantial relationship between size of stability coefficient and time interval between measurement occasions. It is natural to expect such an association for self-esteem as well. In this study, we attempted to estimate the strength and form of this relationship. Olweus also found a positive relationship between size of the stability coefficient for a fixed interval and the subjects' age at the time of first assessment, with less stability or more change for younger subjects (Olweus, 1979, p. 868). The interpretation was made that "the effect, so to speak, of a certain time interval is greater for younger than for older subjects" (p. 868).

The reasoning underlying this interpretation can be somewhat elaborated. An individual's reaction tendencies and/or cognitions within a particular psychological domain (e.g., aggression or self-esteem) are constructed over time. In general, with increasing age, a gradual consolidation of these structures occurs, and later experiences are assimilated into and integrated within the already existing structures. Consequently, a certain set of experiences will have greater impact on an individual's domain-specific structures when the degree of consolidation of these structures is low. In accordance with this gradual consolidation hypothesis, we expect stability coefficients for a fixed time interval to be lower for younger than for older subjects in the area of self-esteem as well.[1]

As part of a construction system, global self-evaluations are expected to have a certain degree of stability (in an absolute sense), helping us to organize our experiences in a meaningful way (see Alsaker, 1987). Under normal circumstances, they are also assumed to continue to develop and change with new experiences across the life span (though generally less so with increasing age). This point of view implies that, other conditions being equal, the highest degree of stability (in both an absolute and a relative sense) is expected in periods with little environmental or maturational change, whereas less stability is anticipated in periods characterized by events that may challenge the individuals' views of themselves. Given the many changes occurring in early adolescence and the general transitional character of this period (Alsaker, 1991; Alsaker & Olweus, in press; Petersen, 1988), it seems natural to hypothesize that the stability of self-esteem may be reduced in certain age periods.

The possible effect of gender on stability of self-esteem has been largely neglected in previous studies, despite the very substantial general interest in gender differences in self-esteem research. Our study provides an opportunity to explore the stability data for sex differences.

The first part of this article contains a description of the methods used, followed by a presentation of the stability coefficients for global self-evaluations. In a subsequent section, results from previously published studies are considered. It is not our aim to provide an exhaustive review of previous studies on the stability of self-esteem, but rather to provide a basis for comparison with our own data. Accordingly, this overview is selective in including only studies that are reasonably comparable to our own study, as specified later.

---

[1]Note that this hypothesis, which also may be regarded as a hypothesis about the gradually decreasing impact of later experiences, may be valid for certain psychological domains and not for others. And different domains may be distinguished by different degrees of consolidation. Presently, there is little knowledge available for further specification of such differentiations. Also, the hypothesis may be reasonably applicable only under typical conditions; age periods or intervals characterized by unusual or extreme events may result in deviations from the expected pattern.

METHOD

Design and Subjects

Data were collected from four large samples of school children from Bergen, Norway. The children who were originally in Grades 4 through 7 came from 112 classes drawn from 28 primary schools and 14 junior high schools. The junior high schools recruited their students to a large extent from the elementary schools represented in the project. A basically random procedure was used in allocating classes to the samples. Consequently, the samples are considered to be largely representative of students in the relevant grades and schools in the community of Bergen and, to a considerable degree, of students in such schools in town communities in Norway. The students were followed for a period of 2½ years. The first measurement was taken in May 1983, when the children's modal ages were 11 (fourth grade), 12, 13, and 14 years, respectively. The data were collected in May 1983, May 1984, May 1985, and October 1985.

Several questionnaires covering a number of different domains (see Olweus, 1987, 1991) were administered to the subjects in their regular classrooms by two research assistants (the teachers were absent). Each measurement session lasted for two or three school periods (45 min each).[2]

At the first measurement point, valid questionnaires were obtained from 2,473 students (94.9% of the participants). Of these students, 86.5% were tested again in May 1984, and 70.6% were still participating in May 1985. In October 1985, the oldest students had finished their compulsory education and thus left the project (compulsory schooling ends with Grade 9, i.e., when the children are about 16 years old). Of the students from the original three youngest cohorts, 59.8% were still participating in the project at the time of the last data collection. Students who moved to the project schools after the project had started were also allowed to participate. Therefore, the number of subjects varies somewhat with the different test-retest intervals. The number of subjects with valid answers for the various time intervals are presented in Table 1.

This design provided us with stability coefficients for test-retest intervals ranging from 5 months (.42 years) through 2 years and 5 months (2.42 years), but due to the nature of the design (generating an

[2]The children in lower grades answered fewer questionnaires than the older children, and only the data collection in May 1985 lasted as long as three school periods. Moreover, efforts were made to diminish subjects' fatigue. For example, a break was included in the middle of the assessment time, and the children were offered peanuts and lemonade. Note that children in Grades 7 through 9 are used to working for several school periods in a row during school tests.

TABLE 1
Raw and Corrected Correlations Between GSE Scores for Different Time Intervals and Reliability Coefficients for Time 1 and Time 2

Time Interval in Years	*Modal Age at Time 1*	*Gender*[a]	*n*	*Raw Correlation*	*Corrected Stability Coefficient*	*Alpha at Time 1*	*Alpha at Time 2*
0.42	13	F	134	.67	.75	.91	.87
		M	149	.64	.73	.88	.87
	14	F	196	.71	.82	.87	.86
		M	187	.70	.84	.85	.81
	15	F	144	.75	.84	.90	.89
		M	132	.72	.85	.83	.87
1	11	F	267	.50	.61	.79	.86
		M	261	.49	.62	.74	.85
	12	F	257	.69	.79	.85	.91
			230	.56	.65	.81	.91
		M	254	.59	.69	.86	.85
			274	.52	.65	.73	.88
	13	F	192	.53	.59	.91	.88
			215	.43	.50	.82	.90
		M	224	.68	.79	.87	.85
			249	.47	.55	.84	.87
	14	F	198	.62	.69	.90	.91
			257	.64	.74	.83	.91
		M	216	.62	.72	.87	.86
			317	.59	.72	.79	.85
	15	F	233	.70	.77	.91	.92
		M	271	.66	.79	.85	.83
1.42	12	F	137	.60	.71	.83	.87
		M	152	.57	.66	.87	.85
	13	F	171	.55	.61	.92	.88
		M	170	.62	.73	.86	.83
	14	F	116	.66	.75	.87	.90
		M	115	.57	.66	.84	.88
2	11	F	245	.39	.46	.78	.91
		M	252	.45	.56	.77	.85
	12	F	192	.34	.41	.79	.88
		M	212	.49	.63	.72	.85
	13	F	205	.42	.49	.82	.91
		M	243	.49	.58	.83	.86
	14	F	242	.47	.53	.85	.92
		M	278	.46	.57	.79	.83
2.42	11	F	134	.31	.39	.73	.87
		M	145	.36	.45	.77	.84
	12	F	165	.45	.53	.81	.89
		M	162	.44	.56	.74	.83
	13	F	129	.42	.50	.79	.90
		M	123	.55	.64	.84	.87

[a]F = female; M = male.

incomplete age–cohort matrix; see Alsaker & Olweus, in press); not all age groups could be represented at all test–retest intervals.

For purposes of clarity, the designations Time 1 and Time 2/retest in this article refer to the particular time interval studied, not to a specific data collection point. For example, data obtained in May 1984 are referred to as Time 1 when compared with data from May 1985, but as Time 2, when compared with data collected in May 1983.

Our analyses of the stability of global self-evaluations were based on 42 coefficients. Females and males were almost equally represented in our samples. Some analyses were conducted on mixed samples of females and males in order to make our results comparable with data from previous studies. Coefficients computed for females and males separately were based on samples ranging from 115 through 317. Students who were in the fourth, fifth, and sixth grades in May 1983 experienced school transition from elementary school (sixth grade) to junior high (seventh grade) sometime during the period.

Measure

We (Alsaker & Olweus, 1986) developed the Global Negative Self-Evaluation Scale (GSE) for use with subjects from 10 years of age (and probably somewhat younger ages) through adulthood. A detailed description of the measure is given in an earlier article (Alsaker & Olweus, 1986). The GSE is a six item, 6-point Likert scale, with four of the items taken from Rosenberg's (1965) Self-Esteem Scale (RSE). The GSE scale is made up of the following items: (a) At times I think I am no good at all; (b) I feel I do not have much to be proud of; (c) I certainly feel useless at times; (d) All in all, I am inclined to feel I am a failure; (e) I would like to change many things about myself; and (f) I have often wanted to be someone else. The response alternatives range from *does not apply at all* (1), *does not apply well* (2), *applies somewhat* (3), *applies fairly well* (4), *applies well* (5), to *applies exactly* (6). Thus, a high score on the GSE scale indicates a high level of negative self-evaluations. (Note that Rosenberg used only four response categories for the RSE.)

As seen from the content of the items, the GSE scale refers to global (negative) self-evaluation and can be considered basically comparable to other scales for this domain, such as the RSE or the general subscale of Harter's (1982) Perceived Competence Scale (PCS). In a previous study, correlation coefficients among the GSE scale, school achievement, and perceived competence were very similar to those obtained with the RSE and the PCS (Alsaker, 1989; Bohrnstedt & Felson, 1983; Harter, 1982).

As previously documented (Alsaker & Olweus, 1986), the GSE scale has displayed good internal consistency and validity. In this article, reliability (internal consistency) coefficients are presented for all subgroups of subjects and for every measurement occasion (range = .72 to .92, see Table 1).

Analyses of the GSE scale scores for females and males of varying ages (10 through 15) revealed very similar patterns of factor loadings (one-factor solution) for the six items making up the scale (Alsaker & Olweus, 1986). This finding is an indication that students from the various age and sex groups interpreted and responded to the items in essentially the same way. Accordingly, possible differences in stability among different age and sex groups cannot be attributed to the scale being inappropriate for measuring global negative self-evaluations in one group or another.

Statistical Analyses

When a number of stability coefficients based on data of varying reliability are to be compared, raw correlation coefficients are usually less comparable than coefficients corrected for measurement error (i.e., disattenuated coefficients; e.g., see Olweus, 1979). In addition, if the researcher's primary interest lies in the relationship among the true rather than the obtained scores (e.g., in the stability of the underlying function in contrast with the actual predictive power of the fallible measurements), a disattenuated coefficient is preferred. For both these reasons, attenuation-corrected stability coefficients should be reported and used as a basis for analysis (in addition to raw correlations) when sufficient information on reliability is available.[3]

In order to determine the extent to which stability (i.e., dependent variable) could be predicted on the basis of the information available, a series of regression analyses were carried out with time interval, age, sex, and their interactions as predictors. Interactions accounting for less than 1.5% of the variance were excluded from the analyses. Because there are dependencies among some of the stability coefficients in that each group (i.e., each grade cohort separated by sex) contributed more than one coefficient,[4] these analyses were conducted for descriptive purposes only and did not include tests for statistical significance.

[3]The formula for disattenuation is $r_{tt} = r_{xy} \times (r_{xx} \times r_{yy})^{-1/2}$, where r_{xx} and r_{yy} are reliability coefficients for the two measurement occasions x and y. The reliability coefficient used here was Cronbach's alpha.

[4]For example, the fourth grade cohort contributed a 1-year coefficient (from May 1983 to May 1984) for subjects aged 11 at the first measurement point. These subjects were assessed again in May 1985; hence, this cohort also yielded a 1-year coefficient for the interval between May 1984 and May 1985. Because the subjects from the fourth grade cohort were about 12 years old in May 1984, this latter coefficient had to be treated as a coefficient coming from 12-year-olds. Accordingly, the fourth grade cohort contributed 1-year coefficients for both 11-year-olds and 12-year-olds. The same principle applies to the other cohorts.

RESULTS FROM THE COHORT LONGITUDINAL STUDY

Results are presented in Table 1 in terms of raw correlations (i.e., stability coefficients), reliability coefficients, and correlations corrected for attenuation, for females and males separately. Raw stability coefficients were also computed for both genders together in order to make them comparable with results from the reviewed studies.

Stability and Time Interval

For an interval of 5 months between Time 1 and Time 2 (retest), the raw stability coefficients displayed in Table 1 ranged between .64 and .75, with an average $r = .70$ ($SD = .04$). For an interval of 1 year, the range was .43 through .70, average $r = .58$ ($SD = .08$). For intervals of 1.42, 2, and 2.42 years, the average raw stability coefficients were .60 ($SD = .04$), .44 ($SD = .05$), and .42 ($SD = .08$), respectively. As expected, there was a trend for stability to decrease as the interval of measurement increased.

The regression of raw stability coefficients on the test–retest interval in years can be described by the equation $y = .74 - .13x$. The standard error of estimate ($s_{y.x}$) was .06, and the correlation between stability coefficients and time interval was −.81. The data were also analyzed in terms of correlations corrected for attenuation for females and males separately. The results are presented in Figure 1 and Table 1.

The regression of size of stability coefficient on time interval (up to 2.42 years) is expressed by the equations $y = .86 - .17x$, $s_{y.x} = .08$ for females and $y = .83 - .12x$, $s_{y.x} = .07$ for males. The correlations between stability coefficient and time interval were −.81 and −.76, respectively. The beta values (unstandardized) indicate a somewhat stronger decrease of the stability coefficients with time interval for females than for males (−.17 and −.12, respectively). As can be seen from Figure 1 and Table 1, both females and males showed high and fairly similar stability levels at relatively short time intervals (i.e., at intervals from 5 months through 1 year and 5 months). For longer time intervals (up to 2.42 years), males showed somewhat higher stability coefficients.

Stability and Age

Averages of the stability coefficients for each age level and time interval were computed. The results are plotted in Figure 2 separately for females and males.

Figure 2 shows that males' stability coefficients tend to increase with age for a particular time interval. This age trend is less marked for

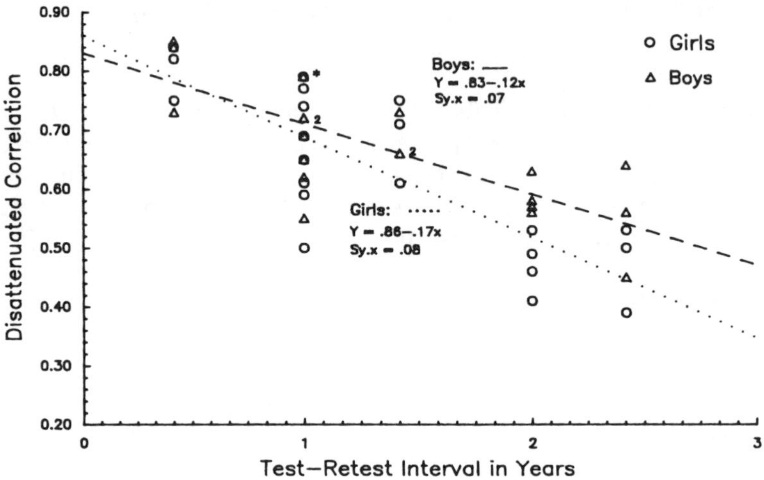

FIGURE 1 Relationship between stability of self-esteem (according to the GSE), in terms of correlation corrected for attenuation, and time interval for our cohort longitudinal study. Forty-two coefficients are plotted. The regression lines for females (dotted line) and for males (dashed line) are shown. [2] represents two coefficients of the same size, * represents two coefficients of the same size for the boys.

females. The correlation between stability and age was .59 for females and .67 for males. Because there was a negative covariation between time interval and age, partial correlations were also computed. When time interval was controlled for, corresponding partial correlations were .42 and .56 for females and males, respectively.

Closer examination of the age-stability relationship for females (Figure 2) reveals that females who were 13 years old at Time 1 showed somewhat lower stability coefficients than other females for time intervals of .42, 1, and 1.42 years, but not for intervals of 2 and 2.42 years.

From the overall covariation between age and stability, one should expect the coefficients to be somewhat higher for the 13-year-olds than for the younger groups and somewhat lower than for the older groups. Figure 2 shows that the average coefficient for the 1-year interval for 13-year-old females was lower than the coefficients for all other groups of females.[5]

[5]On the basis of a multiple regression with time interval and age as predictors of stability, we estimated the predicted value for stability for 13-year-old girls at a 1-year interval. The multiple regression was conducted on all age groups except for the 13-year-olds in order to compare the observed values for the 13-year-old girls with the value we could expect on the basis of the results from the other age groups. The estimated value for 13-year-old girls was .70. The standard error of estimate for the equation was .07. The corresponding observed average value at a 1-year interval for the 13-year-old girls was

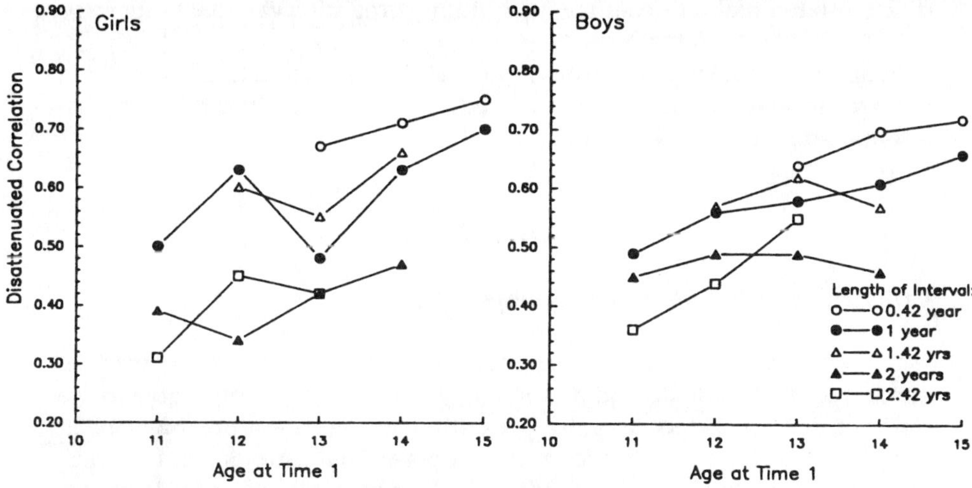

FIGURE 2 Stability of self-esteem (according to the GSE), in terms of correlations corrected for attenuation, for different age groups and different time intervals for females and males separately. Each data point represents an average coefficient for a given age group for a specified time interval. The age groups are based on the subjects' modal ages at Time 1 for each interval.

It is worth noting that the coefficients for the 1-year interval for 13-year-old females came from two different cohorts and that both coefficients (Table 1) were clearly lower than the expected value. There was no indication of such age-specific effects in boys.

Prediction of Stability Coefficients

Hierarchical multiple regression analyses were conducted using disattenuated stability coefficients as the criterion variable and time interval, age, sex, and their interactions as predictors. Entering age after time interval into the model gave an increment of 8.3% in the prediction of stability (from R^2 = .592 to R^2 = .675). Addition of sex and the Sex × Time Interval interaction to the model increased R^2 with 2.8% and 1.9%, respectively.

Separate analyses for females' and males' coefficients showed a smaller increase in predicted variance due to age for females (6.1%) than for males (13.0%). Partial correlations between age and size of

.55 (i.e., 2.14 standard errors below the predicted value). At intervals of .42 years and 1.42 years, the differences between observed and predicted values were small (.74 and .44 standard errors, respectively). These findings suggest that the lower 1-year stability coefficient for 13-year-old girls was not a chance result.

disattenuated stability coefficient, holding time interval constant, were .42 for girls and .56 for boys.

In all, the model including time interval, age, sex, and the Sex × Time Interval interaction was able to predict 72% of the variance in disattenuated stability coefficients.

PREVIOUS STUDIES

Criteria for Inclusion in the Review

Global self-evaluations. As noted previously, this review was restricted to studies that could be considered reasonably comparable to the findings just reported. Results presented in the literature have been based on different definitions and operationalizations of the self-concept. In this article, only studies dealing with global self-esteem are examined.

Several scales of self-esteem such as Coopersmith's (1967) SEI or the Piers–Harris Children's Self-Concept Scale (Piers & Harris, 1969) are quite heterogeneous. Such inventories have been heavily criticized (e.g., Harter, 1982, 1983; Wylie, 1974) and are generally no longer accepted as a measure of global self-esteem. In line with this view, results based on such instruments were not included. Consequently, stability results for Coopersmith's SEI Total scale were excluded from the analyses. However, results for the more circumscribed General subscale from the SEI were included, although this subscale may also be criticized for heterogeneity to some extent.

Similarity of instruments. We also wanted to restrict our review to results based on roughly comparable instruments. Only studies reporting results for self-report instruments using Likert-type scales were reviewed. Results from the studies by Dusek and Flaherty (1981) and by Piotrowski (1983), which were based on the semantic differential technique, were therefore excluded from our analyses.

Stability results reviewed here are based on the RSE, instruments that are adaptations of the RSE (e.g., including some of the RSE's items), the General subscale of the SEI, and the General Self-Worth subscale of the PCS. The RSE was originally designed as a Guttman scale but, in agreement with Rosenberg's (1979) later view, it was used as a Likert scale in most studies. The review and the subsequent comparison with our findings were based on essentially four different instruments. Although this might be considered a methodological limitation to some extent, we emphasize that all of the instruments were derived from a very similar rationale, and some of them included identical or nearly identical items. In addition, inspection of the data presented did not reveal any clear instrument-related differences in stability. Accordingly, it is reasonable to regard the instruments included in the review and in the comparison as fairly equivalent for our purposes.

Sample size. A further criterion for inclusion in the review was sample size. In order to exclude very unreliable findings from our analyses, we decided to consider only studies with a sample size of minimum 50 subjects. Based on this decision, some of the results from the Drummond et al. (1977) study were included, whereas other findings from the same study were not. The sample size of the studies considered in the review varied between 75 and 1,608 (see Table 2).

Time interval between test and retest. Some studies reporting stability coefficients were conducted mainly in order to analyze the reliability of the instrument employed. They typically used short test–retest intervals, such as 2 to 4 weeks. Because reliability per se was not a major focus of this article, we decided to set a lower bound test–retest interval of 4 months. The studies included covered intervals ranging from 5 months to 5 years.

Age at first time of measurement. Because the focus of this article is on early adolescence and adolescence, an upper age limit was set at 18 years. In some studies the age of the subjects was reported, but more often the subjects were characterized according to the school grade they were in. To make results from previous studies and our own data comparable, such information was transformed into approximately modal chronological ages. Some samples included up to four different age groups (e.g., 9th to 12th grade). In such cases, an approximate mean age was used. The age range for the samples was from 7 through 17 (see Table 2).

Results in terms of correlation coefficients. To make findings from different studies reasonably comparable with our own results, only results presented in terms of correlation coefficients were reviewed. In the Method section, we recommended use of correlations corrected for attenuation. However, most authors reported their results in terms of raw correlations, without giving information on the reliability of the measurements. Accordingly, we had to present results from earlier studies in terms of raw correlations. In one study (Harter, 1982), only a

TABLE 2
Review of Longitudinal Studies of Self-Esteem

Study	*Measurement Instrument*	*Gender*[a]	*N*	*Age at Time 1*	*Interval in Years*	*Raw Correlation*
Drummond et al. (1977)	General subscale (GS) from Coopersmith's SEI	FM	75	7–8	0.42	.68
		FM	89	11	0.42	.37[b]
		FM	94	13	0.42	.67
		FM	109	14	0.42	.58
		FM	76	16	0.42	.60
Byrne (1983)	RSE	FM	929	14–17	0.5	.62
	SEI:GS	FM	929	14–17	0.5	.63
Hirsch & Rapkin (1987)	RSE	FM	131	11	0.5	.61
		FM	131	12	0.5	.59
Nottelmann (1987)	PCS:GS	FM	240	11–12	0.5	.55
Harter (1982)	PCS:GS	FM	810	8–11	0.75	.53[c]
Hirsch & Rapkin (1987)	RSE	FM	131	11	1.0	.40
Nottelmann (1987)	PCS:GS	FM	240	11–12	1.0	.51
Simmons & Blyth (1987)	RSE	F	259	11	1.0	.53
		M	294	11	1.0	.46
		F	150	14	1.0	.61
		M	164	14	1.0	.48
O'Malley & Bachman (1983)	RSE type scale	FM	117	17	1.0	.52
					2.0	.59
					3.0	.41
Simmons & Blyth (1987)	RSE	FM	310	11	4.0	.36
Bachmann & O'Malley (1977)	RSE type scale	M	1608	17	5.0	.46

[a]F = females; M = males; FM = mixed group. [b]This coefficient was considered an outlier and was not included in the analyses. [c]Approximation of the raw correlation, computed on the basis of the disattenuated coefficient and the mean reliability coefficient at Time 1 in one sample.

coefficient corrected for attenuation was presented. On the basis of the reliability of the first measurement point, this coefficient was transformed back to an estimated raw correlation.

Some Characteristics of the Reviewed Studies

We started scanning the self literature for articles that might contain stability coefficients for global self-esteem. During the first scanning, 30 studies were found. However, only 8 of them met our criteria. These 8 studies yielded 22 stability coefficients. An overview of the studies, arranged according to length of the time interval between measurement occasions, is presented in Table 2.

Age at first time of measurement. Nine of the 22 coefficients were derived from samples of 11- and 12-year-old children, and 7 were from 16- to 17-year-old children. The remaining 6 coefficients were distributed among five different age groups, varying between 7 and 14 years. Thus, the age distribution yielded roughly two age clusters: subjects younger than 15 and subjects older than 15. In dealing with differences among age groups, a cutoff was placed at 15 years. The younger group is then roughly comparable to our samples.

Gender. Bachman and O'Malley (1977) reported results from a sample of males, and Simmons and Blyth (1987) presented two correlations for males and two for females; all other results were based on mixed samples, containing both females and males. None of the studies reviewed addressed gender differences in relative stability as a major issue.

Results

As shown in Table 2, one of the stability coefficients for the .42-year interval (.37) was much lower than the others. Size of stability coefficients was regressed on time interval excluding this coefficient. The regression equation was found to be $y = .60 - .05x$, with a standard error of estimate $s_{y.x} = .07$. The predicted stability coefficient at .42 years was .58. The coefficient of .37 was thus three standard errors below the predicted value and was considered an outlier. Accordingly, it was not included in the following analyses.[6]

[6]Note that the values obtained when this coefficient was included in the analyses were very similar to the values obtained when the coefficient was excluded. As an example, the regression equation corresponding to the one presented in the text was $y = .58 - .04x$, with a standard error of estimate $s_{y.x} = .08$.

For an interval of 5 to 6 months between Time 1 and Time 2/retest, the coefficients ranged between .55 and .68, with an average of .61 (SD = .04). For an interval of 1 year, the coefficients ranged from .40 to .61, with average r = .50 (SD = .06). Longer time intervals (from 2 to 5 years) were represented by only one coefficient each.

The correlation between size of stability coefficient and time interval was −.65. The linear regression equation for this relationship (just presented) was used to calculate the predicted values of stability for different time intervals. For intervals of 6 months, 1 year, and 3 years, the predicted coefficients were .58, .55, and .45, respectively. For 8- to 15-year-old subjects (n = 14) the equation was $y = .61 - .07x$, $s_{y.x} = .07$, and $r = -.71$.

In order to make the reviewed results more directly comparable with the stability data from our study, the regression equation for all studies with time intervals up to 3 years was calculated: $y = .62 - .07$, $s_{y.x} = .07$. The correlation between size of stability coefficient and time interval was $r = -.58$.

To achieve an even more adequate comparison with our own data, we also calculated the regression equation for younger subjects and for time intervals up to and including 3 years. However, when we examined this data subset, it turned out that all of the stability coefficients were based on intervals of 1 year or less. The regression equation for these data (spanning intervals of up to 1 year) was $y = .71 - .22x$, with a standard error of estimate $s_{y.x} = .06$. The correlation between time interval and stability coefficient was −.74. This equation was based on 13 out of the 14 coefficients available for 8- to 15-year-old subjects. The same analysis was conducted for time intervals up to 1 year using our own data. The regression equation was then $y = .79 - .20x$, $s_{y.x} = .07$, with $r = -.61$.

Entering age after time interval into a regression model gave a variance increase of 4.6% in predicted stability (from $R^2 = .419$ to $R^2 = .465$). The partial correlation of age with size of (raw) stability coefficient with time interval held constant was .31. These analyses were conducted on coefficients derived from samples with males and females combined (with four exceptions, see Table 2).

DISCUSSION

Analyses were based on 42 coefficients from our cohort longitudinal project and 21 coefficients from previous studies. The reviewed studies covered intervals up to 5 years, whereas the longest interval in our study was 2 years and 5 months (2.42 years). The age of the subjects at the first time of measurement varied between 8 and 17 in the studies from the literature and between 11 and 15 in our study. Seventeen of the 21 coefficients from the reviewed studies were obtained from mixed samples, whereas 21 of the 42 coefficients in the current study came from females and 21 from males.

Stability of Self-Esteem and Time Interval

The most adequate comparison of our data with previous studies involves intervals up to and including 1 year. This comparison is based on a restricted subset of coefficients: 13 coefficients from the literature and 11 coefficients derived from our study. For these time intervals, a considerable similarity of results was found in terms of slope (−.22 and −.20), standard errors of estimate (.06 and .07), and correlations between stability coefficient and time interval (−.74 and −.61, respectively). However, coefficients from our study were at a somewhat higher level (e.g., .79 as compared to .71 at the intercept).

Predicted stability coefficients (using the equations just presented) for reviewed studies and our study were .60 and .69, respectively, for a 6-month interval and .49 and .59 for a 1-year interval. Although data on internal-consistency reliability were generally lacking for reviewed studies, it may be speculated whether the somewhat higher level for stability coefficients from our study was a consequence of the relatively high alpha reliabilities (typically in the .80–.90 range, see Table 1). Reliabilities in our study were probably somewhat higher than those of the reviewed studies, something that would make our raw stability coefficients higher even when the underlying "true" relationships were of the same size.

Because our study was much more homogeneous than previous studies in terms of ages, time intervals, and sample composition, it was likely to yield more consistent and dependable results. On the other hand, one may argue that all of the stability coefficients were obtained in the same context and under roughly the same general conditions, a fact that may limit the generalizability of findings from our study. From this perspective, it is reassuring to note that for those time intervals of the reviewed studies (up to and including 1 year) that could be compared directly with our study, there was, for the most part, a striking similarity of findings (as already noted). This result makes it reasonable to assume that the more detailed and extended findings from our study have considerable generality.

Because there was no stability coefficient available in the literature for younger subjects for intervals beyond 1 year, our best estimate of the relationship between stability and longer time intervals (up to and including 2.42 years) for the 11- to 15-year-old age group is derived from our own data. Predicted (raw) stability coefficients for intervals of 6 months, 1 year, and 3 years are .67, .61, and .35, respectively.

When stability coefficients were corrected for differences in reliability between age groups and time intervals, predicted (disattenuated) stability coefficients for females and intervals of 6 months, 1 year, and 3 years were .78, .69, and .35, respectively. For males, corresponding values were .77, .71, and .47, respectively (see Figure 1 and equations presented previously).

On the basis of both raw and disattenuated stability coefficients, we conclude that the expected stability of global self-esteem is high for relatively short time intervals (up to 1 year or so) but that it declines fairly rapidly and is considerably reduced at intervals of approximately 3 years.

As indicated in the introduction, we wanted to compare our results on the stability of global self-esteem with findings from the area of aggression. The regression equation presented by Olweus (1979) on the stability of aggression (relying on several different data sources but excluding self-reports) was used to calculate expected disattenuated stability coefficients for time intervals of 1 and 3 years (for males only). The values were .77 and .73, respectively. For relatively short time intervals, there was a fairly small difference between expected stability coefficients for the areas of aggression and global self-esteem (e.g., .77 vs. .71 for a 1-year interval). The difference in expected stability increased rapidly, however, with longer time intervals, and was fairly substantial at an interval of 3 years (.71 vs. .47). Note that the coefficients for the area of aggression were derived from samples representing a larger age range; however, inspection of the data for more directly comparable age groups (Olweus, 1979, p. 855) yielded very much the same conclusions, with an average value of .74 for the 3-year interval.

We may thus conclude that self-perceptions as expressed in global negative self-evaluations tend to be less stable over time than aggressive behavior. Besides being interesting in their own right, these findings are directly relevant to one of the key issues in the heated person–situation controversy. As noted, it was argued in that debate (Mischel, 1968, 1969) that self-perceptions show considerable stability/continuity (consistency) over time, whereas most noncognitive psychological dimensions, including aggression, evidence no or very little continuity. The latter part of this assertion has already been clearly refuted (e.g., Block, 1977; Epstein, 1979; Olweus, 1979, 1980). The present analysis, however, goes further in showing that global self-perceptions may, in fact, be considerably less stable than social behavior, particularly for somewhat longer time intervals.

Our finding that the stability of global self-esteem decreases fairly rapidly with length of time interval is certainly at variance with the frequently cited test–retest correlation of .70 over a 3-year interval reported by Coopersmith (1967). Recall that Coopersmith's coefficient was based on a sample of only 56 females and males (probably in Grades 5 and 6 at Time 1), and we believe this atypical result may be a consequence of the special nature of the sample employed. It is also worth noting that other studies using the complete SEI scale (e.g., Rubin, 1978) have yielded much lower stability coefficients than that reported by Coopersmith. In any case, .70 should no longer be used as a representative estimate of the degree of stability in self-esteem for longer time intervals.

As mentioned, data from our study suggest that the expected raw stability correlation (for mixed samples) for such an interval would lie in the vicinity of .35. We emphasize, however, that our study was concerned with stability at group level and that we did not examine, for example, the stability of self-evaluations in individuals with extremely poor self-esteem. Remember that we included only a limited set of time intervals and that extrapolations beyond this range should be made with considerable caution. Furthermore, it is possible that the results would have been somewhat different with adult subjects. There is an obvious need for studies including longer time intervals and other age brackets than those represented here.

Stability of Self-Esteem and Age

Age was found to be positively related to degree of stability. With the exception of 13-year-old females in our study, the stability coefficients for adjacent years of measurement showed a fairly regular pattern of a slight increase with age (see Figure 2). Results from hierarchical multiple regression analyses conducted with stability coefficients as criterion variable also showed a clear increment in predicted variance with the introduction of the age variable. In summary, these results indicate that, for a given time interval, the size of the stability coefficient for global self-esteem tends to increase with age, within the ranges represented in the data. There is also some indication that the relationship may be somewhat stronger for males than for females.

The implication of these results is that adolescents' global negative self-evaluations are likely to become relatively more fixed or crystallized with increasing age. The empirical results are thus in agreement with the gradual consolidation hypothesis, implying a generally decreasing impact of later experiences under ordinary conditions. As spelled out in the introduction, periods characterized by changes that may challenge the individuals' perceptions of themselves may result in lower stability. Accordingly, it is possible that we should expect a decrease in stability, for example, during transition to college or in periods involving changes in intimate relationships.

The slow, gradual increase in stability coefficients with age combined with previous findings (Alsaker & Olweus, in press) that normative changes in level of self-esteem across early adolescence are quite small certainly contradicts a discontinuity view of self-esteem development in this period. The pattern of stability coefficients suggested that there were clear intraindividual changes in self-esteem over time, particularly for longer time intervals (as discussed in this article), but they obviously occurred in both positive and negative directions.

At Time 1, 13-year-old females had lower stability coefficients than expected for a 1-year interval. In this article, *age* means modal age for a certain grade and may be replaced by grade. Thus, 13-year-old females are those in the sixth grade at Time 1. This implies that the 1-year interval included a transition from elementary school to junior high (sixth to seventh grade) for these females. It is therefore tempting to speculate whether the lower stability coefficients may partly be a consequence of changes in these young adolescents' social and academic environment (cf. Simmons & Blyth, 1987).

Lower than expected stability coefficients were not obtained, however, for intervals involving retesting 2 months after school transition (a .42-year interval) or 1 year and 2 months after transition (a 1.42-year interval). With such a complex pattern of results, it is difficult to know if the lower stability coefficients for the 1-year intervals were a consequence of the school transition or whether they reflected a specific age effect (or an interaction between transition and age effects). A clear-cut choice between these alternative interpretations would require a different design from the one used here.

Stability of Self-Esteem and Gender

As shown by the regression equations already provided and Figure 1, females evidenced a slightly faster decline than boys in stability of global self-esteem with increasing time interval (slope = $-.17$ for females and $-.12$ for males). For time intervals up to 1 year or so, the difference in disattenuated stability coefficients between the two sexes was negligible (e.g., expected $r = .69$ for females and .71 for males at an interval of 1 year). However, the sex difference was more marked for longer time intervals such as 2 and 3 years: .52 for females and .59 for males, and .35 for females and .47 for males, respectively. Although the data demonstrated a relatively clear main trend, there was also a good deal of overlap in the distributions (e.g., see Figure 1).

Prediction of Stability Coefficients

It is worth emphasizing that the size of a stability coefficient could be predicted from time interval, age, and sex with considerable accuracy, with an R^2 of approximately .70 both in the reviewed studies and in our findings. At the same time, we want to stress that variables, such as time interval and age, in and of themselves, do not carry much psychological meaning and that there is so far relatively little understanding of which factors and events are hidden behind these gross categories. It is an important future task to try to increase our knowledge in these respects. An essential step in this direction would be to delineate consistent intraindividual patterns of consistency or change (individuals with varying degrees of absolute or relative consistency or intraindividual time paths) and to try to identify some of the determinants of such patterns (Olweus & Alsaker, 1991; Rogosa, Brandt, & Zinowski, 1982).

As explained, there are certain advantages to conducting analyses of stability data on disattenuated coefficients. Because the great majority of the reviewed studies did not include reliability information necessary for the estimation of disattenuated coefficients, we encourage authors in this field (as well as in other fields) to report routinely some measure of reliability in connection with stability coefficients. This way, a more adequate body of knowledge can be accumulated over the years to come.

ACKNOWLEDGMENTS

Research reported in this article was supported by grants from the Norwegian Council for Medical Research (RMF-HEMIL) to Françoise D. Alsaker; from the William T. Grant Foundation, the Norwegian Council for Social Research (RSF), and from the Norwegian Ministry of Education to Dan Olweus.

REFERENCES

Alsaker, F. D. (1987). *Research on the self: Need for integrative models* (Mimeo). Bergen, Norway: University of Bergen.

Alsaker, F. D. (1989). School achievement, perceived competence and global self-esteem. *School Psychology International, 10*, 147-158.

Alsaker, F. D. (1991). Utvikling av selvbilde hos barn og ungdom [On the development of self-concept in middle childhood and early adolescence]. In K. I. Klepp & L. E. Aaro (Eds.), *Ungdom, livsstil og helse* (pp. 41-52). Oslo, Norway: Universitetsforlaget.

Alsaker, F. D., & Olweus, D. (1986). Assessment of global negative self-evaluations and perceived stability of self in Norwegian preadolescents and adolescents. *Journal of Early Adolescence, 6*, 269-278.

Alsaker, F. D., & Olweus, D. (in press). Global self-evaluations and perceived instability of self in early adolescence: A cohort longitudinal study. *Scandinavian Journal of Psychology*.

Bachman, J. G., & O'Malley, P. M. (1977). Self-esteem in young men: A longitudinal analysis of the impact of educational and occupational attainment. *Journal of Personality and Social Psychology, 35*, 365–380.

Block, J. (1977). Advancing the psychology of personality: Paradigmatic shift or improving the quality of research? In D. Magnusson & N. S. Endler (Eds.), *Personality at the cross-roads: Current issues in interactional psychology* (pp. 37–63). Hillsdale, NJ: Lawrence Erlbaum Associates, Inc.

Bohrnstedt, G. W., & Felson, R. B. (1983). Explaining the relations among children's actual and perceived performances and self-esteem: A comparison of several causal models. *Journal of Personality and Social Psychology, 45*, 43–56.

Byrne, B. M. (1983). Investigating measures of self-concept. *Measurement and Evaluation in Guidance, 16*, 115–126.

Coopersmith, S. (1967). *The antecedents of self-esteem*. San Francisco: Freeman.

Drummond, R. J., McIntire, W. G., & Ryan, C. W. (1977). Stability and sex differences on the Coopersmith Self-Esteem Inventory for students in grades two to twelve. *Psychological Reports, 40*, 943–946.

Dusek, J. B., & Flaherty, J. F. (1981). The development of the self-concept during the adolescent years. *Monographs of the Society for Research in Child Development, 46*(4, Serial No. 191).

Epstein, S. (1977). Traits are alive and well. In D. Magnusson & N. S. Endler (Eds.), *Personality at the cross-roads: Current issues in interactional psychology* (pp. 83–98). Hillsdale, NJ: Lawrence Erlbaum Associates, Inc.

Epstein, S. (1979). The stability of behavior: I. On predicting most of the people much of the time. *Journal of Personality and Social Psychology, 37*, 1097–1126.

Harter, S. (1982). The perceived competence scale for children. *Child Development, 53*, 87–97.

Harter, S. (1983). Developmental perspectives on the self-system. In P. H. Mussen (Ed.), *Handbook of child psychology: Vol. 4. Socialization, personality and social development* (pp. 275–386). New York: Wiley.

Hirsch, B. J., & Rapkin, B. D. (1987). The transition to junior high school: A longitudinal study of self-esteem, psychological symptomatology, school life, and social support. *Child Development, 58*, 1235–1243.

Lecky, P. (1945). *Self-consistency: A theory of personality*. New York: Island.

Magnusson, D., & Endler, N. S. (Eds.). (1977). *Personality at the cross-roads: Current issues in interactional psychology*. Hillsdale, NJ: Lawrence Erlbaum Associates, Inc.

Marsh, H. W. (1986). Global self-esteem: Its relation to specific facets of self-concept and their importance. *Journal of Personality and Social Psychology, 51*, 1224–1236.

Mischel, W. (1968). *Personality and assessment*. New York: Wiley.

Mischel, W. (1969). Continuity and change in personality. *American Psychologist, 24*, 1012–1018.

Morse, S. R., & Gergen, K. (1970). Social comparison, self-consistency, and the presentation of self. *Journal of Personality and Social Psychology, 16*, 148–156.

Mortimer, J. T., & Lorence, J. (1981). Self-concept stability and change from late adolescence to early adulthood. *Research in Community and Mental Health, 2*, 5–42.

Nottelmann, E. D. (1987). Competence and self-esteem during transition from childhood to adolescence. *Developmental Psychology, 23*, 441–450.

Olweus, D. (1974). Personality factors and aggression: With special reference to violence within the peer group. In J. de Wit & W. W. Hartup (Eds.), *Determinants and origins of aggressive behavior* (pp. 535–565). The Hague, The Netherlands: Mouton.

Olweus, D. (1979). Stability of aggressive reaction patterns in males: A review. *Psychological Bulletin, 86*, 852–875.

Olweus, D. (1980). The consistency issue in personality psychology revisited—With special reference to aggression. *British Journal of Social & Clinical Psychology, 19*, 377–390.

Olweus, D. (1984). Stability in aggressive and withdrawn, inhibited behavior patterns. In R. M. Kaplan, V. J. Konecni, & R. W. Novaco (Eds.), *Aggression in children and youth* (pp. 104–137). The Hague, The Netherlands: Nijhoff.

Olweus, D. (1987). *Bully/victim problems among school children in Scandinavia. An overview* (Mimeo). Bergen, Norway: University of Bergen.

Olweus, D. (1991). Bully/victim problems among school children: Basic facts and effects of a school based intervention program. In D. Pepler & K. Rubin (Eds.), *The development and treatment of childhood aggression* (pp. 411–448). Hillsdale, NJ: Lawrence Erlbaum Associates, Inc.

Olweus, D., & Alsaker, F. D. (1991). Assessing change in a cohort-longitudinal study with hierarchical data. In D. Magnusson, L. Bergman, G., Rudinger, & B. Torestad (Eds.), *Problems and methods in longitudinal research* (pp. 107–132). New York: Cambridge University Press.

O'Malley, P., & Bachman, J. (1983). Self-esteem: Change and stability between ages 13 and 23. *Developmental Psychology, 19*, 257–268.

Petersen, A. C. (1988). Adolescent development. *Annual Review of Psychology, 39*, 583–607.

Piers, E., & Harris, D. (1969). *The Piers-Harris Children's Self-Concept Scale.* Nashville, TN: Counselor Recordings and Tests.

Piotrowski, C. (1983). Reliability of the semantic differential used by children: Evaluation of the evaluative dimension. *Psychological Reports, 52*, 24–26.

Rogers, C. R. (1961). *On becoming a person.* Boston: Houghton Mifflin.

Rogosa, D., Brandt, D., & Zinowski, M. (1982). A growth curve approach to the measurement of change. *Psychological Bulletin, 92*, 726–748.

Rosenberg, M. (1965). *Society and the adolescent self-image.* Princeton, NJ: Princeton University Press.

Rosenberg, M. (1979). *Conceiving the self.* New York: Basic Books.

Rosenberg, M. (1986). Self-concept from middle childhood through adolescence. In J. Suls & A. G. Greenwald (Eds.), *Psychological perspectives on the self* (pp. 107–135). Hillsdale, NJ: Lawrence Erlbaum Associates, Inc.

Rubin, R. A. (1978). Stability of self-esteem ratings and their relation to academic achievement: A longitudinal study. *Psychology in the Schools, 15*, 430–433.

Shavelson, R. J., & Bolus, R. (1982). Self-concept: The interplay of theory and methods. *Journal of Educational Psychology, 74*, 3–17.

Shavelson, R. J., Hubner, J. J., & Stanton, G. C. (1976). Self-concept: Validation of construct interpretation. *Review of Educational Psychology, 46*, 407–441.

Simmons, R. G., & Blyth, D. A. (1987). *Moving into adolescence. The impact of pubertal change and school context.* New York: Aldine de Gruyter.

Wylie, R. C. (1974). *The self concept: Vol. 1. A review of methodological considerations and measuring instruments.* Lincoln: University of Nebraska Press.

Received July 25, 1990
Revision received February 8, 1991
Revision received July 8, 1991
Accepted July 31, 1991

A Longitudinal Study of Consistency and Change in Self-Esteem from Early Adolescence to Early Adulthood

Jack Block and Richard W. Robins
University of California, Berkeley

Block, Jack, and Robins, Richard W. *A Longitudinal Study of Consistency and Change in Self-Esteem from Early Adolescence to Early Adulthood.* Child Development, 1993, **64**, 909–923. In a longitudinal study of 47 girls and 44 boys, developmental change in self-esteem (SE) was examined from early adolescence through late adolescence to early adulthood. Males tended to increase and females tended to decrease in SE over time. There was appreciable rank-order consistency in SE over time. Within each gender, the considerable individual differences in developmental trajectories were coherently related to personality characteristics independently assessed in early adolescence. Boys and girls with high SE possessed quite different personality characteristics in early adolescence; by early adulthood, although important differences remained, the personality characteristics associated with high SE were similar for the 2 sexes. Discussion focuses on the implications of our findings for the "consistency versus change" debate, the influence of gender-role socialization on SE development, and the importance of examining normative, gender-specific, and individual developmental change in SE.

Adolescence is a developmental period marked by rapid maturational changes, shifting societal expectations, conflicting role demands, and increasingly complex relations with the opposite sex (see, e.g., Douvan & Adelson, 1966). Self-esteem plays a critical role in this developmental process (see, e.g., Harter, 1983). Relatively little is known, however, about the developmental path of self-esteem across adolescence and in the transition to adulthood.

To date, a number of useful longitudinal studies of self-esteem development during adolescence have been conducted (Abramowitz, Petersen, & Schulenberg, 1984; Alsaker & Olweus, 1992; Carlson, 1965; Engel, 1959; McCarthy & Hoge, 1982; O'Malley & Bachman, 1983; Savin-Williams & Demo, 1984; Simmons & Blyth, 1987). In the present paper, we seek to add to understanding by describing the developmental change in self-esteem in a sample of girls and boys studied longitudinally from early adolescence (age 14) through late adolescence (age 18) and into early adulthood (age 23). We also examine individual differences in developmental change patterns and explore the correlates of these individual differences, focusing on which personality characteristics at age 14 predict subsequent increases and decreases in self-esteem from age 14 to 23. All analyses are conducted separately for the two sexes in order to evaluate how girls and boys may differ in the ways they develop during adolescence.

Development proceeds through a complex process that involves the mutual influences of a person's innate characteristics, family experiences, peer interactions, social roles, cultural environment, and the fortuities that impinge upon a life. It is during adolescence that the biosocial transition from childhood to adulthood occurs, is experienced, and further influences development. For many decades, developmental psychologists have regarded adolescence as a period of "storm and stress" (Hall, 1904), a time of crisis and psychological upheaval precipitated by biologically driven maturational changes and marked in particular by a questioning of the self and subsequent reformulation of perceptions and evaluations of self. However, the empirical findings of the last 2 decades have not supported the contention that development during adolescence is problematic (Coleman, 1978; Hill,

This research was supported by National Institute of Mental Health grant MH 16080 to Jack and Jeanne H. Block. The second author was supported by a National Science Foundation Graduate Fellowship. Correspondence concerning this article should be addressed to Jack Block or Richard W. Robins at the Department of Psychology, University of California, Berkeley, CA 94720.

1985; Montemayor, 1983; Rutter, Graham, Chadwick, & Yule, 1976). As a corollary, it has been suggested that "adolescence is not a time of upheaval in the self-concept. The person who enters adolescence is basically the same as [the one] who exits it" (Dusek & Flaherty, 1981, p. 39; see also Offer & Offer, 1975; Offer, Ostrov, & Howard, 1981; Savin-Williams & Demo, 1984; Simmons & Blyth, 1987). The present study brings additional evidence to bear on this insufficiently resolved issue.

In the study of developmental change, several facets of this issue must be considered (Block, 1971; Caspi & Bem, 1990; Dusek & Flaherty, 1981; Mortimer, Finch & Kumka, 1982; Simmons & Blyth, 1987). One concern is the direction and amount of age-related change in the level of an attribute. This question typically is posed for the sample as a whole, and is evaluated empirically by examining change in group means over time. The question can also be addressed with regard to subsamples (e.g., males or females) and individual cases. Longitudinal studies of self-esteem development that have examined age-related change in the mean level of self-esteem have tended to find, for the sexes combined, a small, gradual increase in measures of global self-esteem across adolescence (see O'Malley & Bachman, 1983, for a review). Gender differences in age-related changes in self-esteem have been reported by Blyth, Simmons, and Carlton-Ford (1983), who found that, from sixth grade to tenth grade, the global self-esteem of girls decreases while the global self-esteem of boys increases. We know of no longitudinal study that has explored individual differences in developmental change in self-esteem across any time period.

A second developmental question concerns the longitudinal consistency of interindividual differences: to what degree is the ordering of individuals according to their level on a variable maintained over time? Global indices (see below) of self-esteem during adolescence have shown moderate levels of longitudinal ordering consistency. For example, O'Malley and Bachman (1983) found a correlation of .41 across a 3-year period beginning when the subjects were high school seniors. Alsaker and Olweus (1992) and Simmons and Blyth (1987) report similar correlations across similar intervals. These correlations suggest substantial ordering consistency and yet permit considerable individual variations as well. Longitudinal consistency of self-esteem has yet to be examined across a wider range of time, from early adolescence through late adolescence and into young adulthood.

A third, largely unexamined question regarding the development of self-esteem focuses on the consistency of the pattern of relations between self-esteem and other conceptually relevant variables (e.g., personality characteristics). Little is known about the longitudinal consistency of the personality correlates of self-esteem. However, developmentally, it is of interest to examine whether the personality profile of individuals with high (vs. low) self-esteem in adolescence is similar to the personality profile of individuals with high (vs. low) self-esteem in early adulthood.

The three approaches to developmental change described thus far do not provide a complete account of *intra*individual development. Studies of self-esteem change that focus on mean-level changes and on the longitudinal ordering consistency of self-esteem reveal whether variables "behave" consistently across time rather than whether individuals are behaviorally consistent. However, "it is individuals who are stable [or unstable] across time, not variables" (Magnusson, 1990, p. 210), and there has been relatively little inquiry into the variation and the abidingness *within individuals* of their sense of self-worth. Given the myriad influences on self-esteem development during adolescence, it becomes important to examine the extent to which adolescents follow the same developmental path.

Assessing change within individuals therefore also requires a more "person-centered" approach to development (Block, 1961, 1971). Whereas a "variable-centered" perspective presumes that developmental change is much the same for all individuals, a "person-centered" perspective recognizes that individuals may not and often do not all develop in the same way; while some individuals may increase in self-esteem during adolescence, others may decrease in self-esteem, and others may show relatively little change. These observed differences in developmental paths require closer evaluation as to their reliability and significance. In the few instances where different developmental paths taken by individuals have been studied, social-contextual factors and prior personal characteristics have proven influential (e.g., Block, 1971).

In the person-centered study of different developmental paths, the role of gender requires special scrutiny. The characteristics underlying individual differences in self-esteem change in males may differ from the characteristics underlying self-esteem change in females. Although we know of no prior studies that specifically have examined the antecedent correlates of self-esteem change, Ozer and Block (1987) found that males increasing in IQ from age 11 to 18 tended to be shy, anxiety-prone, and non-competitive as children, while females showing IQ increases tended to be socially competent as children. Similarly, Block, Gjerde, and Block (1991) found gender differences in the early childhood antecedents of depression in late adolescence. Mortimer et al. (1982) have identified certain life experiences that *reciprocally* influence the self-concept. Mortimer and Lorence (1981), in an interesting study of males entering college, found that over the subsequent 14-year period a continuing sense of well-being that early was predicated on affectional family support later on was based on the quality of the relationship these men developed with their wives.

In the analyses to be presented, we examine: (*a*) mean-level changes in self-esteem through time; (*b*) the ordering consistency of self-esteem through time, and (*c*) the consistency of the personality correlates of self-esteem through time. To provide a more differentiated, more person-centered account of self-esteem development, all analyses in the present study were conducted separately for females and males and, within each sex, individual differences in age-related changes in self-esteem were examined to identify the personality characteristics predicting appreciable increase versus appreciable decrease in self-esteem from age 14 to age 23.

Conceptualization and Measurement of Self-Esteem

The measurement of self-esteem is inextricably linked to its conceptualization. Not uniquely, we view self-esteem as *the extent to which one perceives oneself as relatively close to being the person one wants to be and/or as relatively distant from being the kind of person one does not want to be, with respect to person-qualities one positively and negatively values*. It follows that the study of self-esteem requires two kinds of assessment: (1) evaluation of the degree of congruence in an individual between the perceived self and the aspired self, and (2) consideration of the specific valued elements or valued criteria in terms of which self-evaluation is referenced. William James (1890), in his seminal formulation, said that self-evaluations depend on the degree to which actual successes coincide with one's goals and aspirations; self-esteem can be defined as "success divided by pretensions" (p. 310). Rosenberg (1965, pp. 243–245) strongly affirms the Jamesian view that it is crucial to know the specific self-values, and their weightings, on which an individual predicates self-esteem. In alternative psychoanalytic terms, an individual's "ego-ideal" provides a polestar—a personal value system—that permits and even compels self-evaluation. Thus, although it is crucial to know the extent to which an individual likes the self perceived, it is also the case that without knowing the particular personal qualities on which an individual "stakes" his or her characterological aspirations, we cannot truly know the meaning or psychological basis of an individual's "claim" to self-esteem.

In the present study, the Q-sort procedure (Block, 1961; Stephenson, 1953)—a different but long-employed approach to the operationalization of self-esteem (e.g., Block & Thomas, 1955; Rogers & Dymond, 1954; Turner & Vanderlippe, 1958)—was employed to assess self/ideal congruence.[1] In the Q-sort procedure, one considers the descriptiveness of a large set of statements, ordering the statements from those most to those least salient or characteristic of oneself or whoever is being described. The number of categories and the number of statements that can be sorted into each category are fixed, and so each respondent offers the same number of discriminations. The procedure is "ipsative," that is, the salience or descriptiveness of each item is evaluated relative to each other item *within* the particular individual being described rather than being evaluated separately, as is the case with most assessment procedures. Because the Q-items "compete" with each other, this approach brings subjects to offer reliable dis-

[1] A number of other investigators representing a variety of theoretical perspectives have worked with self-ideal indices but did not use the ipsative, forced-sort Q-sort approach (e.g., Blatt, Quinlan, Chevron, McDonald, & Zuroff, 1982; Higgins, 1987; Hoge & McCarthy, 1983; Lazzari, Fioravanti, & Gough, 1978; Pelham & Swann, 1989).

criminations among attributes that often would not be offered via other procedures, such as Likert scales or via checklists (Block, 1956; 1961, chap. 6). To develop a self-ideal congruence index, a subject must do a Q-sort description of his or her self and, separately (usually at another time), a Q-sort description of his or her ideal self. The congruence between these two Q-sort descriptions subsequently is calculated by the investigator, and this congruence score becomes the subject's index of self-esteem.

We believe a Q-sort-based self-ideal congruence index, although more cumbersome to implement, has several advantages over the more widely used global self-esteem scales. First, such self-ideal indices are not confounded with individual differences in scale usage because the procedure makes all subjects use the underlying metric commensurately. Incommensurate usage of the underlying dimension because of differences in response tendencies, present in most other self-esteem measures, can be a significant source of bias that renders such self-esteem scores and self-ideal congruence indices not based on Q-sort data sometimes difficult to interpret.

Second, compared with direct approaches to the indexing of self-esteem, Q-sort-based self-ideal indices are indirect and therefore more difficult for subjects to intentionally manipulate in the direction of favorable responses because the self data and the ideal data are collected in more complicated ways, usually on separate occasions, and the subject is unaware of the way these data subsequently will be employed. In contrast, the items used in the direct measurement of self-esteem are patent, even blatant in their content. Individuals can readily discern the underlying measurement intentions and may, ad libitum, manipulate their responses to achieve desired standings on the self-esteem continuum. Although low self-esteem, as reflected by such direct measures, can probably be accepted as such, high self-esteem so measured may not be a genuine expression of the individual's self-view or level of psychological health—contextual circumstances may be motivating and controlling, or the individual, for psychodynamic reasons, may be introspectively unaware (Block & Thomas, 1955).

Third, the self-ideal index provides an operationalization of self-esteem that is consistent with the phenomenological conception of self-esteem advanced by most self-theorists; normative judgments of self-worth are explicitly avoided because the index is based on the congruence between each subject's perceptions of self and his or her personal value system as expressed via the individual's aspirations for an ideal self.

Fourth, besides providing a conceptually satisfactory self-esteem index, the Q-sort approach also permits an analysis of the specific content of the perceived-self and ideal-self perceptions that underlie an individual's self-esteem or lack thereof. Access to the nature of the psychological building blocks on which the edifice of self-esteem is based provides crucial additional information. Besides wanting to know *whether* one likes oneself, it is important to know *why* one likes oneself.

Method

Subjects

The subjects are participants in the Block and Block longitudinal study of personality and cognitive development initiated in 1968 (see J. H. Block & J. Block, 1980, for a comprehensive description of the study). Initially, 128 3-year-olds were studied, coming from two successive cohorts at each of two nursery schools. Subsequently, sample attrition has been low (104 subjects were assessed at age 23). The subjects live primarily in urban settings and are heterogeneous with respect to the social class and educational level of their parents. Approximately two-thirds are Caucasian, one-fourth are African-American, and one-twentieth are Asian-American. There were no significant associations, or even trends toward associations, of our measure of self-esteem with either social class or ethnicity. Although we cannot claim full generalizability of the findings we will report, the sample we have employed, although not strictly representative of the national population, is not special in its characteristics.

The analyses reported in this paper are based on the 44 males and 47 females (N = 91) who, during intensive assessments at about the first year of high school (mean age = 14.80, SD = .54), the last year of high school (mean age = 17.85, SD = .50), and 5 years subsequent to high school (mean age = 23.23, SD = .74), provided complete self- and ideal-self descriptions. It should be noted that, because the same subjects were studied at each assessment period, the developmental changes during adolescence to be reported cannot be attributed to changes in sample composition.

Measuring Self-Esteem: The Self-Descriptive Q-Set

At ages 14, 18, and 23, subjects described themselves (i.e., their perceived-self) and, on another day a week or more later, the person they would ideally like to be (i.e., their ideal-self) using the 43-item Self-Descriptive Q-Set (SQ; J. H. Block & J. Block, 1980). Items on the SQ contain personality-descriptive adjectives and short phrases that are easily understood by adolescents (e.g., "competitive," "affectionate," "responsible," "gets upset easily," "creative"). For both the perceived-self and the ideal-self Q-sorts, subjects sorted the SQ-items into seven categories ranging from Most Undescriptive (1) to Most Descriptive (7), according to a fixed, discrimination-maximizing rectangular distribution (i.e., seven items in the middle category and six items in the remaining six categories).

To index self-esteem, and in accord with our conceptual definition of self-esteem, the congruence between each subject's perceived-self and ideal-self descriptions across the 43 SQ-items was calculated, using the correlation formula to create this score. Higher scores reflect greater congruence and therefore indicate higher levels of self-esteem.[2] The reliability of this self-ideal index was evaluated by applying the Spearman-Brown formula to split-half correlations computed between randomly generated equivalent halves of the 43 adjectives that comprise the SQ (this procedure was repeated three times, and the mean of the three estimates was used). Reliability estimates were computed separately for females and males at each age. The split-half reliability of the self-ideal index at ages 14, 18, and 23 was .88, .81, and .83 for the female sample and .63, .56, and .75 for the male sample, respectively.

Measuring Personality: Encoding Observer Descriptions with the California Adult Q-Set

At ages 14, 18, and 23, the personality characteristics of the subjects were independently described by four psychologists using the California Adult Q-set (CAQ) (Block, 1961). These psychologist judges (doctorates and graduate students in clinical and personality psychology) had each separately and independently observed and interacted with the subjects in the course of administering a wide variety of interviews, cognitive and personality tests, and other assessment procedures, formal and informal. However, they were entirely unaware of the self-esteem scores of the subjects. Each judge sorted the 100 widely ranging descriptive statements of the Q-set into a forced, quasi-normal distribution using nine categories, from *not at all characteristic or salient* to *highly characteristic or salient* of the subject being described. The multiple Q-sort formulations available for each subject were then averaged across corresponding items to form the composite Q-sort descriptions used for the present analyses. The estimated internal consistency reliabilities of the Q items, based on correlations among observers, averaged .72, .59, and .70, at ages 14, 18, and 23, respectively. This approach to personality description previously has demonstrated its usefulness and validity in a variety of contexts (e.g., Block, Block, & Keyes, 1988; Block et al., 1991; Funder & Block, 1989; Kogan & Block, 1991).

Results

Does Self-Esteem Increase or Decrease from Early Adolescence to Early Adulthood?

Mean-level change.—For the combined sample, no age-related changes in the mean level of self-esteem were observed. However, males tended to have higher self-esteem scores than females at every age, and this disparity increased over time. For the males, the self-esteem means (and standard deviations) at ages 14, 18, and 23 were .56 (.20), .59 (.15), and .60 (.19); for the females, the corresponding figures were .53 (.26), .52 (.26), and .48 (.26). Analyses of the simple effects of sex at each age indicate a slight difference favoring the boys at age 14 which does not warrant interpretation ($F < 1$); by age 18, this difference has increased ($p < .07$, one-tailed test); and by age 23, the difference between the sexes in self-esteem has become statistically significant ($p < .005$,

[2] The reader should note that self-esteem, an introspective condition that requires evaluation through self-report measures, stands in no necessary relation to psychological adjustment or mental health. Only when psychological health is evaluated by indices of adjustment not based on self-reports can the empirical connection between self-esteem and psychological health be established (Block & Thomas, 1955).

one-tailed test). In this developmental divergence, males on average increased in self-esteem from age 14 to 23 by about one-fifth of a standard deviation, whereas females on average decreased in self-esteem by about one-fifth of a standard deviation. We evaluated the reliability of this gender divergence in self-esteem using three different analytical strategies: (*a*) a Mann-Whitney analysis of sex differences in raw change scores (self-esteem at age 23 minus self-esteem at age 14) ($p < .03$), (*b*) correlating the sex dichotomy with residualized self-esteem change scores (see below) ($p < .01$), and (*c*) testing the interaction between sex and linear trends in age ($p < .04$) based on the method of orthogonal polynomial contrasts (Keppel & Zedeck, 1989). By all three approaches, the gender divergence in self-esteem levels across time proved to be statistically significant. Blyth et al. (1983) have reported a similar self-esteem divergence in their longitudinal study of sixth graders becoming tenth graders.

The longitudinal consistency of self-esteem.—The longitudinal consistency of individual differences in self-esteem was assessed, for the sexes separately, by intercorrelating the self-esteem scores available at ages 14, 18, and 23 (see Table 1). Because these correlations are attenuated by inevitable measurement error, they provide an underestimate of the true longitudinal consistency of self-esteem. Therefore, the correlations were corrected for unreliability in the self-esteem measures, and these adjusted, theoretically more accurate figures are also shown in Table 1.

Across the 4-year period from age 14 to 18, the adjusted correlations were about .60 for both females and males (.57 and .63, respectively); across the 5-year period from age 18 to 23, the adjusted correlations were .65 for females and .50 for males. Across the entire 9-year period from age 14 to 23, the corrected correlations were .65 for females and .36 for males.

Across the 9-year period from age 14 to 23, the sex difference in the uncorrected correlations (.55 for females, .25 for males) is also quite large, corresponding to a ratio of almost 5 to 1 in variance terms ($p < .05$). The equivalent findings using both the adjusted and uncorrected figures obviates an interpretation that the observed gender difference is a statistical consequence of gender differences in the reliability of our self-esteem measure.

Another possible explanation for the gender difference in longitudinal consistency involves restriction of sample range; the self-esteem measure has less variance in the male sample than in the female sample (which had several outlying self-deprecators), and this difference conceivably may account for the difference between the across-time correlations of the two sexes. To evaluate this possibility, the across-time correlation in the male sample was corrected for range restriction (Hunter & Schmidt, 1990). This correction provides an estimate of what the correlation would have been for the males if the variance in the sample of males had been the same as in the female sample. The corrected correlation estimate was .55 for the females and .40 for the males—a difference of 2:1 in variance terms, which is still substantial considering that the restriction of range correction formula tends to overestimate the true correlation for sample sizes smaller than 50 (Mendoza, Hart, & Powell, 1991).

TABLE 1

LONGITUDINAL CONSISTENCY OF SELF-ESTEEM: CORRELATIONS (and Corrected Correlations) ACROSS AGES 14, 18, AND 23

	INTERVAL ACROSS WHICH SELF-ESTEEM WAS CORRELATED		
	Age 14–18	Age 18–23	Age 14–23
Females	.48 (.57)	.55 (.65)	.55 (.65)
Males	.37 (.63)	.32 (.50)	.25 (.36)
Total sample	.45 (.59)	.50 (.65)	.44 (.55)

NOTE.—For females, $n = 47$; for males, $n = 44$. The correlations in parentheses were corrected for unreliability using Spearman-Brown reliability estimates, computed separately for females and males at each age.

Thus, the greater longitudinal ordering consistency of self-esteem for females across adolescence and the transition to adulthood does not appear to be a statistical artifact. Rather, the greater ordering consistency within the sample of girls implies that, for many girls, personal levels of self-esteem are relatively well established by adolescence, while in our sample of adolescent boys, personal self views are relatively malleable throughout the teen years.

Patterns of individual-level change.— The trends observed in the aggregate analyses reported thus far may not represent the patterns of change existing at the individual level; that is, they may mask individual differences in the direction and magnitude of developmental change. In the following analyses, we examine individual differences in self-esteem change from age 14 to 23.

The nomothetic expectation would be that the trends observed at the sample mean level typify the developmental change patterns exhibited by most of the subjects in the sample. However, substantial individual differences were observed in both the direction and the magnitude of self-esteem change from age 14 to 23. For the males, individual differences in self-esteem change ranged from an increase of .65 to a decrease of −.52 (note that the self-esteem measure has a possible range of −1.00 to +1.00). For the females, individual differences in self-esteem change ranged from an increase of .49 to a decrease of −.60.

In the male sample, from age 14 to 23, 34% decreased in self-esteem (20% by more than one-half a standard deviation, a relatively substantial change), and 64% increased in self-esteem (34% by more than one-half a standard deviation). In the female sample, 57% of the females decreased in self-esteem (49% by more than one-half a standard deviation), and 43% increased in self-esteem (21% by more than one-half a standard deviation). (In the combined sample, more than 60% of the subjects either increased or decreased by more than one-half a standard deviation during the period from age 14 to 23.) For the male and female samples, the proportions decreasing and increasing more than one-half a standard deviation differed significantly ($p < .02$).

These findings indicate substantial individual differences in self-esteem development, with different patterns of change characterizing females and males. They do not, however, provide insight into why some individuals increase in self-esteem from early adolescence to young adulthood while others decrease. Indeed, from a nomothetic viewpoint, these findings might be ascribed simply to random error superimposed upon the increasing gender differences observed over time. But another interpretive possibility is that these individual differences are systematic and are lawfully related to personality characteristics. To address this issue, the relations between personality characteristics existing at age 14 and individual differences in self-esteem change from age 14 to 23 were examined.

Personality Correlates of Self-Esteem Change

The personality correlates of self-esteem change were evaluated using a residualized change index, computed by regressing self-esteem at age 14 onto self-esteem at age 23 and retaining the residuals.[3] This residual index provides a directional measure of individual differences in self-esteem change from age 14 to 23 that is independent of each subject's initial level of self-esteem at age 14 (Cronbach & Furby, 1970; Lord, 1956). The index has a reliability of .70 in the male sample and .71 in the female sample (see Formula 49 in O'Connor, 1972). We correlated this self-esteem change index with each of the 100 CAQ items observers had evaluated as characterizing the subjects at age 14. A positive correlation with a CAQ item indicates that 14-year-olds who were high on the Q-characteristic were more likely to increase in self-esteem from age 14 to 23 than those who were low on the characteristic. Because the observers evaluated these personality characteristics when the subjects were 14 years old, they of course could not have been influenced by the changes in self-evaluation subsequently manifested by the subjects.

Of the 100 CAQ items, 22 were significantly correlated with self-esteem change for females and six were significant for males at the .05 alpha level. The number of correlations well exceeds that expected by chance

[3] We replicated these analyses using a raw change score (self-esteem at age 23 minus self-esteem at age 14) and obtained essentially the same pattern of results but with somewhat weaker relations.

for females but not for males, suggesting that self-esteem change from adolescence to early adulthood may be more lawfully related to personality characteristics for girls than for boys. Although few in number, however, the Q-item correlates of self-esteem change in males display a coherent constellation. Because of the uniqueness and the difficulty of replicating the present longitudinal data and because in an exploratory study such as the present one it makes more sense to increase somewhat the risk of a Type 1 error in order to avoid the more consequential, irretrievable effects of a Type 2 error, we list the Q-items correlating at the .10 alpha level with subsequent self-esteem change for both females and males (see Table 2).

Females who were protective, humorous, sympathetic, and generous at age 14 tended to increase in self-esteem, whereas females who were critical, hostile, irritable, and negative at age 14 tended to decrease in self-esteem. Males who were calm, relaxed, not socially anxious, and who already felt satisfied with themselves at age 14 tended to increase in self-esteem, whereas males who were anxious and who fantasized and daydreamed tended to decrease in self-esteem. Overall, subsequent change in self-esteem among adolescent females seems to be related to an other-orientation, that is, to interpersonal characteristics reflecting warmth and a communal orientation. In contrast, subsequent change in self-esteem in adolescent males seems to derive from a self- rather than an other-orientation, and reflects differential tendencies to experience the personal discomforts of social anxiety.

How Similar Are the Personality Correlates of Self-Esteem Across Time?

In the previous set of analyses, we examined the personality antecedents of *self-esteem change*, rather than the correlates of *self-esteem per se*. We focus here on a different question: Do the character qualities surrounding self-esteem vary from early to late adolescence and into young adulthood or do they remain essentially the same? That is, do observers ascribe the same personality characteristics to individuals with high (vs. low) self-esteem at different developmental periods?

Self-esteem scores at each age were correlated with the 100 CAQ items measured *concurrently*, yielding three sets of 100 Q-item correlations; these three sets or vectors of correlations convey the concomitant relations between self-esteem and personality qualities at ages 14, 18, and 23. We then correlated the vector of 100 Q-item correlation values obtained at one age with the vector of 100 Q-item correlation values obtained at each other age. The resulting correlations between these sets of correlations provide an index of the congruence, or pattern similarity, of the CAQ correlates of self-esteem for the ages being related. A high correlation between two vectors indicates that Q-items more strongly positively (or more strongly negatively) related to self-esteem at one age tend to be more strongly positively (or more strongly negatively) related to self-esteem at the other age. More generally, the correlations between vectors provide an estimate of the similarity at different ages of the personality attributes ascribed by observers to individuals with high (vs. low) self-esteem.

For the female sample, the patterns of Q-correlates of self-esteem were quite similar at ages 14 and 18 (r = .67), age 18 and 23 (r = .68), and across the entire period from 14 to 23 (r = .81).[4] For the male sample, in contrast, the pattern of Q-correlates of self-esteem at age 14 was quite different from the pattern of Q-correlates at age 18 (r = .19) or at age 23 (r = .14); however, the pattern of Q-correlates of self-esteem at age 18 closely resembles the pattern of Q-correlates at age 23 (r = .69). The independently assessed personality profile of a 14-year-old adolescent girl with high self-esteem appears to be already well established because it is quite similar to the personality profile of an 18- or 23-year-old young woman with high self-esteem. In contrast, the personality profile of a 14-year-old adolescent boy with high self-esteem seems not yet firmly formed and is radically different from the personality profile of an 18- or 23-year-old young man with high self-esteem. The transformation in the personality characteristics associated with self-esteem in males appears to occur between age 14 and age 18; by age 18, the pattern of Q-correlates established essentially continues to age 23.

We also evaluated gender similarities at corresponding ages in the Q-item personality patterns surrounding self-esteem. At age

[4] These correlations between vectors of correlations can only be interpreted descriptively; they cannot be referred to sampling distributions for evaluations of their statistical significance.

TABLE 2

PREDICTING SELF-ESTEEM CHANGE: PERSONALITY CHARACTERISTICS MEASURED AT AGE 14 THAT PREDICT INCREASES IN SELF-ESTEEM FROM AGE 14 TO 23

Observer Judgments of Personality at Age 14	Correlation with *Increase* in Self-Esteem[a]
Females:	
Is moralistic	.47**
Responds to and appreciates humor	.46**
Is protective of those close to him/her	.42**
Is turned to or sought out for advice and reassurance	.38**
Is cheerful, happy	.37**
Has a clear-cut personality; is relatively easy to understand	.36**
Behaves in a sympathetic and considerate manner	.36**
Initiates humor; makes spontaneous funny remarks	.34**
Is giving, generous toward others	.34**
It a talkative person	.30**
Has a high aspiration level for self; is ambitious	.30**
Has warmth; has the capacity for close relationships; compassionate	.28*
Compares self to others	.27*
Values intellectual and cognitive matters	.27*
Is productive; gets things done	.25*
Behaves in an ethically consistent manner	.25*
Is critical, skeptical, not easily impressed	−.36**
Has fluctuating moods; moods go up and down	−.34**
Expresses hostility, angry feelings directly	−.34**
Is irritable; overreacts to minor frustrations	−.34**
Is physically attractive; is good looking	−.34**
Is subtly negativistic; tends to sabotage other people	−.33**
Is unpredictable and changeable in attitudes and behavior	−.33**
Communicates through actions rather than words	−.32**
Is condescending to others; acts superior to others	−.31**
Gives up and withdraws in the face of frustration and adversity	−.30**
Has hostility toward others	−.29**
Tends to ruminate and have persistent, preoccupying thoughts	−.28*
Values own independence and autonomy	−.28*
Distrusts people; questions their motivations	−.28*
Feels a lack of meaning in life	−.28*
Keeps people at a distance; avoids close relationships	−.28*
Creates and exploits dependency in people	−.28*
Has a brittle ego-defense system; maladaptive under stress	−.27*
Is guileful and deceitful, manipulative, opportunistic	−.26*
Pushes and tries to stretch limits	−.26*
Is self-defeating	−.25*
Males:	
Socially at ease; has social poise and presence	.36**
Feels satisfied with self; is unaware of self-concern	.34**
Regards self as physically attractive	.33**
Is calm, relaxed in manner	.30**
Behaves in masculine style	.27*
Tends to fantasize, daydream, engage in fictional speculations	−.35**
Is basically anxious	−.30**
Anxiety and stress find outlet in bodily symptoms	−.29*
Tends to ruminate and have persistent, preoccupying thoughts	−.28*
Tends to be self-defensive	−.26*

NOTE.—For females, $n = 47$; for males, $n = 44$.

[a] Correlation between CAQ item at age 14 and residualized change in self-esteem. Positive correlations indicate that the item is more characteristic of individuals whose self-esteem increased from age 14 to 23, controlling for their initial level of self-esteem at age 14.

* $p < .10$ (two-tailed).

** $p < .05$ (two-tailed).

14, the girls and boys showed quite different patterns of Q-correlates ($r = -.05$). However, as the girls and boys proceeded through adolescence to early adulthood, the personality patterns associated with self-esteem became progressively more similar for the two sexes ($r = .41$ at age 18; $r = .76$ at age 23). Thus, the personality profile of a 14-year-old girl with high self-esteem is quite different from the personality profile of a 14-year-old boy with high self-esteem, but there is a convergence over time in the personality profiles associated with self-esteem for the two sexes, although some important differences still remain at early adulthood.

To infuse psychological content into these somewhat abstract congruence coefficients, we report in Table 3 the CAQ items significantly correlated with self-esteem at age 23 for *both* young women and young men. As portrayed by psychologist-observers, and regardless of gender, 23-year-olds

TABLE 3

PERSONALITY CORRELATES OF SELF-ESTEEM AT AGE 23

OBSERVER JUDGMENTS OF PERSONALITY AT AGE 23	CORRELATION WITH SELF-ESTEEM AT AGE 23	
	Females	Males
CAQ items correlated positively with self-esteem:[a]		
Assertive; not afraid to express opinions	.54**	.33**
Is cheerful, happy	.52**	.39**
Feels satisfied with self; is unaware of self-concern	.48**	.54**
Is turned to or sought out for advice and reassurance	.48**	.35**
Socially at ease; has social poise and presence	.46**	.39**
Is productive, gets things done	.38**	.45**
Has a rapid personal tempo; behaves and acts quickly	.36**	.33**
CAQ items correlated negatively with self-esteem:[a]		
Reluctant to commit self; delays or avoids making decisions	−.60**	−.53**
Feels a lack of meaning in life	−.56**	−.47**
Gives up and withdraws in the face of frustration	−.55**	−.46**
Has doubts about adequacy as a person	−.51**	−.44**
Is self-defeating	−.49**	−.50**
Vulnerable to real or fancied threat; generally fearful	−.49**	−.45**
Is basically anxious	−.46**	−.50**
Tends to ruminate; has persistent, preoccupying thoughts	−.45**	−.42**
Has a brittle ego defense system; maladaptive under stress	−.44**	−.49**
Feels cheated and victimized by life; self-pitying	−.43**	−.37**
Has fluctuating moods; moods go up and down	−.39**	−.45**
Is unpredictable and changeable in attitudes and behavior	−.35**	−.30**
Is subtly negativistic; tends to sabotage other people	−.34**	−.30**
CAQ items correlated differently with self-esteem for the two sexes:[b]		
Is a talkative person	.53**	.05
Is sociable, gregarious; emphasizes being with others	.47**	.16
Gives advice; concerns self with other people's business	.46**	.11
Has warmth; has the capacity for close relationships	.43**	.09
Is giving, generous toward others	.31**	−.08
Creates and exploits dependency in others	.27*	−.30**
Is self-dramatizing; histrionic	.21	−.18
Seeks reassurance from others	.01	−.35**
Is physically attractive; is good looking	−.07	.53**
Is an unemotional person; is emotionally bland	−.22	.21
Keeps people at a distance; avoids close relationships	−.49**	−.18

NOTE.—For females, $n = 47$; for males, $n = 44$.

[a] CAQ items that correlate above |.30| ($p < .05$, two-tailed) with self-esteem for both females and males.

[b] CAQ items that have significantly different correlations ($p < .10$, two-tailed) with self-esteem in the female and male samples.

* $p < .10$ (two-tailed).

** $p < .05$ (two-tailed).

with high self-esteem tend to be satisfied with themselves, cheerful, assertive, poised, productive, quick to act, and turned to for advice. They do not delay or avoid action, they do not give up when frustrated, they do not ruminate or have fluctuating moods, they do not feel cheated and victimized by life, and they are not fearful. This is a coherent set of characteristics and there is no conceptual problem in seeing how these personality qualities are conducive to or expressive of a solid sense of self-worth and identity in either sex. This personality core, common to both sexes, underlies the impressive correspondence (.76) between their personality profiles at age 23.

However, it merits mention that, despite their appreciable characterological similarities, young women with high self-esteem also differ from young men with high self-esteem. Reported also in Table 3 are the CAQ items correlating significantly differently with self-esteem for the two sexes. These items suggest that young women with high self-esteem emphasize interpersonal connectedness far more than young men of high self-esteem. They tend to be warm, gregarious, talkative, giving, closely concerned individuals, whereas young men with high self-esteem are relatively unemotional, uninvolved, and independent in distancing ways.

Discussion

In the present paper, developmental change in self-esteem was examined in a cohort of individuals followed longitudinally from age 14 through age 18 to age 23, a period spanning adolescence and the transition to young adulthood. During this cultural time (the decade of the 80s), our subjects confronted a number of important developmental tasks. From age 14 to 18, they were compelled to cope with the pressures and possibilities associated with becoming an adolescent. Puberty had opened the world to them in many alluring but also threatening ways; in junior and senior high school, more was being expected of them cognitively, and how they responded to this press, positively or evasively, had great immediate (and long-term) consequence; deeper and different peer relations were being formed, with many beginning dating; and the possibility of experimentation with sex and drugs was in the atmosphere. From age 18 to 23, our subjects necessarily moved on to begin to meet other demands and expectations associated with becoming an adult: most had finished high school; a fair number had gone to and through college, while others had begun jobs or careers; one was in prison. Some had married or otherwise established enduring relationships; others were in interpersonal limbo. We know of no other study that has longitudinally charted developmental change in self-esteem in the same group of individuals through a time period so long and so developmentally consequential.

What can we now conclude or interpret from our analyses regarding the development of self-esteem during adolescence? Is an individual's sense of self-worth consistent through adolescence or does it exhibit substantial changes?

For the combined sample, the mean level of self-esteem did not change appreciably. Further, there was appreciable longitudinal ordering consistency of self-esteem across the ages 14 to 18, ages 18 to 23, and across the entire 9-year period; individuals relatively high (or low) in self-esteem at age 14 tend to be relatively high (or low) in self-esteem at ages 18 and 23 as well. The notable absence of appreciable age changes in self-esteem, coupled with evidence of considerable levels of longitudinal consistency, might suggest that self-esteem follows the developmental pattern of "sameness," defined by Block (1971) as strong across-time ordering correspondence together with no indication of changes in mean level (p. 62). For the combined sample, then, the results might be said to support the position that the social, emotional, and biological changes occurring during adolescence do not produce normative psychological disturbance.

The magnitude of the across-time correlations was far from unity, however. When more closely analyzed, the "sameness" observed in the combined sample over time did not characterize the developmental trajectories followed by very many of the individuals within the sample or when the combined sample was partitioned according to gender. Although the "average" individual in the total sample showed virtually no change whatsoever, the majority of subjects changed in self-esteem by more than one-half a standard deviation. Moreover, there was a decided tendency for males to increase and females to decrease in self-esteem from early adolescence to young adulthood. These gender differences in self-esteem change were significantly and meaningfully related to coherent patterns of personality in both the sample of girls and the sample of boys. These findings highlight the importance of *not presuming,* without explicit evaluation, that reliable individual differences in development do not exist or are not important.

The findings revealed a number of theoretically provocative differences between females and males. First, longitudinal consistency was appreciably less for males than for females across ages 14 to 23. One conjectural explanation for this observed sex difference stems from the differential socialization experienced by girls and by boys. J. H. Block (1973) noted that socialization processes tend to restrict the range of experience for girls but broaden it for boys. For example, boys are given autonomy earlier than girls and have less constrained opportunities for play outside the home (Hoffman, 1977; Saegert & Hart, 1976). These differences in socialization emphases may produce or permit more diversity in the developmental change patterns of boys as compared to girls. These developmental diversities would produce more changes in the rank-ordering of boys within their peer group, thus decreasing the longitudinal ordering consistency of their self-esteem over time.

Our longitudinal finding that boys tend to increase and girls to decrease in self-esteem during adolescence is consistent with cross-sectional research showing that there are more girls than boys with low self-esteem in early adolescence, and that this difference grows larger by late adolescence (Simmons & Rosenberg, 1975). Further supporting this pattern, girls tend to increase in depressive affect during adolescence, so that by late adolescence they exhibit more depressive affect than boys (Petersen, 1988). Future research, necessarily longitudinal, should attempt to clarify when and why these gender-divergent trends occur. Our own continuing analyses, which will identify, for the sexes separately, the contentual changes from early adolescence to early adulthood in self-images and ideal-self aspirations, may well help our understanding.

Within each gender group, we also examined the relation of prior personality characteristics to the subsequent direction and magnitude of developmental change. Overall, self-esteem change among females seems to be related to prior interpersonal qualities such as warmth and nurturance, whereas self-esteem change among males seems to be more strongly linked to prior self-focused characteristics such as ability to control personal anxiety level.

More generally, our findings suggest that self-esteem development is integrally related to gender differences in the way the cultural press of adolescence is responded to. Sex-role development has been characterized as the process of socializing females to be more communal and males to be more agentic (J. H. Block, 1973); in crasser terms, females are socialized to get along in society and males are socialized to get ahead. Our findings suggest that the ability to relate to other in an interpersonally positive way promotes self-esteem for females. For males, achieving positive interpersonal connections seems less critical; their sense of positive identity seems, instead, to centrally depend on the ability to control social anxiety, thereby enabling them to function effectively.

Finally, we examined whether self-esteem has the same personological implications at early adolescence, late adolescence, and early adulthood. The personality profile associated with self-esteem was quite consistent over time for females but changed dramatically for males. Although the personality characteristics associated with self-esteem in females and males were quite distinct at age 14, these characteristics became progressively more similar over time. Together, these two findings suggest that the introspective criteria for positive self-evaluation are appreciably transformed in the males over the following decade. Thus, in early adolescence and based on analyses to be reported in detail in a later article, boys who regarded themselves highly were characterized by observers as stern, meticulous, humorless, unexpressive individuals lacking in warmth, while the girls with self-esteem were evaluated as cheerful, sociable, expressive, assertive, decisive individuals. By age 23, the young men are radically reordered with regard to their sense of self-worth. The young men now with high self-esteem are much like the young women with high self-esteem in being internally and externally cheerful, interpersonally poised and functionally effective, and consequently somewhat dominant individuals. And yet, despite these impressive personality equivalences in the two sexes during a later and presumably developmentally more mature stage of self-esteem, young women still manifest a greater concern for and effectiveness in achieving intimate interpersonal ties than do young men. Informally, and for ages, women (and men) have had (and have rued) this perception of gender differences. The present study only demonstrates this long-recognized interpersonal asymmetry (Josselson, 1992, chap. 11).

Conclusion

In this study of self-esteem in adolescence and early adulthood, we have examined multiple types of normative developmental change, assessed developmental trends separately for females and males, and conducted person-centered analyses that elucidate the nature of and influences on individual developmental trajectories. Of course, the usual caveats regarding our longitudinal findings apply: our samples of males and of females, although more closely studied than is the case in most psychological inquiries, are nevertheless still relatively small and, conceivably, may be unrepresentative. We do not think our findings are especially sample-dependent, but only subsequent research with other samples can respond to this ineluctable concern.

These reservations having been expressed, the levels of consistency in self-esteem manifested by our longitudinally followed sample impress us as quite remarkable. We are equally impressed by the considerable evidence of developmental change. What then can be concluded about "consistency" and "change?" Like almost any psychological attribute, self-esteem changes in some ways and is continuous in other ways throughout the life course. However, it is too easy to resort to the homily that there is continuity amidst change and change amidst continuity. To go beyond this trivially true, blandly wise response to a simplistically posed question regarding consistency *versus* change, it is necessary to approach the problem in deeper, more differentiated ways. What is needed is further study of the ways in which individuals maintain continuity or change at different periods of their life and the concomitants, consequences, and antecedents of these continuities and changes.

Adolescent self-esteem has important ramifications, both for the developing individual and for society, and therefore warrants further research into the myriad influences—universal, gender-specific, and unique—that lead some individuals to feel good about themselves and others to feel worthless.

References

Abramowitz, R. H., Petersen, A. C., & Schulenberg, J. E. (1984). Changes in self-image during early adolescence. *New Directions for Mental Health Services*, **22**, 19–28.

Alsaker, F. D., & Olweus, D. (1992). Stability of global self-evaluations in early adolescence: A cohort longitudinal study. *Journal of Research on Adolescence*, **2**, 123–145.

Blatt, S. J., Quinlan, D. M., Chevron, E. S., McDonald, C., & Zuroff, D. (1982). Dependency and self-criticism: Psychological dimensions of depression. *Journal of Consulting and Clinical Psychology*, **50**, 113–124.

Block, J. (1956). A comparison of the forced and unforced Q-sorting procedures. *Educational and Psychological Measurement*, **16**, 481–493.

Block, J. (1961). *The Q-sort method in personality assessment and psychiatric research* (reprint ed. 1978). Palo Alto, CA: Consulting Psychologists Press.

Block, J. (1971). *Lives through time*. Berkeley, CA: Bancroft.

Block, J., Block, J. H., & Keyes, S. (1988). Longitudinally foretelling drug use in adolescence: Early childhood personality and environmental precursors. *Child Development*, **59**, 336–355.

Block, J., Gjerde, P. F., & Block, J. H. (1991). Personality antecedents of depressive tendencies in 18-year-olds: A prospective study. *Journal of Personality and Social Psychology*, **60**, 726–738.

Block, J., & Thomas, H. (1955). Is satisfaction with self a measure of adjustment? *Journal of Abnormal and Clinical Psychology*, **51**, 254–259.

Block, J. H. (1973). Conceptions of sex-roles: Some cross-cultural and longitudinal perspectives. *American Psychologist*, **28**, 512–526.

Block, J. H., & Block, J. (1980). The role of ego-control and ego-resiliency in the organization of behavior. In W. A. Collins (Ed.), *Minnesota symposium on child psychology* (Vol. **13**, pp. 39–101). Hillsdale, NJ: Erlbaum.

Blyth, D. A., Simmons, R. G., & Carlton-Ford, S. (1983). The adjustment of early adolescents to school transitions. *Journal of Early Adolescence*, **3**, 105–120.

Carlson, R. (1965). Stability and change in the adolescent's self-image. *Child Development*, **35**, 659–666.

Caspi, A., & Bem, D. (1990). Personality continuity and change across the life course. In L. A.

Pervin (Ed.), *Handbook of personality theory and research* (pp. 549–575). New York: Guilford.

Coleman, J. C. (1978). Current contradictions in adolescent theory. *Journal of Youth and Adolescence*, **7**, 1–11.

Cronbach, L. J., & Furby, L. (1970). How should we measure "change"—or should we? *Psychological Bulletin*, **74**, 68–80.

Douvan, E., & Adelson, J. (1966). *The adolescent experience*. New York: Wiley.

Dusek, J. B., & Flaherty, J. F. (1981). The development of the self-concept during adolescent years. *Monographs of the Society for Research in Child Development*, **46**(4, Serial No. 191).

Engel, M. (1959). The stability of the self-concept in adolescence. *Journal of Abnormal and Social Psychology*, **58**, 211–215.

Funder, D. C., & Block, J. (1989). The role of ego-control, ego-resiliency, and IQ in delay of gratification in adolescence. *Journal of Personality and Social Psychology*, **57**, 1041–1050.

Hall, G. S. (1904). *Adolescence* (2 vols.), New York: Appleton.

Harter, S. (1983). Developmental perspectives on the self-system. In E. M. Hetherington (Ed.), P. H. Mussen (Series Ed.), *Handbook of child psychology: Vol. 4. Socialization, personality, and social development* (pp. 275–385). New York: Wiley.

Higgins, E. T. (1987). Self-discrepancy: A theory relating self and affect. *Psychological Review*, **94**, 319–340.

Hill, J. P. (1985). Family relations in adolescence: Myths, realities, and new directions. *Genetic, Social, and General Psychology Monographs*, **111**, 233–248.

Hoffman, L. W. (1977). Changes in family roles, socialization, and sex differences. *American Psychologist*, **32**, 644–657.

Hoge, D. R., & McCarthy, J. D. (1983). Issues of validity and reliability in the use of real-ideal discrepancy scores to measure self-regard. *Journal of Personality and Social Psychology*, **44**, 1048–1055.

Hunter, J. E., & Schmidt, F. L. (1990). *Methods of meta-analysis: Correcting error and bias in research findings*. Newbury Park, CA: Sage.

James, W. (1890). *Principles of psychology*. New York: Holt.

Josselson, R. (1992). *The space between us: Exploring the dimensions of human relationships*. San Francisco: Jossey-Bass.

Keppel, G., & Zedeck, S. (1989). *Data analysis for research designs: Analysis of variance and multiple regression/correlation approaches*. New York: Freeman.

Kogan, N., & Block, J. (1991). Field dependence-independence from early childhood through adolescence: Personality and socialization aspects. In S. Wapner & J. Demick (Eds.), *Bio-psycho-social factors in the field dependence-independence cognitive style across the life span* (pp. 177–207). Hillsdale, NJ: Erlbaum.

Lazzari, R., Fioravanti, M., & Gough, H. G. (1978). A new scale for the adjective check list based on self versus ideal-self discrepancies. *Journal of Clinical Psychology*, **34**, 361–365.

Lord, F. M. (1956). The measurement of growth. *Educational and Psychological Measurement*, **16**, 421–437.

Magnusson, D. (1990). Personality development from an interactional perspective. In L. A. Pervin (Ed.), *Handbook of personality theory and research* (pp. 193–222). New York: Guilford.

McCarthy, J. D., & Hoge, D. R. (1982). Analysis of age effects in longitudinal studies of adolescent self-esteem. *Developmental Psychology*, **18**, 372–379.

Mendoza, J. L., Hart, D. E., & Powell, A. (1991). A bootstrap confidence interval based on a correlation corrected for range restriction. *Multivariate Behavioral Research*, **26**, 255–269.

Montemayor, R. (1983). Parents and adolescents in conflict: All families some of the time and some families most of the time. *Journal of Early Adolescence*, **3**, 83–103.

Mortimer, J. T., Finch, M. D., & Kumka, D. (1982). Persistence and change in development: The multidimensional self-concept. In P. B. Baltes & O. G. Brim, Jr. (Eds.), *Life span development and behavior* (Vol. **4**, pp. 263–313). New York: Academic Press.

Mortimer, J. T., & Lorence, J. (1981). Self-concept stability and change from late adolescence to adulthood. *Research in Community and Mental Health*, **2**, 5–42.

O'Connor, E. F., Jr. (1972). Extending classical test theory to the measurement of change. *Review of Educational Research*, **42**, 73–97.

Offer, D., & Offer, J. B. (1975). *From teenage to young manhood: A psychological study*. New York: Basic.

Offer, D., Ostrov, E., & Howard, K. (1981). *The adolescent: A psychological self-report*. New York: Basic.

O'Malley, P. M., & Bachman, J. G. (1983). Self-esteem: Change and stability between ages 13 and 23. *Developmental Psychology*, **19**, 257–268.

Ozer, D., & Block, J. (1987, April). *Personality and IQ change from childhood through adolescence*. Paper presented at the meetings of the Society for Research in Child Development, Baltimore, MD.

Pelham, B. W., & Swann, W. B. (1989). From self-conceptions to self-worth: On the sources and structure of global self-esteem. *Journal of Personality and Social Psychology*, **57**, 672–680.

Petersen, A. C. (1988). Adolescent development. *Annual Review of Psychology*, **39**, 583–607.

Rogers, C. R., & Dymond, R. F. (1954). *Psychotherapy and personality change*. Chicago: University of Chicago Press.

Rosenberg, M. (1965). *Society and the adolescent self-image*. Princeton, NJ: Princeton University Press.

Rutter, M., Graham, P., Chadwick, O. F. D., & Yule, W. (1976). Adolescent turmoil: Fact or fiction? *Journal of Child Psychology and Psychiatry*, **17**, 35–36.

Saegert, S., & Hart, R. (1976). The development of sex differences in the environmental competence of children. In P. Burnett (Ed.), *Women in society* (pp. 87–116). Chicago: Maaroufa.

Savin-Williams, R. C., & Demo, D. H. (1984). Developmental change and stability in adolescent self-concept. *Developmental Psychology*, **20**, 1100–1110.

Simmons, R. G., & Blyth, D. A. (1987). *Moving into adolescence*. New York: Aldine De Gruyter.

Simmons, R. G., & Rosenberg, F. (1975). Sex, sex roles, and self-image. *Journal of Youth and Adolescence*, **4**, 229–258.

Stephenson, W. (1953). *The study of behavior: Q-technique and its methodology*. Chicago: University of Chicago Press.

Turner, R. H., & Vanderlippe, R. H. (1958). Self-ideal congruence as an index of adjustment. *Journal of Abnormal and Social Psychology*, **57**, 494–498.

JOURNAL OF RESEARCH ON ADOLESCENCE, 5(4), 451–467

Factors Related to Self-Esteem Among African American Youths: A Secondary Analysis of the High/Scope Perry Preschool Data

Tom Luster and Harriette Pipes McAdoo
Department of Family and Child Ecology
Michigan State University

Data from the Perry Preschool study on 121 African American adolescents were used to explore the correlates of self-esteem. Consistent with Harter's (1990) theoretical integration of the perspectives of William James and Charles Cooley, we expected African American adolescents to be high in self-esteem if they experienced success in areas that were important to them and if they perceived that significant others held them in high regard. Specifically, higher self-esteem scores were expected for youths who had graduated from high school, had positive experiences in school, were moving toward economic self-sufficiency, had positive relationships with their families, and perceived that their families approved of them and what they were doing. The data were consistent with the hypothesis that the effects of the teens' accomplishments and others' appraisals of them are additive.

Adolescent self-esteem is an important developmental outcome that reflects past experience and has implications for future functioning (Mecca, Smelser, & Vasconcellos, 1989). High self-esteem is an indicator of good mental health, and there is some evidence that high self-esteem may be a protective factor for children and adolescents exposed to multiple risk factors (Dubow & Luster, 1990; Rutter, 1987; Werner, 1985). This study examines factors related to individual differences in

Requests for reprints should be sent to Tom Luster, Department of Family and Child Ecology, 101 Morrill Hall, Michigan State University, East Lansing, MI 48824–1030.

self-esteem among African American youths, all of whom were from low socioeconomic status families.

The data used for this study are from the High/Scope Perry Preschool study in Ypsilanti, Michigan. The Perry Preschool children were first studied as disadvantaged preschoolers and follow-up assessments and interviews have been conducted at regular intervals since the start of the study. Self-esteem was assessed when the subjects were 19 years of age; there were marked differences among the Perry Study adolescents in their feelings of self-worth at that time. The central question addressed in this study is: What factors are related to these individual differences in self-esteem? Given that all of these youths would be considered "at risk" for low achievement based on their family backgrounds and early assessments, we are particularly interested in the subsample of youths who had high levels of self-esteem. What set them apart from their peers?

The study of self-esteem has a long history. As Harter (1988) pointed out, the roots of current thinking about the antecedents of global self-esteem can be traced to James (1892) and Cooley (1902). Harter (1988) summarized the difference between the perspectives of Cooley and James succinctly in the following passage:

> For Cooley, the self represented the internalized opinions that we perceive others to hold of us. *Acceptance* and *positive regard* from *others*, therefore, was an important source of one's sense of worth as a person. For James, the evaluation of one's *competence*, one's *achievements*, was a primary determinant of self-worth. More specifically, he postulated that displays of competence in those areas where it was *important* to be *successful* were the most critical to one's overall self-esteem. (pp. 67–68)

Both Harter (1988) and Rosenberg (1979) proposed that Cooley's and James' positions are not antithetical and, rather than thinking of their theories as competing theories, it seems likely that both our beliefs about how positively others perceive us (i.e., reflected appraisals) and our accomplishments in areas considered important are likely to influence our global assessment of self-esteem in an additive way. Rosenberg and others (e.g., Festinger, 1954; Pettigrew, 1967) also emphasized the importance of social comparisons in forming judgments about self-worth. How one feels about oneself is likely to be influenced by how one's competencies and accomplishments compare to others who are used as a reference group.

Much of the research on the self-esteem of African American children and youth has compared their average level of self-esteem with the average for a comparison group of Whites. As Rosenberg (1979) pointed out, both theorists who emphasized the importance of reflected appraisals in the development of self-esteem and those who emphasized social comparison processes expected African American children to have lower levels of self-esteem than White children. Reflected appraisal theorists expected that the negative attitudes of the majority population toward African Americans would be incorporated into African American children's judgments about their self-worth, with the result being relatively low levels of self-esteem. These theorists tended to overestimate the influence of attitudes of people outside the African American community and to underestimate the importance of the reflected appraisal of people in the children's immediate environment, such as parents and other family members. Moreover, these researchers tended to disregard the role of the family in mediating derogatory racial attitudes for their children and instilling in their children a positive sense of ethnic identity (Harrison, 1985). Hypotheses based on the social comparison position held that African American children and youth would have lower levels of self-esteem because they were more likely than White children to come from poor families, to perform poorly in school, and to live in single parent families that were stigmatized by society.

As Rosenberg (1979) noted, much of this research on African American children's self-esteem was based on questionable assumptions (e.g., who African American children use for reference groups) and the data did not support these hypotheses. African American children and adolescents do not have lower levels of self-esteem than White children and adolescents (Cross, 1985, 1991; Graham, 1994; Harrison, 1985; McAdoo, 1985; Rosenberg, 1979; Spencer, 1988; Whaley, 1993).

Rather than focusing on differences in self-esteem between African Americans and Whites, we believe that a more fruitful line of research is to examine factors that contribute to individual differences in self-esteem among African Americans (Graham, 1994). Consistent with Rosenberg's (1979) and Harter's (1988) views, we believe that the theoretical positions of Cooley (1902), James (1892), and the social comparison theorists are germane for studying individual differences in self-esteem among African American youth and should not be dismissed on the basis of the earlier research just described. However, an exploration of the correlates of self-esteem is likely to be more revealing if the focus is on proximal forces (e.g., approval from the family, accomplishments in school relative to classmates) rather than distal forces (e.g., societal attitudes, the school performance of White students outside the community). Put another way, thought must be given to who the significant others are for African American youth (Hughes & Demo, 1989; Rosenberg, 1979).

Consistent with Cooley's (1902) "looking-glass self" (p. 184) conception of the origins of self-esteem, we expected that parents and other family members would be significant influences on the self-esteem of

African American adolescents. If parents convey to their adolescents, either directly or indirectly, that they approve of them and hold them in high regard, this positive appraisal should be reflected in the teens' feelings of self-worth. Harter (1988) found that children between the ages of 10 and 13 who were high in self-esteem perceived that their parents accepted them, supported them, and held them in high regard. Using data from a national sample of African Americans, Hughes and Demo (1989) reported that supportive family relationships were also important for high self-esteem in adulthood.

As James (1892) and others have argued (Harter, 1990; Rutter, 1987), another factor that is likely to influence self-esteem is the degree to which youths are successful in accomplishing important tasks. For most adolescents, the school is one of the most important contexts, aside from the home, that has the potential to influence feelings of worth. In a sample of African American seventh graders, Cauce (1987) found objective indicators of school performance (i.e., grade point average [GPA] and standardized test scores) to be predictive of perceived school competence and feelings of general self-worth. In contrast, Demo and Parker (1987) reported that there was no relation between GPA and global self-esteem among African Americans attending a university. Others have argued that school success may be unrelated to self-esteem among low income African American youth or that those who drop out of school might have higher levels of self-esteem than those who remain in school (Whaley, 1993). Although past research has produced inconsistent results, we expected to find that the Perry Preschool study youths who were successful students (i.e., high achievement test scores, good grades) and who graduated from high school by age 19 would be higher in self-esteem than those who experienced less success in school.

Academic success in school may not be the only way in which the school context contributes to individual differences in self-esteem. Some adolescents who are not stellar students may nevertheless derive satisfaction from other experiences in school. Quinton and Rutter (1988) found that positive experiences in school, broadly defined, were associated with surprisingly favorable outcomes in adulthood among women who had experienced family disruption and institutional rearing in childhood. One possible mechanism—proposed by Quinton and Rutter to explain their results—was that positive experiences in school contributed to high self-esteem, which, in turn, influenced the way the women negotiated the challenges of early adulthood. We know of no other studies that have systematically explored the relation between positive experiences in school and adolescent self-esteem. Data from the Perry Preschool project were available to examine this relation.

The final factor included in this study was the degree to which the youth were self-supporting at age 19. Recently, Harter (1990) proposed that factors that are important in one's self-evaluation are related to age-related developmental tasks. Moving toward financial independence is a developmental task associated with early adulthood; it seems likely that many 19-year-olds would attach some importance to accomplishments in that area. This seems especially likely in African American communities, where rates of unemployment for young adults are often high. Therefore, adolescents who are coping successfully with the task of self-sufficiency were expected to be higher in self-esteem than adolescents who are experiencing less success in that area. Earlier research showed that African American adults tended to have higher levels of self-esteem if they were employed (Hughes & Demo, 1989).

In summary, it is assumed that level of self-esteem, like most other developmental outcomes, has multiple determinants. The factors that influence self-esteem are likely to depend on the developmental tasks with which individuals are dealing at different ages (Harter, 1990). In addition, contextual factors (e.g., family, school, and community characteristics) are likely to influence the way in which developmental tasks are approached and mastered and the reference groups individuals use for assessing accomplishments and self-worth. Several factors that may be related to individual differences in self-esteem during late adolescence are examined in this study. Higher self-esteem scores were expected for youths who had graduated from high school, had positive experiences in school, were moving toward economic self-sufficiency, had positive relationships with their families, and perceived that their families approved of them and what they were doing. In other words, we expected to find support for both the Cooley (1902) and the James (1892) perspectives on the antecedents of self-esteem. Consistent with Harter's (1990) research, we expected the effects of accomplishments and others' appraisals to be additive. Teens are most likely to be high in self-esteem if they are competent in areas that are important to them and if they perceive that significant others think highly of them.

METHOD

Subjects

The Perry Preschool sample includes 123 subjects who were born between 1958 and 1962 and resided in a neighborhood served by the Perry Elementary School in Ypsilanti, Michigan. Ypsilanti is situated close to Detroit, and the economy of the community is dependent to a large degree on the automotive industry. The Perry Elementary School is located on the south side of the city in a predominantly African American neighborhood.

Each child in the study was randomly assigned to attend preschool or to be in a no-preschool control group. The study included 5 cohorts of children who were enrolled in the study from 1962 to 1965. (Two cohorts were recruited in 1962—a group of 4-year-olds and a group of 3-year-olds.) At age 19, those who had attended preschool did not differ significantly from those in the control group in terms of average level of self-esteem.

All of the children in the sample were African American and came from low socioeconomic status (SES) families, as indicated by parental educational level. The average levels of education of the mothers and fathers were 9.4 and 8.6 years, respectively. None of the mothers and only one of the fathers had education beyond high school. The father was present in 53% of the homes at the start of the study and in 46% of the homes at the age 15 follow-up interview. The children had, on average, four siblings at the start of the study.

Fifty-nine percent of the children were male, and 47% attended preschool. At entry, all of the children had Stanford–Binet IQ scores between 60 and 90 ($M = 79$). Comparisons of children and their families in the preschool and control samples showed that the two groups were comparable at the start of the study. Further information on sample characteristics, recruitment, and the effects of the preschool program can be found in earlier publications (Berrueta-Clement, Schweinhart, Barnett, Epstein, & Weikart, 1984; Schweinhart & Weikart, 1980).

Attrition

Relative to other longitudinal studies, the attrition rate in the Perry Preschool study has been low. All but two of the original 123 subjects participated in the 19-year follow-up interview and completed the self-esteem measure. Berrueta-Clement et al. (1984) reported that the median rate of missing data across all measures through age 19 was only 5%. The highest rates of missing data tend to be found for variables concerning the fathers of the subjects. For example, at the age 15 interview, subjects were asked about how close they were to their fathers and data are missing for 56% of the cases on that variable.

Measures

Self-esteem. The outcome of interest in this article, self-esteem, is measured with Rosenberg's (1965) global self-esteem measure. The 10 items of the measure are summed to produce a total score, with higher scores indicating high self-esteem. The mean score for this sample was 30.9 (*SD* = 4.0) and the range was 22 to 40. Cronbach's alpha for this sample was .81. In addition to being used as a continuous variable, self-esteem was converted to a dichotomous variable for some analyses by dividing the sample at the median (*mdn* = 31). Those with scores below the median were designated the low self-esteem group (48.8%), whereas those at or above the median were assigned to the high self-esteem group. The use of the dichotomous outcome variable allowed us to explore further the extent to which various factors (e.g., high school completion) are associated with successful outcomes (i.e., high self-esteem) in African American adolescents from low SES families.

Family support and approval at age 19. The relationship between the youth and his or her family was assessed with three questions at the 19-year interview: (a) How have you been getting along with your family? (on a 3-point scale ranging from 1 [*not too good]* to 3 *[great, no problems]*); (b) How does your family feel about how you are doing? (on a 3-point scale ranging from 1 [*not doing anything worth much*] to 3 [*doing great*]); and (c) Are you turning out to be the kind of person your family expected? (on a 3-point scale ranging from 1 [*not doing as well as expected*] to 3 [*doing better than expected*]). High scores indicate support and approval from the family. A standard score was computed for each of the items, and the three items were then summed to produce an overall score of family support and approval (α = .63).

Family relationships at age 15. At the 15-year follow-up, the teens were asked about how close they felt to their mothers and their fathers. Responses were rated on a 4-point scale ranging from 1 (*not very close*) to 4 (*extremely close*). High scores indicate close relationships. The parent who was interviewed was also asked how close she or he was to the youth. Responses ranged on a 4-point scale from 1 (*not close*) to 4 (*very close*), with high scores indicating greater closeness. The youths were also asked if they were the kind of people that their parents would like them to be. Responses were coded on a 5-point scale ranging from 1 (*never*) to 5 (*always*).

Success in school. Several indicators of success in school were available for this study. Indicators from high school were graduation from high school and GPA. Seventy of the 121 subjects had graduated from high school by age 19 (58%). During the elementary-school years, children were given the California Achievement Tests, and total scores from these assessments are used as indicators of academic performance. They were also given the Stanford–Binet each year from the time they entered the study as preschoolers through the fourth grade and the Wechsler Intelligence Scale for Children (WISC) at the end of the eighth grade.

Positive experiences in school. At the 19-year interview, the youths were asked several questions about their experiences in high school. Seven items were summed to produce the positive experiences in school scale ($\alpha = .81$). Sample items include: (a) Did you feel that you were really part of the school, that you really belonged?; (b) How important was high school to you as a place to be with your friends?; and (c) How many of your high school teachers seemed to really care about students? Each of the seven items was scored on a 3-point scale; higher scores indicate more positive experiences.

Degree of economic independence. The degree to which the youths were self-supporting at age 19 was assessed with a single item: Are you presently supporting yourself on your own earnings and/or those of your spouse? The three possible responses were: (a) *not at all,* (b) *somewhat,* and (c) *completely.* At the 19-year follow-up, 41% of the youths were employed, 52% were not currently working but held a job in the past, and 7% had never been employed.[1]

RESULTS

The extent to which family relationships at age 19 predicted self-esteem scores was examined first. Youths who perceived that their families approved of them and what they were doing tended to have relatively high self-esteem scores (see Table 1 for zero-order correlations). To illustrate this finding in another analysis, the youths were divided into low and high groups based on their self-esteem scores. Sixty-four percent of those who were at or above the median on the family support and approval measure were in the high self-esteem group, compared to 43% of those who received less support and approval from family members, $\chi^2(1, N = 121) = 7.93, p < .05$. The coefficient of contingency was .25.

---

[1]By the age 19 interview, 19 of the youths had attended college and 17 had vocational training. Sixty-nine percent of those who attended college or vocational school indicated that they were somewhat or completely self-supporting, compared to 42% of those who did not have any schooling beyond high school. The 11 youths with postsecondary education who were not self-supporting at all could be viewed as moving toward economic self-sufficiency, but for the purposes of this analysis were classified as not self-supporting.

TABLE 1
Family Relationships and Self-Esteem

Family Relationships	*Correlation With Self-Esteem*	*M*	*SD*
Age 19 interview			
Family approval and support	.40*	0.00	2.27
Age 15 interview			
Closeness to mother	.22*	3.66	0.67
Closeness to father	.24†	2.93	0.93
Parent closeness to teen	.11	3.65	0.54
Kind of person parents want you to be	.25*	3.56	1.27

*$p < .05$. †$p < .10$.

Family relationships at age 15 were also related to self-esteem at age 19. Adolescents who reported feeling closer to their parents and who believed they were the kind of person their parents wanted them to be tended to have higher self-esteem scores. Only 52 of the teens responded to the items on perceived closeness for both mothers and fathers, largely because of missing data for the fathers. When responses for these two items were summed for these 52 teens, the correlation with self-esteem 4 years later was .32 ($p < .05$). In contrast, parents' reports of their closeness to the adolescents at age 15 were not a significant predictor of adolescent self-esteem at age 19. Thus, although the correlations were modest in magnitude, the findings are consistent with the view that levels of self-esteem among African American youths are influenced by the degree to which they perceive that they receive approval and support from family members.

The relation between success in school and self-esteem was examined next. Two indicators of success in high school were used: high school completion and overall GPA. Contrary to expectations, GPA was unrelated to self-esteem, but those who graduated from high school tended to be higher in self-esteem (see Table 2 for zero-order correlations). When self-esteem was used as a dichotomous variable, cross-tabulations revealed that 69% of the graduates, but only 28% of the nongraduates, were in the high self-esteem group, $\chi^2(1, N = 121) = 19.97$, $p < .05$. The coefficient of contingency was .38.

Across the elementary years, positive correlations between scores on the California Achievement Test and adolescent self-esteem were found. The correlations tended to be modest in magnitude, but most were statistically significant. The correlation between Stanford–Binet scores at entry into the study and adolescent self-esteem was not significant ($r = .09$). The correlations between Stanford–Binet IQ from kindergarten through fourth grade and adolescent self-esteem ranged from .34 to .28 and were statistically significant. Youths who scored

TABLE 2
Scholastic Success and Self-Esteem

Scholastic Success	*Correlation With Self-Esteem*	*M*	*SD*
High school accomplishments			
High school graduation	.38*	1.55	.50
Overall GPA	.00	1.89	.70
CAT scores: Elementary grades			
CAT total grade 8	.15	108.80	41.00
CAT total grade 4	.36*	212.78	78.84
CAT total grade 1	.24*	90.35	39.11
Intelligence test scores			
WISC grade 8	.21*	80.86	11.00
Stanford-Binet grade 4	.28*	84.80	11.19
Stanford-Binet grade 1	.34*	89.34	11.14
Experiences in school			
Positive experiences in high school	.35*	13.93	3.84

Note. GPA = grade point average. CAT = California Achievement Test. WISC = Wechsler Intelligence Scale for Children.
*$p < .05$.

higher on the WISC at age 14 also tended to have higher self-esteem scores at age 19. Thus, looking across the various indicators of cognitive ability, children who were more successful students as indicated by achievement tests, IQ tests, and high school graduation tended to have more positive feelings of self-worth by age 19 than did children who experienced less success.

The extent to which the teens had positive experiences while in high school was also evaluated. Adolescents who reported more positive experiences in school tended to be higher in self-esteem, $r = .35$, $p < .05$. In an additional analysis, the sample was divided at the median on the positive experiences in school scale, and the association between this dichotomous measure and the dichotomous self-esteem measure was examined. Sixty-six percent of the youths who had positive experiences in school were high in self-esteem compared to 34% of those with less positive experiences, $\chi^2 = 12.01(1, N = 120)$, $p < .05$. The coefficient of contingency was .30. Other aspects of school life, such as whether the teen had belonged to a club or organization or had been involved in sports, were not directly related to self-esteem. However, teens who were involved in these extracurricular activities reported having more positive experiences in school than those who did not participate.

As one would expect, those who graduated from high school tended to report that they had had more positive experiences in school than those who dropped out (15.1 vs. 12.5), $t = -3.80$, $p < .05$. Given that high school completion and positive experiences in school are confounded, further analysis was done to determine the influence of positive experiences on self-esteem for the subsample of youths who did not finish high school by age 19. Almost half (47%) of the nongraduates who had had positive experiences in school were high in self-esteem. Only 13% of those who had not completed high school and who had not had positive experiences in school were high in self-esteem, $\chi^2 = 7.27(1, N = 50)$, $p < .05$. For this cross-tabulation, the coefficient of contingency was .36.

Another potential predictor of self-esteem that was of interest was the degree to which the adolescents were economically self-supporting at age 19. As expected, teens who were moving toward economic self-sufficiency tended to be higher in self-esteem, $r = .31$, $p < .05$. Sixty-eight percent of those who were somewhat or completely self-supporting were high in self-esteem compared to 34% who were not self-supporting at all, $\chi^2 = 13.92(1, N = 121)$, $p < .05$. The coefficient of contingency was .32.

A one-way analysis of variance (ANOVA), employing a Tukey-B multiple comparison procedure, indicated that the average level of self-esteem of those who were currently employed (32.4) was higher than the average level of those who were employed at one time but were not currently employed (30.2). Those who were employed at one time but were not currently employed, in turn, had higher levels of self-esteem than those who had never held a job (27.2), $F = 8.61$, $p < .05$.

Multiple Influences on Self-Esteem

Both Rosenberg (1979) and Harter (1990) have argued that global self-esteem is likely to be influenced by multiple factors. According to Harter (1990), the number of factors that come into play increases from childhood to adolescence, and domain-specific evaluations collectively influence global self-esteem. Although data were lacking to assess the adolescents' feelings of self-worth in all relevant domains, an attempt was made to assess the collective impact of family approval, success in school, positive experiences in school, and movement toward economic self-sufficiency. We expected that adolescents who experienced success in several areas would be much more likely to be high in self-esteem than adolescents who generally had less positive experiences in these areas. To test this hypothesis, a 5-point index was created. A subject received a score of one for each of the following: (a) graduating from high school, (b) being somewhat or completely self-supporting, (c) having a high score on the positive experiences in school scale (median split), and (d) perceiving that their families were supportive and held them in high regard (median split). Thus, scores on the index ranged from zero to four. The percentage of youths at each level of the index was: zero (18%), one (13%), two (24%), three (32%), and four (14%). All of the measures used in creating the index were based on data collected at the age 19 interview.

The percentage of youths with high self-esteem at each level of the index was then determined; there was a very clear relation between scores on the index and the probability of being in the high self-esteem group. Only 10% of the youths with a score of zero on the index were in the high self-esteem group, compared to 82% of the youths with a score of four (see Figure 1). For youths with intermediate scores of one to three on the index, the percentage with high self-esteem scores was 27%, 45%, and 74% respectively. The chi-square statistic for this analysis was 32.96, $p < .05$, and the coefficient of contingency was .46.

Multiple regression analysis produced results consistent with those just presented. Self-esteem, treated as a continuous measure, was used as the dependent variable. Graduation from high school, degree of economic independence, scores on the positive experiences in school scale, and the youth's perceptions of family support and approval at age 19 were entered simultaneously as predictor variables. Together, the four predictor variables accounted for 30% of the variance in self-esteem scores, $F(4, 115) = 12.36$, $p < .05$. The standardized betas in order of magnitude were: (a) perceptions of parental support and approval

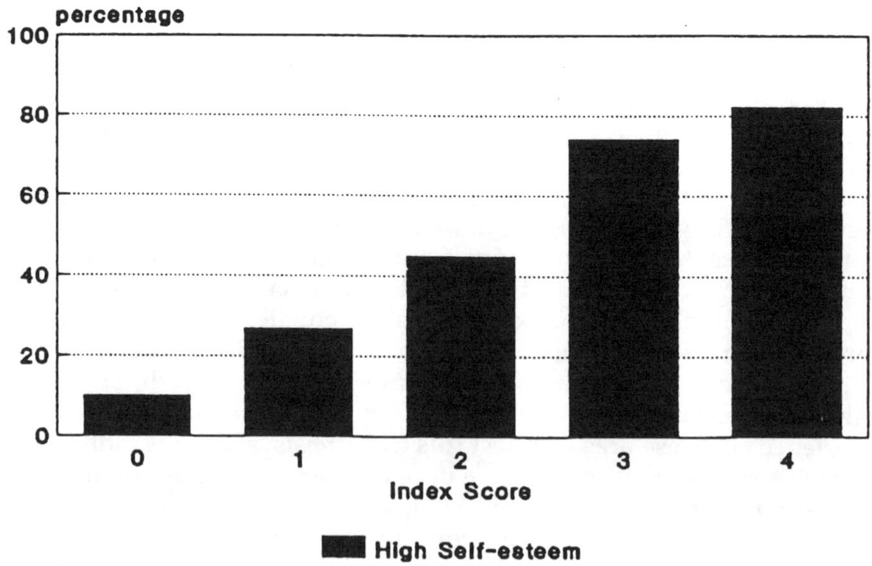

FIGURE 1 Multiple influences on self-esteem.

(.27), (b) high school graduation (.22), (c) positive experiences in school (.18), and (d) economic self-sufficiency (.16). The *t* values for the regression coefficients were significant at the .05 level for family approval and high school completion, and approached significance for positive experiences in school, $t = 1.94$, $p = .05$, and economic self-sufficiency, $t = 1.99$, $p = .05$.

DISCUSSION

The central question addressed in this study was: What factors are related to individual differences in self-esteem among African American adolescents from low SES families? Drawing on the work of Harter (1988), we expected that both the theoretical positions of James (1892) and Cooley (1902) would be useful for understanding individual differences in self-esteem. Consistent with James's emphasis on achievement and competence, we expected to find that adolescents who had successfully completed high school and were moving toward economic independence would tend to be high in self-esteem. The data were consistent with these hypotheses. High school graduates were over twice as likely to be in the high self-esteem group as nongraduates. Likewise, adolescents who were moving toward economic independence were twice as likely as those who depended upon others for economic support to be high in self-esteem.

Consistent with Cooley's (1902) conception of the antecedents of self-esteem, we expected to find the youths' perceptions of the degree of acceptance and support they received from parents and other family members to be predictive of self-esteem. Positive relationships with parents and other family members at age 15 and age 19 were associated with relatively high levels of self-esteem. Despite the hardships associated with poverty, many poor African American parents provide high levels of nurturance for their children and their children flourish with this support. Unfortunately, researchers seldom focus on the positive contributions that poor African American families make to their children's development, and this may contribute to negative stereotypes about African American families.

According to Cooley (1902) and Mead (1934), it is not only parents' approval that influences self-esteem, but also the approval of others. For adolescents, one would expect approval from peers to be important as well. Unfortunately, there were few data available from this data set to explore this possibility. Harter (1988) found in her work that both approval from parents and from peers are related to children's feelings of self-worth.

Given that global self-esteem is likely to be influenced by a host of factors during adolescence (Harter, 1990), there were several other potential influences that merited consideration but that could not be examined because of the constraints of the data set. Among these were the adolescents' sense of ethnic identity, success in establishing intimate relationships with significant others, physical appearance, and athletic competence.

In addition to accomplishments and relationships, positive experiences in school, a potential influence on self-esteem that was suggested by Quinton and Rutter (1988), were examined in this study. To our knowledge, this is the first study to examine systematically the relation between these variables. The data provided support for Quinton and Rutter's hypothesis that those who had positive experiences in school would be higher in self-esteem. Of particular interest was the finding that positive experiences were associated with higher levels of self-esteem among those who dropped out of school. This reinforces the view that schools influence more than children's understanding of academic subjects (e.g., math). Schools are also important contexts for acquiring information about the self. These results suggest that this is an area that merits further study. Additional research is needed to learn more about what kinds of experiences in school contribute to feelings of self-worth and what kinds of schools provide these experiences. In addition, are positive experiences in school particularly important for adolescents from low SES neighborhoods, or are they equally valuable for adolescents from more affluent neighborhoods? To date, we know too little about how schools influence self-concept, but we suspect that schools that provide many ways for students to experience success (not just academic success) help children from low income neighborhoods to cope with the risks they face by bolstering feelings of self-worth and self-efficacy.

Because all of the findings from this study are correlational, obviously, appropriate caution must be used in interpreting the results. Although the data are consistent with the hypotheses, no causal relations can be determined. Indeed, a reasonable argument could be made that high self-esteem may contribute to one's move toward economic independence, rather than being the result of economic self-sufficiency, especially in light of Harter's (1990) work linking self-esteem to motivation and depression. More likely is the possibility that the relationship is bidirectional; high self-esteem may motivate one to persist in seeking employment, and success at finding employment may, in turn, contribute to feelings of accomplishment and positive self-worth. Another important caveat involves the sample; the Perry sample was comprised only of African American youth from low SES families who lived in predominantly African American neighborhoods. Therefore, the extent to which the findings from this study would generalize to African American youths from more affluent families or African American youths who live in predominantly White neighborhoods is not known. Rosenberg (1979) found that African American children who lived in predominantly White neighborhoods in Baltimore tended to have somewhat lower levels of self-esteem, on average, than their peers who resided in predominantly African American neighborhoods. Others, however, found no relation between interracial contact and self-esteem among African Americans (Hare, 1980; Hughes & Demo, 1989).

Although this study contributes to our understanding of the correlates of self-esteem among low income African American adolescents, there is still much that needs to be accomplished in this area of research. In particular, more research is needed to determine to what extent and for what types of outcomes high self-esteem is a protective factor for African American youth exposed to multiple risks. In addition, there is a need to examine other factors (e.g., physical appearance, acceptance by peers, success in athletics and other endeavors) that may contribute to individual differences in self-esteem among African American youth; ideally, these additional factors would be examined in a study that also includes the type of factors assessed in this study (e.g., family approval, school success). Finally, we believe that it is important for researchers to learn more about the relations between experiences in school and self-esteem. We need to look beyond whether children are successful in academic tasks to understand other possible mechanisms by which schools influence adolescent self-concept.

ACKNOWLEDGMENTS

This study was funded by a grant through the High/Scope Educational Research Foundation from the Ford Foundation and the U.S. Administration for Children, Youth and Families.

We are thankful to Stephen Small for his advice on this project.

REFERENCES

Berrueta-Clement, J. R., Schweinhart, L. J., Barnett, W. S., Epstein, A. S., & Weikart, D. P. (1984). *Changed lives: The effects of the Perry Preschool program on youths through age 19.* Ypsilanti, MI: The High/Scope Press.

Cauce, A. M. (1987). School and peer competence in early adolescence: A test of domain-specific self-perceived competence. *Developmental Psychology, 23,* 287–291.

Cooley, C. H. (1902). *Human nature and the social order.* New York: Scribner's.
Cross, W. E. (1985). Black identity: Rediscovering the distinction between personal identity and reference group orientation. In M. B. Spencer, G. K. Brookins, & W. R. Allen (Eds.), *Beginnings: The social and affective development of Black children* (pp. 155–171). Hillsdale, NJ: Lawrence Erlbaum Associates, Inc.
Cross, W. E. (1991). *Shades of Black: Diversity in African-American identity.* Philadelphia, PA: Temple University Press.
Demo, D. H., & Parker, K. D. (1987). Academic achievement and self-esteem among black and white college students. *The Journal of Social Psychology, 127,* 345–355.
Dubow, E. F., & Luster, T. (1990). Adjustment of children born to teenage mothers: The contribution of risk and protective factors. *Journal of Marriage and the Family, 52,* 393–404.
Festinger, L. (1954). A theory of social comparison processes. *Human Relations, 7,* 117–140.
Graham, S. (1994). Motivation in African Americans. *Review of Educational Research, 64,* 55–117.
Hare, B. R. (1980). Self-perception and academic achievement: Variations in a desegregated setting. *American Journal of Psychiatry, 137,* 683–689.
Harrison, A. O. (1985). The Black family's socializing environment: Self-esteem and ethnic attitude among Black children. In H. P. McAdoo & J. L. McAdoo (Eds.), *Black children: Social, educational, and parental environments* (pp. 174–193). Newbury Park, CA: Sage.
Harter, S. (1988). Developmental processes in the construction of the self. In T. D. Yawkey & J. E. Johnson (Eds.), *Integrative processes and socialization: Early to middle childhood* (pp. 45–78). Hillsdale, NJ: Lawrence Erlbaum Associates, Inc.
Harter, S. (1990). Causes, correlates and the functional role of global self-worth: A life-span perspective. In R. Sternberg & J. Kolligian (Eds.), *Competence considered* (pp. 67–97). New Haven, CT: Yale University Press.
Hughes, M., & Demo, D. H. (1989). Self-perceptions of black Americans: Self-esteem and personal efficacy. *American Journal of Sociology, 95,* 132–159.
James, W. (1892). *Psychology: The briefer course.* New York: Holt, Rinehart & Winston.
McAdoo, H. P. (1985). Racial attitude and self-concept of young Black children over time. In H. P. McAdoo & J. L. McAdoo (Eds.), *Black children: Social, educational, and parental environments* (pp. 213–242). Newbury Park, CA: Sage.
Mead, G. H. (1934). *Mind, self, and society.* Chicago: University of Chicago Press.
Mecca, A. M., Smelser, N. J., & Vasconcellos, J. (Eds.) (1989). *The social importance of self-esteem.* Berkeley: University of California Press.
Pettigrew, T. F. (1967). Social evaluation theory: Convergences and applications. In D. Levine (Ed.), *Nebraska symposium on motivation* (pp. 241–311). Lincoln: University of Nebraska Press.
Quinton, D., & Rutter, M. (1988). *Parenting breakdown: The making and breaking of inter-generational links.* Aldershot, England: Avebury.
Rosenberg, M. (1965). *Society and the adolescent self-image.* Princeton, NJ: Princeton University Press.
Rosenberg, M. (1979). *Conceiving the self.* New York: Basic Books.
Rutter, M. (1987). Psychosocial resilience and protective mechanisms. *American Journal of Orthopsychiatry, 57,* 316–329.
Schweinhart, L. J., & Weikart, D. P. (1980). *Young children grow up: The effects of the Perry Preschool program on youths through age 15.* Ypsilanti, MI: The High/Scope Press.
Spencer, M. B. (1988). Self-concept development. In D. T. Slaughter (Ed.), *Black children and poverty: A developmental perspective* (pp. 59–72). San Francisco: Jossey-Bass.

Whaley, A. L. (1993). Self-esteem, cultural identity, and psychosocial adjustment in African American children. *Journal of Black Psychology, 19*, 406–422.
Werner, E. E. (1985). Stress and protective factors in children's lives. In A. R. Nicol (Ed.), *Longitudinal studies in child psychology and psychiatry* (pp. 335–355). New York: Wiley.

Received January 14, 1994
Revision received May 31, 1994
Accepted August 2, 1994

Self-Concept, Self-Esteem, and Body Attitudes among Japanese Male and Female Adolescents

Richard M. Lerner
Pennsylvania State University

Saburo Iwawaki
Chukyo University

Takashi Chihara
Shiga University

Gwendolyn T. Sorell
Pennsylvania State University

LERNER, RICHARD M.; IWAWAKI, SABURO; CHIHARA, TAKASHI; and SORELL, GWENDOLYN T. *Self-Concept, Self-Esteem, and Body Attitudes among Japanese Male and Female Adolescents.* CHILD DEVELOPMENT, 1980, **51**, 847–855. The nature of and interrelations among Japanese male and female adolescents' self-concepts, self-esteems, and ratings of bodily physical attractiveness and physical effectiveness were assessed in a cross-sectional study of 796 Japanese (50.4% female) ranging in educational level from seventh grade through college senior. In comparison to American adolescent data sets, Japanese adolescents are found to have lower self-esteems (more so for females than males), and less favorable views of their bodies' attractiveness and effectiveness. Moreover, sex differences in self-concept account for more variance in the Japanese cohorts than they do in comparative American ones. However, the few instances and types of such self-concept differences are similar in both cultures. Finally, minimal grade differences in the sampled Japanese cohorts are found. Findings are discussed in light of theories which stress necessary linkages between adolescents' self-appraisals and body evaluations; descriptive and explanatory research methods for future investigations are suggested.

Developmentalists from an array of theoretical persuasions believe that adolescence is an ontogenetic period involving changes in self-appraisals, for example, pertaining to self-concept and self-esteem, and that such alterations are related to the bodily changes occurring during this period. For instance, McCandless (1970) argues that "the adolescent is his body, and his body is he," and offers a social learning account of how systems of reward and punishment keyed to the person's sex provide a basis of personality and social development. Similarly, Erikson (1968) stresses that the differential anatomical and reproductive characteristics of male and female adolescents' bodies necessarily foster contrasts in self-esteem, interpersonal orientations, and role behaviors. In turn, dynamic interactional theory (Lerner 1978, 1979; Lerner & Spanier 1980) notes that on the basis of physical (and behavioral) characteristics of individuality, adolescents may elicit differential reactions from socializing others which provide feedback influencing further development.

In a series of studies testing ideas associated with these theoretical positions (Lerner & Brackney 1978; Lerner & Karabenick 1974; Lerner, Karabenick, & Stuart 1973; Lerner, Orlos, & Knapp 1976; Lerner, Sorell, & Brackney, in press), the self-concepts and self-esteems of independent cohorts of male and female late-adolescent American college students have been related to their body attitudes. In all groups of late-adolescent Americans studied, body attitudes (of attractiveness and of effec-

The authors thank Elizabeth Strickler for assistance in data coding. Reprint requests may be sent to Richard M. Lerner, College of Human Development, Pennsylvania State University, University Park, Pennsylvania 16802, or to Saburo Iwawaki, Department of Psychology, Chukyo University, Nagoya 466, Japan.

[*Child Development*, 1980, 51, 847–855. © 1980 by the Society for Research in Child Development, Inc. 0009-3920/80/5103-0026$01.00]

tiveness) were significant predictors of self-concept/self-esteem (Lerner & Spanier 1980). The more attractive or effective the adolescents believed their bodies to be, the more positive was their self-esteem. However, as in other data sets (O'Malley & Bachman 1979), the sexes did not differ in their general level of self-esteem; in addition, few differences were found in the sexes' self-concepts.

The generalizability of these results is limited in some important ways. The above studies provide information only about adolescents in the college milieu. They do not address the question of whether positive associations between self-appraisals and body attitudes occur in age cohorts of adolescents other than late-adolescent, college ones. Thus, in the present study we assess whether self-appraisals are related to body attitudes among younger adolescents, and if such relationships reliably emerge at a particular age level. Second, no studies have investigated the universality of the relations between self-concepts, self-esteems, and body attitudes in adolescents. Are these associations in late adolescents idiosyncratic to America, or are these linkages generalizable across cultural contexts? While Erikson's (1959, 1968) universalistic stage theory would lead to a prediction of generalizability, the contextually sensitive, dynamic interaction position (Lerner 1978, 1979) and the social learning view of McCandless (1970; see also Mussen & Bouterline-Young 1964) would suggest the possibility of intercultural variation.

To provide initial data relevant to assess the implications of age and cultural variation for self-concept, self-esteem, and body attitudes, a descriptive study was undertaken of the interrelations among attitudes of bodily effectiveness, of bodily attractiveness, and of self-concept and self-esteem in male and female Japanese adolescents ranging in grade level from the seventh grade through college. Japanese adolescents were focused on because it was reasoned that the differing histories and traditional value systems of America and Japan constitute a cultural contrast, and because there are existing data sets pertinent to the degree of comparability of Japanese and American adolescents' body attitudes (Iwawaki & Lerner 1974, 1976; Lerner & Iwawaki 1975).

Method

Subjects.—The subjects were 796 Japanese (50.4% female) ranging in educational level from seventh grade through the senior year of college.[1] Tested in the fall and winter of 1977–1978, the precollege students ($N =$ 488; 50% female) were enrolled in public schools in middle-class neighborhoods of Otsu —an urban area—and the college students (N $=$ 308; 51.0% female) were students in either Shiga University (in Otsu) or in Chukyo University (in another urban area—Nagoya). The mean ages of the seventh, eighth, ninth, tenth, eleventh, and twelfth graders were 12.7 years (SD = 0.3 years), 13.7 years (SD = 0.3 years), 14.7 years (SD = 0.3 years), 15.8 years (SD = 0.3 years), 16.8 years (SD = 0.4 years), and 17.8 years (SD = 0.4 years), respectively. The mean age of the college students, who were mostly freshmen (53.9%), was 20.2 years (SD = 1.9 years).

Measures.—The 24-item attractiveness and effectiveness scales and the 16-item self-appraisal scale used in previous research with American samples (Lerner & Brackney 1978; Lerner & Karabenick 1974; Lerner et al. 1973, 1976, in press; Padin, Lerner, & Spiro, Note 1) were translated by two of this study's authors (Iwawaki and Chihara) for use in the present study. The scale evaluating subjects' appraisals of their bodies' physical attractiveness presented a list of 24 body characteristics (e.g., arms, face, profile). Subjects were asked to rate each item in terms of the level of physical attractiveness they assumed to be associated with each of these parts of their own bodies. It was explained that there are many characteristics of the body which one may feel are important to oneself in presenting an attractive physical appearance to members of the opposite sex, and that people may feel that different parts of their bodies are more or less physically attractive than are other parts. Subjects were asked to judge the attractiveness of each of the 24 characteristics of their own bodies and to indicate each response on a five-point Likert scale, with response alternatives ranging from 5 = very attractive through 1 = very unattractive.

The scale evaluating subjects' appraisals of their bodies' physical effectiveness presented

[1] It should be noted that the educational system in Japan differs from the American system. Japanese children are enrolled in compulsory education only through junior high school (i.e., grades 7, 8, and 9). High school (grades 10, 11, and 12) attendance is selective. Of course, college attendance is selective also.

the same 24 body characteristics as in the attractiveness scale. Here, however, subjects were told that there are many characteristics of the body which one may feel are important in making activities in which one engages turn out successfully. It was further explained that different parts of the body may play different roles in helping one to be effective in one's daily functions, and that some body parts may play a very central role in aiding one to function effectively, while other body parts may not play such a central role. Subjects rated the 24 body parts in terms of the effectiveness of these parts of their own bodies, with response alternatives ranging from 5 = very effective through 1 = very ineffective.

Finally, a 16-item scale of bipolar dimensions (e.g., mature-immature, capable-not capable), which are all evaluative in nature, was administered. Six of the items contain bipolar alternatives identified in the sex-role stereotype literature (Block 1973; Broverman, Vogel, Broverman, Clarkson, & Rosenkrantz 1972) as being stereotypically associated with either males or females. For instance, item alternatives, such as independent-dependent, active-passive, and individualistic-conforming, stereotypically differentiating males from females, were included. The remaining items on this scale were not among those found in the sex-role stereotype literature to typically differentiate the male and female stereotypes. Using a five-point Likert format, subjects were asked to select the responses which most accurately reflected how they felt and not how they believed they should feel. Response alternatives ranged from 1 = word on left end of the continuum is most like me, through 5 = word on the right end of the continuum is most like me. Responses were converted in calculation so that for all items, higher scores were toward the positive end of each evaluative continuum. As explained in Lerner et al. (in press), subjects' mean scores across the 16 evaluative items were used as the index of self-esteem, and the vector of responses along the 16 dimensions (i.e., subjects' locations in this multidimensional space) was the index of self-concept.

Data from several studies support the reliability and validity of these scales. Lerner et al. (1976) found that the internal consistency for males' attractiveness and effectiveness ratings was .90 and .90, respectively, and that the corresponding values for females' ratings were .88 and .90. Padin et al. (Note 1) found stability coefficients over a 2-month interval of .89, .70, and .73 for the attractiveness, effectiveness, and self-esteem/self-concept scales, respectively. Finally, responses to each of these scales have been found to bear predicted relations to other self-report measures of body and self-evaluations (Lerner & Brackney 1978; Lerner & Karabenick 1974; Lerner et al. 1973, 1976; Rosen & Ross 1968; Padin et al., Note 1).

Subjects were tested as groups within their classrooms. Each subject was given a test booklet, which included a cover sheet asking for answers to various demographic questions (e.g., age, sex) and the three scales. Subjects' responses were recorded by them on answer sheets enclosed in the booklets.

Results

The purposes of data analyses were to describe the Japanese adolescents' self-esteems, self-concepts, body attitudes, and the interrelations among these self-appraisals in order to evaluate: (1) differences among the sampled Japanese adolescent grade cohorts, and (2) differences between these Japanese data and comparative American data sets.

Relations among self-esteem, physical attractiveness, and physical effectiveness.—The product-moment correlations among the mean physical attractiveness, mean physical effectiveness, and self-esteem (i.e., mean of the 16 evaluative self-ratings) scores for the males and females within each grade level are summarized in table 1, as are the means and standard deviations of the three scores for each grade × sex group.[2] Studies of independent cohorts of American male and female college students (e.g., Lerner & Brackney 1978; Lerner & Karabenick 1974; Lerner et al. 1976; Padin et al., Note 1) have found that self-esteem is positively related to self-ratings of physical attractiveness and effectiveness, and that the relationship between attractiveness and effectiveness is greater for males than for females. As seen in table 1, this pattern of relations was replicated in the sampled cohorts of Japanese college students. Indeed, the absolute levels of the correlations were similar to

[2] Preliminary analyses with the college sample indicated no differences associated with year in college or with age for any variable considered in this study. Therefore, no grade-level differentiation within the college sample is presented in this report.

TABLE 1

MEANS, STANDARD DEVIATIONS, AND CORRELATIONS AMONG SELF-ESTEEM, PHYSICAL ATTRACTIVENESS, AND PHYSICAL EFFECTIVENESS FOR MALE AND FEMALE SEVENTH-GRADE THROUGH COLLEGE JAPANESE ADOLESCENTS

Grade Level and Sex	N	Correlations Among: SE and PA	SE and PE	PA and PE	SE Mean	SE SD	PA Mean	PA SD	PE Mean	PE SD
7:										
Male	38	.13	.30*	.45**	3.2	.4	2.6	.5	3.0	.4
Female	34	.37*	.43*	.66**	2.9	.3	2.7	.4	3.1	.5
8:										
Male	34	.13	.22	.13	3.3	.5	2.3	.8	3.3	.7
Female	38	.11	.08	.21	2.9	.3	2.6	.6	3.2	.5
9:										
Male	30	.33*	.52**	.15	3.1	.4	2.4	.8	3.2	.8
Female	38	.12	.19	.54**	3.1	.3	2.6	.7	2.9	.7
10:										
Male	52	.36**	.47**	.41**	3.2	.3	2.7	.7	3.2	.6
Female	63	.43**	.07	.33**	3.0	.3	2.8	.6	3.1	.5
11:										
Male	57	.41**	.59**	.53**	3.1	.4	2.7	.7	3.0	.6
Female	35	.07	.27	.29*	3.0	.4	2.6	.8	3.2	.6
12:										
Male	33	.05	.59**	.04	3.3	.3	3.0	.4	3.1	.6
Female	36	.19	.12	.45**	3.1	.4	3.0	.5	3.1	.6
College:										
Male	151	.32**	.31**	.35**	3.1	.4	2.8	.6	3.1	.6
Female	157	.18*	.19**	.45**	2.9	.4	2.7	.6	3.0	.6

NOTE.—SE = self-esteem, PA = physical attractiveness, PE = physical effectiveness.
* $p < .05$.
** $p < .01$.

the data reported in studies of American college cohorts.

However, the junior high and high school correlational data presented in table 1 were not generally consistent with either the Japanese college or American college data. Indeed, no consistent interrelational pattern was found either within or between cohorts. The magnitudes of the means and variability associated with these scores were relatively consistent across all Japanese grade cohorts. While the variability associated with these means corresponds quite closely to corresponding data from American college samples (e.g., Lerner et al. 1976; Padin et al., Note 1), the magnitude of corresponding means is discrepant.

For instance, in one study of American college students, the means for self-esteem, physical attractiveness, and physical effectiveness for males were 3.7, 3.7, and 3.6, respectively, and for females 3.7, 3.6, and 3.4, respectively (Lerner et al. 1976). Similarly, in an independent study, these three means for males were 4.8, 3.5, and 3.3, respectively, and for females 4.8, 3.5, and 3.3, respectively (Padin et al., Note 1). Comparisons of corresponding means between the American data sets, on the one hand, and those associated with the Japanese college cohort, on the other, were significant in 92% of the comparisons (all tests were two-tailed t's, $p < .02$ in all significant cases). Across all grade cohorts the Japanese had lower self-esteems and saw their bodies as less attractive and less effective than did the Americans.[3]

The pattern of self-ratings of the sampled Japanese cohorts was also evaluated in three 7×2 fixed-effects analyses of variance. The two between-subjects dimensions in each anal-

[3] "Social desirability" is always a methodological issue in research using self-ratings. It is possible that the lower self-esteem scores for the Japanese cohorts are a product of the differential effects of social desirability on self-ratings between Japan and the United States (e.g., norms for self-presentation may differ in the two cultures). However, there are several data sets indicating that correlations exceeding +.9 exist between American and Japanese college students in their respective social desirability scores on self-report personality inventories (Iwawaki, Okuno, & Cowen 1965; Fujita, Note 2).

ysis were grade level (seventh through college) and sex. The dependent variables for the three analyses were physical attractiveness, physical effectiveness, and self-esteem. Corrections suggested by Overall and Spiegel (1969) were made due to the presence of unequal cell *N*'s.

In the first of these analyses, for physical attractiveness, a main effect for grade, $F(6,782) = 5.9$, $p < .01$, was found (and was the only significant effect). The results of a modified LSD test (Welch 1951) indicated that this effect was primarily attributable to the means of the eighth graders and the twelfth graders, which were, respectively, 0.3 scale points below and 0.3 above the grand mean of 2.7. The amount of variance accounted for by all the differences among the seven means involved in the grade effect was 4.4%, while less than 0.1% of the variance in this analysis was accounted for by the sex dimension.

The second analysis of variance, for physical effectiveness, found no significant effects across these cohorts of Japanese adolescents. Less than 0.9% of the variance was accounted for by the grade dimension in the analysis of the effectiveness scores, while the sex dimension accounted for less than 0.2% of the variance in this analysis.

Significant grade, $F(6,782) = 3.7$, $p < .01$, and sex, $F(1,782) = 45.5$, $p < .01$, effects were found in the analysis of variance for self-esteem scores. The former effect accounted for 2.5% of the variance, while sex accounted for 5.3% of the variance in scores on the self-esteem scale. Moreover, the results of a modified LSD test (Welch 1951) indicated that the grade effect was mostly accounted for by the mean of the college students, which was 0.07 scale points below the grand mean of 3.05, while all other cohorts had means above this overall value. The sex-related variance was attributable to females having a mean score 0.09 scale points below and males having a mean score 0.09 points above the overall mean of 3.05.

Sex differences in self-concept: grade cohort and agency-communion variation.—As noted, the index of self-concept was the vector of responses across the 16 evaluative items. Because of the significant, albeit quite minimal, grade effect found in the self-esteem analysis of variance, the presence of sex differences was assessed within each grade cohort. These analyses involved comparing the male and female vector of means through use of multivariate analyses of variance. The major results of these analyses are presented in table 2, and in different ways they show both consistency and incongruity with comparison American data (i.e., Lerner et al., in press). In the five college cohorts (1973, 1974, 1975, 1976, and 1977) assessed in the Lerner et al. (in press) time-lag study, there was a significant overall discrimination in the multivariate analysis of variance done in each cohort. However, the number of individual items significantly involved in this effect in each cohort were 2, 2, 3, 2, and 5, respectively. Of the six agency-communion-related items included in the measure, there was never more than one item within any cohort which was part of these groups of significant items, and in four of the five cohorts it was the same item (independent-dependent) that discriminated.

In the present Japanese data set, significant overall discriminations occurred in only five of the seven adolescent grade cohorts. As with the American data, it was generally the case that there were few significant individual items involved in within-cohort sex differences.[4] Indeed, in two of the grade cohorts (grades 9 and 10), no individual items had significant univariate *F*'s. Of the remaining grade cohorts, there were two discriminating items involved in three cohorts (grades 7, 8, and 12), one discriminating item involved in another (grade 11), and, somewhat anomalously, seven involved in the last remaining cohort, the college one. However, this number of items was only two above the maximum number found in the American cohorts (Lerner et al., in press). Also as in the American data set, the particular items involved in these significant discriminations tended not to be those related to the agency-communion distinction. Only in the college cohort did such an item enter into the discrimination, and it was the same item as in the American data: independent-dependent. Thus, across a wide age range, male and female Japanese adolescents showed self-concepts that were, along most assessed dimensions, more similar than not; moreover, as in the comparison American data set (Lerner et al., in press), the sexes did not tend to differ

[4] Significance levels were determined by use of the Bonferroni *t* (Kirk 1968), with reduced alpha. That is, an alpha level of .05 was divided by the number of comparisons to be made (i.e., 16), resulting in a minimum acceptable alpha of .0031.

TABLE 2

RESULTS OF MULTIVARIATE ANALYSES OF VARIANCE ASSESSING THE PRESENCE OF SEX DIFFERENCES IN COHORTS OF JAPANESE SEVENTH-GRADE THROUGH COLLEGE ADOLESCENTS

Grade Cohort	Overall Discrimination			Items Having Significant Univariate F's						Estimated Percentage of Variance Accounted for by Total Sex Differences within the Grade Cohort (%)
	F	df	$p <$	Item	F	df	$p <$	Male (Mean)	Female (Mean)	
7	2.32	16,55	.02	Mature-immature	1.91	33,37	.002	3.5	2.8	10.7
				Masculine-feminine	1.77	33,37	.004	4.2	3.6	...
8	2.94	16,57	.002	Masculine-feminine	2.35	39,33	.001	4.5	3.5	13.3
				Intelligent-not intelligent	1.94	39,33	.001	3.3	2.4	...
9	.75	16,49	.75	...	...	...	...	...	...	.8
10	2.59	16,98	.003	...	...	...	...	...	...	7.8
11	1.65	16,75	.08	Successful-unsuccessful	1.82	34,56	.003	3.1	2.5	5.3
12	2.03	16,52	.03	Uninhibited-inhibited	1.87	32,35	.002	2.3	3.0	12.0
				Intelligent-not intelligent	2.08	32,35	.001	3.6	2.6	...
College	5.59	16,291	.001	Mature-immature	1.86	155,151	.002	2.4	2.7	3.2
				Independent-dependent	2.27	155,151	.001	3.0	2.4	...
				Tolerant-intolerant	2.47	155,151	.001	2.4	3.1	...
				Uninhibited-inhibited	1.91	155,151	.001	2.5	2.9	...
				Successful-unsuccessful	1.82	155,151	.002	2.9	2.6	...
				Secure-insecure	2.01	155,151	.001	3.0	2.5	...
				Capable-not capable	1.98	155,151	.001	3.3	2.9	...

along those item dimensions stereotypically associated with sex differences in self-concept (Block 1973; Broverman et al. 1972).

At this point, congruence with the comparison American data ends. On the majority (71%) of the instances of significant-item sex differences across the sampled Japanese grade cohorts, males rated themselves more toward the favorable ends of the item dimensions than did females; this rating difference was a significant basis of the overall self-esteem difference favoring males noted above. Furthermore, the amount of variance accounted for by the total sex differences within each Japanese grade cohort was substantially larger than the percentages found in the Lerner et al. (in press) time-lag study. In that study the percentage of variance accounted for by sex differences within the five college cohorts was 0.5%, 0.1%, 1.8%, 0.1%, and 0.8%, respectively. However, as seen in table 2, the percentages in the Japanese grade cohorts ranged from a low of 0.8% to a high of 13.3%. Thus, the average percentage of variance accounted for across the Japanese grade cohorts (i.e., 7.6%) was 10.9 times greater than in the comparison American data.

In sum, the same types of items, and approximately the same number of items, tended to be implicated in the sex differences in Japanese adolescents' self-concepts, as was the case in comparison American data. However, Japanese females had a pattern of ratings on these items which was consistent with their lower self-esteem; and, in addition, these rating differences accounted for substantially more variance in the Japanese cohorts than in the American ones to which they were compared.

Discussion

The results of the present study indicate that there exist both cultural consistency and inconsistency between Japanese and American data sets. In contrast to American data sets (Lerner & Spanier 1980; Maccoby & Jacklin 1974; O'Malley & Bachman 1979), the self-esteem of Japanese adolescents did show sex differences, in favor of males; this contrast was found to be only somewhat moderated by the grade cohort level of the sex groups, with the primary cohort effect occurring between the college level and the lower grades. Although we will not argue that the total difference of 0.18 scale points between male and female self-esteem means is sufficient to indicate a psychologically significant difference, it is interesting to note the contrast between this finding and those reported with American adolescent samples. Although the data from such samples are not unequivocal (Block 1976), reviews of the literature find most studies reporting no sex differences in self-esteem (e.g., Lerner & Spanier, 1980; Maccoby & Jacklin 1974). However, the studies surveyed in these reviews often involved statistical comparisons with small *N*'s, and thus had little power to reject the null (Block 1976); the conclusion that no overall self-esteem difference exists does not obviate the possibility that the sexes may define themselves quite differently (i.e., have different self-concepts) and yet attain comparable self-esteem scores (Lerner et al., in press).

However, a recent time-lag study of five successive cohorts of American college-level adolescents had *N*'s sufficiently large to afford considerable power, and no sex differences in self-esteem were found (Lerner et al., in press). In addition, few definitional differences in the sexes were found, and these tended not to show intercohort consistency or involve agency-communion items. The present study, then, afforded an opportunity to appraise the nature of sex differences in self-concept with a data set also having an *N* large enough to allow substantial power *and* within a cultural setting having cohorts of female adolescents whose self-esteems were consistently less positive than those of their male counterparts.

Both the sampled Japanese and American cohorts of adolescents had self-concepts showing relatively few sex differences. Moreover, as in comparison American data sets (Lerner et al., in press), Japanese males and females did not tend to rate themselves differently on agency-communion items, that is, those items stereotypically held (Block 1973; Broverman et al. 1972) to differentiate the sexes. However, the few self-concept sex differences that did occur across the sampled Japanese adolescent age range accounted for markedly greater percentages of the variance than was the case in the comparative American data sets.

Across all grade levels Japanese adolescents had relatively consistent scores on the physical effectiveness variable with a modest cohort effect found for the attractiveness variable. Interestingly, although the variability of these scores, as well as for self-concept and self-esteem scores, was comparable to that existing in American data sets (Lerner et al. 1976; Padin et al., Note 1), the mean scores for the Japanese were consistently lower than for American adolescents. Moreover, in American data sets adolescent self-esteem is positively related to ratings of physical attractiveness and of physical effectiveness; although the Japanese college-level data were consistent in both direction and magnitude of relationships with the American pattern (Lerner & Brackney 1978; Lerner & Karabenick 1974; Lerner et al. 1976; Padin et al., Note 1), the data from the other sampled Japanese grade cohorts were not. No interrelation among self-esteem and body attitudes existed across the Japanese noncollege grade cohorts. As such, this data set does not support theories stressing the necessary linkage between self-appraisals and body variables (i.e., Erikson 1968; McCandless 1970).

A universalistic theory, such as Erikson's (1968), might be hard put to parsimoniously account for both the intracultural intercohort variation and the intercultural differences. In turn, the social learning view of McCandless (1970) could account for such differences, probably here on the basis of post hoc assertions of contrasting systems of rewards and punishments existing among cohorts within Japan, and between Japan and America. However, the explanation of the cohort effects might go unspecified in such an account. Because the contextually oriented, dynamic interactional position (Lerner 1978, 1979) is sensitive to the role of such cohort effects, it can—while not necessarily offering predictions or explanations alternative to mechanistic, social learning ones—suggest research designs allowing for an account of the bases of such effects. Indeed, since the present data set provides evidence that the relations of an adolescent's body to his or her self-concept/self-esteem may be neither culturally nor ontogenetically invariant, it is our view that a combination of descriptive, longitudinal sequential designs and simulational explanatory ones, as provided by cross-cultural research (see Baltes, Reese, & Nesselroade 1977), is the methodology of choice in further studies of these components of adolescent psychosocial development.

Reference Notes

1. Padin, M.; Lerner, R. M.; & Spiro, A., III. Stability of body attitudes and self-concept in late adolescence. Unpublished manuscript, College of Human Development, Pennsylvania State University, 1978.
2. Fujita, B. An investigation of the applicability of the Edwards Personal Preference Schedule to a cultural sub-group, the Nisei. Unpublished master's dissertation, University of Washington, 1956.

References

Baltes, P. B.; Reese, H. W.; & Nesselroade, J. R. *Life-span developmental psychology: introduction to research methods.* Belmont, Calif.: Brooks/Cole, 1977.

Block, J. H. Conceptions of sex role: some cross-cultural and longitudinal perspectives. *American Psychologist,* 1973, **28,** 512–526.

Block, J. H. Issues, problems, and pitfalls in assessing sex differences: a critical review of *The Psychology of Sex Differences. Merrill-Palmer Quarterly,* 1976, **22,** 283–308.

Broverman, I. K.; Vogel, S. R.; Broverman, D. M.; Clarkson, F. E.; & Rosenkrantz, P. S. Sex role stereotypes: a current appraisal. *Journal of Social Issues,* 1972, **28,** 59–78.

Erikson, E. H. Identity and the life cycle. *Psychological Issues,* 1959, **1,** 18–164.

Erikson, E. H. *Identity, youth and crisis.* New York: Norton, 1968.

Iwawaki, S., & Lerner, R. M. Cross-cultural analyses of body-behavior relations. I. A comparison of body build stereotypes of Japanese and American males and females. *Psychologia,* 1974, **17,** 75–81.

Iwawaki, S., & Lerner, R. M. Cross-cultural analyses of body-behavior relations. III. Developmental intra- and inter-cultural factor congruence in the body build stereotypes of Japanese and American males and females. *Psychologia,* 1976, **19,** 67–76.

Iwawaki, S.; Okuno, S.; & Cowen, E. L. The social desirability of trait-descriptive terms: sex and cultural differences based on a Japanese arts college sample. *Tohoku Psychologia Folia,* 1965, **24,** 56–64.

Kirk, R. E. *Experimental design: procedures for the behavioral sciences.* Belmont, Calif.: Brooks/Cole, 1968.

Lerner, R. M. Nature, nurture, and dynamic interactionism. *Human Development,* 1978, **21,** 1–20.

Lerner, R. M. A dynamic interactional concept of individual and social development. In R. L. Burgess & T. L. Huston (Eds.), *Social exchange in developing relationships.* New York: Academic Press, 1979.

Lerner, R. M., & Brackney, B. E. The importance of inner and outer body parts attitudes in the self-concept of late adolescents. *Sex Roles,* 1978, **4,** 225–238.

Lerner, R. M., & Iwawaki, S. Cross cultural analyses of body-behavior relations. II. Factor structure of body build stereotypes of Japanese and American adolescents. *Psychologia,* 1975, **18,** 83–91.

Lerner, R. M., & Karabenick, S. A. Physical attractiveness, body attitudes, and self-concept in late adolescents. *Journal of Youth and Adolescence,* 1974, **3,** 307–316.

Lerner, R. M.; Karabenick, S. A.; & Stuart, J. L. Relations among physical attractiveness, body attitudes, and self-concept in male and female college students. *Journal of Psychology,* 1973, **85,** 119–129.

Lerner, R. M.; Orlos, J. B.; & Knapp, J. R. Physical attractiveness, physical effectiveness, and self-concept in late adolescents. *Adolescence,* 1976, **11,** 313–326.

Lerner, R. M.; Sorell, G. T.; & Brackney, B. E. Sex differences in self-concept and self-esteem of late adolescents: a time-lag analysis. *Sex Roles,* in press.

Lerner, R. M., & Spanier, G. B. *Adolescent development: a life-span perspective.* New York: McGraw-Hill, 1980.

McCandless, B. R. *Adolescents.* Hinsdale, Ill.: Dryden, 1970.

Maccoby, E. E., & Jacklin, C. N. *The psychology of sex differences.* Stanford, Calif.: Stanford University Press, 1974.

Mussen, P., & Bouterline-Young, H. Relationships between rate of physical maturing and personality among boys of Italian descent. *Vita Humana,* 1964, **7,** 186–200.

O'Malley, P. M., & Bachman, J. G. Self-esteem and education: sex and cohort comparisons among high school seniors. *Journal of Personality and Social Psychology,* 1979, **37,** 1153–1159.

Overall, J. E., & Spiegel, D. K. Concerning least squares analysis of experimental data. *Psychological Bulletin,* 1969, **72,** 311–322.

Rosen, G. M., & Ross, A. O. Relationship of body image to self-concept. *Journal of Consulting and Clinical Psychology,* 1968, **32,** 100.

Welch, B. L. On the comparison of several mean values: an alternative approach. *Biometrika,* 1951, **38,** 330–336.

Masculinity, Femininity, and Sex Role Attitudes in Early Adolescence: Exploring Gender Intensification

Nancy L. Galambos and David M. Almeida
University of Victoria

Anne C. Petersen
Pennsylvania State University

GALAMBOS, NANCY L.; ALMEIDA, DAVID M.; and PETERSEN, ANNE C. *Masculinity, Femininity, and Sex Role Attitudes in Early Adolescence: Exploring Gender Intensification.* CHILD DEVELOPMENT, 1990, **61,** 1905–1914. This longitudinal study of 200 young adolescent girls and boys (mean age 11.6 years in sixth grade) investigated the hypothesis that differences in masculinity, femininity, and sex role attitudes would intensify across the sixth, seventh, and eighth grades (between 11 and 13 years of age) and that pubertal timing (early, on time, late) would play a role in this intensification. Analyses revealed that sex differences in masculinity and sex role attitudes increased across grades, but not sex differences in femininity. Pubertal timing was not associated with this gender divergence, although the evidence is equivocal for boys. The results provide support for gender intensification, but the role of pubertal timing may not be as strong as previously supposed.

Considering sex differences in adolescence, Hill and Lynch (1983) argued that, with the onset of puberty, boys and girls experience an intensification of gender-related expectations. This "gender intensification hypothesis" posits that behavioral, attitudinal, and psychological differences between adolescent boys and girls increase with age and are the result of increased socialization pressures to conform to traditional masculine and feminine sex roles. Sex roles denote shared expectations for gender-specific sets of behaviors (Worell, 1981), with the masculine role emphasizing instrumental behaviors (e.g., independence) and the feminine role emphasizing expressive behaviors (e.g., nurturance) (Bakan, 1966; Block, 1973). The role that puberty plays in the differentiation of masculine and feminine characteristics may be that it serves as a signal to socializing others (parents, teachers, peers) that the adolescent is beginning the approach to adulthood and should begin to act accordingly, that is, in ways that resemble the stereotypical male or female adult (Hill & Lynch, 1983).

What kind of data constitute evidence for gender intensification in adolescence? First, variables selected for consideration must be gender-salient characteristics on which sex differences already exist before early adolescence. Second, a pattern of increasing differentiation between boys and girls across adolescence must be shown on relevant characteristics. Third, intensification of gender-related attributes should be greatest for those adolescents who have entered puberty, although it is difficult to predict at what point in the pubertal process social pressures and male-female differences will reach their maximum. Will gender-related attributes be most pronounced for those just entering puberty, in the middle of puberty, or when the adolescent clearly resembles an adult (a question of pubertal status)? Furthermore, will increased levels of a given gender-related attribute be greatest for adolescents who are physically on time, early, or late relative to their peers (a question of pubertal timing)?

Gender intensification is evident in the results of several studies, although the role that puberty plays has been considered rarely. Linn and Petersen (1986), for example, reported that during adolescence males gain an advantage over females in certain domains of mathematics achievement. Research on self-image shows that, in early adolescence, girls

This research was supported by a grant from the National Institute of Mental Health (MH 30252/38142) to A. Petersen. The authors thank three anonymous reviewers for their helpful comments on an earlier version of this paper. Address correspondence to: Nancy L. Galambos, Department of Psychology, University of Victoria, Victoria, BC V8W 3P5, Canada.

[*Child Development*, 1990, **61**, 1905–1914. 0009-3920/90/6106-0020$01.00]

are more self-conscious and hold themselves in lower esteem than do males (Rosenberg & Simmons, 1975; Simmons & Rosenberg, 1975). Indeed, Simmons, Blyth, Van Cleave, and Bush (1979) found a significant decrease in self-esteem from the sixth to seventh grades among girls who experienced multiple changes, including pubertal development. In a similar vein, two studies found that depression in girls increases during early adolescence (Hirsch & Rapkin, 1987; Petersen, Sarigiani, & Kennedy, in press). Finally, in a study of adolescents followed from the sixth through tenth grades, the rated importance of not acting like the opposite sex peaked in seventh grade for girls and in ninth grade for boys; differences between the sexes in four body-image variables peaked in ninth grade (Simmons & Blyth, 1987).

Guided by the gender intensification hypothesis, Roberts, Sarigiani, Newman, and Petersen (in press) reasoned that if social pressure to behave according to sex stereotypes increases in early adolescence, then the relation between school achievement and a positive self-image should increase among boys and decrease among girls. This would occur because boys are presumed to be pressured to excel academically whereas girls are presumed to be pressured to excel socially. Indeed, from sixth to seventh grade, the relation between school achievement and a positive self-image increased for boys and decreased for girls. At eighth grade, however, less divergence was evident.

Although these studies offer support for the gender intensification hypothesis, others do not. Hirsch and Rapkin (1987) and Petersen and Ebata (1987), for example, did not find that girls' self-image and self-esteem became less positive as they passed through early adolescence. And, based on a meta-analysis, Linn and Petersen (1985) concluded that where sex differences in spatial ability are detected, they are not more prominent in adolescence than earlier or later in the life span. In the domain of vocational development, adult men and women, on average, experience different career trajectories, making it reasonable to assume that sex differences in educational plans and achievement might be seen in adolescence. Simmons and Blyth (1987), however, did not observe a pattern of increasing divergence between boys and girls across adolescence in future work and educational plans, academic performance, and school problem behavior.

Although some progress has been made in examining gender intensification, there are two major shortcomings in the previous research. First, whether adolescents see themselves in an increasingly sex-typed manner as they pass through early adolescence is unknown—a central assumption of gender intensification. Second, as mentioned previously, little is known about the role of puberty in gender intensification.

The present investigation addresses these concerns by using longitudinal data from a study of adolescents to determine whether gender intensification characterizes the development of self-reported masculinity, femininity, and sex role attitudes in early adolescence. Masculinity and femininity are socially desirable attributes that are stereotypically considered to differentiate males and females. (Spence & Helmreich, 1978). As such, measurement of these attributes in the adolescent would indicate to what extent the adolescent adheres to sex roles. We considered sex role attitudes because males, relative to females, typically have higher approval of the division of labor, responsibilities, and behaviors based on gender (Galambos, Petersen, Richards, & Gitelson, 1985), and it is important to determine whether this sex difference increases in early adolescence. At the same time, we considered the relation between pubertal timing (early, on time, late) and the above sex-typed attributes. Pubertal timing rather than pubertal status is assessed because timing in particular has been associated with perceptions that others hold of the adolescent (Savin-Williams & Small, 1986) and as such may be influential in shaping self-perceptions. The following predictions were made:

1. Sex differences in masculinity, femininity, and sex role attitudes will become larger during early adolescence (or, in analysis of variance terminology, there will be a sex × grade interaction).

2. Early-maturing boys will reach higher levels of masculinity sooner than later-developing boys (a pubertal timing × grade interaction); early-maturing girls will reach their height in femininity sooner than later-developing girls. No prediction was made on the relation between pubertal timing and sex role attitudes.

Method

Sample

The subjects (n = 200; 85 boys, 115 girls) were a subset from a longitudinal study of early adolescence—the Early Adolescence Study (EAS). The design and sample have been described elsewhere (Petersen, 1984; Richardson, Galambos, Schulenberg, & Petersen, 1984). The EAS (N = 335; 182 girls and 153 boys) consists of two successive cohorts of students (birth years: 1967 and 1968) who experienced early adolescence in the late 1970s. They were drawn randomly from the sixth-grade class of two primarily white middle- to upper-middle-class Midwestern suburban school districts. About 80% of targeted students participated, and comparisons revealed that those who did participate were not different on any variable studied (e.g., self-image) from students who did not participate.

The adolescents' average age on January 1 of sixth grade was 11.6 years (SD = .34), with no difference in age between boys and girls. Through interviews and group assessments, data were gathered from subjects twice annually in the sixth, seventh, and eighth grades. A longitudinal sample was defined (n = 253, present for at least four of six interviews and four of six group testing sessions) for purposes of longitudinal data analyses. It did not differ significantly from the full sample on any measure. Only 6% of the original sample dropped out by the eighth grade; none of these are included in the longitudinal sample. Given the few consistent cohort differences, the two cohorts were combined.

Attempts were made to complete two interviews annually, yielding relatively high completion rates (an average of 88% completion across all interviews), but no attempt was made to gather data from those who missed any of the twice-annual group testing sessions (yielding a still-respectable average of 84% completion across all sessions). Despite the limited amount of incomplete data, the longitudinal pattern for any individual is likely to include some missing data. Since these results are missing at random (i.e., there was no systematic pattern of nonresponse), it was appropriate to estimate scores (see Little & Rubin, 1987). Thus, within the longitudinal sample, estimated scores were generated for those subjects missing masculinity, femininity, or sex role attitudes scores on only one occasion; this involved 33 boys and 54 girls, with a nearly equal proportion of boys and girls having nonresponses within each grade. This resulted in a total of 200 subjects with data required for use in this study.

The score for the missing data point was estimated by weighting the group mean within sex on that occasion by the subject's average deviation from the group mean at the other two data points. This estimation procedure might increase cross-year stability but, because the estimates were generated separately by sex, it may decrease the likelihood of divergence, thus providing a conservative test of gender intensification. The means and standard deviations for this subsample of 200 and all those subjects present on any given occasion were nearly identical. The analyses to be reported using the sample of 200 were conducted also with those subjects present on all three occasions; the results were identical, thereby suggesting that the estimation procedure did not bias the findings.

Measures

Pubertal timing.—We measured pubertal timing by using annual height data to assess age at peak height velocity (Bock et al., 1973; Thissen, Bock, Wainer, & Roche, 1976). This maximum-likelihood estimation procedure begins with Bayesian priors based on data from the major growth studies in the United States. Analysis of longitudinal data from these studies has verified the validity of a triple logistic function representing growth in stature from birth (actually conception) to maturity. Although nine parameters are estimated, only one—age at peak height velocity during the adolescent growth spurt—is of interest in the present analysis. Because the estimation begins with Bayesian priors, this measure is useful even for those who do not reach peak growth during the years studied.

The estimates of age at peak height velocity (i.e., age at which growth is fastest) were based on repeated measures of height over the 3 years of the study. However, the nature of the height data differed for the two school districts involved. In one school district, height was measured annually from kindergarten through eighth grade by the school nurse; these data on height, obtained directly from school records, were used to estimate age at peak height velocity. In the other district, objective data on height were not available; therefore, we used the adolescents' self-reports of height to make the estimates. The self-reports were obtained from the adolescents in both school districts as part of the semiannual interviews. Thus, reported and objective values could be compared directly in one of the districts, and these comparisons indicated that the self-report data are valid (median r = 0.94) (Crockett, Schulenberg, & Petersen, 1987). Moreover, the estimates based on objective data and those based on self-report data were virtually identical. Finally, when estimates from the two districts were compared (one set based on objective data, the other on self-reports), no significant differences emerged. Given these findings, we combined the estimates from both districts in the analyses.

To derive pubertal timing categories, the distribution of scores representing estimated age at peak height velocity was trichotomized, with the lower third being classified as "early," the middle third as "on time," and the upper third as "late" maturers. This procedure was carried out separately for boys and girls in order to take into account the sex differences in the age at which puberty begins. (In other samples, the age at peak height velocity is 11 years for girls and 13 years for boys, with the standard deviation usually around 1 year; Bock et al., 1973.)

The mean ages at peak height velocity for the early, on-time, and late-maturing boys were 12.74 (SD = .50), 13.83 (SD = .19), and 14.76 (SD = .51), respectively; these average ages correspond roughly to mid-seventh, -eighth, and -ninth grades, respectively. The mean ages at peak height velocity for the early, on-time, and late-maturing girls were 10.93 (SD = .51), 11.80 (SD = .51), and 12.64 (SD = .54), respectively; these average ages correspond roughly to mid-fifth, -sixth, and -seventh grades, respectively. This measure has been shown to be predictably related to age at menarche in girls, pubertal status scores in boys and girls, and voice change in boys (Petersen & Crockett, 1985; Petersen, Tobin-Richards, & Boxer, 1983). Early-maturing subjects in the present sample, for example, were more advanced physically (as determined by scores on the Pubertal Development Scale, a measure of pubertal status) than on-time adolescents, and on-time adolescents were more advanced than late maturers; these differences were evident in the sixth, seventh, and eighth grades among both girls and boys (see Petersen & Crockett, 1985). Age at peak height velocity is an appropriate measure of pubertal timing because it is *not* dependent on a single event (e.g., menarche) or on the attainment of the full set of secondary sex characteristics, and is relevant for both boys and girls. Age at peak height velocity occurs at about the middle of the pubertal process for girls and close to the end for boys (Marshall & Tanner, 1969, 1970). Thus, from grades 6 through 8, early-maturing girls move from mid- to postpubertal status, on-time girls from early- to late-pubertal status, and late-maturing girls from pre- to mid-pubertal status. Similarly, early-maturing boys move from early- to late-pubertal status, on-time boys from pre- to mid-pubertal status, and late-maturing boys enter early puberty by eighth grade.

Masculinity and femininity.—Items on the short form of the Bem Sex Role Inventory (BSRI) were used to assess the adolescent's view of himself or herself as masculine and feminine (Bem, 1974, 1981). The short form consists of 10 socially desirable adjectives each to measure masculinity (e.g., "self-reliant") and femininity (e.g., "yielding"). Subjects respond to each item, describing themselves on a scale ranging from *never or almost never true* (1) to *always or almost always true* (7). The mean of the items is computed, with higher scores indicating higher masculinity or femininity. Although the BSRI has been used mostly with young adults, Lamke (1982) found it to be useful for research on adolescents. Alpha coefficients for these scales in our sample range in the .70s and .80s for girls and boys across grades. Sixth-, seventh-, and eighth-grade scores were used.

Although Bem (1977) recommended combining the separate masculinity and femininity scores to place individuals in a fourfold classification scheme (resulting in masculine, feminine, androgynous, and undifferentiated categories), the predictive utility of these combinations has been called into question (Deaux, 1984; Taylor & Hall, 1982). More specifically, a comprehensive review of research on psychological androgyny revealed that combinations of masculinity/femininity failed to predict to indices of psychological adjustment above and beyond that predicted by the separate masculinity and femininity scores (Taylor & Hall, 1982). Moreover, Lamke (1982) argued for the importance of using continuous masculinity and femininity scores in research with adolescents. Therefore, masculinity and femininity are treated as independent measures.

Sex role attitudes.—The Attitudes toward Women Scale for Adolescents (AWSA) (Galambos et al., 1985) was used to measure sex role attitudes, or the extent to which the adolescent approves of the gender-based division of roles. The AWSA consists of 12 items (e.g., "Girls should have the same freedoms as boys") to which the subject responds on a four-point scale ranging from *agree strongly* to *disagree strongly.* A total scale score consisting of the mean of the responses is computed, with a higher score indicating less approval of gender differences in roles. Galambos et al. (1985) provided evidence for the scale's psychometric adequacy in several

TABLE 1

INTERCORRELATIONS AMONG MASCULINITY (MASC), FEMININITY (FEM), AND SEX ROLE ATTITUDES (AWSA) BY GRADE AND SEX

Measure	1	2	3	4	5	6	7	8	9
Grade 6:									
1. MASC ...		.49	.11[a]	**.65**	.44	.16[a]	**.61**	.49	.14[a]
2. FEM	.28		.33	.29	**.64**	.42	.30	**.66**	.33
3. AWSA	.05[a]	.01[a]		−.08[a]	.20	**.71**	−.01[a]	.13[a]	**.67**
Grade 7:									
4. MASC ...	**.51**	.22	.17		.43	−.02[a]	**.39**	.38	.05[a]
5. FEM	.27	**.61**	.02[a]	.42		.20	.18	**.54**	.21
6. AWSA	.06[a]	.07[a]	**.66**	.15[a]	.12[a]		−.04[a]	.16[a]	**.60**
Grade 8:									
7. MASC ...	**.56**	.10[a]	.10[a]	**.52**	.21	.12[a]		.39	.08[a]
8. FEM	.13[a]	**.37**	.12[a]	.20	**.40**	.15[a]	.45		.15[a]
9. AWSA	−.08[a]	.06[a]	**.68**	.05[a]	−.01[a]	**.57**	.09[a]	.11[a]	

NOTE.—Correlations for boys (n = 85) are above the diagonal; girls (n = 115) are below. Higher scores on MASC, FEM, and AWSA indicate higher masculinity, higher femininity, and more egalitarian sex role attitudes, respectively. Cross-time stabilities are in bold.

[a] Correlation not significant.

samples, including the present (EAS) one. We use sixth-, seventh-, and eighth-grade scores.

Plan of Analysis

Three 2 × 3 × 3 (sex × pubertal timing × grade) repeated-measures analyses of variance (ANOVAs), with grade as the repeated factor, examined the dependent variables of masculinity, femininity, and sex role attitudes. Linear and quadratic polynomial contrasts were used to test hypotheses about change over time (grade). Although the boys and girls in a given pubertal timing category (e.g., early or on time) were not similar in terms of pubertal status (i.e., *absolute* standing on physical maturation) or average age at peak height velocity, within their same-sex peer group they had the same *relative* standing. Therefore, it seemed reasonable to conduct the above ANOVAs. The confound between sex and pubertal timing, however, is addressed in additional analyses following presentation of the main results.

Results

Intercorrelations among Sex Role Measures

Table 1 presents intercorrelations among the masculinity, femininity, and sex role attitudes measures by sex and grade. The significant autocorrelations indicate that, for both boys and girls, there was stability in masculinity, femininity, and sex role attitudes across grade. The pattern of relations also indicates that, both within and across grade, higher masculinity is associated with higher femininity in boys and girls. Young adolescents who describe themselves as having masculine characteristics are likely to describe themselves as having feminine characteristics as well (with the exception of the girls' sixth/eighth-grade comparisons).

One other pattern is noteworthy. Among boys, most correlations between femininity and sex role attitudes are significant both within and across grades. Boys who described themselves as more feminine had more egalitarian sex role attitudes; that is, they were less likely to approve of the division of roles based on sex. In girls, there was no general relation between sex role attitudes and masculinity or femininity.

Masculinity

The first analysis was a 2 × 3 × 3 (sex × pubertal timing × grade) repeated-measures ANOVA with grade as the within-subjects factor and masculinity as the dependent variable. Table 2 presents the masculinity scores as a function of sex, grade, and pubertal timing. The results showed a significant main effect of sex, $F(1,194) = 23.04$, $p < .001$, with boys more masculine than girls. There was also a significant grade effect, $F(2,388) = 18.91$, $p < .001$, with significant linear, $F(1,194) = 30.68$, $p < .001$, and quadratic, $F(1,194) = 7.97$, $p < .01$, components. These results indicate that masculinity increased across grade, and that the largest increase was between seventh and eighth grade. There was no significant main effect of pubertal timing. There also was a significant sex × grade interaction, $F(2,388) = 3.96$, $p < .05$. Although boys were more masculine at all grade

TABLE 2

MEANS AND STANDARD DEVIATIONS FOR MASCULINITY BY SEX, GRADE, AND PUBERTAL TIMING

Sex and Pubertal Timing	N	Grade 6 M	Grade 6 SD	Grade 7 M	Grade 7 SD	Grade 8 M	Grade 8 SD
Boys:							
Early	28	5.05	.67	5.23	.79	5.51	.80
On time	30	5.07	.89	5.05	.81	5.50	.90
Late	27	5.14	.80	5.08	.77	5.57	.89
Total	85	5.09	.79	5.12	.78	5.53	.85
Girls:							
Early	40	4.85	.62	4.79	.74	4.96	.77
On time	35	4.81	.78	4.76	.74	4.89	.79
Late	40	4.59	.78	4.66	.64	4.85	1.02
Total	115	4.74	.73	4.74	.70	4.90	.86

NOTE.—Higher scores indicate higher masculinity. Possible range: 1–7.

levels than were girls, they were most different in the eighth grade. No other interactions were significant.

Femininity

In order to examine evidence for gender intensification in femininity, a 2 × 3 × 3 (sex × pubertal timing × grade) repeated-measures ANOVA was conducted with grade as the within-subjects factor. The means and standard deviations for femininity by sex, grade, and pubertal timing are presented in Table 3. There was a significant main effect of grade, $F(2,388) = 18.91$, $p < .001$, with a significant linear trend, $F(1,194) = 26.70$, $p < .001$. These results indicated an increase in femininity from sixth to eighth grade. There was also a significant main effect of sex, $F(1,194) = 20.36$, $p < .001$, indicating that girls were more feminine than boys. No other effects were significant.

Sex Role Attitudes

A 2 × 3 × 3 (sex × pubertal timing × grade) repeated-measures ANOVA was conducted to explore whether there was gender intensification of sex role attitudes (AWSA scores). The means and standard deviations on the AWSA by sex, grade, and pubertal timing are seen in Table 4. There was a significant main effect of sex, $F(1,194) = 108.53$, $p < .001$. Girls approved more than boys did of equality between males and females, and given the high means relative to the highest possible score, may be reaching a ceiling effect. There was also a significant sex

TABLE 3

MEANS AND STANDARD DEVIATIONS FOR FEMININITY BY GRADE, SEX, AND PUBERTAL TIMING

Sex and Pubertal Timing	N	Grade 6 M	Grade 6 SD	Grade 7 M	Grade 7 SD	Grade 8 M	Grade 8 SD
Boys:							
Early	28	4.75	.83	5.07	.67	5.12	.84
On time	30	4.88	1.00	5.14	.75	5.26	.96
Late	27	4.83	.98	4.97	1.00	5.35	.97
Total	85	4.83	.93	5.06	.81	5.24	.92
Girls:							
Early	40	5.48	.77	5.57	.83	5.64	.78
On time	35	5.30	.71	5.28	.78	5.51	.62
Late	40	5.37	.68	5.64	.77	5.61	1.05
Total	115	5.39	.72	5.50	.80	5.59	.84

NOTE.—Higher scores indicate higher femininity. Possible range: 1–7.

TABLE 4

MEANS AND STANDARD DEVIATIONS FOR SEX ROLE ATTITUDES BY SEX, GRADE, AND PUBERTAL TIMING

		Grade					
		6		7		8	
Sex and Pubertal Timing	*N*	*M*	SD	*M*	SD	*M*	SD
Boys:							
Early	28	2.79	.50	2.79	.56	2.74	.43
On time	30	2.71	.54	2.71	.47	2.59	.62
Late	27	2.96	.51	2.82	.50	2.74	.47
Total	85	2.82	.52	2.77	.51	2.69	.52
Girls:							
Early	40	3.26	.37	3.38	.32	3.37	.34
On time	35	3.23	.34	3.28	.39	3.38	.35
Late	40	3.25	.35	3.34	.30	3.35	.32
Total	115	3.24	.35	3.34	.34	3.37	.34

NOTE.—Higher scores indicate more egalitarian sex role attitudes. Possible range: 1–4.

× grade interaction, $F(2,388) = 12.70$, $p < .001$. From the sixth to the eighth grades, girls increasingly approved of male-female equality, whereas boys became less approving. There were no main or interaction effects involving pubertal timing.

Additional Analyses

In order to examine whether combining the boys and girls obscured any effects related to pubertal timing (an important issue, given that within the same pubertal timing category, girls were ahead of the boys with respect to average age at peak height velocity), three 3 × 3 (pubertal timing × grade) repeated-measures ANOVAs were conducted separately within sex. These analyses yielded no new information, that is, pubertal timing did not have an effect on the dependent variables when boys and girls were considered separately.

We also performed a set of 2 × 3 (sex × grade) repeated-measures ANOVAs on masculinity, femininity, and sex role attitudes, using only those boys and girls who were *comparable* with respect to age at peak height velocity (early-maturing boys and late-maturing girls; $n = 68$). The results for femininity and sex role attitudes were the same as those found with the larger sample, except that the sex × grade interaction for sex role attitudes failed to reach significance. In this case, failure to reach significance is probably due to the loss in power associated with smaller sample size.

With respect to masculinity, the main effects of sex and grade were significant (as was the case with the total sample). In contrast to the earlier results, however, there was not a significant sex × grade interaction. The pattern of results for this smaller sample was different in that late-maturing girls were less masculine in general than other girls, and early-maturing boys were more masculine in the seventh grade than were other boys.

Discussion

The results provide some support for the gender intensification hypothesis. In particular, across early adolescence, sex differences in masculinity and sex role attitudes increased. Pubertal timing, however, did not play an obvious role in the stimulation of this divergence. Why did initial sex differences in masculinity increase over time? Previous research suggests that masculinity is a critical aspect of self among boys, bearing positive relations to self-esteem and peer acceptance (Lamke, 1982; Massad, 1981). In fact, Massad (1981) argued that there is more social pressure placed on early adolescent boys to conform to the masculine sex role than there is for girls to conform to the feminine sex role. Because masculine behaviors, preferences, and interests are socially valued, it is not surprising that there is an escalation of masculinity among boys as they move toward adulthood. Adolescents see sex roles as flexible, to some extent (Carter & Patterson, 1982), but they still have sex-typed interests, activities, and preferences (Erb, 1983; Huston, 1983; Urberg, 1979). And, despite considerable social change over the last 25 years, there has been little evidence of change since then in attitudes, preferences, and interests among adolescent boys and girls (Lewin & Tragos, 1987; Lueptow, 1984).

Contrary to prediction, there was no escalation of femininity in girls relative to boys (i.e., no sex × grade interaction); rather, the femininity of boys and girls increased in a parallel fashion. Why? One possible explanation derives from longitudinal research showing that boys' and girls' conceptions of femininity become broader across early adolescence, incorporating traditionally masculine attributes along with traditionally feminine attributes (Crockett, Camarena, & Petersen, 1989). With less narrow and rigid definitions of what it means to be feminine, boys might become more comfortable in describing themselves as possessing feminine attributes. Positive correlations between masculinity and femininity among boys and girls in our sample suggest that adolescents have little difficulty in seeing themselves as having both masculine and feminine characteristics. Yet, they still maintain higher levels of sex-typed attributes; that is, girls are more feminine than masculine, and boys are more masculine than feminine.

At the same time, girls may not show dramatic rises in femininity because femininity does not carry with it attributes that are particularly valued or powerful in society (Leahy & Eiter, 1980; Massad, 1981). The disadvantages associated with being female are recognized by adolescent girls—they are more likely than boys to believe that it is hard to be a member of their own sex (Lewin & Tragos, 1987). And girls' recognition of females' relatively inferior position in society may also be seen in the results for sex role attitudes; from the sixth through eighth grades, girls became increasingly egalitarian, and boys became less so. These trends suggest that girls become aware of the personal implications of restrictions placed on them by the feminine sex role, whereas adolescent boys, having limited experience with what it means to be female, may find it easier to adopt less egalitarian attitudes present in society. This is not true for all boys, however; boys who reported having higher levels of feminine attributes were also likely to report more egalitarian sex role attitudes.

Contrary to the gender intensification hypothesis, pubertal timing was unrelated to masculinity, femininity, or sex role attitudes. The possibility remains that pubertal timing may contribute to gender intensification for subjects, especially boys, who are studied beyond the eighth grade. By the end of eighth grade, in contrast to girls, few boys have reached the end of the pubertal process. There might be an effect of pubertal timing among boys, however, once a larger proportion of them experience more of the visible pubertal changes. Indeed, the results of the comparison between early-maturing boys and late-maturing girls on masculinity lead us to suggest that early-maturing boys may be more masculine sooner than later-maturing boys. A fuller test of the gender intensification hypothesis, then, requires an assessment of the effect of pubertal timing as the subjects move through middle adolescence. In this regard, twelfth-grade follow-up data collected on subjects in this study will be useful (Petersen & Ebata, 1987).

Another possible reason for the lack of an effect of pubertal timing is that dimensions of sex typing are shaped by a multiplicity of influences, and despite the prominence of physical characteristics and changes during adolescence, the nature of these other influences on masculinity, femininity, and sex role attitudes may be more powerful. Among the strongest influences are sex role socialization by parents and teachers, messages regarding appropriate behavior as portrayed in the media, and variation in family structure (Huston, 1983). Petersen et al. (1983) argued that behavioral expectations for young adolescents are very much organized around grade in school, and that the experience of puberty is shaped by grade-based experiences. In fact, the most salient aspect of pubertal change for gender intensification may be, not that an individual per se enters puberty, but that a cohort becomes pubertal (Petersen, 1985). With the transition to junior high school for most students, and with successively higher grade levels, the messages regarding sex roles that adolescents receive, observe, and incorporate into their self-concepts may be similar regardless of their outward physical appearance.

Of course, these conclusions should be considered in light of the limitations of the data. The sample is largely middle class and white and consists of adolescents who participated in the study over the course of 3 years. One way in which future investigations could extend the present research is to broaden the age range studied. The present investigation was restricted to early adolescence. Will gender intensification extend into middle adolescence or beyond, or is it limited to early adolescence (see e.g., Petersen & Ebata, 1987)? Could pubertal timing have a more noticeable effect in middle or late adolescence? Another future direction for research is to look at multiple indices of conformity to one's sex role. Huston (1983), for example, discusses many sex-related dimensions that exist, including but not limited to concepts or beliefs about gender, self-perceptions, preferences, and observable behaviors. Through investigation of these issues, we will arrive at a greater understanding of the relation between sex roles and adolescent development.

References

Bakan, D. (1966). *The duality of human existence.* Chicago: Rand McNally.

Bem, S. L. (1974). The measurement of psychological androgyny. *Journal of Consulting and Clinical Psychology,* **42,** 155–162.

Bem, S. L. (1977). On the utility of alternative procedures for assessing psychological androgyny. *Journal of Consulting and Clinical Psychology,* **45,** 196–205.

Bem, S. L. (1981). *Bem Sex-Role Inventory professional manual.* Palo Alto, CA: Consulting Psychologists.

Block, J. H. (1973). Conceptions of sex role: Some cross-cultural and longitudinal perspectives. *American Psychologist,* **28,** 512–526.

Bock, R. D., Wainer, H., Petersen, A., Thissen, D., Murray, J., & Roche, A. F. (1973). A parameterization for individual human growth curves. *Human Biology,* **45,** 63–80.

Carter, D. B., & Patterson, C. J. (1982). Sex roles as social conventions: The development of children's conceptions of sex-role stereotypes. *Developmental Psychology,* **18,** 812–824.

Crockett, L. J., Camarena, P. M., & Petersen, A. C. (1989). *Masculinity and femininity in early adolescence: Developmental change in self-perceptions.* Unpublished manuscript, The Pennsylvania State University.

Crockett, L. J., Schulenberg, J. S., & Petersen, A. C. (1987). Congruence between objective and self-report data in a sample of young adolescents. *Journal of Adolescent Research,* **2,** 383–392.

Deaux, K. (1984). From individual differences to social categories: Analysis of a decade's research on gender. *American Psychologist,* **39,** 105–116.

Erb, T. O. (1983). Career preferences of early adolescents: Age and sex differences. *Journal of Early Adolescence,* **3,** 349–359.

Galambos, N. L., Petersen, A. C., Richards, M., & Gitelson, I. B. (1985). The Attitudes toward Women Scale for Adolescents (AWSA): A study of reliability and validity. *Sex Roles,* **13,** 343–356.

Hill, J. P., & Lynch, M. E. (1983). The intensification of gender-related role expectations during early adolescence. In J. Brooks-Gunn & A. C. Petersen (Eds.), *Girls at puberty: Biological and psychosocial perspectives* (pp. 201–228). New York: Plenum.

Hirsch, B. J., & Rapkin, B. D. (1987). The transition to junior high school: A longitudinal study of self-esteem, school life, and social support. *Child Development,* **58,** 1235–1243.

Huston, A. C. (1983). Sex-typing. In E. M. Hetherington (Ed.), P. H. Mussen (Series Ed.), *Handbook of child psychology: Vol. 4. Socialization, personality, and social development* (pp. 387–467). New York: Wiley.

Lamke, L. K. (1982). The impact of sex-role orientation on self-esteem in early adolescence. *Child Development,* **53,** 1530–1535.

Leahy, R. L., & Eiter, M. (1980). Moral judgment and the development of real and androgynous self-image during adolescence. *Developmental Psychology,* **16,** 362–370.

Lewin, M., & Tragos, L. M. (1987). Has the feminist movement influenced adolescent sex role attitudes? A reassessment after a quarter century. *Sex Roles,* **16,** 125–135.

Linn, M. C., & Petersen, A. C. (1985). Emergence and characterization of sex differences in spatial ability: A meta-analysis. *Child Development,* **56,** 1479–1498.

Linn, M. C., & Petersen, A. C. (1986). A meta-analysis of gender differences in spatial ability: Implications for math and science achievement. In J. S. Hyde & M. C. Linn (Eds.), *The psychology of gender: Advances through meta-analysis* (pp. 67–101). Baltimore, MD: Johns Hopkins University Press.

Little, R. J. A., & Rubin, O. B. (1987). *Statistical analysis with missing data.* New York: Wiley.

Lueptow, L. B. (1984). *Adolescent sex roles and social change.* New York: Columbia University Press.

Marshall, W. A., & Tanner, J. M. (1969). Variations in the pattern of pubertal changes in girls. *Archives of Disease in Childhood,* **44,** 291–303.

Marshall, W. A., & Tanner, J. M. (1970). Variations in the pattern of pubertal changes in boys. *Archives of Disease in Childhood,* **45,** 13–23.

Massad, C. M. (1981). Sex role identity and adjustment during adolescence. *Child Development,* **52,** 1290–1298.

Petersen, A. C. (1984). The early adolescence study: An overview. *Journal of Early Adolescence,* **4,** 103–106.

Petersen, A. C. (1985). Pubertal development as a cause of disturbance: Myths, realities, and unanswered questions. *Genetic, Social, and General Psychology Monographs,* **111,** 205–232.

Petersen, A. C., & Crockett, L. C. (1985). Pubertal timing and grade effects on adjustment. *Journal of Youth and Adolescence,* **14,** 191–206.

Petersen, A. C., & Ebata, A. T. (1987, July). *Gender-related change in self-image during adolescence*. Paper presented at the biennial meeting of the International Society for the Study of Behavioral Development, Tokyo.

Petersen, A. C., Sarigiani, P. A., & Kennedy, R. E. (in press). Adolescent depression: Why more girls? *Journal of Youth and Adolescence*.

Petersen, A. C., Tobin-Richards, M., & Boxer, A. (1983). Puberty: Its measurement and its meaning. *Journal of Early Adolescence*, **3**, 47–62.

Richardson, R. A., Galambos, N. L., Schulenberg, J. E., & Petersen, A. C. (1984). Young adolescents' perceptions of the family environment. *Journal of Early Adolescence*, **4**, 131–153.

Roberts, L. R., Sarigiani, P. A., Newman, J. L., & Petersen, A. C. (in press). Gender differential developmental change over early adolescence in the relationship between school achievement and self-image. *Journal of Early Adolescence*.

Rosenberg, F. R., & Simmons, R. G. (1975). Sex differences in the self-concept in adolescence. *Sex Roles*, **1**, 147–159.

Savin-Williams, R. C., & Small, S. A. (1986). The timing of puberty and its relationship to adolescent and parent perceptions of family interactions. *Developmental Psychology*, **22**, 342–347.

Simmons, R. G., & Blyth, D. A. (1987). *Moving into adolescence: The impact of pubertal change and school context*. New York: Aldine de Gruyter.

Simmons, R. G., Blyth, D. A., Van Cleave, E. F., & Bush, D. M. (1979). Entry into early adolescence: The impact of school structure, puberty, and early dating on self-esteem. *American Sociological Review*, **44**, 948–967.

Simmons, R. G., & Rosenberg, F. (1975). Sex, sex roles, and self-image. *Journal of Youth and Adolescence*, **4**, 229–258.

Spence, J. T., & Helmreich, R. L. (1978). *Masculinity and femininity: Their psychological dimensions, correlates, and antecedents*. Austin: University of Texas Press.

Taylor, M. C., & Hall, J. A. (1982). Psychological androgyny: Theories, methods, and conclusions. *Psychological Bulletin*, **92**, 347–366.

Thissen, D., Bock, R. D., Wainer, H., & Roche, A. F. (1976). Individual growth in stature: A comparison of four growth studies in the USA. *Annals of Human Biology*, **3**, 529–542.

Urberg, K. A. (1979). Sex role conceptualizations in adolescents and adults. *Developmental Psychology*, **15**, 90–92.

Worell, J. (1981). Life-span sex roles: Development, continuity, and change. In R. M. Lerner & N. A. Busch-Rossnagel (Eds.), *Individuals as producers of their development: A life-span perspective* (pp. 313–347). New York: Academic Press.

JOURNAL OF RESEARCH ON ADOLESCENCE, 6(3), 285–308

The Perceived Directionality of the Link Between Approval and Self-Worth: The Liabilities of a Looking Glass Self-Orientation Among Young Adolescents

Susan Harter and Clare Stocker
University of Denver

Nancy S. Robinson
Peabody College
Vanderbilt University

This study examined three orientations toward the relation between peer approval and global self-worth among young adolescents: (a) Self-worth is based upon peer approval of the self, a looking glass self-orientation; (b) self-worth is viewed as preceding approval from others; and (c) no connection is reported between self-worth and peer approval. A number of liabilities of a looking glass self-orientation were hypothesized and supported by the findings. Participants basing their self-worth on peer approval reported the greatest preoccupation with peer approval, they were most likely to be distracted from their schoolwork by peers (according to teachers' reports), they perceived the greatest fluctuations in both classmate approval and their self-worth, and they reported lower levels of classmate approval (confirmed by teachers) and self-worth, compared to those reporting that self-worth precedes approval. Findings were discussed in terms of the need for a model that will elucidate the precursors of these three orientations and their correlates.

Requests for reprints should be sent to Susan Harter, Department of Psychology, University of Denver, 2155 South Race Street, Denver, CO 80208.

Concerns about the self and the approval of others become increasingly salient as one moves into adolescence. Self-awareness, introspectiveness, and preoccupation with one's self-image increase dramatically, in part because of cognitive–developmental advances at this stage (see reviews by Harter, 1990a; Rosenberg, 1986). One particular developmental acquisition involves the ability to form metatheories about the relationship between the self and others. For example, our previous research revealed that young adolescents become capable of formulating theories about the nature of the causal links between perceived appearance and peer approval (Lancelotta, Harter, & Waters, 1993), between perceived appearance and self-worth (Harter, in press) and between self-worth and depression (Harter & Jackson, in press; Harter & Marold, in press). This study focused on another such link, namely, the perceived causal relation between self-worth and approval from *peers*. The developmental increase in the impact of peer support beginning in early adolescence (Brown, 1990; Savin-Williams & Berndt, 1990) makes this a particularly salient source of support. Our interest in the link between approval and self-worth was an outgrowth of our research on formulations that speak to the causes of global self-worth or self-esteem (Harter, 1986, 1987, 1990b, in press). This study addressed young adolescents' metatheories about one such formulation, namely, Cooley's model of the looking glass self.

For Cooley (1902), the self was a social construction, based upon the incorporation of opinions that significant others hold about the self. These others become the social mirror into which one gazes, seeking to determine whether they hold the self in high or low regard. Such reflected appraisals are then internalized as one's own opinion of self, one's global sense of worth as a person. Mead (1934), another symbolic interactionist in the same tradition, elaborated on this theme in his concept of the *generalized other*, which represented the pooled or collective judgments of the significant others in one's life. These formulations received considerable attention in the social psychological literature (see Felson, 1981; Gecas, 1972; Gecas & Schwalbe, 1983; Reitzes, 1980; Shrauger & Schoeneman, 1979).

The programmatic research efforts of Rosenberg (1979, 1986) as well as of our own research group (see Harter, 1986, 1987, 1990b; Harter & Hogan, 1985; Robinson, 1989) revealed that among adolescents, social support from significant others, notably peers and parents, is a strong predictor of global self-worth. In fact, a growing number of studies revealed that self-esteem or self-worth is clearly related to support from parents (Gecas, 1972; Peterson, Schulenberg, Abramowitz, Offer, & Jarcho, 1984), from peers (Buhrmester, 1990; Bukowski & Hoza, 1989; Cauce, 1986), and from both parents and peers (Cauce, Felner, & Primavera, 1982; Cauce, Reid, Landesman, & Gonzales, 1990; Coates, 1985; Furman, 1987; Hirsch & Rapkin, 1987; O'Donnell, 1976). With regard to the particular *type* of support, our own research (Robinson, 1992) demonstrated that support in the form of *approval* from others is most highly correlated with self-worth, which we defined as one's approval and acceptance of the self (Harter, 1982, 1990b). Employing path-analytic techniques, models that specify approval as a predicted *cause* of level of self-esteem provide an excellent fit to the data (Harter, 1986; Harter & Hogan, 1985; Harter, Marold, & Whitesell, 1992).

However, there is reason to be cautious about inferring that the *directionality* of effects postulated in the model reflects individuals' phenomenological experiences of how these components are ordered. Statistical modeling procedures, applied to group data collected at any given point in time, do not necessarily simulate the psychological processes underlying the sequence in which perceptions about the self and others unfold.

Thus, our interest in directionality provoked us to examine what proportion of adolescents *consciously endorse* Cooley's looking glass self-formulation, that is, how many actually acknowledge that one needs the approval of others in order to approve of the self? This issue becomes particularly relevant during the period of adolescence, because, as noted at the outset, at this stage young people begin forming metatheories about the causal nature of the links between constructs that involve the self and others. For example, in our earlier work, we determined that some adolescents felt that their appearance affected their popularity, whereas others reported no such link (Lancelotta et al., 1993). In another study of the perceived directionality of the link between low self-worth and depression, we determined that although approximately half of young adolescents felt that low self-worth precedes depressed affect, the remaining subjects reported that they experienced depressed affect prior to low self-worth (Harter & Jackson, 1993; Harter & Marold, 1993). In a third study (Harter, 1993) on the perceived link between physical appearance and self-worth, one group reported that how they looked determined their self-worth, a second group reported just the opposite directionality, and a third group indicated that there was no connection between appearance and self-worth. Noteworthy is the fact that although the *ability* to formulate theories about the directionality of effects emerges in early adolescence, there are clear individual differences in terms of the particular nature of such connections. These individual differences were the focus of this study, specifically differences in the perceived directionality of the link between approval and self-worth.

In an earlier study, we initially asked adolescents to endorse one of two orientations: (a) If others approve of me first, then I will like myself as a person, or (b) if I like myself as a person, then others will like and approve of me. Across several samples (including middle and high school students), the findings revealed that approximately half endorsed the first, *looking glass self* option, whereas the other half endorsed the second option (Robinson & Harter, 1991).

Moreover, subjects' open-ended verbal descriptions provided converging evidence with regard to the validity of their choices. Looking glass subjects generated explanations such as "If other kids approve of me and say good things about me, then I look at myself and think I'm not so bad, and I start liking myself" and "By having other people approve of you it gives you self-confidence and so you like yourself. If no one liked you, you probably wouldn't like yourself very much." Those for whom self-worth precedes approval from others provided such descriptions as "If I like myself as a person, then I know that the other kids will feel pretty much the same" and "If you like yourself and feel good about yourself, it is easier to make friends and your friends like you more."

Our initial findings also revealed that those endorsing the looking glass self-orientation reported lower self-worth and less approval than did those acknowledging that their level of self-worth determined their level of approval (Robinson & Harter, 1991). These preliminary results, therefore, suggested the potential liabilities of a looking glass self-orientation. Of further interest was the fact that a third orientation emerged among a subgroup of those who selected the second option on our forced two-choice procedure. These individuals wrote that neither orientation really applied because there was no connection between what others thought of them and how much they liked themselves. They provided comments such as "I don't care what other people think of me, it doesn't have anything to do with how much I like myself." It was also noteworthy that in their descriptions, the vast majority of adolescents specifically mentioned *peers* in the plural (e.g., classmates, other kids, friends) or made reference to people in general, suggesting that in pursuing the impact of the generalized other, it would be illuminating to initially focus on peer approval.

In this study, therefore, we first asked young adolescents to endorse one of three possible orientations with regard to the directionality of peer approval and global self-worth: (a) peer approval precedes self-worth, that is, perceptions of peer approval are the basis on which judgments about one's worth as a person are formed; (b) self-worth precedes peer approval, that is, how much one likes oneself as a person will determine how much approval one will receive from peers; and (c) there is no connection between peer approval and self-worth, that is, how much one likes oneself as a person has little or nothing to do with approval from peers.

We viewed these directionality orientations as perspectives, metatheories, or working models that have a number of predictable correlates. These correlates include (a) how much adolescents *think about*, or are preoccupied with, the link between approval and self-worth; (b) the extent to which they are distracted from doing schoolwork by peer concerns; (c) the extent to which adolescents detect or experience *fluctuations* in peer *approval;* (d) the extent to which adolescents experience *fluctuations* in *self-worth;* (e) the *level* of perceived peer *approval;* and (f) the *level* of *self-worth.*

There were certain conceptual and anticipated empirical convergences between our approval to self-worth orientation participants and those prone to high self-monitoring or concern with one's public self (see Buss, 1980; Goffman, 1959). High self-monitors evidence considerable concern about the opinions of others and report frequent fluctuations in the perceptions of these opinions. The characteristics of low self-monitors, however, have been less clearly understood, in that the absence of high self-monitoring might represent either a pattern of defensive avoidance or a more adaptive stance in which one simply is not preoccupied with the opinions of others. The two remaining orientations we discovered, namely, no-connection and the self-worth to approval directionality pattern, may well speak to such a distinction among low self-monitors.

Therefore, the following pattern of predictions was advanced for the three directionality orientation groups, across six correlates:

1. With regard to how much young adolescents *think about* the connection between classmates liking them and liking themselves, we hypothesized that the approval to self-worth group would think the most about this link, the no-connection group would think the least about the link, and the self-worth to approval group would fall in between.
2. Employing teacher ratings, we predicted differences in *social distractibility.* This construct pitted social distractibility by peers against one's ability to attend to or concentrate on schoolwork within the classroom setting. We anticipated that the approval to self-worth orientation might well interfere with one's ability to do the requisite academic tasks at hand. Thus, we hypothesized that the approval to self-worth group would be the most highly distracted, given their general concern over peer approval; the no-connection group would be the least distracted; and the self-worth to approval group would fall in between.
3. Based on the hypothesis that the approval to self-worth group would be the most preoccupied, and therefore the most cognizant of classmate approval, it was predicted that this group would be more likely to detect or experience *fluctuations* in classmate approval, compared to the other two groups.
4. To the extent that the approval to self-worth group would be more likely to detect or experience fluctuations in classmate approval, they would

also report more *fluctuation* in *self-worth* compared to the other groups because by definition they acknowledge that they base their self-worth on peer approval.

5. With regard to the *level* of *peer approval,* it was predicted that the approval to self-worth group would report a lower level of approval than would the self-worth to approval group. Two possible considerations guided this prediction. Lower levels of approval may provoke adolescents to adopt a stance in which they are concerned about approval and its relation to self-worth. It is also possible that individuals in the approval to self-worth group, given their preoccupation with approval, may engage in behaviors that do not garner this type of peer support. For example, they may try too hard to elicit peer approval and in so doing may annoy or alienate their classmates.

6. To the extent that the approval to self-worth group, who by definition base their self-worth on approval, reports lower peer approval, their *self-worth* would also be lower than that of the self-worth to approval group. There is no reason to predict that the no-connection group would have lower self-worth because they are presumably basing their self-worth on other considerations, for example, competence in domains of importance (Harter, 1986; James, 1892). Recent findings (Harter, Simon, & Johnson, 1993) identified a subgroup of middle school adolescents who based their self-esteem primarily on competence considerations rather than on social support.

METHOD

Participants

Ninety percent of the students at a public middle school were included in our initial sample. One third of this population, that is, 147 sixth, seventh, and eighth graders, were administered the measures in this study. In the sixth grade, there were 24 female and 22 male students; in the seventh grade, there were 23 female and 25 male students; and in the eighth grade, there were 28 female and 25 male students. The school was located in a residential neighborhood of lower-middle-class and middle-class families. The majority of parent occupations involved blue-collar, hourly wage, and service positions; a minority had white-collar, managerial, and professional positions. The mean educational level was high school completion, with some college graduates. Eighty-one percent of this particular sample were White,

13% were Hispanic, and the remaining 6% were African American and Asian students.

Procedure

The entire battery of instruments was group administered in classroom units on two consecutive days. Subsequent to obtaining parental and student permission, members of our university research team administered the measures to the students. The instruments were administered to students in their language arts classes, and the language arts teachers served as raters of the students' behavior. From past experience, we found that the language arts teachers in this school were particularly aware of students' thoughts and feelings, based on their knowledge of the students through written and oral exercises and the more interactive, expressive nature of the language arts classes, compared to other school subjects.

Instruments

Directionality measure. Table 1 presents the measure designed to assess the three directionality orientations: (a) Classmate approval leads to approval of the self, (b) approval of self leads to classmate approval, and (c) there is little or no relation between the two. The second set of questions addressed these three orientations with regard to *disapproval.* For each set of three options, participants were asked to indicate which was the most true for them. They were then asked to provide a written example of something that happened to make them feel that way. In a subsequent follow-up study with middle school students, we examined the psychometric properties of a number of measures more thoroughly (Harter & Stocker, 1993). The convergent validity of the directionality measure was demonstrated by administering a separate 18-item rating scale that contained 6 items (3 about approval and 3 about disapproval) on each of three subscales that paralleled the three directionality orientations. A sample item for the approval to self-worth orientation was as follows: "Some kids need to have others tell them they like them in order to like themselves." A sample of an item on the no-connection subscale was "For some kids, whether others disapprove of them doesn't have that much to do with whether they disapprove of themselves." Participants responded to items on a 4-point scale (*really true for me, sort of true for me, not very true for me,* or *not at all true for me*). The 18-item version was administered on a different day than was the global directionality measure. The relations between the initial direc-

TABLE 1
Measure Assessing Directionality Orientation

Which Comes First?

Many middle school students have told us that liking or not liking yourself as a person and having other people like or not like you as a person often go together. We want to know which you feel comes first.

First read all three and then put an "X" in the space to the left of the sentence that is most true for you.

☐ I first feel that my classmates like or approve of me ⟶ and then because of that ⟶ I like or approve of myself.

☐ I first feel that I like or approve of myself ⟶ and then because of that ⟶ my classmates like or approve of me.

☐ How much my classmates like or approve of me and how much I like or approve of myself don't have that much to do with each other.

First read all three and then put an "X" in the space to the left of the sentence that is most true for you.

☐ I first feel that my classmates don't like or approve of me ⟶ and then because of that ⟶ I don't like or approve of myself.

☐ I first feel that I don't like or approve of myself ⟶ and then because of that ⟶ my classmates don't like or approve of me.

☐ How much my classmates don't like or approve of me and how much I don't like or approve of myself don't have that much to do with each other.

Tell us something that made you feel one of the ways you checked. Describe what happened with your classmates.

tionality orientation choice and scores on the corresponding rating scales were highly significant for all three orientations (all $ps < .0001$).

Furthermore, in this study, we performed a content analysis of the examples that participants provided after they selected one of the three directionality orientations (sample descriptions are presented in Table 2). Meaningful responses had to meet the following criteria: (a) They had to match the directionality orientation endorsed; (b) they had to contain both elements, namely, a description of *approval* as well as feelings about the *self;* and (c) the valence could be clearly coded, that is, it had to be either positive or negative in the case of the first two directionality orientations. This analysis revealed that 86% of the participants gave meaningful descriptions

TABLE 2
Examples of Adolescents' Open-Ended Descriptions for Each of the Three Directionality Orientations Involving Approval and Self-Worth

Approval precedes self-worth
"When I meet new kids and they approve of me, then I look at myself and say 'I'm not so bad,' and it makes me feel good."
"They made fun of my clothes. Then I felt stupid like I was an idiot and didn't like myself."
"When other kids make you feel left out you don't feel good about yourself."
"When people praise everything you do, then you start to really like yourself as a person."
"If other people don't like me as a person, then I wonder if I am a good person, I care about what people say about me."
Self-worth precedes approval
"You have to appreciate yourself first, as a person. If you wait for other people to make you feel good, you could be waiting a long time!"
"In seventh grade I didn't like myself as a person, so I didn't have very many friends, but then in eighth grade, I felt confident about myself and then I found that I had many more friends."
"I just like myself, and then other people like me too."
"When I like the way I look, other kids say good and nice things about me."
"The way I figure it, if you can't like the person you are first, then how do you expect other people to like you?"
No connection between approval and self-worth
"When a classmate cuts me down, I don't really care."
"I really don't care if someone doesn't like me because it's their problem."
"Well, somebody said I was stupid. Go ahead, let them think I'm stupid, who cares!"
"The popular people were mean to me, but I kept my head high and ignored it, because I like the way I am, it's me."
"If someone doesn't like me, they can't make me feel bad if I'm confident enough about myself. What they think doesn't matter."

that paralleled the orientations they selected. The remaining 14% provided responses that did not meet the three criteria, and many were also ambiguous or sketchy (e.g., "I got rejected by a girl I had a crush on," "Nobody likes me because I like nerds," "because I might take my anger out on them," and "some like me, some don't").

Preoccupation with the link between classmate approval and approval of self. After providing a written example, students were asked to rate the question "How much do you *think about* the connection between your classmates liking or not liking you and you liking or not liking yourself?" on a 4-point scale: 1 (*hardly ever*), 2 (*not very often*), 3 (*pretty often*), and 4 (*very often*). In our follow-up study a second parallel item was added, yielding an internal consistency reliability of .76 for the two items.

Fluctuations in level of classmate support. Students were given the statement "How my classmates feel about me, how much they like me as a person, usually changes" followed by seven response choices: 1 (*hardly ever*), 2 (*about once a month*), 3 (*several times a month*), 4 (*about once a week*), 5 (*several times a day*), 6 (*about once a week*), and 7 (*several times a week*). Convergent validity was obtained in the follow-up study by demonstrating that the measure used in this study was highly related to scales assessing the frequency with which classmate approval changes. The four response choices from this follow-up measure, and the accompanying fluctuations scores on the 7-point scale, were 1 (*changes a lot;* $M = 6.49$), 2 (*changes pretty much;* $M = 5.54$), 3 (*doesn't change that much;* $M = 4.17$), and 4 (*hardly ever changes;* $M = 2.12$). An analysis of variance (ANOVA) revealed these predicted differences to be highly significant, $F(3, 453) = 42.74$, $p < .0001$.

Fluctuations in level of self-worth. The same format was employed to assess fluctuations in self-worth. Students were given the statement "How I feel about myself, how much I like myself as a person, usually changes," followed by the same seven responses choices described previously.

Level of classmate approval. As part of our standardized battery, students were given an adaptation (see Robinson, 1992) of the Social Support Scale for Children and Adolescents (Harter, 1985b). This instrument identifies three types of support: approval, emotional support, and instrumental support, from four sources: classmates, close friends, parents, and teachers. Theoretically, from a looking glass perspective, *approval* support should be most highly related to self-worth, conceptualized as approval of the self. There is empirical support for this hypothesis (see Robinson, 1992). In this study, only the four-item classmate approval subscale was included. Sample item content included classmates liking you as a person, being proud of you, and wanting you to stay the way you are. Items were presented in a structured alternative format in which participants responded to the following type of question: "Some kids have classmates who like the kind of person they are BUT Other kids have classmates who do not like the kind of person they are." Participants first indicated which of these two statements was more like them and then were asked to decide whether that statement was *sort of true* for them or *really true* for them. Items were scored on a 4-point scale with 4 representing the highest level of approval and 1 denoting the lowest support level. The scale has demonstrated reliability and validity (Harter, 1985b). The internal consistency reliability of the classmate approval scale for this sample was .82.

Global self-worth. As part of the standardized battery, students were also administered the Self-Perception Profile for Children (Harter, 1985a). This instrument taps five specific domains of the self-concept as well as global self-worth, a separate subscale. Only the six-item global self-worth subscale was relevant to this study. A sample item is "Some kids like the kind of person they are BUT Other kids often wish they were someone else." As in the sample question for classmate approval, students select which option is most like them and then indicate whether that statement is *sort of true* or *really true* for them. A score of 4 denotes the highest level of self-worth, and a 1 denotes the lowest level of self-worth. The reliability and validity of this instrument has been amply demonstrated (Harter, 1982, 1985a, 1986, 1990b). The internal consistency reliability of the global self-worth subscale for this sample was .81.

Teacher ratings. The teacher rating scale that accompanies the Self-Perception Profile for Children (Harter, 1985a) was adapted to assess two dimensions involving peer relationships. One two-item subscale tapping peer approval or acceptance was included to assess the convergence between student and teacher judgments. A sample item is "This student is well accepted by classmates OR This student is not that well accepted by classmates." Teachers first decide which statement best describes a given student and then indicate whether that statement is *sort of true* or *really true* for that student. A score of 4 denotes the highest level of approval, a 1 denotes the lowest level of approval. A second two-item subscale to assess peer social distractibility was created for the purpose of this study. A sample distractibility item is "This student is often socially distracted by classmates OR This student concentrates well on schoolwork and class assignments." The internal consistency reliabilities of these two subscales for this sample were .88 and .90, respectively.

RESULTS

Preliminary Analyses

The majority of the participants (74%) selected the same directionality orientation for peer approval and disapproval. We felt that the consistency demonstrated by these participants represented the strongest endorsement of the three orientations and thus restricted our analyses to this group.[1] Thirty-four endorsed the approval to self-worth direction, 23 endorsed the self-worth to approval direction, and 52 reported that there was no connection between approval and their self-worth. No grade or sex differences were predicted. Preliminary chi-square analyses of the distribution of participants in the Grade × Sex × Directionality subgroups were performed. Of the seven possible effects, only one was significant. There was a tendency for more sixth graders to endorse the approval to self-worth directionality orientation, whereas there were somewhat more students in the seventh and eighth grades who endorsed the no-connection orientation, $\chi^2(4, N = 108) = 10.15, p < .05$. This pattern was not predicted and was not replicated in our subsequent work.

With regard to the analyses of the dependent variables (preoccupation, distractibility, fluctuations in peer approval and in self-worth, and level of peer approval and of self-worth), grade and sex were included as independent variables in the preliminary ANOVAs. Of the 35 possible effects tested, only one was significant. Girls reported more classmate approval ($M = 3.11$) than did boys ($M = 2.72$), $F(1, 92) = 11.17, p < .001$, consistent with previous findings (Robinson, 1992). Therefore, because the preliminary analyses (chi-square and ANOVA) revealed negligible differences for either grade or sex, grade and sex were not included in subsequent analyses.

It should be noted that separate one-way ANOVAs for each dependent variable, followed by one-tailed planned comparisons, were performed for comparisons involving all three directionality groups. A multivariate analysis of variance was not appropriate because there were varying *patterns* of group differences across the variables.[2] Moreover, ANOVAs were only performed if predictions involved differences between all three groups. For comparisons in which differences between only two groups were predicted, *t* tests were performed.

---

[1]We did not analyze the inconsistent group ($n = 37$) for several reasons. The participants in each group were too few across the six cells to make meaningful comparisons. Moreover, there was no one type of inconsistency that was significantly more common. A content analysis of these participants' responses was not interpretable. Many participants did not provide a description, and those that did gave comments that did not illuminate their choice with regard to the issue of inconsistency. Sample comments included "I hope my classmates can approve of me," "most of them like me," "because they don't talk to me," and "they ignore me." Finally, analyses of other measures, such as level of approval, where alphas could be calculated, revealed that this group of participants was less internally consistent than were the groups who endorsed the same directionality for both positive and negative questions.

[2]Due to absences and some missing data, the *N*s change slightly from analysis to analysis.

Converging evidence from the descriptions of the three groups

Participants' written descriptions of experiences paralleling the directionality orientation that they selected provided clear evidence that the orientation selected was meaningful.[3] Table 2 presents sample responses from each of the three groups. The most common themes among the students in the approval to self-worth and the self-worth to approval groups were (a) peer social acceptance or rejection of one's behavior or personality (65.1%), (b) peer reactions to their physical appearance and dress (25.9%), and (c) peer evaluations of their competence (7.2%). Among the no-connection group, although the same specific themes did occur, the most striking feature was that 75% of these participants, after paraphrasing the lack of connection between their self-esteem and reactions of others, added that they "didn't care" about the opinions of others.

Of further interest was the fact that, although participants in the approval to self-worth and self-worth to approval groups had the option of describing either a positive event (e.g., a compliment, approval, etc.) or a negative event (e.g., rejection, disapproval, etc.), the approval to self-worth participants cited more negative (59.0%) than positive (34.0%) examples, whereas the opposite was true for the self-worth to approval participants, who were far more likely to give positive (88.9%) than negative (11.1%) examples, $\chi^2(1, N = 46) = 13.36, p < .001$.

Preoccupation with link between approval and self-worth. Figure 1 reveals the predicted pattern for how much adolescents in each of the three groups *think about* the link between approval and self-worth. The approval to self-worth group thought most about the link ($M = 2.63$, $SD = .96$), the no-connection group gave little thought to the link ($M = 1.37$, $SD = 66$), and the self-worth to approval group ($M = 2.22$, $SD = .79$) fell in between, $F(2, 101) = 26.20$, $p < .001$. Contrasts further revealed that the approval to self-worth group was significantly different from the self-worth to approval group ($p < .03$). The no-connection group mean was significantly different from both the approval to self-worth and self-worth to approval group means ($ps < .0001$).

---

[3]The responses to the orientation *selected* appeared meaningful for the vast majority of participants. We did not, however, ask participants to describe or explain the alternative orientations. A reasonable assumption is that because they made a choice, which they justified in their written descriptions, they comprehended the alternatives, an assumption that will be examined in future work.

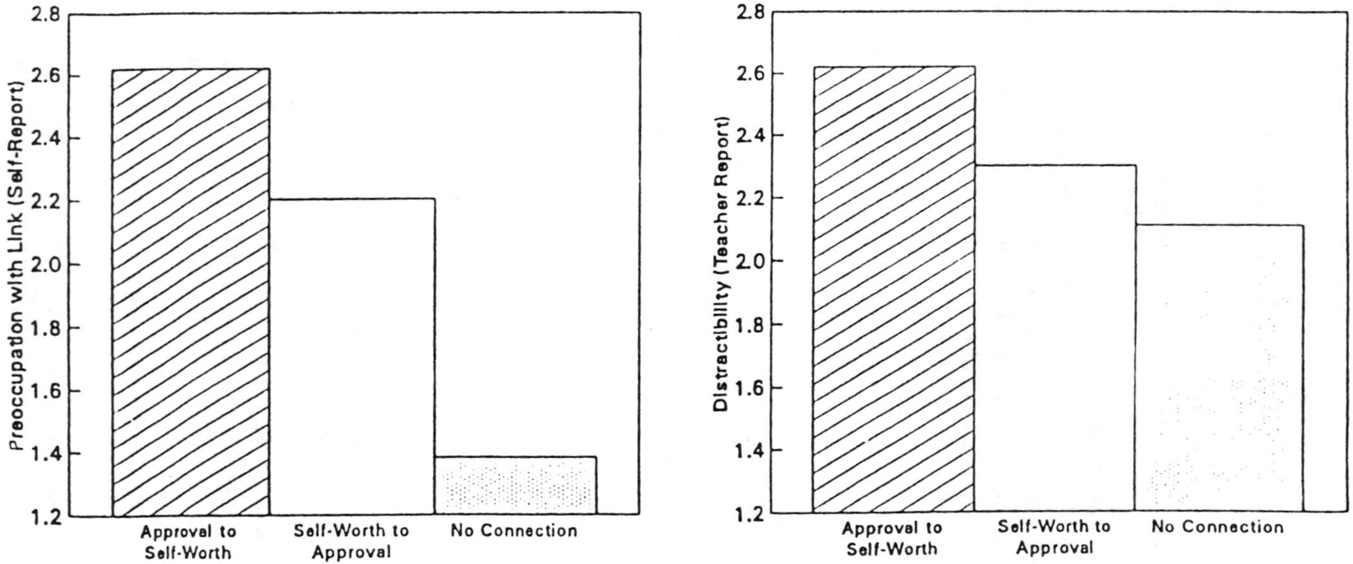

FIGURE 1 Preoccupation with the link between approval and self-worth and distractibility for the three directionality groups.

Distractibility by peers from schoolwork. We asked teachers to rate how much each student was distracted from schoolwork due to his or her competing focus on peers. We hypothesized the approval to self-worth group would be more distracted by peers than would the no-connection group, with the self-worth to approval group falling in between. The results (see Figure 1) confirmed this pattern. The approval to self-worth group was rated as significantly ($p < .05$) more distractible ($M = 2.62$, $SD = 1.09$) than was the no-connection group ($M = 2.11$, $SD = .97$). As predicted, the self-worth to approval group ($M = 2.31$, $SD = 1.01$) fell in between the other two groups, but did not differ significantly from either.

Fluctuations in peer approval and in self-worth. For fluctuations in peer approval as well as in self-worth, a similar pattern was predicted, namely, that the approval to self-worth group would report more fluctuations than would either of the other two groups. This pattern was confirmed by the results presented in Figure 2. With regard to the effects for fluctuations in *classmate approval*, $F(2, 68) = 6.46$, $p < .003$, further contrasts revealed that the approval to self-worth group reported significantly greater fluctuation ($M = 3.95$, $SD = 2.39$) than did the self-worth to approval group ($M = 2.31$, $SD = 2.06$, $p < .009$) or the no-connection group ($M = 1.97$, $SD = 1.71$, $p < .0005$). With regard to the magnitude of change in perceived approval, the approval to self-worth group mean reveals that they felt that the level of classmate approval changed about once a week. For the self-worth to approval group, approval was perceived to change slightly more often than once a month; and for the no-connection group, change was once a month.

A similar pattern was obtained for fluctuations in *self-worth*, $F(2, 91) = 8.85$, $p < .001$, with the approval to self-worth group reporting significantly greater fluctuation ($M = 4.57$, $SD = 2.04$) than did the self-worth to approval group ($M = 2.56$, $SD = 1.85$, $p < .001$) or the no-connection group ($M = 2.63$, $SD = 2.22$, $p < .0001$). Approval to self-worth adolescents reported that their self-worth changed between once and several times a week, in contrast to the other two groups whose mean responses for self-worth change fell between once and several times a month.

Level of peer approval. With regard to perceptions in *level* of approval, the predicted pattern was obtained in that the approval to self-worth group reported lower approval ($M = 2.77$, $SD = .62$) than did the self-worth to approval group ($M = 3.08$ $SD = .56$), $t(49) = 1.80$, $p < .05$. The mean for the no-connection group was 2.84 ($SD = .62$). Teachers' ratings of peer approval revealed the same pattern in that the approval to self-worth group ($M =$

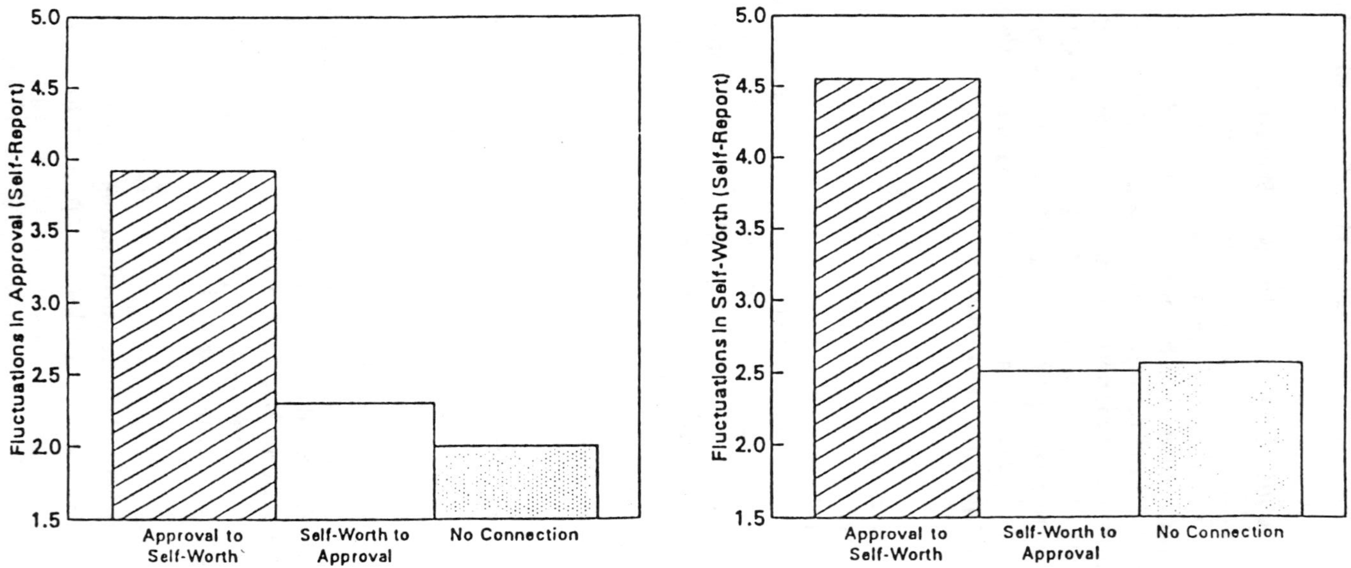

FIGURE 2 Fluctuations in perceived peer approval and in self-worth for the three directionality groups.

2.84, $SD = .72$) was judged to receive less approval than was the self-worth to approval group ($M = 3.31$, $SD = .63$), $t(29) = 1.62$, $p < .055$. The mean teacher rating for the no-connection group was 3.12 ($SD = .82$).

Level of self-worth. For self-worth, we predicted that the approval to self-worth group would have lower self-worth than would the self-worth to approval group. Findings revealed that the approval to self-worth group reported lower self-worth ($M = 3.04$, $SD = .68$) than did the self-worth to approval group ($M = 3.29$, $SD = .63$), $t(51) = 1.37$, $p < .086$. The mean self-worth score of the no-connection group was 3.27 ($SD = .58$).

DISCUSSION

The findings of this study provide compelling evidence that young adolescents endorse particular orientations with regard to the directionality of approval and global self-worth. For young adolescents in general, there is an emerging ability to construct metatheories involving the causal links between constructs involving the self and others (see reviews by Harter, 1990a; Rosenberg, 1986). Of particular interest, however, are the individual differences in how young adolescents conceptualize the nature of the relation between peer approval and self-worth. Each of the three directionality subgroups we identified had clear metatheories about the cause and effect links between approval and self-worth that were corroborated by the descriptions participants reported.

A content analysis of these descriptions revealed that the approval to self-worth and the self-worth to approval groups most frequently provided accounts of peer reactions to their social behavior, personality, and physical appearance. The *valence* of these descriptions was also noteworthy. The approval to self-worth group was more likely to focus on *negative* evaluative reactions by peers, whereas the self-worth to approval group was far more likely to report *positive* evaluations by peers. These findings are consistent with the general pattern revealing more positive outcomes for the self-worth to approval participants, for example, higher levels of approval and more positive feelings of self-worth than was reported by the approval to self-worth participants. The valence of the descriptions of the no-connection group could not be reliably coded because many of these participants indicated that they "didn't care" about the opinions of peers, a finding to which we will return. A major goal of this study was to determine whether these three orientations were associated with a predictable pattern of meaningful correlates. Moreover, we specifically sought to examine the general hypothesis that there were certain liabilities associated with the endorsement of a looking glass self-perspective. The pattern of findings generally supported our predictions. Those endorsing the approval to self-worth directionality reported significantly greater preoccupation with peer approval than did either the self-worth to approval group or the no-connection group, who reported virtually no preoccupation with peer approval.

We also speculated that the approval to self-worth directionality group would report greater perceived fluctuations in peer approval and in self-worth than would either the self-worth to approval or the no-connection group. Although adolescence, as a general developmental period, tends to usher in volatility in the self-concept (Harter, 1986; Harter & Monsour, 1992; Rosenberg, 1986), we obtained predictable individual differences in the extent to which adolescents perceived their self-worth to fluctuate. Those basing their self-worth on peer approval appear to be particularly vulnerable to changes in self-worth because, as our findings suggest, they perceived peer approval to be fluctuating far more than did the other two groups. Given that they are basing their self-worth on such fluctuating approval, it is understandable why their self-worth would fluctuate in tandem. Whether fluctuations in peer approval are observable or are interpretations by these participants is unclear in these findings and is therefore a topic for further study. The approval to self-worth group was clearly more sensitive to peer approval and may therefore be more likely to interpret peer opinions of them as changing.

As hypothesized, the level of peer approval, as reflected in both student and teacher ratings, was significantly lower for the approval to self-worth group, as compared to the self-worth to approval group. Two interpretations are possible, although this study did not provide a test of these alternatives. The first possibility is that if one is perceiving or receiving relatively low levels of support, this in turn may lead to an orientation in which one is concerned about the consequences of low approval for the self. Alternatively, adolescents who endorse the approval to self-worth directionality orientation, and who are preoccupied with peer approval, may have characteristics that cause them to be less likable. For example, they may try too hard to elicit peer approval, may have inappropriate strategies for obtaining such support, or both, which in turn attenuates the support that they actually receive.

Given that the students in the approval to self-worth group (who by definition base their self-worth on approval) reported lower peer support, we hypothesized that their self-worth would also be lower than that of the self-worth to approval group, in particular. The findings were consistent with this prediction. Thus, there appear to be a constellation of negative correlates, involving both self and others, that accompany a looking glass self-orientation.

The liabilities of a looking glass self-orientation manifest themselves in arenas other than self-perceptions, in that teachers observed behavioral ramifications in the classroom. Of particular interest are the implications for a student's ability to function academically. Teachers' ratings revealed that looking glass self students were more likely to be socially distracted from their scholastic activities, which may be due to their preoccupation with peer approval. Their inability to concentrate on the academic demands in the classroom also may have predictable consequences in terms of poorer school performance, a hypothesis we plan to examine in future research.

This study sought, as a first step, to demonstrate correlates of the three orientations identified. Thus, it did not address the issue of the causal links between these correlates, but rather identified a constellation of highly related constructs. Many of these effects may well be bidirectional. One can speculate, however, that the level of support and the need for support may be key mediating variables. For the approval to self-worth directionality group, the fact that both they and their teachers reported that they received lower levels of support may touch off a chain of related reactions. The assumption that this group needs or values support finds confirmation in our follow-up study revealing that the approval to self-worth group reported that peer acceptance was significantly more important (3.6 on a 4-point scale) than did the self-worth to approval group (3.2), who, in turn, reported that peer acceptance was significantly more important than did the no-connection group (2.98). Thus, for the approval to self-worth directionality group, lower levels of desired support may lead to a preoccupation with support and distractibility by peers, which will transfer to a concern about the implications of one's level of support for the self. That is, it will provoke the adoption of the approval to self-worth orientation. Lower levels of support, given this directionality orientation, will also result in lower self-worth. Preoccupation and distractibility, which involve attentiveness to peer behavior, may lead to a greater sensitivity to potential fluctuations in peer approval. To the extent that one perceives greater fluctuations in peer approval, one's self-esteem will fluctuate accordingly. Thus, this is the type of framework that future work will need to address.

Of particular importance are the earlier *developmental* precursors of the three styles identified. Here we share with many developmentalists, particularly those with an attachment perspective, the view that early relationships with caregivers provide working models that children may carry into relationships with peers (Kobak, 1992). With regard to the looking glass self-orientation, we can only speculate that the developmental history of these individuals may have been characterized by more disapproval, inconsistent or fluctuating approval, or support that was *conditional* upon meeting the demands of others (for findings on the negative effects of conditional support among adolescents, see Harter, Marold, & Whitesell, 1992). Such a history could lead to preoccupation and concern over support and perceptions of lower and fluctuating support, which in turn would lead to lower and fluctuating self-worth. A critical assumption is that because such individuals have not received adequate approval of the self from *others*, they did not experience the kind of validating support that could be internalized as approval of the *self*.

In the development of such a hypothesized model, it would thus be assumed that the group of adolescents currently reporting that their self-worth precedes approval from others *did* receive the type and level of approval from caregivers that could be internalized in the form of approval of the self. With regard to the developmental *process* through which one's level of self-worth is initially constructed, we are postulating that, during early and middle childhood, approval that validates the self is a critical precursor of high self-worth. That is, the *formation* of one's level of self-worth proceeded according to a looking glass self-model, a model that has recently been supported in a study of children from 4 to 7 years old (Nikkari & Harter, 1993). A critical assumption, however, is that a more positive history of approval allows the individual to internalize these messages, such that eventually one develops an orientation in which one *perceives* that one's own evaluations of the self precede the evaluative reactions of others.

In constructing a developmental model of the three directionality orientations, it is also necessary to speculate on the caregiving history of those adolescents who reported no connection between others' opinions of them and their opinions of themselves. One hypothesis is that such individuals may have experienced relatively low levels of approval and disapproval. They may have received little attention from socializing agents, ranging from benign to more serious forms of neglect. As noted earlier, many of these individuals insisted that they did not *care* about the opinions of others, suggesting a rather defensive reaction to some form of neglect. It is also likely that there may be subgroups within this particular directionality orientation. For example, within the attachment literature Bartholomew (1990) identified two patterns in which adults avoid intimate relationships. One such style, labeled "dismissing avoidance," would seem to apply to the subgroup within our no-connection participants who reported that they did not care about the opinions of others. This style is one in which there is a defensive denial of the need for social contact, accompanied by a positive view of the self.

However, there may be less defensive stances that lead to the no-connection orientation, leading to another subgroup who may represent a more normative pattern. Such individuals may minimize the need for approval because they are relying on alternative paths to self-esteem. For example, recent findings (Harter, Simon, & Johnson, 1993) on individual differences in the sources of self-esteem revealed three subgroups of young adolescents: (a) those who rely on social support as well as on competence in domains of importance, the hypothesized cause according to James (1892); (b) those who rely on social support only; and (c) those who rely on competence in domains of importance only. It is this third subgroup that may also find membership within the no-connection directionality group. Such subjects place considerable emphasis on personal competence and sense of self-adequacy, which is consistent with the pattern of results obtained for the no-connection participants who were less concerned about approval and less socially distractible in the classroom.

Our analysis places emphasis on the potential developmental histories leading to each of the three directionality orientations. One of several unanswered questions concerns the *stability* of these orientations over time. We do not believe that normative developmental movement through adolescence into adulthood will, in and of itself, provoke changes in one's directionality orientation. However, we also do not believe that these orientations are necessarily stable or intractable. Our hypothesized model of the developmental histories leading to each orientation has certain implications for intervention, given its focus on the role of early approval. Thus, the model implies that one cannot merely alter a given individual's orientation directly, that is, it would be difficult to convince them to adopt another metatheory about the links between approval and self-worth. Rather, one would need to intervene earlier in the hypothesized sequence of events, around issues of approval, for example, with attempts to alter the level and type of such support that are presumed to be the precursors of one's orientation. Thus, for those currently adopting the orientation in which approval leads to self-worth, one would, according to our previous analysis, want to provide more unconditional approval that validated one's worth as a person. Through such an intervention, approval could be internalized, so that eventually the individual would come to switch their orientation toward one in which self-worth was assumed to precede or garner the approval of others.

Finally, the development of a more general model to account for individual differences in orientation must necessarily consider the relation between peer and parental regard. Our findings were based on reports of the relation between peer approval and self-worth because our previous research suggested that peer support provides the best analogue of the *generalized other* (Mead, 1934). However, it is likely that early parental approval provides the psychological building blocks from which self-worth is initially formed. Our own research on the early formation of self-worth among young children revealed that support that validates and enhances the self is critical to the development of high self-esteem (Nikkari & Harter, 1993). Thus, future research needs to examine the relation between parental approval and self-worth, in conjunction with peer approval and self-worth, to determine how the various constructs in this network are related.

ACKNOWLEDGMENTS

The research described in this article was supported by a National Institute of Child Health and Human Development grant awarded to Susan Harter. We thank the school personnel and students at Flood Middle School, Englewood, Colorado, for their cooperation in making this research possible.

REFERENCES

Bartholomew, K. (1990). Avoidance of intimacy: An attachment perspective. *Journal of Social and Personal Relationships, 7,* 147–178.

Brown, B. (1990). Peer groups and peer cultures. In S. S. Feldman & G. R. Elliot (Eds.), *At the threshold: The developing adolescent* (pp. 171–196). Cambridge, MA: Harvard University Press.

Buhrmester, D. (1990). Intimacy of friendship, interpersonal competence, and adjustment during preadolescence and adolescence. *Child Development, 61,* 1101–1111.

Bukowski, W. M., & Hoza, B. (1989). Popularity and friendship: Issues in theory, measurement, and outcome. In T. J. Berndt & G. W. Ladd (Eds.), *Peer relationships in child development* (pp. 15–45). New York: Wiley.

Buss, A. H. (1980). *Self-consciousness and social anxiety.* San Francisco: Freeman.

Cauce, A. M. (1986). Social networks and social competence: Exploring the effects of early adolescent friendships. *American Journal of Community Psychology, 14,* 607–628.

Cauce, A. M., Felner, R. D., & Primavera, J. (1982). Social support in high-risk adolescents: Structural components and adaptive impact. *American Journal of Community Psychology, 10,* 417–428.

Cauce, A. M., Reid, M., Landesman, S., & Gonzales, N. (1990). Social support in young children: Measurement, structure, and behavioral impact. In B. R. Sarason, I. G. Sarason, & G. R. Pierce (Eds.), *Social support: An interactional view* (pp. 64–94). New York: Wiley.

Coates, D. L. (1985). Relationships between self-concept measures and social network characteristics for black adolescents. *Journal of Early Adolescence, 5,* 319–338.

Cooley, C. H. (1902). *Human nature and the social order.* New York: Scribner's.

Felson, R. B. (1981). Social sources of information in the development of self. *Sociological Quarterly, 22,* 69–79.

Furman, W. (1987, April). *Social support, stress, and adjustment in adolescence.* Paper presented at the meetings of the Society for Research in Child Development, Baltimore, MD.

Gecas, V. (1972). Parental behavior and contextual variations in adolescent self-esteem. *Sociometry, 2,* 332–345.

Gecas, V., & Schwalbe, M. L. (1983). Beyond the looking-glass self: Social structure and efficacy-based self-esteem. *Social Psychology Quarterly, 46,* 777–778.

Goffman, E. (1959). *The presentation of self in everyday life* (Rev. ed.). New York: Doubleday.

Harter, S. (1982). The Perceived Competence Scale For Children. *Child Development, 53,* 87–97.

Harter, S. (1985a). *The Self-Perception Profile for Children* [Manual]. Denver, CO: University of Denver.

Harter, S. (1985b). *The Social Support Scale for Children and Adolescents* [Manual]. Denver, CO: University of Denver.

Harter, S. (1986). Processes underlying the construction, maintenance, and enhancement of the self-concept in children. In J. Suls & A. G. Greenwald (Eds.), *Psychological perspectives on the self* (Vol. 3, pp. 137–181). Hillsdale, NJ: Lawrence Erlbaum Associates, Inc.

Harter, S. (1987). The determinants and mediational role of global self-worth in children. In N. Eisenberg (Ed.), *Contemporary issues in developmental psychology* (pp. 219–242). New York: Wiley.

Harter, S. (1990a). Adolescent self and identity development. In S. S. Feldman & G. R. Elliot (Eds.), *At the threshold: The developing adolescent* (pp. 352–387). Cambridge, MA: Harvard University Press.

Harter, S. (1990b). Causes, correlates and the functional role of global self-worth: A life-span perspective. In J. Kolligian & R. Sternberg (Eds.), *Perceptions of competence and incompetence across the life-span* (pp. 67–98). New Haven, CT: Yale University Press.

Harter, S. (1993). Visions of self: Beyond the me in the mirror. In J. Jacobs (Ed.), *Nebraska symposium on motivation* (pp. 99–144). Lincoln: University of Nebraska Press.

Harter, S., & Hogan, A. (1985, March). *A causal model of the determinants and mediational role of global self-worth in middle-school children.* Paper presented at the meetings of the Society for Research in Child Development, Toronto.

Harter, S., & Jackson, B. K. (1993). The perceived directionality of the link between low self-worth and depressed affect among young adolescents. *Journal of Early Adolescence, 33,* 383–407.

Harter, S., & Marold, D. B. (1993). The directionality of the link between self-esteem and affect: Beyond causal modeling. In D. Cicchetti & S. L. Toth (Eds.), *The self and its disorders: Rochester Symposium on Developmental Psychopathology* (pp. 331–370). Rochester, NY: University of Rochester Press.

Harter, S., Marold, D. B., & Whitesell, N. R. (1992). A model of psychosocial risk factors leading to suicidal ideation in young adolescents. *Development and Psychopathology, 4,* 167–188.

Harter, S., & Monsour, A. (1992). Developmental analysis of opposing self-attributes in adolescent self-portrait. *Developmental Psychology, 28,* 251–260.

Harter, S., Simon, V., & Johnson, E. (1993). *Alternative pathways to self-esteem.* Unpublished manuscript, University of Denver, Denver, CO.

Harter, S., & Stocker, C. (1993). *A model of the perceived directionality of the link between approval and self-worth.* Unpublished manuscript, University of Denver, Denver, CO.

Hirsch, B. J., & Rapkin, B. D. (1987). The transition to junior high school: A longitudinal study of self-esteem, psychological symptomatology, school life, and social support. *Child Development, 58,* 1235–1243.

James, W. (1892). *Psychology: The briefer course.* New York: Henry Holt.

Kobak, R. (1992). *Updating working models of self and parents: Implications for adolescent adaptation and psychopathology.* Rochester, NY: Rochester Symposium on Developmental Psychopathology.

Lancelotta, K., Harter, S., & Waters, P. (1993). *Perceptions of the link between physical appearance and popularity among young adolescents.* Unpublished manuscript, University of Denver, Denver, CO.

Mead, G. H. (1934). *Mind, self, and society.* Chicago: University of Chicago Press.

Nikkari, D., & Harter, S. (1993). *Determinants and correlates of presented self-esteem in young children.* Unpublished manuscript, University of Denver, Denver, CO.

Peterson, A. C., Schulenberg, J. E., Abramowitz, R. J., Offer, D., & Jarcho, H. D. (1984). A Self-Image Questionnaire for Young Adolescents (SIQYA): Reliability and validity studies. *Journal of Youth and Adolescence, 13,* 93–111.

Reitzes, D. C. (1980). Beyond the looking glass self: Cooley's social self and its treatment in introductory textbooks. *Contemporary Sociology, 9,* 631–640.

Robinson, N. S. (1989, April). *The impact of different types of parent and peer social support on global self-worth.* Poster session presented at the meetings of the Society for Research in Child Development, Kansas City, MO.

Robinson, N. S. (1992). *Evaluating the nature of perceived support and its relation to perceived self-worth in adolescents.* Unpublished manuscript, Peabody College, Vanderbilt University, Nashville, TN.

Robinson, N. S., & Harter, S. (1991, April). *Which comes first from the adolescent's point of view: Approval from others or liking oneself?* Paper presented at the meetings of the Society for Research in Child Development, Seattle, WA.

Rosenberg, M. (1979). *Conceiving the self.* New York: Basic Books.

Rosenberg, M. (1986). Self-concept from middle childhood through adolescence. In J. Suls & A. G. Greenwald (Eds.), *Psychological perspectives on the self* (Vol. 3, pp. 107–136). Hillsdale, NJ: Lawrence Erlbaum Associates, Inc.

Savin-Williams, R. C., & Berndt, T. (1990). Friendship during adolescence. In S. S. Feldman & G. R. Elliot (Eds.), *At the threshold: The developing adolescent* (pp. 277–307). Cambridge, MA: Harvard University Press.

Shrauger, J. S., & Schoeneman, T. J. (1979). "The symbolic interactionists" view of self-concept: Through the looking-glass darkly. *Psychological Bulletin, 86,* 549–573.

Snyder, M. (1987). *Public appearances, private realities: The psychology of self-monitoring.* New York: Freeman.

Received July 31, 1992
Revision received May 12, 1994
Accepted November 30, 1994

Developmental Psychology
1995, Vol. 31, No. 1, 56–64

0012-1649/95/$3.00

An Exploratory Study of Pubertal Maturation Timing and Self-Esteem Among Gay and Bisexual Male Youths

Ritch C. Savin-Williams
Cornell University

Eighty-three gay and bisexual male youths (17–23 years old) completed questionnaires and a structured interview. Pubertal maturation was associated with self-reported age of first orgasm and homosexual activity and frequency of orgasms during junior high school. Unrelated were age of first same-sex attractions, sexual orientation, age of first heterosexual activity, frequency of orgasms during high school, number of lifetime male and female sex partners, reactions to puberty, and self-esteem. Early and on-time maturers rarely varied from each other on the assessed domains. Youths did not differ in self-esteem level from heterosexual male youths. Gay and bisexual male youths share with heterosexual male youths a similar developmental trajectory in regard to pubertal maturation and self-esteem.

Few empirical studies on adolescence consider the development of gay male, lesbian, and bisexual youths. Those that do tend to focus on the unique, problematic aspects of being a sexual minority in North American culture, such as the effects of prejudice, stigmatization, and harassment on a youth's development (e.g., D'Augelli, 1992; Hunter, 1990; Martin & Hetrick, 1988). Such works often emphasize extreme outcomes, including suicidal behavior, prostitution, running away from home, substance abuse, and HIV infection (reviewed in Savin-Williams, 1994b).

In many important ways, however, lesbian, bisexual, and gay male youths are similar to other adolescents. They experience puberty, friendships, family conflict, peer pressure, and concerns about their future. Undeniably, some encounter developmental issues not faced, at least to the same degree, by heterosexual peers, such as violence, abuse, and rejection from family and peers because of their sexuality. Growing up with forbidden and unacceptable sexual attractions, fantasies, and identity may well alter a youth's developmental trajectory. At the most fundamental level, however, bisexual, lesbian, and gay male youths are, first and foremost, adolescents, sharing with others of their age group basic developmental concerns and processes.

Although it is often assumed that gay male, lesbian, and bisexual adolescents are dissimilar to heterosexual youths in their development and psychological health, relatively little research directly addresses these issues. The present empirical study explored these assumptions by investigating pubertal maturation timing and self-esteem with a sample of gay and bisexual male adolescents. Two fundamental questions are addressed: Do such youths follow the same developmental course as heterosexual youths? and, Do they differ from heterosexual youths in psychological health?

Appreciation is expressed to Val DuMontier for assistance in collecting data, Gary Wetstein for coding data, Haftan Eckholdt for statistical assistance, Kenneth Cohen for editing and manuscript revisions, and the youths who volunteered the data.

Correspondence concerning this article should be addressed to Ritch C. Savin-Williams, Department of Human Development, Martha Van Rensselaer Hall, Cornell University, Ithaca, New York 14853.

Developmental Patterns: Timing of Pubertal Maturation

The developmental literature on pubertal maturation has had a rich, central place in research on adolescence since the 1950s. Various explanations have been offered to explain how pubertal onset affects behavior and psychological functioning (Petersen & Taylor, 1980). In their review of the empirical and theoretical literature on the effects of pubertal maturation, Richards, Abell, and Petersen (1993) noted that one research approach links psychological states and phases of psychological development with pubertal changes in hormone levels. Most frequently, investigations have coupled affective states (e.g., anger, impulse control, and sadness) and sexual behavior (e.g., intercourse and masturbation) with levels of sex steroids and gonadotropins. Although findings associating hormone levels with affective states have been mixed, with greater levels of sex steroids and advanced pubertal development, there is an increased likelihood of sexual behavior occurring.

Another approach noted by Richards et al. (1993) suggests that the psychological effects of puberty are mediated by complex relationships of intervening variables or moderated by contextual factors. The psychological consequences of interindividual variations in the onset of puberty have usually included self-perceptions, developmental status (movement toward maturity), interpersonal relations, and self-concept. For example, it has been hypothesized that puberty changes an adolescent's physical appearance, which in turn influences her or his social status (Jones & Bayley, 1950; Simmons & Blyth, 1987). Thus, because an adolescent looks more like an adult, mature behavior is expected of her or him. Socially shared role and behavior expectations follow, and the adolescent responds accordingly. In regard to male adolescents, research has fairly consistently demonstrated that an early-maturing boy benefits (at least until adulthood) from his advanced maturity. As he becomes more involved in athletics and leadership positions, he experiences a corresponding increase in his social prestige, body image, and self-concept. Late-maturing boys, who are relatively "off-time" in their physical maturity from both male and female peers, score low on these dimensions (Jones & Bayley, 1950; Mussen & Jones, 1957).

A variable that has not, to my knowledge, been investigated in these models is sexual orientation. One explanation for this omission is that there is little biological evidence to support the view that sexual orientation influences the relationship between hormone levels and sexual behaviors (for a review of the similarity in hormone levels between heterosexual and homosexual populations, see Byne and Parsons, 1993). Another view, based in the social and clinical sciences, is that being "off course" from cultural expectations in regard to sexual desires, behaviors, and identity influences the ways in which pubertal timing affects the psychological functioning of bisexual, gay male, and lesbian adolescents. For example, perhaps the advantages of maturation that have been reported with heterosexual male participants are reversed for gay male adolescents. This rationale is reflected in the work of clinicians such as Malyon (1981) and Martin and Hetrick (1988): Early puberty may force a youth to confront a forbidden aspect of himself (i.e., his sexuality) during the time when he is undergoing a "normative" adolescent identity crisis. Indeed, multiple simultaneous transitions during adolescence have been shown in several research studies to place an adolescent at high risk for emotional problems and negative self-perceptions (Richards et al., 1993). In addition, this new information about himself is potentially detrimental to his concept of self during a time when he has limited cognitive skills and little social and emotional support to help him cope with this knowledge. He is seldom given social sanction to behaviorally explore his sexuality, cannot discuss his same-sex attractions with peers or family, and faces peer pressure not to be gay. One effect of these processes is purported to be low self-esteem.

Self-Esteem of Lesbians and Gay Men

An early review of the literature on the psychological adjustment of lesbians and gay men concluded that there are no essential mental health consequences of sexual orientation per se (Gonsiorek, 1977). One dimension of psychological adjustment, self-esteem, has received substantial empirical study. Eight of 16 investigations comparing lesbians and heterosexual women reported that the two groups did not differ; in 6 studies, lesbians had higher self-esteem; and in 2 studies, self-esteem was higher among heterosexual women (Savin-Williams, 1990). Of the 30 studies of men reviewed, 17 reported few differences in global self-evaluation between gay and heterosexual men; in 6 studies, gay men had lower self-acceptance scores; in 4 studies, the reverse was found; and in 3 studies, the results were unclear. Greenberg (1973, pp. 141–142) concluded, "Though feeling alienated from the society in which they lived, [homosexuals] were satisfied with their homosexuality to the extent that they exhibited self-esteem scores that were comparable to heterosexual scores obtained on the same instrument."

None of these studies, however, were conducted with adolescents. Subsequently, in an investigation of 317 lesbian, gay male, and bisexual teenagers and young adults, mean self-esteem score was found to be comparable with that of other samples of high school and college age youths (Savin-Williams, 1990). No direct comparison between gay, lesbian, bisexual, and heterosexual individuals' scores was, however, conducted in the Savin-Williams (1990) study.

Expected Research Findings

If the processes underlying development of gay and bisexual male youths are fundamentally similar to those of other adolescents, then an early onset of puberty will be associated with increased levels of sexual behavior and feelings. In addition, similar to heterosexual populations, early maturation among gay and bisexual male youths will be associated with high levels of self-esteem and positive reactions to puberty. Finally, it can be assumed that gay and bisexual male youths will not differ in their self-esteem levels from heterosexual male peers. Positive findings for these three assumptions will support the view that in fundamental ways, the developmental trajectory and psychological health of gay and bisexual male youths are similar to that of heterosexual adolescents.

Method

Participants

The 83 gay and bisexual male youths who participated in this research ranged in age from 17 to 23 years (M = 20.9 years). Most were university students; the rest graduated from high school but had no college education (12%) or were students at a community college (5%) or high school (2%). The range in education was 11 to 17 years (M = 14.1 years). Sixteen percent are minority youths, including 7 Latinos and 3 African Americans. The youths were diverse in their religious affiliation (28% none, 27% Jewish, 24% Catholic, 18% Protestant, and 4% other) and the community they were reared in, including farm and rural (14%), small town (25%), medium-size towns or suburbs (22%), small cities or large suburbs (17%), and urban (22%). Sixty-three percent of the youths' biological parents remained married to each other; 31% of the parents had divorced or separated; and 6% of the fathers had died.

Procedure

In response to encouragement from class lectures, previous participants, or advertisements placed in local bars, restaurants, and newspapers, participants called the research office to volunteer for a project on "growing up as a gay or bisexual male in the 1980s." The written questionnaires included sociodemographic information, a sexual behavior inventory, and the Rosenberg Self-Esteem Scale. Completing this portion of the project usually required 15 to 20 min. A structured interview followed, consisting of qualitative information about growing up gay or bisexual. The interview was conducted at a location agreeable to the youths, usually the respondent's apartment or the investigator's office.

Measures

Sociodemographic and pubertal onset questionnaire. Similar to a questionnaire used in a previous study (Savin-Williams, 1990), items included age, education level, student status, race, current religion, community size reared in, and parents' marital status.

Onset of pubertal maturation was indicated by each respondent who gave his age and first physical indicators of puberty (e.g., pubic hair, facial hair, body hair, and growth spurt). He also evaluated his feelings about the onset of puberty, from 1 = *extremely negative* to 7 = *extremely positive*.

Sexual behavior questionnaire. Each youth selected the one Kinsey rating (Kinsey, Pomeroy, & Martin, 1948), from *exclusively heterosexual* (0) to *exclusively homosexual* (6), that best described his current sexual orientation. Other questions requested an indication of the number of male and female persons with whom he has had genital sexual relations during his lifetime.

Rosenberg Self-Esteem Scale (RSE). The RSE is a 10-item Likert-type scale that measures global self-esteem (e.g., "On the whole, I am satisfied with myself"; Rosenberg, 1979). On a 4-point scale, from 1 = *strongly agree* to 4 = *strongly disagree*, a respondent indicated the degree to which the 5 positively stated and 5 negatively stated sentences characterize him.

The scoring method used was a four-step system that has been demonstrated to have high interitem and structural reliability and to significantly correlate with other self-report self-esteem scales (Demo, 1985). Test–retest reliability over a 3-month period with another sample of gay male, bisexual, and lesbian youths was .88 (Savin-Williams, 1990).

Interview. During the course of a structured interview, each youth was asked the following:

1. When were you first aware of your attractions to other males?
2. When did you have your first orgasm? How was it achieved?
3. At what age did you have your first homosexual and heterosexual experiences?
4. During your junior and senior high school years, how often did you achieve orgasm? Using the following five outlets—masturbation, homosexual sex, heterosexual sex, wet dreams, and sex with animals—distribute how your orgasms were achieved such that the total equals 100% for each of the two time periods.

Determining Pubertal Maturation Onset and Group

Several studies of male adolescents that have compared adolescent self-reports and physical evidence of pubertal maturation reported reasonable agreement between these measures (Duke, Litt, & Gross, 1980; Morris & Udry, 1980; Schlossberger, Turner, & Irwin, 1992). Schlossberger et al. (1992) noted that researchers must rely on self-reported pubertal maturation because a physical examination of genitalia as part of a research protocol is often unacceptable to participating school staff, parents, and youths. Adolescents are likely to overestimate their development during early stages of maturation and to underestimate pubertal development at later stages. With youths who have essentially completed puberty, as in the present study, "errors due to misinterpretation of an ongoing dynamic process would be minimized; therefore, one would expect agreement between physician and subject regarding pubertal maturation to be high" (Schlossberger et al., 1992, p. 109).

Pubertal onset was defined as the age at which the youths reported that they began puberty. All but 6 youths reported the first sign to be pubic hair growth. The others reported pubertal onset as first ejaculation at age 11 years (n = 3) or 15 years (n = 2) and penis enlargement at age 10 years (n = 1).

For pubertal maturation group analyses, the youths were distributed into one of three groups on the basis of their self-reported ages of pubertal onset and first orgasm. *Early maturers* were defined as those who began puberty at least 1 year before the sample mean age of 12 years and who reported that their first ejaculation occurred before the age of 13. Twelve years is the normative age for the onset of pubic hair among male youths (Tanner, 1962). Thirty-one of the 83 youths (37%) met these two criteria. Six reported that puberty began at age 10 years, and 25 reported that it began at age 11 years. Of these 31, 17 reported an orgasm by their 11th year and 14 during their 12th year.

Late maturers were defined as those who reported an onset of puberty and first orgasm 1 year or longer after the sample mean of these events. The 14 who met these criteria (17%) experienced pubertal onset during the ages of 13 to 15 years and first orgasm between the ages of 13 and 16 years.

On-time maturers were the 38 individuals (46%) who met neither criteria. Age of pubertal onset was reported as occurring between the ages of 11 to 13 years and first orgasm between the ages of 12 and 14 years.

Heterosexual Sample

For comparison of levels of self-esteem, a sample of 403 self-reported heterosexual male youths, ages 17 to 23 years, was included. They were drawn from the same pool as were the gay and bisexual male participants and thus were primarily White and highly educated. They completed the RSE anonymously during university classes on adolescence (N = 198) or introductory psychology (N = 141), a leadership conference for high school students (N = 40), summer college programs for high school youth (N = 13), and a high school biology class (N = 11).

Results

First, descriptive results are presented that characterize the sample. Next, the intercorrelations of the study's variables are reported. Analyses of the three maturation groups amplify the results noted earlier and suggest additional ways in which pubertal timing is associated with psychological and behavioral functioning. Finally, the self-esteem of the study's participants is compared with samples of heterosexual male youths.

Descriptive Characteristics

Seventy-one (86%) of the youths rated themselves as exclusively or predominantly gay (Kinsey score of 6 or 5). The others expressed significant heterosexual and hence bisexual interest: 10% of the youths with a Kinsey score of 4, 2% with a Kinsey score of 3, and 2% with a Kinsey score of 2. The youths reported first feeling same-sex attractions at an average age of 8 years. (See Table 1 for means, standard deviations, and ranges.) Nearly one third (30%) remembered having had these attractions before beginning elementary school. At the other extreme, 15 (18%) did not recall having homoerotic attractions until after pubertal onset.

On average, the 83 male youths reported pubertal onset just before their 12th birthday. First orgasm was recalled to have occurred, on average, 8 months later, primarily by masturbation (71%), with most other first orgasms reported to have been experienced through a nocturnal emission.

During the junior and senior high school years, orgasms were reported to have occurred on average three and four times per week, respectively. Thirty-eight percent of the youths recounted averaging daily orgasms during their junior high school years; this percentage increased to 49% during senior high school. Fourteen percent of the youths recalled having no orgasms during their junior high years. During both the junior (83%) and senior (78%) high school years, the primary means of orgasm was recalled as masturbation. Wet dreams and homosexual sex were reported as secondary sources of orgasms during junior (9% and 7%) and senior (7% and 12%) high school. Although 55% of the youths reported having had heterosexual sex, few of the total number of reported orgasms were achieved by hetero-

Table 1
Means, Standard Deviations, and Ranges of All Study Variables for Total Sample and Pubertal Maturation Timing Groups

Variable	Total sample (*N* = 83)	Early maturers (*n* = 31)	On-time maturers (*n* = 38)	Late maturers (*n* = 14)
Pubertal onset (years)				
M	11.9	10.7	12.2	13.9
SD	1.3	0.5	0.5	0.8
Range	10–15	10–11	11–13	13–15
First orgasm (years)				
M	12.6	11.2	12.8	14.9
SD	1.4	0.7	0.6	0.9
Range	10–16	10–12	12–14	13–16
Sex identity (Kinsey rating)				
M	5.4	5.3	5.5	5.5
SD	0.9	1.0	0.9	0.9
Range	2–6	2–6	2–6	3–6
First gay feelings (years)				
M	7.4	6.6	7.2	9.6
SD	3.9	3.5	4.1	3.8
Range	0–16	0–12	0–16	3–15
First homosexual sex (years)				
M	14.2	12.8	14.6	16.3
SD	4.0	4.4	3.7	2.7
Range	6–21	6–21	6–21	10–19
First heterosexual sex (years)				
M	15.5	15.1	15.8	15.4
SD	2.7	3.1	2.0	3.5
Range	8–20	8–19	13–20	9–20
Junior high orgasms (categories)[a]				
M	3.6	4.6	3.8	1.2
SD	2.0	1.2	1.7	1.9
Range	0–6	1–6	0–6	0–5
Senior high orgasms (categories)[a]				
M	4.4	4.6	4.4	3.9
SD	1.2	1.1	1.1	1.6
Range	1–6	2–6	2–6	1–6
No. of male partners (categories)[b]				
M	4.1	3.8	4.0	4.7
SD	1.9	1.9	2.0	1.9
Range	0–8	0–7	0–8	0–8
No. of female partners (categories)[b]				
M	1.4	1.4	1.4	1.4
SD	1.5	1.6	1.5	1.5
Range	0–5	0–5	0–5	0–4
Reaction to puberty (1–7 scale)				
M	4.5	4.8	4.6	3.6
SD	1.7	1.8	1.6	1.6
Range	1–7	1–7	1–7	1–6
Self-esteem (0–30 scale)				
M	22.4	23.3	21.6	22.4
SD	5.8	4.3	6.5	6.7
Range	6–30	13–30	6–30	8–30

[a] 0 = none, 1 = once or twice per year, 2 = once or twice per month, 3 = once or twice per week, 4 = 2–4 times per week, 5 = daily, 6 = more than daily. [b] 0 = 0, 1 = 1, 2 = 2, 3 = 3–5, 4 = 6–10, 5 = 11–20, 6 = 21–50, 7 = 51–100, 8 = 100+.

sexual sex during the junior (1%) or senior (3%) high school years.

A first same-sex experience was reported to have occurred, on average, 6 years after first homoerotic attractions. The most frequent time reported was during the senior (34%) or junior (23%) high school years. Almost one quarter of the male youths reported prepubertal same-sex activity. For those who reported having had sex with female partners, first heterosexual sex was reported as occurring almost 1.5 years after same-sex activity was initiated. Nearly 70% of these heterosexually experienced youths waited until their high school years or beyond to have heterosexual sex; 7% had prepubertal heterosexual sexual experiences.

At the time of the interview, the youths reported having had,

Table 2
Intercorrelations, Significance Levels, and Sample Size of All Study Variables

Variable	1	2	3	4	5	6	7	8
1. Pubertal onset								
r	—	.83**	.10	.16	.30**	.07	−.46**	−.11
N	83	83	83	83	71	41	80	81
2. First orgasm								
r		—	.05	.27*	.24*	.17	−.62**	−.21†
N		83	83	83	71	41	80	81
3. Sexual identity								
r			—	−.17	.06	−.11	−.06	−.07
N			83	83	71	41	80	81
4. First gay feelings								
r				—	.02	.22	−.29**	−.32**
N				83	71	41	80	81
5. First homosexual sex								
r					—	.20	−.21†	−.02
N					71	41	71	71
6. First heterosexual sex								
r						—	−.14	−.15
N						41	41	41
7. Junior high orgasm								
r							—	.59**
N							80	80
8. Senior high orgasm								
r								—
N								81

† $p < .10$. * $p < .05$. ** $p < .01$.

on average, sex with 8 male partners and 1 female partner. Five youths (6%) reported being "homosexual virgins" and 45% reported being "heterosexual virgins." No youth reported having had sex with more than 20 female partners; 18 (22%) reported having had sex with more than 20 male partners.

Reactions to the physical changes of puberty ranged from very negative, which 4 (5%) youths endorsed, to very positive, endorsed by 12 (14%) youths. Overall, reactions to puberty were slightly more positive than negative. On a scale of 0 to 30, the mean self-esteem level was 22.4.

Correlations Among Study Variables

Intercorrelations among the study variables are presented in Tables 2, 3, and 4. As expected, age and educational level were significantly intercorrelated, older participants reported having had more lifetime sex with both male and female partners, and those who expressed a bisexual orientation reported having had more sex with female partners.

Onset of puberty, age of first orgasm, age of first homosexual sex, and frequency of junior high orgasms were all significantly intercorrelated. In addition, those with an early onset of orgasms reported earlier feelings of being gay, more sex with male individuals, and a higher level of orgasms during senior high school (marginally significant). Those with early homoerotic attractions were more likely to report orgasms during their junior and senior high school years. Youths with many orgasms during early adolescence continued to have a high frequency of orgasms during senior high school. No variable was significantly correlated with reactions to pubertal onset or self-esteem level.

There were several marginally significant ($p < .10$) findings. Those who reported a high number of female sex partners also reported a high number of male sex partners and an early age of first heterosexual and homosexual sex; those who reported many male sex partners tended to rate themselves as more exclusively gay on the Kinsey scale. An early onset of reported same-sex encounters was related to a high number of reported orgasms during early adolescence and advanced educational standing, and an early onset of reported other-sex encounters was related to high self-esteem. Youths who reported many early adolescent orgasms responded positively to their pubertal maturation; those with many reported orgasms during senior high were more highly educated.

Pubertal Maturation Group Analyses

Three pubertal maturation groups were defined on the basis of self-reported pubertal onset and age of first orgasm. Analyses of variance confirmed that this technique significantly differentiated the maturation groups on several variables (see Table 1 for means, standard deviations, and ranges for each group). The three maturation groups did not significantly differ in their self-reported age, educational level, size of community reared in, sexual orientation rating, age of first heterosexual sexual activity, frequency of orgasms during senior high school, number of lifetime male and female sex partners, or self-esteem level. Significant differences were established among the three groups on reported age of first same-sex attractions, $F(2, 80) = 3.02$, $p = .05$; age of first homosexual activity, $F(2, 74) = 4.32$, $p = .02$; and frequency of orgasms during the junior high school years, $F(2, 78) = 21.58$, $p = .001$. Reactions to puberty approached significance, $F(2, 80) = 2.29$, $p = .11$.

Table 3
Intercorrelations, Significance Levels, and Sample Size of All Study Variables

Variable	Pubertal onset	First orgasm	Sexual identity	First gay feelings	First homosexual sex	First heterosexual sex	Junior high orgasm	Senior high orgasm
No. of male partners								
r	.11	.25*	.19†	−.09	−.19	−.05	−.12	.12
N	83	83	83	83	71	41	80	81
No. of female partners								
r	−.08	.04	−.38**	−.10	−.21†	−.26†	.11	.15
N	83	83	83	83	71	41	80	81
Reaction to puberty								
r	−.14	−.17	.00	−.06	−.05	−.09	.19†	−.05
N	82	82	82	82	71	41	80	81
Self-esteem								
r	−.07	.01	.02	.14	.10	−.29†	.02	−.12
N	77	77	77	77	71	41	77	77
Age								
r	.00	.13	.02	.07	−.09	.09	.07	.09
N	83	83	83	83	71	41	80	81
Education								
r	−.03	.01	−.03	.14	−.20†	.03	.12	.18†
N	83	83	83	83	71	41	80	81
Community size								
r	−.01	−.12	.09	−.13	−.14	−.18	.11	.06
N	83	83	83	83	71	41	80	81

† $p < .10$. * $p < .05$. ** $p < .01$.

Post hoc protected *t*-test comparisons revealed that early maturers reported a higher frequency of orgasms than on-time maturers during their junior high school years, $t(64) = 2.09$, $p < .05$; their reported age of first homosexual activity was somewhat younger than on-time maturers, $t(57) = 1.85$, $p < .10$. Both early and on-time maturers reported younger age means than did late maturers on first same-sex attractions, $t(23) = 2.5$, $p < .05$ and $t(25) = 2.0$, $p < .10$, and first homosexual sex, $t(30) = 3.3$, $p < .01$ and $t(30) = 1.7$, $p < .10$; more frequent orgasms during junior high school, $t(18) = 6.1$, $p < .001$ and $t(22) = 4.5$, $p < .001$; and more positive reactions to puberty, $t(28) = 2.1$, $p < .05$ and $t(24) = 1.9$, $p < .10$. Thus, late-maturing adolescents reported a later onset of homoerotic at-

Table 4
Intercorrelations, Significance Levels, and Sample Size of All Study Variables

Variable	1	2	3	4	5	6	7
1. No. of male partners							
r	—	.19†	.02	.11	.37**	.16	−.15
N	83	83	82	77	83	83	83
2. No. of female partners							
r		—	.10	.12	.25*	.08	−.18
N		83	82	77	83	83	83
3. Reaction to puberty							
r			—	.13	−.11	−.14	−.14
N			82	77	82	82	82
4. Self-esteem							
r				—	.14	.10	−.09
N				77	77	77	77
5. Age							
r					—	.67**	.03
N					83	83	83
6. Education							
r						—	.16
N						83	83
7. Community size							
r							—
N							83

† $p < .10$. * $p < .05$. ** $p < .01$.

tractions, a later onset of homosexual sex, fewer orgasms in junior high school, and more negative reactions to puberty than did early and on-time maturing gay and bisexual male youths.

Self-Esteem

The self-esteem of the gay and bisexual male youths (M = 22.4, SD = 5.8) was compared with the self-esteem of 403 self-reported heterosexual male youths (M = 23.2, SD = 4.2). The two groups did not differ in their self-esteem level, $t(481) = 1.17, p > .10$.

Discussion

Although results from the present exploratory study cannot provide a completely satisfactory answer to the question of whether gay and bisexual male youths vary from heterosexual male youths in developmental processes, data from the 83 youths support their similarity to heterosexual male peers in several domains. The findings provided qualified support for the three suppositions that were advanced. Following this discussion, I address limitations of the study and suggest future research directions.

Pubertal Maturation and Sexuality

The study's findings support the association of pubertal development with an increase in homoerotic sexual feelings and behavior. The earlier a gay or bisexual male youth physically matured, the more likely he was to report an early onset of orgasms, frequent orgasms during his junior high school years, and an early age of beginning homosexual activity. Early pubertal development was not, however, related to a generalized onset of sexual encounters but was usually restricted to sexual encounters with other male partners.

This last finding is particularly noteworthy. The social significance of chronological age appeared highly significant in the lives of the gay and bisexual male youths for matters of heterosexual but not homosexual sexual activity. On average, the male youths initiated heterosexual encounters during their 15th year, regardless of their biological age (pubertal maturation). The number of heterosexual partners was also essentially the same for all youths regardless of age of pubertal onset; chronological age was a better predictor than pubertal onset of lifetime frequency of heterosexual sexual activity. Thus, in matters of same-sex attractions and behavior, biology appeared to play a stronger role than chronological age. In matters of social convention and expectation for these youths, such as sexual behavior with female sex partners, chronological age was the best predictor.

Advantages and Disadvantages of Maturational Timing

Although late maturers recalled slightly more negative reactions to the onset of puberty than did early and on-time maturers, there was mixed support for the study's second assumption that an early onset of puberty would be psychologically beneficial and a late onset would be detrimental. Early maturers may have profited from their early pubertal onset during early adolescence, achieving more orgasms, having an earlier onset of first homosexual sex, and reacting to puberty in a more positive way; however, pubertal onset timing was not related to other aspects of sexual and psychological functioning during middle to late adolescence. The maturation groups did not significantly differ in reporting their number of lifetime sexual engagements with male or female sex partners, onset of heterosexual encounters, sexual orientation rating, frequency of senior high school orgasms, or level of self-esteem.

Analyses of the three pubertal maturation groups indicated that differences in pubertal timing can be largely attributed to late-maturing youths. The disadvantages of being late maturing and thus "off time" appear to be greater than the advantages of being early or on-time maturing. Level of self-esteem during young adulthood, however, was not unduly depressed because of late pubertal maturation; indeed, the correlation between reactions to puberty and self-esteem did not approach statistical significance, indicating that later self-esteem level may be relatively independent of reactions to puberty during early adolescence. Once late maturers in the present study "caught up" in terms of pubertal development during middle and late adolescence, few differences remained among the maturation groups.

These results may reflect the methods of defining maturation and maturational groups. This study varied from other strategies commonly used in maturation timing research, such as dividing a sample of youths into three equal pubertal timing groups (e.g., Simmons & Blyth, 1987) or comparing only the extreme early and late maturers of a sample (e.g., Mussen & Jones, 1957). The former assumes that there is a normal distribution of maturational timing within the population sampled and that all those within each group are indeed significantly early, on time, or late on pubertal indicators. The latter approach often ignores on-time maturers by investigating only the most extreme outliers. The empirical literature indicates that pubertal maturation timing effects tend to be relatively minor, except when the most extreme cases—individuals two or three standard deviations above or below the population mean for pubertal onset—are studied and when the outcomes assessed focus largely on how adolescents feel about themselves and relate to others during the time of pubertal inequality. The effects lessen as the distance from puberty increases, that is, as adolescents become adults, and the full range of normative variations in pubertal timing are considered—both of which are characteristic of this study's methodology.

Self-Esteem

The study's third assumption was supported. The mean level of self-esteem in this sample of late adolescents and young adults was not significantly different from that of a comparable sample of heterosexual male youths. Apparently, being gay or bisexual did not depress the youths' self-esteem level. This result counters previous research that has focused primarily on clinical, help-seeking subpopulations of lesbian, bisexual, and gay male youths (see further discussion of this issue in Savin-Williams, 1994b).

Study Limitations

One limitation of this study is the generalizability of the data to other populations of lesbian, gay male, and bisexual youths.

Because of the social stigma attached to same-sex attractions and the resistance of many youths to declare their homoerotic nature to themselves and to others, it is never possible to solicit a random population of gay, bisexual, and lesbian youths. Although the present, nonclinical sample of largely White, small town and suburban, and highly educated youth is distinct from previous studies of youths recruited from urban, social service agencies (e.g., Herdt & Boxer, 1993; Martin & Hetrick, 1988), it too is biased. Thus, caution is advised in generalizing the results to other populations of youths.

In addition, only data from male youths were collected, thus contributing to the male bias in research conducted with sexual minorities. It was a sample of convenience, and no comparable data on lesbian and bisexual female teenagers were available. Samples with lesbian and bisexual female adolescents would be particularly important because research demonstrates that reactions to pubertal timing differ between the sexes (Richards et al., 1993).

Another limitation is that the validity and reliability of the interview measure were not established through standard means. The finding that many of the items that one would expect to be significantly correlated were is thus reassuring. These include age and educational level, age and number of lifetime sex partners, bisexual orientation and sex with female partners, junior and senior high school levels of orgasms, age of first heterosexual encounter and number of female sex partners (negative), exclusively gay sexual orientation and number of male partners, and reactions to puberty and level of orgasms.

The absence of physical confirmation of the youths' self-reported age of pubertal onset was another unavoidable drawback in the study's methodology. Consistent with reports of male adolescents, however, most youths in the study reported onset of pubic hair around ages 11 to 13 years as the marker for puberty.

Some would view the retrospective nature of the study variables as undesirable. Developmental processes can be distorted when data about one time period are gathered when individuals reporting the information are at a different phase of development. Boxer, Cohler, Herdt, and Irvin (1993) discussed the limitations of retrospective bias in research on lesbian, gay male, and bisexual adolescents, concluding that "In short, little is yet known about how they experience their lives as they are living them, rather than as they *remember* them" (p. 265).

Although the study participants were asked to report behaviors and feelings that occurred several months to 2 decades ago, an attempt was made to minimize retrospective bias with respect to the study variables by incorporating face-to-face interviews (Catania, McDermott, & Pollack, 1986; Reinisch, Sanders, & Ziemba-Davis, 1988) and by asking for a description of feelings and behaviors within a concrete, detailed context (Catania, Gibson, Chitwood, & Coates, 1990). (These qualitative data are included in Savin-Williams, 1994a.) For example, youths were requested to specify the circumstances (when, how, where, and why) of their first orgasm; thus, memory recall and accuracy of reporting pubertal onset should have been enhanced. Similarly, they were asked to tell the "story" of their first homosexual and heterosexual encounters and to delineate the frequency and outlet of their adolescent orgasms.

Because of the cross-sectional nature of this study, the immediate effects of pubertal onset could not be assessed. A longitudinal study launched in early childhood could alleviate this problem; however, given current reliance on self-identification of self as lesbian, gay, or bisexual, which is usually a postpubescent event, and the relatively small number of sexual minority individuals in the total population, a longitudinal study commencing in early childhood is unrealistic.

Future Research

Several findings from the present study should be elaborated in future studies. For example, a cluster of highly interrelated variables suggests the existence of a group of adolescents who report an early and highly sexualized life. They had an early onset of same-sex attractions, began puberty early, maintained a high level of orgasms throughout adolescence, began homosexual activity at an early age, and had a large number of lifetime male sexual partners. The developmental antecedents and sequela of these youths could be contrasted with more inhibited youths.

Long-term advantages and disadvantages of maturational timing among lesbian, gay, and bisexual youths could be assessed by including additional measures such as coping strategies, incidence of internalized homophobia, sexual adjustment, and integrated personal identity. The disadvantages of an early recognition of sexual identity, or "homoeroticization" of adolescence, such as being ridiculed by peers, evicted from the home, and denied support when critically needed (Malyon, 1981; Martin & Hetrick, 1988), need to be investigated.

Sample characteristics provided in this report can serve as a comparison for future studies of gay and bisexual male youths and can help correct cultural beliefs regarding the sexual development of gay and bisexual male youths. For example, findings in the present investigation counter the myth that gay and bisexual male adolescents are extremely promiscuous at a very early age. The finding that one quarter of the sampled youths were gay virgins at high school graduation illustrates that self-identification as gay does not require homosexual sex. Also unsupported was the view that individuals "become" gay simply because they did not try heterosexual sex. The majority of the study's youths have had heterosexual experiences and, for the most part, enjoyed them (Savin-Williams, 1994a).

It is difficult to compare many of the study variables with samples of heterosexual youths because relatively little research has thoroughly investigated their sexuality. For example, little is known regarding when heterosexual youths first become aware of heteroerotic attractions, how first orgasm is achieved, the frequency of orgasms during early and middle adolescence, and the first other- and same-sex sexual encounters. Perhaps chronological age dictates same-sex encounters and biology determines heterosexual behaviors and feelings among heterosexual youths. This basic research needs to be conducted.

Results from the present study also further erode the belief that gay and bisexual male youths have defective self-esteem. An earlier review of the extant empirical research (Savin-Williams, 1990) severely questioned this assumption. Although lesbian, gay, and bisexual youths have their difficulties (e.g., keeping their sexual identity hidden from others for fear of verbal and physical retribution), most apparently emerge from adolescence with a positive view of themselves.

References

Boxer, A. M., Cohler, B. J., Herdt, G., & Irvin, F. (1993). Gay and lesbian youth. In P. H. Tolan & B. J. Cohler (Eds.), *Handbook of clinical research and practice with adolescents* (pp. 249–280). New York: Wiley.

Byne, W., & Parsons, B. (1993). Human sexual orientation: The biologic theories reappraised. *Archives of General Psychiatry, 50,* 228–239.

Catania, J. A., Gibson, D. R., Chitwood, D. D., & Coates, T. J. (1990). Methodological problems in AIDS behavioral research: Influences on measurement error and participation bias in studies of sexual behavior. *Psychological Bulletin, 108,* 339–362.

Catania, J. A., McDermott, L. J., & Pollack, L. M. (1986). Questionnaire response bias and face-to-face interview sample bias in sexuality research. *Journal of Sex Research, 22,* 52–72.

D'Augelli, A. R. (1992). Lesbian and gay male undergraduates' experiences of harassment and fear on campus. *Journal of Interpersonal Violence, 7,* 383–395.

Demo, D. H. (1985). The measurement of self-esteem: Refining our methods. *Journal of Personality and Social Psychology, 48,* 1490–1502.

Duke, P. M., Litt, I. F., & Gross, R. T. (1980). Adolescents' self-assessment of sexual maturation. *Pediatrics, 66,* 918–920.

Gonsiorek, J. C. (1977). Psychological adjustment and homosexuality. *JSAS Catalog of Selected Documents in Psychology, 7,* 45.

Greenberg, J. S. (1973). A study of the self-esteem and alienation of male homosexuals. *Journal of Psychology, 83,* 137–143.

Herdt, G., & Boxer, A. (1993). *Children of Horizons: How gay and lesbian teens are leading a new way out of the closet.* Boston: Beacon.

Hunter, J. (1990). Violence against lesbian and gay male youths. *Journal of Interpersonal Violence, 5,* 295–300.

Jones, M. C., & Bayley, N. (1950). Physical maturing among boys as related to behavior. *Journal of Educational Psychology, 41,* 129–148.

Kinsey, A. C., Pomeroy, W. B., & Martin, C. E. (1948). *Sexual behavior in the human male.* Philadelphia: W. B. Saunders.

Malyon, A. K. (1981). The homosexual adolescent: Developmental issues and social bias. *Child Welfare, 60,* 321–330.

Martin, A. D., & Hetrick, E. S. (1988). The stigmatization of the gay and lesbian adolescent. *Journal of Homosexuality, 15,* 163–183.

Morris, N. M., & Udry, J. R. (1980). Validation of a self-administered instrument to assess stage of adolescent development. *Journal of Youth and Adolescence, 9,* 271–280.

Mussen, P. H., & Jones, M. C. (1957). Self-conceptions, motivations and interpersonal attitudes of late- and early-maturing boys. *Child Development, 28,* 243–256.

Petersen, A. C., & Taylor, B. (1980). The biological approach to adolescence: Biological change and psychological adaptation. In J. Adelson (Ed.), *Handbook of adolescent psychology* (pp. 117–155). New York: Wiley.

Reinisch, J. M., Sanders, S. A., & Ziemba-Davis, M. (1988). The study of sexual behavior in relation to the transmission of human immunodeficiency virus. *American Psychologist, 43,* 921–927.

Richards, M. H., Abell, S. N., & Petersen, A. C. (1993). Biological development. In P. H. Tolan & B. J. Cohler (Eds.), *Handbook of clinical research and practice with adolescents* (pp. 21–44). New York: Wiley.

Rosenberg, M. (1979). *Conceiving the self.* New York: Basic Books.

Savin-Williams, R. C. (1990). *Gay and lesbian youth: Expressions of identity.* Washington, DC: Hemisphere.

Savin-Williams, R. C. (1994a). *The sexual lives of gay and bisexual male youths.* Manuscript in preparation.

Savin-Williams, R. C. (1994b). Verbal and physical abuse as stressors in the lives of lesbian, gay male, and bisexual youths: Associations with school problems, running away, substance abuse, prostitution, and suicide. *Journal of Consulting and Clinical Psychology, 62,* 261–269.

Schlossberger, N. M., Turner, R. A., & Irwin, C. E. (1992). Validity of self-report of pubertal maturation in early adolescents. *Journal of Adolescent Health, 13,* 109–113.

Simmons, R. G., & Blyth, D. A. (1987). *Moving into adolescence: The impact of pubertal change and school.* Hawthorne, NY: Aldine de Gruyter.

Tanner, J. M. (1962). *Growth at adolescence.* Oxford, England: Blackwell.

Received April 6, 1993
Revision received January 7, 1994
Accepted January 17, 1994 ■

JOURNAL OF RESEARCH ON ADOLESCENCE, 4(4), 585–600

Adolescents' Affective Experience of Family Behaviors: The Role of Subjective Understanding

Sally I. Powers, Deborah P. Welsh, and Virginia Wright

University of Massachusetts at Amherst

Recent conceptualizations of affect view it as a process of negotiating relations between a person and his or her environment when those relations are important to the person. In this view, cognition and affect are seen as intertwined aspects of the process, which is inherently interpersonal as well as intrapersonal. Thus, a primary aspect of affect is a person's subjective understanding of interpersonal events. Subjective understanding of interpersonal events is multidimensional: It includes feeling states associated with the event, an appraisal of the purpose or intent of the event, and an appreciation of the significance of the event. In this article, we argue that this new definition of affect, with its focus on the subjective understanding of interpersonal events, can be used to expand our models of how observed family behaviors are related to adolescent psychosocial outcomes. We argue that an expanded model of the relations of family behaviors to adolescent outcomes should incorporate the following propositions: (a) adolescents' subjective understanding of family behaviors mediates the impact of those behaviors on adolescents' subsequent functioning and development, and (b) both ecological variables and individual differences influence adolescents' subjective understanding of family behaviors. We contend that this expanded model will increase our ability to find and understand associations between family behaviors and adolescent outcomes and will allow us to study more effectively the diversity of adolescent and family groups. A method for examining adolescents' subjective understanding of family behaviors, the video-recall method, is illustrated in a study of rural adolescents and their families.

Requests for reprints should be sent to Sally I. Powers, Department of Psychology, Tobin Hall, University of Massachusetts at Amherst, Amherst, MA 01003.

Ten years ago, the most prevalent conception of affect[1] was as a person's subjective feeling state (see Campos, Campos, & Barrett, 1989 for a brief overview of the evolution of the definition of affect). This view fostered a dualistic conception of affect and cognition as distinct, although related, aspects of human experience. In contrast, more recent conceptualizations of affect view affect and cognition as intertwined aspects of a unitary process (Campos et al., 1989; Dix, 1991; Fisher & Lamborn, 1989; Frijda, 1986; Hauser & Sayfer, 1994; Thompson, 1985). The primary function of this process is to establish and negotiate relations between the person and his or her environment when those relations are important to the person (Campos et al., 1989; Dix, 1991; Frijda, 1986).

This reconceptualization of affect as a complex, relational process rather than as an intrapersonal state is clearly much broader than previous notions of affect. In their exposition of this new view of affect, Campos and his colleagues (1989) stated:

> Emotion is a single relational process with many facets that act in concert ... The new relational view differs from prior viewpoints in giving equal status (a) to the person's appreciation of the significance of an event, (b) to the individual's feelings, which are now considered to be monitors of the significance of both events and coping potential relative to those events, rather than mere registrations of autonomic or facial feedback, and (c) to the way that a person deals with his or her environment. (pp. 400, 395)

A fundamental facet of affect in this new view is a person's subjective understanding of interpersonal events (Campos et al., 1989; Dix, 1991; Frijda, 1986). A person's subjective understanding of an interpersonal event is multidimensional: It includes feeling states associated with the event, an appraisal of the purpose or intent of the event, and an appreciation of the significance of the event. These dimensions of a person's subjective understanding of the interpersonal event constitute key factors in a person's affective experience of the event. For example, if we are interested in understanding a particular adolescent's (Sharon's) affective experience when her father comments positively on her new shoes, we must assess several dimensions of her subjective understanding of her father's comment. Sharon's subjective understanding of his comment is complex; it includes feelings of embarrassment and pleasure, a judgment that her father is trying to be nice to her, and an appraisal that this comment was very important in

[1]The terms *affect* and *emotion* are used interchangeably in this article.

reestablishing her relationship with her father after an earlier argument. Clearly, the same interpersonal event can be subjectively understood in different ways by different people. Another adolescent's (Judy's) subjective understanding of an identical comment by her father may be radically different, it may include feelings of resentfulness, a judgment that when her father expresses his opinions he is trying to interfere with her freedom to choose her own clothes, and an appraisal that his comment confirms her view of him as trying to keep her from growing up. Likewise, different interpersonal events can be subjectively understood in similar ways by different people (Campos et al., 1989). For example, Sharon and Judy may subjectively understand their mothers' affection for them, although their mothers behave in very different ways: One mother offers her daughter a snack, and the other mother gives her daughter a hug.

This focus on the role of subjective understanding in affect clearly emphasizes the relational nature of affect in interpersonal situations. An individual's subjective understanding is dependent on cues from other persons in two important ways: (a) feeling states are influenced by the affective signals of others through such mechanisms as social referencing (Campos & Stenberg, 1981; Campos et al., 1989) and emotional contagion (Gottman & Fainsilber Katz, 1989; Haviland & Lelwica, 1987); and (b) the purpose and intent of others' behaviors and the significance of those behaviors to the individual are deciphered both by using immediate emotional signals from others (Barrett & Campos, 1987), and by placing immediate behaviors in the context of meaning provided by the history of the relationship (Dix, 1991; Margolin, 1987; Weiss, 1984).

In this article, we argue that this new definition of affect, with its emphasis on the subjective understanding of interpersonal events, can be profitably used to expand current models of how observed family behaviors are related to adolescent psychosocial outcomes. We then present a method for examining adolescents' subjective understanding of family behavior, the video-recall method, as it is used in our longitudinal study of rural adolescents and their families.

AN EXPANDED MODEL OF THE RELATION OF FAMILY BEHAVIOR TO ADOLESCENT OUTCOME

Within the past decade, the majority of scholars reviewing the relations of observed family behaviors to adolescent outcomes has espoused a complex model of these relations (Bronfenbrenner, 1986; Dornbusch,

Petersen, & Hetherington, 1991; Hill, 1987; Powers, Hauser, & Kilner, 1989), perhaps best represented by Bronfenbrenner and Crouter's (1982) person–process–context model. This model asserts that both individual characteristics of each family member (*person variables*) and characteristics of the ecological environment (*context variables*) influence the behavioral patterns of families (*process variables*). The behavioral patterns of families, in turn, then influence adolescent outcomes. Process variables mediate between person and context variables and adolescent outcomes.[2]

We propose an expansion of this model, drawing on the new definition of affect discussed earlier. The expanded model asserts that adolescent affect, particularly that aspect of affect that is an adolescent's subjective understanding of family behaviors, mediates the influence of family behaviors upon adolescent outcomes.[3] This model suggests that investigations of family behaviors have often failed to predict child outcomes because psychologists

> have generally failed to appreciate that the child is always interpreting the actions of parents ... The child's personal interpretation of experience, not the event recorded by camera or observer, is the essential basis for the formation of and change in [the child's] beliefs, wishes, and actions. (Kagan, 1984, pp. 275, 241)

In this model, an adolescent's subjective understanding of his or her family's behaviors is an important determinant of the way that adolescent responds to those behaviors. Differences in adolescents' responses to family behaviors may then be reflected in differences in psychosocial outcomes for the adolescents. For example, in a discussion of their different opinions about the morality of euthanasia, a father comments to his adolescent son that the son's reasoning is flawed—the boy has missed an important logical step in reasoning about the issue. If the son's subjective understanding of his father's comment includes a judgment that his father is showing respect for his intelligence by sparring with him and challenging his thinking, a feeling of excitement

---

[2]The person–process–context model assumes that person and context variables may also have direct effects on adolescent outcomes. The mediating aspect of family behavior is emphasized here because our focus is on the relationship of family behavior to adolescent outcomes.

[3]The investigation of adolescents' perceptions of their family relationships using questionnaires and interviews has a long history. Our emphasis here is on the usefulness of adolescents' understanding of specific observable family behavioral interactions in conceptual models and empirical investigations of the relation of observed family behavior to adolescent outcomes.

and pride, and an appraisal that this interaction matters to their relationship, then the son may respond with increased participation in intellectual discussions with his father. This increased interchange may strengthen the father–son relationship and support the boy's self-esteem. On the other hand, if the son's subjective understanding of his father's comment includes a judgment that his father is dismissing and scornful of his reasoning ability, a feeling of anger and embarrassment, and an appraisal that this interaction is significant, then the son may respond by decreasing his participation in intellectual discussions with his father. Their relationship may, therefore, lose one arena for developing closeness, and the adolescent may feel less confident in other intellectual pursuits.

The importance of assessing the individual's subjective understanding of family behaviors has already been stressed in research on marital interaction. The *communication deficit* explanation of marital distress (Gottman & Porterfield, 1981; Gottman et al., 1976) suggests that distressed couples intend their statements to be received far more positively than they are, in fact, received. The theory suggests, and empirical investigations support, the idea that attributions about and reactions to the spouse's behavior are more important in predicting marital satisfaction than the behavior per se (Gottman & Porterfield, 1981; Gottman et al., 1976; Markman, 1979, 1981). In fact, Gottman (1979) and Margolin, Hattem, John, and Yost (1985) provided evidence that couples with high marital satisfaction develop a private, shared system of understanding marital behaviors. Thus, husband and wife ratings of the meaning of their own behaviors and the behaviors of other couples are more similar to one another than they are to the ratings given to these behaviors by trained observers. Although the study of couples' subjective understanding of their marital behavior has been profitable, this approach has rarely been applied to the study of specific behavioral interactions in families of adolescents (for one exception, see Callan & Noller, 1986).

In our view, assessing adolescents' different subjective understandings of their family behaviors will allow investigators to better understand one of the mechanisms by which family behaviors are related to adolescent psychosocial outcomes. In addition, we propose that including adolescents' subjective understanding in our empirical analyses of the relationship of family behaviors to adolescent outcomes will lead to more consistent and more meaningful associations between family behaviors and adolescent outcomes.

Moderators of Subjective Understanding

As noted previously, there may be individual and group differences in adolescents' subjective understanding of particular behaviors.

Similar behaviors may signify very different things to different adolescents; conversely, very different behaviors may be interpreted similarly by different adolescents. In this model, these adolescent individual and group differences in subjective understanding of behaviors are due to effects of person variables and context variables. That is, person variables (individual differences) and context variables (ecological differences) interact with or moderate an adolescent's subjective understanding of family behaviors.[4]

Individual differences. Individual differences among adolescents (such as level of social–cognitive development, temperament, values, motivation, or psychopathology) moderate the relation of family behaviors to adolescent outcomes by transforming adolescents' subjective understanding of family behaviors. For example, identical family behaviors may be subjectively understood differently by adolescents who are at different levels of ego development (Hauser, Powers, & Noam, 1991; Powers, 1989). Advances in ego development during adolescence typically involve the transition from the preconformist level to the conformist level (Loevinger, 1976). This transition enables the adolescent to better understand the perspective and motives of others. These different interpretations of the meaning of family behaviors may influence how the adolescents respond to these behaviors. Consider the following family interaction: A mother reprimands her two adolescent daughters because they have come home after a designated curfew time. The younger adolescent daughter, who functions at the preconformist level of ego development, subjectively understands her mother's behavior as conflictual, thinking her mother is mean and is trying to restrict her fun and to cause an argument. This daughter responds by making sure that she is more clever in the future about not getting caught when she comes home late. The older adolescent daughter, who functions at the conformist level of ego development, interprets the reprimand very differently: She feels that her mother reprimanded her and her sister because the mother loves her and her sister and wants to make sure they are safe. In this case, the older adolescent understands the mother's reprimand as being a caring and supportive behavior. This adolescent has the capacity to understand her mother's caretaking role and responds by behaving in the future in ways that she hopes will assure her mother that she is a responsible person and can handle a later curfew. Examining the moderating influ-

[4]Although our focus here is on the interaction between subjective understanding and individual and ecological differences, subjective understanding and individual and ecological differences may also have direct influences on adolescent psychosocial outcomes.

ence of individual differences on the meanings that adolescents give to family behaviors should allow a better understanding of variations in the relations between family behaviors and adolescent outcomes.

Ecological differences. This model also proposes that characteristics of the ecological environments in which adolescents reside (such as socioeconomic status, level of social support, cultural traditions, and community safety) will moderate the relation of family behaviors to adolescent outcomes by interacting with the subjective understanding that adolescents have of their families' behaviors. An example of an ecological variable that might interact with the ways in which adolescents subjectively understand their families' behaviors is ethnic background. Kochman (1981) pointed out differences in the ways that many African Americans and European Americans understand interruptions in arguments between intimates. He contrasts the interpretation of interruptions by many European Americans as conflictual and divisive with the interpretation of interruptions by many African Americans as persuasive and signifying "caring about something enough to want to struggle for it" (p. 19). Thus, a mother's interruptions may be interpreted very differently by an African-American adolescent and a European-American adolescent based upon the ethnic context of their community norms regarding styles of interaction.

Assessment of the interaction of ecological differences with adolescents' subjective understanding of behavior has an important benefit: It can facilitate the observational study of a greater diversity of types of families. An often-noted problem with research that investigates the relations of family behaviors to adolescent outcomes is that the vast majority of this research has been primarily restricted to examining one type of family—urban, middle- to high-income, two-parent, European-American families (Bronfenbrenner, 1986; Dornbusch, Petersen, & Hetherington, 1991; Hill, 1987; Spencer & Dornbusch, 1990). As a result, investigators are rarely able to examine the influence of ecological variables, such as socioeconomic status, community, family structure, or ethnic contexts on the relations between observed family behaviors and adolescent outcomes. We cannot assume that the conclusions drawn from research with a single type of family are applicable to adolescents from other populations. Research with more diverse groups of families is necessary to understand the range and variety of ways in which family behaviors are related to adolescent outcomes. We propose that it is especially important to assess adolescents' subjective understanding of family behaviors in populations culturally different from the urban, middle-class, European-American population that has been traditionally studied. Behaviors that seem similar to those observed in European-American families may have characteristically different meanings for adolescents from other ethnic, economic, and regional backgrounds, and may be related in different ways to adolescent outcomes.

In summary, we argue that the newly emerging definition of affect as a relational process (with its emphasis on the role of subjective understanding) provides an extremely useful way of examining the mediating influence of affect on the relations among family behaviors and adolescent psychosocial outcomes. Assessing adolescents' subjective understanding of family behaviors will allow us to better understand one of the mechanisms by which those behaviors are related to specific adolescent outcomes. In addition, we propose that both individual and ecological differences interact with (or moderate) subjective understanding, and thereby affect the impact of family behaviors on adolescent outcomes. It is our belief that including assessments of adolescents' subjective understanding of family behaviors in our theoretical models and empirical investigations will lead to more consistent and meaningful associations between observed family behaviors and adolescent outcomes.

THE MEASUREMENT OF SUBJECTIVE UNDERSTANDING

The Usefulness of Observational Methods

Direct observation of family behaviors is a particularly appropriate methodology for examining adolescent affect with respect to family behavior. This method allows analysis of data sequences that maintain the temporal relationships among adolescent affects (as reflected in adolescents' subjective understanding) and specific family behaviors. As noted earlier, however, adolescents' subjective understanding of their families' behaviors has rarely been studied with observational methods (Callan & Noller, 1986; Margolin, 1987).

Observational studies of adolescents' family behaviors have typically assessed behaviors by having trained observers ascribe one or more specific, preclassified labels to each family behavior (see Markman & Notarius, 1987, and Grotevant & Carlson, 1987, for reviews of the most commonly used interaction coding schemes). These labels assign generic or standardized meanings to the behaviors. That is, the goal of the observers is to assign meanings to a behavior that have a high probability of being assigned to that behavior by any trained observer. The label is, therefore, not simply the observer's subjective understanding of the behavior, or even the observer's hunch about the adolescent's subjective understanding of the behavior, but is, instead, an attempt to assign a generalized understanding of the behavior. For example, if two mothers from different families perform an identical behavior (e.g., interrupting daughter) their behaviors should be given identical codes by trained observers, regardless of the meaning that the behavior had for each particular mother or for her daughter. Interruptions have been traditionally coded as conflict (Holmbeck & Hill, 1991) in standardized coding schemes. In some families, however, interruptions may be a sign of heightened interest and involvement in the daughter's participation, rather than conflict (Kochman, 1981). Assessing an adolescent's subjective understanding of his or her family's behaviors is especially important because these assessments reflect a fundamental aspect of that particular individual's affect in a particular context.

Assessing adolescents' subjective understanding does not, of course, include all relevant ways of understanding family behaviors. There are undoubtably other significant aspects of the family behaviors that adolescents are not able to perceive or express, and these may, nevertheless, have an impact on the adolescent's outcomes. For example, trained observers may be able to interpret family behaviors as conflictual, although those behaviors are not seen as conflictual by the adolescent because he or she is not aware of family conflict. Or an observer may be able to interpret a mother's behavior as signifying ambivalence, although that perception is not available to an adolescent because of his or her level of affective development (Fisher & Lamborn, 1989; Thompson, 1985).

Standardized interpretive labels given to family behaviors by observers have been used quite effectively in analyses to predict a number of adolescent psychosocial outcomes, such as identity development and role-taking skills (Cooper, Grotevant, & Condon, 1983; Grotevant & Cooper, 1985), ego development and psychopathology (Hauser et al., 1984; Hauser et al., 1991; Powers, Hauser, Schwartz, Noam, & Jacobson, 1983), moral development (Powers, 1988, 1989), self-esteem (Isberg et al., 1989), and academic achievement (Welsh et al., 1993). Thus, we do not want to suggest that the standardized labels that observers from outside the family ascribe to family behaviors are unimportant. Multiple assessments of family behaviors, both standardized and subjective, are needed. Our point is that assessing adolescents' subjective understanding of their family behaviors may play a critical role in fully understanding the impact of family behaviors on adolescent outcomes. Too often, researchers are forced to make post hoc explanations for unclear patterns of association between family behaviors and child outcomes. Researchers may more completely tap the explanatory power of observational methods when adolescents' subjective understanding of the observed behaviors are included in observational analyses.

The Video-Recall Procedure

There are currently very few procedures designed to assess subjects' understanding of observed behaviors (Brooks-Gunn, Rock, & Warren, 1989). Our ongoing, longitudinal investigation, the Rural Adolescent and Family Study, employs a method that has been used productively in research with married couples to assess spouses' subjective understanding of their behaviors: the video-recall procedure (Gottman & Levenson, 1985; Levenson & Gottman, 1983, 1985; Margolin, 1987; Weiss, 1984). The purpose of the Rural Adolescent and Family Study is to examine the relationship of a number of aspects of adolescents' family and community environments to adolescents' mental health and adaptive functioning throughout the high school years. The families were drawn from a community population of families with adolescents (ages 14 to 18) from nine rural towns in New England. The nine towns vary in social class and extent of ruralness. Thus, the selection of subjects from these nine towns allows the analysis of the moderating effects of individual and ecological differences on subjective understanding of family behaviors. Our use of the video-recall procedure is described here as an illustration of how this method may be used with adolescents and parents.

Four discussion tasks were videotaped in the adolescent's home. Two discussions took place between the adolescent and mother (or stepmother), and two discussions took place between the adolescent and father (or stepfather). The first discussion task involved negotiating ways of being close to each other, and the second discussion task required negotiating jointly designated areas of conflict. Mothers and adolescents came to the university laboratory within a few days of participating in the original home interaction tasks to view the videotape of their interaction. During this session, they rated and discussed with an interviewer their understanding of the behaviors shown in the videotape.

The video-recall procedure assumes that the ratings obtained while watching the videotapes are accurate representations of the subjective understanding of the subjects during the original discussion. Gottman & Levenson (1985) examined the related assumption that subjects are experiencing similar feeling states in the original interaction and in the recall session by measuring the coherence between physiological responses of the subjects (heart rate, pulse transmission time to the finger, skin conductance level, and general somatic activity) during both sessions. Their results showed that couples' physiological behavior in the recall session closely paralleled that of the interaction session. In fact, subjects appeared to "sweat, change their heart rate, and change their pulse transmission times at nearly the same time points when viewing the videotape of the interaction as they did when they were in the original interaction" (Gottman & Levenson, 1985, p. 157). Further support for this method as a useful assessment of subjects' subjective understanding of behavior comes from evidence that distressed and nondistressed couples differ in their ratings of their behaviors (Notarius, Benson, Sloane, Vanzetti, & Hornyak, 1989) and that their ratings are significantly associated with current and future marital satisfaction (Gottman & Levenson, 1985; Margolin, 1987; Markman, 1981; Weiss, 1984).

The challenge in designing an approach to analyzing videotaped data of adolescents and their parents lay in developing rating procedures that allowed subjects to convey significant aspects of their understanding of their behaviors. Subjective understanding includes judgments about the purpose or intent of the behavior, feeling states associated with the behavior, and appraisals of the significance of the behavior. To capture these different dimensions of subjective understanding, three procedures for collecting data were used. In each case, subjects were asked to give information about their experience when they were in the original interaction and not about the experience of watching themselves on videotape.

First, in a semistructured interview procedure, subjects were asked to identify, in their own words, the dimensions of the observed behaviors that were significant to them. Over the course of viewing 10 min of their 20-min videotaped interaction, the tape was stopped every 30 s, and subjects were asked what they were thinking and feeling during that portion of their interaction. This procedure allowed us to assess subjects' feelings and judgments about the purpose, intent, and significance of behaviors that may have been missed by more structured rating scales (Margolin, 1987).

Information from our interviews revealed that adolescents often had a very different subjective understanding of the videotaped behaviors than did the interviewer. In one example, the adolescent's behavior on the videotape appeared to the interviewer to be extremely passive and disinterested. The interviewer assumed that the adolescent was feeling bored with the interaction and judged that the interaction was unimportant to the adolescent. When asked what she had been thinking and feeling during the original interaction, the adolescent became quite animated and exclaimed, "I was furious! My mother always does that! She always tells me the same thing and nothing I say makes a difference!"

Data from these interviews can also be used to check whether subjects' spontaneously generated understanding of their families' behaviors matches the way they rate their understanding in the more structured procedures described later. By conducting the semi-structured interviews before subjects were asked to rate their interactions, we were assured that the dimensions of understanding represented by the rating scales did not contaminate subject's spontaneous reactions about their behavior. In addition, these interviews allowed subjects time to acclimate to viewing themselves on film and to discuss any extraneous factors, such as their appearance, before beginning the structured ratings of the interaction sessions.

In a second review of the tape, the adolescent and mother were asked to provide a continuous rating of the intensity of their feelings along a positive–negative scale. The continuous rating was obtained by having the family member manipulate a computerized lever that traversed a 180° arc over a 9-point scale, with neutral at 90° (Gottman & Levenson, 1985; Levenson & Gottman, 1983, 1985). The affect dial ratings were averaged across 10-sec time periods.

In two more viewings, the mother and adolescent used six rating scales to describe their understanding of the purpose or intent of behaviors in the family sessions. Two factors were important in designing these rating scales. First, adolescents had to be able to understand the ratings and the rating procedure with minimal instructions, learning the procedure with only a 2-min training session. Second, the number of ratings had to be limited so that the entire procedure was not too time-consuming for families. In the first viewing in this procedure, subjects rated the extent to which their own behaviors were supportive, conflictual, humorous, giving in to the other, and sarcastic. After each 15-s portion, the tape was paused for 15 s, and subjects were asked to complete the rating scales, taking into account the full 15-s segment of the discussion. Subjects were shown 32 such 15-s segments, for a total of 8 min of interaction.[5] Subsequently, the subjects again viewed the same 8-min portion of videotape and repeated the same procedure, this time rating the extent to which the behaviors of the

[5]The first 8 min of the second discussion were shown rather than the entire 20 min because stopping the tape to allow subjects to rate their interaction doubled the time that it took subjects to watch the videotape. Because subjects completed the ratings twice, the rating task took 32 min. If subjects had rated the entire 20 min of interaction, the rating task would have taken 1 hr and 20 min.

family member with whom they were interacting were supportive, conflictual, humorous, giving in to them, and misunderstanding of them.

In addition to subjects' ratings of their family behaviors, trained observers coded the data using both the continuous rating of positive to negative feeling and the rating scales. Subject and observer ratings of these observational data will allow us to examine the assumption that family members' subjective understanding of their behaviors mediate the relation between family behaviors and adolescent outcomes. This assumption will be tested by examining how associations between adolescent outcomes and subjects' ratings differ from the associations between adolescent outcomes and observer ratings. A second assumption that we will be able to test is that individual and ecological differences moderate the meanings of family behaviors to subjects in systematic ways. This assumption will be tested by examining the extent to which subjects' ratings of family behaviors that have previously been identified as equivalent behaviors across the sample (according to the ratings of observers) vary as a result of subjects' levels of ecological or individual differences.

In summary, this article argues that the relations among family behaviors and adolescent psychosocial outcomes may be better understood if adolescents' affective experience of these behaviors is taken into account. The particular facet of adolescent affective experience that is emphasized is the adolescent's subjective understanding of his or her family's behaviors. Subjective understanding is multidimensional and includes feeling states associated with behaviors, judgments of the purpose and intent of the behaviors, and appraisals of the importance of the behavior. The use of the video-recall method and other methods to assess adolescents' affective experiences of their family behaviors may increase our ability to comprehend the associations we find among family behaviors and adolescent outcomes. In addition, including adolescents' affective experience of family behaviors in our theoretical models and empirical analyses should allow us to study more effectively the diversity of adolescent and family groups.

ACKNOWLEDGMENTS

An earlier version of this article was presented at the 1992 National Institute of Mental Health workshop, "Affective Processes in Adolescence," held October 19–20, 1992 in Bethesda, Maryland.

Preparation of this article was supported by a grant from the National Science Foundation to Sally Powers.

We are grateful to the workshop organizers and to Lynne C. Huffman and Stuart T. Hauser, the guest editors of this issue, for helpful comments on an earlier version of this article.

REFERENCES

Barrett, K. & Campos, J. (1987). Perspectives on emotional development: II. A functionalist approach to emotions. In J. Osofsky (Ed.), Handbook of infant development (2nd ed., pp. 555–578). New York: Wiley.

Bronfenbrenner, U. (1986). Ecology of the family as a context for human development: Research perspectives. *Developmental Psychology, 22,* 723–742.

Bronfenbrenner, U. , & Crouter, A. C. (1982). Work and family through time and space. In S. Kamerman & C. Hayes (Eds.), *Families that work: Children in a changing world.* Washington, DC: National Academy of Sciences.

Brooks-Gunn, J., Rock, D., & Warren, M. P. (1989). Comparability of constructs across the adolescent years. *Developmental Psychology, 25,* 51–60.

Callan, V. J., & Noller, P. (1986). Perceptions of communicative relationships in families with adolescents. *Journal of Marriage and the Family, 48,* 813–820.

Campos, J., & Stenberg, C. (1981). Perception, appraisal, and emotion: The onset of social referencing. In M. E. Lamb & L. R. Sherrod (Eds.), *Infant social cognition: Empirical and theoretical considerations* (pp. 217–314). Hillsdale, NJ: Lawrence Erlbaum Associates, Inc.

Campos, J. J., Campos, R. G., & Barrett, K. C. (1989). Emergent themes in the study of emotional development and emotion regulation. *Developmental Psychology, 25,* 394–402.

Cooper, C., Grotevant, H., & Condon, S. (1983). Individuality and connectedness in the family as a context for adolescent identity formation and role-taking skill. *New Directions in Child Development, 22,* 43–59.

Dix, T. (1991). The affective organization of parenting: Adaptive and maladaptive processes. *Psychological Bulletin, 110,* 3–25.

Dornbusch, S. M., Petersen, A. C., & Hetherington, E. M. (1991). Projecting the future of research on adolescence. *Journal of Research on Adolescence, 1,* 7–17.

Fisher, K., & Lamborn, S. D. (1989). Mechanisms of variation in developmental levels: Cognitive and emotional transitions during adolescence. In A. de Ribaupierre (Ed.), *Transitional mechanisms in emotional child development: The longitudinal approach* (pp. 33–67). Cambridge, England: Cambridge University Press.

Frijda, N. (1986). *The emotions.* New York: Cambridge University Press.

Gottman, J. M. (1979). *Marital interaction: Experimental investigations.* New York: Academic.

Gottman, J. M., & Fainsilber Katz, L. (1989). Effects of marital discord on young children's peer interaction and health. *Developmental Psychology, 25,* 373–381.

Gottman, J. M., & Levenson, R. W. (1985). A valid procedure for obtaining self-report of affect in marital interaction. *Journal of Consulting and Clinical Psychology, 53,* 156–160.

Gottman, J. M., Notarius, C., Markman, H., Bank, S., Yoppi, B., & Rubin, M. E. (1976). Behavior exchange theory and marital decision making. *Journal of Personality and Social Psychology, 34,* 14–34.

Grotevant, H., & Carlson, C. I. (1987). Family interaction coding systems: A descriptive review. *Family Process, 26,* 50–72.

Grotevant, H., & Cooper, C. (1985). Patterns of interaction in family relationships and the development of identity exploration in adolescence. *Child Development, 56,* 415–428.

Hauser, S. T., Powers, S. I., & Noam, G. G. (1991). *Adolescents and their families: Paths of ego*

development. New York: Free Press.
Hauser, S. T., Powers, S. I., Noam, G. G., Jacobson, A. M., Weiss, B., & Follansbee, D. (1984). Familial contexts of adolescent ego development. *Child Development, 55*, 195–213.
Hauser, S. T., & Sayfer, A. W. (1994/this issue). Ego development and adolescent emotions. *Journal of Research on Adolescence, 4*, 487–501.
Haviland, J., & Lelwica, M. (1987). The induced affect response: 10-week-old infants' responses to three emotion expressions. *Developmental Psychology, 23*, 97–104.
Hill, J. (1987). Research on adolescents and their families: Past and prospect. *New Directions in Child Development, 37*, 13–32.
Holmbeck, G., & Hill, J. (1991). Conflictive engagement, positive affect, and menarche in families with seventh-grade girls. *Child Development, 62*, 1030–1048.
Isberg, R. S., Hauser, S. T., Jacobson, A. M., Powers, S. I., Noam, G. G., Weiss-Perry, B., & Follansbee, D. (1989). Parental contexts of adolescent self-esteem: A developmental perspective. *Journal of Youth and Adolescence, 18*, 1–23.
Kagan, J. (1984). *The nature of the child*. New York: Basic Books.
Kochman, T. (1981). *Black and white styles in conflict*. Chicago: University of Chicago Press.
Levenson, R. W., & Gottman, J. M. (1983). Marital interaction: Physiological linkage and affective exchange. *Journal of Personality and Social Psychology, 45*, 587–597.
Levenson, R. W., & Gottman, J. M. (1985). Physiological and affective predictors of change in relationship satisfaction. *Journal of Personality and Social Psychology, 49*, 85–94.
Loevinger, J. (1976). *Ego development*. San Francisco: Jossey-Bass.
Margolin, G. (1987). Participant observation procedures in marital and family assessment. In T. Jacobs (Ed.), *Family interaction and psychopathology: Theories, methods, and findings* (pp. 391–426). New York: Plenum.
Margolin, G., Hattem, D., John, R. S., & Yost, K. (1985). Perceptual agreement between spouses and outside observers when coding themselves and a stranger dyad. *Behavioral Assessment, 7*, 235–247.
Markman, H. J. (1979). Application of a behavioral model of marriage in predicting relationship satisfaction of couples planning marriage. *Journal of Consulting and Clinical Psychology, 47*, 743–749.
Markman, H. J. (1981). Prediction of marital distress: A 5 year follow-up. *Journal of Consulting and Clinical Psychology, 49*, 760–762.
Markman, H. J., & Notarius, C. I. (1987). Coding marital and family interaction: Current status. In T. Jacobs (Ed.), *Family interaction and psychopathology*. New York: Plenum.
Notarius, C. I., Benson, P. R., Sloane, D., Vanzetti, N. A., & Hornyak, L. M. (1989). Exploring the interface between perception and behavior: An analysis of marital interaction in distressed and nondistressed couples. *Behavioral Assessment, 11*, 39–64.
Powers, S. I. (1988). Moral judgment development in the family. *Journal of Moral Education, 17*, 209–219.
Powers, S. I. (1989). Family systems throughout the lifespan: Family constellations of development, meaning, and behavior. In K. Kreppner & R. Lerner (Eds.), *Family systems and life-span development* (pp. 271–287). Hillsdale, NJ: Lawrence Erlbaum Associates, Inc.
Powers, S. I., Hauser, S. T., & Kilner, L. (1989). Adolescent mental health. *American Psychologist, 44*, 200–208.
Powers, S. I., Hauser, S. T., Schwartz, J., Noam, G. G., & Jacobson, A. M. (1983). Family interaction and adolescent ego development: A structural–developmental perspective. *New Directions in Child Development, 22*, 5–25.
Spencer, M. B., & Dornbusch, S. M. (1990). Challenges in studying minority youth. In S. Feldman & G. R. Elliott (Eds.), *At the threshold: The developing adolescent* (pp. 255–276). Cambridge, MA: Harvard University Press.

Thompson, A. (1985). The nature of emotion and its development. In I. Fast (Ed.), *Event theory: An integration of Piaget and Freud* (pp. 151–173). Hillsdale, NJ: Lawrence Erlbaum Associates, Inc.

Weiss, R. L. (1984). Cognitive and behavioral measures of marital interaction. In N. S. Jacobson & K. Hahlweg (Eds.), *Marital interaction: Analysis and modification*. New York: Guilford.

Welsh, D. P., Powers, S. I., Stephenson, M., Hauser, S. T., Noam, G. G., & Jacobson, A. M. (1993). *Family interaction and adolescent academic success: Contextual factors.* Unpublished manuscript.

Received December 30, 1992
Accepted February 4, 1994

Contributions of Parental Attachments to View of Self and Depressive Symptoms Among Early Adolescents

Maureen E. Kenny
Donna L. Moilanen
Boston College
Richard Lomax
Northern Illinois University
Mary M. Brabeck
Boston College

Three causal models, examining the relationship of parental attachment to view of self and level of depressive symptoms, were examined for a sample of eighth-grade girls (n = 92) and boys (n = 115). Consistent with the Bowlby construct of the internal working model of self, structural equation modeling provided tentative support for the mediating role of view of self in influencing depressive symptoms. Gender differences were found for levels of depressive symptoms and global self-worth. Longitudinal studies with additional variables and multiple informants are needed to further assess the validity of the proposed model.

Adolescence is characterized as a period of change in parent-child relationships. In contrast with traditional views (e.g., Blos, 1967; Freud, 1969), which emphasized the need for rebellion from parents in fostering psychological growth and autonomy, contemporary models (e.g., Grotevant & Cooper, 1986; Hill & Holmbeck, 1986) suggest that individuation occurs most adaptively within a caring offspring relationship, which is transformed rather than broken during adolescence. Some findings (e.g., Hauser & Bowlds, 1990; Petersen, Sarigiani, & Kennedy, 1991) suggest further that close parental relationships can buffer the negative effects of early adolescent stress and provide a source of comfort and security in the changing adolescent

We would like to gratefully acknowledge the assistance of Sonia Stryker in data entry and management.

Journal of Early Adolescence, Vol. 13 No. 4, November 1993 408-430

world. The study described here examined one psychological process hypothesized to mediate the relationship between parental attachment and the experience of adolescent depression.

Attachment theory (Ainsworth, Blehar, Waters, & Wall, 1978; Bowlby, 1969, 1973, 1980, 1988) has gained increasing theoretical and research attention for its heuristic value in explaining how parental closeness can serve as a protective buffer and source of security throughout adolescence (Ainsworth, 1989; Armsden & Greenberg, 1987; Kenny, 1987; Kobak & Sceery, 1988; Rice, 1990; Ryan & Lynch, 1989). According to attachment theory, a primary role of the parental attachment figure is to provide a secure home base, being available as a source of help when needed, and encouraging the growth of self-reliance in a sensitive manner. In addition to providing a secure base of support, attachment relationships also form the core of internal working models (Bowlby, 1973) or mental representations of the self and others. The dual functions of secure attachments as a base of support and as the source of internal working models of the parental attachment figure and complementary models of the self and others can be conceptualized as protective factors that contribute positively to the psychological well-being of the early adolescent during a period of life change. Conversely, insecure parental attachments, which fail to offer a secure base and contribute to negative internal working models, can be understood as risk factors contributing to psychological distress and depression.

According to the secure-base hypothesis (Ainsowrth et al., 1978; Bowlby, 1988), feelings of security and confidence derive from experience with knowledgeable and responsive attachment figures as a source of comfort and help, if needed. That knowledge enables the individual to explore the environment and take on challenges without excessive anxiety, thereby promoting development of social and intellectual competence. In situations of danger and distress, the comfort provided by the attachment figure reduces distress and restores feelings of psychological well-being. When that source of comfort and support is lacking, risk for psychological dysfunction increases. If parental relationships continue to offer a secure base throughout adolescence (Hartup, 1979), parents may be sought out to provide comfort, support, and advice in meeting the social and developmental challenges of the early adolescent years. Seeking the actual physical presence of attachment figures may not always be necessary because feelings of security may be derived from knowledge that help and support are available, if needed. Some support for the secure-base hypothesis and the role of parental attachments in buffering the effects of emotional distress is provided in existing adolescent research (Armsden & Greenberg, 1987; Kenny, 1987; Papini, Roggman, & Anderson, 1991).

The function of parental attachments as a source of internal working models suggests that attachments have an additional impact on psychological well-being in an indirect way. That is, the internal working model may mediate the relationship between attachment and the experience of psychological distress. According to Bowlby (1969, 1973), the child develops complementary internal working models of the attachment relationship, others, and the self through experiences with attachment figures. Our study focuses on the role of the internal working model of self. The internal representation of the attachment figure is believed to intertwine with one's view of self and to have a pervasive effect on the way in which subsequent information about the self is perceived and interpreted. These internal models are useful in guiding behavior in new situations, so that immediate appraisal of the availability and responsiveness of the attachment figure is unnecessary (Bretherton, 1985). Models of self developed in the context of secure attachment are believed to contribute to feelings of self-worth and confidence and thereby enhance resilience to stress (Bowlby, 1980). When the internal representation of the attachment figure is that of an available, responsive, and reliable person, attachment theory predicts that the individual will develop and maintain an internal model of the self as good, worthy, lovable, capable of getting others' attention, competent, and valuable. Conversely, negative internal working models associated with insecure parental attachments are linked theoretically with negative views of the self and vulnerability to depression. According to Bowlby (1980), a negative internal working model contributed to a predisposition to interpret subsequent losses and disappointments as personal failures, thereby further diminishing feelings of self-worth and increasing vulnerability to depression.

The quality of parental attachments and complementary models of self are relevant to the understanding of emotional development and family relationships in early adolescence. According to attachment theory, internal working models are initially constructed based on early childhood experiences with significant caregivers, but are modified through ongoing interpersonal relationships and increased self-understanding (Bowlby, 1988; Main, Kaplan, & Cassidy, 1985). Kobak, Cole, Ferenz-Gillis, Fleming, and Gamble (1993) suggest that early adolescence is a time of likely change in attachment relationships as adolescents equipped with more sophisticated cognitive skills reflect on and reevaluate models of self and parent and strive to renegotiate an adaptive balance between connection and autonomy. Secure internal working models of attachment and self might be disrupted if the adolescent experiences a loss of parental support, availability, and responsiveness (Kobak, Sudler, & Gamble, 1991).

Whereas a growing body of research has documented a relationship between characteristics of secure parental attachment and adaptive psychological functioning, including self-esteem, among adolescents (Armsden & Greenberg, 1987; Kenny, 1987; Kenny & Donaldson, 1991; Kobak & Sceery, 1988) and between characteristics of insecure attachment and depressive symptoms (Armsden, McCauley, Greenberg, Burke, & Mitchell, 1990; Kobak et al., 1991; Papini & Roggman, 1992), little research has examined the psychological mechanisms through which attachment affects depression. Empirical identification of processes linking the two constructs would strengthen the theoretical model specifying a relationship between attachment and depression (Cummings & Cicchetti, 1990) and provide a better understanding of how parental attachments influence psychological functioning. Such findings would also extend to cognitive models of depression. As Bowlby (1980) points out, his suggestion that cognitive biases (including a negative view of the self) derived from attachment experiences contribute to the risk for depression is consistent with the cognitive model of depression formulated by Beck (1967). Although Beck's theory has been highly influential in the conceptualization and treatment of depression in recent years, its adequacy in explaining depression is limited by the paucity of theoretical and research attention to the environmental and familial precursors of dysfunctional cognitive processes (Bowlby, 1980; Hammen, 1990). Because view of self is a central component of Beck's cognitive triad, examining the relationship between parental attachment, view of self, and depression could contribute to the understanding of family factors associated with a depressogenic view of self. In this study, we examined the role of view of self (internal working model of self) as one psychological process mediating the relationship between parental attachment and depressive symptoms.

This research was also designed to clarify conflicting claims regarding gender differences in attachment, view of self, and depression. According to attachment theory (Ainsworth et al., 1978), secure attachments are equally important to boys and girls as a secure base and source for internal working models, and gender has not been an important focus of research on attachment in infancy and early childhood. However, recent theorists and clinicians (Chodorow, 1978; Gilligan, 1982; Gilligan, Lyons, & Hanmer, 1990; Josselson, 1988; Miller, 1976) have claimed that girls develop stronger attachments to mothers in infancy and childhood than do boys. These relationship theorists maintain that because of different experiences of being mothered and socialization into feminine roles, girls and women develop a self defined by relationships to others and characterized by greater concern for caring about and maintaining relationships (Gilligan & Wiggins, 1988; Jordan, Kaplan,

Miller, Stiver, & Surrey, 1991). Relational theorists argue that during adolescence, girls' identity development and sense of self are fundamentally different from boys. Miller (1991) claims, "Girls are not seeking the kind of identity that has been prescribed for boys, but a different kind, one in which one is a 'being-in-relation,' which means developing all of one's self in increasingly complex ways, in increasingly complex relationships" (p. 21). This orientation toward care and connection has been conceptualized as a source of psychological strength (Miller, 1976, 1991) and self-esteem (Surrey, 1991) for women, but it has also been described as a factor increasing risk for depression when interpersonal relationships are unsatisfying (Kaplan, 1991; McGrath, Keita, Strickland, & Russo, 1990) and as a source of dependency and passivity associated with depression (Gjerde & Block, 1991).

Empirical studies of gender differences in parental attachment in early and middle adolescence have not supported claims of relational theorists that girls develop stronger parental attachments than boys (Armsden et al., 1990; Greenberg, Siegel, & Leitch, 1983; Raja, McGee, & Stanton, 1992; Ryan & Lynch, 1989), and research regarding gender differences in care, connection, or relational identity have been conflicting (see Brabeck, 1989). Evidence does indicate that in adolescence, males show higher self-esteem than females (Freiberg, 1991; Keltikangas-Jarvinen, 1990; Richard, Gitelson, Petersen, & Hurtig, 1991) and that adolescent girls, to a greater degree than boys, are at risk for depression (e.g., Allgood-Merten, Lewinsohn, & Hops, 1990; Baron & Peixoto, 1991; Petersen, Sarigiani, & Kennedy, 1991).

However, researchers have paid little attention to whether or not the relationship between early adolescent girls' and boys' parental attachments has a different impact on the view of self or psychological well-being. Some research (Bronfenbrenner, 1961; Cooper, Grotevant, & Condon, 1983) suggests that family relationships that foster autonomy in girls and connectedness in boys may lead to healthier identity development for girls and boys. Other research on late adolescents (Kenny & Donaldson, 1991; Palladino & Blustein, 1991) suggests that parental attachment may be associated with psychological functioning for college-age women, but not for men. This work suggests that although girls and boys may not differ in parental attachment per se, these relationships may have a different impact on one's view of self and, in turn, on psychological well being (e.g., depression). Our research tested hypothesized models of the relationships among parental attachments, view of self, and development of depression among a group of boys and a group of girls.

In sum, this study sought to examine the empirical plausibility of a theoretical model linking parental attachment, view of self, and depressive symptoms. We sought first of all to replicate previous findings (e.g., Armsden & Greenberg, 1987; Papini & Roggman, 1992; Papini et al., 1991) with our sample by examining a direct model assessing the role of parental attachments as determinants of view of self and depressive symptoms. Based on the understanding of parental attachments as a secure base of support and source of internal working models, we hypothesized, consistent with previous findings, that characteristics of secure parental attachment would be significantly associated with a positive view of self and significantly and negatively associated with level of depressive symptoms. Second, based on the role of parental attachments in influencing the internal working model of self, we sought to test a mediating model in which parental attachment is viewed as a determinant of view of self, which in turn contributes to level of depressive symptoms. Based on theory concerning the formation and the role of the internal working model of self, we hypothesized that parental attachment would be significantly associated with a positive view of self, which in turn would be significantly and negatively associated with depressive symptoms. Finally, the large body of theory suggesting that interpersonal and family relationships may be more critical to the well-being of females, the substantial evidence that girls report more depressive symptoms and lower self-esteem than boys during the adolescent years, and the emerging attention to gender differences in adolescent familial relationships (Steinberg, 1987) warrant attention to gender in our analyses. Our interest was not in replicating previous studies of gender differences in parental attachment, self-esteem, or depression. Rather, we investigated a model of the differential impact of adolescent boys' and girls' parental attachments on their view of self and depression. To examine gender differences in the hypothesized relationships among attachment, view of self, and psychological functioning, analyses were completed separately for boys and girls.

METHOD

Participants

The participants were 207 (boys = 115, girls = 92) eighth-grade students attending a public middle school in a suburban community 30 miles south of Boston. The student body is primarily White and middle class. Participants were recruited in the fall of 1990 (n = 108; 58% of all eighth graders in the school system) and the fall of 1991 (n = 99; 51% of all eighth graders in the school system) for a longitudinal study concerning students' ability to cope effectively with the stresses of growing up, through enhanced self-esteem and freedom from depression. The longitudinal phase of this study is in progress.

Procedure

The proposal for this study was developed in close collaboration with a district school psychologist, the middle school guidance counselor and principal, and a group of teachers. The proposal was approved by a university ethics committee; school administrators (superintendent, assistant superintendent, principals), and the school committee. A letter describing the purposes of the research and requesting consent for participation from students and their parents was distributed to students by eighth-grade homeroom teachers. Students were asked to give the letter to their parents, discuss the content of the letter with them, and return the signed form of informed consent to their homeroom teachers within one week.

In the fall of 1990, all students who had returned the forms of informed consent were asked to report to the cafeteria for a group testing session. All questionnaires, distributed in four different versions to control for order effects, were completed within the first two class periods of that day. Several additional measures, including the Defining Issues Test (Rest, 1979), the Social Interest Scale (Crandall, 1975) and the Mehrabian-Epstein Empathy Scale (Mehrabian & Epstein, 1972), not of interest for the present study, were included in the questionnaire packets. School teachers, administrators, and the team of researchers and their assistants were present to answer student questions and monitor the assessment process. In the fall of 1991, questionnaires were completed during social studies classes on two consecutive days of the same week. Other procedures were the same as the fall of 1990.

Measures

Attachment. The 55-item Parental Attachment Questionnaire (PAQ) (Kenny, 1987) was designed to assess security of attachment by adapting the Ainsworth et al. (1978) conceptualization of attachment for use with adolescents and young adults. The PAQ contains three scales, Affective Quality of Attachment, Parental Fostering of Autonomy, and Parental Role in Providing Emotional Support, which we derived from factor analysis. Respondents are asked to answer each item on a 5-point Likert-type scale, ranging from 1 = *not at all* to 5 = *very much.* The instrument was initially constructed requesting a single rating for both parents, but was recently modified by Kenny to request separate ratings for each parent.

Kenny (1987) assessed the reliability of the original attachment measure, which assessed attachment to both parents with a single rating, through test-retest and internal consistency methods. Test-retest reliability over a 2-week interval was .92 for the measure as a whole and ranged from .82 to .91 for the three scales derived from factor analysis. Cronbach's coefficient alpha was .96 for Affective Quality of Attachment and .88 for both the Parental Fostering of Autonomy and Parental Role in Providing Emotional Support scales. Internal consistency for the entire measure is Cronbach's alpha of .93 for male college students and .95 for female college students. Although the PAQ measure requesting separate mother and father ratings was used, we did not make any specific hypotheses in this study concerning the differential role of mothers and fathers. For that reason, we decided to calculate each of the three PAQ scales by combining the mother and father ratings. We assessed internal consistency for the modified (mother and father scores added together) version of the PAQ with the eighth-grade sample and obtained Cronbach's alphas of .95 for combined maternal and paternal Affective Quality of Attachment, .88 for combined maternal and parental Parental Fostering of Autonomy and .83 for combined maternal and paternal Role in Providing Emotional Support. With respect to validity (Kenny & Donaldson, 1991), PAQ subscales have been found to correlate moderately with conceptually relevant subscales of the Family Environment Scale (FES) (Moos & Moos, 1986). In addition, the factor structure of the PAQ (Kenny, 1990) is theoretically consistent with the Ainsworth et al. (1978) conceptualization of attachment as an enduring affective bond, which serves as a secure base in providing emotional support and in fostering autonomy and mastery of the environment.

View of self. The Self-Perception Profile for Adolescents (SPPA) (Harter, 1988) assesses eight specific domains of perceived competence, as well as the global perception of one's worth as a person. However, we administered only six of the SPPA scales that correspond with the scales of the Self-Perception Profile for Children (SPPC) (Harter, 1985), a downward extension of the SPPA. We piloted our instruments prior to beginning this research and were told by eighth-grade students that some of the items, especially those from the Romantic Appeal and Job Competence subscales of the SPPA, were not relevant for them. Harter (1988) acknowledged that the adolescent measure may not be appropriate for some seventh and eighth graders and suggested use of the child form in those cases. We believed that our participants would respond more favorably to items that asked about adolescents rather than younger children, so we decided to administer the six scales of the SPPA that are also included on the SPPC. Of the six scales administered, we decided to use the Global Self-Worth, Social Acceptance, Behavioral Conduct, and Scholastic Competence subscales as the measures of view of self for this study. Attachment theory (Bowlby, 1973, 1980) suggests that the quality of parental attachments affects one's sense of acceptability to the attachment figure and promotes the development of social and intellectual competence through interaction with the environment. Individuals who view themselves as acceptable in the eyes of the attachment figure would furthermore be likely to view themselves as generally worthy, behaving in socially and morally acceptable ways, and capable of academic success and would expect to be accepted by others, including peers. We did not include Athletic Competence and Physical Appearance in this study because the theoretical association with parental attachment was not as strong. Each subscale contains five items. Subjects respond to each item by selecting which of two descriptions is more true of them and then rating that description as either "sort of true for me" or "really true for me." Internal consistency reliabilities, as reported by Harter (1988), ranged from .80 to .89 for Global Self-Worth, from .77 to .90 for Social Acceptance, and from .77 to .91 for Scholastic Competence based on results from four samples, and was .78 for Behavioral Conduct, based on data from one sample. The eight subscales of the SPPA emerged as separate scales in a series of factor analyses (Harter, 1988).

Depressive symptoms. The Children's Depression Inventory (CDI; Kovacs, 1983) is a 27-item self-report measure designed to assess the severity of depressive symptomatology in children and adolescents and assesses a broad range of cognitive, affective, and behavioral symptoms. Each item consists of three statements reflecting different levels of severity and is scored on a scale from 0 to 2. Subjects are instructed to select the one statement that best describes how they have felt during the past 2 weeks. Scores on the CDI range from 0 to 54, with higher scores indicative of greater severity of symptoms. Kovacs reported the internal consistency (based on coefficient alpha) to be .86 for a diagnostically, heterogeneous psychiatric sample of 8- to 13-year-olds, .71 for an outpatient medical pediatric sample, and .87 for a large sample of Toronto public school students. Test-retest reliability of .54 was reported for an outpatient sample of youth tested 1 month apart (Weiss & Weisz, 1988), and test-retest reliabilities of .76 and .84 were reported for student samples tested at 3 weeks and 9 weeks, respectively (Kovacs, 1983). With respect to validity, the CDI has been found to correlate in the expected direction with children's depression and psychiatric ratings in the Dysthymia Checklist (Haley, Fine, Marriage, Moretti, & Freeman, 1985), as well as with depression-related constructs such as low self-esteem and self-concept (Kovacs, 1985; Saylor, Finch, Baskin, Furey, & Kelly, 1984).

RESULTS

Preliminary Analyses

Table 1 presents means and standard deviations for each variable for the boys and girls separately. Because the parental attachment and psychological functioning (view of self and depressive symptom) variables were viewed as theoretically distinct, we completed two multivariate *t* tests to assess gender differences on those variables. A multivariate main effect was found for the measures of psychological functioning, Hotellings' $t = .11$, $F(5, 203) = 4.87$, $p < .001$. Univariate *F*s indicated significant gender differences for depressive symptoms ($F[1, 207] = 6.74, p < .01$) and for Global Self-Worth ($F[1, 207] = 5.73, p < .02$), with girls reporting a higher level of depressive symptoms and lower level of self-worth. The main effect for the multivariate *t* test examining gender differences on the attachment scales was not significant (see Table 1).

Description and Evaluation of Models

The intercorrelations among the measures are presented separately for boys and girls in Table 2. These matrices served as the data for the structural equation iterations in subsequent analyses.

We used structural equation modeling (LISREL VII; Jöreskog & Sörbom, 1988) to test the theoretical models assessing the relationship between parental attachment, view of self, and depressive symptoms. Prior to conducting these analyses, we examined all variables for level of skewness. The values were not sufficiently large (< 1.2 in the current sample) to require transformations of the variables or modifications in the analyses. According to Muthen and Kaplan (1985), skewness of less than two is not of concern in structural equation modeling.

Figure 1 presents the standardized solution for the structural equation model specifying parental attachment as a direct determinant of view of self and depressive symptoms. The first step in evaluating the model was to assess the fit between the hypothesized model and the data. The goodness-of-fit index (GFI), which is interpreted similarly to a correlation coefficient in terms of desirable values, is considered a reasonable statistic for this purpose

TABLE 1: Means and Standard Deviations for Adolescent Boys and Girls on Measures of Parental Attachment, View of Self, and Depressive Symptoms

	Boys (n = 115)			*Girls (n = 93)*		
	$\bar{X}$	SD	*Range*	$\bar{X}$	SD	*Range*
Parental Attachment						
Affect	181.55	29.83	90-228	177.92	35.12	74-228
Autonomy	106.48	15.51	54-134	105.35	19.70	43 -134
Support	90.30	15.61	42-124	89.40	18.22	25-119
View of Self						
Global Self-Worth*	3.34	.65	1-4	3.13	.63	1-4
Social Acceptance	3.22	.60	1-4	3.13	.68	1-4
Behavioral Conduct	2.96	.58	1-4	3.11	.59	1-4
Scholastic Competence	3.25	.67	1-4	3.10	.66	2-4
Depressive Symptoms						
Children's Depression Inventory**	6.53	5.35	0-25	8.63	6.34	0-25

*$p < .02$; **$p < .01$.

because the chi-square statistic is easily distorted by large sample sizes (Fassinger, 1987). The adjusted goodness-of-fit index (AGFI) is the goodness-of-fit index adjusted for degrees of freedom and the root mean square residual (RMSR) is the average of the mean square of the residuals. Evaluative standards for interpretation of the GFI, AGFI, and RMSR are not empirically determined because statistical distributions and hence probability values for these indexes are unknown. GFI values above .90 and AGFI values above .80, however, are often cited as criteria for acceptable fit (e.g., Long, Kahn, & Schutz, 1992; Quintana & Lapsley, 1987). Low values for the RMSR are desirable. The GFI and AGFI indexes, presented in Figure 1, suggest that the model provides a reasonable fit to the data for both boys and girls. The second step in evaluating the model was to observe the relationship between each construct and its indicators. The standardized coefficients representing factor loadings between the indicators and the constructs are presented in Figure 1 and indicate that each indicator has a positive and statistically significant ($p < .05$) loading on the relevant construct.

Support for the model was also assessed by examining the standardized path coefficients (analogous to standardized beta weights in multiple regression) along the paths connecting the constructs. The pathways linking parental attachment with view of self and depressive symptoms are statistically significant for both boys and girls. We tested both pathways for gender

TABLE 2: **Correlations Among All Measures for Boys and Girls**

	1	*2*	*3*	*4*	*5*	*6*	*7*	*8*
Parental Attachment (mother and father)								
1. Quality Affect	—	.71**	.79**	.27*	.27*	.34**	.43**	–.51**
2. Facilitates Autonomy	.84**	—	.54**	.25*	.35**	.39**	.32**	–.53**
3. Provides Emotional Support	.83**	.76**	—	.20*	.15	.30*	.32**	–.39**
View of Self								
4. Global Self-Worth	.40**	.31*	.34**	—	.43**	.39**	.35**	–.59**
5. Social Acceptance	.22*	.12	.27*	.64**	—	.13	.33**	–.46**
6. Behavioral Conduct	.48**	.44**	.36**	.45**	.51**	—	.45**	–.43**
7. Scholastic Competence	.30*	.33**	.20*	.50**	.22*	.39**	—	.36**
Depressive Symptoms								
8. Children's Depression Inventory	–.48**	–.40**	–.45**	–.70**	–.51**	–.43**	–.43**	—

NOTE: Boys = above diagonal; girls = below diagonal.
*$p < .05$; **$p < .001$.

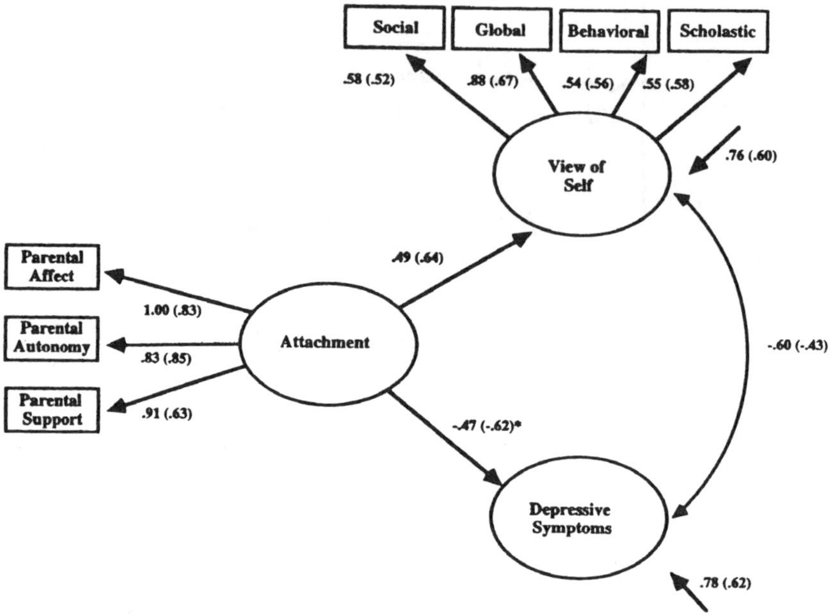

Figure 1: Structural Equation Model 1
NOTE: Girls = no parentheses, boys = in parentheses; standardized solution; all paths significant ($p < .05$). $X^2(16df) = 23.71$ (25.00); GFI = .94 (.94); AGFI = .86 (.86); RMSR = .06 (.06).
*Path coefficients differ by gender.

differences and found statistically significant gender differences for one pathway, indicating that the relationship between parental attachment and depressive symptoms is stronger for boys than for girls. The final step in evaluating the model was to examine the total amount of variance in each criterion variable that was explained by the predictor variable (parental attachment). This was assessed by observing the values for zeta (amount of variance not explained) and 1 – zeta (amount of variance explained). Parental attachment explained 40% of the variance in view of self for boys and 24% for girls and 38% of the variance in depressive symptoms for boys and 22% for girls.

The pathway shown in Figure 1 between view of self and depressive symptoms indicates the correlation between the residuals of those variables or, in other words, the relationship between the variance in self not explained by parental attachment and the variance in depression not explained by parental attachment. Several explanations can be considered in interpreting that correlation. One possibility is that other factors, not included in this

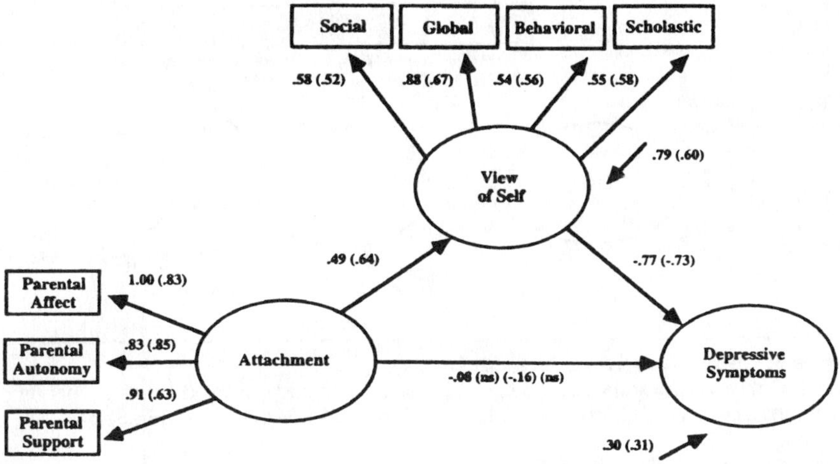

Figure 2: Structural Equation Model 2
NOTE: Girls = no parentheses, boys = in parentheses; standardized solution. All paths significant ($p < .05$) unless indicated (ns). $X^2(16df) = 23.71$ (25.00); GFI = .94 (.94); AGFI = .86 (.86); RMSR = .06 (.06).

model, account for that shared variance. A second possibility is that at least some part of that shared variance can be explained by the influence of view of self on depression. That second possibility is explored in the model illustrated in Figure 2. In addition to testing the direct paths between attachment and depression and attachment and view of self specified in Model 1, Model 2 includes an additional path between self and depressive symptoms, which assesses the role of self as mediating the relationship between attachment and depression.

The GFI and AGFI, as indicated in Figure 2, suggests an acceptable fit between hypothesized Model 2 and the data. The relationships between all constructs and their indicators were positive and statistically significant. The pathways between attachment and view of self and between view of self and depressive symptoms were statistically significant for both genders, but the direct pathways between attachment and depressive symptoms were not significant for either boys or girls. No statistically significant gender differences were found for any of the path coefficients linking the variables. Of the variance in depressive symptoms, 69% for boys and 70% for girls were explained by the combined direct and indirect pathways.

Because the pathway between attachment and depression was not significant in Model 2, we decided, in efforts to achieve a more parsimonious solution, to evaluate a third model (illustrated in Figure 3), which eliminated

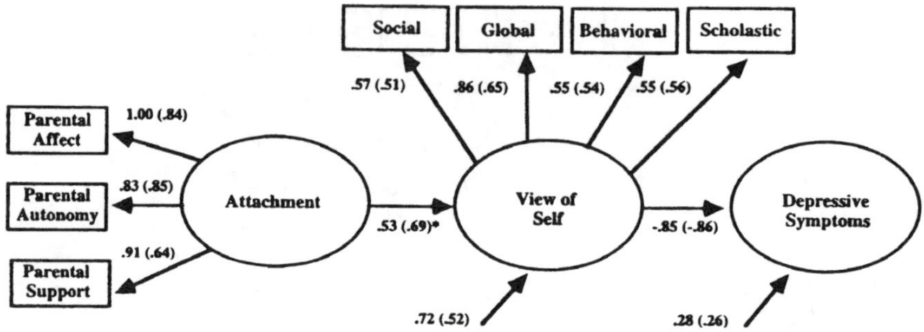

Figure 3: Structural Equation Model 3
NOTE: Girls = no parentheses, boys = in parentheses; standardized solution. All paths significant ($p < .05$). $X^2(17df) = 24.37$ (25.85); GFI = .94 (.94); AGFI = .86 (.87); RMSR = .06 (.06).
*Path coefficients differ by gender.

the direct pathway between attachment and depression. This model assessed only the indirect influence of parental attachment on depressive symptoms through view of self. As with the previous two models, the GFI and AGFI indicate an acceptable fit and the indicators met the statistical criteria as measures of the constructs. The pathway linking parental attachment with view of self and that linking view of self with depressive symptoms were both statistically significant. A statistically significant gender difference was found for the path coefficients linking attachment with view of self, with a stronger relationship between the variables measured for the boys. Parental attachment accounted for 48% of the variance in view of self for boys and 28% of the variance for girls. Of the variance in depressive symptoms, 74% for boys and 72% for girls was explained by the predictors with view of self mediating the effects of parental attachment.

Statistical tests were completed to determine whether the three models differed in overall fit for either boys or girls and to determine whether there were differences in fit between boys and girls for each individual model. Findings indicated that there were no differences in fit among the three alternate models for either boys or girls. In addition, there were no differences in fit between boys and girls for each of the individual models.

DISCUSSION

Our results add to the growing body of research documenting a relationship between attachment security and psychological functioning among adolescents (Armsden & Greenberg, 1987; Armsden et al., 1990; de Jong, 1992; Kenny & Donaldson, 1991; Kenny & Hart, 1992; Kobak & Sceery, 1988; Kobak et al., 1991; Lapsley, Rice, & Fitzgerald, 1990; Papini & Roggman, 1992; Papini et al., 1991; Raja et al., 1992). Our findings also provide tentative support for the role of an internal working model of self in mediating the relationship between parental attachment and depression.

We evaluated three models depicting both direct and indirect relationships between parental attachment and level of depressive symptoms. Each model provides a reasonable and almost identical fit with our data. Structural equation modeling provides an opportunity to disconfirm models that do not fit the data, but cannot positively confirm a model (Fassinger, 1987). Consequently, based on fit statistics, we cannot disconfirm any of the models and find tentative support for all three models. The finding of a reasonable fit for each model is consistent with our hypotheses, with previous findings, and with the roles of parental attachment as a secure base and foundation for internal working models of self.

The strengths and weaknesses of each model can be further evaluated by attention to theory and other statistics provided as part of the structural equation solution. Although Model 1 provides a reasonable fit with the data, the clarity of the model is somewhat limited from a theoretical perspective. As expected, the pathway between parental attachment and depressive symptoms is significant, as is the pathway linking view of self and depression. The psychological mechanisms underlying the relationship between attachment security and depression, however, are not clear in this model. Theoretically, secure attachment may mitigate against depressive symptoms by providing a secure base of support, by contributing to a secure and competent sense of self, or by other facets of internal working models described by Bowlby (1973), such as view of others, which were not explored in this study. All of these understandings are consistent with the hypothesized model and are supported by the statistical solution.

Model 2 offers several theoretical and empirical strengths in comparison with Model 1. From a theoretical perspective, Model 2 provides support for the internal working model of self, which was hypothesized to influence the relationship between attachment and depression. With the introduction, in comparison with Model 1, of an additional pathway by which attachment influences depressive symptoms through self, the direct relationship between attachment and depression was no longer significant. From a statistical perspective, Model 2 differs only by the introduction of one additional pathway, so it is not surprising that the overall fits of the models are similar. In comparison with Model 1, Model 2 accounts for a greater proportion of the variance in depressive symptoms and thus provides a more complete statistical explanation for depression. Our third model, like Model 2, evaluates and supports the role of an internal working model of self but provides a more parsimonious solution. With parsimony as a criteria for the strength of a model, Model 3 eliminated the nonsignificant direct path between attachment and depressive symptoms without cost to the overall fit. Thus, according to the criteria of theoretical clarity, consistent with Bowlby's construct of the internal working model of self and parsimony, Model 3 has strengths in comparison with the other models evaluated.

This research also examined gender differences in levels of psychological functioning and parental attachment and was designed to assess whether attachment and psychological functioning are related in gender specific ways. With respect to gender differences in levels of psychological functioning, our findings provide additional support for the well documented assertion (e.g., Allgood-Merten et al., 1990; Baron & Peixoto, 1991; Nolen-Hoeksema, 1987; Petersen, Kennedy, & Sullivan, 1991) that early adolescent girls are at risk in comparison with early adolescent boys for the development of depressive symptoms. Both for boys and girls on the average, however, depressive symptoms were below levels characteristic of clinical depression. The finding of no gender differences on the attachment measure supports the preponderance of previous research assessing parental attachment in early adolescence and suggests that early adolescent girls and boys view the affective quality of their parental relationships as equally positive, view their parents as encouraging their independence to a similar degree, and view their parents as similarly available as sources of support.

With respect to gender differences in the relationships between parental attachment and measures of psychological functioning, we obtained two unexpected findings that counter the claims of relational theorists. Although the relationships between attachment security and self were positive and significant for both boys and girls in all three models, the magnitude of that relationship was significantly greater for boys than for girls in Model 3. When the direct relationship between parental attachment and depressive symptoms was assessed, as shown in Figure 1, the magnitude of the negative relationship between attachment security and depressive symptoms was stronger for boys. These findings are intriguing, need to be replicated in future samples, and indicate the need for further testing of causal models separately for boys and girls. They support earlier assertions that healthy identity development for boys is achieved through greater parental attachment (Bronfenbrenner, 1961; Cooper et al., 1983; Grotevant & Cooper, 1986). The conceptualization and measure of parental attachment used in this study emphasize both the support-providing and autonomy-facilitating components of parental attachment. Because structural equation modeling provided an assessment of the effects of these components combined, further clarification of possible gender specific relationships between parental attachment and psychological functioning might be gained by examining the separate effects of each attachment component. This may be important in future investigations of the relationship between parental attachment and the claims of relational theorists that girls develop a self in relationship, which they suggest is different from an autonomous self.

This study represents an initial effort at examining the psychological processes that influence the relationship between parental attachments and psychological functioning during the early adolescent period. Support for the mediating model and the finding that a direct relationship between attachment and depression is not significant once the mediating role of self is introduced make sense from a psychological perspective. Internal working models have been considered salient when discussing parental attachment in the adolescent period (Armsden & Greenberg, 1987; Kobak & Sceery, 1988; Kobak et al., 1991). For the adolescent whose cognitive and emotional resources far exceed those of the younger child, the internal working model of self may be relied on more than actual or even symbolic contact with the attachment figure during situations of stress.

Our study has methodological and theoretical limitations and the results do not provide definitive conclusions. The findings, however, support further investigation of the role of internal working models and suggest many directions for further model building and testing. Future research that addresses the limitations of this study may serve to cross-validate our findings and add to the understanding of the psychological processes that influence the relationship between attachment and psychological functioning. In terms of methodological limitations, this study included only one measure of depression, which presents a measurement limitation in structural equation modeling. As the Children's Depression Inventory (CDI) was the only indicator of depression, it was assumed to assess depression without measurement error in terms of construct validity and reliability. The use of multiple indicators in structural equation modeling allows for examination of the psychometric properties of the indicators through the estimation of factor loadings and measurement error variance. Based on reliability and validity evidence for the CDI (i.e., Haley et al., 1985; Kovacs, 1983, 1985; Saylor et al., 1984; Weiss & Weisz, 1988), measurement error would be small, and its impact on other estimates in the structural equation model would also be small (Hayduk, 1987). Nevertheless, future research needs to include additional measures of depression and might also consider additional areas of symptomatology, in addition to depression, to determine whether the model is specific for depression or fits equally as well in explaining other psychological symptoms. The selection of measures that do not rely on self-report would help to control for self-report bias. Exclusive reliance on self-report in the measure of attachment could be problematic, as Bowlby (1980) suggests that defensive processes may distort awareness and memory of parental rejection.

Although the models evaluated in this article specified causal paths from parental attachments to view of self and depressive symptoms, directions of causal effects cannot be determined from these data. It is equally plausible that depressed mood contributed to negative cognitive appraisals of the self and parental relationships, and that depressed individuals elicit negative responses from their surroundings. The latter interpretation is consistent with interpersonal models of depression (Gotlib, 1992). Whereas a transactional relationship among these and other variables is also likely (Cicchetti & Schneider-Rosen, 1986), direction of causality can be more adequately tested in longitudinal research. We expect to test alternate models assessing direction of causality when we have collected longitudinal data.

The models tested in this study provide incomplete explanations for variance in view of self and depressive symptoms. Because many factors, including life stress, gender role, peer support networks, pubertal status, and body image, among other factors, have been implicated in adolescent depression (Allgood-Merten et al., 1990; Petersen, Sarigiani & Kennedy, 1991), it is not surprising that parental attachment provides an incomplete explanation of depressive symptoms. Future research might consider additional variables that would explain additional variance in depression and view of self. The obtained goodness-of-fit indexes indicated acceptable but not excellent fit between the data and the hypothesized models. Reliable measures of additional variables not included in this model, the addition of some measures that do not rely on self-report, and further testing with a new sample may contribute to models that provide a more complete understanding of the experience of adolescent depression and result in strong fit indexes.

Attachment theory provides additional suggestions for building on the model set forth in this study. We considered the impact of one cognitive process, the internal working model of the self, on depressive symptoms. Bowlby (1973, 1980) suggested that the quality of parental attachment effects cognitive processes in additional ways that contribute to vulnerability or resilience to depression. The absence of sensitive and responsive caretaking, for example, may contribute to an internal working model of others as not helpful or even hostile. Similarly, because one's efforts to obtain help have not been responded to by sensitive caretakers, expectations for accomplishing change and enjoying a more positive future may be low. Testing of causal models that account for these and other cognitive processes is needed to gain a more complete understanding of the psychological mechanisms that mediate the relationship between attachment quality and depressive symptoms during the adolescent years.

REFERENCES

Ainsworth, M.D.S. (1989). Attachments beyond infancy. *American Psychologist, 44,* 709-716.

Ainsworth, M.D.S., Blehar, M. C., Waters, E., & Wall, S. (1978). *Patterns of attachment: A psychological study of the strange situation.* Hillsdale, NJ: Lawrence Erlbaum.

Allgood-Merten, B., Lewinsohn, P., & Hops, H. (1990). Sex differences in adolescent depression. *Journal of Abnormal Psychology, 99*(1), 55-63.

Armsden, G. C., & Greenberg, M. T. (1987). The inventory of parent and peer attachment: Individúal differences and their relationship to psychological well-being in adolescence. *Journal of Youth and Adolescence, 16,* 427-454.

Armsden, G. C., McCauley, E., Greenberg, M. T., Burke, P. M., & Mitchell, J. R. (1990). Parent and peer attachment in early adolescent depression. *Journal of Abnormal Child Psychology, 18,* 683-697.

Baron, P., & Peixoto, N. (1991). Depressive symptoms in adolescence as a function of personality factors. *Journal of Youth and Adolescence, 20,* 493-500.

Beck, A. (1967). *Depression: Causes, treatment, and theoretical aspects.* New York: Harper & Row.

Blos, P. (1967). The second individuation process of adolescence. *Psychoanalytic Study of the Child, 72,* 162-186.

Bowlby, J. (1969). *Attachment and loss: Vol. 1. Attachment.* New York: Basic Books.

Bowlby, J. (1973). *Attachment and loss: Vol. 2. Separation.* New York: Basic Books.

Bowlby, J. (1980). *Attachment and loss: Vol. 3. Loss.* New York: Basic Books.

Bowlby, J. (1988). *A secure base: Parent-child attachment and healthy human development.* New York: Basic Books.

Brabeck, M. (Ed.). (1989). *Who cares? Theory, research and educational implications of the ethic of care.* New York: Praeger.

Bretherton, I. (1985). Attachment theory: Retrospect and prospect. *Monographs of the Society for Research in Child Development, 50*(1-2, Serial No. 209).

Bronfenbrenner, U. (1961). Some familial antecedents of responsibility and leadership in adolescents. In L. Petrullo & B. Bass (Eds.), *Leadership and interpersonal behavior.* New York: Holt, Rinehart & Winston.

Chodorow, N. (1978). *The reproduction of mothering.* Berkeley: University of California Press.

Cicchetti, D., & Schneider-Rosen, K. (1986). An organizational approach to childhood depression. In M. Rutter (Ed.), *Depression in young people.* New York: Guilford.

Cooper, C., Grotevant, H., & Condon, S. (1983). Individuality and connectedness in the family as a context for adolescent identity formation and role-taking skill. In H. Grotevant & C. Cooper (Eds.), *Adolescent development in the family* (New Directions for Child Development, Series No. 22). San Francisco: Jossey-Bass.

Crandall, J. (1975). A scale for social interest. *Journal of Individual Psychology, 31,* 187-195.

Cummings, E. M., & Cicchetti, D. (1990). Towards a transactional model of relations between attachment and depression. In M. Greenberg, D. Cicchetti, & M. Cummings (Eds.), *Attachment in the preschool years*. Chicago: University of Chicago Press.

de Jong, M. (1992). Attachment, individuation, and risk of suicide in late adolescence. *Journal of Youth and Adolescence, 21*, 357-373.

Fassinger, R. (1987). Use of structural equation modeling in counseling psychology research. *Journal of Counseling Psychology, 34*, 425-436.

Freiberg, P. (1991). Self-esteem gender gap widens in adolescence. *APA Monitor, 22*(4), 29.

Freud, A. (1969). Adolescence as a developmental disturbance. In G. Kaplan & S. Lebovici (Eds.), *Adolescence: Psychosocial perspectives*. New York: Basic Books.

Gilligan, C. (1982). *In a different voice*. Cambridge: Harvard University Press.

Gilligan, C., Lyons, N. P., & Hanmer, T. J. (Eds.). (1990). *Making connections: The relational world of adolescents at Emma Willard School*. Cambridge, MA: Harvard University Press.

Gilligan, C., & Wiggins, G. (1988). The origins of morality in early childhood relationships. In C. Gilligan, J. V. Ward, & J. M. Taylor (Eds.), *Mapping the moral domain*. Cambridge, MA: Harvard University Press.

Gjerde, P. F., & Block, J. (1991). Preadolescent antecedents of depressive symptomatology at age 18: A prospective study. *Journal of Youth and Adolescence, 20*(2), 217-232.

Gotlib, I. H. (1992). Interpersonal and cognitive aspects of depression. *Current Directions in Psychological Science, 1*, 149-154.

Greenberg, M., Siegel, J., & Leitch, C. (1983). The nature and importance of attachment relationships to parents and peers during adolescence. *Journal of Youth and Adolescence, 12*, 373-386.

Grotevant, H. D., & Cooper, C. R. (1986). Individuation in family relationships. *Human Development, 29*, 82-100.

Haley, G.M.T., Fine, S., Marriage, K., Moretti, M. M., & Freeman, R. J. (1985). Cognitive bias and depression in psychiatrically disturbed children and adolescents. *Journal of Consulting and Clinical Psychology, 53*, 535-537.

Hammen, C. (1990). Cognitive approaches to depression in children. In B. Lahey & A. E. Kazdin (Eds.), *Advances in clinical child psychology: Vol. 13*. New York: Plenum.

Harter, S. (1985). *Manual for the Self-Perception Profile for Children*. University of Denver.

Harter, S. (1988). *Manual for the Self-Perception Profile for Adolescents*. University of Denver.

Hartup, W. (1979). The social worlds of childhood. *American Psychologist, 34*, 944-950.

Hauser, S. T., & Bowlds, M. K. (1990). Stress, coping and adaptation. In S. Feldman & G. Elliot (Eds.), *At the threshold: The developing adolescent*. Cambridge, MA: Harvard University Press.

Hayduk, L. A. (1987). *Structural equation modeling with LISREL*. Baltimore, MD: Johns Hopkins Press.

Hill, J. P., & Holmbeck, G. N. (1986). Attachment and autonomy during adolescence. *Annals of Child Development, 3*, 145-189.

Jordan, J., Kaplan, A., Miller, J. B., Stiver, I., & Surrey, J. L. (Eds.). (1991). *Women's growth in connection: Writing from the Stone Center*. New York: Guilford.

Jöreskog, K. G., & Sörbom, D. (1988). *LISREL VII: A guide to the program and applications*. Chicago: SPSS, Inc.

Josselson, R. (1988). The embedded self: I and thou revisited. In D. K. Lapsley & S. M. Quintana (Eds.), *Self, ego, and identity: Integrative approaches*. New York: Springer.

Kaplan, A. G. (1991). The "self-in-relation": Implications for depression in women. In J. Jordan, A. Kaplan, J. B. Miller, I. Stiver, & J. L. Surrey (Eds.), *Women's growth in connection: Writing from the Stone Center*. New York: Guilford.

Keltikangas-Jarvinen, L. (1990). The stability of self-concept during adolescence and early adulthood: A six-year follow-up study. *Journal of General Psychology, 117*(4), 361-368.

Kenny, M. (1987). The extent and function of parental attachment among first-year college students. *Journal of Youth and Adolescence, 16*, 17-27.

Kenny, M. (1990). College seniors' perceptions of parental attachments: The value and stability of family ties. *Journal of College Student Development, 31*, 39-46.

Kenny, M., & Donaldson, G. (1991). Contributions of parental attachment and family structure to the social and psychological functioning of first-year college students. *Journal of Counseling Psychology, 38*, 479-486.

Kenny, M., & Hart, K. (1992). Relationship between parental attachment and eating disorder symptoms in an inpatient and a college sample. *Journal of Counseling Psychology, 39*, 521-526.

Kobak, R. R., Cole, H., Ferenz-Gillis, R., Fleming, W., & Gamble, W. (1993). Attachment and emotion regulation during mother-teen problem solving: A control theory analysis. *Child Development, 64*, 231-245.

Kobak, R. R., & Sceery, A. (1988). Attachment in late adolescence: Working models, affect regulation, and representation of self and others. *Child Development, 59*, 135-146.

Kobak, R. R., Sudler, N., & Gamble, W. (1991). Attachment and depressive symptoms during adolescence: A developmental pathways analysis. *Development and Psychopathology, 3*, 461-474.

Kovacs, M. (1983). *The Children's Depression Inventory. A self-rated depression scale for school-aged youngsters.* Unpublished manuscript, University of Pittsburgh School of Medicine.

Kovacs, M. (1985). The Children's Depression Inventory. *Psychopharmacology Bulletin, 21*, 995-999.

Lapsley, D. K., Rice, K. G., & Fitzgerald, D. P. (1990). Adolescent attachment, identity, and adjustment to college: Implications for the continuity of adaptation hypothesis. *Journal of Counseling and Development, 68*, 561-565.

Long, B., Kahn, S., & Schutz, R. (1992). Causal model of stress and coping: Women in management. *Journal of Counseling Psychology, 39*, 227-239.

Main, M., Kaplan, N., & Cassidy, J. (1985). Security in infancy, childhood and adulthood: A move to the level of representation. *Monographs of the Society for Research in Child Development, 50*(1-2, Serial No. 209).

McGrath, E., Keita, G. P., Strickland, B. R., & Russo, N. F. (1990). *Women and depression: Risk factors and treatment issues.* Washington, DC: American Psychological Association.

Mehrabian, A., & Epstein, N. (1972). A measure of emotional empathy. *Journal of Personality, 40*, 525-543.

Miller, J. B. (1976). *Toward a new psychology of women.* Boston, MA: Beacon.

Miller, J. B. (1991). The development of women's sense of self. In J. Jordan, A. Kaplan, J. B. Miller, I. Stiver, & J. L. Surrey (Eds.), *Women's growth in connection: Writing from the Stone Center.* New York: Guilford.

Moos, R., & Moos, B. (1986). *Family Environment Scale manual.* Palo Alto, CA: Consulting Psychologists Press.

Muthen, B., & Kaplan, D. (1985). A comparison of some methodologies for the factor analysis of non-normal Likert variables. *British Journal of Mathematical and Statistical Psychology, 38*, 171-189.

Nolen-Hoeksema, S. (1987). Sex differences in unipolar depression: Evidence and theory. *Psychological Bulletin, 101*(2), 259-282.

Palladino, D. E., & Blustein, D. L. (1991, August). *Contributions of family relationship factors to the identity formation process.* Paper presented at the annual meeting of the American Psychological Association, San Francisco, CA.

Papini, D. R., & Roggman, L. A. (1992). Adolescent perceived attachment to parents in relation to competence, depression, and anxiety: A longitudinal study. *Journal of Early Adolescence, 12*, 420-440.

Papini, D. R., Roggman, L. A., & Anderson, J. (1991). Early adolescent perceptions of attachment to mother and father: A test of the emotional-distancing and buffering hypothesis. *Journal of Early Adolescence, 11*, 258-275.

Petersen, A. C., Kennedy, R. E., & Sullivan, P. (1991). Coping with adolescence. In M. E. Colten & S. Gore (Eds.), *Adolescent stress: Causes and consequences*. New York: Aldine.

Petersen, A. C., Sarigiani, P. A., & Kennedy, R. E. (1991). Adolescent depression: Why more girls? *Journal of Youth and Adolescence, 20*(2), 247-271.

Quintana, S. M., & Lapsley, D. K. (1987). Adolescent attachment and ego identity: A structural equations approach to the continuity of adaptation. *Journal of Adolescent Research, 2*, 393-409.

Raja, S. N., McGee, R., & Stanton, W. R. (1992). Perceived attachments to parents and peers and psychological well-being in adolescence. *Journal of Youth and Adolescence, 21*, 471-485.

Rest, J. (1979). *Revised manual for the Defining Issues Test: An objective test of moral judgment development*. Minneapolis, MN: Moral Research Projects.

Rice, K. G. (1990). Attachment in adolescence: A narrative and meta-analytic review. *Journal of Youth and Adolescence, 19*, 511-538.

Richard, M. H., Gitelson, I. B., Petersen, A. C., & Hurtig, A. L. (1991). Adolescent personality in girls and boys: The role of mothers and fathers. *Psychology of Women Quarterly, 15*, 65-81.

Ryan, R. M., & Lynch, J. H. (1989). Emotional autonomy versus detachment: Revisiting the vicissitudes of adolescence and young adulthood. *Child Development, 60*, 340-356.

Saylor, C. F., Finch, A. J., Baskin, C. H., Furey, W., & Kelly, M. M. (1984). Construct validity for measures of childhood depression: Application of multitrait-multimethod methodology. *Journal of Consulting and Clinical Psychology, 52*, 977-985.

Steinberg, L. (1987). Recent research on the family at adolescence: The extent and nature of sex differences. *Journal of Youth and Adolescence, 16*(3), 191-197.

Surrey, J. (1991). The "self-in-relation": A theory of women's development. In J. Jordan, A. Kaplan, J. B. Miller, I. Stiver, & J. L. Surrey (Eds.), *Women's growth in connection: Writing from the Stone Center*. New York: Guilford.

Weiss, B., & Weisz, J. R. (1988). Factor structure of self-reported depression in clinic-referred children versus adolescents. *Journal of Abnormal Psychology, 97*, 492-495.

Requests for reprints should be addressed to Maureen Kenny, Department of Counseling, Developmental Psychology and Research Methods, Boston College, Campion 305D, Chestnut Hill, MA 02167.

*Ethnicity, Ethnic Identity, and Competence Formation: Adolescent Transition and Cultural Transformation**

Margaret Beale Spencer, Dena Phillips Swanson, and Michael Cunningham, *Emory University**

As a point of transition, adolescence is heavily influenced by what comes before in addition to the effects of current experiences. It also undergirds the expected quality of the adult outcomes that follow. This transition occurs in particular contexts. When the effects of race and ethnicity are factored in, significant symbolic and structural variations become evident in both the quality of problems encountered and the objective outcomes experienced across *settings* (e.g., school and peer group). For African American and other ethnic minority group adolescents, the patterned nature evident for some (e.g., teen pregnancy, youth incarceration, male aggression, school failure) has influenced both the types of research questions pursued, the specific scientific studies conducted, the interpretations of empirical data made, and the policies initiated from research findings.

The pursuits of young people and the developmental stages these pursuits represent are quite different from those expected of adults. Thus, it is critical to examine ethnic minority youth from a perspective that considers both their unique structural and symbolic experiences. Generally, the nature of these experiences has important implications for the critical identity processes that occur during the adolescent stage. However, given adolescents' unique developmental placement and dependency status, their experiences must be disentangled from those of adults.

The issue of an interactive ethnic influence on identity and competence processes during adolescence is under-studied and frequently misunderstood. Relative to the social sciences, DeVos and Romanucci–Ross (1982, p. vii) note that many methods of classification within societies have been stressed. From kinship systems of simple preliterate, prein-

*Support for this article was provided through grants from the Spencer Foundation, the Ford Foundation, and the Trust Fund of Georgia.

Journal of Negro Education, Vol. 60, No. 3 (1991)

dustrial societies to the stratified economic classes of complex industrial societies, each has enjoyed significant attention. On the other hand, ethnic divisions have generally remained unnoticed, thereby reinforcing the assumption that societies are unitary and possess homeostatic cultural traditions that represent the norm. However, as indicated for American ethnic minority adolescents (particularly those from disfavored ethnic/racial groups, e.g., African Americans, Chicanos, and Native Americans), all show significant and patterned outcomes. These outcomes are often different from those of nonminority or Anglo-American (Anglo) youth although not unlike the outcomes described by Ogbu (1985) for parallel disfavored groups in other countries. (Notably, these outcomes are significantly influenced by a group's visibility due to skin color.) Such patterned adolescent outcomes are important in that they shape, undergird, and texture the most protracted period of the life course: adulthood (Lerner & Spanier, 1980). While stressing the importance of phenotypical visibility, Mithun (1983) suggests that the structure of opportunity and the degree of discrimination, prejudice, and identity difficulties encountered by a minority group also serves a deterministic function.

The resurgent and continued interest by researchers in the history of adolescence is not surprising. What is unexpected is the invariant limitation of the research questions generated for the purpose of examining nonminority ethnic group youth unless the research is concerned with deviance, identity confusion, assimilation efforts, school failure, or premature sexuality. This limitation has led to implicit linkages between ethnicity and pathology and to assumptions that cultural difference implies cultural deviance.

Ethnicity and Culture

A basic question researchers continue to ponder regards the source of human behavior and development. When posed for ethnic minority youth, however, a priori assumptions too often affect the specific issues raised and the interpretations made of observed behavior. Generally, neither sociocultural (e.g., racism or oppression) nor psychocultural variables (e.g., chronic stress) are considered as possible mediating processes or mechanisms. Too often the available literature on ethnic minority youth is either lacking in quantity and breadth or is inadequately conceptualized and interpreted. Although there has been a virtual 50-year period of developmental research on nonminority youth, relatively minimal and selective attention has been paid to examining ethnicity from a developmental perspective as it relates to the organism-environment "fit" experienced by minority youth.

For the most part, the more general ethnicity-focused research can be categorized as taking one of three approaches. The first approach is an outcome-oriented perspective (e.g., focussing on teen pregnancy, aggression, deviancy, school failure, etc.). This approach generally ignores the mechanisms, mediating processes, or "cultural clashes" experienced both structurally and symbolically by minority youth and their families. The second approach is a developmental one that focuses on processes but seldom includes an examination of context or sociocultural variables. Third, ethnographic or empirical studies describe or report phenomena; yet, more often than not they bypass the construction of psychological theoretical frameworks that might aid in operationalizing underlying mechanisms, which have implications for teaching, parenting, and more general service delivery.

Notwithstanding, it is virtually impossible to understand the experience of ethnicity without also addressing culture. Ethnicity refers to the customs, language, and social views usually associated with a particular ethnic group. By customs one generally refers to the mode of behavior that is relatively permanent, stable, and characteristic of a society; or to the complex habits or patterns individuals within societies learn during the course of acculturation. Ordinarily, members of ethnic groups share a common sense of identity that is often associated with a common place of origin (such as African Americans, Polish Americans, Irish Americans, American Indians, or Swedish Americans). Also shared might be religion (such as Jewish Americans) or race (such as Black Americans or White Americans). However, both rational and irrational components of ethnic identity exist (DeVos & Romanucci–Ross, 1982); yet, the presence of both components in the larger society's reaction to and ultimate treatment of ethnic minorities, at both the symbolic and structural levels, is generally not discussed. Both the reason for group identification and the choice or option to identify with a group are important considerations. For instance, White Americans often elect to identify with a particular European ethnic group, the so-called "Anglo-American" ethnic group. This choice may affect their family's traditions, holidays, food preferences, and world views (Slavin, 1988). Because of the commonality experienced due to race, most Whites are readily absorbed into the mainstream of American society unless they make a proactive decision to remain autonomous; that is, they accept autonomy and its corresponding potential for marginality or biculturality as a matter of conscious choice (e.g., Jews, Mormons). Furthermore, the issue of visibility is extremely important, as is the value associated with a group's physical features.

Given the broadening social contexts and peer relations that characterize the present period, aspects of ethnicity and ethnic identity have profound implications for the ongoing experiences of minority youth. These aspects become increasingly salient during adolescence because this period represents the developmental stage wherein insecurity about the "self" characterizes the normative state of feelings and associated experiences for *all* adolescents, independent of their group's unique cultural experiences or social status. While the biological experience of puberty supersedes all group characteristics, membership in a disfavored group typically exacerbates puberty-linked insecurities.

For visible minorities (those physically distinct from the majority) from disfavored groups, the qualitative experience of ethnicity has special implications for ethnic identity formation processes. Traditionally, the cultural experience of minorities in the United States requires they become not only marginal persons but also bicultural ones capable of demonstrating competence both in the larger society and within their own ethnic community. The experience of functioning in two cultures results in dual responses or what DuBois (1903/1970) describes as a "double-consciousness." This duality of response does not necessarily suggest duality in personality or a kind of schizophrenia; rather, learning two ways of coping with the tasks, expectations, and requirements of society based on one's ethnic minority status becomes essential for manifest competence and psychological health (Chestang, 1972, p. 7). Thus, the issue of choice in cultural identification has important implications for (1) the experiences of the group, (2) the economic successes and security achieved by members of the group, (3) the availability of models and apprenticeship opportunities for the youth of the group, and (4) the general quality and outcomes of identity pursuits experienced by the youth.

Although he refers specifically to the African American experience, the issues raised by Chestang are apropos to other visible ethnic minorities. His perspective suggests the lack of a good match between the self and the environment (i.e., the concept of "the goodness of fit" suggested by Lerner [1982]). According to Chestang, the special environmental conditions that minority youth are forced to confront include (1) social injustice, (2) societal inconsistency, and (3) denied personal efficacy (or impotence). Each of these conditions has implications for the social experiences and treatment of ethnic minority youth and their responses to same, particularly during puberty when salient affective, cognitive, and physical developments are also underway. (The latter aspect is of special importance for the experiences of physically mature, dark-skinned adolescent males given the persistent stereotypes concerning all things "dark," and the societal penchant to view such early maturing males not as youth but instead as threatening adult males to be feared.) Chestang's analysis is particularly useful in elucidating the experiences of African Americans, Chicanos, Native Americans, and many Asian Americans, although Asian Americans as a group may suffer less handicapping than the other groups due to positive stereotyping.

As described by Chestang, the denial of legal rights is generally described as social injustice, or the violation of the social agreements that represent group consensus. Whether or not it occurs in an informal or formal caste system, social injustice is hypothesized as having the effect of threatening both a group's or an individual's feelings of confidence and personal security. Individual effects, however, are mediated through the group and experienced as diffused rather than direct effects. Accordingly, damage to the individual is shared by the group, thus diminishing the personally weathered stress of group-experienced aggression.

The second hypothesized characteristic of the ethnic experience for minority youths is societal inconsistency. Societal inconsistency, which is more closely aligned with the experience of chronic frustration, is the institutionalized disparity between what is said and what is actually done in or by societies. According to Chestang it is "social immorality perpetrated on the oppressed by the manners, morals, and traditions of the majority" (p. 3). This phenomenon is particularly important for ethnic minority youth because it represents individual-level expressions of the majority group's rejection. Given their chronic exposure to race-linked daily hassles or "microaggressions," minority adolescents, particularly those without group support (i.e., in predominantly White settings), experience societal inconsistency subjectively (and often in isolation) as personalized injustice. This individualized expression suggests that minority adolescents should be culturally prepared for such encounters as a means of preventing psychological damage.

The experience of social inconsistency is potentially devastating because it expresses informal and unofficial rejection of a group in ways that often leave its victims without recourse to regulatory agencies and courts of law for remedy. As Chestang notes, there are no laws ruling dark skin unattractive, Black art unaesthetic, Black culture uncivilized, or Black persons unworthy of respect (p. 3). As subjectively experienced and cognitively processed by ethnic minorities, many expressions of the manners, morals, and traditions of Anglo-American culture held as the "model" or "norm," may be interpreted by minority youth as representing subtle and overt rejection of themselves and their group. Ethnic minority adolescents must cope with expressions of group rejection in addition to the more generic, puberty-linked insecurities and identity pursuits characteristic of the developmental experience of adolescence. Nonetheless, it must also be remembered that individuals may be affected by the special conditions of the social system but not necessarily shaped by them, a phenomenon suggested by the work of Powell and Fuller (1970) in their descriptions of the effects of desegregation on the self-concepts of African American youth.

Social inconsistency is manifested interpersonally by superficiality and artificiality in interracial transactions and the resulting distrust and suspicion between races. For example, as Chestang attests, the 1954 *Brown v. Board of Education* ruling did not offset the development of cynicism among Blacks; that the goals of the *Brown* decision remain as yet unrealized represents proof to many that cynicism among African Americans is warranted. Moreover, societal inconsistency is erosive and destructive to individual identity processes because it is related to the personal experience of frustration, confusion, and bewilderment. It occurs in a transaction between two persons, and assaults on a group are perceived by individual group members as direct attacks. A wide array of individual consequences may thus result because such realization necessitates the individual's use of psychic energy to demonstrate his or her equality, competence, and humanity. Chestang suggests that the resulting feelings of anger, distrust, and suspicion require adaptive modes of protection; however, he warns that adaptation may give rise to either personality integration or maladaptive defenses.

Societal inconsistency in school settings is effectively communicated by teachers' categorization of students. In this regard the comparison of subgroupings of Chicano adolescents and Japanese American students by Matute–Bianchi (1986) is especially instructive. Matute–Bianchi's ethnographic study indicates differences in academic expectations of Japanese American versus Chicano youth at various levels of acculturation. The group image projected by teachers and school personnel for adolescents of Japanese descent generally provided these youth the opportunity to disengage themselves from an ethnically explicit identity. That is, although the Japanese American students were conscious of their own cultural uniqueness and identifiability due to their distinct physical attributes, they were also aware that to be identified as Japanese American meant that they were considered "smart," "hardworking," "well behaved," and "studious" regardless of individual academic prowess. Equally important was the finding that the Japanese American adolescents in Matute–Bianchi's study saw themselves and were seen by others as being virtually indistinguishable from the successful, accomplished, and well-dressed Anglo students in the school (p. 253). On the other hand, the comparable level of psychic energy used by the Chicano students to cope with their phenotypic uniqueness was quite different. Because individual Chicano students, whether they performed well or poorly, did not benefit from a positive group image, they had to negotiate an identity that necessitated "the crossing of cultural boundaries" and the taking on of "Anglo behaviors" or the adoption of what Ogbu (1985) calls "school oppositional mannerisms" to gain acceptance. Such forced choice dilemmas were not found to represent the experiences of the Anglo-American adolescents in Matute–Bianchi's study.

The ethnographic observations of Matute–Bianchi parallel those of Fordham and Ogbu (1986) for African American adolescent high school students. In both studies the outward appearance of diminished achievement orientation was believed to be associated with minority students' efforts to maintain their cultural identity. However, the patterns of school failure that emerged for disadvantaged, disparaged, and disfavored minority group members suggest a reactive process, and thus an intensive intragroup reliance in the development of collective identity.

Although described in various ways by a plethora of theorists from Erikson (1966) and Pettigrew (1964) to Kardiner and Ovesey (1951), the general assumption undergirding personality theorizing for minorities has been one of personality disorganization (McCarthy & Yancey, 1971). Implicit in this perspective has been the idea that members of minority groups suffer from a loss of autonomy, a diminished sense of self-worth, and low self-esteem. Because all minority group members are similarly categorized in the bulk of this research without regard for their personal attainments, income, or other criterion whereby recognition is extended, these feelings are believed to transcend social class (Chestang, p. 6). According to Chestang, feelings associated with the objective state of denied efficacy include fear, inadequacy, and insecurity. This results in diminished potential for ego enhancement because personal recognition is always preceded by the minority person's questioning whether or not his or her acknowledged personal competence is due to individual contributions or to expediencies such as institutional needs to comply with affirmative action guidelines. As suggested by Bradley (1982), there are few opportunities where one's pigmentation is of incidental relevance.

Approaches to Ethnicity

The central task for all adolescents is successful identity formation; thus, developmental tasks for racial and ethnic minority youth are more likely linked to their racial or ethnic status. In the following sections I will explore these linkages both conceptually and theoretically.

The historical treatment of the social construction of adolescence has special meaning for ethnic minorities. Generally, with regard to colonized groups (e.g., American Indians and Chicanos) and the special involuntary situation of African Americans, youthful members of these groups are neither treated nor studied in a scientific manner *as children*. Instead they are interacted with and viewed as if they are adult members of their group rather than youth engaging in preparatory behaviors for anticipated adult roles.

Modell (1990) suggests that adolescence is characterized by an organized set of expectations linked to structural aspects of the culture into which youth must fit and assume their expected adult roles. In this regard the unique history of an individual's group has significant implications for the individual's perceptions of his or her daily treatment by others throughout the life course. The historical interaction of minorities with other colonized or (voluntarily or forcibly) migrated groups is also a significant factor influencing the treatment and perspectives of minority adolescents.

Although Brooks–Gunn and Reiter (1990) indicate that social conditions and interactions may possibly affect adolescent behavior, they do not describe precisely what shape those conditions, interactions, and behaviors may take. However, these issues are particularly salient for the experiences of early-maturing ethnic minority male youths during the late primary grades or middle school years, especially as these youth relate to their White female teachers and vice-versa. Some theorists lean toward sexually based interpretations of instructional patterns that seem to disparage minority male adolescents (Stember, 1976). For instance, as indicated by Dweck's (1978) early study, female teachers more often show differential interaction and feedback patterns for boys and girls. Adolescents' perceptions and interpretations of these differences in feedback require the use of cognitive processes not available to them at earlier developmental periods; yet, independent of the motivation for differential interactional patterns between teachers and students, adolescents' more abstract cognitive capabilities make their stress response unavoidable. Anxiety about discriminatory cross-sex and interracial interaction patterns between teachers and students have undergirded a portion of the concern that minority neighborhoods build strong community-based (and controlled) institutions (Woodson, 1988).

Descriptive Models of Developmental Experiences

Identity processes are fundamental to the more general issue of competence. Like all adolescents, the major developmental task for minority youth is the achievement of an identity which serves as the basis for the development of a competent self. It is not unexpected that second to the achievement and deviance literature, the majority of research conducted on adolescents focuses on personal or group identity outcomes. With but a few exceptions the models or perspectives purporting to represent minority adolescence (which continue to guide empirical research and its interpretation) generally have been problem (outcome) focused or deviance oriented. However, other models are available that are more conceptually complete, that consider psychocultural and/or sociocultural factors, and that are integrative in approach.

The Life Span Perspective

The incorporation of the life span perspective (Lerner & Spanier, 1980; Elder, 1974; Riley, 1979) with notions concerning the importance of a "goodness of fit" between organism and environment (Lerner, 1982) afford greater conceptual breadth in exploring adolescent development. These perspectives and their associated components place individuals in the context of their time and place as well as provide a useful heuristic device for understanding minority adolescent experiences. Too frequently, researchers look to psychological outcomes only. A life course perspective allows a concurrent analysis of other factors, and therefore helps to untangle developmental processes and enhance our understanding of psychological outcomes. A life span human developmental perspective is also well suited for application to the experiences of minority youth because it is multidisciplinary and thus increases one's ability to account for change.

The issue of discontinuity is especially important to this discussion. Because traditional developmental theory holds that development is more singularly viewed as emanating from biological determinants, theorists have stressed continuity. On the other hand, a life span perspective speculates about multiple determinants presented in diverse forms and operating at varying levels of the ecosystem. As indicated by Brim and Kagan (1980), individuals who appear quite similar on the surface may show extremely different outcomes that are best explored and explained from a life span perspective. These issues are of special importance in light of Werner's (1982) description of resilient youth and their unexpected characteristics, and with the taxonomy of risk and vulnerability described by Anthony (1974). Of special importance is Anthony's psychiatric perspective, which links environmental risk with individual vulnerability as a method of determining the source of disturbance too often assumed the norm for minority youth. Moreover, the life span approach underscores the problems associated with Ogbu's (1985) perspective, which ignores diverse outcomes for "castelike minority" youth from similar backgrounds.

The ontogeny of the self system represents the continual and interactive effects of all processes across time. Given the issue of pubertal development it represents more than the emergence of puberty as a biological event; however, the biological events of puberty and adolescence are linked to particular sociocultural processes and social structural conditions for young people of disfavored minority groups. For example, their particular sociocultural experiences may correlate with an increased likelihood of having experienced inadequate nutritional and medical care. Further, as suggested by Hammond and Ladner (1969), the contextual experiences of lower income African American female youths may expose them to at-risk conditions promotive of early sexuality, inadequate sex education information, and unplanned pregnancies. For other minority youth, observations by Matute–Bianchi (1986) suggest that those from poor migrant families, regardless of their family demographic characteristics, experience very different sociocultural conditions and varying psychological, identity-linked outcomes compared to either acculturated Chicano or Japanese American adolescents. Because minority adolescents experience environmental effects which are often distinctly different from those of Anglo or nonminority youth, the need to incorporate contextual effects into any analysis is essential. Besides having psychological importance, the experiences of ethnic minority adolescents are also inextricably linked to historical, environmental, and sociocultural conditions.

In particular, the biological outcome of early maturation may produce very different schooling experiences for ethnic minority males than for similarly developing nonminority or Anglo males. Although it has been shown that the maturation rates of boys generally lead to varying social appraisals, very little is known about the implications of these diverse outcomes for minority male youth. Speculations by McGhee (1984), however, suggest that environmental influences on minority male youth are often perilous at best.

Ecological Approaches

The environmental experiences of minority youth and especially lower income adolescents are important factors that interact with psychological characteristics (given developmental status) and together produce unique behavioral products. Early studies by Barker and Wright (1954) and the later research of Bronfenbrenner (1972) and Garbarino (1982) are especially useful for bringing attention to the effects of environmental contexts on the lives of children. However, studies that explore contextual effects are seldom conducted on minority youth. Nonetheless, there are a few recent exceptions (Taylor, 1976; Bell–Scott & Taylor, 1989). Additionally, although it focuses on late primary school African American youth, the work of Holliday (1985) incorporates both ecological and life span notions to explain the academic outcomes of this group. Holliday's findings suggest that environmental factors produce different behavioral effects for competence (i.e., children who appeared competent at home, with their peers, and at church were evaluated as generally incompetent in the school environment). Simpkins et al. (1973) describe this phenomenon in African American youth as a school-based, "six-hour" mental retardation. Certainly, the disproportionate number of Black male students labeled as either behaviorally disordered or mentally retarded confirm the Simpkins et al. analysis of the academic mislabelling problem. Hare and Castenell's (1985) work on African American males is also instructive in its suggestion that the inference-making processes engaged in by African American boys in the school environment tend to reinforce a particular school-linked identity that diminishes the importance of the school setting and encourages a greater focus on peer relations. Hare and Castanell further suggest that such youth, although they perform extremely poorly in school, nevertheless demonstrate positive (and area-specific) self-esteem. Their analysis thus aids researchers in improving interpretations of African American male adolescents' patterned school-related outcomes. Although designed as ethnographic studies, Matute–Bianchi's (1986) research and that of Ogbu (1984) and Fordham and Ogbu (1986) also suggest differential perceptions of the school setting by Chicano, Japanese American, and African American adolescents, respectively.

According to Garbarino (1983), the microsystem level represents that aspect of the environment in which individuals have direct (physical) contact, while the mesosystem represents the relationships between settings. Ogbu's (1984) ethnographic study of children in Stockton, California, suggests that the involvement of parents at the mesosystem level has profound effects on the success of minority youth in school. For youth of Japanese descent, however, Matute–Bianchi reports that parental participation at the mesosystem level appears less salient than the individual social images held of Japanese Americans by teachers or the available at-home resources (e.g., role model availability). This is attributed to the positive social image of their group and the higher level of home-based support indicated for Japanese-descent students. As stated by an Asian American subject in Matute–Bianchi's study: "They [the school/community] think we're all smart and quiet. We're not, but they think we are" (p. 246). Another Japanese American student indicated that Asians "have a reputation for being really good in science and math"; still another revealed that he was not particularly "good" in math, but "the teacher expected me to do good in it" (p. 247). Thus, for these students, beliefs at the macrolevel of the environment, which represent and convey societal ideologies (or, in this case, social stereotypes), appear most predictive of success.

The exosystem to which Garbarino (1982) refers is the level of the environment wherein policy that affects the experiences of minority adolescents is made, though the youth themselves are not directly involved in the policy-making process. The perspective offered by Fillmore and Britsch (1988) provides another illustration of exosystem effects that is both instructive and relevant for language-different minority youth independent of developmental stage. They note that placing children in academic situations that result in the loss of "home" language has implications for family unity, closeness, and parental respect. This issue is also raised by Matute–Bianchi, who describes the disruptive role acculturation plays when visible and supportive role models are not available to help minority youth with the important adolescent processes of ego identity and group identity development. Similarly, Powell's (1982) work suggests the impact of desegregation legislation on African American youths' school experiences and psychological functioning. Further, Powell and Fuller (1970) suggest that television programming (and thus, media policy) provide another source of psychological impact, although it is rarely discussed as such. Implicit in each of these illustrations of environmental effect is an emphasis on the role of social structure.

Current Models of Minority Adolescent Outcomes

The Influence of Family, Race, and Education on Competence-Related Outcomes

Nearly 150 years following Horace Mann's 1848 report to the Massachusetts Board of Education, the nation continues to struggle with the issue of quality education for minorities. According to Mann, education:

> beyond all other devices of human origin, represents the great equalizer of the conditions of men—the balance-wheel for the social machinery. . .it gives each man the independence and the means by which he can resist the selfishness of others. It does it better than to disarm the poor of their hostility toward the rich; it prevents being poor. (pp. 59–60)

Mindful of that legacy of faith in American education Kenniston (1978) identifies two perspectives that generally describe the American approach to the problem of educating oppressed minorities. The first perspective proclaims that something is wrong with the schools; the second, that something is wrong with minority youth.

In contrast to either approach Ogbu's (1978, 1985) model seeks to move the inequality and opportunity debate concerning African Americans beyond a domestic context by examining parallel experiences of minority youth in other countries. His research suggests that the position of Blacks in the American system of caste or racial stratification contributes to their poorer school performance. Further, Ogbu's provocative and controversial interpretation of research findings suggests that African Americans and similarly placed minority groups often reject the idea of academic competition with members of the dominant group. Additionally, Johnson (1988) suggests that in the process of transmitting culture African American families are particularly vulnerable to the ecological stress factor of racism; what is transmitted, and how, is very much dependent on the coping strategies and perceptions of specific environmental demands. This latter view is consistent with that of Pierce (1989) who writes: "being Black in America means being stressed more because you are Black" (p. 298).

Competence, Social Cognition, and Identity Processes

Theoretical discussion of competence is evident in the writings over three decades ago of Robert White (1959, 1960) and Foote and Cottrell (1955). The discussion continued into subsequent decades with the work of Smith (1968) and DeCharms (1968) as well as more recent work by Harter (1978, 1981, 1983), who has been particularly helpful both in explicating theoretical bridges and providing empirical support for its component domains (e.g., academic, social) (Harter, 1982; Harter & Connell, 1982). Anderson and Messick (1973) were among the first to discuss the implications of the social competence construct's multidimensionality with regard to the experiences of specific subgroups of children (i.e., Head Start's minority and/or poor children) and implications for program content and goals.

The issue of ethnic identity appears critical for explaining competence and/or competence-linked outcomes for youth of diverse cultures. One could infer from the research by Arce (1981) with Chicanos and by Hsu (1983) and Sung (1985) with Asian Americans that issues of immigration, assimilation, identity, and stereotyping remain focal issues for research and theorizing regarding these two groups. However, the more theoretical issue concerning the relationships of these variables to the ontogeny of competence for youth from disfavored groups has been virtually ignored. The more recent ethnographic research on Chicanos and Asian Americans by Matute–Bianchi, DeVos, and others, although identity focused, also has very important implications for explicating the development of competence and efficacious functioning among ethnic and racial minority youth.

Research on African American youth suggests that the lack of achievement outcomes and of a more widespread competence orientation are due to the reluctance of minority youth to "act white" by demonstrating an achievement orientation (Fordham & Ogbu, 1988). On the other hand, as suggested by Johnson's (1988) empirical findings and by the several reports of Slaughter and Johnson (1988) on African American youth attending private schools, doing well academically does not necessarily imply that youth from disfavored groups perceive themselves as having crossed cultural boundaries. Despite differences in resource availability (Spencer, 1983; 1990; Allen, 1985; Matute–Bianchi, 1986) and in the level of exposure to risk of children from poor minority families (Spencer, Dobbs, & Swanson, 1988; Spencer, Kim, & Marshall, 1987), minority parents have been found to express hopes, dreams, and expectations for their children similar to those of Anglo parents (Brookins, 1988; Spencer, 1983). Exploratory research on suburban African American youth suggests that not only are these youth performing satisfactorily but they manifest an own-group identity as well (Banks, 1984). Nonetheless, Banks's study produced several unexpected findings that require further examination. For example, he notes that adolescent African American girls appear to have more problems adjusting to predominantly White environments than do African American boys; moreover, older suburban Black boys tend to feel less positive about their suburban communities and about Blacks in general.

Parents also play an important role. Allen's (1985) research findings for African American and Anglo-American parents of male adolescents suggest that African American fathers use written child-rearing resources least often, while Anglo-American mothers reported the highest use of such books and magazines. Findings reported by Matute–Bianchi (1986) indicate similar differential resources: Japanese American parents have greater access to child-rearing resources and role models than do Chicano youth who showed least academic competence. Recent data by social status show similar differences in resource use for African American families (Spencer, 1990).

Routine educational approaches might also be involved in the manifestation of competence orientations and outcomes (see Irvine, 1990). Erickson (1987) portends that in the case of disfavored groups routine educational approaches may require transformation to arrive at a culturally responsive pedagogy with the potential to enhance the academic outcomes and competence of minority youth. Further, Shade (1987) suggests that culturally specific learning patterns have been ignored. Boykin (1986) enjoins that the study of academic competence among African American youth specifically and disfavored minorities more generally demands the crossing of disciplinary boundaries. According to Boykin, unless the boundaries crossed are psychology and biology or the psychological and social outcomes of topical interest focus on either intelligence or deviance, the more integrative approach is utilized too infrequently. However, crossing disciplinary boundaries without an awareness of the role of structural and sociocultural factors (including differential exposure to risk factors) is not necessarily promotive of more informed analyses of particular patterned outcomes. For example, a study by Newcomer and Udry (1984) purporting a genetic linkage between the sexual behaviors of mothers and their teenage children is illustrative of interdisciplinary efforts that ignore the more structurally related and environmentally linked explanations for adverse youth outcomes.

ETHNICITY, ETHNIC GROUPS, AND ETHNIC IDENTITY

Mithun's (1983) definition of an ethnic group suggests that members of such groups share a sense of tradition that may be derived from common religious, physical, linguistic, aesthetic, or historical origins. Borrowing from the ideas of DeVos and Romanucci–Ross (1975), Mithun clarifies her interpretation by explaining the critical term "belonging" as having to do with factors of sex, biological features, time and place of birth, and descent. Subsequent identification with such basic traits may be due to the particular individual, the ethnic group itself, and external factors (DeVos & Romanucci–Ross, p. 204). More recent work approaching the issue from a sociocognitive, developmental perspective includes analysis of the role of undergirding cognitive structures (Alejandro–Wright, 1985; Semaj, 1985; Spencer, 1985, 1988).

Ethnic identity processes are usually relegated to the affective domain; however, the same rules by which the child comes to know the world of objects are also used to determine and understand the affective status of self and others. Models of ethnic identity generally suggest that initial awareness occurs between five to seven years of age, although ethnic attitudes, concepts, and preferences become evident much earlier, by age three (see Spencer, 1982a). Children's undergirding sociocognitive inference-making processes make the awareness of race unavoidable (Alejandro–Wright, 1985; Semaj, 1985; Spencer, 1982b, 1984, 1985). This concept of supportive sociocognitive processes is important because it allows one to understand within-age-group variation as well as the effects and effectiveness of socialization practices.

From an historical perspective, Frazier (1968) perceives color and race at once among the most important and most enigmatic categories. Although inadequately conceptualized and integrated into theories of development, ethnicity and race continue to be of significant importance. As Cooley (1902) notes: ". . .the thing that moves us to pride or shame is not the mere mechanical reflection of ourselves, but an imputed sentiment, the imagined effect of this reflection upon another's mind" (p.

152). Yet, the role of adolescent cognitive structures in the reflection processes suggested by Cooley is very often ignored.

Chestang's conceptual formulation of ethnic minorities' experiences suggests that the trilogy of experiences of injustice, societal inconsistency, and denial of personal efficacy are linked to racial and ethnic minority status. However, especially with regard to the role of social stereotyping, this approach fails to address developmental and psychological processes. Several different perspectives on the problem of stereotyping are helpful in unraveling these processes. For instance, the findings from an analysis of National Opinion Research Center (NORC) data from 1958 to 1978 by Smith (1985) have implications for Chestang's analysis. Smith's findings suggest that during this period changes occurred in the overall levels of racial tolerance at both the upper and lower ends of a tolerance spectrum and thus in the degree of social stereotyping. Differential effects were shown to be dependent upon cohort and level of education. The most conservative end of the spectrum was slightly affected (an eroding effect of tolerance) by the respondents' increased educational attainment. Independent of position in the spectrum, tolerance change was most often due to more general respondent changes in all cohort and educational groups. Simply put, Whites are more tolerant now than in the past, and changes in the racial attitudes of Whites stem from changes across all education and cohort groups.

Other theorists suggest that it is not the issue of racial tolerance that is important but rather the value characteristics of the group (Mithun, 1983). Mithun suggests that the cultural content of the experiences of Chicanos, Puerto Ricans, and African Americans is very different in several dimensions from that of Anglos. She asserts that for these American minority groups, with their cultural emphasis on the supernatural, the values of the White Anglo-Saxon Protestant (WASP) ethic—aggressiveness, competitiveness, self-reliance, self-sufficiency, and individualism—are not primary; nor are thrift, sobriety, and goal- and future-oriented behavior guiding tenets (although Mithun notes that the Chinese and the Jews share with Anglos a similar emphasis on self-reliance and self-sufficiency). Additionally, the diffuse sexuality *that is assumed to permeate minority cultures* not only diametrically opposes but directly confronts the traditional tenets of mainstream Anglo–American culture (pp. 218–219).

Further, DeVos (1980) indicates that acculturation on the part of minorities may be accompanied by problems. That is, instrumental advantages may be offset by affective arousal due to the expenditure of inevitable internal conflict which accompanies some aspects of acculturation or upward social mobility or change in ethnic identity (p. 115). Acculturation into the dominant group might increase intracultural marginality. Such issues are of particular salience for social development during the pre- and post-pubescent periods due to the importance of the peer group in bolstering social self-identity during those stages. The processes and unique requirements of cultural socialization are indeed complex. Parental cultural socialization varies significantly and often may not be available as a source of "individualized or personalized" protection or buffer against individual expressions of the group's rejection. As indicated by the child-rearing research on African American parents by Spencer (1983; 1990) and Bowman and Howard (1985), and on youth of Mexican descent by Matute–Bianchi (1986), minority parents seldom raise cultural concerns with their adolescents unless requested to do so by their youth. The peer group may thus serve a greater protective role for ethnic minority youth. Research regarding African American youth (Fordham and Ogbu, 1986; Spencer, 1983; Howard & Bowman, 1985; Sager et al., 1983) along with Deyhle's (1986) research on American Indian youth together suggest the potential mediator effects of parents and peers and proposes a much more complex process.

Ego Identity Processes and Ethnic Identity Formation

As suggested by Devereux (1975), identity represents an individual's absolute uniqueness. Identity formation processes, as either the development of a "self theory" or of an acquired identity, are issues confronted by all youth. Erikson's (1968) description of the seven parts of the adolescent identity crisis have important implications for youth of disfavored groups. For example, acquisition of a sense of self-certainty versus a sense of self-consciousness is more difficult when one is visibly and culturally different. Sager et al (1983) found their sample of sixth grade youth to interact primarily with others of their own race and sex. However, African American youth were twice as likely as Whites to be the initiators of cross-racial interactions, and generally African American boys interacted more across racial lines than did African American girls. Gender aggregation was also less pronounced among Black youth than Whites. Significant sex differences have been found by others who emphasize the importance of analyzing data by sex, class, and race to enhance knowledge of the more precarious social situation of specific subgroups (Scott–Jones & Clark, 1986). Although Gibbs (1989) suggests that Black adolescent males are routinely exposed to multiple risk factors, Sager et al. conclude that conditions for Black female adolescents necessitate greater coping skills. Among Black female youth, coping with inequities caused by race and social class is apparently of at least comparable importance as those inequities fostered by sex bias alone.

The identity formation processes of minority youth are much more critical due to the environmental risk factors that accompany minority status. As Spencer and Markstrom–Adams (1990) report, however, repeated efforts have been made to address the many barriers to identity formation encountered by minority youth which require very different intervention strategies (see Markstrom–Adams & Spencer, in press). The improved educational methods described by Irvine (1988) and the contextual inferences offered by Powell (1985), Verna and Runion (1985), and Fillmore and Britsch (1988) all facilitate the resolution of the self-certainty versus self-consciousness crisis as one aspect of ego identity formation for minority youth.

Barriers to self-certainty for ethnic and racial minority youth may well emanate from teacher characteristics and minority teacher shortages. Irvine (1988, 1990) analyzes the implications of the shortage of minority teachers on youth outcomes and teacher performance, and concludes that methods aimed at diminishing the possibility of societal inequities being perpetrated through schooling experiences demand that *all* teachers and principals—Black (or other minorities) and White—acquire the skills necessary to educate America's increasingly multiethnic school populations. Her analyses suggest that teachers and principals of all ethnic groups may require motivational incentives to obtain the skills and knowledge to teach Black (and other) inner-city youth. Teacher preparation programs must provide prospective teachers with reliable tests and affective techniques for maximizing instruction for all children (Irvine, 1988). All of the training needs noted are research-dependent. Comparable ideas have been expressed by Fillmore and Britsch (1988) regarding language- and culturally different youth. The variety of contextual effects possible may be further attenuated as a function of social class (Holliday, 1985). Comer's (1988) ideas for effective educational techniques and his successful efforts with lower-income African American youth in New Haven (CT) also implicate the importance of parental support and school-home partnerships for enhancing minority youth's academic competence.

Implications, Conclusions, and Policy Recommendations

Although presented in a very skeletal form, the theoretical approaches discussed herein for exploring the interactive relationship between ethnicity, identity, and competence for minority youth affords an initial step toward a reconceptualization of the experiences of these adolescents. As a more inclusive perspective of human development, these approaches should result in the development of more comprehensive models. Specifically, the use of a more culturally informed conceptual framework by teachers and all youth-focused service providers should accomplish the following goals:

- increased awareness of the importance of constructing environments and formulating incentives that will keep ethnic minority youth in school and academically oriented, especially because education continues to serve as the variable of importance for offsetting socioeconomic disadvantage;
- heightened consciousness of the importance of mental and physical health across the life course;
- affirmation of the importance of constructive social networks and support systems for minority youth (especially males);
- the development of methods to assure and support minority parents in their role as cultural transmitters;
- the promotion of a cultural emphasis that affirms the group identity of Anglo and ethnic minority youth alike; and
- the provision of incentives for the development and utilization of more culturally sensitive teaching techniques.

Additionally, the described multicultural approach should generate several types of research and information that can be used by practitioners, service providers, policy analysts, and other researchers for multiple purposes. Such data should then lead to more comprehensive, culturally responsible, and sensitive theories and serve as guides for reformulating current developmental models of risk and coping. It would also form the basis for proposing and implementing unique prevention strategies and intervention models and ultimately for upgrading the struggles of ethnic minorities to obtain educational and social equity.

REFERENCES

Alejandro–Wright, M. N. (1985). The child's conception of racial classification: A socio-cognitive developmental model. In M. B. Spencer, G. K. Brookins, & W. R. Allen (Eds.), *Beginnings: The social and affective development of Black children* (pp. 185–200). Hillsdale, NJ: Erlbaum.

Allen, W. R. (1985). Race, income and family dynamics: A study of adolescent male socialization processes and outcomes. In M. B. Spencer, G. K. Brookins, & W. R. Allen (Eds.), *Beginnings: The social and affective development of Black children* (pp. 273–292). Hillsdale, NJ: Erlbaum.

Anderson, S., & Messick, S. (1973). *Social competency in young children* [Report prepared under Office of Child Development Grant Number H-2993 A/H]. Princeton, NJ: Educational Testing Service.

Anthony, E. J. (1974). Introduction: The syndrome of the psychologically vulnerable child. In E. J. Anthony and C. Koupernik (Eds.), *The child in his family: Children at psychiatric risk* (pp. 3–10). New York: Wiley & Sons.

Arce, C. (1981). A reconsideration of Chicano culture and identity. *Daedalus, 110*(2), 177–192.

Banks, J. A. (1984). Black youths in predominantly White suburbs: An exploratory study of their attitudes and self-concepts. *Journal of Negro Education, 53*, 3–17.

Barker, R. G., & Wright, H. F. (1954). *Midwest and its children: The psychological ecology of an American town*. Evanston, IL: Row, Peterson.

Bell–Scott, P., & Taylor, R. L. (1989). Introduction: The multiple ecologies of Black development. *Journal of Adolescent Development* (Special edition on Black adolescents). Newbury Park, CA: Sage.

Bowman, P. J., & Howard C. (1985). Race-related socialization, motivation and academic achievement: A study of Black youths in three-generation families. *Journal of the American Academy of Child Psychiatry, 24*, 134–141.

Boykin, A. W. (1986). The triple quandary and the schooling of Afro-American children. In U. Neisser (Ed.), *The school achievement of minority children* (pp. 57–92). Hillsdale, NJ: Erlbaum.

Bradley, D. (1982, May). Black and American, 1982. *Esquire*, pp. 58–71.

Brim, O., & Kagan, J. (1980). *Constancy and change in human behavior*. Cambridge, MA: Harvard University Press.

Bronfenbrenner, U. (1979). *The ecology of human development: Experiments by nature and design*. Cambridge, MA: Harvard University Press.

Brookins, G. K. (1988). Making the honor roll: A Black parent's perspective on private education. In D. T. Slaughter & D. J. Johnson

(Eds.), *Visible now: Blacks in private schools* (pp. 12–20). New York: Greenwood Press.
Brooks–Gunn, J., & Reiter, E. O. (1990). The role of pubertal processes. In S. S. Feldman & G. R. Elliott (Eds.), *At the threshold* (pp. 16–53). Cambridge, MA: Harvard University Press.
Chestang, L. W. (1972). *Character development in a hostile environment* (Occasional Paper No. 3). Chicago: University of Chicago Press.
Comer, J. P. (1986). Parent participation in the schools. *Phi Delta Kappan, 67*, 442–446.
Cooley, C. H. (1902). *Human nature and the social order*. New York: Scribner & Sons.
DeCharms, R. (1968). *Personal causation: The internal affective determinants of behavior*. New York: Academic Press.
Devereux, G. (1982). Ethnic identity: Its logical foundation, and its dysfunction. In G. DeVos and L. Romanucci–Ross (Eds.) *Ethnic and identity* (pp. 42–70). Chicago: University of Chicago Press.
DeVos, G. A. (1980). Ethnic adaptations and minority status. *Journal of Cross-Cultural Psychology, 11*(1), 101–124.
DeVos, G., & Romanucci–Ross, L. (1982). Preface. In G. DeVos & L. Romanucci–Ross (Eds.), *Ethnicity and identity* (pp. 11–27). Chicago: University of Chicago Press.
Deyhle, D. (1986). Break dancing and breaking out: Anglos, Utes, and Navajos in a border reservation high school. *Anthropology and Education Quarterly, 17*, 111–127.
DuBois, W. E. B. (1970). *The souls of Black folk*. Greenwich, CT: Fawcett. (Original work published 1903)
Dweck, C. S. (1978). Achievement. In M. Lamb (Ed.), *Social and personality development* (pp. 114–130). New York: Holt, Rinehart.
Elder, G. H., Jr. (1974). *Children of the great depression*. Chicago: University of Chicago Press.
Erikson, E. (1968). *Identity, youth and crisis*. New York: W. W. Norton.
Erikson, E. H. (1966). The concept of identity in race relations: Notes and queries. *Daedalus, 95*, 145–171.
Erickson, F. (1987). Transformation and school success: The politics and culture of educational achievement. *Anthropology and Education Quarterly, 18*, 335–356.
Fillmore, L. W. & Britsch, S. (1968). *Early education for children from linguistic and cultural minority families.* A paper prepared for the Early Education Task Force of the National Association of State Boards of Education.
Foote, N., & Cottrell, L. S. (1955). *Identity and interpersonal competence: A new direction in family research*. Chicago: University of Chicago Press.
Fordham, S., & Ogbu, J. U. (1986). Black students' school success: Coping with the "burden of acting White." *Urban Review, 18*, 176–206.
Franklin, J. H. (1968). Introduction. In J. H. Franklin (Ed.), *Color and race* (pp. ix–xvii). Boston: Beacon.
Garbarino, J. (1982). *Children and families in the social environment*. New York: Aldine.
Gibbs, J. T. (1989). Black American adolescents. In J. T. Gibbs & L. Huang (Ed.), *Children of color* (pp. 179–223). San Francisco: Jossey–Bass.

Hammond, B., & Ladner, J. A. (1969). Socialization into sexual behavior. In C. Broderick & J. Bernard (Eds.), *The individual and sex: Background readings for sex education*. Baltimore, MD: Johns Hopkins University Press.

Harter, S. (1978). Effectance motivation reconsidered: Toward a developmental model. *Human Development, 1*, 34–64.

Harter, S. (1981). Model of intrinsic mastery motivation in children: Individual differences and developmental changes. In W. A. Collins (Ed.), *Minnesota symposium on child psychology: Volume 14* (pp. 215–255). Hillsdale, NJ: Erlbaum.

Harter, S. (1982). The perceived competence scale for children. *Child Development, 53*, 87–97.

Harter, S. (1983). Developmental perspectives on the self system. In P. H. Mussen (Ed.), *Child psychology* (pp. 275–385). New York: Wiley.

Harter, S., & Connell, J. P. (1982). A comparison of alternative models of the relationship between academic achievement and children's perceptions of competence, control and motivation orientation. In J. Nicholls (Ed.), *The development of achievement-related cognitions and behavior*. Greenwich, CT: JAI Press.

Hilliard, A. G. (1983). Psychological factors associated with language in the education of the African-American child. *Journal of Negro Education, 52*(1), 24–34.

Hilliard, A. G. (1988). Public support for successful instructional practices for at-risk students. In Council of Chief State School Officers (Ed.), *School success for students at risk* (pp. 195–208). Orlando, FL: Harcourt Brace Jovanovich.

Holliday, B. G. (1985). Towards a model of teacher-child transactional processes affecting Black children's academic achievement. In M. B. Spencer, G. K. Brookins, & W. R. Allen (Eds.), *Beginnings: The social and affective development of Black children* (pp. 117–130). Hillsdale, NJ: Erlbaum.

Hsu, J. (1983). Asian family interaction patterns and their therapeutic implications. *International Journal of Family Psychiatry, 4*, 307–320.

Irvine, J. J. (1988). Disappearing Black educators. *Elementary School Journal, 88*, 503–513.

Irvine, J. J. (1990). *Black students and school failure*. New York: Greenwood Press.

Johnson, D. J. (1988). Racial socialization strategies of parents in three Black private schools. In D. T. Slaughter & D. J. Johnson (Eds.), *Visible now: Blacks in private schools* (pp. 251–267). New York: Greenwood Press.

Kardiner, A., & Ovesey, L. (1951). *The mark of oppression: Explorations in the personality of the American Negro*. New York: W. W. Norton.

Keniston, K. (1978). Foreword. In J. Ogbu (Ed.), *Minority education and caste*. New York: Academic Press.

Lerner, R. (1982). Children and adolescents as producers of their own environments. *Developmental Review, 2*, 342–370.

Lerner, R., & Spanier, S. (1980). *Adolescent development: A life span perspective*. New York: McGraw–Hill.

Mann, H. (1848). *Twelfth annual report to the board of education.* Boston, MA: Dutton & Wentworth.
Markstrom-Adams, C., & Spencer, M. B. (in press). *Interventions with minority cultures.* In S. Archer (Ed.), Interventions for adolescent identity development. Beverly Hills, CA: Sage.
Matute-Bianchi, M. E. (1986). Ethnic identity and patterns of school success and failures among Mexican descendant and Japanese American students in a California high school: An ethnographic analysis. *American Journal of Education, 95,* 233–255.
McCarthy, J., & Yancey, W. (1971). Uncle Tom and Mr. Charlie: Metaphysical pathos in the study of racism and personal disorganization. *American Journal of Sociology, 71,* 648–672.
McGhee, J. (1984). *Running the gauntlet: Black men in America.* Washington, DC: National Urban League Research Department.
Mithun, J. S. (1983). The role of the family in acculturation and assimilation in America: A psychocultural dimension. In W. C. McCready (Ed.), *Ethnicity and identity: Current issues in research.* New York: Academic Press.
Modell, J., & Goodman, M. (1990). Historical perspectives. In S. S. Feldman & G. R. Elliott (Eds.), *At the threshold* (pp. 93–122). Cambridge, MA: Harvard University Press.
Newcomer, S. F., & Udry, J. R. (1984). Mothers' influence on the sexual behavior of their teenage children. *Journal of Marriage and the Family, 46,* 477–485.
Ogbu, J. (1974). *The next generation: An ethnography of education in an urban neighborhood.* New York: Academic Press.
Ogbu, J. (1978). *Minority education and caste.* New York: Academic Press.
Ogbu, J. (1985). *A cultural ecology of competence among inner-city Blacks.* In M. B. Spencer, G. K. Brookins, & W. R. Allen (Eds.), *Beginnings: The social and affective development of Black children* (pp. 45–66). Hillsdale, NJ: Erlbaum.
Pettigrew, T. F. (1964). *A profile of the Negro American.* Princeton, NJ: Van Nostrand.
Pierce, C. M. (1989). Unity in diversity: Thirty-three years of stress. In G. L. Berry & J. K. Asamen (Eds.), *Black students: Psychosocial issues and academic achievement* (pp. 296–312). Newberry Park, CA: Sage.
Powell, G. J. (1982). The impact of television on the self-concept development of minority group children. In G. L. Berry & C. Mitchell-Kernan (Eds.), *Television and the socialization of the minority child* (pp. 105–131). New York: Academic Press.
Powell, G. J. (1985). Self-concepts among Afro-American students in racially isolated minority schools: Some regional differences. *Journal of the American Academy of Child Psychiatry, 24*(2), 142–149.
Powell, G. J., & Fuller, M. (1970). Self-concept and school desegregation. *American Journal of Orthopsychiatry, 40,* 303.
Riley, M. W. (1979). Introduction: Life-course perspectives. In M. W. Riley (Ed.), *Aging from birth to death* (pp. 3–14). Washington, DC: Westview Press.
Sager, A., Schofield, J. W., & Snyder, H. N. (1983). Race and gender barriers: Preadolescent peer behavior in academic classrooms. *Child Development, 54,* 1032–1040.

Scott-Jones, D., & Clark, M. (1986). The school experiences of Black girls: The interaction of gender, race and SES status. *Phi Delta Kappan, 67*, 520–526.
Semaj, L. (1985). Africanity, cognition and extended self-identity. In M. B. Spencer, G. K. Brookins, & W. R. Allen (Eds.), *Beginnings: The social and affective development of Black children* (pp. 173–184). Hillsdale, NJ: Erlbaum.
Shade, B. J. (1982). Afro-American cognitive style: A variable in school success? *Review of Educational Research, 52*, 219–244.
Simpkins, G., Gunnings, T., & Kearney, C. (1973). The Black six-hour retarded child. *Journal of Non-White Concerns in Personnel and Guidance, 2*(1), 29–34.
Slaughter, D. T., & D. J. Johnson (1988). *Visible now: Blacks in private schools*. New York: Greenwood Press.
Slavin, R. E. (1987). Cooperative learning and the education of Black students. In D. S. Strickland & E. J. Cooper (Eds.), *Educating Black children: American's challenge* (pp. 63–68). Washington, DC: Bureau of Educational Research, Howard University School of Education.
Smith, A. W. (1985). Cohorts, education, and the evolution of tolerance. *Social Science Research, 14*, 205–225.
Smith, M. B. (1968). Competence and socialization. In J. A. Causen (Ed.), *Socialization and society* (pp. 270–320). Boston: Little, Brown.
Spencer, M. B. (1982a). Personal and group identity of Black children: An alternative synthesis. *Genetic Psychology Monographs, 103*, 59–84.
Spencer, M. B. (1982b). Preschool children's social cognition and cultural cognition: A cognitive developmental interpretation of race dissonance findings. *Journal of Psychology, 112*, 275–286.
Spencer, M. B. (1983). Children's cultural values and parental child rearing strategies. *Developmental Review, 3*, 351–370.
Spencer, M. B. (1984). Black children's race awareness, racial attitudes, and self-concept: A reinterpretation. *Journal of Child Psychology and Psychiatry, 25*(3), 433–441.
Spencer, M. B. (1985). Cultural cognition and social cognition as identity correlates of Black children's personal-social development. In M. B. Spencer, G. K. Brookins, & W. R. Allen (Eds.), *Beginnings: The social and affective development of Black children* (pp. 215–230). Hillsdale, NJ: Erlbaum.
Spencer, M. B. (1988). Self-concept development. In D. T. Slaughter (Ed.), *Perspectives on Black child development: New directions for child development* (pp. 59–72). San Francisco: Jossey–Bass.
Spencer, M. B. (1990). Parental values transmission. In J. B. Stewart & H. Cheatham (Eds.), *Interdisciplinary perspectives on Black families* (pp. 111–130). New Brunswick, NJ: Transactions.
Spencer, M. B., Dobbs, B., & Swanson, D. P. (1988). Afro-American adolescents: Adaptational processes and socioeconomic diversity in behavioral outcomes. *Journal of Adolescence, 11*, 117–137.
Spencer, M. B., Kim, S., & Marshall, S. (1987). Double stratification and psychological risk: Adaptational processes and school experiences of Black children. *Journal of Negro Education, 56*, 77–86.

Spencer, M. B., & Markstrom-Adams, C. (1990). Identity processes among racial and ethnic minority children in America. *Child Development, 61*(2), 290–310.
Stember, C. H. (1976). *Sexual racism.* New York: Elsevier.
Sung, B. L. (1985). Bicultural conflicts in Chinese immigrant children. *Journal of Comparative Family Studies, 16*(2), 255–270.
Taylor, R. L. (1976). Psychosocial development among Black children and youth: A re-examination. *American Journal of Orthopsychiatry, 46,* 4–19.
Verna, G. B., & Runion, K. B. (1985). The effects of contextual dissonance on the self-concept of youth from a high versus low socially valued group. *The Journal of Social Psychology, 125*(4), 449–458.
Werner, E. E., & Smith, R. S. (1982). *Vulnerable but invincible.* New York: McGraw–Hill.
Woodson, R. (1988, July 31). Building a new base for Black prosperity. *Atlanta Journal-Constitution,* p. D-4.

Developmental Psychology
1982, Vol. 18, No. 3, 341–358

0012-1649/82/1803-0341$00.75

Identity Development From Adolescence to Adulthood: An Extension of Theory and a Review of Research

Alan S. Waterman
Trenton State College

Those aspects of Erikson's theory of psychosocial development concerning the formation of a sense of personal identity are examined in light of research evidence. When the Stage 5 component is considered as a bipolar dimension, the expectation is that the transition from adolescence to adulthood involves a progressive strengthening in the sense of identity. When the identity construct is expanded to include the processes by which an identity is formed, it is hypothesized that over time there will be progressive developmental shifts in identity status, that is, from the identity diffusion status into either the foreclosure or moratorium status, from the foreclosure into the moratorium status, and from the moratorium into the identity achievement status. The circumstances associated with progressive shifts, regressive changes, and reentry into an identity crisis are discussed. The review of the literature focuses on questions of the direction and timing of identity development, sex differences in development, and the identification of antecedent conditions relating to the choice of developmental pathways.

Erikson's (1963, 1968) construct of identity has become the principal tool for understanding the development of personality from adolescence into adulthood:

> The wholeness to be achieved at this stage I have called a sense of inner identity. The young person, in order to experience wholeness, must feel a progressive continuity between that which he has come to be during the long years of childhood and that which he promises to become in the anticipated future; between that which he conceives himself to be and that which he perceives others to see in him and to expect of him. Individually speaking, identity includes, but is more than, the sum of all the successive identifications of those earlier years when the child wanted to be, and often was forced to become, like the people he depended on. Identity is a unique product, which now meets a crisis to be solved only in new identifications with age mates and with leader figures outside of the family. (Erikson, 1968, p. 87)

Erikson has identified several developmental issues that may become the focus of an identity crisis. There is the choice of an occupation that is both socially recognized and personally expressive. Another is the development of an ideological world view that is worthy of a personal commitment. Such an ideology may be either religious or political in nature. Other questions involve sex role appropriate behavior and sexual orientation. Here too the task is to find modes of expression that reflect intrinsic inclinations and for which sufficient sources of social support exist within the individual's cultural milieu.

Since the construct of identity was introduced for purposes of clinical analysis, whether of individuals or of cultures, its definition could remain richly associative without being precisely specified. The impact of Erikson's clinical interpretations rests, in part, on his capacity to persuade the reader that quite diverse forms of behavior are accountable for in terms of a limited number of concepts. However, the absence of a definitive statement of the boundaries of the identity construct has posed a problem for researchers attempting to develop operational definitions that cover the range of aspects attributed to it. The assessment instruments that have been developed have usually focused on some combination of the following facets of identity: (a) a clear sense of self-definition; (b) the presence of commitments regarding goals, values, and beliefs; (c) the existence of activity directed toward the implementation of commitments; (d) the consideration of a range of identity alternatives; (e) the extent of self-accep-

Requests for reprints should be sent to Alan S. Waterman, Department of Psychology, Trenton State College, Hillwood Lakes, CN 550, Trenton, New Jersey 08625.

tance; (f) a sense of personal uniqueness; and (g) confidence in one's personal future. Among the global paper-and-pencil instruments with items tapping different combinations of these themes are Rasmussen's (1961) Ego Identity Scale, Dignan's (1965) Ego Identity Scale, the Ego Identity–Incomplete Sentences Blank (Marcia, 1966), the Inventory of Psychosocial Development (Constantinople, 1969), and the Identity Achievement Scale (Simmons, 1970).

Such a global approach to assessment permits a determination of the extent to which a person has established a clear sense of identity but does not provide information on the processes by which identity elements were developed. In writing on the processes of development, Erikson (1958) used William James's distinction between those who are once born and those who go through a second birth or growth crisis in the shaping of their identity. The former experience no difficulties in fitting themselves into their society. They translate their childhood identifications into adult experience without serious doubt or conflict. In contrast, the twice born undergo a crisis of purpose or faith in which their adult commitments are formed as an act of personal choice.

Marcia (1966) constructed a semistructured interview by which to assess both the clarity of personal identity and the process by which it develops. The classification system used is composed of four ego identity statuses: (a) identity achievement, (b) moratorium, (c) foreclosure, and (d) identity diffusion. These statuses are defined in terms of two dimensions: crisis and commitment. "Crisis" refers to a period of struggle or active questioning in arriving at such aspects of personal identity as vocational choice and ideological beliefs. "Commitment" involves making a firm, unwavering decision in such areas and engaging in appropriate implementing activities.

An *identity achiever* is someone who has gone through a period of crisis and has developed relatively firm commitments. The term *moratorium* is used to refer to a person who is currently in a state of crisis and is actively seeking among alternatives in an attempt to arrive at a choice. A person is classified as a *foreclosure* if he or she has never experienced a crisis but is nevertheless committed to particular goals, values, or beliefs. The commitments that foreclosures have made generally reflect the wishes of parents or other authority figures. The category of *identity diffusion* includes individuals who do not have firm commitments and who are not actively trying to form them. They may never have been in crisis, or they may have had a period of questioning and been unable to resolve it, subsequently emerging without having made a decision.

There have been several recent reviews of the research literature on identity (Bourne, 1978a, 1978b; Marcia, 1980, Note 1) evaluating the validity of the various assessment techniques and documenting the broad range of variables to which identity is related. The more limited focus here is on theory and research pertaining to questions of identity formation. Specifically, the issues to be discussed are (a) the direction and timing of identity development, (b) sex differences in development, and (c) antecedent conditions relating to the choice of developmental pathways.

Developmental Hypotheses

Direction and Timing of Development

At its simplest, the basic hypothesis of identity development is that the transition from adolescence to adulthood involves a progressive strengthening in the sense of identity. It is this hypothesis that has been tested in numerous studies using paper-and-pencil measures of identity.

Because Marcia's identity interview procedure involves categorizing individuals according to their strategy for handling the task of identity formation and does not yield a single continuous measure, a more complex set of developmental patterns can be identified. A schematic presentation of the pathways of identity status formation consistent with Erikson's theory is given in Figure 1.

A person who is in the identity diffusion status may (a) become a moratorium by beginning to seriously explore a variety of identity alternatives (D → M); (b) become a foreclosure by latching on to the first real possibility that is presented without ever evaluating other courses of action (D → F);

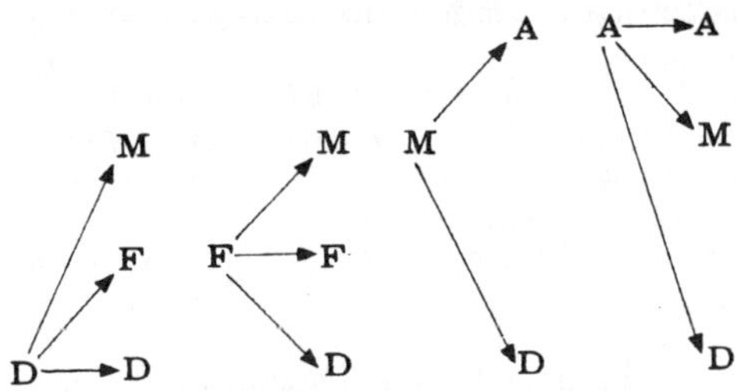

Figure 1. A model of the sequential patterns of ego identity development. (D = identity diffusion; F = foreclosure; M = moratorium; A = identity achievement.)

or (c) continue indefinitely in the diffusion status, never making a serious effort to work out identity issues (D → D).

A person who is in the foreclosure status may (a) become a moratorium if the early commitments are challenged in a way that requires the consideration of alternative possibilities (F → M); (b) continue as a foreclosure, carrying into adulthood commitments to the goals and values that were developed prior to or during adolescence (F → F); or (c) become a diffusion if the initial commitments gradually become less meaningful without steps being taken to revise or replace them (F → D).

A person who has entered the moratorium status may (a) become an identity achiever by establishing firm, meaningful commitments to specific goals and values (M → A) or (b) become an identity diffusion by giving up on the efforts to find something worthwhile to which to become committed (M → D).[1]

A person who has become an identity achiever may (a) continue as an achiever, maintaining the commitments to the goals and values that were worked out during the identity crisis (A → A); (b) again become a moratorium, reentering crisis if the earlier resolution proves unsatisfactory in some way (A → M); or (c) become a diffusion if the commitments that were established gradually lose their vitality without triggering a new crisis (A → D).

Of the changes in status just described, the following constitute progressive developmental shifts: from the identity diffusion status into either the foreclosure or moratorium status, from the foreclosure into the moratorium status, and from the moratorium into the identity achievement status. Each represents movement involving either the initiation of reflective consideration of identity alternatives or the development of personally meaningful commitments. A change into the identity diffusion status from any of the other statuses can be viewed as developmentally regressive, since it involves a putting aside of identity concerns, at least temporarily, without having established a satisfactory resolution. The shift from the identity achievement to the moratorium status might more appropriately be considered as the resumption of a crisis rather than a developmental regression. It reflects a continuation of the identity formation process, an attempt to make more rewarding choices, not a renunciation of identity concerns.

The above constitutes a descriptive model rather than a theory of development, since there are virtually no patterns of identity status change inconsistent with it. The utility of the model rests in the opportunity it affords to study the relative frequency of the different developmental paths and the circumstances that influence their adoption. It thus becomes possible to compare the patterns of development among various groups within a population (and between populations) and to identify the impact of sociohistorical conditions on identity formation.

The basic hypothesis of identity development may now be phrased: Movement from adolescence to adulthood involves a preponderance of changes in identity status which can be characterized as progressive developmental shifts.

There are two questions related to the direction of identity development about which little a priori theorizing has been done. One concerns the relative stability of the various identity statuses. It can be antici-

[1] Continuing in the moratorium status is not included here, since indefinitely maintaining an identity crisis is highly improbable (although theoretically possible). Moving from the moratorium (or achiever) status to the foreclosure status is not a theoretical possibility. Once a person has undergone an identity crisis, he or she no longer can meet the definition of a foreclosure, even if he or she goes back to the same goals and values that were held before the crisis.

pated that the moratorium category will be the least stable of the statuses, since it is associated with an expressed desire to make changes in one's life. Further it is difficult for individuals to sustain the subjective discomfort usually associated with identity crises. If a successful resolution cannot be achieved, the person is likely to eventually renounce the task as unresolvable. However, it is unclear as to which status will be the most stable. While both the foreclosure and identity achievement statuses involve commitments, the stability of either type of commitment may be influenced by a wide variety of life events. The lack of commitment characteristic of the identity diffusion status may or may not prove to be a relatively stable developmental quality. Further, it is possible that the relative stability of the various statuses will vary by the topic area in which identity is considered.

The other question best approached in empirical fashion concerns the timing of identity changes. In his discussion of the epigenetic principle, Erikson (1959) refers not only to a proper sequence of stage development but to a proper rate. Stage 5 in his theory can be presumed to cover much or all of the period from puberty through the college years. He does not, however, suggest a timetable of the ages at which particular identity issues are most likely to arise, become a focus of development, and reach eventual resolution. Although wide individual differences in the timing of identity development may be expected, it should be of interest to determine if there are characteristic times (or developmental settings) associated with the greatest probability of change.

Sex Differences in Identity Development

Since Erikson (1963, 1968, 1975) wrote extensively on the differences in psychological functioning between the sexes, it might be expected that he would anticipate sex differences in the patterns of identity formation. It is questionable, however, as to whether he intended such a hypothesis. Before addressing that question, it is helpful to look at the differences that he does describe.

Working from his experience with the play constructions of preadolescent participants in a long-term development study, Erikson discussed differences between the sexes in the real and symbolic use of space. He drew an association between the play constructions and anatomically based genital modes. Males, with external genital organs, erectable and intrusive, developed play construction characterized by height and downfall, strong motion and its channelization or arrest. Females, with internal genital organs having vestibular access, constructed static interiors that were open, simply enclosed, and peaceful or intruded upon. However, Erikson did not conclude that intrusion and enclosing were the exclusive prerogatives of males and females, respectively. Rather, these differences were seen as ones of "predisposition and prediliction." He wrote that where cultural and historical conditions permit, each sex may be led "to make use of, to share, and at times to imitate, the configurations most typical of the other sex" (Erikson, 1975, p. 233).

The emphasis Erikson (1975) placed on the presence of anatomically based sex differences in behavior reflects an effort to counter the assertions made by some that all sex differences are learned. He did not postulate different developmental processes for males and females. Thus, while biological predispositions may be expected to play some role regarding the content of identity choices, they would not necessarily be involved in the processes by which identity elements are selected. Both sexes may undergo comparable experiences of crisis and commitment. It should be recognized that any sex differences observed in the frequency of presence in the different identity statuses can be interpreted as a function of cultural influences, not a result of the unfolding of different developmental capabilities.

Antecedent Conditions Relating to Identity Development

The choice of a developmental pathway for identity formation may be expected to be influenced by a variety of interrelated variables. The following is a summary presentation of hypotheses relating antecedent conditions to the course of identity development.

1. The greater the extent of identification with parents prior to or during adolescence, the greater the likelihood will be of forming and maintaining personally meaningful commitments. With strong identification, entrance into, and maintenance of, the foreclosure status appears most probable.

2. Differences in parenting styles (Becker, 1964) will be reflected in differences in pathways of identity formation. Individuals with permissive, neglecting, or rejecting parents may be expected most frequently to be identity diffuse and to have difficulty in successfully resolving identity crises should they occur. Those from authoritarian families may take either of two quite divergent paths, becoming foreclosed on parental choices or rebelling and going through an identity crisis, perhaps of quite strenuous proportions. The former alternative should be more common under circumstances where an adolescent is able to earn parental respect, whereas the latter should more frequently occur where parental approval cannot be gained. Both protective and indulgent parenting styles may be expected to yield outcomes characterized either by relative insecurity (identity diffusion) or by docile conformity (foreclosure). Finally, democratic parenting should be relatively conducive to the consideration of identity alternatives and the forming of personal commitments (identity achievement). Presence in the foreclosure status may also be expected where any early decisions are functional for the adolescent and meet with parental support.

3. The greater the range of identity alternatives to which an individual is exposed prior to or during adolescence, the greater the likelihood will be of undergoing an identity crisis. Thus, homogeneous communities may be conducive to the forming and maintaining of foreclosure commitments, whereas more heterogeneous communities may serve to facilitate the entrance into an identity crisis.

4. The greater the availability of model figures perceived as living successfully, the greater the probability will be that a person will form meaningful commitments. This should have particular relevance for the likelihood of successfully resolving an identity crisis, since successful adult models may serve as examples of how to cope with difficulties and may suggest identity content alternatives that can be profitably explored. Similarly, the parents' own identity statuses may influence the process of identity development through the model value they have for the adolescent.

5. The nature of the social expectations pertaining to identity choices arising within the family, the schools, and the peer group will contribute to the particular identity development pathways employed. Where one is exposed to social groups that seldom question received authority, an identity crisis would appear less probable than among groups where questioning is more common and even encouraged.

6. Consistent with the epigenetic principle, it is anticipated that to the extent that preadolescent personality provides an appropriate foundation for coping with identity concerns (i.e., there are sufficient levels of basic trust, autonomy, initiative, and industry), the more successfully identity development is likely to proceed. Similarly, success in such other aspects of development as formal operations and moral reasoning may also contribute to advances in identity formation.

Research Evidence

Direction and Timing of Development

Development prior to and during the high school years. Prior to the high school years, there appears to be little interest in identity-related questions. Ciaccio (1971) used a Thematic Apperception Test-type story-telling projective instrument to assess the extent of concerns associated with each of the first five stages described by Erikson. The samples consisted of males at three age levels: 5, 8, and 11 years. The results of a "unit utterance" scoring procedure indicated that the 11-year-old boys were beginning to evidence identity concerns, but the frequency of such concerns was far lower than for concerns associated with the earlier stage components of industry and initiative. Similarly, in two studies using the ego identity interview with 11- to 13-year-olds (Meilman, 1979; Archer, Note 2), the identity achievement status was observed in less than 4% of the topic area scoring decisions.

The results of cross-sectional studies of development during the high school years using paper-and-pencil instruments have revealed only limited differences. Pomerantz (1979) found twelfth-grade females to score significantly higher than eighth-grade females on the Rasmussen Ego Identity Scale, but the difference for males, though in the expected direction, was not significant. La Voie (1976) studied high school sophomores, juniors, and seniors of both sexes using Marcia's Ego Identity–Incomplete Sentences Blank and found a nonsignificant increase with increasing grade level. Similarly, Howard (1960), in a comparison of sophomore and senior high school girls, found a nonsignificant increase in scores on her own identity questionnaire.

Cross-sectional studies involving the ego identity interview were conducted by Meilman (1979) and Archer (Note 2). The participants in Meilman's study were college-bound males aged 12, 15, and 18 years.[2] Those in Archer's study were males and females from Grades 6, 8, 10, and 12, without restriction as to future plans. In both studies, at the youngest age level virtually all participants were in the foreclosure and/or identity diffusion statuses. The foreclosure status was more frequent in the areas of sex role attitudes (included only in Archer's study), avocational choice (included only in Meilman's study), and religious beliefs (included in both studies), and the identity diffusion status was most frequent in the area of political ideology (included in both studies). In comparison, the oldest high school samples evidenced more instances of the identity achievement status in both studies, and these increases with age were distributed across all content areas. There were corresponding decreases in instances of the identity diffusion status, also distributed across the various content areas. The frequencies of the moratorium and foreclosure statuses did not change substantially during the period considered here.

Hauser (1971) conducted a longitudinal study with a small sample of white and black male high school students from lower socioeconomic status backgrounds. He used a combination of interview and Q-sort procedures over a 3-year period. He found the white adolescents to show a pattern of "progressive identity formation" characterized by frequent changes in self-concept during the early high school years followed by increasing consistency and stability as the person approached high school graduation. In contrast, the black adolescents showed a general stability in their identity elements over the entire study period, a pattern Hauser termed "identity foreclosure." He interpreted this lack of change as reflecting a problem in development in that important developmental issues had been dodged rather than resolved. Many of the stable identity elements were defined in the negative; that is, the adolescent knew what he did not want to become rather than what alternative he actively wanted to pursue. The result was a rigid and impoverished self-definition.[3] Hauser speculated that these racial differences may have resulted from greater discrimination directed toward poor blacks than toward whites from the same background.

Development during the college years. It is during the college years that the greatest gains in identity formation appear to occur. College environments provide a diversity of experiences that can serve both to trigger consideration of identity issues and to suggest alternative resolutions for identity concerns. The results of numerous studies confirm that, in general, senior men and women have a stronger sense of personal identity than do their freshman counterparts and that the identity commitments held as seniors are more likely to have been arrived at through the successful resolution of identity crises.

Cross-sectional studies using paper-and-pencil measures of identity yield a consistent pattern of findings, with high scores associated with advancing age and/or years in

[2] Meilman (1979) also included samples of males aged 21 and 24 years.

[3] In Marcia's (1966) classification system, such individuals would probably have been termed identity diffuse.

college. Such results have been found for the Dignan Ego Identity Scale (Dignan, 1965; Stark & Traxler, 1974; Thompson, 1963) and the Stage 5 scale of the Inventory of Psychosocial Development (Constantinople, 1969; Whitbourne, Jelsma, & Waterman, 1982), though the effects were not always statistically significant.[4] Longitudinal studies using the Inventory of Psychosocial Development provide further evidence of identity development during the college years (Constantinople, 1969, 1970; Whitbourne et al., 1982). Fry (1974) found significant gains on the Stage 5 components for a sample of college students from rural backgrounds but a retrogressive shift for those from urban backgrounds.

There have been three longitudinal studies tracing identity development among college students using the ego identity interview procedure. Adams and Fitch (in press) interviewed males and females from different college cohorts at a state university in successive years. In the other studies, changes from the freshman to the senior year were assessed among male students at a technological institute (Waterman & Waterman, 1971; Waterman, Geary, & Waterman, 1974) and at a private liberal arts college (Waterman & Goldman, 1976). In each of the studies, the interview covered the areas of vocational choice, religious beliefs, and political ideology. The results from the three schools were quite similar.

1. College clearly facilitates identity development in the area of vocational plans. In both studies covering the 4-year period from the freshman to the senior year, there were significant increases in the frequency of students in the identity achievement status and decreases in the frequency of students in the moratorium status. In addition, there was a decrease in the frequency of students in the identity diffusion status at the liberal arts college. In the 1-year study, there was a significant decrease in the frequency of identity diffusions and a nonsignificant increase in the frequency of identity achievers.

2. College experiences appear to undermine traditional religious beliefs without necessarily helping the students to establish alternate belief systems. At all three colleges there were significant decreases in the frequency of students in the foreclosure status. At the state university there was an increase in the frequency of students in the identity achievement status, and at the technological school there was an increase in the frequency of identity diffusions.

3. Although the development of new, clearer commitments in the area of political ideology was observed to occur during the college years, a substantial proportion of the students demonstrated little interest in the topic. Significant increases in the frequency of the identity achievement status were observed over 1 year at the state university and over 4 years at the technological institute. At the state university there was also a significant increase in the frequency of the moratorium status. Significant decreases were found for the identity diffusion status at the state university and the foreclosure status at the technological institute. No systematic changes were found for the students at the private liberal arts colleges. In both 4-year studies, more than half of the participants were approaching graduation without clear beliefs in this area and without trying to form any commitments.

The patterns of identity development observed were relatively consistent across the three studies, but some differences were evident. The differences may have been due to the distinctive characteristics of the student populations at the three schools. Differences in the timing of the studies may also have affected the results, particularly in the area of political ideology. For example, the first 4-year study was conducted at the technological institute from 1968 to 1972 during the height of the antiwar protest. The second study, conducted at the private liberal arts college, took place from 1970 to 1975, with the senior-year interviews conducted after the issue of the war had largely subsided and following the Watergate scandal. It should also be noted that in all three studies, follow-up data were only obtained from individuals

[4] Protinsky (1975) found a similar difference in a comparison of junior high school students and college students for the Stage 5 items of the Rasmussen Ego Identity Scale. However, the broad age range of the participants in the study does not permit a determination as to the timing of development.

who continued at their respective schools throughout the period of the research. As yet, nothing is known about the patterns of development of those who withdraw from college.

Development during the adult years. To date only limited research has been conducted concerning identity among adults. Waterman and Waterman (1975) compared the distribution of the identity status of college males and their fathers. They found that the fathers (men between the ages of 40 and 65 years) were more frequently in the foreclosure status in the three topic areas covered in the interview (vocational choice, religious beliefs, and political ideology). Their sons were more likely to be in the moratorium and identity diffusion statuses. A very high percentage of foreclosures was also found in a sample of married adult women between the ages of 23 and 50 years (Waterman, Note 3). All of the women were from middle-class communities, were in their initial marriage, and had at least one child aged 17 years or less living at home. The greatest concentrations of foreclosure decisions were in the topic areas of family/career priorities, religious beliefs, and sex role attitudes. It seems reasonable to suggest that the high percentage of foreclosures among these adult men and women were a function of the societal conditions that were present when they were in the stages of adolescence and youth (e.g., the depression, World War II, or the Korean War). These studies may tell us more about the impact of sociohistorical events than about ontogenetic development.

O'Connell (1976) conducted a retrospective study of identity synthesis in married women with school-aged children. The women were classified as traditional (full-time homemakers), neotraditional (having resumed a career after an interruption for child bearing), or nontraditional (continuously committed to their careers). On the Sense of Identity Inventory, women in all samples indicated they had experienced an increasingly strong sense of identity as they moved from adolescence through the periods when they were first married, had their first child, and their children were of preschool age, to the point where their children were of school age. O'Connell observed that after marriage "traditional and neotraditional women's sense of identity seems to undergo a moratorium [i.e., a hiatus] which is not terminated until the school children stage of the life cycle, while nontraditional women develop their sense of identity in a more straightforward progression" (p. 683).

Two longitudinal studies have traced identity development from the college years into adulthood. Whitbourne and Waterman (1979), using the Inventory of Psychosocial Development, conducted a follow-up with male and female college alumni 10 years after they had completed the instrument as undergraduates. A significant increase was found for the Stage 5 scale assessing identity versus identity diffusion. Marcia (1976), using the ego identity interview, followed up on 30 men who had originally been interviewed 6 years earlier while in college. All were living within a 50-mile radius of the city in which their college was located. The results were reported in terms of changes in overall identity status, a judgment arrived at by combining information from the vocational, religious, and political content areas of the interview. The identity statuses, aside from the moratorium status, were fairly stable (70%). The individuals in the foreclosure and identity diffusion statuses were found to be more stable than were those in the identity achievement status. Six of the 7 identity achievers at the time of the first interview were committed, as well, in the follow-up. However, 3 of the men were classified as foreclosures. These must be considered as anomolous changes, since once a person goes through an identity crisis, he or she can no longer fit the technical definition of the foreclosure status.[5] Five of the 7 moratoriums in college had firm commitments at the follow-up, and 2 had become diffuse. Only 1 of the 16 participants who were foreclosed or diffuse at the beginning of the study had become an identity achiever, while 2 others were going through an identity crisis 6 years later. Thus it appears that the adult years

[5] Waterman et al. (1974) analyzed instances of anomolous scoring and found them due to (a) respondents' failing to report some significant piece of information in one interview that was reported in another interview and (b) inconsistent application of the scoring standards.

are a period of strengthening of identity but not a time when many new identity issues are raised or novel possibilities considered.[6]

Comparative Stability of the Identity Statuses

The three longitudinal studies of identity development during the college years have also provided data on the relative stability of the identity statuses. Comparisons of relative stability can be made for a 1-year period at the state university (Adams & Fitch, in press) and for a 4-year period at the technological institute (Waterman & Waterman, 1971; Waterman et al., 1974) and the private liberal arts college (Waterman & Goldman, 1976). Table 1 contains the percentage of instances in which an individual was in the same identity status at both the beginning and end of the study period in a particular content area of the interview.[7]

As expected, the moratorium status was the least stable of the four statuses across the period from the freshman to the senior year and was the second least stable status in the shorter study. In the two 4-year studies, there were 34 instances of identity crises in particular interview areas found at the start of the freshman year. Not one of these crises was continuing during the senior year. Of these crises over three quarters ended in the formation of clearly defined, personally meaningful commitments. At the technological institute 76% of the moratoriums had become identity achievers, and the corresponding figure at the private liberal arts college was 85%. Considering only those instances in the 1-year study in which the person had emerged from the moratorium status, in 85% of cases firm commitments had been developed. Thus, there is a very high probability that identity crises experienced in college will be successfully resolved.

The stability of the other identity statuses was generally comparable. It was evident that in instances where individuals had firm commitments at the start of the study, approximately one third to one half were no longer in the same identity status by the time of the follow-up. This finding for the identity achievement status makes it clear that the successful resolution of an identity crisis does not give a permanence to the commitment formed. Although the achievement status is slightly more stable than the foreclosure status, both statuses are affected by factors leading to the initiation of a crisis or to regression.

When the comparative stability data are analyzed separately for the different content areas of the interview, some differences emerged. The identity achievement and foreclosure statuses were more stable in the area of vocational plans than in the other topic areas. Conversely, the identity diffusion status was more stable in the areas of religious beliefs and political ideology than in the area of vocational plans. The moratorium status was highly unstable in all interview areas.

Sex Differences in Identity Development

The paper-and-pencil measures of the identity construct indicate few differences between males and females. Sex differences have not been found on the identity items of the Inventory of Psychosocial Development (Constantinople, 1969; Waterman & Whitbourne, 1981; Whitbourne & Waterman, 1979); the Identity Achievement Status Scale (Simmons, 1970); the Texas Psychosocial Identity Scale (Dunivant & Bieri, Note 4); the Objective Measure of Ego Identity Status (Adams, Shea, & Fitch, 1979); Rasmussen's Ego Identity Scale (Pomerantz, 1979); or Marcia's Ego Identity–In-

[6] The limited number of instances in which the adult men (Waterman & Waterman, 1975) and adult women (Waterman, Note 3) were found to be in the identity achievement status for the most part did involve crises occurring during the adult years. Because these frequencies were small, however, the findings can be viewed as consistent with the conclusion that the adult years do not constitute a period of extensive redirection of identity choices. In this regard, the phenomenon of midlife crisis should be studied from an identity status perspective. If such crises are or become frequent within the society, and if such crises entail the reflective consideration of identity alternatives, the above stated conclusion will have to be modified.

[7] The relative stability percentages reported here are underestimates of the actual extent of change, since individuals who went through several changes during the study period and who resumed the same status they were in initially would be counted as stable. The content of the identity elements at the second interview may have been the same or different from their initial ideas.

Table 1
Percent Stability of the Ego Identity Statuses in Longitudinal Research

Identity status	1-year stability at state university[a]	4-year stability at technological institute[b]	4-year stability at private liberal arts college[c]
Identity achievement	68	59	54
Moratorium	50	9	0
Foreclosure	61	44	46
Identity diffusion	42	50	67

[a] Data from Adams and Fitch, in press.
[b] Data from Waterman and Waterman, 1971, and Waterman, Geary, and Waterman, 1974.
[c] Data from Waterman and Goldman, 1976.

complete Sentences Blank (La Voie, 1976). Dunivant and Bieri (Note 4) did find females to score higher than males on Gruen's (1960) Ego Identity Scale and Block's (1961) Role Consistency Index.

At least 10 studies have been conducted that can be used for comparisons of the distribution of the various identity statuses between males and females. Two involved samples of high school upperclassmen or recent high school graduates (Waterman & Archer, 1979; Grotevant, Note 5); six involved college samples (Adams & Fitch, in press; Hodgson & Fisher, 1979; Orlofsky, 1978; Poppen, 1974; Waterman & Nevid, 1977; Rothman, Note 6); one involved a sample of 17- to 18-year-old Danish students (Matteson, 1977); and one involved adults (Tesch, 1980). Some differences emerged in particular content areas.

Vocational choice. No sex differences were observed in either high school sample or in five of the six college samples. In one college sample, males were more frequently in the identity achievement status, and females were more frequently foreclosed or diffuse (Hodgson & Fisher, 1979). Also, the Danish males showed more exploration of occupational alternatives than did the females (Matteson, 1977). No difference was found for the adult sample.

Religious beliefs. Among the high school students, Waterman and Archer (1979) found that males were disproportionately present in the foreclosure category and females were overrepresented in the identity diffusion status. Grotevant (Note 5) found no difference in this area. At the college level, two studies indicated tendencies for males to more likely be identity achievers (Adams & Fitch, in press; Hodgson & Fisher, 1979); one showed a significant effect for females to be more frequently in the achiever status (Orlofsky, 1978); and three revealed no differences (Poppen, 1974; Waterman & Nevid, 1977; Rothman, Note 6). The adult sample did not yield a significant difference.

Political ideology. Prior to the college years, Grotevant (Note 5) found males to be more frequently in the identity achievement status and females more often in the moratorium status. In contrast, Waterman and Archer (1979) found males to be overrepresented in the foreclosure category and females to be more frequently diffuse. Significant differences were also observed in two of the college studies, with males more often in the identity achievement status and females overrepresented in the foreclosure status (Adams & Fitch, in press; Hodgson & Fisher, 1979). No differences were found in the other four college studies, nor were any found in the study of adults.

Attitudes toward premarital intercourse. In three of the five college studies that included this topic area, females were found to be more frequently reported as identity achievers than were males, whereas the males were more frequently foreclosed or diffuse (Orlofsky, 1978; Poppen, 1974; Waterman & Nevid, 1977). Rothman (Note 6) found the identity achievement status to be the most frequent for both males and females, with males more likely to be in the moratorium status and females more likely to be foreclosed. No differences were found by Hodgson and Fisher (1979). Matteson

(1977) reported that among Danish students, females were more likely than males to undergo exploration of sexual identity alternatives.

Sex role attitudes. At the high school level, no sex differences were observed in either study. Only one of the college studies included the topic of sex roles, and as in the area of sexual attitudes, females were more likely to be in the identity achievement and moratorium statuses, whereas the males were more likely to be foreclosed or diffuse (Hodgson & Fisher, 1979). Tesch (1980) found a trend toward a sex difference in this area for adults, with females somewhat more likely to be in the moratorium status and males overrepresented in the foreclosure category.

Psychological significance of the identity statuses for males and females. The results of these analyses for sex differences suggest that in most interview topic areas, males and females undergo similar patterns of identity development. Only in the area of attitudes toward sexual behavior was there general, though not complete, consistency among the studies, indicating the use of different processes. (Not enough research on sex role attitudes has been conducted to reach a conclusion regarding this topic.) It is clear that males and females are more similar than different in their use of developmental processes, but there is reason to believe that the identity statuses may nevertheless have different psychological implications for the sexes (Marcia, 1980). For both sexes, the identity achievement status is associated with relatively good adaptive capacities, whereas the identity diffusion status is often associated with difficulties in coping. For the moratorium and foreclosure statuses, however, sex differences emerge. Among males, individuals in the moratorium status look generally similar in behavioral traits to identity achievers, and both stand in contrast with males in the foreclosure and identity diffusion statuses. Among females the patterns are more complex, with women in the foreclosure and identity achievement statuses looking most similar on some qualities, while on others it is the identity achievement and moratorium women who appear most similar. Marcia (1980) suggests that "the relative adaptiveness of the Moratorium and Foreclosure status for women is a function both of the dependent variables used in a particular study and of the existing cultural supports for women's explorations of alternatives" (p. 175).

Antecedent Conditions Relating to Identity Development

A large number of hypotheses were offered regarding variables that may contribute to determining the course of identity development, but only a few have been investigated. The search for antecedent influences has focused on family variables, developmental characteristics believed to be hierarchically related to identity, and personal activities and interests.

Family variables. Considerable attention has been directed toward identifying the nature of differences in family relationships and parenting styles characteristic of individuals in the various identity statuses. Since Marcia (1980) has reviewed this literature in some detail, only a brief summary of the findings will be presented here.

As would be expected, foreclosures have been found to have the closest relationships with their parents. Both sons and daughters evaluate their parents most favorably and describe their families as child centered. The fathers of foreclosures are seen as relatively possessive and intrusive toward their sons while being more supportive and encouraging of their daughters. In turn, foreclosure sons are the most willing to involve their families in making important life decisions. In contrast, identity diffusions of both sexes reported the most distance from their families. The parents of identity diffusions were seen as indifferent, inactive, detached, not understanding, and rejecting. Both males and females in the moratorium and identity achievement statuses were relatively critical of their parents and were likely to report themselves to be in conflict with their families. Sons in these statuses were not likely to turn to their families when making important life decisions. This tension within the family appears related to ambivalence on the part of both parents and offspring over the latter's attempts at individuation. With the successful resolution of an identity crisis, better family relationships may be established. Finally, there is evidence that, in general, the nature of the relationship with the parent of the same sex is more strongly related to identity status than is the relationship with the opposite-sex parent.

It is an attractive hypothesis that parental behavior contributes to identity formation, and the pattern of research results obtained provides readily interpretable links between family functioning and the various identity statuses. However, for both methodological and conceptual reasons, it cannot be concluded that the family variables studied actually do influence the process of identity development. In most studies, the researchers have relied solely on verbal report measures obtained from adolescent or youth respondents. These measures are subject to errors of memory, defensive distortion, and conscious impression management. The same problems exist in those studies where information was obtained from the parents. Even if the accuracy of the reports were assumed, it would still not be possible to reach a conclusion concerning any causal contribution of family variables. The type of behavior shown by a son or daughter may well have elicited particular responses from the parents, which could account for the observed relationships. It is far easier to provide a supportive, child-centered environment when children identify strongly with the parents and follow family traditions without questioning. In contrast, the ambivalence and conflict found in the family backgrounds of moratoriums and identity achievers may be a response to the sometimes extreme shifts in behavior engaged in by a son or daughter going through a stressful, and stressing, identity search. Similarly, it is possible that the lack of involvement shown by the parents of identity diffusions may be at least partially the result of a child's giving few strongly directed behavioral stimuli to which the parents can respond. It is probably not possible to entirely unravel the complex causal effects present in any relationship of long duration. Long-term, longitudinal, predictive studies appear necessary if any meaningful evaluation is to be made of the likelihood that parenting behaviors contribute to the process by which identity is formed.

Along another line, Waterman and Waterman (1975) hypothesized that parents may serve as role models for the type of decision-making processes involved in identity formation. However, they found no relationship between the identity statuses shown by a sample of fathers and their college-attending sons.

Variables relating to family stability have also been investigated as possible contributors to identity development with conflicting results to date. Oshman and Manosevitz (1976) found that a sample of college males who experienced father absence from an average age of about 10 years had significantly lower full scale scores on the Rasmussen Ego Identity Scale than did samples from intact families and families in which the mothers had remarried. The directions of differences were the same on all Ego Identity Scale stage scales, but the effect for the Stage 5 (identity vs. identity diffusion) items was not significant. Jordan (1970) found that college males in the identity diffusion status were more likely to have come from broken homes than were those in the other statuses. In contrast, St. Clair and Day (1979) reported that in a sample of high school females, two thirds of the students in the identity achiever status came from homes disrupted by divorce or the death of one parent, whereas less than one fifth of the students in each of the other statuses were from broken homes. Also, Grossman, Shea, and Adams (1980) found that male college students with a history of parental divorce scored higher on Marcia's Ego Identity-Incomplete Sentences Blank than did males from intact families or females from either divorced or intact families.

Developmental characteristics. One test of the epigenetic principle—that the successful resolution of the crisis associated with each of the earlier stages of psychosocial development provides the foundation for the successful development of identity—is furnished by the pattern of intercorrelations among the stage scales of the Inventory of Psychosocial Development (Constantinople, 1969). This instrument is designed to assess the personality components associated with each of the first six stages in Erikson's theory. As expected, the scores on the Stage 5 scale for identity versus identity diffusion have been shown to yield significant correlations with each of the earlier stage scales in samples of undergraduates drawn from five colleges and a sample of adult college alumni (La Voie & Adams, in press; Waterman, Buebel, & Waterman, 1970; Waterman & Whitbourne, 1981). Marcia and Miller (Note 7), working with a sample of adult women, compared the identity statuses, as assessed by the ego identity interview, with regard to scores from the Inventory of Psychosocial Development. Women in the identity achievement status had the highest scores on each of the early stage scales, whereas those in the identity diffusion status consistently had the lowest scores. Rothman (1978) conducted a similar study with a college student sample using the Rasmussen Ego Identity Scale instead of the Inventory of Psychosocial Development. Again the identity diffusion status was associated with the lowest scores on each of the early stage scales, but no clear pattern existed among the other statuses. The stage components of autonomy and industry most clearly discriminated among the statuses.

Ego identity has also been presumed to rest upon a developmental foundation provided by other aspects of ego functioning than those focused on by Erikson. Efforts have been made to relate progress in identity formation to Loevinger's ego stages, Kohlberg's stages of moral reasoning, and Piaget's stages of cognitive functioning. In each instance there is a possibility that a certain level of stage functioning may constitute a necessary but not sufficient condition for adopting a particular path of identity formation.

A positive relationship between identity and Loevinger's ego stages was obtained by Adams and Shea (1979) in a sample of male and female college students. They reported that while 20% of individuals in the identity diffusion status were in the Δ stage of self-protective functioning (the lowest stage observed in the sample), less than 4% of those in each of the other statuses were at that level. In contrast, only 5% of identity diffusions were at or above the I-4 stage of conscientious functioning; the corresponding percentages for the other status were 19% for foreclosures, 29% for moratoriums, and 37% for identity achievers. The only two individuals at the I-6 stage of integrated functioning were in the identity achievement status. These data suggest that the attainment of Stage I-4 could constitute a necessary but not sufficient condition for movement out of the identity diffusion status. (The few exceptions found in the study may have been a function of measurement error on either variable.) The possibility also exists that Stage I-6 is a necessary condition for becoming an identity achiever, but the extremely small sample involved renders such a relationship highly speculative.

Adams and Fitch (1981) conducted a 1-year follow-up with the sample from the previous study. They found considerable change in both identity status and ego stage. Cross-lagged correlations using continuous measures on both variables yielded evidence of contemporaneous change but not sequentiality. (It should be noted that the continuous measure of identity did not preserve the uniqueness of the different identity statuses.)

A positive relationship between identity status and level of moral reasoning was obtained in three studies of college samples using Kohlberg's interview procedure or a modification of it (Podd, 1972; Poppen, 1974; Rowe & Marcia, 1980). The identity achievement status was most strongly associated with postconventional moral reasoning, whereas the foreclosure and identity diffusion statuses were overrepresented at the preconventional and conventional levels. Cauble (1976) did not find a difference between the combined identity achievement and moratorium statuses and the combined foreclosure and identity diffusion statuses using Rest's Defining Issues Test as the measure of moral reasoning. The study by Podd provided data in a form most suitable for determining whether the postconventional level of reasoning serves as a necessary but not sufficient condition for entering the moratorium and/or identity achievement statuses. He found 51% of the participants in the identity achievement status to be functioning at the postconventional level. The corresponding percentages for the other statuses were 31% for moratorium, 12% for foreclosure, and 9% for identity diffusion. Thus, although a relationship between the two developmental schemes is apparent, postconventional reasoning does not serve as a necessary condition for entering or successfully resolving an identity crisis.

It has also been hypothesized that formal operational thought is related to the likelihood of undergoing and resolving an identity crisis (Inhelder & Piaget, 1958; Kohlberg & Gilligan, 1971). However, the research results obtained to date have been largely negative. Neither Berzonsky, Weiner, and Raphael (1975) nor Cauble (1976) have obtained support for the hypothesis. Rowe and Marcia (1980) obtained supportive results, but their sample size was too small for meaningful statistical analysis. Marcia (1980) suggested that methodological problems in the earlier research may account for the negative results.

Since virtually all of the research on developmental characteristics has involved assessment at only a single point in time, it is not possible to conclude that these variables actually constitute antecedents of progress in identity formation. The associations observed could be operating in either direction, or the change may be occurring simultaneously rather than sequentially. Again, longitudinal research is needed to establish whether any of the stage constructs are predictive antecedents of identity development.

Interests and activities. A large number of correlates of the identity statuses have been identified, any of which might contribute to the process of identity development; however, in only a couple of instances is there reason to believe that a sequential arrangement may exist. In the longitudinal studies conducted at the technological institute and the private liberal arts college (Waterman & Waterman, 1971; Waterman et al., 1974; Waterman & Goldman, 1976), the College Student Questionnaire–Part 1 (Peterson, 1965) was given to all participants at the beginning of their freshman year. The Cultural Sophistication scale, which taps an interest in such areas as art, music, literature, and foreign films, was found to be predictive of identity formation. At both schools, freshmen who were identity achievers scored higher on the scale than did freshmen who were not identity achievers. More importantly, students who became identity achievers during their college years had more cultural interests as freshmen than did students who did not enter the status. Cultural interests may contribute either to the creation of identity crises and/or their resolution. The exposure to new ideas through cultural media may serve to challenge the views with which a person was raised and suggest more promising identity alternatives to which commitments can be formed.

A possibly related variable shown to be associated with identity development is expressive writing activity. Among samples of both high school and college students, males and females who wrote poetry were far more likely to be in the identity achievement status than were students who had never written poetry (Waterman & Archer, 1979; Waterman, Kohutis, & Pulone, 1977). No differences were found between students who had kept a personal journal or diary and those who had not. Since expressive writing was found to have started relatively early in adolescence, the poetry writing activities were almost certainly antecedent to the achieving of a stable sense of identity.

It had been originally expected that poetry writing and journal keeping would yield similar results. The differences may be explained in terms of the ways in which the students approached the two types of expression. Both groups saw their writings as helping to increase their level of self-understanding, but there were differences in the themes written about and in the perceptions of the functions the writing served (Waterman & Archer, 1979). Journal keeping appeared to be used primarily for making a record of current activities and for describing relationships with friends and parents. In contrast, poetry writing was seen as a vehicle for the creative expression of more abstract, emotional concerns. Further, poetry writers were much more likely to want to share their writings than were journal keepers. Thus, poetry writing may be a technique that is instrumental in working through an identity crisis by aiding in the exploration of possible identity alternatives and by serving as a means for gaining feedback from others.

Rather than there being a direct, facilitative connection between cultural interests, poetry writing, and identity formation, it is possible that all three may relate to some common underlying psychological quality involving curiosity and exploration. The impetus to explore the realm of ideas and feelings through cultural media and personal emotional states through poetry writing may also be involved in the tendency to consider a variety of identity alternatives.

One other variable that may serve as an antecedent of identity formation is the individual's work history. Munro and Adams (1977) reported a comparison of the distribution of the identity statuses between samples of college students and working youth of equivalent age. They found the working sample to be more frequently in the identity achievement status and the college sample to be more often in the identity diffusion status. The groups differed significantly with respect to identity status in the areas of religious beliefs and political ideology but not with respect to vocational choice. Munro and Adams (1977) suggested that full-time employment "might stimulate rapid movement toward identity formation, while college attendance might be seen as an extended moratorium period" (p. 523).

Concluding Comments

The basic hypothesis embodied in Erikson's theory of identity development—that movement from adolescence to adulthood involves changes in identity that can be characterized as progressive developmental shifts—fares very well in empirical studies. Substantial evidence exists for both an increased probability that consideration will be given to identity alternatives and an increased probability that personally meaningful commitments will be formed. With respect to the timing of development, it appears that only limited changes occur prior to or during the high school years. The most extensive advances in identity formation occur during the time spent in college. (Not enough research has been conducted with noncollege samples of equivalent age to determine the relative contribution of ontogenetic and situational variables to such changes.) The period immediately after college appears most often to involve a consolidation of the sense of identity rather than the continued exploration of identity alternatives.

Of the topic areas that may become the focus of identity concern, the greatest documentation of progressive developmental shifts exists for vocational choice. Identity questions concerning sexual expression have not been studied longitudinally, but the high probability of the identity achievement status, at least among women, indicate similar progress in this area. Less consistency has been observed for the patterns of identity change in the areas of religious beliefs and political ideology, perhaps as a function of differences in the background characteristics of the participants in various studies or changing sociohistorical conditions.

Comparisons of the patterns of identity formation shown by males and females yield far more evidence of similarities than differences. With respect to the processes of development, the sexes show generally similar probabilities of consideration of identity alternatives and establishment of commitments. Only in the area of attitudes toward premarital sexual activity are differences evident. Here, females appear more likely to go through a period of moratorium and achieve identity commitments; males are more likely to maintain the early commitments on which they had foreclosed. The similarities between the sexes in developmental processes do not contradict the substantial evidence from other research that males and females differ in the content of their identity choices (Frieze, Parsons, Johnson, Ruble, & Zellman, 1978).

To date the research has yielded only limited information with regard to the antecedents of developmental change. Although the findings concerning the relationship between parental behavior and the identity statuses of sons and daughters are consistent with theoretical expectations, there are a number of alternative explanations available that do not involve a causal influence of the parental variables. Similarly, extensive data that are consistent with a hierarchical arrangement of Erikson's psychosocial stages exist, but the methodological limitations of the research do not permit a determination of the direction of effect. Only a couple of personality or activity variables have been identified as predictive of the direction of future identity formation.

What is needed at the present time is research that traces identity development over a relatively broad range of ages. In particular, more information is needed about both the roots of identity in the years before and during high school and the nature of identity changes during the adult years. In addition, developmental research is particularly needed on samples that do not attend college. The use of cohort-sequential methodology (Schaie, 1965, 1970) would aid in the identification of the generality of developmental patterns across cohorts. It is also recommended that longitudinal studies on identity development include the assessment of possible predictor variables of identity change.

Reference Notes

1. Marcia, J. E. *Studies in ego identity.* Unpublished manuscript, 1976. (Available from J. E. Marcia, Department of Psychology, Simon Fraser University, Burnaby, British Columbia, Canada V5A 1S6.)
2. Archer, S. L. *Ego identity development among early and mid-adolescents.* Paper presented at the meeting of the Eastern Psychological Association, New York, April 1981.
3. Waterman, A. S. *Ego identity status among married, adult women.* Paper presented at the meeting of the Eastern Psychological Association, Hartford, Connecticut, April 1980.
4. Dunivant, N., Jr., & Bieri, J. *A multimethod comparison of various measures of Erikson's concept of ego identity.* Paper presented at the meeting of the Southwestern Psychological Association, Dallas, Texas, April 1973.
5. Grotevant, H. D. Personal communication, April 7, 1981.
6. Rothman, K. M. Personal communication, February 14, 1980.
7. Marcia, J. E., & Miller, E. C. *Ego identity in mature women.* Paper presented at the meeting of the Eastern Psychological Association, Hartford, Connecticut, April 1980.

References

Adams, G. R., & Fitch, S. A. Ego stage and identity status development: A cross-lag analysis. *Journal of Adolescence*, 1981, *4*, 163–171.

Adams, G. R., & Fitch, S. A. Ego stage and identity status development: A cross-sequential analysis. *Journal of Personality and Social Psychology*, in press.

Adams, G. R., & Shea, J. A. The relationship between identity status, locus of control, and ego development. *Journal of Youth and Adolescence*, 1979, *8*, 81–89.

Adams, G. R., & Shea, J., & Fitch, S. A. Toward the development of an objective assessment of ego-identity status. *Journal of Youth and Adolescence*, 1979, *8*, 223–237.

Becker, W. C. Consequences of different kinds of parental discipline. In M. L. Hoffman & L. W. Hoffman (Eds.), *Review of child development research.* New York: Russell Sage Foundation, 1964.

Berzonsky, W. M., Weiner, A. S., & Raphael, D. Interdependence of formal reasoning. *Developmental Psychology*, 1975, *11*, 258.

Block, J. Ego identity, role variability and adjustment. *Journal of Consulting Psychology*, 1961, *25*, 392–397.

Bourne, E. The state of research on ego identity: A review and appraisal. Part I. *Journal of Youth and Adolescence*, 1978, *7*, 223–251. (a)

Bourne, E. The state of research on ego identity: A review and appraisal. Part II. *Journal of Youth and Adolescence*, 1978, *7*, 371–392. (b)

Cauble, M. A. Formal operations, ego identity, and principled morality: Are they related? *Developmental Psychology*, 1976, *12*, 363–364.

Ciaccio, N. V. A test of Erikson's theory of ego epigenesis. *Developmental Psychology*, 1971, *4*, 306–311.

Constantinople, A. An Eriksonian measure of personal development in college students. *Developmental Psychology*, 1969, *1*, 357–372.

Constantinople, A. Some correlates of average level of happiness among college students. *Developmental Psychology*, 1970, *2*, 447.

Dignan, M. H. Ego identity and maternal identification. *Journal of Personality and Social Psychology*, 1965, *1*, 476–483.

Erikson, E. H. *Young man Luther*. New York: Norton, 1958.

Erikson, E. H. Identity and life cycle: Selected papers. *Psychological Issues*, 1959, *1*(1), 1–171.

Erikson, E. H. *Childhood and society* (2nd ed.). New York: Norton 1963.

Erikson, E. H. *Identity: Youth and crisis.* New York: Norton, 1968.

Erikson, E. H. *Life history and the historical moment.* New York: Norton, 1975.

Frieze, I. H., Parsons, J. E., Johnson, P. B., Ruble, D. N., & Zellman, G. L. *Women and sex roles: A social psychological perspective.* New York: Norton, 1978.

Fry, P. S. Developmental changes in identity status of university students from rural and urban backgrounds. *Journal of College Student Personnel*, 1974, *15*, 183–190.

Grossman, S. M., Shea, J. A., & Adams, G. R. Effects of parental divorce during early childhood on ego development and identity formation of college students. *Journal of Divorce*, 1980, *3*, 263–272.

Gruen, W. Rejection of false information about oneself as an indication of ego identity. *Journal of Consulting Psychology*, 1960, *24*, 231–233.

Hauser, S. T. *Black and white identity formation*. New York: Wiley-Interscience, 1971.

Hodgson, J. W., & Fischer, J. L. Sex differences in identity and intimacy development in college youth. *Journal of Youth and Adolescence*, 1979, *8*, 37–50.

Howard, L. P. Identity conflicts in adolescent girls. *Smith College Studies in Social Work*, 1960, *31*, 1–21.

Inhelder, B., & Piaget, J. *The growth of logical thinking from childhood to adolescence*. New York: Basic Books, 1958.

Jordan, D. *Parental antecedents of ego identity formation*. Unpublished master's thesis, State University of New York at Buffalo, 1970.

Kohlberg, L., & Gilligan, C. The adolescent as a philosopher: The discovery of self in a postconventional world. *Daedalus*, 1971, *100*, 1051–1086.

La Voie, J. C. Ego identity formation in middle adolescence. *Journal of Youth and Adolescence*, 1976, *5*, 371–385.

La Voie, J. C., & Adams, G. R. Erikson developmental stage resolution and attachment behavior in young adulthood. *Adolescence*, in press.

Marcia, J. E. Development and validation of ego-identity status. *Journal of Personality and Social Psychology*, 1966, *3*, 551–558.

Marcia, J. E. Identity six years after: A follow-up study. *Journal of Youth and Adolescence*, 1976, *5*, 145–160.

Marcia, J. E. Identity in adolescence. In J. Adelson (Ed.), *Handbook of adolescent psychology*. New York: Wiley, 1980.

Matteson, D. R. Exploration and commitment: Sex differences and methodological problems in the use of identity status categories. *Journal of Youth and Adolescence*, 1977, *6*, 353–374.

Meilman, P. W. Cross-sectional age changes in ego identity status during adolescence. *Developmental Psychology*, 1979, *15*, 230–231.

Munro, G., & Adams, G. R. Ego-identity formation in college students and working youth. *Developmental Psychology*, 1977, *13*, 523–524.

O'Connell, A. N. The relationship between life style and identity synthesis and resynthesis in traditional, neotraditional, and non-traditional women. *Journal of Personality*, 1976, *44*, 675–688.

Orlofsky, J. L. Identity formation, nAchievement, and fear of success in college men and women. *Journal of Youth and Adolescence*, 1978, *7*, 49–62.

Oshman, H. P., & Manosevitz, M. Father absence: Effects of stepfathers upon psychosocial development in males. *Developmental Psychology*, 1976, *12*, 479–480.

Peterson, R. E. *Technical manual: College Student Questionnaires*. Princeton, N.J.: Educational Testing Service, 1965.

Podd, M. H. Ego identity status and morality: The relationship between two developmental constructs. *Developmental Psychology*, 1972, *6*, 497–507.

Pomerantz, S. C. Sex differences in the relative importance of self-esteem, physical self-satisfaction and identity in predicting adolescent satisfaction. *Journal of Youth and Adolescence*, 1979, *8*, 51–61.

Poppen, P. J. *The development of sex differences in moral judgment for college males and females*. Unpublished doctoral dissertation, Cornell University, 1974.

Protinsky, H. O., Jr. Eriksonian ego identity in adolescents. *Adolescence*, 1975, *10*, 428–432.

Rasmussen, J. E. An experimental approach to the concept of ego identity as related to character disorder. *Dissertation Abstracts*, 1961, *22*, 1711–1712. (University Microfilms No. 61-3723)

Rothman, K. M. Multivariate analysis of the relationship of psychosocial crisis variables to ego identity status. *Journal of Youth and Adolescence*, 1978, *7*, 93–105.

Rowe, I., & Marcia, J. E. Ego identity status, formal operations, and moral development. *Journal of Youth and Adolescence*, 1980, *9*, 87–99.

Schaie, K. W. A general model for the study of developmental problems. *Psychological Bulletin*, 1965, *64*, 92–107.

Schaie, K. W. A reinterpretation of age related changes in cognitive structure and functioning. In L. R. Goulet & P. B. Baltes (Eds.), *Life-span developmental psychology: Research and theory*. New York: Academic Press, 1970.

Simmons, D. D. Development of an objective measure of identity achievement status. *Journal of Projective Techniques and Personality Assessment*, 1970, *34*, 241–244.

Stark, P. A., & Traxler, A. J. Empirical validation of Erikson's theory of identity crises in late adolescence. *Journal of Psychology*, 1974, *86*, 25–33.

St. Clair, S., & Day, H. D. Ego identity status and values among high school females. *Journal of Youth and Adolescence*, 1979, *8*, 317–326.

Tesch, S. A. *Intimacy and identity development in early adulthood*. Unpublished doctoral dissertation, University of Rochester, 1980.

Thompson, M. St. G. *Modifications in identity: A study of the socialization process during a sister formation program*. Unpublished doctoral dissertation, University of Chicago, 1963.

Waterman, A. S., & Archer, S. Ego identity status and expressive writing among high school and college students. *Journal of Youth and Adolescence*, 1979, *8*, 327–341.

Waterman, A. S., Geary, P. S., & Waterman, C. K. A longitudinal study of changes in ego identity status from the freshman to the senior year at college. *Developmental Psychology*, 1974, *10*, 387–392.

Waterman, A. S., & Goldman, J. A. A longitudinal study of ego identity development at a liberal arts college. *Journal of Youth and Adolescence*, 1976, *5*, 361–369.

Waterman, A. S., Kohutis, E., & Pulone, J. The role of expressive writing in ego identity formation. *Developmental Psychology*, 1977, *13*, 286–287.

Waterman, A. S., & Waterman, C. K. A longitudinal study of changes in ego identity status during the freshman year at college. *Developmental Psychology*, 1971, *5*, 167–173.

Waterman, A. S., & Whitbourne, S. K. The Inventory of Psychosocial Development: A review and evaluation. JSAS *Catalog of Selected Documents in Psychology*, 1981, *11*, 5. (Ms. No. 2179)

Waterman, C. K., Buebel, M. E., & Waterman, A. S. The relationship between resolution of the identity crisis and outcomes of previous psychosocial crises. *Proceedings of the 78th Annual Convention of the American Psychological Association*, 1970, *5*, 467–468. (Summary)

Waterman, C. K., & Nevid, J. S. Sex differences in the resolution of the identity crisis. *Journal of Youth and Adolescence*, 1977, *6*, 337–342.

Waterman, C. K.,.& Waterman, A. S. Fathers and sons: A study of ego identity across two generations. *Journal of Youth and Adolescence*, 1975, *4*, 331–338.

Whitbourne, S. K., Jelsma, B. M., & Waterman, A. S. An Eriksonian measure of personality development in college students: A reexamination of Constantinople's data and a partial replication. *Developmental Psychology*, 1982, *18*, 369–371.

Whitbourne, S. K., & Waterman, A. S. Psychosocial development during the adult years: Age and cohort comparisons. *Developmental Psychology*, 1979, *15*, 373–378.

Received June 4, 1981 ■

Journal of Personality and Social Psychology
1966, Vol. 3, No. 5, 551–558

DEVELOPMENT AND VALIDATION OF EGO-IDENTITY STATUS [1]

JAMES E. MARCIA

State University of New York at Buffalo

4 modes of reacting to the late adolescent identity crisis were described, measured, and validated. Criteria for inclusion in 1 of 4 identity statuses were the presence of crisis and commitment in the areas of occupation and ideology. Statuses were determined for 86 college male Ss by means of individual interviews. Performance on a stressful concept-attainment task, patterns of goal setting, authoritarianism, and vulnerability to self-esteem change were dependent variables. Ss higher in ego identity performed best on the concept-attainment task; those in the status characterized by adherence to parental wishes set goals unrealistically high and subscribed significantly more to authoritarian values. Failure of the self-esteem condition to discriminate among the statuses was attributed to unreliability in self-esteem measurement.

Ego identity and identity diffusion (Erikson, 1956, 1963) refer to polar outcomes of the hypothesized psychosocial crisis occurring in late adolescence. Erikson views this phase of the life cycle as a time of growing occupational and ideological commitment. Facing such imminent adult tasks as getting a job and becoming a citizen, the individual is required to synthesize childhood identifications in such a way that he can both establish a reciprocal relationship with his society and maintain a feeling of continuity within himself.

Previous studies have attempted to determine the extent of ego-identity achievement by means of an adjustment measure and the semantic differential technique (Bronson, 1959), a *Q*-sort measure of real-ideal-self discrepancy (Gruen, 1960), a measure of role variability based on adjective ranking (Block, 1961), and a questionnaire (Rasmussen, 1964). While these studies have investigated self-ratings on characteristics that should follow if ego identity has been achieved, they have not dealt explicitly with the psychosocial criteria for determining degree of ego identity, nor with testing hypotheses regarding direct behavioral consequences of ego identity.

To assess ego identity, the present study used measures and criteria congruent with Erikson's formulation of the identity crisis as a *psychosocial* task. Measures were a semistructured interview and an incomplete-sentences blank. The interview (see Method section) was used to determine an individual's specific identity status; that is, which of four concentration points along a continuum of ego-identity achievement best characterized him. The incomplete-sentences blank served as an overall measure of identity achievement. The criteria used to establish identity status consisted of two variables, crisis and commitment, applied to occupational choice, religion, and political ideology. Crisis refers to the adolescent's period of engagement in choosing among meaningful alternatives; commitment refers to the degree of personal investment the individual exhibits.

"Identity achievement" and "identity diffusion" are polar alternatives of status inherent in Erikson's theory. According to the criteria employed in this study, an identity-achievement subject has experienced a crisis period and is committed to an occupation and ideology. He has seriously considered several

[1] This paper is based in part on a doctoral dissertation submitted to the Ohio State University (Marcia, 1964).

The author is indebted to D. P. Crowne, director of the dissertation, and to G. A. Kelly for their guidance and criticism during various phases of the research. The author also wishes to thank D. P. Crowne and L. H. Ford for their helpful comments concerning portions of the final manuscript. To the confederate experimenters from Hiram College, particularly to M. B. Herzbrun who served as research assistant, the author expresses his gratitude.

Parts of the research were reported in a paper read at the 1965 Midwestern Psychological Association convention.

occupational choices and has made a decision on his own terms, even though his ultimate choice may be a variation of parental wishes. With respect to ideology, he seems to have reevaluated past beliefs and achieved a resolution that leaves him free to act. In general, he does not appear as if he would be overwhelmed by sudden shifts in his environment or by unexpected responsibilities.

The identity-diffusion subject may or may not have experienced a crisis period; his hallmark is a lack of commitment. He has neither decided upon an occupation nor is much concerned about it. Although he may mention a preferred occupation, he seems to have little conception of its daily routine and gives the impression that the choice could be easily abandoned should opportunities arise elsewhere. He is either uninterested in ideological matters or takes a smorgasbord approach in which one outlook seems as good to him as another and he is not averse to sampling from all.

Two additional concentration points roughly intermediate in this distribution are the moratorium and foreclosure statuses. The moratorium subject is *in* the crisis period with commitments rather vague; he is distinguished from the identity-diffusion subject by the appearance of an active struggle to make commitments. Issues often described as adolescent preoccupy him. Although his parents' wishes are still important to him, he is attempting a compromise among them, society's demands, and his own capabilities. His sometimes bewildered appearance stems from his vital concern and internal preoccupation with what occasionally appear to him to be unresolvable questions.

A foreclosure subject is distinguished by not having experienced a crisis, yet expressing commitment. It is difficult to tell where his parents' goals for him leave off and where his begin. He is becoming what others have prepared or intended him to become as a child. His beliefs (or lack of them) are virtually "the faith of his fathers living still." College experiences serve only as a confirmation of childhood beliefs. A certain rigidity characterizes his personality; one feels that if he were faced with a situation in which parental values were nonfunctional, he would feel extremely threatened.

Previous studies have found ego identity to be related to "certainty of self-conception" and "temporal stability of self-rating" (Bronson, 1959), extent of a subject's acceptance of a false personality sketch of himself (Gruen, 1960), anxiety (Block, 1961), and sociometric ratings of adjustment (Rasmussen, 1964). Two themes predominate in these studies: a variability-stability dimension of self-concept, and overall adjustment. In general, subjects who have achieved ego identity seem less confused in self-definition and are freer from anxiety.

Four task variables were used to validate the newly constructed identity statuses: a concept-attainment task administered under stressful conditions, a level of aspiration measure yielding goal-setting patterns, a measure of authoritarianism, and a measure of stability of self-esteem in the face of invalidating information.

The hypotheses investigated were these:

1. Subjects high in ego identity (i.e., identity-achievement status) will receive significantly lower (better) scores on the stressful concept-attainment task than subjects lower in ego identity. Subjects who have achieved an ego identity, with the internal locus of self-definition which that implies, will be less vulnerable to the stress conditions of evaluation apprehension and oversolicitousness (see Method section).

2. Subjects high in ego identity will set goals more realistically than subjects low in ego identity on a level of aspiration measure. The increment to overall ego strength following identity achievement should be reflected in the ego function of reality testing.

3. Subjects in the foreclosure status will endorse "authoritarian submission and conventionality" items to a greater extent than subjects in the other statuses.

4. There will be a significant positive relationship between ego identity measures and a measure of self-esteem.

5. Subjects high in ego identity will change less in self-esteem when given false information about their personalities than subjects low in ego identity.

6. There will be a significant relationship between the two measures of ego identity: the identity-status interview and the incomplete-sentences blank.

METHOD

Subjects

Subjects were 86 males enrolled in psychology, religion, and history courses at Hiram College.

Confederate Experimenters

Due to the possibility of contamination by subject intercommunication on a small campus, the study employed 10 confederate (task) experimenters who administered the concept-attainment task in one 12-hour period to all subjects. These task experimenters, 7 males and 3 females, were members of the author's class in psychological testing and had taken three or more courses in psychology. They had previously assisted in a pilot study and had been checked twice by the author on their experimental procedure. The use of a sample of experimenters, none of whom were aware of the subjects' standings on crucial independent variables, also has advantages in terms of minimizing the effects of experimenter bias (Rosenthal, 1964).

Identity status. Identity status was established by means of a 15–30 minute semistructured interview. All interviews followed the same outline, although deviations from the standard form were permitted in order to explore some areas more thoroughly. In most cases, the criteria for terminating an interview involved the completion of the prescribed questions as well as some feeling of certainty on the interviewer's part that the individual had provided enough information to be categorized. Interviews were tape-recorded and then replayed for judging. Hence, each interview was heard at least twice, usually three or four times.

A scoring manual (Marcia, 1964) was constructed using both theoretical criteria from Erikson and empirical criteria from a pilot study. Each subject was evaluated in terms of presence or absence of crisis as well as degree of commitment for three areas: occupation, religion, and politics—the latter two combined in a general measure of ideology. The interview judge familiarized himself with the descriptions of the statuses provided in the manual and sorted each interview into that pattern which it most closely resembled. Analysis of interjudge reliability for the identity statuses of 20 randomly selected subjects among three judges yielded an average percentage of agreement of 75. One of the judges was essentially untrained, having been given only the scoring manual and the 20 taped interviews.

A sample question in the occupational area was:

> How willing do you think you'd be to give up going into ______ if something better came along?

Examples of typical answers for the four statuses were:

> [Identity achievement] Well, I might, but I doubt it. I can't see what "something better" would be for me.
>
> [Moratorium] I guess if I knew for sure I could answer that better. It would have to be something in the general area—something related.
>
> [Foreclosure] Not very willing. It's what I've always wanted to do. The folks are happy with it and so am I.
>
> [Identity diffusion] Oh sure. If something better came along, I'd change just like that.

A sample question in the religious area was:

> Have you ever had any doubts about your religious beliefs?
>
> [Identity achievement] Yeah, I even started wondering whether or not there was a god. I've pretty much resolved that now, though. The way it seems to me is . . . .
>
> [Moratorium] Yes, I guess I'm going through that now. I just don't see how there can be a god and yet so much evil in the world or . . . .
>
> [Foreclosure] No, not really, our family is pretty much in agreement on these things.
>
> [Identity diffusion] Oh, I don't know. I guess so. Everyone goes through some sort of stage like that. But it really doesn't bother me much. I figure one's about as good as the other!

Overall ego identity. The Ego Identity Incomplete Sentences Blank (EI-ISB) is a 23-item semistructured projective test requiring the subject to complete a sentence "expressing his real feelings" having been given a leading phrase. Stems were selected and a scoring manual designed (Marcia, 1964) according to behaviors which Erikson (1956) relates to the achievement of ego identity. Empirical criteria were gathered during a pilot study. Each item was scored 3, 2, or 1 and item scores summed to yield an overall ego-identity score. Two typical stems were: If one commits oneself ——, and, When I let myself go I——. Scoring criteria for the latter stem are:

> 3—Nondisastrous self-abandonment. Luxuriating in physical release. For example, have a good time and do not worry about others' thoughts and standards, enjoy almost anything that has laughter and some physical activity involved, enjoy myself more.
>
> 2—Cautiousness, don't know quite what will happen, have to be careful. Defensive or trivial. For example, never know exactly what I will say or do, sleep, might be surprised since I don't remember letting myself go.
>
> 1—Goes all to pieces, dangerous, self-destructive, better not to. For example, think I talk too much about myself and my personal interests, tend to become too loud when sober and too

melodramatic when drunk, sometimes say things I later regret.

Analysis of interscorer reliability for 20 protocols among three judges yielded an average item-by-item correlation of $\bar{r} = .76$, an average total score correlation of $\bar{r} = .73$, and an average percentage of agreement of 74.

Measures of Task Variables

Concept Attainment Task performance. The Concept Attainment Task (CAT) developed by Bruner, Goodnow, and Austin (1956) and modified by Weick (1964), requires the subject to arrive at a certain combination of attributes of cards. The subject may eliminate certain attributes by asking whether a card is positive or negative for the concept and he may guess the concept at any time. He is penalized 5 points for every request, 10 points for every guess, and 5 points for every 30 seconds that passes before he attains the concept. Level of aspiration was obtained by informing the subject of his previous time and asking him to estimate his time on the next problem.

Quality of performance on the CAT was assessed by the following measures: overall CAT scores (points for time plus points for requests and guesses), points for time alone, points for requests and guesses alone, number of "give-ups" (problems which the subject refused to complete). The main level of aspiration measure was attainment discrepancy or *D* score, the algebraic average of the differences between a subject's stated expectancy for a problem and his immediately preceding performance on a similar problem.

A combination of two stress conditions (stress defined here as externally imposed conditions which tend to impair performance) were used: evaluation apprehension and oversolicitousness. Evaluation apprehension refers to a subject's feeling that his standing on highly valued personal characteristics is to be exposed. The characteristic chosen for this study was intellectual competence, unquestionably salient for college students. Oversolicitousness was chosen as a logical complement to evaluation apprehension. It was assumed that unnecessary reassurance would validate and, hence, augment whatever anxiety the subject was experiencing.

Pilot study data indicated that the stress conditions were effective. Using the same task experimenters as in the final study, 56 subjects (27 males and 29 females) took the CAT under stress and nonstress (i.e., stress omitted) conditions. Each experimenter ran about 3 stress and 3 nonstress subjects. Stressed subjects performed significantly more poorly than nonstressed ones ($t = 2.61$, $df = 54$, $p < .02$).

Self-esteem change and authoritarianism. The Self-Esteem Questionnaire (SEQ-F) is a 20-item test developed by deCharms and Rosenbaum (1960) on which the subject indicates his degree of endorsement of statements concerning general feelings of self-confidence and worthiness.

In addition, statements reflecting authoritarian submission and conventionality, taken from the California F Scale (Adorno, Frenkel-Brunswik, Levinson, & Sanford, 1950), which were originally filler items, are used here as a dependent variable. The SEQ-F was administered twice, the first time in a classroom setting, the second, during the experimental situation following an invalidated self-definition.

The treatment condition of "invalidated self-definition" (ISD) followed the CAT and directly preceded the second administration of SEQ-F. It consisted of giving the subject false information concerning the relationship between his alleged self-evaluation and his actual personality.

Procedure

Following is the experimental procedure: Subjects completed the EI-ISB and SEQ-F in class. Each subject was interviewed to determine his identity status. (This interviewing period lasted about 2 months.) On the day of the experiment, each subject went through the following conditions: (*a*) Administration of the CAT under stress by the task experimenter. *Evaluation apprehension* was created by the task experimenter's saying:

> By the way, I thought you might be interested to know that this test is related to tests of intelligence [2] and that it's been found to be one of the best single predictors of success in college. So of course, you'll want to do your very best.

Oversolicitousness was created during CAT performance by the task experimenter's hovering over the subject, asking him if he were comfortable, advising him not to "tense up," not to "make it harder on yourself." (*b*) Following the CAT, the subject was seated in the author's office where he was given either a positive or negative (randomly assigned) invalidated self-definition. The subject found the experimenter intently scanning a data sheet and was told:

> I've been looking over some of the data and it seems that while you consider yourself less [more] mature than other subjects, you actually come out as being more [less] mature. Is there any way you can account for this discrepancy? [Pause for the subject's response.] This seems to hold up also for self-confidence. It seems that you consider yourself as having less [more] self-confidence than other subjects, yet you actually come out having more [less].

(*c*) The subject was then sent to another room where he took the SEQ-F for the second time. The following day, each subject received a postcard from the experimenter explaining the false information.

[2] In fact, intelligence test scores gleaned from the subjects' college files did correlate significantly with CAT performance ($r = .55$, $df = 82$, $p < .0005$). However, no significant relationship was found between intelligence and identity status.

TABLE 1

DIFFERENCES BETWEEN IDENTITY STATUSES IN CAT PERFORMANCE

	N	*M* time	*SD*	*M* requests + guesses	*SD*	*M* overall score	*SD*	*t*
Identity status								
Identity achievement (A)	18	18.17	7.94	599.17	186.63	791.94	244.15	
Moratorium (B)	22	24.50	15.77	807.14	495.58	1024.82	612.04	
Foreclosure (C)	23	34.20	13.84	875.82	285.44	1147.83	407.98	
Identity diffusion (D)	21	29.73	18.52	767.38	266.43	1078.57	352.38	
Groups compared								
Time								
A versus D								2.39*
A versus B + C + D								2.41**
A versus C								2.90***
A + B + D versus C								2.24*
Requests + guesses								
A versus D								2.19*
A versus B + C + D								2.28*
A versus C								3.47***
A + B + D versus C								1.69
Overall score								
A versus D								3.47***
A versus B + C + D								2.45**
A versus C								3.19***
A + B + D versus C								1.63

* $p \leq .05$.
** $p \leq .02$.
*** $p \leq .01$.

RESULTS

Performance on CAT

The relationship between the identity statuses and CAT performance was investigated by means of individual *t* tests. These are found in Table 1 and support the hypothesis of significant differences in CAT performance between subjects high and low in ego identity.

For all three indices of CAT performance identity-achievement subjects perform significantly[3] better than identity-diffusion subjects (*p*'s ranging from .01 to .05), and identity-achievement subjects perform significantly better than the other three statuses combined (*p*'s ranging from .02 to .05).

Data involving the number of problems on which the subjects in the different identity statuses gave up are presented in Table 2.

Comparing identity-achievement subjects with other subjects, significantly fewer instances of giving up on CAT problems are found for the identity-achievement subjects. This, together with the previous findings concerning the relationship between identity status and CAT performance under stress, provides substantial confirmation of Hypothesis 1.

[3] All significance levels for *t* tests are based on two-tailed tests.

TABLE 2

NUMBER OF CAT PROBLEMS ON WHICH SUBJECTS IN EACH IDENTITY STATUS GAVE UP

	Identity status				
	Identity achievement	Moratorium	Foreclosure	Identity diffusion	All other
Give-ups	1	7	13	11	31
Completions	107	125	131	109	365
	$\chi^2 = 8.93$*				$\chi^2 = 5.69$**

* $p < .05$.
** $p < .02$.

An interesting supplementary finding is that moratorium subjects were significantly more variable in overall CAT scores than subjects in the other three statuses combined ($F_{max} = 2.62$, $df = 21/61$, $p < .05$; see McNemar, 1955, pp. 244–247).

Correlations between all three CAT performance measures and the EI-ISB, while in the expected direction, failed to reach significance. The Pearson r between overall CAT performance and EI-ISB scores was $-.14$ ($df = 82$).

Level of Aspiration

The *D*, or attainment discrepancy score, reflects the difference between a subject's aspirations and his actual performance. An overall positive *D* score means that the subject tends to set his goals higher than his attainment; a negative *D* score means the opposite.

Inspection of original data revealed that no status obtained a negative average *D* score, the range being from 3.60 for identity achievement to 5.06 for foreclosure. Analysis of variance indicates a significant difference among statuses in *D* score ($F = 5.10$, $df = 3/80$, $p < .01$). The *t* tests presented in Table 3 show the foreclosure subjects exhibiting higher *D* scores than identity-achievement subjects ($t = 3.35$, $df = 38$, $p < .01$) and higher *D* scores than the other statuses combined ($t = 3.70$, $df = 82$, $p < .001$). It appears that foreclosure subjects tend to maintain high goals in spite of failure.

TABLE 3

DIFFERENCES IN *D* SCORE BETWEEN IDENTITY STATUSES

	N	*M*	*SD*	*t*
Identity status				
Identity achievement (A)	18	3.60	.80	
Moratorium (B)	22	4.11	.72	
Foreclosure (C)	23	5.06	1.65	
Identity diffusion (D)	21	3.91	1.49	
Groups compared				
C versus A				3.35*
C versus A + B + D				3.70**
B versus A				1.90
C + B + D versus A				.57

* $p \leq .01$.
** $p \leq .001$.

TABLE 4

DIFFERENCES IN F SCORES BETWEEN IDENTITY STATUSES

	N	*M*	*SD*	*t*
Identity status				
Identity achievement (A)	18	34.28	8.99	
Moratorium (B)	23	37.57	8.05	
Foreclosure (C)	24	45.17	9.01	
Identity diffusion (D)	21	38.67	10.19	
Groups compared				
C versus A				3.88*
C versus A + B + D				3.75*
D versus A				.44
B versus A				1.20

* $p \leq .001$.

Authoritarian Submission and Conventionality (F)

The *t* tests presented in Table 4 show that foreclosure subjects received significantly higher F scores than identity-achievement subjects ($t = 3.88$, $df = 38$, $p < .001$) and also significantly higher F scores than the other statuses combined ($t = 3.75$, $df = 82$, $p < .001$).

Self-Esteem

The significant relationship found here was between EI-ISB scores and the initial SEQ ($r = .26$, $df = 84$, $p < .01$). No significant differences among identity statuses for SEQ were found ($F = .66$, $df = 3/82$, *ns*). In addition, self-esteem appeared to be unrelated to authoritarian submission and conventionality ($r = -.03$, $df = 84$, *ns*) and to CAT performance ($r = -.03$, $df = 82$, *ns*).

Change in SEQ following ISD

Although differences in the expected direction were found (i.e., identity achievement changed less than identity diffusion), these were not significant ($t = 1.39$, $df = 37$, $p < .20$). Observer ratings of subjects' reactions to the invalidated self-definition indicated that this treatment condition was effective. The failure to obtain significant results may have been due to unreliability in the self-esteem measure engendered by the 2-month span between the first and second administration. There was a tendency for foreclosure subjects given negative informa-

TABLE 5
DIFFERENCES BETWEEN IDENTITY STATUSES IN EI-ISB SCORES

	N	*M*	*SD*	*t*
Identity status				
Identity achievement (A)	18	48.28	5.10	
Moratorium (B)	23	48.09	4.23	
Foreclosure (C)	24	46.17	4.62	
Identity diffusion (D)	21	43.33	3.52	
Groups compared				
A versus C				1.37
B versus C				1.41
B versus D				3.94*
A versus D				3.89*
A + C + B versus D				3.61*

* $p \leq .001$.

tion to show a greater decrease in self-esteem than identity-achievement subjects under similar conditions ($t = 2.60$, $df = 19$, $p < .02$).

No relationship was found between EI-ISB scores and self-esteem change ($r = .001$, $df = 84$, *ns*).

EI-ISB Scores and Identity Status

Two techniques were employed to assess the relationship between overall ego identity as measured by EI-ISB and identity status. These were an analysis of variance among the four statuses ($F = 5.42$, $df = 3/82$, $p < .01$), and *t* tests among the individual statuses. The latter are found in Table 5.

Identity-achievement subjects received significantly higher EI-ISB scores than did identity-diffusion subjects ($t = 3.89$, $df = 37$, $p < .001$), and the first three identity statuses taken together received significantly higher EI-ISB scores than did identity diffusion ($t = 3.62$, $df = 84$, $p < .001$). Thus, the distinctive group with respect to EI-ISB scores appears to be identity diffusion. These findings lend some support to the hypothesized relationship between overall ego identity and identity status.

DISCUSSION

Of the two approaches to the measurement of ego identity, the interview, based on individual styles, was more successful than the incomplete-sentences test, which treated ego identity as a simple linear quality.

Particularly interesting was the relationship between such apparently diverse areas as performance in a cognitive task and commitment to an occupation and ideology. The interview and the CAT tapped two prime spheres of ego function: the intrapsychic, seen on the CAT which required the individual to moderate between pressing internal stimuli (stress-produced anxiety) and external demands (completion of the task), and the psychosocial, seen in the interview which evaluated the meshing of the individual's needs and capabilities with society's rewards and demands. The relationship between these two spheres contributes validity to both the identity statuses and to the generality of the construct, ego.

No confirmation of the hypothesis relating ego identity to resistance to change in self-esteem was obtained, possibly because the length of time between the first and second SEQ administration was 2 months. The variability in subjects' self-esteem over this period of time may have obscured differences due to treatment alone.

Following are experimentally derived profiles of each status:

1. Identity achievement. This group scored highest on an independent measure of ego identity and performed better than other statuses on a stressful concept attainment task—persevering longer on problems and maintaining a realistic level of aspiration. They subscribed somewhat less than other statuses to authoritarian values and their self-esteem was a little less vulnerable to negative information.

2. Moratorium. The distinguishing features of this group were its variability in CAT performance and its resemblance on other measures to identity achievement.

3. Foreclosure. This status' most outstanding characteristic was its endorsement of authoritarian values such as obedience, strong leadership, and respect for authority. Self-esteem was vulnerable to negative information and foreclosure subjects performed more poorly on a stressful concept-attainment task than did identity-achievement subjects. In addition, their response to failure on this task was unrealistic, maintaining, rather than moderating, unattained high goals. This behavior pattern is referred to by Rotter

(1954) as "low freedom of movement [and is associated with] the achievement of superiority through identification [pp. 196–197]"—an apt description for one who is becoming his parents' alter ego.

4. Identity diffusion. While this status was originally considered the anchor point for high-low comparisons with identity achievement, it occupied this position only in terms of EI-ISB scores. CAT performance was uniformly poorer than that of identity achievement, although not the lowest among the statuses. The identity-diffuse individuals to which Erikson refers and identity-diffusion subjects in this study may be rather different with respect to extent of psychopathology. A "playboy" type of identity diffusion may exist at one end of a continuum and a schizoid personality type at the other end. The former would more often be found functioning reasonably well on a college campus. While having tapped a rather complete range of adjustment in the other statuses, the extent of disturbance of an extreme identity diffusion would have precluded his inclusion in our sample. Hence, it is the foreclosure, and not the identity-diffusion, subject who occupies the lowest position on most task variables.

In conclusion, the main contribution of this study lies in the development, measurement, and partial validation of the identity statuses as individual styles of coping with the psychosocial task of forming an ego identity.

REFERENCES

Adorno, T. W., Frenkel-Brunswik, E., Levinson, D. J., & Sanford, R. N. *The authoritarian personality.* New York: Harper, 1950.

Block, J. Ego identity, role variability, and adjustment. *Journal of Consulting Psychology,* 1961, **25**, 392–397.

Bronson, G. W. Identity diffusion in late adolescents. *Journal of Abnormal and Social Psychology,* 1959, **59**, 414–417.

Bruner, J. S., Goodnow, I. J., & Austin, G. A. *A study of thinking.* New York: Wiley, 1956.

deCharms, R., & Rosenbaum, M. E. Status variables and matching behavior. *Journal of Personality,* 1960, **28**, 492–502.

Erikson, E. H. The problem of ego identity. *Journal of the American Psychoanalytic Association,* 1956, **4**, 56–121.

Erikson, E. H. *Childhood and society.* (2nd ed.) New York: Norton, 1963.

Gruen, W. Rejection of false information about oneself as an indication of ego identity. *Journal of Consulting Psychology,* 1960, **24**, 231–233.

Marcia, J. E. Determination and construct validity of ego identity status. Unpublished doctoral dissertation, Ohio State University, 1964.

McNemar, Q. *Psychological statistics.* (2nd ed.) New York: Wiley, 1955.

Rasmussen, J. E. The relationship of ego identity to psychosocial effectiveness. *Psychological Reports,* 1964, **15**, 815–825.

Rosenthal, R. Experimenter outcome-orientation and the results of the psychological experiment. *Psychological Bulletin,* 1964, **61**, 405–412.

Rotter, J. B. *Social learning and clinical psychology.* Englewood Cliffs, N. J.: Prentice-Hall, 1954.

Weick, K. E. Reduction of cognitive dissonance through task enhancement and effort expenditure. *Journal of Abnormal and Social Psychology,* 1964, **68**, 533–539.

(Received March 19, 1965)

Developmental Psychology
1971, Vol. 5, No. 1, 167–173

A Longitudinal Study of Changes in Ego Identity Status during the Freshman Year at College

ALAN S. WATERMAN[1]
Rensselaer Polytechnic Institute
Troy, New York

AND

CAROLINE K. WATERMAN
State University of New York at Albany

Erikson described adolescence as the period of the life cycle when an individual's ego identity is most likely to undergo significant change. A longitudinal study involving 92 male college freshmen was conducted to assess the pattern of changes in ego identity status during the freshman year. Possible antecedent conditions associated with changes in status were also investigated. A positive developmental shift was observed for changes in identity status in the area of occupation while a retrogressive shift was found with regard to ideology. In addition, the hypotheses concerning psychological differences between individuals who changed their identity status and those that did not were supported. These differences involved personality characteristics which predated any of the observed changes in status.

Erikson (1959, 1968) conceptualized psychological growth in terms of the development of a series of ego components which are determined by the manner of resolution of successive psychosocial crises. An individual's resolution of each stage-specific crisis is described in terms of his position along the bipolar continuum used to define the relevant ego component. For the adolescent, the stage-specific crisis involves the establishing of a stable sense of identity, and the relevant bipolar continuum is termed identity-identity diffusion. In our society, the adolescent must make meaningful decisions about his occupational future and is also expected to develop a stable set of beliefs, for example, about religion and politics. The successful handling of these socially posed problems has been referred to as the "achieving" of an ego identity while the general absence of stable commitments is the hallmark of identity diffusion.

Based on Erikson's theory, Marcia (1966) has devised an interview technique to assess four possible positions on the identity-identity diffusion continuum: (*a*) identity achievement, (*b*) moratorium, (*c*) foreclosure, and (*d*) identity diffusion. According to Marcia, these various identity statuses can be defined on the basis of two dimensions: crisis and commitment. The term crisis is used to refer to a period of struggle or active questioning in arriving at a set of beliefs and a vocational choice. Commitment is defined as a firm unwavering decision regarding occupational plans and belief systems.

An identity achiever is someone who has gone through a period of crisis and has developed relatively firm commitments. The term moratorium is used to refer to a person who is currently in a state of crisis and is actively seeking among alternatives in an attempt to arrive at a choice. A person is classified as a foreclosure if he has never experienced a crisis but nevertheless is committed regarding occupation and beliefs. The commitments which have been made are generally ones which reflect the wishes of his parents or other authority figures. The category of identity diffusion includes individuals who are not committed to anything and who are not actively trying to make a commitment. These people may never have been in crisis, or they may have had a period of questioning but were not able to resolve it and subsequently emerged without making a choice.

While a considerable body of data is available regarding the correlates of these four

[1] Requests for reprints should be sent to Alan S. Waterman who is now at the Department of Psychology, Hartwick College, Oneonta, New York 13820.

identity statuses (Marcia, 1966, 1967; Waterman & Waterman, in press) and of identity as measured by a variety of paper-and-pencil tests (Block, 1961; Dignan, 1965; Heilbrun, 1964), only one previous study has been conducted in which the nature of developmental changes in levels of this construct was investigated. Constantinople (1969), using scales to separately assess both levels of identity and identity diffusion, found that college students showed an increase in identity and a decrease in identity diffusion as they moved from their freshman to their senior year.

In the present study, a longitudinal design was employed to assess changes in the four ego identity statuses described by Marcia over the course of students' freshman year at college. The use of the four-category classification system allows for greater specificity in describing the nature of the changes and permits a determination of the relative stabilities of the various categories of ego identity. In addition, this study was designed to yield information about personality differences between students who change their identity status and students who remain in the same category throughout the year. If antecedent conditions associated with changes in status can be identified, then future prediction of individual changes in status will become possible. Thus, this investigation was conducted in an attempt to answer the following questions: (*a*) What is the pattern of changes in ego identity status during the freshman year at college? (*b*) Are there differences in the stability of the four identity categories? (*c*) Are there specifiable personality characteristics which predate developmental changes in status?

Regarding predictions about the probable pattern of changes in identity status that would occur during the freshman year, it is clearly implied in Erikson's theory that, over time, individuals will progress from the developmentally lower end of the identity-identity diffusion continuum toward the more positive end of that continuum. This type of change is consistent with what would be expected on the basis of Sanford's (1962) view of the stimulus properties of college. He describes college as a setting in which the student is exposed to a variety of new ideas and behavior patterns that can serve to challenge his previously established ideas or stimulate him to think about questions never before considered. To the extent that this situation prevails, it is expected that there will be an increase in the frequency of students in the moratorium category and a decrease in the number of students in the foreclosure and identity diffusion statuses.

With respect to the relative stability of the various identity statuses, it was hypothesized that identity achievers will be more likely to maintain their initial status than will students in the other categories. Since identity achievers have already been through a period of crisis and have selected among various alternatives, they will, presumably, be less likely to encounter ideas not previously considered. No prediction was made as to which status would be least stable.

The predictions concerning the possible antecedents of changes in identity status were based on the findings of several studies which showed that, for a given vocational field, students who change out of that field differ in their attitudes and interests from those students who had selected the same field and do not change their plans (see Feldman & Newcomb, 1969). In other words, there is a tendency toward increased homogeneity of personality characteristics within occupational fields because many individuals who are atypical for a given vocation switch to a different field. If this generalization is applicable to the broader construct of ego identity, then the following hypothesis can be drawn: Students who change out of a given identity status will show traits and interests that are inconsistent with those usually associated with that status, while students who continue to remain in that category will show traits generally found to be associated with the particular status in question.

Preliminary analyses of the data from the subjects in this study indicated a relationship between ego identity status and two scales of the College Student Questionnaires (Peterson, 1965). The two scales were Family Independence and Cultural Sophistication. For both of these variables, subjects in the foreclosure category were consistently found to score low while identity achievers generally yielded high scores. Therefore, it was predicted that identity achievers who switched out of that status during the course of their freshman year would have *lower* scores on Family Independence and Cultural Sophistication than would students who remained in the achiever category throughout the year. Using the same line of reasoning, it was expected that students who were initially foreclosures and who changed out of that category would show *higher* scores for both variables than would subjects who did not change from their initial foreclosure status. Since the subjects' scores for these two personality variables were obtained before any assessments of ego identity were made, confirmation of the hypotheses would indicate the existence of antecedent conditions associated with developmental changes in status.

Method

Subjects

Subjects were 92 male freshmen enrolled at Rensselaer Polytechnic Institute. All but two of the subjects were white; the two others were of oriental ancestry. The students were mainly from lower-middle-socioeconomic-class backgrounds. In many instances these subjects were from families where the parents had never attended college. They were all above average in mathematical skills (average Scholastic Aptitude Test Quantitative score: 684.67) and most were above average in verbal skills (average Verbal score: 595.16). In addition, all of the subjects had originally applied to Rensselaer for the engineering program.

Measures of Ego Identity Status

Each subject's ego identity status was assessed by means of a semistructured interview which took between 15 and 30 minutes to conduct. The form of the interview was the same as that described by Marcia (1966) including questions pertaining to the student's choice of an occupational field and the nature and content of the religious and political belief systems. The questions were designed to elicit information concerning the presence or absence of a crisis in each of these areas and to permit a determination of the subject's degree of commitment to his ideas.

All interviews were taped and scored independently by at least two judges. For each subject, separate decisions were made as to his identity status in the areas of occupation and ideology. The latter judgment involved a pooling of the material gathered about his religious and political views. In addition, each subject was given a designation of an overall identity status which was derived from all of the information obtained in the interview. The average rate of interjudge agreement was approximately 72%.

In those instances where the two judges differed in their categorization for any of the three decisions, the tape was submitted to a third judge for scoring. Agreement by two of the three judges was considered sufficient for assigning the subject to an identity status. In any instance where this criterion was not met, that part of the interview was termed unscorable.

Measures from the College Student Questionnaire—Part 1

The two scales from the College Student Questionnaire—Part 1 which were considered likely to yield antecedents of changes in status were Family Independence and Cultural Sophistication. Family Independence refers to the student's degree of closeness with his parental family and the importance that parental expectations have for him. Cultural Sophistication refers to the student's degree of interest and pleasure in various areas of the humanities including literature, poetry, music, and philosophy. Both scales are composed of 10 four-alternative Likert-type items. The reliability and validity of each scale is discussed by Peterson (1965). The finding, referred to above, that identity achievers are high on Family Independence while foreclosures are low, provides further validation for that scale.

Procedure

All subjects were initially reached through the office of the dean of freshmen and asked to participate in the study. The College Student Questionnaire—Part 1 was administered during the first week of the fall semester. The initial identity status interviews were conducted during the first 5 weeks of the fall term and the follow-up interviews took place during the last 8 weeks of the spring semester. The same individual conducted all of the interviews. All of the interviewing and judging was done without knowledge of the scores on the College Student Questionnaire—Part 1. Since the hypotheses are concerned with changes in ego identity status, only data from subjects who provided scorable material from *both* the fall and spring interviews could be used to test the predictions. Seventy-seven subjects provided scorable data for occupational status on both interviews. The corresponding figure for ideological status was 80 subjects.[2]

[2] Subjects providing scorable and unscorable interviews for occupational status were compared for scores on Family Independence and Cultural Sophistication and for freshman year grade point average. The corresponding analyses were conducted for subjects who were scorable and unscorable for ideology. For none of the differences did the results approach significance. Thus, the unscorable subjects do not appear to differ in any systematic ways from those providing scorable interview data.

Results

All analyses were performed separately for occupational and ideological status because, as discussed below, the developmental patterns of changes in status were different for occupation and ideology. The use of overall status would have obscured these differences.

Changes in Status

The number of subjects in each of the four identity statuses in the areas of occupation and ideology can be seen in Table 1. This table also contains the number of freshmen changing into and out of each category over the course of the freshman year. The McNemar test for the significance of changes (see Siegel, 1956) was used to evaluate the frequency of changes for each ego identity status. Regarding occupational status, these analyses reveal a significant increase in the number of moratoriums ($\chi^2 = 6.37$, $p < .05$) and a significant decrease in the number of identity diffusions ($\chi^2 = 5.76$, $p < .05$). This pattern of changes is clearly consistent with Erikson's theory and can be viewed as a positive developmental trend. For ideology, on the other hand, there was a significant increase in the number of identity diffusions ($\chi^2 = 6.76$, $p < .01$). This change was unanticipated and represents a retrogressive shift within an Eriksonian framework.

Stability of Initial Status

For each of the initial identity statuses, derived from the fall semester interviews, the number of students who remained in the category at the second interview and the number who switched out of the category are reported in Table 2. It was found that approximately 44% of the students changed status for occupation and just over 51% did so for ideology. Chi-square analyses failed to confirm the hypothesis that the identity achievement status would be more stable than the other categories.

Antecedents of Changes in Status

It was hypothesized that subjects who changed out of a given status would indicate levels of various personality traits that were inconsistent with the levels usually associated with that status. On the other hand, subjects who remained stable in a given status would be expected to show scores on personality scales consistent with the levels generally found for that status. To test these hy-

TABLE 1

NUMBER OF SUBJECTS IN EACH OCCUPATIONAL AND IDEOLOGICAL IDENTITY STATUS AND THE NUMBER OF SUBJECTS CHANGING OUT OF AND CHANGING INTO EACH STATUS DURING THE FRESHMAN YEAR

Status	Fall interviews	Spring interviews	Changed out of status	Changed into status	χ^2
		Occupation			
Identity achievement	11	12	6	7	.08
Moratorium	11	22	4	15	6.37*
Foreclosure	23	22	8	7	.07
Identity diffusion	32	21	16	5	5.76*
		Ideology			
Identity achievement	20	14	13	7	1.80
Moratorium	8	8	6	6	.00
Foreclosure	38	31	16	9	1.96
Identity diffusion	14	27	6	19	6.76**

* $p < .05$.
** $p < .01$.

TABLE 2

NUMBER OF SUBJECTS IN EACH OCCUPATIONAL AND IDEOLOGICAL IDENTITY STATUS WHO REMAINED IN THEIR INITIAL STATUS AND WHO CHANGED OUT OF THEIR INITIAL STATUS

Status	Occupation		Ideology	
	Remained in initial status	Changed out of initial status	Remained in initial status	Changed out of initial status
Identity achievement	5	6	7	13
Moratorium	7	4	2	6
Foreclosure	15	8	22	16
Identity diffusion	16	16	8	6
Total	43	34	39	41
	$\chi^2 = 2.00$		$\chi^2 = 4.99$	

potheses, those subjects who remained in the identity achievement status were compared to those who changed out of that status, for their scores on the Family Independence and Cultural Sophistication scales of the College Student Questionnaire—Part 1. Students who remained stable were expected to show the higher scores for both variables. The corresponding comparisons were made between foreclosures whose statuses remained stable and foreclosures whose statuses changed during the freshman year. In this instance, students who changed were predicted to yield the higher scores. The data for the identity achievement status can be found in Table 3, while the corresponding data for the foreclosure status are presented in Table 4.

The *t*-test comparisons reveal that, consistent with the hypothesis, those identity achievers who remained achievers on ideology were significantly higher on both Family Independence ($t = 2.69$, $df = 18$, $p < .05$) and Cultural Sophistication ($t = 2.50$, $df = 18$, $p < .05$) than those who changed out of the achiever status. Neither of the differences for occupation approached significance.

TABLE 3

MEAN FAMILY INDEPENDENCE AND CULTURAL SOPHISTICATION SCORES FOR THOSE IDENTITY ACHIEVERS WHO REMAINED IN THAT STATUS AND THOSE WHO CHANGED

Scale	Remained in status	Changed out of status	*t*
Identity achievers for occupation			
Family Independence	20.60	23.17	−1.30
Cultural Sophistication	23.20	20.50	.80
Identity achievers for ideology			
Family Independence	27.86	21.69	2.69*
Cultural Sophistication	27.00	21.46	2.50*

* $p < .05$.

TABLE 4

MEAN FAMILY INDEPENDENCE AND CULTURAL SOPHISTICATION SCORES FOR THOSE FORECLOSURES WHO REMAINED IN THAT STATUS AND THOSE WHO CHANGED

Scale	Remained in status	Changed out of status	t
	Foreclosures on ideology		
Family Independence	22.07	24.50	1.74*
Cultural Sophistication	17.07	22.13	3.33***
	Foreclosures on ideology		
Family Independence	21.35	24.67	2.70**
Cultural Sophistication	17.33	20.33	2.10**

* $p < .10$.
** $p < .05$.
*** $p < .01$.

Regarding foreclosures, the expected tendency for those who left that status to be higher in family independence than those who remained foreclosures approached significance on occupation ($t = 1.74$, $df = 20$, $p < .10$) and attained significance for ideology ($t = 2.70$, $df = 33$, $p < .05$). Furthermore, foreclosures who left the status were higher in cultural sophistication than those who stayed in that status, and this effect was significant for both occupation and ideology ($t = 3.33$, $df = 20$, $p < .01$; $t = 2.10$, $df = 34$, $p < .05$, respectively).

Discussion

While most of the results of this study are consistent with Erikson's theory, a few of the findings are apparently incompatible with it. For example, the increase in the frequency of subjects in the moratorium category for occupation and the corresponding decrease for the identity diffusion category represents a predictable pattern of psychological growth within an Eriksonian framework. On the other hand, the significant increase in the number of identity diffusions for ideology was unexpected and can be viewed as retrogressive within the context of Erikson's theory. While it had been anticipated that the stimulus properties of college would lead to an increase in the number of students questioning their ideological beliefs, this was not the case. The topics of religion and politics appeared to be less salient for the subjects at the time of the spring interviews than they had been during the fall.

It is possible that these divergent trends for occupation and ideology reflect the relative importance of these two areas to the students. The fact that all of the subjects had selected a major field (i.e., engineering) before starting college suggests the importance of occupational questions for them. The shift toward noncommitment on matters of ideology might be due to the demands of college further diverting their attention toward vocational problems and away from questions of religion and politics. This suggests that there may be a limit to the number of areas that can be of simultaneous focus in the formation of an ego identity. Presumably, when the concerns in the area of vocational choice have been resolved, these students will be increasingly likely to try to work through problems in the general area of ideology. However, the question of whether the divergent trends found here are a function of the type of subjects studied or whether they reflect a more general phenomena, must be considered as open. It is plausible to expect that for students who consider concerns in the ideological area to be of greater importance, opposite trends might be found.

A second unanticipated aspect of the data

was the relatively large proportion of subjects who changed status in each of the areas of occupation and ideology. The fact that more than 75% of the students changed status in one or both areas suggests that either the characteristics of identity for students just beginning college are particularly unstable or that the college experiences during the freshman year are very effective in instigating change. The failure to confirm the hypothesis that the identity achievement status would be more stable than the other categories carries the implication that any resolution of the identity crisis while in high school can only be regarded as tentative. It is possible that the consideration of various alternatives while in high school makes the identity achievers receptive to new viewpoints when they are exposed to them at college which results in a reconsideration of their ideas, despite the fact that this occurs in an area that had previously been worked through.

While the general instability of the various identity statuses is high, the results of this study support the view that the changes are not random in direction and are orderly in terms of the characteristics of those individuals who change and those who remain stable. The findings, in general, supported the hypothesis that subjects who change their category have scores on personality scales inconsistent with the scores usually associated with their particular identity status. While the variables of Family Independence and Cultural Sophistication of the College Student Questionnaire—Part 1 were found to relate to changes in status for the sample employed here, it is possible that for different subject populations other variables may be involved. On the basis of the results obtained here, it can be suggested that, for any given population, the traits most likely to relate to changes in status will be those for which significant differences between the various identity statuses exist. The identification of specific antecedent conditions associated with status changes opens the possibility of eventual systematic prediction of such changes.

REFERENCES

BLOCK, J. Ego identity, role variability, and adjustment. *Journal of Consulting Psychology,* 1961, **25,** 392–397.

CONSTANTINOPLE, A. An Eriksonian measure of personality development in college students. *Developmental Psychology,* 1969, **1,** 357–372.

DIGNAN, M. H. Ego identity and maternal identification. *Journal of Personality and Social Psychology,* 1965, **1,** 476–483.

ERIKSON, E. H. Identity and the life circle. *Psychological Issues,* 1959, **1,** 1–171.

ERIKSON, E. H. *Identity: Youth and crisis.* New York: Norton, 1968.

FELDMAN, K. A., & NEWCOMB, J. M. *The impact of college on students.* San Francisco: Jossey-Bass, 1969.

HEILBRUN, A. B. Conformity to masculinity-femininity stereotypes and ego identity in adolescents. *Psychological Reports,* 1964, **14,** 351–357.

MARCIA, J. E. Development and validation of ego-identity status. *Journal of Personality and Social Psychology,* 1966, **3,** 551–558.

MARCIA, J. E. Ego identity status: Relationship to change in self-esteem, "general maladjustment," and authoritarianism. *Journal of Personality,* 1967, **35,** 118–133.

PETERSON, R. E. *Technical manual: College student questionnaires.* Princeton, N. J.: Educational Testing Service, 1965.

SANFORD, N. Developmental status of the entering freshman. In N. Sanford (Ed.), *The American college.* New York: Wiley, 1962.

SIEGEL, S. *Nonparametric statistics for the behavioral sciences.* New York: McGraw-Hill, 1956.

WATERMAN, A. S., & WATERMAN, C. K. The relationship between ego identity status and satisfaction with college. *Journal of Educational Research,* in press.

(Received April 22, 1970)

Identity Processes among Racial and Ethnic Minority Children in America

Margaret Beale Spencer
Emory University

Carol Markstrom-Adams
Utah State University

SPENCER, MARGARET BEALE, and MARKSTROM-ADAMS, CAROL. *Identity Processes among Racial and Ethnic Minority Children in America*. CHILD DEVELOPMENT, 1990, **61**, 290–310. A synthesis of the literature related to identity processes among American ethnic and racial minority children and adolescents is presented. In general, ethnic and racial identification, preferences, and attitudes have been studied among younger children, while the constructs of ego identity and ethnic identity have been generally studied among adolescents. The literature is unequally distributed across ethnic groups, with more research on African Americans and American Indians, and on Hispanics and Asians. Methodological concerns, such as problems of nonequivalence across groups, are identified in the conduct of research on ethnic and racial minorities. The synthesis concludes with an identification of intervention efforts along with an articulation of conceptual issues salient for promoting and theorizing about identity development processes among ethnic and racial minority children and adolescents.

In this article we present a synthesis and overview of the literature on identity development during childhood and adolescence for ethnic and racial minority groups in the United States. The establishment of identity is a major developmental task for all adolescents (Erikson, 1968). As a psychosocial task, striving for a sense of unification and cohesiveness in the self provides meaning, direction, and purpose while also serving a critical function for the individual's manifest competence and adaptive functioning (Allen & Majidi-Ahi, 1989).

While identity development is a complex task for all youths, it is particularly complicated for children and adolescents belonging to ethnic and racial minority groups in the United States. Minority-focused mental health research has identified several ways in which ethnicity and race affect psychological well-being. However, less attention has been given to their influences on the developing child and adolescent (Gibbs & Huang, 1989, p. 8). Specifically, the complexity of identity formation may increase as a function of color, behavioral distinctions, language differences, physical features, and long-standing, although frequently unaddressed, social stereotypes. Further, these factors operate, to varying degrees, between minority groups. For example, the issue of color may be more salient for African Americans and American Indians than it is for other minority groups (e.g., Hispanic and Asian). The persistence of color stereotyping and color bias results in the potential for unique identity formation processes for both monoracial and biracial youth (i.e., children of interracial unions). Finally, for the dimensions of color and language differences, the socialization efforts required of significant others (e.g., parents, teachers, and child-care providers) necessitate different and greater burdens and responsibilities for obtaining a maximum individual-environment fit and thus competent individual life-course outcomes (Fillmore & Britsch, 1988).

The scope of this review of the literature, then, encompasses the issues raised above. This review and synthesis of identity formation processes for racial and ethnic minority

We are appreciative of Beverly O'Shea, Dionne Thompson, and Ellen Pasco for their assistance in the preparation of this manuscript and the support of Dena Swanson and our colleagues Gerald Adams and Roger Bakeman who read an early draft. Reprint requests should be sent to Margaret Beale Spencer, Division of Educational Studies, Emory University, 201 Fishburne Building, Atlanta, GA 30322.

[*Child Development*, 1990, **61**, 290–310. 0009-3920/90/6102-0021$01.00]

children and youth is presented in four sections.

First, we begin with a statement about the relation of identity to other constructs of the self system. This initial section also includes a statement of our theoretical perspective, which "drives" the review and synthesis. In addition, we offer a brief description of the major ethnic/racial groups included in the review along with comments about each group's unique features as well as characteristics and experiences shared with other groups.

Second, we move to a review of available research on identity processes among ethnic and racial minority children. We begin the section by defining the construct of identity, for the purposes of this article, and delineating its relation to other components of the self system. We then present childhood precursors to identity formation of adolescents. In keeping with the focus of the special issue, the studies reviewed focus on those carried out on minority children and adolescents in the United States (Canadian studies of American Indians are included). Issues of ethnic and racial identification and ethnic and racial behavior in children are included.

Third, the focus turns to adolescence, where the broader constructs of ego identity and ethnic and racial identity have received more attention. Although many of the research studies reviewed consider African American and American Indian children and adolescents (and to a lesser degree Hispanic and Asian Americans), many of the issues and questions they raise are applicable to Hispanic and Asian Americans as well. For Hispanic and Asian minority groups, the available literature is both sparse in quantity and conceptually shows important continuities and discontinuities to previous decades' research on African American youth (DeVos & Romanucci-Ross, 1982a; Gibbs, Huang, & Associates, 1989).

Fourth, the final section presents issues pertinent in the field and proposes specific interventions. Barriers to identity development and psychological well-being among minorities and associated methodological problems in ethnic and racial minority research are identified. The article concludes with suggestions for improved prevention and intervention models for promoting an achieved identity, group pride, and manifest competence for American minority group youth.

Relations among Constructs, Definitions, Theoretical Orientation, and Demographic Characteristics for Each Ethnic Group

Relation of Identity to Other Constructs of the Self System

In approaching the study of identity as a broad construct, it is possible to relate identity to other components of the self system. The self system includes dimensions of self-development and self-perception, such as self-recognition, self-awareness, self-esteem, and locus of control (Harter, 1983). Erikson's (1963, 1968) writings provide some clarification of the relation between identity and other components of the self system. However, it is important to first define the role of the ego in identity formation.

The psychological nature of the ego is readily identified in the concept of ego identity. Ego identity, as presented in this review, is characterized by the attainment of an ever-revised sense of psychological reality that is supported by a social reality. The ego and its functions, although operating primarily unconsciously, possess the capacity for synthesis and resynthesis, differentiation and integration, and the psychological sequences of interjection and identification that undergird identity formation.

Erikson provides an interesting view of the relation between ego identity and other constructs of self-perception. On the one hand, Erikson (1968) states, "Identity in its vaguest sense suggests, of course, much of what has been called the self by a variety of workers, be it in the form of a self-concept, a self-system, or in that of fluctuating self experience" (pp. 208–209). In more specific terms, however, Erikson argues that components of the self system, in particular, self-esteem and self-concept, are operative prior to ego-identity formation and later become part of the identity. Thus, according to this conceptualization, ego identity is a broader construct than other components of the self system.

In studies on U.S. minorities, both the broader notion of ego identity and its specific components (e.g., self-esteem and self-concept) have been studied. Numerous articles are available on such topics as self-esteem, self-concept, locus of control, and other aspects of self-perception among minority children and adolescents. Fewer articles pertaining directly to the construct of ego identity are available.

Precursors to Identity Formation of Minority Group Members

We affirm that *all* adolescents are faced with the task of identity establishment. However, along with the developmental precursors identified by Erikson (1968), minority group members are confronted with additional important childhood precursors. Constructs of ethnic and racial identification, ethnic and racial preference, ethnic and racial attitudes, and reference group orientation (e.g., racial attitudes and preferences or group-identity studies) are examples of precursors reflecting the multifaceted nature of identity. Since these terms are often erroneously treated as synonyms, definitions are warranted.

Ethnic and racial identification implies a consciousness of self within a particular group. Rotheram and Phinney (1987) define self-identification as "the accurate and consistent use of an ethnic label, based on the perception and conception of themselves as belonging to an ethnic group" (p. 17). Further, 50 years ago, Clark and Clark (1939) suggested that racial identification is indicative of a particularized self-consciousness. More recent social cognitive theorizing would imply that cognitive processes undergird the identification process, and are different from preferences and attitudes (see Alejandro-Wright, 1985; Semaj, 1985; Spencer, 1985).

Ethnic and racial preferences are indicative of group pride. Race or ethnic pride functions to bolster self-respect and to reinforce the self-concept (DeVos & Romanucci-Ross, 1982b).

Ethnic and racial attitudes are often treated as synonymous with ethnic and racial preference. However, while we define preferences as the manner in which a minority group views itself, *attitudes* refers to the view of minorities reflected in society at large. We believe that attitudes are related to the notions of identification and preference, and studies have demonstrated that attitudes are well formed by age 3 (see Spencer & Horowitz, 1973). An attitude suggests an implied response believed to be socially significant in the individual's society (Doob, 1947, p. 144). Rotheram and Phinney (1987) suggest that self-attitudes are generally studied in two areas: "children's preferences or liking for their own or another ethnic group, and their negative attitudes toward other groups (that is, prejudice)" (p. 19).

Reference group orientation, or group identity studies (Cross, 1985; Spencer, 1988), generally refers to the studies conducted on African American children and youth. Racial attitudes (i.e., race stereotypes), racial preferences, and color concept connotations are constructs within this area.

Before proceeding, the relation between race and ethnicity as reviewed in this article requires clarification. As a term, ethnicity refers to a characteristic of shared unique cultural traditions and a heritage that persists across generations. It is not identical to race (DeVos, 1982). Race and ethnicity may overlap, as seen with African Americans and Chinese Americans. In addition, Hispanics are distinguished by their shared language (Spanish) although they may differ by race (i.e., white, black, or Indian) (Gibbs & Huang, 1989, p. 9). Ethnic group membership accords the individual a cultural identity, a sense of belonging and group pride, and a set of prescribed norms, values, and social behaviors (DeVos, 1982; Gibbs & Huang, 1989). Specifically, Gibbs and Huang (1989) propose that an ethnic identity affords a framework for acquiring a view of the self, the world, and future opportunities, while also providing a structure for interpersonal relations and subjective experiences (p. 9); in other words, ethnic identity has the potential of providing a conceptual framework for interpreting the ongoing experience or "fit" between self and the environment.

Theoretical Orientations

There are three major theoretical orientations or perspectives that we feel are particularly suited to the study of racial and ethnic minority groups. Each perspective affords special insights into the unique ecological experiences and adaptive responses to race and ethnicity.

Developmental theoretical perspectives. —The theoretical framework of Erikson (1959) is important for understanding the developing individual generally but takes on additional meaning when race and ethnicity are considered. Researchers in the social sciences have demonstrated wide ethnic variations in maturational processes (Rotheram & Phinney, 1987). Each of the five psychosocial stages between birth and later adolescence in Erikson's (1959) epigenetic model represents a conflict that must be resolved in a positive manner for a desirable element or virtue to be incorporated into the psyche. The probability of obtaining a positive outcome may be compromised for minority children by prejudice, discrimination, relocation, and acculturation between generations, and/or culturally linked methods of coping. For example, for the latency-aged child or adolescent, the stress-related experience of relocations or migrations is experienced directly and may be perceived as a significant loss, and may result in temporary instability and uncertainty. As suggested by Huang and Ying (1989) in their review of Asian Americans, the experience of anxiety and depression with immigration may initially offset the appeal and fascination associated with the move and affect age-appropriate psychosocial outcomes (p. 40).

Concerns about identity formation are often associated with mental illness. The unique psychosocial problems of African Americans are described as often reflecting a misdiagnosis or undetected condition. It is reported that African American juvenile delinquents have elevated levels of depression and neurological symptoms when compared with white juvenile delinquents (Gibbs, 1989a, p. 189). Undetection or misdiagnosis results in a pattern that routes African American youth to the justice system while the mental health system serves white youth (Gibbs, 1989a). This disparate structural pattern is described by Chestang (1972) as representing a societal inconsistency (i.e., structural disparity between public policy and social practice) that contributes to personal impotence.

Life span perspective.—This perspective is structured for evaluating the social experience, psychosocial processes, and behavioral outcomes of minority youth in examining the effects of historical, sociocultural, psychological, and biological factors. Work that exemplifies this category includes Nagata's (1989) review of Japanese American families in light of the historical/social impact of the internment experience; the examination of the intergenerational communication dilemma involving language experience and various Hispanic populations (Fillmore & Britsch, 1988; Inclan & Herron, 1989; Ramirez, 1989); Gibbs's (1989b) review of cultural conflict in biracial children who have ties to more than one social viewpoint; and work that reveals how biological events, particularly the onset of sexual maturity, help build or damage psychological well-being (Huang & Ying, 1989).

Ecological perspective.—The works of Bronfenbrenner (1979) and Garbarino (1982) provide mechanisms for examining the interaction of the individual and the various levels of the environment. The largest environment, the macrosystem, contains some of the most important but difficult factors to assess in ways related to individual outcomes (e.g., attitudes, values, ideologies, and beliefs). The stereotypes that accompany minority-group status most often emanate from this macrolevel and are given structure and reality as they permeate the various levels of the ecosystem within which minority youth and their families must operate (e.g., microsystem). The implications for clinical treatment of African American children are illustrated by Allen and Majidi-Ahi (1989), who suggest that to work effectively with such children, mental health workers must be sensitive to the ecological context of their clients, which means, for example, that they recognize that there is no single entity called "the black family" (p. 154). They suggest that families vary significantly in their backgrounds, economic and social situations, values, and degree of acculturation to the norms and values of mainstream America. On the other hand, as a function of color and "easy identifiability," there are within- and between-group commonalities of experience that emanate from the macrosystem's devaluation of African American people (p. 154). In addition, at the microsystem level (e.g., peers, church, school, and family), significant differences may exist in the preparation of African American children for macrosystem-derived devaluation at the level of child rearing in the family (Bowman & Howard, 1985; Spencer, 1983) or at the level of the school (Brookins, 1988; Johnson, 1988). That is, parents or teachers may focus on their child-rearing and teaching tasks as if they are socializing "human beings" *only*, versus particular socialization efforts in support of African American youth who need to struggle with identity processes under dissonance-producing or stereotype-imbued contexts. As indicated by Epps (1988), "Put simply, such institutions [schools] continue to reflect historical values and beliefs, including racial stereotypes and prejudice" (p. 86). The black family (Allen, 1985) and black community (Barnes, 1972) have shown constancy in their inculcation of expected and traditional beliefs and values as child-rearing agents. The question implied by Epps (1988) is whether the efforts are explicit and direct enough. In other words, given the level of institutionalized (and often covert) practices, are traditional child-rearing methods adequate?

In contrast, for Asian Americans, youth may struggle at the microsystem level under different effects emanating from the macrosystem. Although generally positive, Asian American–linked stereotypes provide a significant source of stress. Japanese American youth are often stereotyped as obedient and educationally successful. However, unique cultural and sociohistorical factors have implications for mental health (Nagata, 1989). The stress associated with living up to the "achieving Asian" social stereotype along with parental pressures for excellence in school performance result in potentially adverse individual psychosocial developmental experiences.

Differential rates of acculturation at the microsystem level have a significant impact on Mexican American families' use of support services (Ramirez, 1989). As an effective buffer between the child and the larger society, at certain levels of acculturation, Mexican American families may be less effective than other families for whom issues of acculturation, migration, and "worldview" are less salient (p. 234).

In sum, like the developmental and life span perspectives, the integration of an ecological approach offers another method for understanding individual (e.g., identity formation) and family processes and outcomes for culturally diverse groups. As indicated, even within ethnic and racial groups, there may be significant differences and commonalities as a function of migration history, language variations (e.g., there are 200 distinct languages for American Indians), color, social stereotypes, acculturation, and worldview.

Descriptive Profile of Racial and Ethnic Minorities in America

Although this article reflects the greater availability of empirical data on aspects of psychosocial functioning of African American and American Indian children and adolescents, studies concerning Asian American and Hispanic youth are also included. Together, the four major groups represent the largest minority groups with the longest period of residence in the United States. They represent a range of acculturation situations, linguistic diversity, and family structures. Each group's history in this country varies from the indigenous (American Indians) to those Japanese and Chinese Americans who were imported as laborers (Gibbs & Huang, 1989). Blacks were imported in large numbers as slaves, although Van Sertima (1977) asserts their presence in ancient America before Columbus. In addition to the wide variation among groups, there is also great diversity within each ethnic group (Gibbs & Huang, 1989, p. xvii).

Huang and Ying (1989) describe the Chinese American minority as relatively older (median age of 29.6), with 30% of its population represented by youth. The process of migration interfered with the extended family structure, although there have been attempts to restore family relationships (Huang & Ying, 1989, pp. 32–36).

Educationally, Japanese Americans, like Chinese Americans, are above the national norm. The identification of generations is important when examining Japanese culture (e.g., the immigrant "Issei," the American born "Nisei," and the second generation of American-born Japanese called "Sansei" [Nagata, 1989, p. 67]). With the approach of the twenty-first century, Asian American (excluding Japanese American) growth rates are expected to exceed the present populations by at least 10% (Nagata, 1989). Nagata's (1989) review indicates that Japanese Americans have an out-marriage rate of 60% and have assimilated well into American mainstream society. DeVos and Romanucci-Ross's (1982b) analysis, however, suggests that the assimilation pattern and out-marriage rates in and of themselves suggest major psychosocial conflicts.

A recent review of American Indians (LaFromboise & Low, 1989) defines the group as all North American native people, including Indians, Alaska Natives, Aleuts, Eskimos, and Metis, or mixed bloods (p. 115). The majority of American Indians are considered young (i.e., average age of 20 for American Indians and 18 for Alaska Natives) when compared with the national average of 30 (LaFromboise & Low, 1989). The 517 federally recognized native entities and 200 distinct tribal languages actively spoken make this group one of the most diverse. Substandard living conditions, poverty, and chronic unemployment place its youth at risk for school failure and poor health.

As indicated by the reviews of African Americans by Allen and Majidi-Ahi (1989), Gibbs (1989a), and Jackson, McCullough, and Gurin (1988), identity-focused variables more often have been studied for this group. However, the literature suggests continued controversy surrounding assumptions about personality organization. As a group, African Americans have shown strengths under conditions of adversity and poverty (Hill, 1972), although the conduits that have afforded adaptation and adjustment have seldom been examined. Allen and Majidi-Ahi (1989) note that the risk factors of poverty and racial oppression remain a part of the social ecology of black children. In fact, it is suggested that the status of African Americans is attributable to four primary social and historical factors: slavery, segregation and discrimination, poverty, and urbanization (Gibbs, 1989a, p. 182). Color makes identification and subsequent discrimination virtually unavoidable. Like other minority groups, there is diversity among group members (Gibbs, 1989a).

Ramirez's (1989) review cites a 22% growth of Mexican Americans in the United States between 1980 and 1987. They are much younger than other groups (average age of 23.3 years as compared with 24.3 years for Puerto Ricans, 39.1 for Cuban Americans, and 31.9 years for non-Hispanics). With a high fertility rate, low educational attainment, and large extended families, Mexican Americans also show great diversity in that both traditional and contemporary patterns are found (Ramirez, 1989, p. 227). Puerto Rican youth are reported to show many identity conflicts, and as a group generally reside in the metropolitan New York area (Inclan & Herron, 1989). Mental health data for Puerto Ricans are generally sparse, and the identity conflicts experienced are contributed to by migration and transculturation (p. 256). With this background information, we now turn our attention to the empirical literature.

Identity Formation in Childhood

A commonly used procedure in studying ethnic and racial identification, preference, and attitudes is to present a child with dolls and pictures that are representative of his or her own group and of the majority group. Annis and Corenblum (1987), Beuf (1977), Corenblum and Wilson (1982), and Hunsberger (1978) examined ethnic identification among children through the presentation of Indian and white dolls. Using this procedure, questions were posed to subjects related to their preferences toward and identification with the different dolls. Taken together, these studies show that preschool and young school-age children demonstrate a white bias. Beuf (1977) found this to be the case with both rural and urban American Indian children. Furthermore, Aboud (1977) and Annis and Corenblum (1987) report that most of the children in their studies could correctly identify Anglos and Indians in the pictures, but a smaller number of American Indian children correctly identified which pictures they themselves resembled. These findings are disturbing; however, certain qualifiers are required. For example, Corenblum and Wilson (1982) found that race of subject and race of experimenter need to be considered in conducting these studies. In a study conducted in Canada, Annis and Corenblum (1987) found that American Indian children show greater preferences for their own race when tested in their native language.

A similar racial attitude, preference, and color connotation study by Spencer and Horowitz (1973) with African American and Anglo preschool children indicated an unexpected effect by experimenter's race. Independent of the child's race, socioeconomic status, sex, and age (3, 4, or 5), baseline data obtained by Spencer (1970) and reported by Spencer and Horowitz (1973) indicated a significant pattern of negative connotations associated with the color black and African American people. Social (puppet and token) reinforcers were effective for reversing the baseline pro-white pattern for the study's experimental subjects. For the experimental condition, following the collection of (pro-white patterned) baseline data, all experimental subjects were trained for new values through the use of social reinforcements. Both black and white experimental subjects of the study were taught that the color black and black persons were positive and that the color white and white persons were negative. The experimental condition required that the traditional (pro-white, generally) attitudes, connotations, and references be experimentally reversed by introducing and reinforcing *new learning*. The subjects trained by the white experimenter showed a pattern of enhanced learning (of a pro-black bias) when compared with subjects trained by a black experimenter. In sum, response trends suggested that, at baseline, the color white and white persons were more valued. However, independent of the child's race (i.e., for the experimental pro-white training condition), the equally well-trained white experimenter was more reinforcing of the child's acquisition of new pro-black color connotations, attitudes, and preferences when applied to white and black *persons* (i.e., representative stimuli or pictures). Taken together, the studies cited indicate that preschool and young school-age children demonstrate a (pro) white bias in ethnic and racial preference, attitudes and identification, and reference group orientation unless an intervention (i.e., treatment) is introduced (Cross, 1985; Spencer, 1985, 1988).

Other studies of Anglos and American Indians (Aboud, 1977; Annis & Corenblum, 1987) as well as northern and southern African American children (Spencer, 1977, 1982a, 1986) suggest children's early awareness of ethnic and racial differences. The studies of racial identification for African Americans have generated the most controversy. The findings of *misidentification* raise other concerns.

Conceptual and methodological problems have been associated with these studies (Banks, 1976; Brand, Ruiz, & Padillo, 1974). Generally, the research approach follows from the early studies on African American children for whom questions of identification were initially posed (e.g., Clark & Clark, 1939, 1940). Specifically, the large body of racial attitude, preference, and identification studies does not make clear the sources of or reasons for the findings of misidentification (Banks, 1976; Brand et al., 1974; Cross, 1985; Spencer, 1988). Are experimental stimuli of nonwhite groups less attractive? When forced to respond to extreme stimuli, are children noting their knowledge concerning "how the world is organized and run"? Are children reporting their understanding of "power" positions? Or are minority group children offering their knowledge of connotative meanings associated with specific groups as a function of their own level of cognitive development? Are the findings "chance" response patterns? Do the patterned findings represent context or situational variables? Put another way, do children respond from a position of perceived power and/or implicitly understood stereotyped preferences versus an actual "other-group" orientation or out-group values internalization and rejection of the self?

These questions are more than rhetorical when studies of racial identification, preference, or attitudes (i.e., the more "specific" aspects of identity processes) are compared with the more broadly conceptualized "self" studies (i.e., either self-concept measures or self-esteem instruments). As indicated by data for African American preschool and primary school children (e.g., Spencer 1982a, 1985, 1988), the relation between the broader construct or self system and the more specific identity construct (i.e., ethnic or racial identification, attitudes, or racial preference) has been either negative, nonlinear, or, in fact, independent, depending on the age range of the subjects or stage of cognitive development (Banks, 1976; Cross, 1985; Spencer, 1985).

Several relevant studies were designed to explore the role of cognitive processes for social-emotional functioning during the preschool and early school years among African American children. The theorizing also appears appropriate for American Indian and Hispanic children. As indicated from the empirical findings by Alejandro-Wright (1985), Semaj (1985), and Spencer (1982b, 1985, 1988), cognitive awareness appears to support the acquisition of pro-majority group or Caucasian-oriented attitudes among racial or ethnic minority children. Such results may not necessarily suggest misidentification or self-rejection in the case of very young children. Given the more positive attributes credited to white stimuli, instead, the response pattern may reflect young children's identification (of the self) with the (perceived) more valued stimuli. The interpretation is consistent both with a pro-white bias *and* the findings of high self-esteem among African American children (Powell, 1985) and cognitive egocentrism during the preschool years. The latter supports the acquisition and maintenance of dissonant-appearing information. That is, young egocentric children may report on both their self-esteem *and* knowledge of (negative) social stereotypes (Spencer, 1982b).

Black children's tendency to misidentify has been viewed as supporting assumptions of personal disorganization. However, empirical findings for both attitude/preference *and* self-concept suggest the presence of positive self-esteem and pro-white attitudes/preferences. Consistent with our combined use of developmental, ecological, and life span theories, at least during the preschool and early school years, we believe that African American children's pro-white racial attitude and preference patterns appear to represent cultural-ecological variables (i.e., negative social stereotypes about blacks) and not psychological characteristics.

Environmental and family influences have seldom been considered in previous research on black youths' personal and group identity (Jackson et al., 1988). Stereotypes and attitudes represent infrequently considered factors of special importance for children of stigmatized groups. Strongly negative or discomfort-producing attitudes are often associated with minorities, while positive attitudes (or at least more balanced perceptions) are associated with whites. Thus, the ecological niche for minority youth is different from that of nonminority youth. American Indian, African American, and Hispanic youth, unlike Anglo youth, are presented a basically negative image about the reference group. Accordingly, white youth are less likely to experience the chronic stress and problems associated with an implied group deviance or, at best, group invisibility (Gougis, 1986; Moritsugu & Sue, 1983). Beuf (1977) reports that around age 10, American Indian children begin to show a greater preference toward and identification with their own group. This response pattern occurs with increasing age for children in the concrete stage of cognitive development—roughly between ages 7 and 11. A parallel pattern of own-group preference has been described by Spencer (1982b) for older (ages 10 and 12) African American children. Such advances in cognitive skills are perhaps reflected in a more realistic assessment of oneself and one's group and a greater consciousness of the "referent other" used for comparison purposes when evaluating the self. The more "reference group other"-oriented perspective has been discussed in detail by Cross (1985) for African American youth as reference group orientation studies.

In summary, several constructs—identification, preference, and attitudes—have been more commonly studied among younger children than among older children and adolescents. Evidence suggests that young ethnic and racial minority children are likely to demonstrate a white bias for these constructs. Reasons for these findings remain unclear, although ecological and cognitive maturation explanations are plausible. Normative cognitive limitations of younger children along with ecological factors may complicate and confuse the task of interpreting their ethnic and racial misidentification.

Identity Formation in Adolescence

Ego Identity

Although ethnic and racial identification, preference, and attitudes have commonly been studied in childhood, identity formation becomes particularly salient in adolescence. Identity formation has been regarded by Erikson (1968) as the fifth stage in psychosocial development. From this framework, identity development is not only dependent on an individual's developmental history but is also linked with the historical period of which the individual is a product. According to Erikson (1968), identity "contains a complementarity of past and future both in the individual and society; it links the actuality of a living past with that of a promising future" (p. 310). Implicit in the identity construct is an awareness of the sameness and continuity of the self in time and space. The continuity of these ideas is apparent in Erikson's assertions of successful identity formation being mediated by resolutions of earlier developmental tasks. One might add to these assertions that the outcome to younger children's establishment of ethnic and racial identifications, preferences, and attitudes also contributes to adolescent identity formation. Furthermore, the success or failure of adult developmental tasks is heavily dependent on the outcome of the identity crisis in adolescence. Essentially, the adolescent identity resolution sets the stage for the quality of later identity-focused conflicts (e.g., career decisions, marriage, and retirement [disengagement]).

The development of identity, in an Eriksonian sense, has been minimally researched among minorities. However, Marcia (1966) provides a model useful in such research. He conceives of identity as four "statuses" (achievement, moratorium, foreclosure, and diffusion) which have been explored to some degree. Identity achievement is characterized by exploration of and commitment to an identity; moratorium status exists when the individual, having explored an identity, remains uncommitted to one; foreclosed status refers to prematurely closed off exploration; and diffused status is an inability to reconsolidate the ego. Accordingly, both "foreclosed" and "diffused" adolescents have not fully explored potential identity options, although for different reasons. Foreclosed adolescents, however, have committed to an identity, while diffused adolescents have not.

There has been some research carried out with American minority adolescents based on Marcia's (1966) identity status model. It has been reported in these studies that minority adolescents tend to score higher in foreclosure than white adolescents. Streitmatter (1988) examined ethnicity as a variable in a study of ego identity carried out among 367 white and minority (i.e., Hispanic, African American, American Indian, Asian, and other) adolescents in the southwestern United States. The Anglo adolescents scored significantly lower than the minority adolescents on foreclosure in both interpersonal and ideological components of identity. In terms of significant gender and ethnicity differences, white males scored lower on ideological and interpersonal measures than Anglo females and minority males and females. Minority males scored significantly higher on ideological diffusion than minority females and Anglo males and females. From an ecosystem analysis, the findings are consistent with the macro-level beliefs, stereotypes, and attitudes surrounding minority status youth and the perceptions and values associated with females.

Abraham (1986) found Mexican American adolescents more foreclosed in ideological identity than their white American counterparts. Similarly, with respect to ideological identity, Markstrom (1987) found American Indian adolescents (along with Mexican Americans and black Americans to a lesser degree) to score higher on foreclosure, in contrast to Anglos. Hauser (1972a, 1972b) also found the identity pattern of African American adolescents to be characterized by foreclosure. However, it should be noted that, although Hauser purported to study equivalent groups of lower-income boys, the family background characteristics were not the same. Hauser's study was designed significantly better than other comparative studies of blacks and whites; lower-income boys of both groups were compared. However, his sample contained lower-income African American boys who more often than the whites came from single-parent homes, which, by definition, are accompanied by great economic and social hardships and chronic stress.

Exploration is a key ingredient for identity-formation processes. Furthermore, as supported by a level of cognitive awareness not possible earlier (i.e., social cognition), minority adolescents are faced with an assumed consciousness of prejudicial attitudes and discriminatory practices of the majority group (Gougis, 1986; Spencer, 1982b; Spencer, Dobbs, & Swanson, 1988). The relation for minorities is compounded as a function of color. Color plays an important role, although its effect is seldom addressed either empirically or conceptually. The overall effect may be one of discouragement from involvement with those outside of one's own reference group and/or a subsequent diminished level of exploration during childhood and use of academic and apprenticeship opportunities during adolescence, which may have life-course implications (Ogbu, 1983; Spencer, Kim, & Marshall, 1987). For example, Nagata's (1989) description of Japanese American adolescents would suggest that parental pressure for academic excellence may not necessarily be accompanied by opportunities to explore options fully. Minority parents vary in their access to resources for buffering the effects of stigmatization (Spencer, in press).

A confounding factor in these studies may be between ethnicity and socioeconomic status (SES). The SES of subjects in Streitmatter's (1988) study is unknown. In Abraham's (1986) study, a greater number of the Anglo subjects' parents had completed college degrees as compared to the parents of Mexican American subjects. Thus, it is likely that the Anglo subjects were of higher SES. Markstrom's (1987) and Hauser's (1972a, 1972b) subjects, both minority and Anglo, were from lower-income families. However, it has been noted that the African American boys in Hauser's studies were more likely to come from single-parent homes. Both SES and family constellation then may be important confounding factors in studies on ego identity of minority adolescents. To obtain a true picture of whether the high level of foreclosure of these groups can be attributed to ethnicity or some other factor, it will be important in future studies to match Anglo and minority subjects on both SES and family configuration.

An alternative explanation to the above results is that some minority groups, by certain preferences in life-style, migration, or acculturation rates, may foster greater foreclosure. Further, foreclosure may be an adaptive identity status for these youths (in the short run). For example, American Indian adolescents reared on reservations, where the adherence to cultural norms is encouraged and exploration discouraged, might, quite adaptively, hold a foreclosed identity. Similar arguments may be made for Hispanic youths living in predominantly Hispanic communities, and so on. The point is that exploration of identity may not be desirable for such youth when social and ideological roles are clearly defined by the community. Foreclosure may foster greater social recognition by one's ethnic community and impart a sense of well-being to the individual (DeVos & Romanucci-Ross, 1982b).

Ethnic or Racial (Group) Identity

Ethnic or racial (group) identity and self-image.—One aspect of identity that has been indirectly explored among American Indians and other minority groups is ethnic identity. Ethnic identity refers to "one's sense of belonging to an ethnic group and the part of one's thinking, perceptions, feelings, and behavior that is due to ethnic group membership" (Rotheram & Phinney, 1987, p. 13). This is different from ethnic identification in that identification implies that one has the ability to define him/herself as a member of a certain group. With identity, an internalization of identification has occurred. Aboud (1988) describes ethnic self-identification as a narrower concept and ethnic identity as a broader concept. In addition, as indicated by Cross's (1985) review, reference group orientation (RGO) or the construct "group identity" refers to a specific construct that addresses the central issue of color and race. The issue of group identity, either as ethnic identity or one's RGO, represents an important domain, particularly for minority group members. An intriguing model of ethnic identity development has been proposed by Phinney and Tarver (1988). They assert that, although ethnic identity has not been studied from an Eriksonian perspective, models of ethnic identity development have been presented by others (Atkinson, Morten, & Sue, 1983; Cross, 1978). Phinney and Tarver (1988) note several of the similarities between these models and Marcia's identity statuses. The models of ethnic identity suggest that movement begins from a point of an unexamined ethnic identity (similar to Marcia's identity diffusion and foreclosure statuses). Following that, an encounter experience occurs that promotes exploration (similar to the moratorium status). Finally, after searching, a commitment is made to an identity (achievement status).

Drawing on this conceptual framework, Phinney and Tarver (1988) examined the processes of search and commitment in ethnic identity among 24 black and 24 white, middle-class eighth graders. Subjects were interviewed and then rated from 1 (none) to 4 (high) on both search and commitment. While no significant differences were found between the two groups, there was evidence that ethnic identity begins to form as early as the eighth grade. However, a qualitative analysis of the transcribed interviews revealed that blacks had a better understanding of prejudice and had greater understanding of their own culture than did whites. The researchers argue that the experience of prejudice might foster the need for greater understanding of one's culture. The perspective is consistent with the theorizing about ethnicity by DeVos and Romanucci-Ross (1982b), which incorporates the views of the symbolic interactionist G. H. Mead (1934).

Identity is said to be a process occurring in the core of the individual and in his or her communal culture. In a discussion of racial identity, Erikson (1968) speculates that minority and oppressed individuals may be prone to develop a negative identity as a result of *accepting* negative self-images projected onto them, not only by the larger society, but by their own group as well. This perspective focuses primary attention on identity as a *product* (i.e., the "what" of behavior) as opposed to addressing the multiple ways in which identity represents developmental *processes*. The process perspective has been taken with respect to personality theorizing about nonminority youth; the emphasis for minority youth, however, has remained riveted on the "what" as opposed to the "why" and the "how," thus evading questions about the mechanisms of identity formation. Accordingly, the potential sources of negative stereotypes and the Eriksonian assumptions of a negative identity among minority youth must be clarified.

As an organizing device for describing the several sources of adverse (minority youth) stereotypes, we consider the ecology. Ecological models (Bronfenbrenner, 1979; Garbarino, 1982) serve as instructive and important explanatory mechanisms for highlighting the lack of "goodness of fit" between organism and environment for many ethnic minority youth. Although referring to behavioral mismatches between the social setting or context and sex, body type, or facial attractiveness, the "goodness of fit" model proposed by Lerner (1982) has special relevance given the issues of color and ethnicity. As indicated, the macrosystem level of the environment represents societal-level attitudes, beliefs, and ideology that are assumed to be linked with the quality, duration, and content of long-term interracial contacts. Such an approach supports an "unpackaging" or improved clarity about possible sources of interracial conflicts along with deeply ingrained reference group stereotypes. History also serves an important function.

Only a brief look at the 500 years of interaction between American Indians and whites is required to see the recurrence of events in which negative images of American Indians were perpetuated (Deloria, 1969). Similarly, the long-standing patterns of interaction between Hispanic Americans and African Americans with Anglo Americans reflect a legacy of extreme stereotyping of both minority groups. At the turn of the century, there were numerous examples of minority group attempts at self-definition and self-determination (Hill, 1983), none of which received high visibility during a period of increased (i.e., particularly southern) racial violence (Franklin, 1985; Williamson, 1984).

Throughout the nation over the last 200 years, the experiences of Hispanics, American Indians, and African Americans are consistent in one respect: The children of each group have been exposed to negative imagery and a nascent sense of *invisibility* in school materials. A recent review suggests the absence may have implications for schooling, and that it is important for minorities to internalize and maintain traditional values for maximizing educability beginning at the preschool level for both cultural and language-different minorities (Fillmore & Britsch, 1988).

According to Erikson (1968), the development of identity is a process involving personal reflection and observation of oneself in relation to others. The individual examines him/herself as others might judge the self in relation to themselves (Erikson, 1968). The individual then evaluates the judgments made by others about the self and compares the self with others. Identity develops, in part, out of this process of judgments and comparisons. This perspective has strongly influenced personality theorizing about minority group members. The major problem with this analysis, when compared with the available empirical evidence on child rearing, is that the subtle reflective processes of evaluations, comparisons, inferences, and judgments suggested require higher levels of reasoning than those available to young children. In fact, most of our empirical work is on young, cognitively egocentric children. Empirical studies are needed that simultaneously explore cognitive processes with the child's emergent ethnic and racial concepts during early childhood, middle childhood, and the adolescent years.

In response to this need, cognitive developmental perspectives have recently been introduced with African American children and group identity variables (Alejandro-Wright, 1985; Semaj, 1985; Spencer, 1982b, 1985). Several findings suggest that inference-making abilities are related to an awareness of race as a social-biological category (Spencer, 1982b). The awareness of race itself is related to the child's knowledge of *stereotypes;* children with greater inference-making skills seemingly have more information about the world, including knowledge of (learned) attitudes and stereotypes concerning groups. In addition, the child's inference-making skills appear related to performance on both intellectual measures and self-esteem scales. Children who perform most competently on intellectual outcome measures and manifest higher levels of self-esteem perform better at inference-making processes. The findings are consistent with conclusions from symbolic interactionists (e.g., Mead, 1934).

Writings by early symbolic interactionists were the first to integrate notions of role taking in self development. Cooley's (1902) "looking glass self" is defined as the process in which children define themselves by taking the perspectives of important others and then reflecting on the self from these perspectives. Likewise, the development of Mead's (1934) "generalized other" contributes to a sense of self. These ideas are quite similar to those of Erikson. This line of theorizing on defining the self according to the perceptions of others is studied to some degree among American Indians. Although identity has not been explored explicitly in this regard, several researchers have been interested in attitudes toward the self evolving out of minority status and acculturation experiences.

For example, self-esteem has also been examined as a function of degree of acculturation among two branches of the Florida Seminole Tribe (Lefley, 1976). The Miccosukees, a less acculturated tribe, had higher self-esteem than the Seminoles, a more acculturated tribe. In contrast, Cockerham (1979) found both positive and negative self-attitudes to exist among Indians who had varying degrees of contact with whites. Fuchs and Havighurst (1972) found that, when American Indian teenagers were the majority in their schools, self-esteem was higher than when they were in the minority. In contrast to the findings by Fuchs and Havighurst (1972), American Indian adolescents attending high school as minorities were found to have higher self-esteem than youth attending all-Indian schools (Cockerham, 1979). But the latter may have been referred to the all-Indian schools due to problematic behavior, and thus their low self-esteem may have been independent of their school's configuration. Cockerham (1979) argues, in conclusion, that not all American Indians accept the negative attitudes directed toward them by the dominant culture.

Perhaps negative self attitudes are generated by some other means than internalization or acceptance of negative stereotypes (Erikson, 1968). There is no reason to assume that "the referent other" for comparison purposes is someone other than a minority group person. Indeed, Rosenberg (1981) makes a similar argument and cites empirical evidence from Rosenberg and Simmons (1972) to support such a claim, stating: "What the child believed his parents, teachers, and friends thought of him and his own self-esteem was very strong for both black and white children and was, in fact, slightly stronger among the black children" (Rosenberg, 1981, p. 605). The finding is consistent with speculation by Barnes (1972) about the "buffering" role provided by the black community and DeVos's

(1975) perspective concerning the nurturing function of ethnicity (p. 386).

Levels of esteem among senior high school students who were either black, Indian, or white and living in the same county were examined by Barkley (1985). Each group esteemed itself more highly than the other groups. However, the Indian females were not significantly higher in their esteem of American Indian people than of people of the other two groups. In studies reported by Markstrom (1987) and Markstrom and Mullis (1986), adolescent American Indian females also reported more disturbing aspects of self-perception in contrast to their male counterparts and in contrast to Anglo adolescents of both sexes. True sex differences are not unusual findings. It may be that American Indian girls define themselves in terms of external (white) characteristics (which include standards of beauty and associated insecurities) to a greater extent than Anglo youth. In any event, a combined ethnic/racial group and gender-discrimination effect may characterize minority females' development of self-esteem.

Research on African American and white adolescents by Hare and Castenell (1985) does suggest that self-perceptions may be area specific. For example, Hare and Castenell (1985) used an area-specific self-esteem measure and obtained sex differences that were not consistent across domains (e.g., home, school, peer, and self). African American males who performed least well on indicators of educational attainment obtained the highest peer self-esteem score but the lowest scores for general, school, and home self-esteem.

The study by Hare and Castenell (1985) raises the issue of a possible area-specific self-esteem and introduces the problem of uninterpretable data without greater sociocultural information. The studies on American Indians noted by Markstrom (1987) and Markstrom and Mullis (1986) were carried out with different American Indian tribes. Findings indicated that the troubling aspects of self-perception of American Indian female adolescents are not unique to one Indian tribe. The combination of being *both* female and a minority group member may be especially problematic for these females. It is impossible to say exactly what value-laden features are associated with beauty or more general attractiveness for female Indian youth. Or, as argued by Lewis (1975) relative to black-white comparative studies, sex differences among nonminority or white children may not predict differences among African Americans. The same caution may also be applicable for other minority groups.

In sum, traditional personality theorists (e.g., Erikson, 1968) conclude that minority and oppressed individuals are expected to internalize negative images. Yet available empirical data suggest otherwise. The processes of identity formation may be more complex than previously thought. Undoubtedly, identity processes for minority group youth are diverse. Alternative formulations require consideration of previously unaddressed concerns. Topics in need of future study across ethnic and racial groups include: (*a*) the link between efforts by minority youths to maintain traditional values and developmental outcomes; (*b*) methods to determine mediating roles for developmentally determined cognitive processes; (*c*) attempts to understand identification processes when "own-group referent others" are used for comparison purposes; (*d*) obtaining more precise, socioculturally sensitive interpretations of unexpected findings supported by area-specific self-esteem results; and (*e*) exploration of the confounding effects of gender and race/ethnicity since the study of sex differences among whites may be an inadequate model for racial and ethnic minority youth.

Barriers, Methodological Issues, and Recommended Interventions

Barriers to Identity Formation

Many researchers have addressed the factors that interfere with the identity formation of minority youth. Often a child confronts conflicting values—those of the larger society and those of the reference group—from which he or she must choose in forming an identity (see DeVos & Romanucci-Ross, 1982a). Such conflicts among American Indian adolescents have been noted by a number of individuals (Berlin, 1986; Bryde, 1971; Burgess, 1980; Fillmore & Britsch, 1988; Katz, 1981; Sue, 1978). American Indians value autonomy, and youngsters are expected to operate semi-independently and to make their own decisions. The child-rearing style supports freedom to experiment and the natural consequences of those choices (LaFromboise & Low, 1989, p. 122). Tribal spirituality remains important among American Indian people. Adolescents and children are expected to participate in ceremonies that often violate attendance policies of Anglo-operated schools (LaFromboise & Low, 1989, p. 123). For the American Indian adolescent, the task of sorting out the traits of two sets of cultures is formidable, and one which may result in rejection by the tribe if the expected traditional role is not assumed. Many American Indian youth swing back and forth between an Anglo identity and a tribal identity without ever forming a coherent blend of the two (Katz, 1981). This task is further hindered by a lack of adequate adult role models, limited opportunities for identity exploration (such as those that work experience might provide), and early developmental failures (Berlin, 1986).

Identity conflicts for Mexican American adolescents have been reported by Mendelberg (1986), who shows that Mexican American youngsters are presented with an image of Anglos as being powerful, advanced, and positive, whereas Mexican Americans are stereotyped as powerless, primitive, and negative. Adoption of such negative stereotypes by the Mexican American adolescent may well lead to a sense of futility in exploring life possibilities. Exposure alone may cause psychological dissonance and discomfort, which keep adolescent students off [academic] task. Mendelberg (1986) states: "Identification with members of outside groups appears to be blocked for minority members, and identification with their own group is fraught with difficulties" (p. 223).

For Japanese Americans, their identification pattern has been described as an identification with the aggressor (DeVos, 1982). That pattern may be associated with the high out-group marriage rate (Nagata, 1989). Of course, the group's assimilation pattern also may support the academic prowess of its youth, which may be accompanied by significant stress.

Ramirez and Castaneda (1974) identify the melting-pot philosophy as a major barrier against minority group members adopting an adaptive ethnic identity. The historical argument of this philosophy, as interpreted and reviewed by Ramirez and Castaneda (1974), was that by the conglomeration of all races in the United States, a new, superior race would be formed. The melting pot has not come to be, yet the approach taken by many educators toward minority children is that such a reality exists. Thus, Ramirez and Castaneda (1974) argue that for Mexican American children, the values presented at school are in direct conflict with those presented at home. Indeed, Ramirez (1969) identified two groups of Mexican American adolescents: those who embraced Anglo values and those who continued to adhere to their traditional culture. Ramirez and Castaneda (1974) state that, ideally, children should be allowed to develop a bicultural identity that consists of a dual identification. Biculturalism for many is hindered by peer pressure (Matute-Bianchi, 1986) and made more complex because of within-group color preference (DeVos & Romanucci-Ross, 1982b). For example, Mexicans rank themselves according to skin color and physical types. At the top are the most Caucasian looking and at the bottom the most "Indian" in appearance (DeVos & Romanucci-Ross, 1982b, p. 377).

Achieving group identity is difficult without the consistent guidance of important socializing agents (Spencer, 1983, 1985). African American parents, relatives, and teachers must actively and continually struggle to present evidence to children that confirms the worth of black culture and people as a mechanism for offsetting cultural identity confusion. The difficulties acknowledged may emanate from the fact that many of the child's socializing adults themselves have "diffused extended identities" marked by lack of a consistent pattern of Afrocentricity (Semaj, 1985).

Similarly, from a psychiatric perspective, Westermeyer (1979a) has noted ethnic identity problems among American Indians. He suggests that identity problems are no more common among American Indians than the rest of the population, but, instead, a unique problem to be contended with is "negative or ambivalent feelings regarding their own racial and ethnic identity" (Westermeyer, 1979a, p. 188).

Westermeyer (1979b) also describes an "apple Indian syndrome" for American Indians who show a cultural preference for the larger Anglo society; it is suggested that such individuals are red on the outside and white on the inside. Individuals identified by Westermeyer (1979b) as being prone to this syndrome had a childhood history of childrearing experiences in non-Indian homes and communities. Such environments did not appear problematic until adolescence, when issues related to identity became salient. At the same time, these Indian adolescents became cognizant of discrimination. Further, society forced an unfamiliar stereotyped identity upon them. The results of these experiences were exhibited in problems such as substance abuse, psychiatric disorders, and legal and other behavior problems. Many of Westermeyer's patients ultimately rejected the Anglo culture, but did not immediately replace it with an internalized American Indian identity aside from adopting overt behavioral indicators of Indianness. Means (1980) noted the same "apple identity" problem for other minority group members. He described the parallel confusion of identity for Hispanics as a "coconut syndrome," for Asians the "banana syndrome," and for African Americans the "Oreo syndrome."

Another barrier to identity formation may come from within the family. Too often minority status parents may not discuss ethnic or racial issues with their children since the adults themselves remain uncomfortable with issues having to do with either race or ethnicity. Research studies suggest a general reluctance by African American parents to broach the issue of race unless the subject is raised first by their children since many parents assume that the 1960s took care of the significant issues (Spencer, 1983, 1988). A parallel trend has been obtained for a national sample of African Amerian parents (Bowman & Howard, 1985). Responses indicate a parental focus on the rearing of "human beings" versus the more reality-based conclusions that they are socializing human beings who happen also to be people who are negatively stereotyped by the larger society as a function of color, racial group membership, or ethnicity. It is argued that this reluctance may reflect a defensive strategy on the part of the parents that leaves their children exposed to the continuing problem of racial intolerance, albeit expressed in subtle forms.

Several factors thus complicate the task of identity formation among minority youth. The value conflicts that exist between cultures, the lack of identity-achieved adult role models, and the lack of culture-focused specific guidance from the family represent ongoing issues. The preponderance of negative stereotypes about minorities in general is also counterproductive to acquiring a solid sense of self.

Methodological Problems

There are several problems associated with the measurement of identity, or for that matter any other psychosocial construct, among American minorities. One difficulty is that most instruments are administered in English, which is a major problem for minorities for whom English is a second language (e.g., many American Indian tribes, Hispanics, and Asian Americans). Even if the individual has some knowledge of the English language, there is still a problem of nonequivalence for minority and nonminority children in items, words, and performance requirements (Beiser, 1981). Instruments are generally designed for and normed on the middle-class Anglo population. Even when a minority child or adolescent has learned English as a first language, cultural biases remain. Further, when any form of subjective scoring is involved, there may be cultural biases if Anglos are judging minority children according to Anglo standards.

Not only may items lack equivalence across ethnic groups, but often there is lack of continuity within ethnic groups. For example, there are more than 300 American Indian tribes in the United States alone (May, 1987). Vast cultural, geographic, linguistic, and economic differences exist among tribes. A pan-Indian assumption cannot be made when conducting or interpreting American Indian studies. Likewise, Asian Americans exhibit within-group diversity, and a similar argument applies to various subgroups within Hispanic culture. Assumptions of similarity have also plagued African Americans. For example, within-group diversity derives from the presence of Caribbean and African families who are minimally identifiable from African American families.

A related problem is that the constructs selected for measurement may represent attributes that are desirable in the dominant Anglo society but not in a particular minority culture (e.g., independence may be less important than interdependence for Asian Americans). Another issue involves generalizability of psychological laws and theories across cultures (Lonner, 1987). In an attempt to investigate similar notions among American Indians, Bienvenue (1978) proposed a dual-socialization model. According to this model, socialization of minorities encompasses both local cultural values and those of the dominant culture. Thus, in assessing self-evaluation, both models require careful consideration. Indeed, Bienvenue (1978) found that Canadian Indian high school students evaluated the self more positively from the standpoint of their own cultural values (e.g., friendly and unselfish). On the other hand, self-evaluations were lower on such white traits as achievement and success. In the case of African Americans, the need for a dual consciousness has been discussed for nearly a century by DuBois (1896/1963).

A different issue concerns the adequacy of the identity construct itself. This construct may be inadequately conceptualized. Although the work by Erikson (1959, 1968) serves as a convenient heuristic device for understanding identity processes for Anglo youth, there remains a dearth of conceptual formulations for these processes among American minority youth. Ogbu's (1983) typology (e.g., castelike, immigrant, and autonomous) for describing minority youth has been illuminating but remains inadequate for linking internal psychological processes with environmental effects. The typology links the individual's status with the group's structural experiences as minority group members. However, it does not account for individual social successes (Trueba, 1988). The psychological processes alluded to are those that relate to developmental tasks generally and others linked to adaptations required as a function of specific sociocultural conditions. New conceptual frameworks shaped by models of normal developmental processes are needed (i.e., as opposed to deviance- and deficit-dependent formulations). Racial and ethnic groups have heretofore been examined through pathology-driven models.

For many minority youth, traditional models of self or identity development (*a*) ignore sociocognitive developmental processes, (*b*) assume homogeneity among group members, (*c*) overlook patterns of coping and adaptation, (*d*) fail to link unique ecosystem or multileveled environmental experiences with life-course models (which integrate historical, sociocultural, biological, and psychological components with behavioral response patterns), and, as a consequence, (*e*) ignore the opportunity of furthering or broadening the knowledge extant on resilience and risk for youth whose normative experiences require ongoing adaptive coping strategies as a function of race, ethnicity, and/or color. These problems suggest the need for alternative conceptual approaches.

A multifaceted theoretical formulation for understanding developmental processes for minority status youth is required. As indicated elsewhere (see Spencer, 1988), an inclusive framework of development would account for identity-formation *processes* and would respond to several needs, which include: (1) delineation of the role of status characteristics (e.g., race/ethnicity, color, sex, and economic status) for later life-course outcomes; (2) addressing the subjective experience of stress and probable responses; (3) exploring several intermediate processes that reflect perceptual organization (and thus the role of cognition); (4) accounting for mediating problem-solving patterns, such as coping strategies that are accompanied by or linked to observed identity orientations or adaptive responses; and, finally, (5) linking the antecedent factors (i.e., minority status and the experience of stress) and the perceptually undergirded mediating processes described (i.e., points 2–4 above) with specific behavioral outcomes.

As suggested by competence theorizing (e.g., White, 1959), an established or manifested *identity* is associated with either adverse or productive life-course experiences. We believe that an alternative formulation, as noted, would address several of the issues and concerns alluded to previously and which follow. First, it is our position that traditional approaches have not been developmental. Interpretations of child outcomes (e.g., patterns of preference behavior) have been made as if youth were short black persons as opposed to African American children. Adult cognitions were inferred from young children's response patterns (e.g., traditionally, internalized self-hatred has been concluded vs. a consideration of findings as egocentric [childhood] responses about social "knowledge").

Second, the research has been generally reactive in quality. Early research (Clark & Clark, 1939, 1940; Goodman, 1952) on young African American children generated empirical and conceptual reactions during subsequent decades. On the other hand, nonminority research approaches have explored the processes of human development across broad topics. Specifically, from about 1933 to the early 1960s, white American children were the objects of broad scientific study and research by developmentalists (see Slaughter & McWorter, 1985, p. 6). African American (and other minority) youth were seldom included in these studies (Guthrie, 1976).

For language and cultural minorities, the approach to research taken, the empirical questions posed, the study designs, and the interpretations made have been often skewed to respond to a priori negative assumptions (e.g., Guthrie, 1976; Slaughter & McWorter, 1985). Most amazing has been the third major trend. Social science research findings or perspectives that run counter to the more traditional deviance- or deficit-linked conclusions are infrequently cited or considered (e.g., Billingsley, 1968; Hill, 1972; Ladner, 1971). Alternative formulations that interpret psychological processes for minority youth should inform developmental theorizing as well as integrate the nature of environmental experiences both for the socializing agent and the object of socialization. Recent minority-focused reports are useful in structuring specific interventions (Boykin, 1986; Gibbs, Huang, & Associates, 1989) targeted for racial and ethnic minority children and families.

Prevention and Intervention Efforts to Enhance Identity Formation among Ethnic Minorities

The research reviewed here has shown that identity formation among ethnic and racial minority children and adolescents is problematic and complex. Specific barriers to the process of identity formation for minorities have been described. Given that, it is imperative to identify specific prevention and intervention strategies that can be utilized with minority children and adolescents. Alternative identity-focused intervention and prevention efforts for African Americans, Hispanic, and American Indian children, youth, and their families overlap somewhat and move us to present several prescriptions.

1. Methods should be proposed to keep minority youth in school and academically oriented since their lack of education continues to serve as a condition that virtually guarantees a life course of socioeconomic disadvantage.

Economically disadvantaged minority youth perform less well on standardized achievement tests, in credits earned toward graduation, or in grade-point averages when compared with their nonminority peers (Gibbs & Huang, 1989, p. 18). Problems and controversy remain about the inappropriate use of tests with minority youth (Samuda, 1975). In addition, minority youth are frequently "token" members of groups that produce prestige and promote competence in them and their parents (Gibbs & Huang, 1989). Often, these experiences are compromised by a lack of acculturation (Matute-Bianchi, 1986). On the other hand, the extreme stress placed on Sansei children by their Nisei parents may undermine academic performance for some Japanese youth (Nagata, 1989, p. 76). Fordham and Ogbu (1986) suggest that bright black youth may behave in ways to avoid perceptions of "acting white" or being seen as "brainiacs." Similar patterns have been noted by Matute-Bianchi (1986) for Mexican-American youth.

2. Efforts are required to heighten health consciousness (chronic health problems confound identity processes). Several strategies have been found to be effective for promoting the utilization of mental health services. For example, a friendly style (called *personalismo* by Hispanics) has been found to defuse anxiety and establish rapport (Gibbs & Huang, 1989). Clinicians are encouraged to offer a brief explanation of therapy and to point out its link to the familiar role of healer in the minority culture (e.g., *curandero*, medicine man) (Gibbs & Huang, 1989, p. 23). Although the general health of Americans has improved, the physical health of African American (Carter, 1983), Mexican American (Solis, 1983), and American Indian (Brown & Hernasy, 1983) children continues to lag behind.

3. The importance of constructive social networks and support systems should be affirmed. Minority families differ widely in the quality and breadth of social support. For lower-income African Americans, the church, although important, is not viewed as an important resource for child rearing (Spencer, in press). Extended kin networks often provide an alternative and temporary source of support for African Americans (McAdoo, 1981). However, reinforced mutual assistance may also serve as a source of stress. Extended kin in rural areas often afford a respite for troubled teens and their families (Gibbs, 1989a). For American Indians, uncles and aunts are important teachers who share wisdom and impart values (LaFromboise & Low, 1989).

4. Methods should be proposed to support parenting efforts as cultural transmitters. Families vary greatly in their ability to serve as cultural transmitters. Findings for African American youth suggest that parents do not emphasize cultural values (Bowman & Howard, 1985; Spencer, 1983). For Mexican American families, the cultural transmission emphasis may vary by level of acculturation and the family's immigration history (Ramirez, 1989), and for Japanese families, family structure (e.g., generational changes and outmarriages) would affect the content and form of cultural transmission. In addition, the Japanese internment (generally not discussed) resulted in many parents opting to raise their children to be as "American" as possible (Nagata, 1989, p. 82).

5. Proposals are needed to offer a compensatory (media-focused) cultural emphasis that affirms group identity for all youth and thus enhances ego-identity processes and group pride. The process of changing images may be less straightforward for specific groups. Filipino Americans experience a mixture of stereotypes. Although thought of as hospitable, neat, hard-working, patient, docile, and bright, they are also stereotyped as sneaky, dishonest, lazy, and social climbers

(Santos, 1983, p. 138). The stereotype of Japanese-American youth as "model Americans" is also stress producing. The negative stereotypes associated with African Americans, Mexican Americans, and American Indians are pervasive and often linked to color connotations and long-standing social stereotypes.

6. Methods to promote the teaching in schools of native languages and cultures (particularly for American Indian tribes who appear most at risk of losing their heritage) are needed. Creativity will be required to encourage biculturalism while preserving (identity-linked) cultural traditions.

7. Providing a mechanism for the special training of teachers of ethnic minority students is critical. This would include sensitizing teachers to the customs, traditions, communication patterns, and, sometimes, the language of ethnic minorities. Teacher accountability should be built into the process.

8. Child-rearing support by way of teaching parenting skills that promote the parents' sense of ethnic pride and enhance "home-school partnership bonds" is essential. The Yale-New Haven Primary Prevention Program (Comer, 1985) provides an important model. Serving children and families from kindergarten through the fourth grade, the program is based on an ecological model and "focuses on creating a desirable climate or social environment in schools through application of mental health principles in a way that effects a coordinated management, curriculum, and staff development" (p. 155).

9. Improved methods of training for mental health workers who specifically serve an ethnic minority population should be required.

In summary, we believe that an overall system-wide intervention with multiple components is needed. For example, in many American Indian tribes the support of tribal leaders and training of indigenous social workers and therapists can foster ethnic pride and may provide support for youth currently struggling with developing a sense of identity (LaFromboise & Low, 1989). The developmental needs of African American and Hispanic youth are similar to those of other minorities and, in fact, to those of white youth. However, given particular structural conditions, ethnic and racial sensitivity must be added to the training of professionals, and accountability must be included. Service providers must dismantle barriers that reinforce negative images of minority youth, undermine manifest competence of service providers, diminish positive identity outcomes for minority youth, and offer incomplete analyses (as theories) of human development.

Finally, from a theory-generating and empirical research perspective, an alternative, ongoing, and developmental approach to the life-course experiences of minority youth should provide important information of several types to be used for multiple purposes. For example, research would afford information: (*a*) for generating more comprehensive theories, (*b*) for reformulating developmental models of risk and coping, (*c*) for proposing and implementing programs of intervention, and (*d*) for increasing efforts aimed at equity in a more overt or concrete manner. Combined efforts such as the ones proposed would influence and broaden conceptualizations of psychosocial processes. Minority youth generally (and male minority youth specifically) should, from the early toddler and preschool years, believe that they can have a positive impact on the world. Environments could be restructured to support children's acquisition of a sense of personal efficacy and thus the ontogeny of a more constructive identity and the perception and experience of a competent self.

References

Aboud, F. E. (1977). Interest in ethnic information: A cross-cultural developmental study. *Canadian Journal of Behavioral Science*, **9**, 134–146.

Aboud, F. E. (1988). *Children and prejudice*. New York: Basil Blackwell.

Abraham, K. G. (1986). Ego-identity differences among Anglo-American and Mexican-American adolescents. *Journal of Adolescence*, **9**, 151–166.

Alejandro-Wright, M. N. (1985). The child's conception of racial classification: A socio-cognitive developmental model. In M. B. Spencer, G. K. Brookins, & W. R. Allen (Eds.), *Beginnings: The social and affective development of black children* (pp. 185–200). Hillsdale, NJ: Erlbaum.

Allen, L., & Majidi-Ahi, S. (1989). Black American children. In J. T. Gibbs & L. N. Huang (Eds.), *Children of color* (pp. 148–178). San Francisco: Jossey-Bass.

Allen, W. R. (1985). Race, income and family dynamics: A study of adolescent male socialization processes and outcomes. In M. B. Spencer, W. R. Allen, & G. K. Brookins (Eds.), *Beginnings: The social and affective development of black children* (pp. 273–292). Hillsdale, NJ: Erlbaum.

Annis, R. C., & Corenblum, B. (1987). Effect of test

language and experimenter race on Canadian Indian children's racial and self-identity. *Journal of Social Psychology*, **126**, 761–773.

Atkinson, D., Morten, G., & Sue, S. (1983). *Counseling American minorities: A cross-cultural approach*. Dubuque, IA: William C. Brown.

Banks, W. C. (1976). White preference in blacks: A paradigm in search of a phenomenon. *Psychological Bulletin*, **83**, 1179–1186.

Barkley, K. L. (1985). Inter- and intra-group levels of esteem among three ethnic groups. *Journal of Negro Education*, **54**, 56–70.

Barnes, E. (1972). The black community as the source of positive self-concept for black children: A theoretical perspective. In R. Jones (Ed.), *Black psychology* (pp. 166–192). New York: Harper & Row.

Beiser, M. (1981). Mental health of American Indian and Alaska Native children: Some epidemiological perspectives. *White Cloud Journal*, **2**, 37–47.

Berlin, I. N. (1986). Psychopathology and its antecedents among American Indian adolescents. In B. B. Lahey & A. E. Kazdin (Eds.), *Advances in clinical child psychology* (Vol. **9**, pp. 125–152). New York: Plenum.

Beuf, A. H. (1977). *Red children in white America*. University Park: Pennsylvania State University Press.

Bienvenue, R. M. (1978). Self-evaluations of native and Euro-Canadian students. *Canadian Ethnic Studies*, **10**, 97–105.

Billingsley, A. (1968). *Black families in white America*. Englewood Cliffs, NJ: Prentice-Hall.

Bowman, P., & Howard, C. (1985). Race-related socialization, motivation, and academic achievement: A study of black youth in three-generation families. *Journal of the American Academy of Child Psychiatry*, **24**, 134–141.

Boykin, A. W. (1986). The triple quandary and the schooling of Afro-American children. In U. Neisser (Ed.), *The school achievement of minority children: New perspectives* (pp. 57–92). Hillsdale, NJ: Erlbaum.

Brand, E. S., Ruiz, R. A., & Padillo, A. M. (1974). Ethnic identification and preference: A review. *Psychological Review*, **81**, 860–890.

Bronfenbrenner, U. (1979). *The ecology of human development*. Cambridge, MA: Harvard University Press.

Brookins, G. K. (1988). Making the honor role: A parent's perspective on private education. In D. T. Slaughter & D. J. Johnson (Eds.), *Visible now: Blacks in private school* (pp. 12–20). New York: Greenwood.

Brown, A. D., & Hernasy, K. W. (1983). The impact of culture on the health of American Indian children. In G. J. Powell (Ed.), *The psychosocial development of minority children* (pp. 39–48). New York: Brunner/Mazel.

Bryde, J. F. (1971). *Indian students and guidance*. Boston: Houghton Mifflin.

Burgess, B. J. (1980). Parenting in the Native-American community. In M. D. Fantini & R. Cardenas (Eds.), *Parenting in a multi-cultural society* (pp. 63–73). New York: Longman.

Carter, J. H. (1983). Vision or sight: Health concerns for Afro-American children. In G. J. Powell (Ed.), *The psychosocial development of minority children*. New York: Brunner/Mazel.

Chestang, L. W. (1972). *Character development in a hostile environment*. Occasional Paper No. 3. Chicago: University of Chicago.

Clark, K. B., & Clark, M. K. (1939). The development of consciousness of self and the emergence of racial identity in Negro children. *Journal of Social Psychology*, **10**, 591–599.

Clark, K. B., & Clark, M. K. (1940). Skin color as a factor in racial identification of Negro preschool children. *Journal of Social Psychology*, **11**, 159–169.

Cockerham, W. C. (1979). Interactional considerations in studying American "Indians": The case of adolescent self-esteem. *Symbolic Interaction*, **2**, 43–57.

Comer, J. (1985). The Yale-New Haven Primary Prevention Project: A follow-up. *Journal of the American Academy of Child Psychiatry*, **24**, 154–160.

Cooley, C. H. (1902). *Human nature and the social order*. New York: Charles Scribner's Sons.

Corenblum, B., & Wilson, A. E. (1982). Ethnic preference and identification among Canadian Indian and White children: Replication and extension. *Canadian Journal of Behavioral Science*, **14**, 50–59.

Cross, W. E. (1978). The Thomas and Cross models of psychological nigrescence: A literature review. *Journal of Black Psychology*, **4**, 13–31.

Cross, W. E. (1985). Black identity: Rediscovering the distinction between personal identity and reference group orientation. In M. B. Spencer, G. K. Brookins, & W. R. Allen (Eds.), *Beginnings: The social and affective development of black children* (pp. 155–172). Hillsdale, NJ: Erlbaum.

Deloria, V. (1969). *Custer died for your sins*. New York: Avon.

DeVos, G. (1982). Ethnic pluralism: Conflict and accommodation. In G. DeVos & L. Romanucci-Ross (Eds.), *Ethnic identity: Cultural continuities and change* (pp. 5–41). Palo Alto, CA: Manfield.

DeVos, G., & Romanucci-Ross, L. (1982a). *Ethnic identity*. Chicago: University of Chicago Press.

DeVos, G., & Romanucci-Ross, L. (1982b). Ethnicity: Vessel of meaning and emblem of contrast. In G. DeVos & L. Romanucci-Ross (Eds.), *Ethnic identity* (pp. 363–390). Chicago: University of Chicago Press.

Doob, L. W. (1947). The behavior of attitudes. *Psychological Review*, **54**, 135–156.

DuBois, W. E. B. (1963). *An ABC of color*. Berlin: Seven Seas Books. (Original work published in 1896)

Epps, E. E. (1988). Summary and discussion. In D. T. Slaughter & D. J. Johnson (Eds.), *Visible now: Blacks in private school* (pp. 86–89). New York: Greenwood.

Erikson, E. H. (1959). Identity and the life cycle. *Psychological Issues* (Selected papers), Monograph I.

Erikson, E. H. (1963). *Childhood and society* (2d ed.). New York: Norton.

Erikson, E. H. (1968). *Identity: Youth and crisis*. New York: Norton.

Fillmore, L. W., & Britsch, S. (1988, June). *Early education for children from linguistic and cultural minority families*. Unpublished paper prepared for the Early Education Task Force of the National Association of State Boards of Education.

Fordham, S., & Ogbu, J. U. (1986). Black students' school success coping with the burden of acting white. *Urban Review*, **18**, 176–206.

Franklin, V. P. (1985). From integration to black self-determination: Changing social science perspectives on Afro-American life and culture. In M. B. Spencer, G. K. Brookins, & W. R. Allen (Eds.), *Beginnings: The social and affective development of black children* (pp. 19–28). Hillsdale, NJ: Erlbaum.

Fuchs, E., & Havighurst, R. J. (1972). *To live on this earth*. New York: Doubleday.

Garbarino, J. (1982). *Children and families in the social environment*. New York: Aldine.

Gibbs, J. T. (1989a). Black American adolescents. In J. T. Gibbs & L. N. Huang (Eds.), *Children of color* (pp. 179–223). San Francisco: Jossey-Bass.

Gibbs, J. T. (1989b). Biracial adolescents. In J. T. Gibbs & L. N. Huang (Eds.), *Children of color* (pp. 322–350). San Francisco: Jossey-Bass.

Gibbs, J. T., & Huang, L. N. (1989). A conceptual framework for assessing and treating minority youth. In J. T. Gibbs & L. N. Huang (Eds.), *Children of color* (pp. 1–29). San Francisco: Jossey-Bass.

Gibbs, J. T., Huang, L. N., & Associates (Eds.). (1989). *Children of color*. San Francisco: Jossey-Bass.

Goodman, M. E. (1952). *Race awareness in young children*. New York: Crowell-Collier.

Gougis, R. A. (1986). The effects of prejudice and stress on the academic performance of black Americans. In U. Neisser (Ed.), *The school achievement of minority children: New perspectives* (pp. 145–158). Hillsdale, NJ: Erlbaum

Guthrie, R. (1976). *Even the rat was white*. New York: Harper & Row.

Hare, B. R., & Castenell, L. A. (1985). No place to run, no place to hide: Comparative status and future prospects of black boys. In M. B. Spencer, G. K. Brookins, & W. R. Allen (Eds.), *Beginnings: The social and affective development of black children* (pp. 185–200). Hillsdale, NJ: Erlbaum.

Harter, S. (1983). Developmental perspectives on the self-system. In E. M. Hetherington (Ed.), P. H. Mussen (Series Ed.), *Handbook of child psychology: Vol. 4. Socialization, personality, and social development* (pp. 275–385). New York: Wiley.

Hauser, S. T. (1972a). Black and white identity development: Aspects and perspectives. *Journal of Youth and Adolescence*, **1**, 113–130.

Hauser, S. T. (1972b). Adolescent self-image development. *Archives of General Psychiatry*, **27**, 537–541.

Hill, R. (1972). *The strengths of black families*. New York: Emerson-Hall.

Hill, R. A. (1983). *The Marcus Garvey and Universal Negro Improvement Association Papers* (Vol. 1). Berkeley: University of California Press.

Huang, L. N., & Ying, Y. (1989). Chinese American children and adolescents. In J. T. Gibbs & L. N. Huang (Eds.), *Children of color* (pp. 30–66). San Francisco: Jossey-Bass.

Hunsberger, B. (1978). Racial awareness and preference of white and Indian Canadian children. *Canadian Journal of Behavioral Science*, **10**, 176–180.

Inclan, J. E., & Herron, D. G. (1989). Puerto Rican adolescents. In J. T. Gibbs & L. N. Huang (Eds.), *Children of color* (pp. 251–277). San Francisco: Jossey-Bass.

Jackson, J. S., McCullough, W. R., & Gurin, G. (1988). Family, socialization, environment, and identity development in black Americans. In H. P. McAdoo (Ed.), *Black families* (2d ed., pp. 252–263). Newbury Park, CA: Sage.

Johnson, D. J. (1988). Racial socialization strategies of parents in three black private schools. In D. T. Slaughter & D. J. Johnson (Eds.), *Visible now: Blacks in private school* (pp. 251–268). New York: Greenwood.

Katz, P. (1981). Psychotherapy with native adolescents. *Canadian Journal of Psychiatry*, **26**, 455–459.

Ladner, J. (1971). *Tomorrow's tomorrow: The black woman*. New York: Doubleday.

LaFromboise, T. D., & Low, K. G. (1989). American Indian children and adolescents. In J. T. Gibbs & L. N. Huang (Eds.), *Children of color* (pp. 114–147). San Francisco: Jossey-Bass.

Lefley, H. P. (1976). Acculturation, child-rearing,

and self-esteem in two North American Indian tribes. *Ethos*, **4**, 385–401.

Lerner, R. M. (1982). Children and adolescents as producers of their own development. *Developmental Review*, **2**, 342–370.

Lonner, W. J. (1987). Introduction to the special issue. *Journal of Cross-Cultural Psychology*, **18**, 379–382.

Marcia, J. E. (1966). Development and validation of ego identity status. *Journal of Youth and Adolescence*, **13**, 419–438.

Markstrom, C. A. (1987, April). *A comparison of psychosocial maturity between four ethnic groups during middle adolescence*. Paper presented at the biennial meetings of the Society for Research in Child Development, Baltimore, MD.

Markstrom, C. A., & Mullis, R. L. (1986). Ethnic differences in the imaginary audience. *Journal of Adolescent Research*, **1**, 289–301.

Matute-Bianchi, M. E. (1986). Ethnic identity and patterns of school successes and failures among Mexican-descent and Japanese-American students in a California high school: An ethnographic analysis. *American Journal of Education*, **95**, 233–255.

May, P. A. (1987). Suicide and self-destruction among American Indian youths. *American Indian and Alaska Native Mental Health Research*, **1**, 52–69.

McAdoo, H. P. (1981). *Black families*. Newbury Park, CA: Sage.

Mead, G. H. (1934). *Mind, self and society*. Chicago: University of Chicago Press.

Means, R. (1980). Fighting words on the future of the earth. *Mother Jones*, **5**(10), 12–38.

Mendelberg, H. E. (1986). Identity conflict in Mexican-American adolescents. *Adolescence*, **21**, 215–222.

Moritsugu, J., & Sue, S. (1983). Minority status as a stressor. In R. Felner, L. Jason, J. Moritsugu, & S. Farber (Eds.), *Preventive psychology: Theory, research and practice* (pp. 3–10). Elmsford, NY: Pergamon.

Nagata, D. (1989). Japanese American children and adolescents. In G. T. Gibbs & L. N. Huang (Eds.), *Children of color* (pp. 67–113). San Francisco: Jossey-Bass.

Ogbu, J. (1983). Crossing cultural boundaries: A comparative perspective on minority education. *Race, class, socialization and the life cycle*. Symposium organized in honor of Allison Davis, John Dewey Professor Emeritus, University of Chicago.

Phinney, J. S., & Tarver, S. (1988). Ethnic identity search and commitment in black and white eighth-graders. *Journal of Early Adolescence*, **8**, 265–277.

Powell, G. J. (1985). Self-concepts among Afro-American students in racially isolated minority schools: Some regional differences. *Journal of the American Academy of Child Psychiatry*, **24**, 142–149.

Ramirez, M., III. (1969). Identification with Mexican-American values and psychological adjustment in Mexican-American adolescents. *International Journal of Social Psychiatry*, **15**, 151–156.

Ramirez, M., III, & Castaneda, A. (1974). *Cultural democracy, bicognitive development, and education*. New York: Academic Press.

Ramirez, O. (1989). Mexican American children and adolescence. In G. T. Gibbs & L. N. Huang (Eds.), *Children of color* (pp. 224–250). San Francisco: Jossey-Bass.

Rosenberg, M. (1981). The self-concept: Social product and social force. In M. Rosenberg & R. H. Turner (Eds.), *Social psychology* (pp. 593–624). New York: Basic.

Rosenberg, M., & Simmons, R. G. (1972). *Black and white self-esteem: The urban school child*. Washington, DC: American Sociological Association.

Rotheram, M. J., & Phinney, J. S. (1987). Introduction: Definitions and perspectives in the study of children's ethnic socialization. In J. S. Phinney & M. J. Rotheram (Eds.), *Children's ethnic socialization* (pp. 10–28). Newbury Park, CA: Sage.

Samuda, R. (1975). *Psychological testing of American minorities: Issues and consequences*. New York: Dodd, Mead.

Santos, R. (1983). The social and emotional development of Filipino-American children. In G. J. Powell (Ed.), *The psychosocial development of minority children* (pp. 131–146). New York: Brunner/Mazel.

Semaj, L. T. (1985). Afrikanity, cognition, and extended self-identity. In M. B. Spencer, G. K. Brookins, & W. R. Allen (Eds.), *Beginnings: Social and affective development of black children* (pp. 173–184). Hillsdale, NJ: Erlbaum.

Slaughter, D. T., & McWorter, G. A. (1985). Social origins and early features of the scientific study of black American families and children. In M. B. Spencer, G. K. Brookins, & W. R. Allen (Eds.), *Beginnings: Social and affective development of black children* (pp. 5–18). Hillsdale, NJ: Erlbaum.

Solis, F. (1983). Factors relating to the health status of Mexican-American children. In G. J. Powell (Ed.), *The psychosocial development of minority children* (pp. 26–38). New York: Brunner/Mazel.

Spencer, M. B. (1970). *The effects of systematic social (puppet) and token reinforcement on the modification of racial and color concept-attitudes in preschool aged children*. Unpublished master's thesis, University of Kansas, Lawrence.

Spencer, M. B. (1977). The social-cognitive and personality development of the black preschool child: An exploratory study of developmental process (Doctoral dissertation, University of Chicago). *Dissertation Abstracts International,* **38.**

Spencer, M. B. (1982a). Personal and group identity of black children: An alternative synthesis. *Genetic Psychology Monographs,* **103,** 59–84.

Spencer, M. B. (1982b). Preschool children's social cognition and cultural cognition: A cognitive developmental interpretation of race dissonance findings. *Journal of Psychology,* **112,** 275–286.

Spencer, M. B. (1983). Children's cultural values and parental childrearing strategies. *Developmental Review,* **3,** 351–370.

Spencer, M. B. (1985). Cultural cognition and social cognition as identity factors in black children's personal-social growth. In M. B. Spencer, G. K. Brookins, & W. R. Allen (Eds.), *Beginnings: The social and affective development of black children* (pp. 215–230). Hillsdale, NJ: Erlbaum.

Spencer, M. B. (1986). Risk and resilience: How black children cope with stress. *Social Science,* **71,** 22–26.

Spencer, M. B. (1988). Self concept development. In D. T. Slaughter (Ed.), *Black children in poverty: Developmental perspectives* (pp. 59–72). San Francisco: Jossey-Bass.

Spencer, M. B. (in press). Parental value transmission: Implications for black child development. In J. B. Stewart & H. Cheatham (Eds.), *Interdisciplinary perspectives on black families.* Atlanta, GA: Transactions.

Spencer, M. B., Dobbs, B., & Swanson, D. P. (1988). Afro-American adolescents: Adaptational processes and socioeconomic diversity in behavioral outcomes. *Journal of Adolescence,* **11,** 117–137.

Spencer, M. B., & Horowitz, F. D. (1973). Racial attitudes and color concept-attitude modification in black and caucasian preschool children. *Developmental Psychology,* **9,** 246–254.

Spencer, M. B., Kim, S., & Marshall, S. (1987). Double stratification and psychological risk: Adaptational processes and school experiences of black children. *Journal of Negro Education,* **56,** 77–86.

Streitmatter, J. L. (1988). Ethnicity as a mediating variable of early adolescent identity development. *Journal of Adolescence,* **11,** 335–346.

Sue, S. W. (1978). World views and counseling. *Personnel and Guidance Journal,* **56,** 458–462.

Trueba, H. T. (1988). Culturally based explanations of minority students' academic achievement. *Anthropology and Education Quarterly,* **19,** 270–287.

Van Sertima, I. (1977). *They came before Columbus: The African presence in ancient America.* New York: Random House.

Westermeyer, J. (1979a). Ethnic identity problems among ten Indian psychiatric patients. *International Journal of Social Psychiatry,* **25,** 188–197.

Westermeyer, J. (1979b). The apple syndrome in Minnesota: A complication of racial-ethnic discontinuity. *Journal of Operational Psychiatry,* **10,** 134–140.

White, R. (1959). Motivation reconsidered: The concept of competence. *Psychological Review,* **66,** 297–333.

Williamson, J. (1984). *The crucible of race.* New York: Oxford University Press.

INTERNATIONAL JOURNAL OF BEHAVIORAL DEVELOPMENT, 1991, *14* (2), 165–193

Adolescent Ego Development within the Family: Family Styles and Family Sequences

Stuart T. Hauser, John Houlihan, Sally I. Powers, Alan M. Jacobson, Gil G. Noam, Bedonna Weiss-Perry, Donna Follansbee, and Barbara K. Book

We describe a series of analyses that were carried out using the Constraining and Enabling Coding System (CECS). This scheme was specially constructed to identify family interactions conceptually relevant to adolescent ego development. We present results based on the application of these scales to observations of 80 families, consisting of two parents and an adolescent drawn from closely matched high school and psychiatric populations. The families are predominantly upper middle and middle class. Each family member completed the Loevinger Sentence Completion Test and then participated in a revealed-differences task, using responses to Kohlberg Moral Dilemmas as discussion stimuli. Transcripts of these audio-recorded discussions form the database for our family analyses. The family analyses were of two general types. First, we examined relations between *family style* and the ego development of each family member. The style analyses were based on aggregate scores for each of the enabling or constraining behaviours. After controlling for patient status, adolescent age, and family social class, adolescent and parent ego development scores

---

The addresses of the authors are as follows: *Stuart T. Hauser*, Department of Psychiatry, Harvard Medical School, Massachusetts Mental Health Center, and Joslin Diabetes Center. *John Houlihan*, Academic Computing Center, Boston University. *Sally I. Powers*, Department of Psychology, University of Massachusetts, Amherst; Department of Psychiatry, Harvard Medical School. *Alan M. Jacobson*, Department of Psychiatry, Harvard Medical School, Massachusetts Mental Health Center, and Joslin Diabetes Center. *Gil G. Noam*, Department of Psychiatry, Harvard Medical School; McLean Hospital. *Bedonna Weiss-Perry*, Northwestern University. *Donna Follansbee*, Harvard Medical School, Judge Baker Guidance Center. *Barbara K. Book*, Department of Psychiatry, Harvard Medical School; Massachusetts Mental Health Center.

Requests for reprints should be sent to Dr Stuart T. Hauser, Adolescent and Family Development Project, Harvard Medical School, 74 Fenwood Rd., Boston, MA 02115, U.S.A.

This article is a revision of a paper presented at SRCD meetings, 25 April 1985, Toronto, Canada; and at the Pre-conference Workshop on Family Contexts of Adolescent Development, Society for Research on Adolescence, 20 March 1986, Madison, Wisconsin, U.S.A.

contributed to explained variance in these family style behaviours. Parental style behaviours, especially of mothers, were also significantly associated with parent ego development as well as adolescent ego development. We then examined *family sequences* in terms of their links with adolescent ego development. Through these process-oriented analyses, we discovered that the intensity of turn taking and reciprocal enabling (mutual enabling) interactions between mothers and adolescents were significantly enhanced by the ego development of the mother. Such associations between reciprocal interactions and parental ego development were not present for mutual enabling pairings between fathers and adolescents. In our discussion we consider the importance of adding these sequence analyses to our studies, as one more way of exploring relations between family factors and adolescent development.

INTRODUCTION

In this paper we report new directions in our studies of family contexts of adolescent ego development. The key questions we pursue involve how adolescent and parent characteristics influence their interactions with one another, and how parent-adolescent interactions may contribute to adolescent development. We use two analytic perspectives. The first perspective, *interaction style*, refers to the level of a particular behaviour that a parent or adolescent expresses within the family. The second perspective, *interaction sequence*, describes moment to moment family processes, such as mutuality. The introduction of sequence analyses represents a new approach in our analyses: 15 years ago, Mishler and Waxler (1975, p. 17) commented: "The vast amount of research on interaction in . . . families would be summarized with fair accuracy by the statement that there has been almost exclusive emphasis on summary or aggregate measures of behaviors, that is, on measures of behavior summed and averaged across an interval of time to provide overall indices." Such a generalisation also applies to most current studies of interactions in families with adolescent members, and studies of the possible connection of these interactions with the development of the adolescents themselves. Although we believe that much can be learned by looking at overall indices of behaviours (family style) during family discussions, we think that it may be enlightening to also identify key processes, *moment-to-moment* behaviours occurring between family members during ongoing discussions.

Emphasising the importance of "dynamic" data in contrast to more trait-like data is hardly news to clinically informed observers. Most of our clinical colleagues, regardless of their persuasion, would insist that such phenomena as the processes of family life, or the sequential verbal associations of an individual, provide some of the most important clues to understanding the nature of family life or of the individual's internal life.

Until recently, it has not been possible to apply such a widely accepted clinical insight to more quantitative empirical studies of family interaction. Methodological developments have now made it possible to undertake rigorous empirical analyses of interaction sequences within families (e.g. Mishler & Waxler, 1975; Sackett, 1980, 1987; Bakeman, 1978; Gottman, 1979; Bakeman & Gottman, 1986a, 1986b).

We extend our previous studies (Hauser et al., 1984; Powers et al., 1983) in several ways. Using a larger sample, we ask a series of related questions: (1) Does an adolescent's ego development level predict his or her behaviours within the family? (2) Do parental family behaviours predict the adolescent's level of development? (3) Do parents' ego development levels predict their family behaviours? (4) Does the adolescent's gender influence these development/family relationships? We consider these four questions in terms of family "style" dimensions, that is aggregate indices based on measures of specific behaviours summed and averaged across a period of time (a family discussion).

We then consider two final questions that address *specific sequences* between parent and adolescent. The first question focuses on whether certain theoretically important sequences, such as mutual enabling behaviours between mothers and their sons, are linked with their levels of development. In addition to this substantive question, there is an important methods one: What additional understandings about family processes and individual development do we gain through the new "window" provided by sequence analyses?

CONCEPTUAL BACKGROUND

Ego Development

The aspect of adolescent development that we follow is ego development. This construct plays a central role in many theoretical and clinical discussions of adolescence. Yet it is only recently that systematic empirical studies have included this concept, a welcome advance largely prompted by the important theoretical and psychometric contributions made by Loevinger and her colleagues (Loevinger, 1976; Loevinger & Wessler, 1970; Loevinger, Wessler, & Redmore, 1970). In tracing adolescent ego development, we incorporate this theoretically guided assessment approach.

At the most general level, ego development refers to the *framework of meaning* that the individual imposes upon his or her experience. The sequence of ego development stages, defined independently of age, have much relevance to psychosocial issues encountered during adolescent years. Each of these stages differs from the others along intrapsychic and interpersonal dimensions. In brief, individuals at the earliest stages are wary, impulsive, demanding, and concrete. In addition, they express stereotyped cognitive styles, and exploitative or dependent interpersonal behaviours. The three stages that share these characteristics are the "pre-conformist" ones.

A second set of stages is referred to as the "conformist" level. Inner-states are verbally expressed at these stages. Yet the individual's mode of expression is, for the most part, in terms of clichés, stereotypes, and moralistic judgements. Nonetheless, there is a gradual increase of self-awareness and an appreciation of multiple possibilities in different situations. This increasing self-awareness is most prominent at the advanced or "post-conformist" stages. At this highest level of development, individuals cope with inner-conflict through more intensive self-perception, show much cognitive complexity, and have interpersonal styles that emphasise mutuality, autonomy, empathy, and the cherishing (not merely accepting) of individual differences. These telegraphic descriptions of the ego development levels are intended to convey basic features that distinguish adolescents from the earliest stages to the most advanced ones. Table 1 presents a more detailed description of the stages.

Family Processes and Ego Development

Our central interest is in understanding bi-directional relations between family dimensions (style and sequence) and ego development: How family processes may play a role in advancing as well as delaying or arresting the individual in this line of development; *and* how families may be influenced/changed by transformations in ego development. With respect to family processes that are broadly relevant to considering adolescent ego development, there is an extensive empirical and clinical literature (cf. Hauser et al., 1984, 1985, 1991, for reviews of this literature). Although rich and interesting, this work, with the exception of the contributions of Cooper and Grotevant (Cooper, Grotevant, & Condon, 1983; Grotevant & Cooper, 1986), has limited direct relevance for our studies. First of all, many of the central constructs are developed largely to explain how severe psychiatric disturbance (e.g. schizophrenia) might be the product of specific family factors or patterns. Secondly, the database for these family concepts consists primarily of clinical observations of psychiatric patients, and thus represents a skewed sample.

Our conceptualisation of relevant family processes was sparked by Stierlin's (1974) formulations of how parental interactions influence adolescent maturation. The major theme of his theoretical framework is that disturbed families are distinctive, in the light of the numerous attempts that parents make to interfere with the autonomous functioning of children and adolescents. Among these impediments to independent perceptions and cognitions are *binding* interactions, through which parents actively resist the differentiation of their adolescent child. We have expanded this framework in several ways: First, we distinguish among several types of "binding". Secondly, and perhaps most significantly, we look at *enabling* interactions, ways in which family members encourage or support the expression of more independent perceptions and behaviours from one another. And thirdly, we take account of *reciprocal* effects, how adolescents may evoke parental behaviours as well as how parents influence adolescents. These family behaviours refer to two large descriptive domains of family variables: cognitive/attentional and affective/relational (Wynne, Jones, & Al-Khayyal, 1982). Within each of these realms are family interactions that can impede and undermine (constrain) ego development, as well as those that can assist and facilitate (enable) this development. Among the constraining behaviours are distracting, devaluing, and withholding. Enabling behaviours include focusing, explaining, and accepting. Table 2 presents the entire array of constraining and enabling variables.

In a previously reported study (Hauser et al., 1984), we examined how these family dimensions were linked with adolescent ego development. In those first analyses (with a smaller sample), we studied family enabling and constraining behaviours in terms of their average expression by each family member (e.g. father's aggregate cognitive enabling score divided by father's total speeches). These scores can be viewed as "family style" variables, as they reflect the given family member's pattern that is expressed throughout a family discussion. Using this new scoring system, we reported theoretically meaningful correlations between family members' enabling and constraining styles and individual ego development of both the adolescent and his or her parents (Hauser et al., 1984).

Now, through our larger sample of 80 families, we investigate relations between ego development and family variables with respect to: (1) individual family member styles; and (2) bi-directional sequences between adolescents and their parents.[1] Our overall aim is to delineate those family dimensions that contribute to, and are influenced by, variations in individual ego development. This aim leads us to the study of *sequential patterns*, linked family behaviours involving reciprocity, mutuality, or asynchrony. Through conceptualising and then assessing such family processes, we move one step closer to examining important *causal* questions, such as: Do adolescents at certain levels of development elicit particular behaviours (e.g. accepting) from their parents who may also be functioning

[1]In a future paper we will report interparental sequences and individual (parent and adolescent) ego development.

TABLE 1
Loevinger's Stages of Ego Development (from Loevinger, 1976)

Stage	*Impulse Control "Moral" Style*	*Interpersonal Style*	*Conscious Preoccupations*	*Cognitive Style*
Preconformist				
Presocial (I–1)	—	Autistic	Self vs. non-self	—
Symbiotic (I–1)	—	Symbiotic	Self vs. non-self	—
Impulsive (I–2)	Impulsive, fear	Receiving dependent, exploitive	Bodily feelings, especially sexual and aggressive	Stereotypy, conceptual confusion
Self-protective Δ	Fear of being caught, externalising blame, opportunistic	Wary, manipulative, exploitive	Self-protection, wishes, things, advantages, control	—
Transition from self-protective to conformist (Δ/3)	Obedience and conformity to social norms are simple and absolute rules	Manipulative, obedient	Concrete aspects of traditional sex roles, physical causation as opposed to psychological causation	Conceptual simplicity, stereotypes
Conformist				
Conformist (I–3)	Conformity to external rules, shame, guilt for breaking rules	Belonging, helping, superficial niceness	Appearance, social acceptability, banal feelings, behaviour	Conceptual simplicity, stereotypes, clichés
Transition from conformist to conscientious; self-consciousness (I–3/4)	Dawning realisation of standards, contingencies, self-criticism	Being helpful, deepened interest in interpersonal relations	Consciousness of the self as separate from the group, recognition of psychological causation	Awareness of individual differences in attitudes, interests and abilities; mentioned in global and broad terms

Post-conformist				
Conscientious (I–4)	Self-evaluated standards, self-criticism	Intensive, responsible, mutual concern for communication	Differentiated feelings, motives for behaviour, self-respect, achievements, traits, expression	Conceptual complexity, idea of patterning
Transition from conscientious to autonomous	Individuality, coping with inner conflict	Cherishing of interpersonal relations	Communicating, expressing ideas and feelings, process and change	Toleration for paradox and contradiction
Autonomous (I–5)	Add:* Coping with conflicting inner needs	Add: Respect for autonomy	Vividly conveyed feelings, integration of physiological and psychological causation of behaviour, development, role conception, self-fulfilment, self in social context	Increased conceptual complexity; complex patterns, toleration for ambiguity, broad scope, objectivity
Integrated (I–6)	Add: Reconciling inner conflicts, renunciation of unattainable	Add: Cherishing of individuality	Add: Identity	—

*"Add" means in addition to description applying to previous level.

TABLE 2
Constraining and Enabling Variables

Enabling	*Symbol*	
Explaining	Exp	
Problem Solving	Prob	*Cognitive Enabling*
Focusing	Foc	
Curiosity	Cur	
Accepting	Accep	*Affective Enabling*
Empathy	Emp	
Constraining		
Distracting	Dist	
Withholding	With	*Cognitive Constraining*
Judgmental	Jud	
Devaluing	Deval	
Indifference	Ind	*Affective Constraining*
Gratifying	Grat	

at these levels? Are there certain helpful behaviours that adolescents at higher levels of development express in response to the parents' more problematic behaviours (e.g. attacking or indifferent speeches)? On the other hand, are some parental behaviours (e.g. devaluing) so powerful that they uniformly influence an adolescent's family behaviours, regardless of his or her level of development? These questions reflect our expectation that sequence analyses can provide an important addition to analyses based only on style dimensions. Taken together, data gained from *both* levels of analysis are likely to further illuminate how family forces underlie or are reactive to adolescent ego development.

METHODS

Subjects

Eighty, two-parent families were drawn from two populations: high school students ($n = 40$) and a psychiatrically hospitalised ($n = 40$) group. The high school students were volunteers attending a suburban high school. The psychiatric subjects were volunteers from successive admissions to a private hospital children's unit. All patients diagnosed as having a thought disorder or organic brain damage were excluded from the sample. The mean age for all subjects was 14.5 (STD 0.85). Subjects and their families were paid $30 for participating in the family discussion sessions. The 80 families analysed in this paper are predominantly upper middle and middle class subjects who participated in the first year of a larger longitudinal project in which we are following adolescents and their families (one and two parent) from psychiatric and non-patient samples (Hauser et al., 1983, 1984, 1991; Powers et al., 1983; Jacobson, Hauser, Powers, & Noam, 1985).

The rationale for sampling from these contrasting populations was based on our expectation that many of the patients would be functioning at lower levels of ego development. By selecting from the psychiatric population, we reasoned that we would be more likely to obtain adolescents with ego development arrests (subjects at low ego stages upon entering the study who would probably not increase over the several years of the study). In sharp contrast, we predicted that the student sample would include many adolescents showing progressive ego development over time. We knew from our previous work that we would have less chance of finding such a range of ego development levels by using the more traditional and ideal method of randomly sampling a larger (e.g. entire high school population). In an earlier study of 100 upper and middle class girls we found that fewer than 10% were at the lowest (pre-conformist) level (Hauser, 1978).[2] Thus, while we did not rule out the presence of adolescents at lower ego development levels in the high school sample, we expected to find fewer such adolescents within a single high school freshman class.

We matched the samples as closely as possible for age, gender, and social class. As can be seen in Table 3, the matching was fully accomplished on all variables except social class (SES). Using the Hollingshead two-factor Index (Hollingshead, 1957), we found upper middle and middle class families predominated in both samples, as well as a greater spread of lower middle and working class families in the psychiatric sample.[3]

---

[2]Block (1971) refers to the need for such a strategy in discussing the problem of "defining the universe of subjects for a longitudinal study". He comments that random selection from a definable universe may not be "necessarily the most efficient strategy for developing understanding. Randomness, unaided, cannot be depended upon to represent sufficiently often certain types of individuals who, although not numerically frequent, are nevertheless of great conceptual significance" (p. 23). A similar point could be made for sampling techniques in clinical research (e.g. successive admissions of patients in a given diagnostic category).

[3]Data reported by Holt (1980) reveal significant correlations between social status (indexed through occupation and education) and Loevinger ego development scores in a cross-national sample of 501 men and women. In addition, Weinstock's (1967) ego processes study, and Miller and Mishler's discussion paper (1959) emphasises that for ego processes and mental illness the critical social class difference is that between lower class and middle/upper classes. Jacob (1974) makes a similar distinction of his family interaction analyses of social class. In the light of this, it is important to note that the SES differences in our subsamples involve primarily the middle classes. Nonetheless, as noted later, we control for social class in our multiple regression analyses.

TABLE 3
Demographic Characteristics of the Adolescent/Family Samples

Variable[a]	*Total*	*Psychiatric*	*High School*
Gender			
Male	36	18	18
Female	44	22	22
Age[b]			
Adolescent	14.5 (0.85)	14.4 (1.06)	14.5 (0.56)
Mother	42.6 (4.97)	42.1 (5.57)	43.0 (4.29)
Father	45.5 (6.40)	44.7 (7.23)	46.3 (5.37)
SES[c]			
Upper middle and middle	54 (66.2%)	18 (45.0%)	35 (87.5%)
Lower middle	16 (20.0%)	12 (30.0%)	4 (10.0%)
Working and lower	11 (13.8%)	10 (25.0%)	1 (2.5%)

[a]All comparisons between psychiatric and high school groups were non-significant, except for SES ($\times^2$ (1) = 15.9; $P < 0.0009$).
[b]All values are based on average age; numbers in parentheses are standard deviations.
[c]SES based on Hollingshead's (1957) two-factor index.

Another set of analyses compared the samples in terms of ego development. As expected, the psychiatric adolescents had significantly lower ego development scores, and (unexpectedly) parents of psychiatric patients had lower ego development scores. In addition, girls had higher ego development levels, in terms of both stage and item sum scores. (Definitions of both types of scores are provided in the Methods section below.) The overall sample had an average ego stage score of 3.2 (between self-protective and conformist). Table 4 summarises the ego development scores for adolescents and parents from each of the samples.

In the light of these sample differences, analyses of relations between ego development and family dimensions (style and sequence) statistically control for psychiatric status as well as social class through hierarchical multiple regressions. Our general strategy, then, is to use the psychiatric sample to "generate" many of the low ego development scores, while the high school sample provides the adolescents at the upper end of the developmental spectrum.

Setting and Timing

Individual adolescent subjects and families were seen at their hospital (patients and families) or at their school (non-patients and families). At each of these sites, we used private interview rooms and a larger meeting

TABLE 4
Ego Development Scores

Ego Development	*Total*	*Psychiatric*	*High School*	F *Variable*
Adolescent stage score	3.2 (1.8)	2.0 (1.1)	4.5 (1.5)	76.8[a]
Adolescent item sum score	139.6 (29.4)	118.2 (19.7)	160.9 (20.8)	93.42[a]
Mother stage score	5.0 (1.3)	5.2 (1.4)	5.8 (1.0)	5.27[b]
Mother item sum score	179.2 (23.0)	74.5 (24.3)	183.8 (20.9)	3.28[c]
Father stage score	5.5 (1.0)	5.3 (1.2)	5.8 (0.8)	5.58[b]
Father item sum score	182.2 (20.9)	177.9 (23.8)	186.7 (16.5)	3.56[c]

Numbers in parentheses are standard deviations.

Significance for the adolescent ego development differences were calculated using two-way ANOVAs, with psychiatric status and gender as independent variables. Significant gender differences were found for item sum scores ($F = 4.97^b$) and stage scores ($F = 5.90^b$) revealed girls to show higher ego scores, with no significant interactions between gender and psychiatric status.

Parent analyses are based on one-way ANOVAs, with psychiatric status (of adolescent) as the independent variable. There were no significant differences between mothers and fathers.

$^aP < 0.0001$; $^bP < 0.05$; $^cP < 0.10$.

room for the family session. Separate sites were required because of geographic considerations, and concerns regarding the impact of a new "laboratory" on patients or non-patients.[4]

In preceding sessions, the adolescent subjects completed the ego development test. Approximately two months later, the family (adolescent and parents) met with two experimenters for the family session. Experimenters were blind to the subjects' ego levels and to the study's hypotheses.

Family Procedure

Our family procedure is described in some detail in other papers reporting this family coding system (cf. Hauser et al., 1984, 1985). In brief, the basic

[4]It is, of course, possible that testing families in two different sites could have created a confound. The fact that the psychiatric and normal families showed minimal differences in family styles (Hauser et al., 1984) suggests that the different testing sites did not contribute to varying family findings.

features of our methods of collecting and analysing our family observations are:

1. A standard procedure to generate family discussion data. This method of "revealed differences" (Strodtbeck, 1958) requests family members to discuss known differences of opinion. Family members were brought together and their different moral judgement responses (based on Kohlberg Moral Judgement Interviews [Colby et al., in press]) revealed. For each of the differences, family members were asked to both defend their individual positions and then attempt to reach a consensus representing the whole family.
2. Discussions took place in the two settings described, and were taperecorded. Experimenters presented the family differences, but were not present during the actual discussion. The recordings were of high quality, and the transcripts used for coding were carefully made with notations of pauses, interruptions, and other speech disruptions.
3. The coding system that was developed and independently applied to the speeches was the Constraining and Enabling one, described earlier. The coding reliability, using Cohen's Kappa (1960) was favourable, as reported in Hauser et al. (1984).
4. For coding with the Constraining and Enabling Coding System, all successive speeches (turn taking occasions) were numbered. Each of these speeches was then rated by trained coders using the Constraining and Enabling Coding System Manual (Hauser, Powers, & Noam, 1991). While a speech might be sufficiently complex that it could receive a constraining as well as an enabling code, there were mutual exclusion rules regarding specific codes within the cognitive and affective subtypes of constraining and enabling. Each speech could receive only one score from cognitive and affective categories of constraining and enabling. Where codes were of equal strength, specific hierarchy rules were used by the coders.[5]

Elsewhere, we have more fully described the content of these family discussions that were based on Kohlberg moral dilemmas (Hauser et al., 1987b, 1991). Using these materials for family interaction raises the concern as to how much we limit the generality of our family findings. We have been impressed with the intensity shown by adolescents, and their parents, as they grapple with one another in defending positions, question-

[5]A step of "collapsing" codes was taken for the sequence analyses because of the special requirements of mutually exclusive coding. For instance, if a speech received both constraining and enabling, it was re-coded as ambivalent, and treated as having *only* that score in sequence analyses. In a similar fashion, speeches could receive *only* enabling *or* constraining classifications, regardless of the subtype (e.g. "cognitive enabling").

ing, challenging, and sometimes attacking others; seriously searching for levels of agreement, or repetitively confusing and fragmenting their discussions. Often families spontaneously remarked, "This is just like dinner conversation." These observations suggest that the discussions touch meaningful issues within the family, eliciting various aspects of the family's interaction styles and sequences.

Family Interaction Data Analyses

All of the preceding taped discussions were transcribed, preserving interruptions, simultaneous speech, and other nonverbal cues such as hesitation, laughter, and stutters. Explicit transcribing instructions and training exercises were used to underscore the importance of both preserving nonverbal events and minimising inferences about them. (The transcribing rules are available from the senior author.)

In addition to the data-preparation rules, there are specific coding rules governing the application of the CECS. The rules are summarised later, and are available as a manual from the senior author (Hauser et al., 1991).

The data reported in this paper are derived from the scoring of all speeches of 80 triadic family discussions with the Constraining and Enabling Coding system (CECS; Hauser et al., 1984, 1985, 1987a, 1987b). The raters were blind to the study's hypotheses, family member ego development levels, and the subsample source (psychiatric or high school) of each transcript. The transcript was unitised, as described earlier. All speeches were scored according to the CECS manual (Hauser et al., 1991). This manual consists of conceptual definitions of each code, with multiple scoring examples, for each level (low or high). As noted above, parent and adolescent speeches can receive a score on one scale from each of the constraining categories (affective and cognitive) as well as from one scale from each enabling category (affective and cognitive). In addition, the source and object of each speech was scored, for example, father to son, son to mother, mother to father, and so on.

Inter-rater reliabilities for source and object of speeches were 99% and 84%, respectively.[6] Inter-rater reliabilities using the Kappa statistic (Cohen, 1960) were applied to a speech-by-speech comparison of ratings by pairs of coders (cf. Hauser et al., 1984). The 80 transcripts were scored by three coders whose reliability was checked at two early and later points

[6]Eighty-four per cent represents the average interrater agreement for object. In terms of the *k* index, reliabilities for object of speech varied from 0.49 to 0.83. The 1% of disagreement regarding "speaker" represents errors of a clerical type. These few errors were discovered in preparing the data for reliability analyses and subsequently corrected prior to computing the reliabilities.

in the coding process to evaluate rater decay. Re-analyses of reliabilities have shown continued acceptable levels. Each of the three raters coded a set of transcripts that were a mix of adolescent ego levels and subsamples. This mix was generated by a research assistant who removed all identifying data (e.g. special site numbers).

Assessments

To measure ego development we used Loevinger's sentence completion test (Loevinger & Wessler, 1970; Loevinger et al., 1970), with the scoring based on the recommended methods published by Loevinger and her group through both the original scoring manual and more recent mimeographed manuals provided for male stems that were not included in the originally published work. Stage scores were calculated for each of the 237 subjects (adolescents and parents) using ogive rules (Loevinger & Wessler, 1970). A second score, the Item Sum Score (ISS) was obtained by summing the 36 item scores. Although we present both ego development scores in Table 4, it is the second set (ISS) that we use in the correlational and multiple regression analyses reported in this paper. Three trained coders scored the items, separated from their protocols, before reassembling them to generate each subject's score. Inter-rater reliabilities (using intra-class correlations) ranged from 0.70 to 0.80. Coders were blind to the identity of subject (adolescent or parent) and site (psychiatric or high school).

Family style analyses were conducted to see the extent to which these variables were predicted by each member's ego development (e.g. adolescent ego development and adolescent cognitive enabling), and the extent to which adolescent ego development could be predicted by parent family style. These correlational and regression analyses were based on the total frequency that a given code was expressed by a family member, e.g. adolescent cognitive enabling. To permit inter-family comparisons, this frequency was then standardised, by dividing it by the family member's total number of speeches.[7]

Family sequence analyses were performed to determine whether selected reciprocal and non-reciprocal sequences could be characterised as shaped by the ego development of the participating speakers. The scores entered into these correlational and regression analyses were derived for specified pairs of family members who immediately followed or preceded one another (lag-1) in the flow of the family's discussion. Four dyadic sequences were examined: mother-adolescent, adolescent-mother, father-

---

[7]These proportions were then transformed to normal distribution using an arcsin transformation.

adolescent, adolescent-father. These sequences, based on three possible, mutually exclusive, speech scores (enabling, constraining, or ambivalent [= enabling + constraining]) trace the potential influence of one speaker on the subsequent speaker. For example, the sequence score ("z score") for adolescent enabling following mother enabling is a value which indexes the extent to which knowing that mother expressed an enabling speech adds to our ability to predict that the next speaker (here the adolescent) will express the same type of speech (cf. Asarnow, 1983). Although we initially considered numerous possible sequences for each parent-adolescent pairing, including such theoretically interesting ones as mutual constraining, considerations of minimum frequency reduced the number of sequence variables that could be included in our analyses. Families that did not meet a minimum occurrence criterion of eight occurrences for a given sequence variable (e.g. father enabling followed by adolescent enabling eight times) were omitted from analyses. Correlational and regression analyses of these family variables with ego scores were then performed for those sequences where there was an adequate sample of families that had met the minimum occurrence criterion. Table 5 presents those sequence variables that were included in these later analyses.

The method for calculating these scores is based on the lag-sequential approach first introduced by Sackett (1977), and used since then to study marital interaction (Gottman, 1979), early child-mother interaction

TABLE 5
Family Sequence Variables

Sequence	*Family Behaviours*	*Participants*
Turn taking	SP → SP	M → A A → M F → A A → F
Mutual enabling	EN → EN	M → A A → M F → A A → F
Facilitating	CON → EN	M → A A → M F → A A → F
Undermining	EN → CON	M → A A → M F → A A → F

(Bakeman & Brown, 1980), friendship interactions among children (Gottman, 1983), and, most recently, sequences between caregivers and hospitalised children (Susman & Hollenbeck, 1984). Our calculation of the sequence scores utilised the formula given by Gottman (1980a), which includes the corrected standard error term discussed by Allison and Liker (1982; cf. Hauser et al., 1987b, for further discussion and examples of these analyses applied to family data).

In summary, the findings that we present in this paper refer to relations between ego development (of adolescent and parent), and two types of family dimensions: family styles (aggregate scores for individual members); and family processes (sequences between members). The style analyses examine two classes of variables: (1) overall (macro) categories, such as total enabling, total constraining, and enabling balance (enabling minus constraining); and (2) subcategories, such as cognitive enabling or cognitive constraining. In contrast, the sequence analyses are based exclusively on specific pairings of the macrocategories.[8] Although our style findings for the "whole" categories (e.g. overall enabling) overlap with those of the subcategories (e.g. cognitive enabling), these results are nonetheless presented to permit comparison with the subsequent sequence analyses, which are completely based on "whole" categories.

RESULTS

Family Style

1. *Prediction of Adolescent Family Style from Adolescent Ego Development Levels*

Several findings point to linkages between the adolescent's ego level and his or her family style. For the pooled sample, Pearson correlation analyses revealed numerous significant associations between adolescent ego development score and family style, as detailed in Table 6. It is of interest that boys and girls show virtually identical associations between their ego development and their family styles.

All of the associations are in theoretically expected directions (e.g. positive correlations with enabling, and negative ones with constraining) and are identical for the normal and psychiatric groups (results not shown on table). Given the possible impacts of psychiatric status and social class

---

[8]This strategy of examining summary categories differs from our previous analyses (Hauser et al., 1984, 1985), where we also studied the more discrete categories, such as explaining or devaluing. We now look at these larger codes in the light of the requirements of mutual exclusiveness of codes for sequence analyses.

TABLE 6
Correlations between Adolescent Ego Development and Adolescent Family Style

Style Variable	*All Adolescents*	*Boys*	*Girls*
Overall enabling	0.48[a]	0.42[c]	0.53[a]
Cognitive enabling	0.54[a]	0.45[b]	0.61[a]
Affective enabling	0.19[e]	0.17	0.20
Overall constraining	−0.18	−0.24	−0.16
Cognitive constraining	−0.14	−0.19	−0.11
Affective constraining	−0.36[b]	−0.39[d]	−0.38[d]
Enabling balance	0.34[b]	0.34[d]	0.35[d]
Number of speeches	0.08	0.01	0.10

All significance levels are for 2-tailed tests of significance.
[a]$P < 0.0002$; [b]$P < 0.003$; [c]$P < 0.01$; [d]$P < 0.05$; [e]$P < 0.10$.

on both the adolescent and family, and the known influences of age on ego development (Hauser, 1976), we next examined the effects of ego development independently of these other variables. To accomplish this, hierarchical multiple regressions were carried out, with psychiatric status and age entered first, followed by social class and gender; with ego development score entered as the final term. Adolescent ego scores contributed significantly to adolescent constraining and enabling styles (e.g. 16.7% for cognitive enabling; $P < 0.001$). As can be seen in Table 7, using this more stringent test, overall enabling, cognitive enabling, affective constraining, and enabling balance continue to be predicted by adolescent ego development.

2. *Prediction of Adolescent Ego Development from Parent Family Style*

These analyses take up relations between parents' interactions and their adolescent's ego development, with the aim of discerning how parental styles may predict adolescent ego development.

Mothers For the pooled sample, several of mothers' enabling and constraining scores were associated with adolescent ego development. As can be seen in Table 8, significant and marginally significant correlations were found for affective enabling (accepting, empathy), overall constraining, and cognitive constraining. These variables were not significant predictors of the pooled sample adolescent ego development when entered in multiple regression analyses.

TABLE 7
Prediction of Adolescent Family Style From Adolescent Ego Development: Multiple Regressions

Style	R^2 *age status*	R^2 *SES*	R^2 *sex*	R^2 *ego*	*Increment*[a] *in* R^2	F[b]	β[c]
Overall enabling	0.13	0.19	0.19	0.33	0.15[d]	15.8	0.60
Cognitive enabling	0.16	0.19	0.19	0.36	0.17[d]	19.0	0.65
Affective enabling	0.12	0.17	0.17	0.17	0.003	0.22	0.08
Overall constraining	0.07	0.07	0.08	0.08	0.002	0.17	−0.07
Cognitive constraining	0.07	0.07	0.07	0.07	0.000	0.01	−0.02
Affective constraining	0.09	0.10	0.10	0.20	0.10[d]	7.50	−0.49
Enabling balance	0.12	0.12	0.13	0.17	0.04[e]	3.89	0.33
Number of speeches	0.01	0.02	0.06	0.06	0.000	0.003	−0.01

[a]Increment in R^2 after adolescent item sum score is entered; [b]F, the increment in R^2; [c]β, the association between ego score and the given style variable.
[d]$P < 0.009$; [e]$P < 0.05$.

When the correlations were separately calculated for each sex, only constraining ones remained significant for boys. In other words, when mothers expressed more distracting and opinionated speeches, their sons who were participating in these discussions were at higher ego development levels. On the other hand, when mothers were more affectively constraining (devaluing, gratifying), their daughters who were participating in the project were at lower ego development levels.

Fathers For the pooled sample, there were several positive correlations between fathers' family styles and adolescent ego development: Affective enabling and cognitive constraining are especially noteworthy (Table 9). It is of interest that fathers' empathy and accepting were strongly associated with the ego development of their adolescents, especially sons participating in the discussions.

When the more stringent hierarchical regressions were carried out, father's cognitive constraining explained a significant amount of the adolescents' ego score for the pooled sample, and overall enabling contributed marginally to ego development.

TABLE 8
Correlations Between *Mother* Family Style and Adolescent Ego Development

Style Variable	*All Adolescents*	*Boys*	*Girls*
Overall enabling to adolescent	−0.01	0.16	−0.08
Cognitive enabling to adolescent	−0.16	0.06	−0.24
Affective enabling to adolescent	0.22[b]	0.18	0.21
Overall constraining to adolescent	0.21[c]	0.25	0.21
Cognitive constraining to adolescent	0.32[a]	0.37[c]	0.27[b]
Affective constraining to adolescent	−0.21	−0.05	−0.39[b]
Enabling balance to adolescent	−0.14	−0.08	−0.19
Number of speeches to adolescent	0.01	0.03	−0.04

[a]$P < 0.007$; [b]$P < 0.05$; [c]$P < 0.10$.

TABLE 9
Correlations Between *Father* Family Style and Adolescent Ego Development

Style Variable	*All Adolescents*	*Boys*	*Girls*
Overall enabling to adolescents	0.19[c]	0.10	0.25[c]
Cognitive enabling to adolescents	0.08	0.02	0.10
Affective enabling to adolescents	0.35[a]	0.42[b]	0.29[c]
Overall constraining to adolescents	0.17	0.18	0.21
Cognitive constraining to adolescents	0.36[a]	0.32[c]	0.38[b]
Affective constraining to adolescents	−0.07	0.07	−0.12
Enabling balance to adolescents	0.05	0.05	0.09
Number of speeches to adolescents	0.06	−0.12	0.14

[a]$P < 0.002$; [b]$P < 0.01$; [c]$P < 0.10$.

3. *Prediction of Parent Style from Parent Ego Development*

This third set of style analyses considers the extent to which parents' ego development may account for their interaction styles within the family.

Mothers In the pooled sample, we find several significant and trend level correlations between mothers' family style dimensions and their ego development (cf. Table 10). These include overall enabling, affective enabling, and enabling balance.

There are also numerous significant relations between mothers' ego development and their family styles with daughters participating in the discussions (e.g. overall enabling, affective enabling, and enabling balance). In contrast, however, there are no significant correlations between mothers' ego development and their interaction styles with their sons.

Multiple regression analyses looking at the predictive strength of mothers' ego development, while controlling for psychiatric status, social class, and gender, reveal that mothers' ego development contributes significantly and marginally to predicting overall enabling, cognitive enabling, enabling balance, and number of speeches with both sons and daughters (Table 11).

TABLE 10
Correlations Between *Mother* Ego Development and Mother Family Style

Style Variable	*All Adolescents*	*Boys*	*Girls*
Overall enabling to adolescent	0.34[a]	0.17	0.44[a]
Cognitive enabling to adolescent	0.19[c]	0.24	0.17
Affective enabling to adolescent	0.22[b]	−0.06	0.42[a]
Overall constraining to adolescent	−0.05	−0.04	−0.03
Cognitive constraining to adolescent	0.13	0.13	0.15
Affective constraining to adolescent	−0.21	−0.28	−0.13
Enabling balance to adolescent	0.23[b]	0.11	0.33[b]
Number of speeches to adolescent	0.22[c]	0.20	0.20

[a]$P < 0.006$; [b]$P < 0.05$; [c]$P < 0.10$.

TABLE 11
Predictions of Mother Family Style to Adolescent from Mother Ego Development: Multiple Regressions

Variable	R^2 *age status*	R^2 *SES*	R^2 *sex*	R^2 *ego*	*Change*[a] *in* R^2	F[b]	β[c]
Overall enabling	0.010	0.066	0.069	0.170	0.101[d]	8.63	0.336
Cognitive enabling	0.037	0.094	0.094	0.128	0.034[e]	2.73	0.194
Affective enabling	0.075	0.088	0.104	0.125	0.021	1.72	0.154
Overall constraining	0.075	0.171	0.176	0.176	0.000	0.001	−0.004
Cognitive constraining	0.109	0.130	0.130	0.144	0.014	1.01	0.124
Affective constraining	0.004	0.150	0.173	0.180	0.008	0.49	−0.096
Enabling balance	0.061	0.175	0.180	0.219	0.039[e]	3.28	0.210
Number of speeches	0.003	0.003	0.035	0.075	0.040[e]	3.09	0.212

[a]Increment in R^2 after mother ego development is entered; [b]F, change in R^2; [c]β, relationship between mother ego score and given family style variable.
[d]$P < 0.005$; [e]$P < 0.10$.

In summary, there are several ways that mothers' ego development contribute to their family styles; but most striking are the gender difference findings, suggesting that the link between mother ego development and family style is stronger when they are speaking with their daughters.[9]

Fathers Associations between fathers' ego development and their family styles show a similar pattern, again being most prominent for affective enabling (Table 12). When viewed separately by sex of the adolescent who was participating in these discussions there were stronger associations with sons. Multiple regression analyses reveal that in the pooled sample fathers' overall enabling was marginally predicted by their ego development.

Summarising the parent ego development findings, we see that there are significant relations between parents' ego development and their family behaviours. Moreover, these relations are strongest when parents are

[9]These findings must be viewed as suggestive only, because when specific correlations are compared between boys and girls (through multiple regression interaction terms), these correlations do not significantly differ from each other.

TABLE 12
Correlations Between Father Ego Development and Father Family Style

Style Variable	*All Adolescents*	*Boys*	*Girls*
Overall enabling to adolescent	0.27[b]	0.37[b]	0.18
Cognitive enabling to adolescent	0.23[b]	0.35[b]	0.08
Affective enabling to adolescent	0.35[a]	0.44[a]	0.26[c]
Overall constraining to adolescent	−0.07	−0.003	0.16
Cognitive constraining to adolescent	0.07	−0.003	0.16
Affective constraining to adolescent	−0.20	0.24	−0.04
Enabling balance to adolescent	0.22[c]	0.31[c]	0.09
Number of speeches to adolescent	0.16	0.09	0.15

[a]$P < 0.009$; [b]$P < 0.05$; [c]$P < 0.10$.

speaking with a same-sex child: mothers with daughters, fathers with sons. Having separately reviewed the contributions of adolescent and parent ego development to their family styles, we are now in a position to take up the joint contribution of these developmental variables to family discourse through examining interaction sequences.

Family Sequences

To what extent do individual ego development levels influence specific, conceptually relevant, sequences of speeches between adolescents and their parents? As described in an earlier section, the scores used in these analyses are those of macrocategories. For instance, in tracing mutual enabling between mother and daughter, we look at all mother enabling and daughter enabling speeches, rather than separate "affective" or "cognitive" enabling speeches. We set a minimum of eight relevant "matches" (e.g. mother constraining following adolescent constraining) to permit calculations of a stable sequence index (z). When fewer than 20 families displayed this minimum number of matches, non-parametric analyses (Spearman correlations) were used to calculate associations of interest (e.g. between participants' ego development levels and family processes).

In parallel with our family style analyses, we examine these sequences in terms of their relation to individual ego development. Now, however, the analyses involve two participants. We explore simple correlations and, where appropriate, consider the strength of adolescent and parent ego development as predictors of a given sequence, after controlling for influences of psychiatric status, family social class, adolescent sex, and adolescent age.

1. *Turn Taking*

At the most general level, we can ask about turn taking (cf. discussion of this dimension by Sackett, 1980). To what extent does a family member's (e.g. mother) ego development level influence the likelihood of her first speaking or responding to her son or daughter, regardless of the type of speech either has expressed? As can be seen in Table 13, when mothers were at higher levels of ego development they were more likely to initiate speaking with their sons and daughters. Multiple regression analyses reveal that this association remains a significant one, after controlling for age, gender, and social class. In contrast, there is a marginally significant association indicating that mothers at higher levels of ego development are less likely to respond to adolescents' speeches. With respect to fathers, adolescents are marginally more likely to respond to them when at higher levels of ego development.

2. *Mutual enabling*

Turning to more specific sequences, the strongest results again involve mothers. At higher levels of ego development, in parallel with turn taking, mothers are more likely to engage in reciprocal enabling with their sons

TABLE 13
Correlations between Ego Development and Family Sequences: All Adolescents

Sequence Variable	*Adolesc. Ego*	*Parent Ego*	*Sequence Variable*	*Adolesc. Ego*	*Parent Ego*
1. *Turn taking*			3. *Facilitating*		
M → A	0.13	0.35[a]	M → A	−0.04	−0.18
A → M	0.05	−0.20[c]	A → M	0.14	−0.15
F → A	0.21[c]	0.07	F → A[d]	−0.10	0.53[c]
A → F	0.11	0.16	A → F	−0.13	0.16
2. *Mutual enabling*			4. *Undermining*		
M → A	0.21[c]	0.33[a]	M → A	−0.39[b]	−0.17
A → M	−0.03	0.22[c]	A → M	0.14	−0.15
F → A	0.07	−0.02	F → A	−0.09	0.34[c]
A → F	−0.01	0.12	A → F[d]	0.07	0.05

[a]$P < 0.002$; [b]$P < 0.05$; [c]$P < 0.10$.
[d]These values represent Spearman correlations, as cell sizes were lower than 20.

and daughters (cf. Table 13). Multiple regression analyses, controlling for influences of psychiatric and demographic factors, revealed that mothers' ego development was a significant predictor of mutual enabling between them and their adolescent sons and daughters, accounting for 12% ($P < 0.005$) of the variance when they initiated these sequences, and 10% ($P < 0.01$) when they responded to the adolescents' enabling.

With respect to gender-specific patterns, the strongest associations are between mothers' ego development and mutual enabling with their daughters. Mothers at higher levels of ego development are more likely to initiate and respond in reciprocal enabling sequences when interacting with their daughters ($r = 0.40, 0.35$).[10]

3. *Facilitating*

In this sequence, one partner (adolescent or parent) expresses an enabling speech (e.g. accepting) after the other has been constraining (e.g. devaluing). In the pooled sample, we find that when fathers are at higher ego development levels, adolescents are more likely to be facilitating towards them (Spearman $r = 0.53$; $P < 0.10$). In the light of the relatively small sample sizes (e.g. $n = 15$) for this sequence, and the following one, separate correlations for boys and girls were not carried out for these variables.

4. *Undermining*

In this sequence, one partner expresses a constraining speech (e.g. judgemental) after the family member with which he or she is speaking has been enabling (e.g. explaining). Adolescents at higher levels of ego development are unlikely to follow mothers with such opposing speeches (Table 13). This was not true for sequences with fathers, where we see that fathers at higher levels of ego development are marginally more likely to initiate these sequences.

DISCUSSION

Through these style and sequence analyses we have launched new probes about the interplay between family processes and ego development—of adolescents and their parents—using the Constraining and Enabling cod-

[10]Although this association is especially strong for mothers when initiating and responding to their daughters, it is important to recognise that further analyses did not show a statistically significant interaction between adolescent gender and mothers' ego development for this sequence.

ing system. We began with a strong interest in adolescent ego development. Yet logic urges the idea that a parent's level of development will likely influence interactions with his or her adolescent, interactions that may be highly relevant to that adolescent's development. Besides our increased emphasis upon the contribution of parent development, a second thrust of these new analyses is their continued highlighting of bidirectional contributions. Thus, in one set of analyses we traced how an individual's ego development influenced his or her family styles, while other analyses examined the contribution of parent style to adolescent ego development.

In many ways, the preceding results confirm our previous report (Hauser et al., 1984). Once again, we find that individual ego development predicts numerous aspects of adolescents' and mothers' family styles. Moreover, these relations between mothers' ego development and their family behaviour were magnified when they were interacting with their daughters.

Puzzling and intriguing are the findings that seemingly contradictory parenting styles—affective enabling, cognitive constraining—were associated with adolescent ego development. The affective enabling findings were most apparent when fathers were speaking to their sons. We interpret this observation as reflecting father's reacting to their sons, expressing more empathy and accepting to sons who are at higher levels of ego development.

A second new finding, that cognitive constraining (primarily distracting) of both parents is associated with higher adolescent ego development, can also be best understood in terms of a reactive effect. Adolescents functioning at higher levels of ego development may elicit more interruptions and intense participation from their parents. From this vantage point, then, interruptions—a major component of distracting codes—may be secondary to heated discussions; and perhaps ultimately stimulate higher levels of ego development.

A third set of results points to differences between mothers and fathers. In a study that specifically focused on parent and adolescent sex differences (Hauser et al., 1987a), we found that, when compared with mothers, fathers spoke in consistently more enabling ways. In interpreting this pattern we argued that the powerful demands of this discussion task—defending a position, abstract moral reasoning, bringing together opposing moral views—may have been more congenial to fathers, thereby eliciting a higher level of participation from them (with reciprocally high levels of participation from their sons and daughters towards them). In the light of these previous observations and interpretations, our new findings are especially interesting, suggesting that mothers' involvements in these discussions are driven by their ego development; when it is higher, they will participate more fully, being more accepting and more "tuned in" from moment to moment. This point clearly emerged in the sequence analyses as we observed that mothers at higher levels of ego development initiated more turn taking sequences and engaged (initiated and responded) in more mutual enabling with their sons and daughters. Fathers, on the other hand, appear to be more driven by the very nature of the task itself, which virtually overshadows any contribution of their ego development in specific interactions with their sons.

Yet why is this "ego effect" on mothers even more pervasive when mothers are interacting with their daughers? We can envision several paths from maternal development to the family system. A circuitous route would be through mother's transactions with her husband, who then responds differentially to the adolescent son or daughter, influencing his or her subsequent interactions with mother. In addition, there may be certain contextual conditions, imposed by the nature of our family task: Specific pairings, such as mother opposed to the other members being especially well suited to higher levels of her ego development, as she now can defend and clarify her differences with her husband and/or youngster. Our results already highlight one context "enhancer", the presence of a daughter. Through our sample of one-parent families (primarily mothers and adolescents), we will be able to more fully examine how the presence of sons or daughters may moderate how mothers' ego development influences their maternal family interactions.

Remaining directions point toward the need to elucidate—on theoretical and empirical levels—how parent and child characteristics (ego development, self-esteem, authority orientations) may shape family system dimensions. A second direction of much interest involves how parental compatibility (in terms of their ego development) may underlie their interactions with one another, with their adolescent, and ultimately how this aspect of their relationship may contribute to their son or daughter's ego development (Rogell, 1990). Finally, given our longitudinal data base, we can pursue questions of continuity and discontinuity. How do these individual and relationship features, assessed in mid adolescence, influence later family functioning and development in late adolescence and early adulthood? It will be especially interesting to trace the theme of parental relationships and developmental differences, because these sometimes subtle differences may have important, yet unnoticed, long-term effects on adolescent development.

ACKNOWLEDGEMENTS

This study was supported through a Research Scientist Award No. 5K-05-07-MH-70178 (Stuart T. Hauser) from the NIMH, and a grant from the National Institute of Child and Human Development (NICHD, No. 5R01 HD18684-02).

Barbara Turner, Eydie Kasandorf, Dena Grossier, and Stephanie Bukema assisted in data collection. Daranee C. Rajapark valuably contributed to recent supervision of family interaction coding and training of coders, while Richard Rasulis and Robin Bliss provided major assistance in the data management and aspects of computer programming. Numerous discussions with our colleague, Elliot Mishler, were most helpful in the various considerations that have gone into the carrying out of these new sequence analyses. Finally, discussions with colleagues at the 1987 Family Processes Workshop of the Society for Research in Adolescence were of major help in clarifying a number of issues involved in the sequence analyses.

Manuscript received May 1987
Revised manuscript accepted under the editorship of Harry McGurk, May 1990

REFERENCES

Allison, P. D. & Liker, J. K. (1982). Analyzing sequential categorical data on dyadic interaction: A comment on Gottman. *Psychological Bulletin, 91*(2), 393–404.

Asarnow, J. R. (1983). Children with peer adjustment problems: sequential and non-sequential analyses of school behaviors. *Journal of Consulting and Clinical Psychology, 51*, 709–717.

Bakeman, R. (1978). Untangling streams of behavior: Sequential analysis of observational data. In G. Sackett (Ed.), *Observing Behavior*. Vol. 2, *Data collection and analysis methods*. Baltimore: University Park Press.

Bakeman, R. & Brown, J. (1980). Analyzing behavioral sequences: Differences between pre-term infant mother dyads in the first months of life. In D. Sarvin, R. Hawkins, L. Walker, & J. Penticuff (Eds), *Exceptional infant*, Vol. 4. New York: Brunner-Mazel.

Bakeman, R. & Gottman, J. (1986a). Applying observational methods: a systematic view. In J. Osofsky (Ed.), *Handbook of infant development*, 2nd edn. New York: John Wiley.

Bakeman, R. & Gottman, J. (1986b). *Observing interaction*. Cambridge University Press.

Bateson, G., Jackson, D., Herley, J., & Weakland, J. (1956). Toward a theory of schizophrenia. *Behavioral Science, 1*, 252–264.

Block, J. (1971). *Lives through time*. Berkeley: Bancroft Books.

Cohen, J. (1960). A coefficient of agreement for nominal scales. *Educational and Psychological Measurement, 20*, 37–46.

Colby, A., Kohlberg, L., Candee, D., Gibbs, J. C., Hewer, A., Kaufman, K., Power, C., & Speicher-Dubin, B. (in press). *Assessing moral judgements: A manual*. Cambridge University Press.

Cooper, C., Grotevant, H. D., & Condon, S. M. (1983). Individuality and connectedness in the family as a context for adolescent identity and role-taking skills. In H. D. Grotevant & C. R. Cooper (Eds), *Adolescent development in the family. New directions for child development*. San Francisco: Jossey-Bass.

Gottman, J. M. (1979). *Marital interaction: Experimental investigations*. New York: Academic Press.

Gottman, J. M. (1980a). Analysing for sequential connection and assessing interobserver reliability for the sequential analysis of observational data. *Behavioral Assessment, 2*, 361–368.

Gottman, J. M. (1980b). Consistency of non-verbal affect and affect reciprocity in marital interaction. *Journal of Consulting and Clinical Psychology, 48*, 711–717.

Gottman, J. (1983). How children become friends. *Monographs of Society in Research and Child Development, 48*, 2.

Gottman, J. (1987). The sequential analysis of family interaction. In T. Jacob (Ed.), *Family interaction and psychopathology: Theories, methods, and findings*. New York: Plenum.

Grotevant, H. D. & Cooper, C. R. (1986). Individuation in family relationships. *Human Development, 29*, 82–100.

Hauser, S. T. (1976). Loevinger's model and measure of ego development: A critical review. *Psychological Bulletin, 33*, 928–955.

Hauser, S. T. (1978). Ego development and interpersonal style in adolescence. *Journal of Youth and Adolescence, 7*, 333–352.

Hauser, S. T., Jacobson, A., Noam, G., & Powers, S. (1983). Ego development and self-image processes in early adolescence: Longitudinal studies of diabetic and psychiatric patients. *Archives of General Psychiatry, 40*, 325–332.

Hauser, S. T., Powers, S., Jacobson, A., Noam, G., Weiss, B., & Follansbee, D. (1984). Family contexts of adolescent ego development. *Child Development, 55*, 195–213.

Hauser, S. T., Weiss-Perry, B., Follansbee, D., Powers, S., Jacobson, A., & Noam, G. (1986). Adolescent development and family transactions. In S. Sugarman (Ed.), *Family therapy and individual therapy: Critical issues at the interface*. Rockville, MD: Aspen Collections in Family Therapy.

Hauser, S. T., Book, B. K., Houlihan, J., Powers, S. I., Weiss-Perry, B., Follansbee, D., Jacobson, A. M., & Noam, G. (1987a). Sex differences within the family: Studies of adolescent and parent family interactions. *Journal of Youth and Adolescence. 16*, 199–220.

Hauser, S. T., Houlihan, J., Powers, S. I., Jacobson, A. M., Noam, G., Weiss-Perry, B., & Follansbee, D. (1987b). Interaction sequences in families of psychiatrically hospitalised and non-patient adolescents. *Psychiatry, 50*, 308–319.

Hauser, S. T., Powers, S. I., & Noam, G. (1991). *Adolescents and their families: Paths of ego development*. New York: Free Press.

Hauser, S. T., Powers, S., & Noam, G. (in press). *Separating and connecting: The family nexus of adolescent development*. New York: Free Press.

Hollingshead, A. B. (1957). *Two factor index of social position (mimeographed)*. New Haven: Yale University.

Holt, R. R. (1980). Loevinger's measure of ego development: Reliability and national norms for male and female short forms. *Journal of Personality and Social Psychology, 39*, 909–920.

Jacob, T. (1974). Patterns of family conflict and dominance as a function of child age and social class. *Developmental Psychology, 10*, 1–12.

Jacobson, A. M., Hauser, S. T., Powers, S., & Noam, G. (1985). The influence of chronic illness and ego development on self-esteem in diabetic and psychiatric adolescent patients. *Journal of Youth and Adolescence, 13*, 489–507.

Loevinger, J. (1976). Ego development: Conceptions and theories. San Francisco: Jossey-Bass.

Loevinger, J. & Wessler, R. (1970). *Measuring ego development*. Vol. I. San Francisco: Jossey-Bass.

Loevinger, J., Wessler, R., & Redmore, C. (1970). *Measuring ego development*, Vol. II. San Francisco: Jossey-Bass.

Miller, S. M. & Mishler, E. (1959). Social classes and mental illness and American psychiatry: An expository review. *Millbank Memorial Fund Quarterly, 37*, 174–199.

Mishler, E. G. & Waxler, N. E. (1968). *Interaction in families*, New York: John Wiley.

Powers, S., Hauser, S. T., Schwartz, J., Noam, G., & Jacobson, A. (1983). Adolescent ego development and family interaction: A structural-developmental perspective. In C.

Cooper & H. Grotevant (Eds), *Adolescent development and family interactions. New directions in child developments*. San Francisco: Jossey-Bass.
Rogell, D. (1990). *Ego development and communication patterns in the marital dyad*. Honors Dissertation, Psychology Department, Harvard University.
Sackett, G. P. (1987). The lag sequential analysis of contingency and cyclicity in behavioral interaction research. In J. Osofsky (Ed.), *Handbook of infant development*. New York: Wiley.
Sackett, G. P. (1980). Lag sequential analysis as a data reduction technique in social interaction research. In D. Sarvin, R. Hawkins, L. Walker, & J. Penticuff (Eds), *Exceptional infant*, Vol. 4. New York: Brunner-Mazel.
Stierlin, H. (1974). *Separating. Parents and adolescents*. New York: Quadrangle.
Strodtbeck, F. L. (1958). Husband–wife interaction and revealed differences. *American Sociological Review*, *16*, 468–473.
Susman, E. & Hollenbeck, A. (1984). Sequential variations in the interactions of caregivers and hospitalised seriously ill children and adolescents. *International Journal of Behavior Development*, *7*, 385–421.
Weinstock, A. (1967). Longitudinal study of social class and defense preferences. *Journal of Counceling Psychology*, *31*, 539–541.
Wynne, L., Jones, J., & Al-Khayyal, M. (1982). Health family communication patterns: Observations in families "at risk" for psychopathology. In F. Walsh (Ed.), *Normal family processes*. New York: Guilford.

JOURNAL OF RESEARCH ON ADOLESCENCE, 4(4), 487–502

Ego Development and Adolescent Emotions

Stuart T. Hauser
Department of Psychiatry
Harvard Medical School
and
Department of Psychology
Boston University

Andrew W. Safyer
Boston University School of Social Work

In this article, we investigate associations between ego development and emotion communication during adolescence, using a newly constructed coding system for scoring these affect dimensions from clinical research interviews with early adolescent subjects. One overarching question frames our inquiry: How does an adolescent's ego development influence his or her communication of emotional experience? To follow special combinations of emotion communications, diversity of communication and conflict within communication were operationally defined. Findings revealed that both these more complex combinations were present in a higher number of speeches for adolescents at higher levels of ego development. In terms of specific emotions, Pearson correlation analyses indicated that enthusiasm, affection, anxiety, and neutrality were directly associated with higher stages, whereas sadness and anger were inversely correlated with ego development. These associations were similar for both genders. The findings are discussed in terms of the implications of ego development stages for the individual's experience and understanding of different affect states and intersections of ego development trajectories with emotional communication during adolescence.

Requests for reprints should be sent to Stuart T. Hauser, Department of Psychiatry, Harvard Medical School, 74 Fenwood Road, Boston, MA 02115.

Affects and their many vicissitudes are often the centerpiece of clinical observations and theories of adolescent development. Yet our understanding of emotional development in adolescence—beyond clinical theory—is limited, representing virtually uncharted territory (Haviland & Kramer, 1991). In this article, we consider the relation between ego development and emotion communication during adolescence and connections between emotional life and relationships during this phase of development. One overarching question frames our inquiry: How does adolescent development influence the communication of emotional experience?

At the outset, it is important to note that there is a major question we do not tackle: How do emotions influence aspects of development during adolescence? This important issue was explored by Haviland and Kramer (1991) in their diary study of Anne Frank, and by Hauser and Smith (1991), who argued that unique emotional currents may function as possible elicitors and organizers of adolescent experience and developmental change.

EGO DEVELOPMENT AND EMOTIONS: CONSTRUCTS AND MEASURES

Adolescence has been traditionally described by psychoanalytic observers as a period of emotional turbulence, as adolescents respond to major biological and psychological changes: the onset of puberty, striking reductions in psychological dependency on parents, psychological separation from the family, and navigation of the complex transition to adult life (Blos, 1962; Erikson, 1959, 1964, 1968; Freud, 1946, 1958). Although many researchers now agree that adolescence is a period of development requiring multiple changes—biological, social, and psychological—it is clear that adolescence cannot be described exclusively as a time of severe dysfunction or vulnerability (Powers, Hauser, & Kilner, 1989). For instance, epidemiological studies indicate that about 10% to 20% of adolescents exhibit some type of severe emotional disturbance (as defined by descriptive diagnostic criteria); this is approximately the same proportion as reported in similar surveys of the adult population (Offer, Ostrov, & Howard, 1981; Petersen, 1988). Within developmental psychology, many contemporary studies of adolescent development clearly conceptualize diverse patterns of adolescent adaptation and growth (e.g., Brooks-Gunn, Rock, & Warren, 1989; Collins, 1991; Collins & Gunnar, 1989; Hauser & Bowlds, 1991; Petersen, 1988). Often theoretically guided, these empirical studies trace biological, dispositional, and contextual aspects of adolescence. Such attention to individual differences is pertinent to our thinking about emotional development during adolescence.

In our research program, we continue this focus on individual differences in development as we follow stages and paths of adolescent ego development. Based on clinical and theoretical understandings (which are detailed later), there are strong grounds for expecting that this line of development shapes the growing adolescent's communication of his or her emotion experience. Consequently, through observing how ego development unfolds during the adolescent years, we can delineate an important set of templates shaping emotional life during this era.

Ego Development

Ego development represents an important perspective for illuminating several interconnected aspects of adolescence. As conceptualized by Loevinger and colleagues (Loevinger, 1976; Loevinger & Wessler, 1970; Loevinger, Wessler, & Redmore, 1970), ego development is an evolving framework of meaning that is imposed by the individual upon his or her inner experiences and perceptions of people and events. Implicit in this view, then, is the assumption that each person has a customary orientation to himself or herself, and to the world, and that there is a continuum (ego development) along which these frames of reference can be arrayed (Hauser, 1976).

Each of the ego development stages differs from the others along the dimensions of impulse control, conscious concerns, and interpersonal and cognitive style (Loevinger, 1976). In brief, early stages of ego development are marked by a sense of control by external forces, an egocentric view of the environment, and a limited ability to relate to others. The two stages and the transition phase that share these characteristics comprise the *preconformist level.*

A second set of stages comprises the *conformist* level. Individuals at these stages are concerned with social acceptance and approval. An understanding of mutuality begins to emerge, although relationships are largely seen along the lines of concrete events and actions, rather than clear feelings or motives. Most adolescents and adults eventually advance to a transitional phase, *self-aware,* marked by a growing realization that the right ways of living are relative to situations. As self-awareness grows, so, too, does access to a broader, more complex repertoire of experienced emotions and understandings of others' emotions.

In the next, *conscientious,* stage, there is consolidation of the changes begun during the self-aware transition. Rigid stereotypes are now fading; a growing and increasingly sustained interest in differences among people becomes salient. Relationships are now seen and understood along the lines of feelings and intricate connections, rather than simply as collections of actions and events (Hauser & Levine, 1993). In the later stages (*autonomous* and *integrated*), there is increasing respect for individuality and inner experience, and a growing interpersonal sensitivity to relationships. This set of stages (beginning with conscientious) forms the *postconformist* level of ego development.

We can also think about these stages and transitions in terms of their patterns of change and stability over time (Hauser, 1991). Adolescents can be classified with respect to their varied ego development paths, based on repeated observations of their stages of development (Hauser, 1991). The eight ego development paths that we can identify are analogous to a range of adolescent growth curves (Figure 1).

Profoundly arrested teenagers remain at a preconformist stage throughout their adolescence. They have a limited range of emotional responses to people and events and are restricted in their perceptions and expectations. Adolescents who reach and remain at a conformist stage express socially acceptable feelings and respond in socially ap-

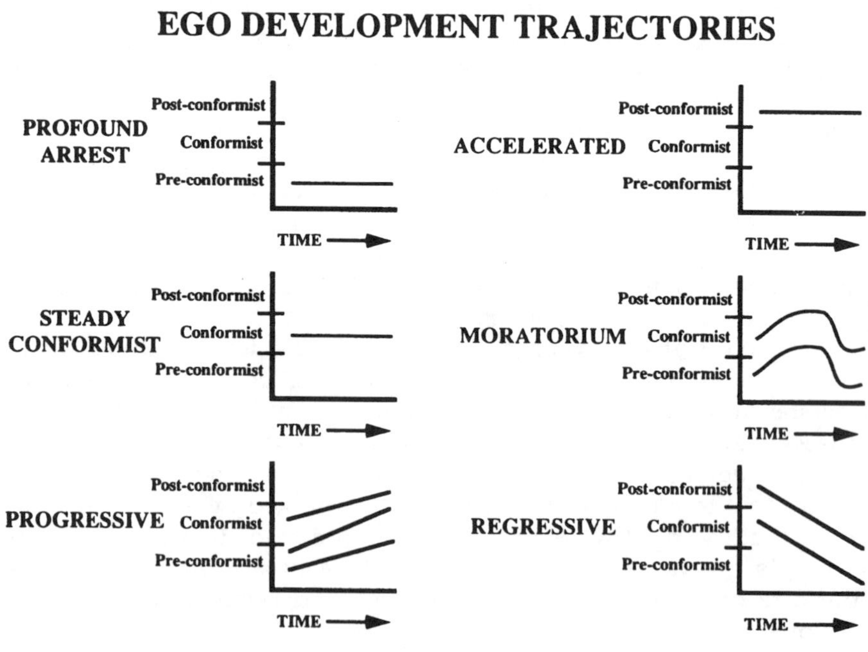

FIGURE 1 Ego development paths.

propriately ways to the feelings of others. These *steady conformist* adolescents are at times aware of inner feelings, but they usually speak about them in relatively bland terms, or as clichés.

Another group of adolescents clearly progress in their ego development as they begin at either very low (preconformist) or intermediate stages (conformist), and within subsequent years are functioning at unmistakably higher stages. There is a family of progressions—*early progression, advanced progression,* and *dramatic progression.* Noteworthy change is characteristic of these paths. Transformations in self-understanding and views of friends and parents are visible, associated with recognition and expression of a greater range of feelings. Teenagers following early progression paths advance from more concrete, often one-dimensional views to socially acceptable, yet less simplified views. Those characterized by advanced progression move from conventional understandings and beliefs to beliefs based on self-derived inner principles. Accompanying this change is their enhanced appreciation of individual differences. Adolescents demonstrating dramatic progression, within a brief span of time, leap from wary perceptions of feelings (many unacceptable and attributed to others) to awareness of subtle emotional states in themselves and in others.

Unusually mature adolescents—those following the *accelerated* trajectory—speak with precocious insight about themselves and their surroundings. They are surprisingly attuned to others' feelings. Far earlier than most of their peers, they perceive the complexity of personal relationships and attend to subtle aspects of their inner lives. The emotional life of these adolescents is highly differentiated and sensitively responsive to different settings and relationships.

There is also a *regressive ego development* trajectory, in which an adolescent moves unexpectedly downward in his or her level of development (e.g., from conformist to preconformist). Finally, there is a trajectory that we term (after Erikson, 1964) *psychosocial moratorium,* in which a teenager vacillates in his or her levels of ego development. Accompanying these often precipitous swings are striking changes in the adolescent's understandings of others' affective states and expressions of his or her own feelings. Such oscillations are sometimes considered to reflect experimentation by an adolescent, as he or she tries out new roles and/or enacts conflicting, yet personally prized, ideals and wishes.

Framing development in terms of multiple pathways of perception and cognition provides one entrée to understanding how emotional development is intertwined with types of adolescent intrapsychic organization. Yet this way of conceptualizing adolescent development does not posit that cognitive processes, in the final analysis, underlie and structure affective development. Rather, we view affective experience as reflecting closely related components (e.g., interpersonal style, impulse control, cognitive complexity) of ego development stages and paths. We are not arguing for the causal superiority of either affect or cognition.[1]

Studying Adolescent Ego Development

Using Loevinger's model and assessment of ego development, our research group studied stages and paths of ego development as they unfold during the adolescent years. In an ongoing longitudinal project, we follow the psychosocial development of 146 predominantly middle-class White boys and girls from a public high school and inpatient psychiatric hospital through adolescence and into young adulthood. The psychiatric sample is included to enable study of a wide range of developmental trajectories. Although the hospitalized adolescents were not psychotic, there were strong reasons to expect that most of them would be developmentally impaired in terms of their perceptions of others, interpersonal styles, understanding of their surroundings, and impulse control (Weiner, 1970). In contrast, we expected that the high school freshmen, having no apparent psychiatric problems, would include many teenagers with progressive or accelerated ego development.

The psychiatrically hospitalized adolescents were consecutive admissions to the children's unit of a private university teaching hospital between autumn 1978 and winter 1980 who agreed to participate in the study. Their diagnoses included disruptive behavior disorders, affective disorders, and anxiety- and stress-related disorders. The average age of patients and students was 14.4 years on entering the study; subjects were equally divided by gender.

Shortly after agreeing to participate, the subjects and their parents filled out the Washington University Sentence Completion Test (WUSCT) assessing individual ego development (Loevinger & Wessler, 1970). The projective nature of this test enables identification of underlying developmental structures in an individual's responses. This 36-item measure, with favorable reliability and validity, has been used in over 200 published analyses (Cohn, 1991). Coders, trained to reliability and blind to the identity of the subject, rated the ego development

[1]This issue of cognitive primacy over emotional development is discussed at greater length in Hauser and Smith (1991).

stages using the recommended methods (Hauser et al., 1984; Loevinger & Wessler, 1970; Loevinger et al., 1970).

Emotion Communication

These considerations regarding ego development and emotions, together with our increasing interest in relationship development (Hauser & Levine, 1993), have led to a new initiative in our project, to identify adolescent emotion communications. This assessment requires a newly constructed assessment approach based on the view that these communications represent discrete states (sadness, anger), varying in more ways than hedonic tone (i.e., positive or negative) or level of arousal (Safyer & Hauser, 1994). Distinctly different functional, phenomenological, and expressive features characterize these communications, which are activated in response to significant events in the internal or interpersonal environments (Campos, Campos, & Barrett, 1989, p. 398). We use the term *emotion communication,* rather than *emotion expression,* because we consider emotions to be closely linked with relational processes, not merely the outward signs of some internal essence. Relevant to our thinking here is the recent work of Campos and colleagues (1989), conceptualizing emotions as processes involved in "establishing, maintaining, or disrupting the relations between the person and the internal or external environment, when such relations are significant to the individual" (p. 395).

Studying Adolescent Emotion Communications

One month after responding to the WUSCT, each subject met with a clinical research interviewer for his or her annual semistructured interview. Several topics were always covered, in whatever order seemed most natural: school experience, peer and family relationships, family history, illness experience, wishes and fantasies about the future. Two questions cutting across all of these topics concerned the adolescent's experiences of conflict within the self and with others, and how he or she handled these experiences. These interviews, taped and then transcribed, provide the data base for our analyses of adolescent emotional life.

Our approach for analyzing these interviews, the Adolescent Emotion Coding System (AECS), differs from other measures of adolescent emotions in its reliance on observed discourse, rather than on conscious self-reports. By using voice cues and speech content, we assume that we are detecting emotion communications that are likely to be observable by others, yet often out of the speaker's awareness. The specific coding criteria builds on Gottman's Specific Affect Coding System (Gottman, 1988), used for assessing communications in marital interactions. With some revisions, we extend this approach to adolescents. Other important influences on the construction of the AECS are Scherer's (1988) analysis of vocal indicators of emotional state, and Shaver and colleagues' hierarchical organization of emotion terms (Shaver, Schwartz, Kirkson, & O'Connor, 1987). The coding system and its psychometric properties are described in an earlier manual and article (Safyer & Hauser, 1992, 1994).

Raters, trained to reliability (average $\kappa = .71$), first classified a speech turn (everything the adolescent said between the immediately prior interview question or comment and before the interviewer spoke again) as positive, negative, or neutral in tone. If the speech was positive or negative, it was then scored in terms of five specific emotions—enthusiasm, affection, sadness, anger, and anxiety. The raters had not participated in any interviews and were blind to all research questions or hypotheses. They also had no information about results of other adolescent or family assessments. The total interview occurrence for each emotion was then determined. To allow for comparisons across subjects, all raw scores were standardized by dividing the individuals' emotion scores by their total number of speeches.

FINDINGS

First analyses are based on our application of the AECS to audio tapes and transcripts of 73 clinical research interviews (32 male and 41 female subjects from 2-parent families), a subsample of the 146 adolescents from the first year of a larger longitudinal study. The mean age of the sample was 14.5 years (SD = .80). Thirty-three of these subjects were patients at the time of the interviews.

Intersections between ego development and emotion communications were explored in several ways. First, we addressed the theoretically inspired question of whether ego development stages are associated with different ways of communicating emotions. Based on the preceding theoretical discussion, we expected that adolescents at higher stages of ego development would more likely communicate several emotions, as well as conflicting emotions, when reflecting on and describing their interpersonal relationships and other significant experiences. To study these predictions, two new variables—*diverse emotions* and *conflicting emotions*—were empirically defined. Conflicting emotions refers to the presence of positive (enthusiasm and/or affection) and negative (anger, sadness, anxiety) emotions in the same

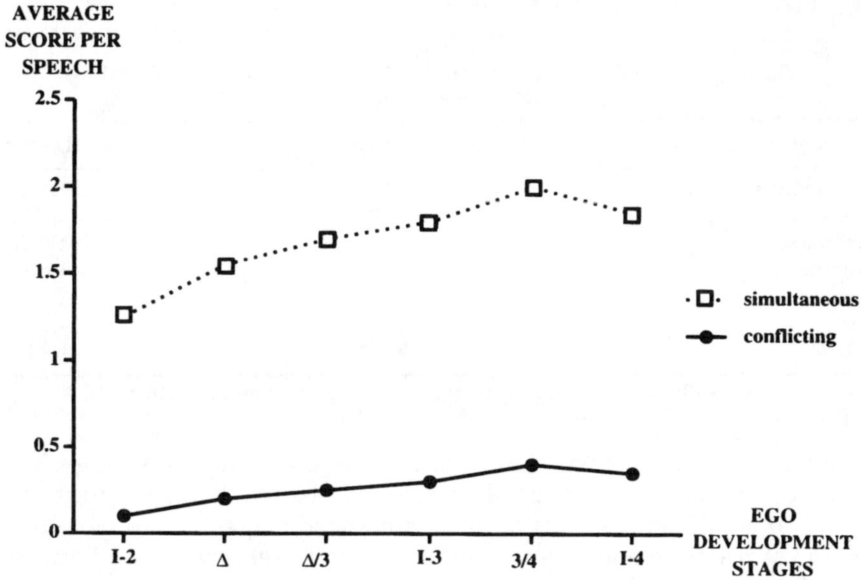

FIGURE 2 Conflicting and simultaneous emotions in adolescent speeches: Variations by ego development stage.

speech turn. Diverse emotions refers to the number of different emotions expressed, regardless of whether they are positive or negative, in a speech turn. As expected, conflicting and diverse emotion communications were significantly correlated with adolescent ego development stages, a pattern consistent for male and female subjects and remaining significant after controlling for psychiatric status (Figure 2).

These results are based on first-year interviews and, thus, examine associations between stages of ego development and emotion communications. What about paths of ego development? Are there any early signs of developmental trajectory differences in these very first interviews? Trajectory comparisons, using one-way analyses of variance, suggest that, early on, emotion communications of several groups are already distinct (Table 1). Adolescents who eventually follow steady conformist and accelerated paths show significantly higher levels of conflicting emotions than those who remain profoundly arrested over the years, $F(5, 67) = 5.27$, $p < .001$. In addition, steady conformists, accelerated, and moratorium adolescents show significantly higher levels of diverse emotions than those who remain arrested, $F(5, 67) = 4.97$, $p < .001$.

In contrast to emotion diversity and conflict, we had no theoretically or clinically generated predictions about how communication of spe-

TABLE 1
Conflicting and Simultaneous Emotion Communications in Speeches and Ego Development Trajectories

Trajectory	*Conflicting*	*Diverse*
profoundly arrested	0.017_a	1.49_a
steady conformist	0.326_b	1.980_b
accelerated	0.277_b	1.912_b
progressive	0.174	1.644
moratorium	0.221	1.868_b
regressive	0.257	1.824
$F(5, 62)$	5.27*	4.97*

Note. Values with different subscripts significantly differ from each other.
$^*p < .001$.

cific emotions would vary with adolescent ego development stage. Yet these new data give us a special opportunity to ask this new question. For instance, do adolescents at more advanced stages of ego development express more enthusiasm and affection in relationships? Exploratory Pearson correlation analyses reveal that enthusiasm, affection, anxiety, and neutrality are directly associated with higher stages. On the other hand, sadness and anger are inversely correlated with ego development (Table 2; Figure 3). These associations are similar for both genders. When psychiatric status is controlled, correlations between ego development and enthusiasm, affection, and anxiety remain significant, indicating that these observed relationships cannot be wholly explained by severe psychopathology.

DISCUSSION

In these first analyses of adolescent emotion communication and ego development, we found that greater emotion diversity and emotion conflict were linked with higher levels of ego development. These results were anticipated because individuals functioning at more advanced ego development stages are aware of many differences among individuals and within their interpersonal relationships (Hauser, 1993). In addition to being consistent with understandings of ego development, these findings provide further support for the view that adolescents are a diverse group, leading us to be wary when describing the emotional states or experiences of all adolescents. Petersen (1993) speaks directly to this point in her recent presidential address to the Society for Research on Adolescence: "it is clear that there is more than one healthy way to traverse the adolescent decade" (p. 2).

Petersen's comment leads to another question: What about relations between emotions and dysfunctional processes in adolescent development? Do psychiatrically impaired adolescents experience different patterns of conflicting and diverse emotions than nonpatients? Or is it a matter of different frequency and intensity, with their emotion com-

TABLE 2
Correlations Between Specific Emotions, Emotion Diversity, and Emotion Conflict and Year 1 Ego Stages

Specific Emotion and Emotion Pattern	*Ego Development Stage*
Enthusiasm	.62***
Affection	.38**
Neutral	.37**
Sadness	−.24*
Anger	−.33**
Anxiety	.59***
Conflict	.61***
Diverse	.63***

*$p < .05$. **$p < .01$. ***$p < .0001$.

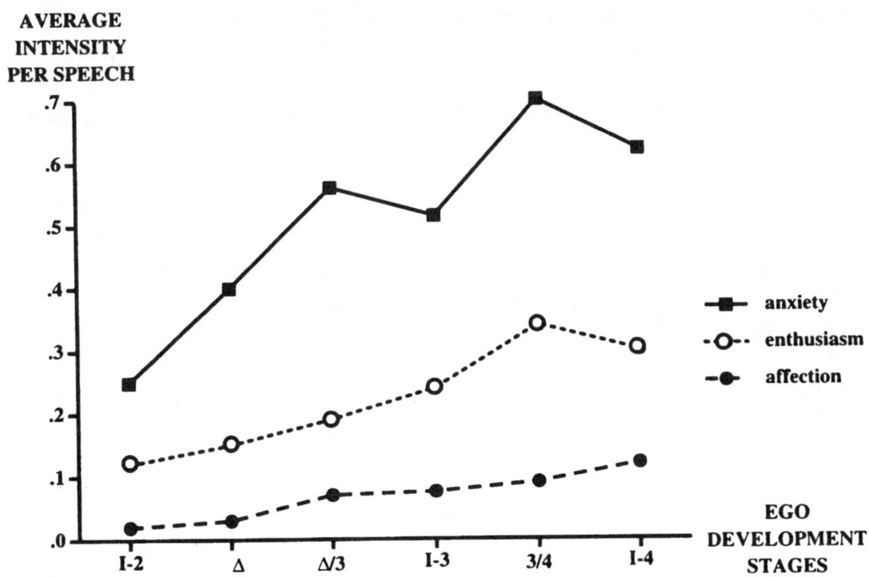

FIGURE 3 Specific emotions and adolescent ego development.

munications tied to clearly different internal and interpersonal events? These are important and timely questions, in light of the increasing interest in adolescent mental health and the development of preventive interventions (Kazdin, 1993). At this point, we know more about affective disorders in adolescence and their risk factors but less about specific emotional processes, as well as links between emotions, cognitions, and actions for these more vulnerable adolescents (Gore & Colten, 1991). Future analyses of our more enlarged sample are pertinent to these questions. But on a broader canvas, and with more diverse samples, studies traversing the more traditional boundaries between clinical and developmental psychology will undoubtedly engage these questions, as the realm of developmental psychopathology continues its active growth (e.g., Rolf, Masten, Cicchetti, Nuechterlein, & Weintraub, 1990).

Our second set of findings was surprising, revealing that adolescents at more advanced ego development stages communicated higher levels of several specific emotions during their interviews. Because the analyses took the number of adolescent speeches into account, we know that these findings do not simply result from the fact that these higher stage adolescents were more loquacious. Nonetheless, it is possible that adolescents functioning at higher ego stages are interested in disclosing more information about their emotional experiences as they engage more fully with the interviewer's queries about their relationships with family peers and other adults (teachers, counselors, employers).

Yet, why should adolescents at higher ego development levels report so much more anxiety in comparison to the other specific emotions? It is of interest that new data about these same adolescents as young adults reveal a similar pattern. Preliminary analyses of their friends' descriptions of them indicates that those young adult subjects at higher ego development levels are also seen by their friends as being more anxious (Hauser & Allen, in press). One reason for this higher anxiety may be that it is characteristic of individuals at higher ego development stages to have a greater awareness of complexities and uncertainties, involving themselves as well as the envisioned future. A cost of this heightened awareness could be more anxiety. Although we do not fully understand these differences in specific emotions, such findings certainly emphasize the fact that advancing ego development cannot be considered equivalent to diminished suffering or increasingly optimal mental health.

More complete explanation of these connections between ego development and anxiety will require more extensive analyses, probing in finer detail the interpersonal contexts of these emotion communications. Are the anxiety communications of adolescents at higher stages associated, for instance, with certain experiences they have had with significant others, or with insights about these relationships? Or are their anxieties tied to imagining their futures, anticipating dangers overlooked by adolescents at lower stages?

A recurrent theme threading through this discussion has been the interplay between emotional processes and interpersonal relationships. From direct experience, as well as from clinical observations, connections between relationships and emotions are well known. Studies of adult attachment, with their many references to separation, loss, and conflicted ties with representations of significant others, further highlight these ties (e.g., Main, Kaplan, & Cassidy, 1985). But systematic empirical studies of close relationships and emotional processes are few, in contrast to the large number of such reports in the clinical literature (e.g., Kernberg, 1991; Ross, 1991). This gap points to yet another research direction: synchronously focusing on the nature of unfolding relationships, and the emotions associated with these relationships, through conceptual and empirical approaches.

Finally, we must underscore our view that there are other ways to study emotions, in particular those emotions not so readily observable (Furth, 1991). Anne Frank's diary, filled with her spontaneous references and descriptions of her inner experiences in adolescence, reminds us of these emotions—ones not so readily coded from interviews and other observed behaviors. Besides recognizing alternate sources of data about the individual's emotion experiences and communications, we need to take seriously alternate approaches for assessing emotions, ones that can complement " ... coding and summing ... hardly an unambiguous indication of emotional experiences" (Furth, 1991, p. 161). Commenting on Haviland and Kramer's innovative treatment of Anne Frank's diary, Furth (1991) urges that they expand their methodology in other directions, namely " ... a qualitative treatment of the text" (p. 162). By this, Furth reminds us of the fact that interviews can be analyzed in terms of their narrative characteristics: the themes, the unfoldings of emotions, the pervasive emotional tones that accompany hot or cold issues in a subject's life and (using longitudinal interviews) how such themes and evolving patterns shift over time.

These first explorations, then, have launched our interpretations and future agendas in several directions: connections of emotion processes with psychopathology; more intensive analyses of interview texts; use of other texts (autobiographical materials, family interviews, attachment interviews); and consideration of other ways to aggregate our current codes. Surely these results and reflections underscore the already strong arguments for merging the very best of quantitative and qualitative methods to study so central an experience in the lives of adolescents.

ACKNOWLEDGMENTS

This article was produced as a result of the National Institute of Mental Health (NIMH) workshop "Affective Processes in Adolescence," held October 19–20, 1992 in Bethesda, Maryland.

Preparation of this article was supported, in part, by grants from the NIMH (Research Scientist Award #K-0570178-07) and The John D. and Catherine T. MacArthur Foundation (#8900078) to Stuart Hauser while he was a Fellow at the Center for Advanced Study in the Behavioral Sciences, Stanford, California, and by an NIMH Faculty Scholar Award (#MH 19144) to Andrew Safyer.

REFERENCES

Blos, P. (1962). *On adolescence: A psychoanalytic interpretation*. New York: Free Press.

Brooks-Gunn, J., Rock, J., & Warren, M. (1989). Comparison of pubertal constructs across the adolescent years. *Developmental Psychology, 25*, 51–60.

Campos, J. J., Campos, R. G., & Barrett, K. C. (1989). Emergent themes in the study of emotional development and emotional regulation. *Developmental Psychology, 25*, 394–402.

Cohn, L. (1991). Sex differences in the course of personality development: A meta-analysis. *Psychological Bulletin, 109*, 252–266.

Collins, W. A. (1990). Parent–child relationships in the transition to adolescence: Continuity and change in interaction, affect, and cognition. In R. Montemayor, G. R. Adams, & T. P. Gullotta (Eds.), *Advances in adolescent development: Vol. 2. From childhood to adolescence: A transitional period?* (pp. 85–106). Newbury Park, CA: Sage.

Collins, W. A., & Gunnar, M. (1989). Social and personality development. *Annual Review of Psychology, 41*, 387–416.

Erikson, E. H. (1959). Identity and the life cycle. *Psychological Issues, 1*, 1–171.

Erikson, E. H. (1964). *The challenge of youth*. New York: Anchor.

Erikson, E. H. (1968). *Identity: Youth and crisis*. New York: Norton.

Freud, A. (1946). *The ego and mechanisms of defense* (C. Baines, Trans.). New York: Internet Universities Press.

Freud, A. (1958). *Adolescence. Psychoanalytic study of the child: Vol. 13*. New York: Basic Books.

Furth, H. (1991). Commentary. *Human Development, 34*, 160–162.

Gore, S., & Colten, M. E. (1991). *Adolescent stress: Causes and consequences*. New York: Aldine de Gruyter.

Gottman, J. (1988). *Specific affect coding system manual*. Unpublished manuscript, Univer-

sity of Washington, Seattle, WA.
Hauser, S. T. (1976). Loevinger's model and measure of ego development: A critical review. *Psychological Bulletin, 83,* 928–955.
Hauser, S. T. (1993). Loevinger's model and measure of ego development: A critical review II. *Psychological Inquiry, 83,* 928–955.
Hauser, S. T., & Allen, J. P. (in press). Exceptional outcomes: Negotiating a perilous adolescence. Cambridge, MA: Harvard University Press.
Hauser, S. T., & Bowlds, M. K. (1991). Stress, coping, and adaptation. In S. Feldman & G. Elliot (Eds.), *At the threshold: The developing adolescent* (pp. 388–413). Cambridge, MA: Harvard University Press.
Hauser, S. T., & Levine, H. A. (1993). Relatedness and autonomy in adolescence: Links with ego development and family interactions. In S. C. Feinstein & R. C. Marohn (Eds.), *Adolescent psychiatry* (Vol. 19, pp. 185–227). Chicago: University of Chicago Press.
Hauser, S. T., Powers, S. I., Noam, G. G., Jacobson, A. M., Weiss, B., & Follansbee, D. (1984). Familial contexts of adolescent ego development. *Child Development, 55,* 195–213.
Hauser, S. T., & Smith, H. F. (1991). The development and experience of affect in adolescence. *Journal of the American Psychoanalytic Association, 39,* 131–165.
Haviland, J., & Kramer, D. (1991). Affect–cognition relationship in adolescent diaries: The case of Anne Frank. *Human Development, 34,* 142–159.
Kazdin, A. (1993). Adolescent mental health: Prevention and treatment programs. *American Psychologist, 48,* 127–141.
Kernberg, O. (1991). The psychopathology of hatred. *Journal of the American Psychoanalytic Association, 39,* 209–238.
Loevinger, J. (1976). *Ego development.* San Francisco: Jossey-Bass.
Loevinger, J., & Wessler, R. (1970). *Measuring ego development* (Vol. I). San Francisco: Jossey-Bass.
Loevinger. J., Wessler, R., & Redmore (1970). *Measuring ego development* (Vol. II). San Francisco: Jossey-Bass.
Main, M., Kaplan, N., & Cassidy, J. (1985). Security in infancy, childhood, and adulthood: A move to the level of representation. In I. Bretherton & E. Waters (Eds.), Growing points of attachment theory and research. *Monographs of the Society for Research in Child Development, 50* (1–2, Serial No. 209).
Offer, D., Ostrov, E., & Howard, K. (1981). *The adolescent: A psychological self-portrait.* New York: Basic Books.
Petersen, A. C. (1988). Adolescent development. *Annual Review of Psychology, 39,* 583–607.
Petersen, A. C. (1993). Creating adolescents: The role of context and process in developmental trajectories. *Journal of Research on Adolescence, 3,* 1–18.
Powers, S. I., Hauser, S. T., & Kilner, L. (1989). Adolescent mental health. *American Psychologist, 44,* 200–208.
Rolf, J., Masten, A. S., Cicchetti, D., Nuechterlein, K. H., & Weintraub, S. (1990). *Risk and protective factors in the development of psychopathology.* Cambridge, England: Cambridge University Press.
Ross, J. M. (1991). A psychoanalytic essay on romantic, erotic love. *Journal of the American Psychoanalytic Association, 39,* 439–474.
Safyer, A. W., & Hauser, S. T. (1992). *Coding manual for the Adolescent Emotion Coding System (AECS).* Unpublished manuscript.
Safyer, A. W., & Hauser, S. T. (1994). A microanalytic method for exploring adolescent emotional expression. *Journal of Adolescent Research, 9,* 50–66.
Scherer, K. (1988). *Facets of emotion.* Hillsdale, NJ: Lawrence Erlbaum Associates, Inc.

Shaver, P., Schwartz, J., Kirkson, D., & O'Connor, C. (1987). Emotion knowledge: Further exploration of a prototype approach. *Journal of Personality and Social Psychology, 52,* 1061–1086.
Weiner, I. (1970). *Psychological disturbance in adolescence.* New York: Wiley.

Received December 6, 1993
Accepted February 24, 1994

Acknowledgments

Baltes, Paul B., and John R. Nesselroade. "Cultural Change and Adolescent Personality Development: An Application of Longitudinal Sequences." *Developmental Psychology* 7 (1972): 244–56. Copyright 1972 by the American Psychological Association. Reprinted by permission.

Tubman, Jonathan G., and Richard M. Lerner. "Continuity and Discontinuity in the Affective Experiences of Parents and Children: Evidence from the New York Longitudinal Study." *American Journal of Orthopsychiatry* 64 (1994): 112–25. Copyright 1994 by the American Orthopsychiatric Association, Inc. Reprinted by permission.

Tubman, Jonathan G., Richard M. Lerner, Jacqueline V. Lerner, and Alexander von Eye. "Temperament and Adjustment in Young Adulthood: A 15-Year Longitudinal Analysis." *American Journal of Orthopsychiatry* 62 (1992): 564–74. Copyright 1992 by the American Orthopsychiatric Association, Inc. Reprinted by permission.

Damon, William, and Daniel Hart. "The Development of Self-Understanding from Infancy Through Adolescence." *Child Development* 53 (1982): 841–64. Reprinted with the permission of the Society for Research in Child Development.

Bandura, Albert. "Perceived Self-Efficacy in the Exercise of Personal Agency." *The Psychologist* 2 (1989): 411–24. Reprinted with the permission of the British Psychological Society.

Alsaker, Françoise D., and Dan Olweus. "Stability of Global Self-Evaluation in Early Adolescence: A Cohort Longitudinal Study." *Journal of Research on Adolescence* 2 (1992): 123–45. Reprinted with the permission of Lawrence Erlbaum Associates Inc.

Block, Jack, and Richard W. Robins. "A Longitudinal Study of Consistency and Change in Self-Esteem from Early Adolescence to Early Adulthood." *Child Development* 64 (1993): 909–23. Reprinted with the permission of the Society for Research in Child Development.

Luster, Tom, and Harriette Pipes McAdoo. "Factors Related to Self-Esteem Among African American Youths: A Secondary Analysis of the High/Scope Perry Preschool Data." *Journal of Research on Adolescence* 5 (1995): 451–67.

Reprinted with the permission of Lawrence Erlbaum Associates, Inc.

Lerner, Richard M., Saburo Iwawaki, Takashi Chihara, and Gwendolyn T. Sorell. "Self-Concept, Self-Esteem, and Body Attitudes Among Japanese Male and Female Adolescents." Child Development 51 (1980): 847–55. Reprinted with the permission of the Society for Research in Child Development.

Galambos, Nancy L., David M. Almeida, and Anne C. Petersen. "Masculinity, Femininity, and Sex Role Attitudes in Early Adolescence: Exploring Gender Intensification." *Child Development* 61 (1990): 1905–14. Reprinted with the permission of the Society for Research in Child Development.

Harter, Susan, Clare Stocker, and Nancy S. Robinson. "The Perceived Directionality of the Link Between Approval and Self-Worth: The Liabilities of a Looking Glass Self-Orientation Among Young Adolescents." *Journal of Research on Adolescence* 6 (1996): 285–308. Reprinted with the permission of Lawrence Erlbaum Associates, Inc.

Savin-Williams, Ritch C. "An Exploratory Study of Pubertal Maturation Timing and Self-Esteem Among Gay and Bisexual Male Youths." *Developmental Psychology* 31 (1995): 56–64. Copyright 1995 by the American Psychological Association. Reprinted by permission.

Powers, Sally I., Deborah P. Welsh, and Virginia Wright. "Adolescents' Affective Experience of Family Behaviors: The Role of Subjective Understanding." *Journal of Research on Adolescence* 4 (1994): 585–600. Reprinted with the permission of Lawrence Erlbaum Associates Inc.

Kenny, Maureen E., Dena L. Moilanen, Richard Lomax, and Mary M. Brabeck. "Contributions of Parental Attachments to View of Self and Depressive Symptoms Among Early Adolescents." *Journal of Early Adolescence* 13 (1993): 408–30. Reprinted with the permission of Sage Publications, Inc.

Spencer, Margaret Beale, Dona Phillips Swanson, and Michael Cunningham. "Ethnicity, Ethnic Identity, and Competence Formation: Adolescent Transition and Cultural Transformation." *Journal of Negro Education* 60 (1991): 366–87. Reprinted with the permission of Howard University.

Waterman, Alan S. "Identity Development from Adolescence to Adulthood: An Extension of Theory and a Review of Research." *Developmental Psychology* 18 (1982): 341–58. Copyright 1982 by the American Psychological Association. Reprinted by permission.

Marcia, James E. "Development and Validation of Ego-Identity Status." *Journal of Personality and Social Psychology* 3 (1966): 551–58. Copyright 1966 by the American Psychological Association. Reprinted by permission.

Waterman, Alan S., and Caroline K. Waterman. "A Longitudinal Study of Changes in Ego Identity Status During the Freshman Year at College." *Developmental Psychology* 5 (1971): 167–73. Copyright 1971 by the American Psychological Association. Reprinted by permission.

Spencer, Margaret Beale, and Carol Markstrom-Adams. "Identity Processes Among Racial and Ethnic Minority Children in America." *Child Development* 61 (1990): 290–310. Reprinted with the permission of the Society for Research in Child Development.

Hauser, Stuart T., John Houlihan, Sally I. Powers, Alan M. Jacobson, Gil G. Noam, Bedonna Weiss-Perry, Donna Follansbee, and Barbara K. Book. "Adolescent Ego Development Within the Family: Family Styles and Family Sequences." *International Journal of Behavioral Development* 14 (1991): 165–93. Reprinted with the permission of Taylor and Francis Ltd.

Hauser, Stuart T., and Andrew W. Safyer. "Ego Development and Adolescent Emotions." *Journal of Research on Adolescence* 4 (1994): 487–502. Reprinted with the permission of Lawrence Erlbaum Associates, Inc.